Studies
in Scottish
Literature

Copyright © G. Ross Roy 1971

Published in Columbia, S. C., by the
UNIVERSITY OF SOUTH CAROLINA PRESS, 1971

International Standard Book Number: 0-87249-209-5
Library of Congress Catalog Card Number: 73-138822

Manufactured by
VOGUE PRESS, INC.
Columbia, S. C.

CONTENTS

INTRODUCTION

It is over ten years since I conceived the idea of a scholarly journal devoted to Scottish literature. Most of those to whom I made my suggestion were enthusiastic, but there were those who felt that such a publication would be too specialized. "You will never get enough good articles," I was told. I am happy that I did not heed this well-intentioned warning which events have shown to have been quite wrong.

And so with plenty of enthusiasm, but without the slightest idea about how to found a journal, the idea of *Studies in Scottish Literature* was born. It was to be nearly three years before the idea became a reality. Any such hazardous undertaking must be attended by considerable good fortune if it is to prosper, and mine was soon evident in the selection of an Editorial Board. I determined to keep its number to a minimum. One of the most obvious choices was Professor A. L. Strout, an internationally known American scholar with wide connections in Scotland. With his unfailing enthusiasm Professor Strout, who was later to be my colleague, threw himself into the project. Dr. Kurt Wittig was asked to serve because of his "world view" of the literature of Scotland, a view which he had ably set forth in *The Scottish Tradition in Literature.* Finally, "Hugh MacDiarmid" responded with his usual enthusiasm when asked to serve. Professor David Daiches and Dr. A. M. Kinghorn, who need no introduction to students of Scottish literature, were equally willing to serve when it was decided, shortly after the initial publication, to enlarge the Editorial Board.

The response from scholars who were approached for contributions to the early issues was equally gratifying—almost unanimously their replies were affirmative. Other than these few requests *SSL* has never solicited articles, and we have been for some time in the (at least partially) enviable position of having more good material on hand than we can publish—a situation which may cause us to re-evaluate our function and consider the advisability of increasing our size. From its first issue scholars and the informed public have recognized the importance of *SSL* and the quality of its contents—in fact this journal, almost from its first issue, claimed a place in the forefront of Scottish journals, and is still without peer in the field of Scottish literature.

Although specialized publications such as this one appeal to a limited audience, it is gratifying to note that *SSL* has enjoyed an increasingly wider circulation. Almost all of the major research libraries in the English-speaking world, as well as a significant number of European libraries, now subscribe. Because the early issues are out of print, and in response to inquiries for them, the University of South Carolina Press decided to reprint the first eight issues of *SSL* in bound form. Subsequent volumes will be reissued as demand arises.

G. ROSS ROY

STUDIES IN SCOTTISH LITERATURE

VOLUME 1   *NUMBER* 1   *JULY* 1963

CONTENTS

STUDIES IN SCOTTISH LITERATURE

EDITED BY PROFESSOR G. ROSS ROY
TEXAS TECHNOLOGICAL COLLEGE

EDITORIAL BOARD:

HUGH MACDIARMID (Dr. C. M. GRIEVE)
PROFESSOR A. L. STROUT - Dr. KURT WITTIG

STUDIES IN SCOTTISH LITERATURE is an
independent quarterly devoted to all aspects of
Scottish literature. Articles and notes are welcome.
Subscriptions are available at $5.00 U.S. per annum in the
United States and Canada, elsewhere 30 shillings.
All communications should be addressed to the
Editor, Department of English, Texas Technological College.
Lubbock, Texas, U.S.A.

PUBLISHED BY TEXAS TECHNOLOGICAL COLLEGE
AND PRINTED BY WILLIAM MACLELLAN
240 HOPE STREET, GLASGOW, C.2., SCOTLAND

EDITORIAL

The launching of any new journal is a precarious operation; when it is an unsubsidized scholarly journal the venture might well appear foolhardy. Not only is there the financial aspect of publication, but the very real problem of the availability of suitable material. If we have not yet solved the first of these problems, we have been greatly encouraged by the response of scholars in submitting articles.

Studies in Scottish Literature was founded with the idea of creating a common meeting ground for work embracing all aspects of the great Scottish literary heritage. It is not the organ of any school or faction; it welcomes all shades of opinion. It will publish articles on Scottish authors, including biographical studies or appreciations; or their influence on others; or trends in the literary history of Scotland, including aesthetics. As a journal devoted to a vigorous living literature it will carry studies of contemporary authors.

The question as to whether or not another scholarly journal is justified must find its answer in the future. The editorial board, those who have submitted articles, our advertising patrons and our subscribers obviously feel that it is. One thing is certain: considering the importance of Scottish literature there is not enough space available for publishing articles and notes on the subject.

A word about the future. It is planned to add reviews shortly in order to bring to the attention of our readers expert evaluations of recent Scottish literature. There will be reviews of critical works, biographies, poetry and fiction. At a later date it is hoped that an annual bibliography of Scottish literary studies can be added.

[3]

CONTRIBUTORS
TO THIS ISSUE

Nelson S. BUSHNELL: Robert Professor of English, Emeritus, at Williams College (Litt.D., Williams, 1959). In the 1930's his step-by-step reconstruction of Keats' tour of Galloway, the Western Isles and the Highlands introduced him to research in Scottish subjects; his latest publication in that field is *William Hamilton of Bangour, Poet and Jacobite*. At present Mr. Bushnell is examining the novels of Scott and of Susan Ferrier in the course of a study of the novel of manners.

Thomas CRAWFORD: Educated Dunfermline High School and University of Edinburgh; has lived in New Zealand since 1948, where he has worked in Adult Education, and as a Civil Servant and University teacher. At present Senior Lecturer in the Department of English Language and Literature at the University of Auckland. Author of *The Edinburgh Review and Romantic Poetry* (1955) and *Burns: A Study of the Poems and Songs* (1960) Was a Carnegie Senior Research Fellow in Edinburgh in 1960; at present preparing a general study of Scottish Popular Lyrics before Burns.

Francis R. HART: Assistant Professor of English at the University of Virginia, having received his degrees at Harvard and having taught previously at Harvard and Ohio State. He has published articles and reviews in *Victorian Newsletter, TLS, ELH* and *Studies in Bibliography*. His interest in ⸻ Literary traditions derive originally from the study of biographical theory and practice, 1790-1840, with special reference to Boswell, Scott, Lockhart and Carlyle. He is writing a book-length critical description and assessment of the Waverley Novels, and a series of essays on 20th century Scottish fiction.

Alexander Manson KINGHORN: Lecturer in Mediaeval Literature at the University of the West Indies; educated University of Aberdeen and Pembroke College, Cambridge. Co-editor (with Alexander Law, O.B.E.) of the Scottish Text Society's edition of Allan Ramsay's *Works*; editor of Barbour's *Bruce* in the Saltire Classics series; contributor to learned journals for the past ten years (British, American, Canadian and European).

Tom SCOTT: Educated Hyndland Academy, Madras College, University of Edinburgh (M.A. with Honours in English Literature). Began publishing poems in 1941; published *Seven Poems o Maister Francis Villon: Made Oure intil Scots* (1953); *An Ode til New Jerusalem* (1956) and has in press (O.U.P.) *The Ship and Other Poems*. Presently taking a Ph.D. at Edinburgh University with a thesis on Dunbar's poems. Received an Atlantic Award in 1950 and travelled in France, Italy and Sicily during which time he became interested in Scots literature. Has had poems published in British magazines and in *Poetry* (Chicago) and broadcast over the B.B.C. Has written several book-length poems (unpublished), and has recently turned to the writing of satirical pamphlets.

TOM SCOTT

Observations
on Scottish Studies

THIS periodical is a most welcome and necessary contribution to Scottish studies. No such publication exists in
Scotland and no Scottish university has a Department of
Scottish Studies, literary or otherwise. Glasgow has a
readership in Scottish literature, held by Mr. Alexander Scott,
attached to the Department of Scottish History. This about sums
up the ghastliness of the position here in Scotland where Scottish
literature is reckoned to belong to the past, not the present and
the future: and Professor Roy's admirable enterprise in Canada
puts Scottish universities to shame. Here in Edinburgh, it is true,
we have. nominally, a "School of Scottish Studies." While Vice-
Principal Sir Edward Appleton has put Scotland eternally in his
debt by the creation of this school, it must be said that it is, as
at present constituted, a misnomer: since it is concerned only
with folklore studies, it would be more properly called "The
School of Folklore Studies in Scotland," as such central areas of
study as literature and language are not included; even such as
it is, Sir Edward's school is harassed by lack of financial support.

Perhaps I had better make it clear from the outset that I
have no pretentions to academic detachment in this matter. I
am as disinterested as a husband who sees his wife slowly flogged
to death under his captive eyes. Since the late 13th century,
Scotland has been oppressed by a neighbour, England, whose
amiable intentions towards Scotland have been, and are consistently. those of cultural and political genocide. The Treaty
of Union of 1707 gave England the perfect weapon with which
to achieve these aims, and the state of Scottish studies today,
literary and otherwise, is indicative of the degree of success
achieved by the English and the Anglo-Scots. This simple fact,
however incredible it may seem to countries outside the circle
of English domination, is the first thing to be grasped by any

[5]

student or would-be student of Scottish matters of any sort whatsoever. The so-called Union of 1707 was an " incorporative " one — that is, one that allowed the devouring of Scotland by England, under the euphemism " Britain," which invariably means " England," as " British " means " English."

The first problem of Scottish literary studies is the problem of texts and their availability. Much good work has been done in the past by such clubs as the Bannatyne and the Spalding, and and the Scottish Text Society is still doing admirable work. But these scholarly editions are not easily available to the general public, and above all, to students in universities and elsewhere. There is therefore a great need for the publication of cheap one-volume texts, such as the Oxford University Press Standard Authors series. The immediate need is for some publisher or publishers — why not the combined university presses? — to make available in such format all texts already printed by the Scottish Text Society, and other such editions. The bulk of Scottish mediaeval poetry, for instance, is to be found in the Maitland and Bannatyne MSS. These have been published by the Scottish Text Society — they should be made available as soon as possible in cheaper editions.

One of the first things to strike a student of Scottish literature is the failure to develop a Scots prose. This has been ascribed, of course, to the passing of the homogeneous literary language under the impact of the Kirk's adoption of the Sudron versions of the Bible, as part of their anglicising New Alliance; and to the passing of the Scottish Court to London in 1603 when James VI decided to rule his two kingdoms from London instead of from Edinburgh, with the consequent anglicisation of the court and official writings. Yet before 1603 there was a great deal of Scots prose of considerable quality: had it been developed, I would not be writing this article in the *lingua franca* of Standard. There is need to publish such prose as there is: Murdoch Nisbet's *New Testament* for example, and the works of Buchanan, Bellenden, Major, Pitscottie and others, as well as the magnificent *Complaint of Scotland*. The easy circulation of such works might lead to a prose revival similar to the present poetic one, and to the much - to - be - desired creation of a Scots critical prose.

Perhaps the most fertile ground for students intending to do work of thesis length is the 17th century. It is usual to regard the Scottish seventeenth century as a bleak time for creative literature, an era of religious strife, in which little was written but tracts and sermons. Poetry had gone underground together with the native language, except for such poetasting anglicisers as Drummond of Hawthornden, and when it re-emerged in the eighteenth century it was a folksy vernacular poetry culminating in Burns. The truth is that little is really known about this period in literature, and diligent research might produce a very different picture from this current one — and in any case the ecclesiastical literature wants looking into. There is still room for standard editions of the works of such men as Knox, Calderwood, Spottiswoode and others. Certainly the seventeenth century in Scotland is a field that is well worth the tillage of pioneering scholars.

The problem of available texts does not apply to literature written after 1707; compared to the greater age of Scots literature, there is almost an abundance, although even here the quality leaves much to be desired. Certainly Fergusson has been shabbily treated, and a standard edition of his works (taken from the S.T.S. edition by Professor Matthew MacDiarmid) is long overdue, and should lead to the clear recognition that this boy who died aged twenty-four was no mere "precursor" of Burns but a major poet in his own right, and in certain respects even more important to Scottish poetry than Burns. There is still room also for thoroughly scholarly texts of Scott. Much is available through such series as the Everyman, but there is room for improvement here too — glossing is particularly bad in popular editions. One would hope that the appearance of the *Scottish National Dictionary* and the *Dictionary of the Older Scottish Tongue* will make paucity in this regard less excusable than at present. There is much here for Scottish presses to get down to.

The two dictionaries I have mentioned above are each rather more than half-way through the alphabet, and each has already published paperback volumes suitable for binding when complete. This work is of an importance impossible to exaggerate yet each is run on a skeleton staff of no more than the editor and one or two assistants, and each is constantly under sentence of financial death. These dictionaries, housed in the same building in George Square as the School of Scottish Studies, under the aegis of Edinburgh University, will ultimately run to some ten volumes each, comparable to the *Oxford English Dictionary*. It is clear that such an edition will not be easily available to the public, and few who have not been regular subscribers will be able to possess them. It is therefore of prime importance that there should be, now that each is in its latter half, competent staffs already at work compiling shorter versions to be published in one volume for sale to the general public and students. At present there is not the slightest sign of this being done, and indeed, the very continuation of the full - scale dictionaries is, as I have said, problematical.

The School of Scottish Studies is itself in desperate need of hard cash. In one small building, formerly an eighteenth-century dwelling-house, next door to where Walter Scott once lived, in George Square, there are housed collections of Gaelic song, verse, tales, and music; a large library of tape collections; Mr. Hamish Henderson's collection of (mainly Scots) folk-songs, ballads and tales; a place-name survey; a material culture section; the Scottish linguistic survey of dialects of both Gaelic and Scots from all parts; an Orkney and Shetland culture section; a very fine library of folklore and other studies; and a transcription section. All this is supported on a shoe-string. More money is spent on the Gaelic side of this work than on Scots — indeed, the major and lowland culture is grossly neglected — partly, it is argued, because Gaelic is disappearing faster, and therefore needs collecting and recording more urgently. This may be so—but it points to the utterly wrong and inadequate attitude underneath the whole concept: that of collecting museum specimens of a supposedly dying culture before it is too late, instead of rushing in to keep the patient alive. We need doctors and medicines, and what we get is an undertaker. The School does publish an admirable magazine twice yearly, but of all the masses of work collected, nothing is being printed or otherwise reissued to the nation from which it is gathered. The heart of the School of Scottish Studies is all in-beat and no out-beat — a mortal abnormality. But of course there is no money for publication— the patient is less expensive dead than alive, a coffin less costly than a living house. The School should engage a financier with the task of digging up money for its maintenance and expansion —he would be well worth it.

But the work of the School of Scottish Studies, as we have seen, is not strictly relevant, since it bypasses the greatest study of all — literature, which is my concern here. Yet the Scottish universities, and perhaps Edinburgh, my own alma mater, in particular, are better placed than ordinary commercial firms for the production of critical editions of standard authors. Not only have they the appropriate scholastic authority and connections, but they are in the position to raise funds (to cover possible losses) from such sources as the Carnegie Trust. It is long past time that we had an E.U.P. series of standard Scottish authors comparable to that series of the O.U.P. standard authors mentioned above, and well-known to students and lay readers alike. If the project seems too challenging for one university press to undertake, surely all the Scottish universities could combine resources over a period of time — say ten years — to float the venture. I for one will not be fobbed off with the usual excuse that "there is no money." The money is there — let the universities demand it.

The real trouble is not money, in this regard, but will. There is far too little sense of urgency among the Scottish or Anglo-Scottish academics. Most of these latter whom I have talked to harm the culture they are supposed to advance, having been taught to regard it with a sneer as something inferior to that of our sudron neighbours. In America, in Canada, in many parts of the world, there is great interest in Scottish literature; but when students come to Scotland to follow up this interest they too often meet with ignorance, prejudice, and downright obstructionism. The students therefore starting off with eagerness and enthusiasm, are gradually scunnered and depressed by these defeatists, and lose heart and interest. Sometimes they give up and go home. I have heard of one such going back to America after three months of obstructionism in this country, and saying of a certain professor who had helped to defeat him: "That man is ASHAMED of being a Scot." As long as Scottish literature is treated as an inferior branch of English literature, and as long as universities hold out no education in their own traditions to Scotsmen, offering them nothing better than to become honorary Englishmen, so long will Scottish professors be encouraged to feel ashamed of being Scots, and so long will the Scottish universities fail those overseas students who are more interested in Scottish literature than English. After all, Shakespeare apart, the most influential "English" writers abroad have been Scott, Byron, and "Ossian" Macpherson — Scotsmen all. One of the tasks before students of Scottish literature is to sort out how many writers disguised under the name of English are in fact Scots. So far as I know, T. S. Eliot's trenchant observation that Byron is an instance of Scottish genius achieving itself as best it may in the

[9]

foreign medium of English has not been taken up by any Scottish critic.

I know of a case of a Scottish professor who applied for a literature chair in one of our universities — a chair of English, of course, there being no such thing as a Scottish one. He is a man of international repute as a critic of Scottish literature, apart from his work as a teacher in English and American universities. When asked what he would do with his chair if he got it, he replied that he would make this university the world centre of Scottish literary studies, and when he went on to outline his plan, remarking on the acute interest in Scottish studies in America, he was made so uncomfortable that he had to leave. This is the position here today. No Scots academic who has contributed anything to Scottish literature holds a chair in Scotland. The three most prominent men in this regard have their chairs in English universities — redbrick of course. Another is in Ireland. This is part of what seems to be the English policy of getting all potential Scottish leaders out of Scotland and keeping them out, so that the people and their natural leaders are kept apart. Fortunately there are signs that the Scots may wake up in time to save the nation. Every student of Scottish matters should constantly bear such facts in the forefront of his mind.

My own interest being chiefly in Scots, which is the central literature, I can say little about the Gaelic. Such editions of the Gaelic Text Society as Watson's edition of the *Book of the Dean of Lismore,* which contains Ossianic fragments among two hundred-odd poems, are excellent. Much of what I have said in regard to Scots literature is even more true of the Gaelic. It is too little realized that Scottish literature does not begin with Barbour's *Brus* in the fourteenth century, but with the Erse and Latin hymns of Columba in the sixth. A true survey of Scottish literature would include work in Irish, Gaelic (a development from Irish), Welsh (Taliessin and Aneurin), Latin (Buchanan and Johnston), Scots and English.

If in the course of this article I have concentrated mainly on publishing problems, I hope it is clear that this is because publishing *is* the main problem at the moment. Without textbooks, what can students do? Postgraduate men may be able to come over and specialize in Edinburgh, which, having the School of Scottish Studies, however inadequate, plus the magnificent Advocates' Library (now the National Library), ought certainly to be the world centre of Scottish studies. But these are specialists, and it is of the essence of these studies that less specialized readers and undergraduates should have access to what writers have bequeathed and scholars made available, but which has not yet been published. The truth is that the state of Scottish publishing is so bad that it is past time for the nation to consider whether this essential service to the community and to humanity can be left any longer in private hands. It is ironic that the greatest ballad authority up to date should have been Professor Child, and that his great collection should have been published at Harvard. The tunes to these ballads, collected and edited by Bronson, have also been published at Harvard. Almost the whole history of the Scottish Renaissance has been one of works printed cheaply and almost clandestinely, as if it were a dirty secret, by jobbing printers. The latest disgrace is that the *Collected Poems* of Hugh MacDiarmid (and only now in his seventieth year) have been published in New York and not by any Scottish publisher. Goodsir Smith still awaits collection, and the great Gaelic poet Sorley MacLean goes almost unread now in his own lifetime, although he is a major poet by international standards, and as deserving attention as, say, Dylan Thomas.

Scotland is probably the richest country in Europe for folklore, excepting Hungary: but where is our Bartok? And who would publish him if he came? Harvard? Yale? Oxford? or is there any chance that our Scottish universities might wake from their sleep of centuries to some sense of their responsibility to the Scottish nation and its culture? Here in Edinburgh recently has been published by the Edinburgh University Press a book by a member of the staff of the Department of Philosophy, Dr. George Davie. It is called *The Democratic Intellect,* and has been described by Hugh MacDiarmid as the most important book to be published in Scotland in his lifetime. It is a book of immense erudition, a product of the phenomenon which gives the book its title, and which Scotland and Scottish education gave to the world, and an exemplar of the kind of broad general Scottish education the slow but sure destruction of which by Anglicisers throughout the nineteenth century is its main subject. Yet I have never heard any Edinburgh academic remark on this book except in the most superficial and defensive manner. The Anglicisation has done its work of corruption only too thoroughly, and taught the child to despise the father. It is no consolation to us in Scotland, as we see our own university traditions crumble and decay, to witness also the signs of a

[11]

similar fate, in part government - engineered, overtaking the English universities. Yet the publication of Davie's book has given. I understand, a new lease of life to Saunders's *Scottish Democracy in the Nineteenth Century*, by creating a revived demand for it.

Occasionally one comes across certain *really* disinterested English scholars who promote Scottish studies despite their national background. One of these seems to me to be Professor Croft-Dickinson (died May 1963) of the History Department in Edinburgh, and his editions of historical documents and other works are of great value. What is needed now, in the matter of history, is a thorough study of the Union since 1707 from a Scottish point of view, doing for the nation as a whole (saving the word) what Davie has done for the universities. Edinburgh also boasts Professor T. B. Smith, a man dedicated to the independence of Scottish Law, always menaced by English Law, and whose publications, especially of institutional writings, are compulsory reading. *Scottish Manuscript Sources*, by Dr. William Montgomerie, is a must for the advanced students. But without publication, as Dr. David Craig has recently pointed out, there can be no writing and no reading; it is today and its work on which all else depends.

The supremacy of our own time is paramount not only in relation to the literature of our own time, but also in relation to the literature of the past; the present is not so if it is not forward-looking. So far I have been concerned chiefly with texts and their availability, because that is the first condition of literary studies of any sort. But after the textual problem comes that which interests me most (after creative writing): criticism. As Professor David Daiches has pointed out in his essay on the subject, in his *Collected Essays*, the first need of Scottish literary criticism is for full-length works on individual authors, periods, trends, and the like, as the ground work of a critical history of Scottish literature. Apart from Burns and Scott, and perhaps not even excluding them, the whole of this work remains to be done. This does not mean that nothing at all has been done: a good deal has, but almost entirely worthless. Academic theses which go in for such harmless sports as source hunting, or proving that a mediaeval poet is a mediaeval poet, or that James I had read his Chaucer, or that Dunbar was or was not Dunbar, are so much waste product of literature. Like the examination papers to which they bear so much resemblance, their proper goal is the

[12]

waste paper basket. It does not matter so much whether Dunbar did or did not write a certain poem; it does matter whether the poem was worth writing by Dunbar or anybody else, and that means not whether it is an example of the ballade at its best but whether it embodies values which can help us today, and our children tomorrow, to lead better lives. To decide this, we must ourselves have a vision of human life *sub specie aeternitatis* to which all literature of any age can be referred, and by which the critic must judge it, while acknowledging that his own vision will itself be judged by reality itself. Anything else is not criticism but at best idle and harmless doodling. "Why should I read Dunbar at all?" said an English undergraduate to me once. That is a serious question and one which every reader ought to ask, and not be fobbed off with humbug for an answer.

To answer this question in relation to any piece of literature under his study is the minimal task of the critic. This involves, not merely presenting facts and leaving the educated reader to draw his own conclusions: it is precisely those who cannot draw their own conclusions who most need critical help — the uneducated. This is particularly true today when the future of the race and the welfare of society depend on the rising proletariat. It is for them, the best of them, that we write particularly, and our work must be at once a critique, an interpretation, an evaluation, and a teaching. The people must NOT be left to draw their own conclusions—they must be told in no uncertain terms, where possible, exactly what is going on in a given work, and its significance for them today. No risk is too daring in the attempt to accomplish such a task, and the critic must fearlessly confront the sacred cows of establishments and drive them out of his path where necessary, and smash idols and destroy their temples where necessary, in his pursuit of true value. Anything less belongs in Swift's Academy.

It is my belief that the bulk of Scottish literature has much to give the present day in terms of life more abundant, and is thoroughly permeated by a spirit of genuine, as distinct from nominal, democracy. It is our task as students and critics to prove this to our fellow men to the best of our ability.

UNIVERSITY OF EDINBURGH

[13]

NELSON S. BUSHNELL

Walter Scott's Advent
as Novelist of Manners

ON New Year's Day of 1829 the world's most prominent novelist, in a letter to the Bishop of Llandaff, gave his reasons for *not* writing a story about Owen Glendower. Sir Walter Scott, by that time the acknowledged author of some two dozen novels published during the preceding fifteen years, began by praising the suggested subject: it provided a contrast between British and Norman cultures, a warrior " assuming the character of a Necromancer," and a " gallant resistance " affording " as many grand situations as the romantick country which they inhabit contains beautiful localities all of which . . . are perhaps a little in my way."

Here in brief was the popular conception of what a historical novel should be. " But," the novelist continued, " the misfortune is that I am totally ignorant on the subject not merely of Welch history . . . but the far more indispensible peculiarities of language habits and manners . . . . If we have not a full and clear view of ones subject . . . we may perhaps be able to sketch out an outline of a story but I should doubt extremely the possibility of being able to colour it according to nature so as to acquire that distinctive individuality which ought to distinguish so interesting a topick . . . . I am no longer as at 25 years old ready to walk thirty miles a day or ride a hundred to get hold of an old ballad or tradition and without such exertions one can do little for it is in out of the way corners and among retired humourists that men find whatever can be found of national manners."[1]

A sharp distinction is sometimes attempted beween the " romantic " historical novel and the " realistic " novel, of

---

[1] *The Letters of Sir Walter Scott*, edited by H. J. C Grierson (12 volumes. London, 1932-7), XI, 85 f. Cf. Scott's similar reason for rejecting Alfred the Great as subject for a poem, 12 March 1813, *Letters*, III, 234.

[15]

manners.[2] Scott, though traditionally the father of the former type, is credited with occasional excellence in the "manners" style, and his remarks to the bishop recognize the mastery of manners as prerequisite to success in his special field. Thus it becomes desirable to scrutinize his purposes and initial achievements in the area of manners.

Unfortunately, scrutiny is at the outset clouded by confusion as to what the term "manners" actually denotes. Everybody talks about the "novel of manners," but almost no one attempts to define it. And it cannot safely be assumed that there is any tacit consensus that makes definition unnecessary. If there exists anywhere an analysis of the methods and function of the novel of manners as a literary type, it seems to have been generally overlooked. Without attempting any universal definition, we may at least inquire what Scott himself meant by "manners," whence he derived his conception of the importance of manners to the novel, and what contributions manners made to his own first novel, over and above the "distinctive individuality" which he later specified. On the many occasions when Scott writes the word "manners," it is clear that he is referring to attributes not of an individual as such but as a member of a society — for example, the society of the Highland clans as it survived to the middle of the eighteenth century. The frequent linking of "manners" with some other term suggests that the category of social attributes must be broad enough to include particulars of economic, political, and social organizations.[3] "Manners" are paralleled to "domestic customs" and "usages;" they are perhaps reflected superficially in the typical "costume" of a people, but they also seem to extend their influence inward to affect "habits of thinking" and "traits of . . . characters," and thus become extremely relevant to the purposes of the serious

2 Scott himself insists on distinguishing between "Novels" and "Romances and Tales." *Letters*, II, 119.

3 Scott's early (1789) "essay on the origin of the feudal system" was entitled "On the Manners and Customs of the Northern Nations," according to J. G. Lockhart, *The Life of Sir Walter Scott, Bart.* (New Popular Edition, London, 1893), p. 47. Four decades later, Scott described his "Essay on Clanship, etc." as an "essay on highland Manners"—*Letters*, X, 231 and n. 2. This essay, in *The Miscellaneous Prose Works of Sir Walter Scott* (28 vols., Edinburgh, 1834-6), XX, 1-93, originated in a published review of *The Culloden Papers*, in 1816; it deals with the history, customs, and organization of the Highlands and of clanship, and provides an extended illustration of what Scott meant by "manners."

novelist.[4] " Manners " derive their peculiarity, their distinction, from the particular time, place, and culture in which they develop; in Scott's practice that time is almost always in the past; and (at least throughout his early career) he felt that first-hand knowledge of the local language and terrain was a prerequisite to a satisfactory grasp of " manners." [5]

The examples of his use of the term justify the conclusion that by " manners " Scott meant the activities, behaviour, and attitudes of members of a distinct social group. " Manners " in this sense suggest the Latin " mores," the French " moeurs," though Scott almost always avoids any suggestion that they are to be used as a basis for moral judgments. The works of Maria Edgeworth, Jane Austen, and other writers whom he admired, as well as his own novels, are brimming with examples of such " manners." One of many definitions to be found in the *New English Dictionary* comes close to confirming Scott's use: "The modes of life, customary rules of behaviour, conditions of society, prevailing in a people." Lionel Stevenson, in his recent *The English Novel* (Boston, 1960), consistently writes " manners " to indicate such phenomena, and it is thus that the term is to be understood in the following pages.

Scott had recognized the importance of manners as an ingredient in his particular brand of poetry,[6] and it has been made clear that he later realized that a mastery of manners was likewise essential to success in prose fiction. In the works of those novelists, past and contemporary, whom he singles· out for praise, or whose influence is flatteringly apparent in his own works, the exploitation of manners is often a dominant characteristic even where he does not specifically refer to it. Some of these, to be sure, subject manners to moral valuation, or highlight them as a source of comedy or satire in the style of certain examples of the dramatic comedy of manners. Among others, manners are displayed for their own sake, or as an aid to suspension of disbelief, or as a determining influence on

4 *Letters*, III, 115. f., 427, 457. 502. See also *The Journal of Sir Walter Scott*, edited by J. G. Tait and W. M. Parker (Edinburgh, 1950), p. 103.

5 *Letters*, I, 303, 343, 347; III, 104; IV, 166, 292 f., 318; XII, 278 f.

6 E.g., on 26 April 1808, referring to *Marmion* and other poems: " My plan . . . has always been . . . to exhibit ancient costume, diction, and manners "—*Letters*, II, 55. A week later George Ellis wrote to Scott of the poet's " intention . . . of making that story [*Marmion*] subservient to the delineation of the manners which prevailed at a certain period of of our history "—*Lockhart*. p. 152.

character. But whatever the motive, they are there, and there Scott saw them.

Of his predecessors in prose fiction, and of those contemporaries who published early enough, nine at least may be named whose writings won Scott's regard and influenced his theory and practice of the novel: Defoe, Fielding, Smollett, Walpole, Fanny Burney, Charlotte Smith, Maria Edgeworth, Jane Austen, and Susan Ferrier. In view of a notion current today that Scott's claim to dubious fame rests on his development of the historical novel from the eighteenth century Gothic romance, it is surprising to note the absence from this list of such names as Clara Reeve, Ann Radcliffe, and M. G. Lewis.[7] In their place we find a group of writers (the latter five—all women) whom we should label primarily novelists of manners, while of the others the three earliest all incorporate large swatches of manners material in their narratives, and Scott himself repeatedly insists that a prime object of Walpole in *The Castle of Otranto* was " to draw such a picture of domestic life and manners during the feudal times, as might actually have existed." [8]

---

[7] There is a passing complimentary reference to Reeve and Radcliffe in the memoir of Charlotte Smith prepared by Scott for John Ballantyne's projected *Novelist's Library*—*Miscellaneous Prose Works*, IV, 69. But in essays specifically devoted to each of them in the same series, Scott is critical of their achievements: " In *The Old English Baron* . . . all parties speak out much in the fashion of the seventeenth century. . . . It cannot compete with that [interest] which arises out of . . . a strict attention to the character and manners of the middle ages." " The species of romance which Mrs Radcliffe introduced, bears nearly the same relation to the novel that the modern anomaly entitled a melodrame does to the proper drama."—*Miscellaneous Prose Works*, III, 332 f., 359. Scott's choice of authors for representation in the *Novelist's Library*, avowedly a money-making scheme, is not necessarily evidence of his critical regard. Note, for example, his actual contempt for Cumberland, and his comment on Richardson: " a heavy dog, but I fear we cannot do without him "— *Letters*, II, 170, 176, f. and n. 1; VII, 15.

Miscellaneous Prose Works, III, 313-24. A selection, by no means exhaustive, of explicit statements of Scott's regard for each of the nine novelists is given below. While reading this evidence, it is well to bear in mind that Scott's loyalty toward friends and compatriots frequently betrayed him into an uncritical admiration for their writings. On a later page of this article there will be a further treatment of the influence of Walpole and Edgeworth, in greater detail.

Defoe — " Peculiar charm . . . carries the reader through . . . De Foe's compositions, and inspires a reluctance to lay down the volume till the work is finished; . . . the desire, not generally felt in the perusal of works of fiction, to read every sentence and word upon every leaf." *Miscellaneous Prose Works*, IV, 261. See also John R. Moore, " Defoe and Scott," *Publications of the Modern Language Association of America*, LVI (1941), 710-35

Scott's recognition of the manners elements in the works of these novelists—and in many others with which he was familiar —is a reflection of his inveterate personal respect for " the ordinary business of the world, . . . the exercise of the useful and domestic virtues, . . . the temper of well-ordered and well-educated society, . . . the career of simple and commonplace duty." [9] This respect is of course reflected in his preferred way of life at Abbotsford and in Edinburgh:

> I wish you could . . . light on us in an Abbotsford evening with cousins by the score & piper and dancers and old songs & a little good claret and whisky punch & people contented to be happy as their fathers were before them upon the same occasion. [10]

The same reverence for established manners underlies the whole massive structure of loyalties—family, feudal, religious; economic social, political—through which his personal integrity operated; it even penetrates his most intimate relationships, as on the occasion of Lady Scott's death:

> The Highlanders speak of their dead children as freely as of their living, and mention how poor Colin or Robert would have acted in such or such a situation. It is a generous and manly tone of feeling—and, so far as it may be adopted without affectation or contradicting the general habits of society, I reckon on observing it. [11]

And of course it predetermined the whole line of his literary development from antiquary to poet to novelist.

Scott's youthful raids on Border territory were inspired by a mixture of motives: love of exercise, adventure, and fun; pride

Fielding—" While passing from the high society to which he was born, to that of the lowest and most miscellaneous kind to which his fortune condemned him, . . . he acquired the extended familiarity with the English character, in every rank and aspect, which has made his name immortal as a painter of national manners. . . . *Joseph Andrews* continues to be read. for the admirable pictures of manners which it presents." *Miscellaneous Prose Works*, III, 78, 94.

Smollett—" *Roderick Random* may be considered as an imitation of Le Sage, as the hero flits through almost every scene of public and private life, recording, as he paints his own adventures. the manners of the times. . . . The wonderful knowledge of life and manners . . . is evinced in the tale of *Count Fathom*. as much as in any of Smollett's works." *Miscellaneous Prose Works*, III, 126, 137.

Walpole—" We refer the reader to the first interview of Manfred with the Prince of Vicenza, where the manners and language of chivalry are finely painted. . . . The applause due to . . . a of race and region; thirst for glamour; inquisitiveness as to an outmoded culture. Much of the booty he brought home was later (1802) incorporated in *Minstrelsy of the Scottish Border.* For this collection he wrote a lengthy " Introduction," beginning with a summary of Border history, of which he says:

> In these hasty sketches of border history, I have endeavoured to select such incidents, as may introduce to the reader the character of the march-men, more briefly and better than a formal essay upon their manners. . . . It is, therefore, only necessary to notice, more minutely, some of their peculiar customs and modes of life.

Here follow twenty-two thoroughly documented pages descriptive of Border manners. At the end of his "Introduction" Scott mentions the critical apparatus designed to accompany the ensuing ballad selections:

> In the notes and occasional dissertations, it has been my object to throw together . . . a variety of remarks, regarding popular superstitions, and legendary history, which, if not now collected, must soon have been totally forgotten. By such efforts . . . I may contribute somewhat to the history of my native country; the peculiar features of whose manners and character are daily melting and dissolving into those of her sister and ally.[12]

Obviously, the material that went into the editorial apparatus shared Scott's enthusiasm equally with the ballads themselves, and George Ellis quickly pointed out to the editor that Scott had taken advantage of his own " Introduction " to present a

tone of feudal manners and language . . . must be awarded to the author of *The Castle of Otranto." Miscellaneous Prose Works*, III, 323 f.

Fanny Burney—" Evelina and Cecilia are uncommonly fine compositions." *Letters*, III, 465. " A plan different from any other that the author [Scott] has ever written, although it is perhaps the most legitimate which relates to this kind of light literature . . .—to give an imitation of the shifting manners of our own time, . . . daily passing round us. . . . Formidable competitors have already won deserved honours in this department. The ladies. . . . gifted by nature with keen powers of observation and light satire, . . . from the authoress of Evelina to her of Marriage, . . . including the brilliant and talented names of Edgeworth, Austin, Charlotte Smith, . . . have appropriated this province of the novel." *The Works of Sir Walter Scott, Bart.* (London, Nelson, 1901), Vol. XVII, *St. Ronan's Well*, " Introduction," pp. v f.

body of documentary evidence in support of " your view of the state of manners among your Borderers, which I venture to say will be more thumbed than any part of the volume." [13]

In the meantime Scott had begun (c. 1799) his attempts at prose fiction with " the ambitious desire of composing a tale of chivalry, which was to be in the style of the Castle of Otranto, with plenty of Border characters, and supernatural incident." [14] These first attempts—a fragmentary " Chapter I " of *Thomas the Rhymer*, and *The Lord of Ennerdale*—in which, incidentally, manners are pretty well ignored except in the rituals of knightly service, were quickly abandoned, and he next tried his hand at sustained narrative composition in the verse of *The Lay of the Last Minstrel* (1805), which " is intended to illustrate the customs and manners which anciently prevailed on the Borders of England and ˙Scotland. . . . The description of scenery and manners was more the object of the Author than a combined and regular narrative." [15] But Scott had not renounced " the idea of fictitious composition in prose, though [he] determined to give another turn to the style of the work." By the time of his next attempt, his " early recollections of the Highland scenery and customs," along with his personal acquaintance " with many of the old warriors of 1745," had naturally suggested to him " that the ancient traditions and high spirit of a people, who, living in a civilized age and country, retained so strong a tincture of manners belonging to an earlier period of society, must afford a subject favourable for romance. It was with some idea of this kind that, about the year 1805, I threw together about one-third part of the first volume of *Waverley*, . . . having proceeded as far, I think, as the Seventh Chapter; . . . not . . .

Charlotte Smith—" We must have as many of Charlotte Smith's novels as we can compass—the ' Old Manor House ' in particular." " We should have all Charlotte Smith's very entertaining novels which are not property." " I thought of Charlotte Smith whom I admire very much." *Letters*, II, 120; VII, 15; X, 95.

Maria Edgeworth—" I liked Patronage excessively. . . . It will perhaps on the whole be less poignant, than some of her other works . . .—but in other respects I think it fully equals, and even in some degree excells it's admirable Predecessors—Indeed this Lady is one of the wonders of our age." " There is no person in the world of literature for whose name I have more sincere respect. . . . You have had a merit transcendent in my eyes." " I will never believe but what she has a wand in her pocket and pulls it out to conjure a little before she begins to write those very striking pictures of manners." *Letters*, III, 445; V, 142; VIII, 56. " Reading at intervals a novel . . . of that very difficult class which aspires to describe beyond the departure of the hero for Scotland." [16] *Waverley* was soon laid aside, and for some years Scott's chief creative energy was expended in long verse narratives, while the dream of recording Highland manners in verse continued to obsess him, even after *The Lady of the Lake* (1810).[17] Meanwhile, two circumstances nourished and conditioned in Scott the impulse toward prose fiction: the "well-merited fame of Miss Edgeworth, whose Irish characters have gone so far to make the English familiar with the character of their gay and kind-hearted neighbours of Ireland;" and Scott's undertaking (1807-8) to write a conclusion to Joseph Strutt's *Queen-Hoo-Hall*, a work "written to illustrate the manners, customs, and language of the people of England during" the reign of Henry VI. "This concluding chapter . . . was a step in my advance towards romantic composition." In his continuation Scott has gone a considerable way to carry out Strutt's intentions with respect to manners: for instance, the description of the gathering for the stag-hunt, the "lost" account of the wedding with "running at the quintain, and other rural games practised on the occasion," and the mock sermon introduced "in compliance with Mr. Strutt's plan of rendering his tale an illustration of ancient manners." But the "indifferent reception" of *Queen-Hoo-Hall* taught Scott to avoid "language too ancient" and "antiquarian knowledge too liberally" displayed, and persuaded him "that the manners of the middle ages did not possess the interest which I had conceived"—obviously, he was otherwise persuaded before undertaking *Ivanhoe*—and led him "to form the opinion that a romance, founded on a Highland story, and more modern

the actual current of society, whose colours are so evanescent that it is difficult to fix them on the canvas. . . . The women do this better—Edgeworth, Ferrier, Austen have all had their portraits of real society, far superior to anything Man, vain Man, has produced of the like nature." *Journal*, p. 144.

Jane Austen—"Miss Austen, the faithful chronicler of English manners, and English society of the middling, or what is called the genteel class." *Miscellaneous Prose Works*, IV, 69. "Miss Austen's [novels] are inimitable." *Letters*, X, 96. "Keeping close to common incidents, and to such characters as occupy the ordinary walks of life, she has produced sketches of . . . spirit and originality. . . . The turn of this author's novels . . . affords . . . a pleasure nearly allied with the experience of [the reader's] own social habits." Walter Scott, review of *Emma*, *Quarterly Review*, XIV (1815), 193, 200.

Susan Ferrier—"The living excellence of . . . the Authoress of *Marriage* and the *Inheritance*." *Miscellaneous Prose Works*, IV, 69. "He spoke with praise of Miss Ferrier as a novelist." *Lockhart*, p. 738.

events, would have a better chance of popularity."[18] In 1810, therefore, he revived the project of *Waverley;* the title was included in John Ballantyne and Co.'s list of " New Works and Publications for 1809-1810;" but James Ballantyne's lukewarm enthusiasm for the 1805 fragment of six chapters only — oddly enough, he found the " air of antiquity . . . too great " for a mere " sixty years since " — was insufficient to rouse Scott to carry on the endeavour.[19]

But all during this time, a nagging desire " to say something about poor Charley " was haunting Scott's consciousness;[20] until, apparently around Christmas-time, 1813, the impulse was re-inforced by economic pressure, the chance recovery of the abandoned fragment, and (possibly) the impending anniversary of the first Jacobite rising; and the first volume (Chapters I-XXIII) of *Waverley* was completed. Although publication of the complete novel was announced on 1st February, 1814, Scott was distracted by other commitments and did not write the remaining two volumes until June of the same year—in three weeks. The whole was published on 7th July, 1814.[21]

Our response to Scott's own account of his emergence as novelist outlined above as found, mainly, in his " General Preface " ("Abbotsford, 1st January, 1829 ") to the Waverley novels, is at first one of scepticism, so pat does his hindsight appear. But his circumstantial story of the recovery of the abandoned fragment of *Waverley,* the contemporary evidence supplied in " Appendix No. I " and " Appendix No. II," and his observations elsewhere on *The Castle of Otranto* and on the novels of Maria Edgeworth are very compelling. And the

9 *Letters*, II, 278.
10 *Letters*, X, 144 f. See also *Lockhart*, pp. 423, 428, 435, 443.
11 *Journal*, p. 173.
12 Walter Scott, *Minstrelsy of the Scottish Border* (London, 1839), " Introduction," pp. xxix f., lvii f.
13 *Lockhart*, p. 95.
14 He writes in the " General Preface " of 1829. " About this time (now, alas! thirty years since); . . . the commencement of the inundation which had so nearly taken place in the first year of the century being postponed for fifteen years later [i.e., 1814]; . . . the time of composition . . . about the end of the eighteenth century." *Works*, I, *Waverley*. " General Preface " and " Appendix No. 1," pp. xvii, xxxiii-xlix.
15 *The Poems and Ballads of Sir Walter Scott* (6 vols., Boston, 1900), " Preface." I, xxxvii. Scott's basic pre-occupation was immediately confirmed in the *Annual Review*, 1804: " The chief excellence of *The Lay* consists in the beauty of the descriptions of local scenery, and the accurate picture of customs and manners among the Scottish Borderers at the time it refers to." *Poems*, I, xxxvii, n. 1.

K

implication of these testimonies is increasingly clear: that Scott was preparing himself for the rôle of novelist of manners.

We have seen that Scott's earliest avowed model for prose fiction was Horace Walpole's notorious novel. Now the author of that preposterous concoction had from the first insisted on the importance therein of the manners ingredient:

> Belief in every kind of prodigy was so established in those dark ages, that an author would not be faithful to the manners of the times who should omit all mention of them.[22]

In the "Preface" to the second edition, published in the following year, Walpole lays claim to having created

> a new species of romance, . . . an attempt to blend the two kinds of romance: the ancient and the modern. . . . In the latter, nature is always intended to be . . . copied with success. . . . The great resources of fancy have been damned up, by a strict adherence to common life.

But the effect of common life is achieved, it appears, through the plausibility of the characterization:

> The author . . . wished to conduct the moral agents in his drama according to the rules of probability; in short, to make them think, speak, and act, as it might be supposed mere men and women would do in extraordinary positions.[23]

The claim of novelty is immediately repeated in a letter to Joseph Warton:

> I am not quite sure whether its [*The Castle's*] ambition of copying the manners of an age which you love, may not make you too favourable to it. . . . In fact, it is but partially an imitation of ancient romances; being rather

16 *Waverley*, "General Preface," pp. xvii f. Scott is guilty of a rather unusual inaccuracy when he states here that the favourable impression made by *The Lady of the Lake* (not published till 1810) was partly responsible for his first attempt at *Waverley*.
17 *Letters*, I, 303, 312 f., 324, 347; II, 26; III, 115 f.; XII, 278 f., 284, 286.
18 *Waverley*, "General Preface," pp. xix-xxi; "Appendix No. II," pp. l-lxv.
19 *Letters*, III, 456, n. 1; *Lockhart*, p. 202.
20 *Letters*, I, 341-3; II, 37, 177, 425.
21 *Lockhart*, 255 f.
22 Horace Walpole, *The Castle of Otranto*, in *Shorter Novels, Vol. III, Eighteenth Century* (Everyman's Library). "Preface to the First Edition," p. 100, first issued in Dec., 1764.
23 *The Castle of Otranto*, pp. 106, 102.

intended for an attempt to blend the marvellous of old story with the natural of modern novels.[24]

In Walpole's actual narrative, however, the jaded twentieth-century eye recognizes precious little human nature, and of manners in our sense the only examples to be found are in the herald's challenge, the retinue of the Knight of the Gigantic Sabre, and the table manners at the ensuing feast — unless the comic relief of the servants' behaviour be admitted as representative of " common life."

A dozen years later, however, Clara Reeve presented her *Old English Baron* as a follower of *The Castle* in terms that indicate that she has swallowed Walpole's prospectus whole.

> This Story is the literary offspring of the Castle of Otranto, written upon the same plan, with a design to unite the most attractive and interesting circumstances of the ancient Romance and modern Novel; . . . a picture of Gothic times and manners. . . . The Castle of Otranto . . . is an attempt to unite the various merits and graces of the ancient Romance and modern Novel. . . . There is required . . . enough of the manners of real life, to give an air of probability to the work. . . . The book . . . is excellent in [this respect].[25]

It would appear that Scott in his turn was more influenced by what had been claimed for *The Castle of Otranto* than by what had been actually illustrated in it. Scott's interest in Walpole's book as a specimen of prose fiction—already aroused in 1799, as we have seen above—was sustained over a long period. In 1811 he published a critical " Introduction " to a new edition of *The Castle*,[26] containing the following glowing tributes:

> Mr. Walpole's purpose was . . . to draw such a picture of domestic life and manners, during the feudal times, as might actually have existed. . . . It seems to have been Walpole's object to attain, by the minute accuracy of a fable, sketched with singular attention to the

24 *The Letters of Horace Walpole*, edited by Mrs. Paget Toynbee (16 vols.. Oxford, 1903-5), VI, 198; see also 201.

25 Clara Reeve, *The Old English Baron* (Revised and re-titled edition, London, 1778). " Preface," pp. iii, v.

26 " A finely printed Copy of the Castle of Otranto (1811) which was printed by the Ballantynes here & to which at their request I wrote a hasty sort of a preface," *Letters*, II, 499. Presumably this is " Sir Walter Scott's Introduction " included in Caroline F. E. Spurgeon's edition of *Otranto* (New York, n.d.) from which I quote, pp. xxxiii, xxxv f., xl, xliv, xlvi f.

costume of the period in which the scene was laid, that
same association which might prepare his reader's mind
for the reception of prodigies congenial to the creed and
feelings of the actors. . . . The remote and superstitious
period, . . . its Gothic decorations, the sustained, and,
in general, the dignified tone of feudal manners, prepare
us gradually for the favourable reception of prodigies.
. . . The bold assertion of the actual existence of
phantoms and apparitions seems to us to harmonize
. . . naturally with the manners of feudal times.
. . . [Walpole's plan was] calculated . . . to exhibit a
general view of society and manners during the times
which the author's imagination loved to contemplate.
. . . We refer the reader to the first interview of Manfred
with the Prince of Vicenza, where the manners and
language of chivalry are finely painted. . . . The applause
due to . . . a tone of feudal manners and language . . .
must be awarded to the author of the Castle of Otranto.
Seven years later, in reviewing a collection of Walpole's letters,
Scott was less enthusiastic:

His Castle of Otranto, notwithstanding the beauty of
the style, and the chivalrous ideas which it summons
up, cannot surely be termed a work of much power.[27]
But the " Dedicatory Epistle " to *Ivanhoe* (1819) is somewhat
more favourable: " Horace Walpole wrote a goblin tale which
has thrilled through many a bosom;" [28] and the biographical
memoir of Walpole which Scott prepared for Ballantyne's
Novelist's Library (1821-4) [29] is a mere expansion of the 1811
" Introduction " to *Otranto,* incorporating all the high praise of

[27] *The Quarterly Review* (New York reprint, 1819), XIX (1818), 122.
This number, dated " April," was not actually published till September
of the same year. The review is identified as Scott's in *Letters*, V.
109 and n. 3, 130 and n. 1, 136, 140; see also 169 and n. 1.

[28] *Ivanhoe* (London, Nelson, 1905), p. xxiii.

[29] *Miscellaneous Prose Works*, III (1834), 299-324. The memoir of Clara
Reeve in the same collection again praises Walpole's mastery of
manners: " In what may be called the costume, or keeping, of the
chivalrous period in which the scene of both is laid, the language
and style of Horace Walpole, together with his intimate acquaintance
with the manners of the middle ages, form an incalculable difference
betwixt *The Castle of Otranto* and *The Old English Baron.* . . . In
the present day, . . . authors . . . are obliged to make attempts
. . . to imitate the manners . . . of the times in which the scene
is laid. . . . It is not improbable that the manner in which Walpole
circumscribes his dialogue . . . within the stiff and stern precincts
prescribed by a strict attention to the manners and language of the

that novel's manners detailed above. Under these circumstances it seems fantastic to deny Walpole's contribution to Scott's evolution as a novelist of manners.[30]

The influence of Strutt's *Queen-Hoo-Hall* does not seem to have continued operative upon Scott very long, except as we have seen in persuading him to abandon for a decade the middle ages as a source for the manners which he held to be so essential to prose fiction. But there was another literary source of *Waverley* which Scott specified in the " General Preface " and in the pages of the novel itself. He—like most critics since—recognised the Irish novels of Maria Edgeworth [31] as important because of their revelation of manners. The first — and probably the most important for Scott's purposes — announces its function in its " Preface ':

> Those who were acquainted with the manners of a certain class of the gentry of Ireland some years ago, will want no evidence of the truth of honest Thady's narrative. . . . The manners depicted in the following pages are not those of the present age.[32]

Within the brief compass of the novel itself there are some two dozen passages illustrative of distinctively Irish manners in the eighteenth century—in dress, entertainment, eating, drinking; in education; in tenancy; even in burial; in fact, in practically every type of activity that the Irishman practised jointly with his fellows. These examples are reinforced by copious footnotes, and in later editions by a " Glossary " of notes, one-fourth as long as the narrative itself—apparatus prophetic of that which was to encumber Scott's own novels.

times, is the first instance of such restrictions. . . . *The Old English Baron* . . cannot compete with that [interest] which arises out of . . . a strict attention to the character and manners of the middle ages." *Miscellaneous Prose Works*, III, 332 f.

30 But cf. Stephen Gwynn, *The Life of Horace Walpole* (Boston, 1932), pp. 192 f.: " It is really pushing the claims for this fantasy much too far to say, as Miss Dorothy Stuart does [in her *Horace Walpole* (EML series, New York, 1927), p. 104; see also her *Sir Walter Scott. Some Centenary Reflections* (The English Association Pamphlet No. 89, London, 1934], that Horace Walpole by his authorship of *The Castle of Otranto* was the progenitor of Walter Scott. . . . In prose, there is not the shadow of a trace that Sir Walter was conscious of the least debt to this pioneer of romance."

31 *Castle Rackrent*, 1800; *Ennui*, 1809; *The Absentee*, 1812. The last of the series, *Ormond*, was not written till three years after *Waverley*.

32 Maria Edgeworth, *Tales and Novels* (London, 1857), IV, v f.

Ennui is cluttered with moral purpose [33] and with a complicated plot—the hero turns out to be a changeling. Many of the characters, titled and Anglicized, lack the distinctively regional quality of those in *Rackrent*; nevertheless, there are extensive passages, notably in Chapters VI and VII, detailing the typical behaviour of groups of the peasantry. Although by its title *The Absentee* indicates its special concern with a phenomenon proverbially central in Irish social and economic organization, Richard Edgeworth's "Preface to the First Edition" [34] points out that the novel is more concerned with the behaviour of Irish landlords in London than it is with conditions in Ireland, where in fact only seven of its seventeen chapters are placed. But here again we find examples of distinctively Irish manners, and the novel closes with Larry Brady's delightful account of the tenantry's reception of the absentees returning to their ancestral estate.

During the period when *Waverley* was awaiting and achieving completion, Scott records his admiration for two of Miss Edgeworth's Irish novels; [35] and his tributes to her influence indicate a special personal motive for his own exploitation of Scottish manners, the motive of patriotism. The first circumstance that

> recalled my recollection of the mislaid manuscript [*Waverley*] . . . was the extended and well-merited fame of Miss Edgeworth, whose Irish characters have gone so far to make the English familiar with the character of their gay and kind-hearted neighbours of Ireland, that she may be truly said to have done more towards completing the Union than perhaps all the legislative enactments by which it has been followed up.
>
> Without being so presumptuous as to hope to emulate the rich humour, pathetic tenderness, and admirable tact which pervade the works of my accomplished friend, I felt that something might be attempted for my own country, of the same kind with that which Miss Edgeworth so fortunately achieved for Ireland — something which might introduce her natives to those of the sister kingdom, in a more favourable light than

---

[33] "The present volumes are intended to point out some of those errors to which the higher classes of society are disposed"—*Tales and Novels,* IV. "Preface" by Maria's father, 211.

[34] *Tales and Novels,* V. 237.

[35] *Ennui,* in *Letters,* II, 511; *The Absentee, Letters,* III, 269 f., 454.

they had been placed hitherto, and tend to procure sympathy for their virtues and indulgence for their foibles. I thought, also, that much of what I wanted in talent might be made up by the intimate acquaintance with the subject which I could lay claim to possess, as having travelled through most parts of Scotland, both Highland and Lowland; having been familiar with the elder, as well as more modern race; and having had from my infancy free and unrestrained communication with all ranks of my countrymen, from the Scottish peer to the Scottish ploughman. Such ideas often occurred to me, and constituted an ambitious branch of my theory, however far short I may have fallen of it in practice. . . . The triumphs of Miss Edgeworth . . . worked in me emulation.[36]

For the purpose of preserving some . . idea of the ancient manners of which I have witnessed the almost total extinction, I have embodied in imaginary scenes, and ascribed to fictitious characters, a part of the incidents which I . . . received from those who were actors in them. . . . The Lowland Scottish gentlemen, and the subordinate characters, are not given as individual portraits, but are drawn from the general habits of the period, of which I have witnessed some remnants in my younger days, and partly gathered from tradition.

It has been my object to describe these persons, not by a caricatured and exaggerated use of the national dialect, but by their habits, manners. and feelings; so as in some distant degree to emulate the admirable Irish portraits drawn by Miss Edgeworth.[37]

The author [of *Waverley*] must have had your inimitable Miss Edgeworth strongly in his view, for the manner is palpably imitated while the pictures are original.[38]

Before proceeding to an analysis of the manners elements in *Waverley* it is well to take account of a remark of Scott's which appears in the very first-written pages of the novel:

By fixing, then, the date of my story Sixty Years before this present 1st November 1805, I would have my readers

36 *Waverley*, "General Preface," p. xix.
37 *Waverley*, "Chapter LXXII, A Postscript, Which Should Have Been a Preface." pp. 554 f.
38 *Letters*, III, 465.

understand that they will meet in the following pages
neither a romance of chivalry nor a tale of modern
manners. . . . From this my choice of an era, the understanding critic may further presage that the object of my
tale is more a description of men than manners.[39]

This remark has been cited in support of a somewhat baffling
statement: "He expressly separated [*Waverley*], when accounting for its qualities, from the novels of manners."[40] In its context,
however, the Scott passage patently refers only to contemporary
(1805) manners: "modern manners, . . . the present fashion of
Bond Street, . . . a modern fashionable." The section of the
"General Preface," pp. xvii f., quoted above has already made
clear the importance that Scott ascribed to the manners motive for
first embarking on *Waverley;* furthermore he was (in 1814) to
describe the novel as a "slight attempt at a sketch of ancient
Scottish manners;" and he was (in 1829) to excuse its haphazard
structure on the ground that it permitted him "to introduce
some descriptions of scenery and manners." [41]

Another passage from "Chapter I. Introductory" is more
puzzling in that Scott here argues that "a tale of manners to be
interesting, must either refer to antiquity, . . . or . . . those
scenes which are passing daily before our eyes." Furthermore,
he questions the interest of costumes of the period of George II,
and of the manners of the last generation (for example, apparently, "the splendid formality of an entertainment given Sixty
Years since"). This contention is so obviously and immediately
demolished in the pages of the novel itself [42] that one is forced
to conclude that Scott is for the moment adopting the pose of
that master ironist whom he knew and admired so well.

39 *Waverley*, "Chapter I. Introductory," p. 11.
40 Ernest Rhys, "Introduction" to *Waverley* (Everyman's Library, London,
1906), p. viii.
41 *Waverley* (London, Nelson, 1904), "Preface to the Third Edition," p.
i; "General Preface," p. xxi f. Oddly enough, the specific sections
of the narrative for which Scott apologizes—"the whole adventures of
Waverley, in his movements up and down the country with the Highland cateran Bean Lean"—constitute in fact only three chapters (XVII
and XXXVI f.) and are practically barren of manners material.
42 Note especially "Chapter LXXII. A Postscript . . ." p. 554: "For
the purpose of preserving some idea of the ancient manners of which
I have witnessed the almost total extinction, I have embodied in
imaginary scenes, and ascribed to fictitious characters, a part of the
incidents which I then received from those who were actors in them"
—that is to say, precisely "Sixty Years since" and in "the period of
George II."

It was through the publication and success of *Waverley* that the Great Unknown was created and in the process committed to the basic formula of his future novels. But the function of manners in this formula is, in spite of Scott's repeated assertions, only partially revealed in the course of his first completed prose narrative. In the seventy chapters that actually tell the story of Waverley (omitting " I. Introductory" and " LXXII. A Postscript ") there are some three dozen passages, ranging in length from one sentence to a couple of pages, presenting examples of manners. One is immediately struck by the fact that none of these examples is to be found within the first six chapters of the novel, written in 1805, and that almost half of them appear in Chapters VII-XXIII, written when work was first resumed, in 1813. Over half of the "Notes explanatory of the ancient customs and popular superstitions "[43] added in later editions are based on the same section, just one-quarter of the entire novel. We have already seen what had occurred within the years between 1805 and 1813 to give a new direction to Scott's pen: his reading of the manners novels of his predecessors and contemporaries, his critical assessment of them in preparation for editing a series of British Novelists,[44] and his avowal of the determination to record Highland manners. He had also become middle-aged, a laird, and a prominent public figure; and he had lived (and was continuing to live) through critical years of egalitarian and Napoleonic threats to the status quo. These later circumstances create an added motive for affirming established manners, to which *Waverley* itself points.[45]

The manners passages in *Waverley* can be roughly assigned, according to their function, among several different categories, whose limits are of course loosely defined and often overlapping.

---

43 *Waverley*, "Advertisement," p. xi.

44 which he was planning in collaboration with John Murray as early as 1808 (*Lockhart*, pp. 160, 168; *Letters*, II, 114, 119), though only in 1821 did the project begin to be realized.

45 On p. 30: " to perpetuate a great deal of what is rare and valuable in ancient manners:" p. 46: to maintain " the natural dependence of the people upon their landlords," and (p. 554) " disinterested attachment to the principles of loyalty." Scott's sympathy for the Jacobites was undoubtedly enhanced by the fact that theirs was that "party, which . . . long continued to pride themselves upon maintaining ancient Scottish manners and customs"—p. 553. He affirms the importance of the manners motive in *Waverley* in letters of July, 1814: " It was a very old attempt of mine to embody some traits of those characters and manners peculiar to Scotland the last remnants of which vanished during my own youth." " It may really boast to be a tolerably faithful portrait of Scottish manners." *Letters*, III, 456 f., 478.

Some examples of manners appear to have been introduced primarily to gratify Scott's private antiquarian tastes — for instance, the Scotch breakfast at Tully-Veolan (Ch. XII), the morning dram (Chs. XVIII, XLIV), the Highland practice of medicine (Ch. XXIV); or his dilettantism; [46] or his appetite for glamour and his sense of the comic.[47] These same passages, however, have some slight relevance to the business of the novel, in filling out " an outline of a story " by colouring " it according to nature.[48]

Obviously more organic are examples of manners which predetermine the course of the action, or assist its progress. The business of the stirrup cup involves Waverley in his minor conflict with Balmawhapple, and along with the code of the duel,[49] blackens the blot on his reputation in Gardiner's regiment. The Highland habits of cattle-lifting and the Lowland response in protection-money serve to get Waverley involved in the great adventure of his life, while the whole inception, progress, and collapse of the Rising are predicated to a considerable extent on the structure of clan society and the relations in which the Chieftain is involved with the paramount government, with his peers, and with his followers of varied degree; that is to say, in the field of manners with which Scott is primarily concerned throughout the whole novel. It appears that Scott himself was brought to see the necessity of integrating his manners scenes with the action of his story; the elaborate description of that Highland stag-hunt in which Waverley got his ankle sprained (and was thereby kept in ignorance of the extent of the Rising till it was too late for him to extricate himself) is further justified (if somewhat inadequately) by Scott's addition of a footnote in later editions, pointing out that such a hunting-party had in fact prepared for the prior rebellion, of 1715.[50]

46 And note Frank Stanley's infection, in his turn, with the virus of Waverley's " tartan fever," Chs. LXII, LXXI.
47 E.g., the feudal homage of personal service to the sovereign—pulling off his boots (Ch. XLVIII), a custom converted to serious uses (in Ch. L) when it is included among " acts of feudal homage " recalling " the ties which united to the Crown the homage of the warriors by whom it was repeatedly upheld and defended."
48 Letters, XI, 85 f.
49 Chs. XI and XIV. The latter subject impinges on the action again in the abortive squabble between Fergus and Waverley (Ch. LVII), where Scott adds his own comic interpretation—in spite of which he himself was seriously disposed to play the part of principal in an " affair of honor " as late as 1827, see Lockhart, pp. 665-7.
50 Waverley, p. 195 n.

The critic who feels that the chief concern of the novel as a literary type should be with individual human character, as it interacts with conduct, will observe that much of the manners material is applied to the determining or illustrating of the personalities of the actors. The background of Highland manners, so influential on the action, also serves to explain vivid and serviceable minor participants like Donald Bean Lean, or Brad-wardine (surely one of Scott's most plausible, lovable, and memorable achievements), as well as Fergus and Flora, who perhaps best represent as much of the technical "antagonist" of the plot as is external to Waverley himself. Fergus, a creature of some complexity, capable of extraordinary energy and of a charm reflecting, flickeringly, his Prince's, becomes really almost believable in the light of the almost unbelievable, but true, account of the manners out of which he sprang.

It appears as if Scott, having by 1813 made up his mind as to the importance of manners to his programme, utilized them to the utmost in those first seventeen chapters (VII-XXIII) immediately following his resumption of work on *Waverley,* and then, having set his scene, established his main characters, and got his action well launched, relegated manners to a slighter rôle in the carrying out of his narrative. But the effects of the manners earlier presented continue operative, so that one might say that the prime narrative function of manners in *Waverley* is to get the hero himself (granted his romantic disposition, which is of course given to him in Don Quixote fashion, in order to minister to this function) involved with the 'Forty-five and with Flora, entanglements essential, respectively, to the historical and the sentimental plots.

In addition, the manners serve a deeper and more pervasive purpose in providing material for the thematic conflict between the antique and the contemporary, the dilemma between charm and utility that generates Scott's creative activity and persistently underlies his subsequent work as a novelist and his life as a man. Yet when all (perhaps too much) has been made of *Waverley* as a novel of manners, there remain potentialities of the genre still untapped. If we seek that affirmation of manners which may be a legitimate part of the novelist's business, we find that Scott has not paid them the supreme compliment of taking them for granted — though that is hardly possible when the particular manners are chosen partly because they are unfamiliar.

What Scott might have done, however, is to make the manners themselves the real bone of contention, to be jeopardized by the villain and maintained by the hero. But this possibility is fatally obstructed by Fergus's rôle as villain when he is in fact the chief advocate of the old clan life. Conversely, Bailie Macwheeble, who will have no truck with the carryings-on of the wild Hielan' men, is on the side of the angels throughout. Furthermore, any attempt to centre the technical conflict on the value of the manners would be frustrated by the fact that Edward Waverley (and the reader) have to cope with two very distinct types of antique behaviour; the manners of Tully-Veolan, and the manners of Glennaquoich. Though the two are first presented in conflict, in the affair of the creagh, they are harmonized by the exigencies of the Rising, and both apparently suffer defeat with it. But then we discover that while Fergus goes to the block, Tully-Veolan is reprieved after all, as symbolized in the return of the Blessed Bear.

Although Scott failed in *Waverley* to take full advantage of the possibilities inherent in the novel of manners, the triumph of his 'prentice-work demonstrated his right to respectable rank among the practitioners of that type, and committed him to further efforts in it. He did not know that the financial success of this first novel and of its offspring was to lead to the ultimate disaster of a Tully-Veolan attempted at Abbotsford.

WILLIAMS COLLEGE

A. M. KINGHORN

Literary Aesthetics and the Sympathetic Emotions—a Main Trend in Eighteenth Century Scottish Criticism

I N his *Lectures*, first published in 1783, Hugh Blair summed up contemporary Scots critical opinion by assessing the value of a literary work according to the degree of emotional response it evoked. His declaration that

> we are pleased with ourselves for feeling as we ought, and for entering, with proper sorrow, into the concerns of the afflicted.[1]

reads rather quaintly now as an example of the way in which the self-consciously upright members of the *literati* tried to combine the offices of art critic and moral adviser in their efforts to discover a general criterion on which aesthetic judgments could be made. This muddling of aesthetics and ethics was the result of a development of the idea that " taste," that is, the power of judging, was a purifying influence upon mankind. Moral philosophers, nourished in an atmosphere of Newtonian scientism, invariably analysed the feelings in their quest for the Good, and those who sought the Beautiful relied a great deal on the methods and findings of the moralists, justifying their dependence by identifying the Beautiful with the Good and the True. Francis Hutcheson's version of the humanitarian doctrine of the Cambridge neo-Platonists, first made into a system by Shaftesbury,[2] gave encouragement to the idea that the sharing of others'

---

1 *Lectures on Rhetoric and Belles-Lettres* (6th ed. London, 1796, 3 vols). III. 294. Blair's conclusion is clearly derived from Hutcheson's *Inquiry* (vide n. 2, infra) and probably owes something to Steele's article on the drama of sensibility in *Spectator* No. 502, Oct. 6th, 1712.
2 *An Inquiry into the Original of our Ideas of Beauty and Virtue* (1725). Reference should be made here to Professor R. S. Crane's paper: " Suggestions Toward a Genealogy of the Man of Feeling," prepared in April. 1934. and later published in *Studies in the Literature of the Augustan Age* (Michigan 1952), 207-208. The anti-Stoical sermons and writings of

emotions might give pleasure, and Hume, Kames, Campbell, Beattie, Blair and other " emotional logicians " all admitted that a man might feel joys and sorrows with his neighbours no less acutely than on his own account.

This stress on the sympathetic feelings in connection with art found popular expression in Adam Smith's *Theory of Moral Sentiments* (1759),[3] which, like Hutcheson's *Inquiry,* drew upon Shaftesbury's extension of the creed of universal benevolence. Benevolism urged men to sympathise with the feelings of others regardless of self-interest and, in terms of literary criticism, had a much more powerful appeal than any abstract theory of aesthetics—everyone founded on a " sense of beauty " capable of development in every individual. Henry Mackenzie's *Man of Feeling* dealt with tears and a code of moral behaviour " delightfully intermingled "— in other words, it moved the reader and taught him simple ethical principles, without setting up any intellectual barrier to the right kind of appreciation. Blair, referring to the moral reformation in the English theatre, mentions Steele's *Conscious Lovers* as a comedy which

> aims at being sentimental, and touching the heart by means of the capital incidents; it makes our pleasure arise, not so much from the laughter it excites, as from the tears of affection and joy which it draws forth.[4]

Adam Smith explained many kinds of emotion with reference to this doctrine of sympathy, and his pronouncement on the function of poetry is typical of the vague theorising which the so-called philosophy of the sentiments encouraged in critics. He declared that

> Poetry . . . is capable of expressing many things fully and distinctly . . . such as the reasonings and judgments of the understanding; the ideas, fancies and suspicions of the imagination; the sentiments, emotions and passions of the heart.[5]

mid-seventeenth-century Latitudinarian divines in England and the wide dissemination of translations of French Courtesy books throughout Europe after 1670 anticipated Shaftesbury's *Characteristicks* by nearly half a century. The Scots critics, however, took their cue from Hutcheson, himself a disciple of Locke. *Vide* also Ernest Tuveson, " The Importance of Shaftesbury," *English Literary History,* XX, (1953), 267-299.

3 With reference to the start of the Blair-Kames-Beattie trend, readers should note the 30 MS *Lectures* (1748-1751) by Adam Smith which were discovered and edited by J. M. Lothian of King's College, Aberdeen University [for publication by Nelsons].

4 *Lectures,* ed. cit., III, 356.

5 *Essay on the Imitative Arts.*

The argument that poetry is " to the heart," if argument it may be called, occurs again and again in the criticism of the period. It is perhaps the most characteristic motif in the works of the Scots and " sentimental logic " forms the basis for their theory of taste from Kames and Gerard to Beattie and Blair. Newton's " science of nature " became Kames' " science of mind ", that is to say, an empirical psychology rooted in the old theory of associative attraction. To say that a poem affected the heart was simply a loose way of approving the poet's understanding, intuitive or calculated, of human emotional experience, particularly of the softer emotions like joy and grief.

Scots theories of tragedy, for example, starting with that of Hume in Book II of the *Treatise of Human Nature,* all indicate a growing insistence on extending the scope of the emotions traditionally associated with tragedy and on softening them. Those of pity and fear lost much of their violence and concentration and were multiplied into those connected with fellow-feeling. Beattie, in his *Essay on Poetry,*[6] held that one cause of the pleasure of tragedy is the fact that we tend to heighten our own emotions by sympathising with those of the audience — a common eighteenth-century idea which rested communion among men upon a combination of sympathy and self-assertion. Blair made the same point when he asked

> Is not real distress often occasioned to the Spectators by the Dramatic Representations at which they *assist*? [7]

Henry Mackenzie found that the modern tendency was to emphasise love: [8] Corneille and Dryden had first argued that love made tragedy less morbid but subsequently modified their views on the ground that love and heroic qualities did not mix. Mackenzie saw that the passion of love on the stage had become a convention which made the hero forget his more responsible kingly or patriotic duties — a sequence of events which, in Mackenzie's opinion, was likely to compel a young mind to believe that successful love is the only felicity in life. What really disturbed him was the possibility that the power of poetry and the eloquence of sentiment might mesmerise a youthful spectator into mistaking " wrong " for " right " so that the stage would cease to be a reliable instrument of moral education.

6 *Essays: on Poetry and Music as they affect the Mind: on Laughter and Ludicrous Composition* (1776).
7 *Lectures,* III, 293.
8 " Essay on the Moral Effects of Tragedy," *Lounger,* Nos. 27 and 28.

Arguments of this kind must be absorbed against the background of the time, when the " live " theatre was by no means free from the " Devil's taint ' and moderates like Mackenzie and Blair felt that they had to be on the defensive against implied charges of immorality. Hence they were continually issuing pompous warnings against the substitution of impulse in the place of higher principles of conduct based on reason or reflection. Kept in its place, love was accepted as a legitimate element of tragedy; what the critics insisted upon was that it should be disciplined and not allowed to usurp the place of " nobler " elements. The character thus endowed would then illustrate, as in their opinion it should, a balance between feeling and reflection and so become a visual aid to morality. Thus we have William Richardson describing Lear as a " man of mere sensibility " whose complete reliance on feeling had encompassed his own destruction and Hamlet as a man with an acute sense of virtue totally out of key with the intriguing Machiavellian type of society in which he had been brought up.[9]

These critics went a step further than Kames and his school, for they perceived the shortcomings of a psycho-sociological criticism which measured the mental qualities of others by our own. Shakespeare in fact provided an ideal example of minds different from our own, at least in degree; the murderer driven by ambition and a desire to live up to his own image of himself, the gullible man, the noble mind in decay and so on, and his plays showed that an academic knowledge of internal feelings was insufficient to allow a critic complete insight into human nature. With the notable exception of Hume, the Scots assumed that the realm of art was also that of real life so that art implied an attempt to create real emotions.[10] The characters in a play were therefore liable to judgment on moral grounds and such a process was considered an aesthetic process, in spite of the fact that it neglected dramatic form. The tragic heroes supposedly illustrated relations between self-interest and society, so that *Hamlet,* for example, showed the manner in which temperament could bring

[9] *Essays on Shakespeare's Dramatic Characters* (1784), 58-9: & *vide* " Essay on the Character and Tragedy of Hamlet " *Mirror* 99 & 100. [April 18 & 22, 1780], by Mackenzie. Ernest Tuveson's " The Importance of Shaftesbury " (cf. n. 2, *supra*), discusses the critics' particular interest in *Hamlet,* a play which fitted in well with their theories.

[10] In this connection *vide* Ralph Cohen, " The Transformation of Passion: a Study of Hume's Theories of Tragedy " *Philological Quarterly,* XLI (April, 1962), 450-464.

about a lack of balance between the "moral sense" and the emotions. Hamlet's tragic situation was brought about by his inability to master powerful feelings and not by any chance external grouping of hostile forces. Kames disapproved of *Romeo and Juliet* because its catastrophe relied on blind chance, hence destroying the chain of "ideas." *Othello*, on the other hand, is logically developed and he praises it.[11] Beattie's disapproval of tales of calamity was less theoretical; he said that they fatigued and overwhelmed the soul and had a bad effect upon readers especially when innocent characters are made to suffer. Both critics object to the offence against moral justice and Kames makes it clear that attention to the principles of emotional logic would ensure morality. On such a theory, the didactic possibilities of the plays were endless; Shakespeare, who filled his works with a multitude of examples of the variability of human nature, provided the critics with a test-case on which to try out their "science of mind" and speculate on the ethics of man in society.

Most discussions of tragedy were supported by a solid reading of neo-classic commentators on the subject; Hume, Kames, Campbell, Beattie, Blair, Mackenzie and Richardson were all well-versed in past theory [12] and tried with some success to make fresh contributions to the existing fund of ideas. The same cannot be said, however, for their examinations of the comic, which in general contrived to conceal their lack of depth behind a skilful handling of previous theory.[13] Beattie's was typical and as might be expected, confined itself to a treatment of "sympathetic" laughter. Everyone had the power to appreciate humour "sentimentally," according to Beattie, because its result "is at once both natural and innocent." [14] His illustrations from comic literature bear out that his own test for the comic is its power to appeal to the natural human emotion that makes a man laugh.

---

11 Henry Home, Lord Kames, *The Elements of Criticism* (1762: 5th ed. Lond 1774, 2 vols.), II, 381.

12 *Vide* Earl R. Wasserman, "The Pleasures of Tragedy," *English Literary History*, XIV (1947), 283-307. This deals with Hume's predecessors in the field.

13 Addison discussed Hobbes' theory in *Spectator*, No. 47 (April 24, 1711) and Hutcheson modified it in his *Essay on Laughter*, contributed to the *Dublin Journal*, reprinted in 1729 and again in 1734, latterly as *Hibernicus' Letters (made by James Arbuckle)*. These discussions provided most of the material drawn upon by subsequent eighteenth-century investigators.

14 *Essay on Laughter and Ludicrous Composition* (3rd ed., corrected, London, 1779), 303.

Unfortunately, he does not define this emotion and is content to declare that the kind of stimuli required to excite it are con- tained in such incidents as are designed to bring out the charms of virtue and the odiousness of vice. Mackenzie's assertion that the subject of modern comic writing is " the history of the human heart in trying situations "[15] summed up the attitude of all "enlightened" readers. For him the appeal of a character like Falstaff lay in a peculiar combination of humour and grossness, which draws sympathy from the audience.[16] The elder Warton had made a similar observation with regard to Caliban in whom, according to the writer, Shakespeare had succeeded in creating a convincing character outside the bounds of human experience by attending judiciously to detail and mingling human and sub- human characteristics.[17] What both Mackenzie and Warton meant, although they did not express it very well, was that the human elements in Falstaff and Caliban rendered these characters acceptable in terms of human sympathies.

Blair takes the familiar line that humour is an instrument of moral censure and ultimately of moral education, and claims that its inclusion in a work of literature is justifiable only if it accomplishes this end. Campbell had stated, unoriginally, that the object of laughter was invariably a group of things " in which there is some striking unsuitableness."[18] Blair applies this Hutchesonian theory to comedy which, he claims, should hold up to ridicule the parts of men's characters

> . . . which raise in beholders a sense of impropriety, which expose them to be censured; and laughed at by others, or which render them troublesome in civil society.[19]

This unenlightening statement is as far as any of the Scots goes towards working out a comprehensive theory of comedy; like the *Mirror* essayists Blair approved of the stage and the novel only so far as they were intended to purge society of its ills and encourage in an audience the emotions of goodwill.

---

[15] " Essay on Comedy," *Lounger*, Nos. 49 & 50 (January 7 & 14, 1785).
[16] " Essay on the Character of Falstaff," *Lounger*, Nos. 29 & 30 (May 20 & 26, 1786).
[17] *Adventurer*, No. 97 (October 9, 1753)
[18] George Campbell, *The Philosophy of Rhetoric* (1776: 2nd ed., London, 1801, 2 vols.), I, 79. Campbell is following Hutcheson, whose ex- planation was founded on the notion of contrast or incongruity.
[19] *Lectures*, III, 332.

The implication behind this view of the function of the writer is more complex than at first sight appears. In his *Essay on Poetry*, Beattie starts off by asking the old question of whether the end of poetry is pleasure or instruction and answers it by stating that a poem ought to succeed in both respects before it merits the highest praise. Like Blair, Beattie did not believe that a poet ought to aim deliberately at instruction and ignore the reader's pleasure for he states clearly that if a poem does not please it has failed in its purpose. He qualifies this view by adding that in most cases a poet must introduce an element of instruction into his work if the general taste, that is, the preference of the majority of trained minds, is to be gratified. This amounts to a distinction between a poem's end as a literary achievement and its end as a social product for, if Beattie's theory is to be accepted, a poem, as a poem, need inculcate no moral values, though as a social force it should do so. The writer seems to imply that good poetry is not necessarily "good" by itself, but becomes wholly admirable only if it be also on the side of virtue, the natural disposition of the human mind. He exclaims:

> So true it is, that the bard who would captivate the heart must sing in unison to the voice of conscience.[20]

This is another recurrent theme in Scots criticism. Since poetry was supposed to be the voice of nature uncorrupted by custom, anything which touched the heart was endowed with virtue and therefore carried instruction along with it. Critics like Dryden and Johnson failed to explain whether the "instruction" which poetry ought to provide was instruction in the truth of human nature, virtuous and vicious alike, or whether it was moral instruction on ideal conduct. The argument of Beattie and other followers of Shaftsbury and Hutcheson, which was dependent on a purely hypothetical proneness of the human constitution to virtue, provided only a theoretical solution to this problem, by enlarging the meaning of the term "instruction." For the philosophers it meant not only the communication of fresh knowledge, but also that

> . . . which awakens our pity for the sufferings of our fellow creatures; promotes a taste for the beauties of nature: makes vice appear the object of indignation and ridicule; inculcates a sense of our dependence upon

20 *Essay on Poetry*, ed. cit., 16-17.

Heaven; fortifies our minds against the evils of life; or promotes the love of virtue and wisdom, either by delineating their native charms, or by setting before us in suitable colours, the dreadful consequences of imprudent and immoral conduct.[21]

It thus became possible for critics to praise style and condemn matter in the same work; Kames and Blair object to Milton's picture of Sin and Death although they praise his power of description in painting it and all the Scots who wrote on Homer condemn the behaviour of his characters. Beattie himself attacked *Gulliver's Travels* because Swift's imagery was frequently " filthy and indecent " and, what was in his view worse, because " human nature itself is represented as the object of contempt and abhorrence." [22] That Swift was a moralist whose social ideals made him an ironic critic of things as he saw them was a possibility that never occurred to Beattie, who considered *The Tale of a Tub* to be without equal as a piece of humorous writing but observed sadly that it had a tendency " to produce, in the mind of the reader, some very disagreeable associations of the most solemn truths with ludicrous ideas." [23] Again, with reference to Smollett's *Roderick Random* and *Peregrine Pickle,* Beattie states that they are

> . . . two performances, of which I am sorry to say, that I cannot allow them any other praise, than that they are humorous and entertaining.[24]

At first reading such a statement appears to reflect no more than the fatuousness of the writer, but it nevertheless illustrates his consistent critical principle that literature must do more than please. If the function of literature were simply to please and nothing else, criticism like this ought to be favourable to any novelist. Beattie disapproved of Smollett because his two novels did not instruct as well as entertain; he did not consider that they might be included in the category of works depicting " the dreadful consequences of imprudent and immoral conduct," although this would surely have been permissible in the light of their matter. Criticism of fiction seems to have been based on different criteria from that of poetry probably because all the Scots started off under the disadvantage of believing that the

---

21 *Ibid.,* 120.
22 *Dissertations, Moral and Critical* (1783), 515-516.
23 *Ibid.,* 516.
24 *Ibid.,* 570.

novel, like the theatre, was a potential threat to morality. Both Beattie and Blair adhered to the neo-classic notion that the literary "kinds" were distinct from one another but neither explained why this should be. It seems evident, though, that the position of a literary *genre* in the hierarchy was determined by the extent of its capacity to draw out the sympathetic emotions. On such a scale, the dramatic and especially the tragic was placed highest and the novel lowest. Few allowances were therefore made for fiction which, at its best, would have been considered a stylised product of modern urban society, itself corrupt and remote from nature.

Another feature of Scots criticism at this time was its lack of a pronounced bias of the sophisticated kind such as existed during the sixteenth and seventeenth centuries and the way in which it related poetic simplicity and moral purity. "Only an innocent mind can relish the effusions of real unaffected simplicity" exclaimed an anonymous contributor to the Edinburgh *Weekly Magazine*,[25] while another, writing to the *Scots Magazine,* informs his readers that

> Simplicity is the native dress of truth, and a sincere love of the latter is seldom without a taste for the former.[26]

This links up with the Scots quest for original genius. When these critics sought a genius, they were inclined to look for him either in the remote past, or in a modern unsophisticated environment to which urban decadence had not penetrated. The notion that inspiration was more at liberty to function when human nature was uncorrupted by sophisticated customs led Beattie and his contemporaries to regard purity and simplicity of poetic language as an ideal genuine emotional expression, unattainable by the educated writer.[27] For this reason "correct" qualities were not expected of primitive poets, nor of modern poets with untutored ability whose natural origins and environment had preserved their sublime imaginations.

---

25 *Weekly Magazine or Edinburgh Amusement*, XXIV, (April 14, 1774) by "A Lover of Poetry."

26 "On Taste and Elegance," *Scots Magazine*, LV, (June, 1793).

27 Mackenzie, who succeeded Hume as a patron of "original genius" and wrote one of the earliest reviews of Burns' Kilmarnock volume, said in a letter to Elizabeth Rose: "One great excellence of (ancient compositions) is a certain manly unaffected simplicity which we do not always find in our best modern performances. We are often obliged to resort to Expression for that energy which they found in Idea." December 22, 1776: (MS 647, National Library of Scotland).

This seeking after simplicity brought the critics to the ballads; even a critic as far back in time as Addison had been fascinated by the "natural" qualities of ballads and the second half of the century saw a growing interest in folk-poetry which was not merely the result of a focus on the past. Percy summarised the literary interests of many of his contemporaries when he wrote

> In a polished age, like the present, I am sensible that many of these reliques of antiquity will require great allowances to be made for them. Yet have they, for the most part, a pleasing simplicity, and many artless graces, which in the opinion of no mean critics, have been thought to compensate for the want of higher beauties, and if they do not interest the imagination, are frequently found to interest the heart [28]

and, speaking of Scots music and ballads, David Herd asserted that

> the characteristic excellence of both . . . is a forcible and patriotic symplicity, which at once lays strong hold on the reflections, so that the heart itself may be considered as an instrument which the Bard or Minstrel harmonises, touching all its strings in the most delicate and masterly manner.[29]

Both Beattie and Blair drew attention to the qualities inherent in simple music and verse which made them dear to the heart of the Scot and they noted that the inspiration behind the ballads (under which general head they included genuine or spurious ballads, songs and in fact any poem written in short stanzas) was the same inspiration as that which gave expression to great poetry and consisted of the urge of strong emotions. The "anonymous" verse on the title-page of the Kilmarnock edition of Burns's poems displayed such clear prejudices in favour of the natural origin of poetry as to suggest a calculated approach to the critics:

> The Simple Bard, unbroke by rules of Art,
> He pours the wild effusions of his heart;
> And, if inspir'd, 'tis Nature's pow'rs inspire
> Her's all the melting thrill, and her's the
> [kindling fire.[30]

[28] *Reliques of Ancient English Poetry* (1767: pref.)
[29] *Ancient and Modern Scots Songs, Heroic Ballads* (Edinburgh, 1769), pref. iii.
[30] Robert Burns, *Poems, Chiefly in the Scottish Dialect,* (Kilmarnock, 1786).

As theory, this strongly emotional criterion was a convenient generalisation which enabled a "romantic" or subjective judgment of literature to support or even at times to supersede a neo-classic or formal method of assessment. It did not take into account the possibility that literature might have certain effects not connected with the rousing of emotions, nor did it consider that a given work might not necessarily affect every individual to the same emotional extent. On such a standard of judgment, there was a danger of placing inferior works, which had no other aim than that of being sentimental, above masterpieces of wider scope in which the rhetorical evocation of such emotion was not the outstanding quality. Application of this standard failed to enlighten readers as to why a poet like Milton was of the first rank; in fact, the versifiers of the eighteenth-century, like Logan, Michael Bruce or Wilkie, to cite but three, were dubbed "geniuses" with less hesitancy than Milton was, since their appeal to the sympathetic emotions was more obvious and immediate. If a poet wrote "to the heart" and supplied incidents calculated to affect the tender sentiments of the reader, then he was sure of praise from the critics. Such an approach to criticism had been carefully worked out in theory, but in practice it became loose and careless, partly because of its limited emotional concerns and partly because of the critics' failure to build up a vocabulary of precise terminology by which the complicated effects of literature could be accurately described. Periodical reviewers during the last quarter of the century habitually appraised insignificant poets in the same terms as were customarily applied to Spenser and Milton. At the same time, there was no proper outlet for appreciation of new and original poetic work, such as that of Fergusson and Burns in Scots. The critics were instead bemused by Macpherson's "Ossian" poems. Blair observed that the outstanding characteristic of Ossianic poetry was the mingling of heroic and elegiac elements, the paradox of joy in tears—"the joy of grief"—when the very sadness of the world encouraged the benevolent emotions and the recurrent theme was that of the pathos of youth in love together with the eternal loneliness and transience of all creatures. The "joy of grief" was the highest joy which life held for Fingal and was a most powerful emotional expression, precisely, in fact, what critics were looking for in poetry. Their hearts were touched by the VIth Book of *Fingal*:

> 'Swaran,' said the king of hills, 'today our fame is greatest. We shall pass away like a dream. No sound

will remain in our fields of war. Our tombs will be lost
in the heath. The hunter shall not know the place of
our rest. Our names may be heard in song. What
avails it, when our strength hath ceased?'
or by the conclusion of the *Songs of Selma*:
>Why does Ossian sing? Soon shall he lie in the narrow
>house, and no bard shall raise his fame! Roll on, ye
>dark-brown years; ye bring no joy on your course! Let
>the tomb open to Ossian, for his strength has failed.

Taking such fustian as an example, it is historically clear
that the question which "Ossian" raises in connection with
literary criticism concerns the relationship of the poems to the
critical and psychological requirements of the time; in other
words, one must wonder to what extent Macpherson conditioned
the practical criticism of Blair and his school and *vice-versa*. It
is evident that Macpherson wished to please the critics and that
he wrote his poetry accordingly, for *Fingal* reflects many, if not
all, of the prejudices of the *literati;* in it, and in the remainder
of the Ossianic "fragments," we find what amounts to a testi-
monial to their author's capacity to know his public. Ossian's
"characteristic excellence,' according to Blair, lay in his ability
to "paint to the heart' and the *Critical Dissertation* is mainly
concerned with pointing out this quality in the light of Blair's
theory of "simple" poetic origins. In the works of Ossian we
find, states Blair

>tenderness and even delicacy of sentiment . . . our
>hearts are melted with softest feelings, and at the same
>time elevated with the highest ideas of magnanimity
>generosity and true heroism [31]

qualities which are found in Homer, Virgil, Dante, Tasso
Shakespeare and Milton. Michael Bruce and Burns were later
revealed to the public in the same terms; they understood the
sentimental side of human nature and their poetry excelled in
the pathetic.

Yet the theory was significant, even if the manner of its
practice was not. Wordsworth's main idea regarding the nature
of the imagination was that it consisted in seeing everything in
its human relations or sympathies; the possession of such power,
according to both Wordsworth and Coleridge, distinguished
imagination from mere fancy. The Scots were thus expressing
an idea which was to become fundamental in nineteenth-century

[31] *A Critical Dissertation on the Poems of Ossian.* (1763), 11.

criticism when they demanded of a poet that he should " paint to the heart as well as to the fancy." Such an approach to the mind of the poet, denying or distrusting his artifice and applauding his " sincerity," may strike the modern analytic critic as naïve, but it comes at least as near as he does to understanding the success of a poet like Burns. Burns touched a chord which his rivals failed to touch and no amount of descriptive criticism will explain exactly what it was that Burns's verses did to their early readers.

Henry Mackenzie's words of encouragement to his cousin Elizabeth Rose:

> You need not be in the smallest degree afraid of pronouncing on the merit of Poetry . . . it is felt, and therefore it is excellent. 'Tis but a cold-blooded quality that first discovers its excellence, and then pronounces it to be felt [32]

relegates the " science of mind " to a secondary position and, by extolling the superiority of " men of feeling," makes known a conception of the critic's art which, in spite of its psychological origins in the theories of literary aestheticians, is anti-intellectual. Obsession with the virtue of the romantic ideal from Sidney onward was not favourable to the development of sound theory, wedded to equally sound practice, particularly since the majority of the theorists did not themselves cultivate the art which they professed to discuss. The gradual movement towards simplicity and naturalness of situation and language which their essays reveal led inevitably to the poetic manifesto of the *Lyrical Ballads*, which, with the *Preface*, transformed the theories of Beattie and Blair into a more practicable scheme of things without, in fact, adding very much to what the latter had said. The Scots critics seem to have had a clearer notion of what the romantic poem was to be like than any of their English contemporaries, and within their rather severe limitations they tried very hard to define or at least describe it.

UNIVERSITY OF THE WEST INDIES

---

[32] 12 May, 1770 (*MS 647*, National Library of Scotland).

Scottish Popular Ballads and Lyrics of the Eighteenth and Early Nineteenth Centuries: Some Preliminary Conclusions

ANY discussion of Scottish lyrical poetry in the 18th and early 19th centuries must be based on three types of source-material: (a) manuscripts; (b) printed broadsides, chapbooks and slips; (c) printed song-books, with or without music. For the sake of convenience, I have restricted myself to sources which were written or printed in Scotland, and chosen 1786 as the terminal date for printed material, and 1825 for MSS. This limitation has the disadvantage of excluding Thomson's *Orpheus Caledonius* of [?1726] and 1733, and Ritson's *Scotish* [sic] *Songs* of 1794, simply because they were printed in England. Nevertheless, the general conclusions which emerge from an examination of the primary sources are not affected by the omission of these and similar works.

The most important of the existing manuscripts [1] are:

(1) Elizabeth Cochrane's Song Book [ca. 1730]. Harvard College Library, MS Eng. 512.

(2) Agnes Thorburn Creighton: A Collection of Old Songs [1818]. Ewart Pubic Library, Dumfries.

(3) David Herd's MSS [1766]: British Museum Add. MSS 22311-2. One folio of these MSS is in the Edinburgh University Library, La. II. 358. 2.

(4) Robert Jamieson's Brown MS [1783]. Edinburgh University Library, La. III. 473.

(5) William Motherwell's MSS [ca. 1825]. 6vo. All in Glasgow University Library, except for one ballad note-book in the possession of Sir John Stirling Maxwell.

---

[1] Listed by William Montgomerie, "Bibliography of the Scottish Ballad Manuscripts 1830-1825," unpublished Ph.D. thesis (Edinburgh, 1954); and in part by Francis James Child, *The English and Scottish Popular Ballads*, 5 vols. (Repr. New York, 1957), V, pp. 397-399.

(6) A Miscellaneous Collection of MSS in the National Library of Scotland. MS 893, bound in one volume.

(7) The Miscellanies of Sir Walter Scott in the National Library of Scotland, and other MSS of Scott in the N.L.S. and at Abbotsford.

(8) "The Collection of an old lady's complete set of ballads" [Sir Walter Scott's Title, 1805-7 and 1818]: at present in Broughton House, Kirkcudbright.

(9) Thomas Mansfield's Manuscript [1770-80]: lost for much of this century, at present in Broughton House, Kirkcudbright.

(10) Thomas Percy's Papers (MSS sent from Scotland to Bishop Percy after 1765) Harvard College Library.

(11) Thomas Wilkie's MS Notebooks [1813-15]. National Library of Scotland, MSS 121-3; 877.

(12) William Tytler's Brown MS [1783]. Aldourie Castle.

Nos. 4 and 12, the Jamieson Brown MS and the Tytler Brown MS, record part of the repertoire of a particular singer, Mrs. Brown of Falkland.

These twelve MSS have authority primarily for the history of individual songs. With the possible exception of David Herd's MSS, they do not add significantly to our knowledge of the *types* of song current in Scotland during this period; and even in this solitary instance, of the 370 items in Herd's MSS, only seven remain unprinted either

(1) By Herd himself, in *Scottish Songs* [1st. edn. 1769, 2nd edn. 1776],

(2) by Francis James Child, in *The English and Scottish Popular Ballads,* 5 vols., 1882-98.

or (3) by Hans Hecht, Songs from David Herd's Manuscripts, Edinburgh 1904.[2]

Although the Mansfield MS is of great importance for those investigating the sources of Burns's songs in that it preserves a number of otherwise unknown versions of songs later touched up or transformed by Burns, it contains few songs of which we have no other record; and most of the remaining eleven MSS are of value mainly to the student of the Child Ballads. It would appear, then, that MS material is not of primary concern to those whose main interest is in Scottish sung lyrics of the 18th century,

[2] See William Montgomerie. "Some Notes on the Herd Manuscripts." *Edinburgh Bibliographical Society Transactions (1948-55),* III (1957).

and whose purpose is to formulate general "literary - historical" conclusions about Scottish song during its golden age. The grounds on which this conclusion is based can best be exhibited in relation to a single typical MS, Mrs. Creighton's Collection of 1818. At first sight, the MS appears to have the authenticity of a direct transcript of a folk-singer's words: the title page states that it is "written from the memory of Mrs. Creighton by her daughter, Agnes Thorburn Creighton, January 31st MDCCCXVIII," and this suggests that the words were taken down from Mrs. Creighton's recitation or singing. But the MS is obviously a fair copy, behind which there must lie a rough draft of some kind. The rough draft may have been in A.T.C.'s hand, the transcript of material orally transmitted by her mother; or it may even have been in her mother's hand, for that is surely one possible interpretation of "written from the memory of Mrs. Creighton"—Mrs. Creighton's memory prompted her own rough copy. In either case, there was nothing to prevent A.T.C. from collating the final draft with printed texts, where these were available, and indeed there is some evidence which suggests that this happened, at any rate with certain pieces. Mrs. Creighton's collection contains Scott's *Young Lochinvar*, Burns's *The Soldier's Farewell*, a parody of the ballad *William and Margaret*, and *Alcanzor and Zaida*: a *Moorish Tale* of 104 lines, all of which must at some stage have had printed texts behind them: at the very least, they must have been originally *learnt* from print.

At the same time, many of the other texts exhibit variations from other versions of the songs concerned, which can best be explained by their having passed through Mrs. Creighton's memory, as the title-page claims. It seems probable that she knew by heart all or most of the 106 pieces in the MS; that she had learnt many, perhaps most, of them from a printed source, often a broadside or chapbook; and that some, but by no means all, of the songs and poems may have been collated with a printed source before the MS was copied into its present form. The Creighton MS has thus some of the attributes of a commonplace book; it is valuable primarily as an indication of late eighteenth and early nineteenth century taste; and the probability that the proximate sources of many pieces appear to have been song-books, chapbooks and broadsides, seems to lessen the authority of this MS and elevate that of the printed sources themselves. Now what I have just said about the Creighton MS is equally true of much, but not all, of the *song* material in the other MSS, although it does not apply to the traditional ballads (Child Ballads) in such MSS as the two Brown MSS or the Thomas Wilkie MSS, and others like them, which formed the basis of the great printed ballad collections of the nineteenth century, including Child's own.

It follows, then, that we shall be wise to devote our main attention to printed sources. Of these, the most interesting, and the most difficult to cover with any approach to completeness, are the white-letter broadsides, chapbooks containing ballads and songs, and the song sheets, the latter being sometimes " slips " or galley " pulls " containing one or more songs. It seems evident that broadsides and chapbooks printed by the popular printers of Aldermary Churchyard, London, and such northern English centres at Newcastle-on-Tyne and York, were widely circulated by itinerant pedlars and ballad-singers. It is often impossible to state when or where a broadside or chapbook was printed because of the lack of a date or printer's name, and the inclusion of specifically Scottish songs is by no means an infallible guide, since these were often printed in London chapbooks or sheets, presumably for sale in both Scotland and London. Furthermore, since Scottish popular printers included a fair proportion of English songs in their productions, and since Irish collections printed both Scots and English songs, one is led to conclude that the popular song market was at this time an all-British one. As the eighteenth century advanced, broadsides and chapbooks printed in Scotland itself became increasingly common. Many song chapbooks were issued by the printers J. & M. Robertson of Glasgow between 1780 and 1810,[3] and other printers in Paisley, Falkirk, Stirling, Dumfries, Edinburgh and elsewhere exploited the popular market at about the same time. Material originating in English black-letter broadsides of the seventeenth century was reprinted in Scottish chapbooks of the early nineteenth century, such as those printed by T. Johnston of Falkirk and M. Randall of Stirling (c. 1815). For example, one Randall chap includes *The Maid's Complaint for Jockey* (l.1. " Love did first my thoughts employ "), a pseudo-Scots song of the type published in London by Thomas Durfey in the late seventeenth century; in another, *The Frigate Well-Mann'd* (l.1. " In blows a fresh and pleasant gale "), a woman is compared to a frigate in a way that

---

[3] See W. Walker. *Peter Buchan and Other Papers on Scottish and English Ballads and Songs* (Aberdeen, 1915), pp.272 ff.

was standard in Durfey's time. These correspondences could be multiplied, and they help to document the close connection between Scottish song and the English broadside tradition.

There may well be, as is often claimed, a specific "broadside" or "stall" type of song; but its existence did not preclude the appearance of other kinds of song in the printed material sold at stalls and carried into the countryside by travelling packmen. This is well illustrated by a collection of 42 whiteletter broadsheets in the British Museum,[4] which can be proved to have been printed at Aberdeen, and which bear the dates 1775 or 1776. They contain a fairly high proportion of comic songs, including some of the "Merry Muses" type; many Scottish songs, some of which have a specific Aberdeen reference, and quite a large number of English ones. One broadsheet prints the English *Blind Beggar's Daughter of Bethnal Green* (l.1. "It was a blind beggar had long lost his sight"), together with the Scottish *Bonny Highland Lad* (l.1. "Down by yon shady grove"). Two more of these Aberdeen broadsides were reprints of well-known English productions, *The Berkshire Lady's Garland: Or Bachelors of Ev'ry Station* and *The Bristol Garland: Or The Merchant's Daughter of Bristol*. Of the few Child Ballads in this Aberdeen series, one is *Barbara Allen*, widely distributed throughout the British Isles and America; another is the English *Chevy Chase*. Finally, and even more typically, *The Roving Maids of Aberdeen's Garland*, dated 30 Jan. 1776, contains as its third song the English *Golden Grove* (l.1. "A wealthy young squire of Tamworth we hear.").

Now Aberdeenshire has for centuries been one of the main centres of balladry and popular song in the British Isles. A surprisingly large number of Child's "A" texts (his main or favoured texts) turn out to be Aberdeenshire ones, and at the present day the North East is richer than any other part of Scotland in the remains of the old popular song. Of some 10,000 variants of Lowland Scottish songs recorded by the School of Scottish Studies since 1945, several thousand are from the Aberdeen area alone. Many songs in the repertoire of present-day Aberdeen folk-singers are of English or Irish origin, and there seems to be a fairly common impression that such borrowing took place mainly during the nineteenth century. The existence of these late eighteenth century broadsides, however, documents

4 1346 m.7, *Ballads.*

[53]

the popularity of English material in this area as early as 1775, and one may well suspect that songs and ballads from the English broadsides entered oral tradition in Aberdeenshire at least a hundred years before this. It is perhaps significant that the first song book ever printed in Scotland, Forbes' *Cantus* of 1662,[5] was an Aberdeen production. It is a learned, not a popular song-book; and with perhaps one or two exceptions, all its songs are English. Thus, in all probability, the song culture of Aberdeenshire was not simply all-Scottish, but an all-British, at quite an early date.

Broadsides and chapbooks, then, are sometimes the closest we can get to popular tradition, and often have at least as much authority as manuscripts. They sometimes contained songs which their printers acquired from oral tradition; while, conversely, townsfolk and country people might learn songs from printed copies, only to transmit them to others by oral communication, thus initiating the "folk process," in the course of which some stanzas would disappear, and others perhaps be modified beyond all recognition.

The last primary sources to be considered are the printed song books. Collections of words without music far outnumber those which print the music, and most of the former are 12mo, 16mo, or 18mo volumes ranging from about 100 pp. to 400 pp. in length, with an elaborate title-page (often engraved) and an index of first lines. Even when known, authors' names are often suppressed; where possible, the titles of well-known tunes to which the songs can be sung are mentioned; and sometimes the song books will give the name of a well-known professional singer into whose repertoire the song has passed, such as " Mrs. Catley" or "Signor Tenducci." Song books with music were often of folio or quarto size, and finely engraved. The *Perth Musical Miscellany* of 1786, 12mo, 347 pp., was the first pocket-book with music to be printed in Scotland, so far as I am aware. The best bibliography of Scottish song books is that in J. C. Dick, *The Songs of Robert Burns: now first printed with the melodies for which they were written*, London 1901, but is far from complete. Some sixty-five song books, with or without music, are known to have been published in Scotland before 1786. They contain between them approximately 2,500 separate songs. A first line index is in course of preparation, which will

---

[5] The only known copy is in the Huntington Library. There is a photostat copy in the National Library of Scotland.

classify them according to *genre* and linguistic category, but until this is completed it is impossible to say more than that (a) songs written by Englishmen appear to outnumber those of Scottish origin; (b) a large number of songs composed in Scotland are linguistically indistinguishable from English songs on the printed page; (c) the pieces in the song books are broadly speaking the same *sort* of songs as those in the chapbooks, slips, broadsides or manuscript collections. The song books appear to print a larger number of Art songs than do other source-groups.

The pieces in the song books, chapbooks, broadsides and manuscripts fall into four generally recognized types or *genres,* which we may designate (1) Traditional (" Child ") Ballads (2) Folk Songs (3) Broadside Ballads (4) Art Songs. Although it is natural to associate each of these types with its own class of source material, the correspondences are at best merely approximate. Manuscripts may contain laboriously copied broadsides; art songs circulated in chapbooks cheek by jowl with examples of gross popular drollery; " folk songs " and traditional ballads were printed in the song books. Nevertheless, when every allowance has been made for the difficulty of classifying individual songs, it is possible to formulate certain general characteristics of matter and style which apply to each of these four types.

There is surely no need to quote a traditional ballad in full: all that is necessary is to mention three titles, *Lord Randal, Sir Patrick Spens, The Wife of Usher's Well.* A lyrical folk-song is a song like this one from the Thomas Wilkie MS:[6]

> Where will bonny Ann lie
> Where will bonny Ann lie
> Where will bonny Ann lie
> I' the cauld nights o' winter.
>
> Where but in the hen bauks
> Where but in the hen bauks
> Where but in the hen bauks
> Amang the rotten timmer oh.
>
> There shall bonny Ann lie
> There shall bonny Ann lie
> There shall bonny Ann lie
> Till the warm nights o' simmer.

MS 122, National Library of Scotland : *Old Scots Songs etc. Collected mostly in Roxburghshire, Berwickshire, and Selkirkshire :* by Thomas Wilkie (ca. 1814), p. [i].

Wha d'ye think will cuddle her
Wha d'ye think will cuddle her
Wha d'ye think will cuddle her
A' the cauld nights o' winter o

Wha but Patie o' the glen
Wha but Patie o' the glen
Wha but Patie o' the glen
Will cuddle bonny Annie O'!

Or else it's a song like this one, from the Mansfield MS.—the source of Burns's " Comin' Thro' the Rye " :[7]

Jennys a' wet, poor Body
Coming frae the Kye
Jennys a' wet, poor Body
Coming frae the Kye
She draggled a' her petticoat
She draggled a' her petticoat
She draggled a' her petticoat
And Jennys never dry.

Typical of the Stall Ballad is a whole class of ballads purporting to be the last words of a criminal, such as *The Last Words of James Mackpherson, Murderer* [8] (the source of Burns's " MacPherson's Farewell ")—a broadside preserved in the Roseberry Collection in the National Library of Scotland, and apparently printed in the early eighteenth century; or such a comic ballad as *An Excellent new Ballad, intituled, The Four Drunken Wives that live at Belsiehill,* to the tune of the Four Drunken Maidens at the Nether-bow. Edinburgh, 1710.[9] And typical, too, of the broadside and chapbook type is a well-known series of political ballads, Jacobite and anti-Jacobite, on events from 1689 to 1741, such as *Killiecrankie* (l.1. " Clavers and his Highlandmen ") [10] or *Tranent Muir* (l.1. " The Chevalier being void of fear ").[11] The author of the last song is known, and we may prefer to classify it as a popular art song, even although it

---

[7] Frank Miller, *The Mansfield Manuscript : An old Edinburgh Collection of Songs and Ballads* (Dumfries, 1935), p.19; MS, p.36.
[8] In *Broadsides and Ballads,* National Library of Scotland, Ry III. a. 20(29).
[9] In *Old Scotch Ballads etc.* 1679-1730, National Library of Scotland Ry. III. a. 10(82).
[10] Herd, *Scots Songs* (Edinburgh, 1776), I, p.10.
[11] *Ibid.,* I, p. 109 (by Adam Skirving).

was repeatedly printed as a broadside. There are also two quite separate types of song which might well be termed Stall Songs— (1) fairly lengthy expansions of a lyrical theme, sometimes written for a political purpose, such as some of the early broadsides of *Auld Lang Syne*,[12] and (2) comic songs of a brash plebian type, like *Crooked Shoulder*,[13] the source of Burns's *Willie Wastle*, where the balladist is being funny at the expense of a deformed wife. It was a persistent habit of chapbook and broadside printers to issue lengthy, padded versions of well-known lyrics. *The Birks of Abergeldy, A New Song, to its Own Proper Tune*[14] expands a brief folk-song, occupying two stanzas in Herd's *Scottish Songs* 1776,[15] to five stanzas and prints a " Second Part " of seven stanzas " to the same tune," while an undated [? 1785] chapbook in the National Library of Scotland[16] swells out *The Flowers of the Forest* to ballad proportions: it takes fourteen stanzas of hack writing before we reach Jean Elliot's l.1. "I have heard a lilting at our ewes milking." When Burns's songs were issued in chapbooks in the early nineteenth century, they were often expanded in a similar way. An undated chapbook entitled *Three Excellent New Songs*,[17] Printed at Edinburgh by J. Morren, gives Burns's *The Soldier's Return* (l.1. "When wild war's deadly blast was blown "), followed by a doggerel *Answer to the Soldier's Return*, quite in the tradition of the English broadside printers of the seventeenth century.

For Art-Song, one need go no further than Robert Crawford's *The Bush Aboon Traquair*, in Ramsay's *Tea-Table Miscellany*;[18] it was reprinted time and time again in the course of the century. The last stanza is sufficient to convey the flavour of the whole:

> Ye rural pow'rs who hear my strains,
>   Why thus should Peggie grieve me?
> Oh! make her partner in my pains;
>   Then let her smiles relieve me.

12 e.g. the versions (l.1. " O Caledon, O Caledon ") in National Library of Scotland, MS 2960. fol.33 and Ry. III. a. 10(71).
13 In *The Nightingale* (Edinburgh, 1776), p.36.
14 In *Old Scottish Ballads, etc., 1679-1730*, National Library of Scotland, Ry. III. a. 10(57).
15 II. p.221.
16 Ry. III. e. 16(9).
17 In Glasgow University Library.
18 2 vols. (Repr. Glasgow, 1871, from 14th Ed.), I, p.2 (l.1, " Hear me, ye nymphs, and ev'ry swain ").

If not, my love will turn despair:
My passion no more tender;
I'll leave the bush aboon Traquair
To lonely wilds I'll wander.

Yet much Scottish art-song was in a folk or even a broadside tradition: one has only to think of the works of those remarkable eighteenth century women, Lady Grisell Baillie (author of *Werena my heart licht I wad dee*). Jean Adam (herself a wandering hawker and author of *There's nae luck aboot the hoose*), Lady Anne Barnard, whose *Auld Robin Gray* is in two parts, just like a broadside, and Baroness Nairne (author of *The Land o' the Leal, Caller Herrin', The Laird o' Cockpen,* and the most popular set of *Charlie is my Darling*—l.1. "'Twas on a Monday morning ").[19] The productions of these women are generally more finished, more "artistic," and sometimes more sentimental than folk-song proper; while those of Allan Ramsay, Crawford, and their school often unite European conceptions of pastoral with a rather clammy sensuality, lip-service to "Virtue," and a preoccupation with the comedies of love and marriage.

In his *Schottische Volkslyrik in James Johnson's The Scots Musical Museum*, Berlin 1920. E. Schwebsch attempts to draw distinctions of form and treatment between these four *genres* in a more precise and rigid manner than the evidence perhaps warrants. He states that the lyrical folk-song is generally shorter than a ballad, and that it does not tell a story, though in actual practice it often possesses a narrative content, ever so lightly sketched in. It is often the expression of a *persona,* as in the overheard laments of young girls; or a dialogue with narrative background, as in many songs of the " night visit " type; or the development by means of incremental repetition of a situation and sentiments indicated in the first stanza. In Schwebsch's view, when folk song deals with nature at all, it does so in broad, powerful images which are at once stereotyped and unrealistic. With much, perhaps most, of this we can all agree. Schwebsch thinks that the folk song does not employ a conscious rhetorical art, or rather that, because the stanza-sequence is often so uncertain, it is impossible to say whether it does or not: for him, the folk-song has " laws of its own," determined by its generic character, not by any individual purpose. At this juncture,

19 See S. Tytler ond J. L. Watson, *The Songstresses of Scotland,* 2 vols. (London, 1871).

however, Schwebsch betrays more than a trace of that irrationality, that folk-song *mystique* which has bedevilled discussion of the topic from Herder and Carl Engel to the present day. According to Schwebsch, folk song and the traditional ballad are distinguished from art song by their lack of individuation as well as the existence of many variants actually sung among the people. The street or broadside ballad is distinguished by its presentation of characters from all walks of life, these being seen mostly from the point of view of household servants; and it generally exhibits a greater realism. Street and broadside ballads often arrange events in chronological order and employ a longer line than common metre; they are often tedious, pedantic, moralising, erotic, obscene, and comical; they love what he calls " cock and bull stories," and are sometimes decked out with " rags of erudition." The " pure lyric," lacking even the faintest shadow of narrative or dramatic content, is almost certain to have an " art song " behind it; a long lyric generally indicates a broadside origin; and the folk-song is usually serious in tone, often tragic, with a pronounced tendency towards sentimentality, though not towards crude insipidities and obscenities. Above all, it is seldom humorous: comic song, for Schwebsch, is almost always either art or street song.[20]

As I have said, the insufficiencies of Schwebsch's approach are due to his uncritical adherence to a romantic, primitivist concept of folk-song. Even Gavin Greig, the greatest of all twentieth century song collectors in Scotland, did not succeed in escaping from it. Here is how Greig defined Folk-Song in 1909: " It may be taken to mean, briefly, that body of minstrelsy which circulates among the common people and has originated among them . . . It is of the very essence of folk-song that its origin cannot be traced." Greig, like so many of his German predecessors, was a " communalist ": he said that " it " [i.e. folk-song] . . . " is communal in origin, evolution and character." [21] Greig drew a firm distinction between folk-song and book-song; to him, none of Burns's songs were folk-songs, but, on the contrary, all were book-songs; similarly, the lyrics of Hogg, Tannahill, Ramsay, Baroness Nairne and the other women writers I have mentioned were book-songs.

20 pp. 208-218.
21 In *Folk-Song of the North-East. Articles contributed to the " Buchan Observer " from December, 1907, to September, 1909,* (Peterhead, 1909) I, p.1; IX, p.2.

It should be pointed out, however, that it is possible to adopt another sort of classification of the songs in the song-books, a classification according to content, of the sort employed by Angellier in his *Robert Burns: la vie, les oeuvres*, Paris 1893, and further developed in my own *Burns: a Study of the Poems and Songs*, Edinburgh 1960.[22] Such a classification cuts completely across the divisions of "art," "folk," and "stall" song. Furthermore, when the tunes to which the songs are set are considered, it is seen that from Ramsay onwards poets wrote "art" songs for traditional tunes; and so, too, did the writers of broadsides. It is surely quite impossible to isolate a given melody and say: "this is a typical broadside *tune*," or, alternatively, "this is a typical folk (as opposed to broadside) tune." But it *is* possible to say that *See the Conquering Hero Comes* and *Rule Britannia*, both reprinted frequently in the song books, and songs with melodies by Dr. Arne or J. C. Bach, are quite different from songs that can be traced back — via, perhaps, the *Orpheus Caledonius* — to early eighteenth century musical MSS, such as the Agnes Hume MS (1704), the Margaret Sinkler MS (? 1698-1710), and Mrs. Anne Crookshank's MS (slightly later than the Sinkler MS), all in the National Library of Scotland.[23]

The distinction that is of the greatest value in the study of Scottish song literature before and immediately after Burns's time is the distinction between popular and artificial. By artificial song I mean a particularly insipid variety, often sung by professional singers at the public gardens of Ranelagh and Vauxhall, and at their northern counterparts in Edinburgh and Aberdeen. Such *artificial* songs were a peculiar sub-class of art song, by no means identical with the whole of art song; they were associated with a particular social group, the "polite," and above all with the women of that group; and their idea content was often that of the mid-eighteenth century cult of sentiment. One Scotswoman who enjoyed and herself wrote this kind of artificial song was Burns's "Clarinda"—Mrs. Agnes McLehose: her relations with Burns were nothing more nor less than an attempt to *live* according to the cult of sentiment.

All the other songs in the song-books may be subsumed under the single category of "popular song." By "popular song" I mean a generic term which will cover (1) composed songs by

22 pp. 281 ff.
23 MSS 5.2.17 and Glen 143(1). The Crookshank and Sinkler MSS are bound together.

popular writers of certain conventional types, sung to Scots or popular English tunes; (2) slip or chapbook songs, generally shorter than broadside ballads and often printed under such titles as *Three Excellent New Songs, Seven Excellent New Songs,* etc.; (3) " broadside " or " stall " ballads — *i.e.* songs with a considerable narrative content, generally fairly long, and often showing signs of sheer padding; (4) folk songs, as defined below; (5) traditional ballads of the type collected by Child. The dividing line between (4) and (5) is exceedingly difficult to draw, but it nevertheless exists: the Child ballad seems to have originated either in feudal society or in the frontier clan society of the Scottish borders, and to have become part of the traditional culture of post-Reformation agricultural communities, transmitted from one part of the country to another by such wanderers as tinkers and cattle-drovers. Lyrical folk-song, in contrast, does not *necessarily* embody, even in a romanticised form, the values of pre-capitalist society, and indeed—as the work of Alan Lomax and A. L. Lloyd has shown—lyrical folk-song is still being composed at the present day. Broadside ballads and stall songs, unlike the Child ballads, are in the first instance popular artforms of the towns, and above all of capital cities; in some ways they look back to the jest books of the sixteenth century and the attitudes of the medieval fabliaux, in others they anticipate the sensationalism and scandalmongering of the modern popular press.[24] Although it is necessary to distinguish between these five types of song for certain critical and literary-historical purposes, it is also necessary to realise that, taken together, they formed a single eighteenth-century popular lyrical culture. Furthermore the dividing line between this popular culture and " official " literature is in Scotland peculiarly difficult to draw. From the early eighteenth century until Scott's time, imaginative literature in Scotland was on the whole more popular in character and inspiration than that of England. Watson and Allan Ramsay published broadsides for sale in the streets; Burns, whose poems were early printed in chapbook form, based his work on every kind of *popular* tradition, including the broadside tradition; all Walter Scott's creative work was in a sense an extension of his early ballad-collecting, and he too did not disdain to take hints from chapbooks and broadsides; Hogg's tales — especially his most popular one, *The Long Pack* — were sold by hawkers at

[24] See V. de S. la Pinto, " The Street Ballad in English Poetry," *Politics and Letters*, Nos. 2 and 3 (Winter-Spring, 1947-48) 34-46.

the cottage-door. This, of course, was probably the result of the more homogeneous nature of Scottish society, and of the democratic system of village education, under which the laird's son and the peasant's son often sat at the feet of the same dominie.

The most important general conclusion—and I would stress that it is at best an extremely tentative one — to emerge from this preliminary survey concerns the necessity for a new approach to folk-song, which would replace the old dichotomies between folk-song and broadside, folk-song and *composed* popular song, by the realization that folk-song is from one point of view simply a species of a wider genus of popular song. Most definitions of folk-song speak of a song current among " the people." I suggest replacing the vague term " people " (" das Volk ") by a *series* of terms emphasizing the possibility of different societies and social groups producing different types of song. An improved definition of folk-song might run something like this: " A folk-song is a song current among the members of some national, tribal, regional, urban, village, occupational or other community or group, transmitted orally from one generation to another, and subject to the laws that govern oral transmission — namely the co-existence for long periods of a fixed norm with spontaneously occurring variations." This recognizes that the folk process—the process of oral transmission — is the result of the interplay of two tendencies: a tendency to preserve, and a tendency to alter, to innovate, to " ad lib." Now the definition I have just given is a definition of what may be called " pure " folk-song, and is therefore, a definition of something that does not exist at the present day, and perhaps did not exist in the eighteenth century either. As soon as a sizeable minority of the " lower orders " is able to read and write, the possibility arises of singers noting down their words as an aid to memory, and this immediately interferes with the folk process by fossilizing some songs in the singer's repertoire and by encouraging him to improve others in the very act of writing them down. Once these improvements are committed to paper they acquire all the authority of the written word, and are less liable to spontaneous variation in future. From the sixteenth century onwards in England, and from the late seventeenth century in Scotland, printed broadsides and chapbooks, originating in the towns, were circulating in the villages and influencing local folk-song in a way that Shakespeare documented once and for all in a well-known scene (IV, iii) between Mopsa and Autolycus in *The Winter's Tale*. The next step was that the folk-singer became a popular poet, the self-conscious composer of an art song on a traditional theme, employing conventional phrases and even whole stanzas learnt from other sources, but nevertheless still an art song—or, if you like, still a popular song. The folk-singer is metamorphosed into an artist in folk-song, or an artist who uses folk-song; he becomes an Allan Ramsay, a Skinner, or, if he happens to be at the same time a genius, a Robert Burns.

UNIVERSITY OF AUCKLAND

[The above article is based on a paper read before the 8th Congress of the Australasian Universities Languages and Literature Association held in Canberra, 15-21 August, 1962.]

FRANCIS R. HART

The Hunter and the Circle:
Neil Gunn's Fiction of Violence

A S a contemporary British novelist, to be a regionalist, we are told, is to be unread. "Regionalism is dead," pronounced V. S. Pritchett, optimistically some years ago. Thus, the connoisseur of cosmopolitan letters may be regaled with any number of assertions that Neil Gunn is "by far the most considerable novelist who has ever worked beyond the, Highland line," that he has "a strong sense of the organic rhythms of the old Highland life," that in fact his work is the highest peak of achievement in modern Scottish fiction[1]—he may hear all of these and still confess his complete ignorance without shame, with resolve.

Such assertions, though true, are unfair. To see only the Highland novelist is to miss the essential Neil Gunn, whose characteristic fictive manoeuver has been to rescue pastoral from the regionalist, just as it has been to rescue what is valid primitive experience from misguided primitivism. Indeed, in his latest book, Gunn is ironic at the expense of both:

> There are those beyond the urban walls who live in the depths of the country. From their dark dens they stalk, inarticulate, across the sombre landscape of the regional novel. The old barbarian is the new moron, and the new moron is the peasant, the archetype of the brutal before the brutal got brains. His hunger is in his prowl, his covetous-

---

[1] J. M. Reid, *Modern Scottish Literature*, Saltire Pamphlets No. 5 (Edinburgh, 1945), p.18; D. Daiches, *The Present Age After 1920* (London, 1958), p.283. For convincing and admiring appraisals of his importance as a modern Scottish novelist, see K. Wittig, *The Scottish Tradition in Literature* (Edinburgh, 1958), pp. 333-339, and S. Angus, "The Novels of Neil Gunn," *Scottish Periodical*, Vol. I, No. 2 (Summer, 1948), pp. 94-103.

E

ness in his eye, his greed in the dark impenetrable intricacies of his bowels where all that matters is digested until the plot requires indigestion.[2]

For Gunn, as for comparable pastoralists such as Wordsworth and Frost, the regional landscape is setting for the discovery of the "primordial," the "given," in human nature and experience. For him, every fictional event awakens the sense he attributes to far-flung Highland families: the "sense of the ends of the earth and of human beings inhabiting the earth, one with another."[3] Every event comes to full realization only as myth or apocalytic parable: "All stories . . . meet in one story," states the narrator of the latest novel; and elswhere, "Of all the stories man had made only two were immortal: the story of Cain and the story of Christ."[4] But how do such stories find their way out of the crofting communities of Sutherland and Caithness, and in doing so, how do they justify the claims made for Gunn as a serious artist in modern fiction?

To begin an answer I have chosen three of the eight novels he has published since World War II. The choice is variously motivated. For one thing it has proved too easy to praise Gunn as recounter of Highland boyhood—as in *Morning Tide* (1931), *Highland River* (1937), *Young Art and Old Hector* (1942)—and prejudge as failures his later experiments with adult experience and sophisticated points of view. For another, it can be argued that the latest of Gunn's twenty novels (in twenty-nine years) are in many ways the best—most universal, most timely, most mature philosophically and artistically. If this has any truth, then we can achieve an initial appreciation of his work without confronting the special problems raised by the earlier books. We can, for the moment, sidestep those in which the "Highland question" bulks large: *Butcher's Broom* (1934), *The Silver Darlings* (1941); or those which evoke, with a sometimes burdensome poetic pathos, the doomed Celtic soul, and which led the disappointed Angus MacDonald in 1933 to cite "Fiona MacLeod" as the damaging inspiration:[5] *Grey Coast* (1926), *The Lost Glen* (1932),

---

2 *Atom of Delight* (London, 1956), p. 218; cf. p 298 : "As experts, the old primitives would not have been impressed by the new."
3 *Bloodhunt* (London, 1952), p.231.
4 *The Other Landscape* (London, 1954), pp. 294-295; *Bloodhunt*, p. 233. Cf. *Atom*, p. 183 : "what was told was the story of someone at some time, and the eye saw destiny last year, or last century, or any time beyond. A thousand years made no difference."
5 In "Modern Scots Novelists," *Edinburgh Essays on Scots Literature*, pref. by H. J. C. Grierson (Edinburgh, 1933), pp. 161-162.

Sun Circle (1933). Not that these problematical strains have vanished in the later books; rather, they have been adapted to more fundamental concerns, to popular plot motifs and contemporary themes. We shall see how in *The Key of the Chest* (1945), *The Shadow* (1948), *and Bloodhunt* (1952).

At the end of his elusive apologia, *Atom of Delight* (1956), Gunn defines the quest which evidently informs the three novels: "an examination of those destructive or disintegrating forces that seem so wantonly to destroy delight in living; and . . . means for countering them." Earlier in the same book, in a passage which catalogues the major symbols of all his fiction, he draws in sharp outline the myth by which the examination could proceed. At its center is a kind of seeing, a wholeness and immediacy of vision grounded in a wholeness of being which for Gunn is always the primary given need of the essential human self.

> When he encountered the birches on Hampstead Heath he saw them all in a moment, from within the circle around the second self. That kind of seeing is never lost. It may seem to be lost, then instantly it is there. Where all is food for life, this is food of the living tree. The tap root of the tree is watered by the well, with the circle around it that the serpent made. In our most modern moment we are back in the Garden where the Devil entered into the serpent and broke the circle (pp. 304, 222).

In our three novels we are not quite back in the Garden, though all three have their political and symbolic source in Gunn's magnificent Edenic anti-utopia, *The Green Isle of the Great Deep* (1944). We are, however, in a world stalked by the figure of Cain.

The novels share a central event: a murder. Each proceeds, sketching the interplay of a community touched by this act of personal violence, to explore the given event as a symptom of the murderousness of the modern world. Each relates external violence to the inward violence of personality that has lost its wholeness and turned through deprivation or perversion to destructiveness. Each envisions the possibility of recovery through a variety of means. There is the temporary "escape" of Frost's "Directive," back to the restorative confrontation of an unsentimentalized pastoral ideal, a vision of individual and social wholeness. There is self-renewal through mythic self-discovery, a vision of one's nature and destiny in archaic or archetypal turns. "Man must for ever move," says Gunn, "like a liberator, through his own unconsciousness" (*KC*, p.196). He does so by the gesture

Gunn has likened to the fisherman's backward cast, by assuming what Thomas Mann calls the " archaizing attitude." Archaic man, says Mann, " searched the past for a pattern into which he might slip as into a diving-bell," in order to find reanimation in " life in the myth, life as a sacred repetition " or " eternal return."[6] This, the function of myth as defined by Joseph Campbell, is the reanimating experience of Gunn's people. There is, finally, a willed ceremony of affirmation, a rite of passage to recovered innocence and delight. As one puts it, in *The Lost Chart* (1949), " The darkness creates drama ready-made for man; but man has to create his own drama of the light " (p.178).

The drama begins, however, with particulars. The regional landscape is real enough before the " other landscape " begins, by a variety of means, to declare itself.

I I

Gunn as narrator reminds one of the Marlow of *Heart of Darkness*: " to him the meaning of an episode was not inside like a kernel but outside, enveloping the tale which brought it out." The " episode " of *The Key of the Chest* is the death by strangulation of a Swedish seaman during his rescue from a freighter sinking in a storm off the Highland coast. The rescuer, Charlie, suspected of his murder, and his brutish shepherd of a brother, Dougald, suspected of stealing money from the dead man's chest (to which the key cannot be found), live geographically and morally on the outskirts of their community. Their position is the more debatable for a long standing conflict with the minister, the local spiritual overlord, a paternalist perverted to destructiveness, a repressive will against whom life has taken its revenge by awakening a love for his daughter that is both incestuous and idealizing — a curious variant of Aschenbach's love for Tadzio

---

6 " Freud and the Future," *Essays of Three Decades*, trans. H. T. Lowe-Porter (N.Y., 1947), p. 424; cf. Mircea Eliade, *Cosmos and History* [*The Myth of the Eternal Return*], trans. W. R. Trask, Torchbooks (N.Y., 1959), p. 5; Joseph Campbell, *The Hero with a Thousand Faces*, (Meridian N.Y., 1956), pp. 17, 385-91. Mann recalls Ortega's figure of the bull-fighter's gesture for archaic man's backward step, with which cf. Gunn, *Atom*, p. 9: " though the general direction, as in any sport, is forward, clues can be picked up by a cast back. But the backward cast becomes entirely nostalgic unless the clues are used in an actual hunt to-day and to-morrow "; and p. 283 : " *Reculer pour mieux sauter* is a normal procedure for the athlete about to take a jump or putt the shot."

in *Death in Venice*. Charlie is his rival. During an ill-fated period at Edinburgh University, Charlie has entangled his own academic disgrace with an imprudent love affair with the minister's daughter Flora. When, home again, they begin meeting once more at the time of the mysterious death, the minister sacrifices his whole position to pursue a deathhunt to drive Charlie to destruction. Charlie and Flora attempt to flee, are rescued by a community that favors them over the minister; the minister is chastened. The novel ends with the hint that the lovers will emigrate together, "leaving the shadow on the land. The shadow from the passing of the bright ones" (p.262).

The Shadow's title refers to the shadow of violence cast upon another Highland village by the robbery and murder of an old hermit. The episode occurs early in the convalescence from nervous collapse of a young woman who has been almost destroyed spiritually by the London "blitz" and has come to her Aunt Pheemie's Highland farm to rest, only to have "the living figure of destruction . . . come away from the city where he has been impersonal and many-shaped, shapes flying across the sky, come at last to the country, to the quiet countryside, to prowl around on two feet and smell out a poor old man and murder him for his money" (p.26). The result of her new and personal encounter with destructiveness is given in the title of the second of three parts: "Relapse." Her "Recovery," Part Three, is the outcome of a complex inner war of light and health against darkness and disorder, and of an equally complex parallel outer war among friends, lovers, relatives who would all claim her spirit on behalf of their conflicting visions of the nature of her illness and the world's illness it embodies. Her recovery, a pastoral ceremony of reanimation, allows her to return to London transformed.

Bloodhunt, the latest of the three, is as narrative simplest and perhaps most perfect. Here, too, the aftermath of the murder is what matters. The bloodhunt is for the murderer, a likeable young man who has killed the rival who got his girl pregnant; the bloodhunter, a policeman, is the murdered man's brother. Once again, an obscurely defined, powerful brother-bond is at the center of the "kernel." But the story is mainly of an old man, a retired seaman living in peaceful isolation on the edge of the community, and of how, for all his determination not to become involved, he becomes "secret sharer" of his young friend's guilt: "it was not Allan himself, not the old friendliness between them, that moved him now, though they were in him, but the thought of the lad being tried and hanged. Somehow *that* he could not stomach. It tied life's tap-root in a knot. It was an obstacle in front of him, between him and death " (p.166). Sandy tragicomically intrigues to hide and feed the fugitive, has his own absurd accidents, nearly dies, resists the invasions of a " well meaning " widow from the next farm, and finally accepts and protects the pregnant girl. Meanwhile, the hunt goes on; the hunter is brutalized; the fugitive, weak and ill, is caught and killed. Sandy, knowing all, remains silent and thus calls an end to violence, and finds new life in Liz and her new baby, born suddenly in Sandy's barn. As Sandy sees them in their mythic aspect, the events are a " sacred repetition ": " The manger and the hay and life's new cry; beyond it, that hunt. Of all the stories man had made only two were immortal: the story of Cain and the story of Christ " (p.233). Sandy chooses his story, as it were, and thus enacts his own " drama of the light."

Conrad wrote, " All my concern has been with the *ideal* value of things, events, and people." Gunn's interest in the three murders is, likewise, ideal — is in what they epitomize of a destructiveness that is timeless in nature and man, and of the growing murderousness of the modern world. Old Sandy contemplates the hunted Allan's plight and sees a symptom:

More and more . . . nearer and nearer . . . violence upon violence, increasing violence . . . until the teeth champed and the juices ran about the gums . . . Then satisfaction, the satisfaction after the orgy . . . until the hunt did not need a murderer, could substitute something else, an *ism* or *ology* that stood for the murderer, providing a wider hunt, a greater kill, more blood (p.99).

The urbane onlookers speculate broadly, in *The Key*, on the desire to destroy in a world that is a " desert," a " dark wood," of nihilism. Aunt Pheemie, in *The Shadow*, watches Nan struggle against her own absorption in the world's violence, and comes to this remarkable vision:

The child, wandering up through the daylight fields, trying to clean the shadow from its world. . . . The thistledown, the soft eager balls, seeds on the wing — changing into the grey steady eyes, the searching eyes of the policeman. Changing, in his turn, into the youth with the tommygun on his knees and the cigarette in his mouth, while love in its naked family waited in the trench; he mowed them down as a pernicious corn (p.207).

But his interest is "ideal" in another way, too. The destructiveness he portrays is "ideal" — of the mind. For Gunn, even a natural violence has, like Conrad's typhoon, a personifying malevolence: "they all listened to the wind outside and heard the whine and snarl in its throat, but also they heard, streaming away into the moor, the cry of anguish, of the unutterably lost that was at its heart, that is always at the heart of great violence." [7] And like Conrad's typhoon, it is essentially a "disintegrating power," an anguished self-destructive agency seeking to destroy man's wholeness, or murder by dissection his essential nature. The Gunn protagonist facing the threat of violence has a sense of imminent personal disintegration; the hero of *Wild Geese Overhead* (1939) "felt himself disintegrating, and fought to keep the strands of his body together" (p.115). Gunn's archetypal murderer is one who seeks, by intellectual disintegration, to destroy his victim spiritually. The boy-hero of *Morning Tide* (1931) fights to defend the essential privacy of his brother and his brother's girl friend against intellectual violation: "For he knew there were minds that could think any thing. But not the brave fine minds that were secretive and strong and kind" (p.113). Here are the lines of the psychological warfare of which Gunn's fiction is made. The minds "that could think any thing" assume their most menacing form as the police-state utopians of *The Green Isle of the Great Deep*, who seek to "find out everything" in the "brave fine minds," who enjoy "teasing the human mind into its strands, of combing the strands, and leaving them knotless and gleaming and smooth over one's arm or the back of a chair" (p.78).

These are the intellectual murderers of Gunn's fiction, those who "entered into the serpent and broke the circle." In *The Lost Chart* the hero's antagonist's mouth has "a disintegrating effect" (p.35) — and we anticipate at once that Basil is to be one with "a very considerable analytical power — when it comes to things touching the mind. He's got a certain watching cuteness. He's like a weasel. He knows the holes in the dyke" (p.86). Geoffrey of *Second Sight* (1940) is the same: "It's something in Geoffrey's spirit — I don't know what it is — something that disintegrates." Geoffrey's "may be the advanced sort of analytic mind that we're not ready for. He disintegrates — without integrating" (p.171). In *Wild Geese Overhead*, the hero's newspaper friend Mac has a "satiric face, now openly sneering and disintegrating . . . the face of a man, thwarted himself, warped and thwarted in his spirit, pursuing him, Will, slowly, remorselessly, until he would break his resistance, bit by bit, get him down to his own level and then dominate him with a devil's satisfaction" (p.44). His "destructive annihilating mind" makes him one of those "who took life's central purpose of delight and smothered it, out of fear and self-importance and egotism, and the devil's thrill of power over others. . . . Even his animosity felt like a snake-bite" (pp.63, 75).

Such are the "sly destructive ones," the diabolical analysts of *The Shadow*. Nan's lover Ranald, with his logical utopian rigidity a descendant of the Green Isle "managers," can easily qualify. In argument he "gets pale . . . and logical in a remorseless way." On one occasion, Nan recalls, he tore his opponent's "mind into small bits — and showed him the bits" (p.192). Pheemie, pondering Nan's illness, visualizes her own analytic interest as a "remorseless white face, like Ranald's face. . . . This white taut face watched until sympathy was slain, until emotion withered. It's the slayer's face, thought told her in silence, and she was aware of being between the thought and the face, like a soul in an experiment" (p.127).

The soul in experiment of *The Key of the Chest* is the energetic, wealthy young game lord, Michael Sandeman; he, too, has a capacity for destructiveness: "When the ego gets going like that, one feels in it — something destructive — a sort of teasing out that cares nothing for another's feelings — a tearing down to the root, a tearing out" (p.205). He is saved by his impulsive creativity, and by the faculty we perceive on first meeting him: "an intuitive apprehension of the nature of wild life" (p.37), an intuition that carries him far toward a creative awareness of the "mystery of the individual personality," "the one whole being," before his soul's experiment ends. The truly "destructive one" of *The Key* is the minister, and of *Bloodhunt*, the policeman; but their destructiveness is of a different sort from those mentioned above, and before speaking of them, it may be well to clarify the general attitude these characterizations imply — that is, what appears to be Gunn's primitivistic anti-rationalism.

His intellectual destroyers murder spontaneity, murder to dissect. A facile classification would place him with earlier deplorers of the "false secondary power" and "Newton's sleep" — Wordsworth and Blake; with Lawrence, who, he said, "endeavoured to give back its own delight to the body made disgusting or impotent by intellect" (*Atom of Delight*, p.301); and with Eugen Herrigel's Zen master in archery, another defender of the body's wisdom against the pretensions of analytic reason (*Atom*, chap. 18). But any such classification should be reviewed in the light of Nan's cry: "We have to rescue the intellect from the destroyers. They have turned it into death rays, and it should be the sun" (p.42). "Reason" — culture *more geometrico*, in Ortega's terms—is his destroyer: "Reason's noise. One who makes too much noise will never see a fawn in a glen. But there are fawns in glens" (*Atom*, p.210). "Reason," he says, "has tended to collar intellect in our time"—intellect, that is, as the "Old schoolmen" used it to denote the action or apprehension of the "second self," which "reason calls non-rational" (*Atom*, p.291). But to try to save Reason from itself, or to save *Vernunft* from *Verstand*, is "not to disparage reason or intellect and opt wholly for the dark gods, the irrational flesh" (p.289). Gunn, like Thomas Mann, moves only experimentally among the anti-intellectuals. He must have shared the concern of, for instance, Mann and Ortega, over the miserable effects on modern Europe of an anti-intellectualism that saw *Der Geist als Widersacher der Seele*, divorced culture—Geist—and spontaneity —Leben, and opened the way to a bloodhunt for the primitive.[8] The end, to which Gunn's seemingly extravagant primitivism is only the means, is most fully articulated by Michael in *The Key*:

> Back into the primitive? . . . no, back into themselves. That
> was the search. For oneness. Searching, with paint, for the
> primitive where wholeness began, but finally here, on the sea,
> in the leap, with death as life's shadow, under the sun, against
> the gale, the body whole and singular, with warmth in it, for
> one other, for others, for all. Man's strangely tragic story,
> so full of wonder and light (p.238).

The dark gods belong at last to the destroyers. The destroyers may be more than intellectual in their violence.

The minister's destructiveness, in *The Key*, is a peculiarly Scottish conception, but one easily comprehensible to readers of

---

8 While the analogy with Mann is offered merely as opening speculation, the chapter on "Myth and Psychology" in Henry Hatfield's *Thomas Mann* (N.Y., 1951) and F. C. Sell's essay, "The Problem of Anti-Intellectualism," in *The Stature of Thomas Mann*, ed. C. Neider (N.Y., 1947), are interesting glosses on Gunn's fictional manoeuvres *vis à vis* primitivism. For Ortega on the divorce, see *The Modern Theme*, trans. J. Cleugh (N.Y., 1933), p. 53 and elsewhere.

Hawthorne. He is the destroyer in whom life has been thwarted
and perverted into sadistic violence. His daughter recognizes
" something dark in her father, full of flesh and blood, . . . that
went beyond religion and all things of the mind " (p.90). Others
" had seen the minister's face as he walked restlessly and softly,
like a caged animal " (p.101), but for Flora, " he inhabited the
back regions of her mind, an imminent deadly menace " (p.114),
and " she knew only the awful menace of her father and of his
anger. It was of the spirit, not of the flesh. The anger of the
unknowable god that destroys " (p.118). He belongs to the same
devil-ridden tradition that fostered the diabolism of Burns and
Byron, and produced Hogg's Justified Sinner and Muriel Spark's
Calvinist monomaniac Miss Jean Brodie in her prime. But he
recalls Lawrence in a curious way. The connection of his
" menace " with a " deep incestuous motive " is perhaps incidental, but it does have a suggestive parallelism with the relationship of Nan and Ranald. In both, the menace of disintegration
is associated with illicit sexuality. In both, sexuality is literally
incidental; what is not incidental is the way all of Gunn's
destroyers wear an aura of sexual menace, are potential ravishers,
violators, dividers of spiritual wholeness. " To feel whole,"
postulates Gunn (*Atom*, p.264), " is a primary need of the self."
In evoking moments of felt wholeness, he makes frequent use of
the word *intact,* and speaks of the primitive fear of *touching* as
a violation of individual safety. For the boy or adult seeking to
preserve himself whole, " to withdraw intact was the great thing "
(p.84). The object, then, in resisting the disintegrative effects of
the destroyer is to preserve intact the curious kind of spiritual
virginity that characterizes Gunn's triumphant heroes and heroines: to prevent the devil-perverted serpent of life from breaking
one's circle. Here, Gunn is a kind of anti-Lawrence.

The main metaphor for the relation of destroyer to victim in
most of Gunn's fiction is not, however, sexual, though traditionally associated with sexual pursuit. It is the Hunt. The relation
of Hunter to Hunted is, for Gunn, more " primordial " than any
other. The dominance in the relationships and motivations of
which his novels are made of the hunter-hunted motif makes this
metaphor the key to the formal and symbolic integrity of his
fiction. *Bloodhunt* alone gives it titular prominence, and the full
and starkly simple articulation, within the limits of old Sandy's
consciousness, of the titular symbol has much to do with the
arguable superiority of this, the latest of the three novels. And as

we trace this organizing motif it will be useful to experiment with comparative evaluation and thus single out Gunn's characteristic achievement.

III

The destroyer in *Bloodhunt*, Nicol Menzies the policeman, like Spenser's Malbecco and Milton's Satan, becomes the embodiment of his own obsession. He who begins as avenger of his brother's death carries at last the mark of violence against his brother, the mark of Cain. At the beginning he has "a good-looking face but without something, without light" (p.30). Later, "his face seemed not only thinner but darker in a disturbing avid way. He had taken the night in with him; and then Sandy realized that it was not the dark night outside, but the dark inner world in which the fellow now lived" (p.214). But the story is Sandy's, and fittingly, it is his inner world, the "secret country of his mind" (p.22), that sees the war between darkness — analytic withdrawal — and light — the self-commitment to the law older than crime and punishment, the law that is "the warm feeling at life's real core" (p.126). An alien being inside, with ironic eye, drives him toward disengagement, peace, nothingness; but life is Sandy's bloodhunter and it keeps breaking in upon him, trapping him. The old man's complex flight from this hunter gives the tragicomedy its symbolic unity and significance. On the level of character and situation Sandy's battle is to preserve Allan and the unwed mother from the laws of the tribe, and to preserve his own privacy. But in "the other landscape" the war is between "Nothingness . . . participation. The twins" (p.140), and between two visions of the law of the tribe. At last Sandy accepts that law as a law of love, and rejects the law behind it, the law of Cain and the bloodhunt. It is remarkable how wide a vision of human alternatives is embodied in this concrete parable, and how much is implied in the shift of Sandy's deepest allegiance from the fugitive murderer to the guilty girl and her bastard, the girl who has sought him out, trapped him in his home, in his self and life, while outside, in ritual circles, the older hunt, the death hunt, draws to its own destruction. The novel is remarkable for the coherence and economy with which it develops its titular symbol.

In Gunn's world, every relationship has, in a sense, its basic element of hunter-hunted. Every individual constitutes something of a threat to the autonomy, the "delight," of every other; hence every encounter has an element of menace, and every conversation, as Dr. Wittig has noted,[9] is a subtle manoeuvering, a stalking exercise, a game of self-preservation against the threat of penetration, against the hunter that seeks out the self in the thicket of its secretive circle. In *The Shadow*, all hunts are potentially destructive, except for the last (Nan's search for the "true Ranald"); but by ironic inversion, some transcend their own destructiveness. Such is the source of this book's coherence.

Part of its economy is a peculiar structure. The first section is made up of Nan's letters to Ranald concerning her convalescence. She is seeking to rediscover an instinct for life, and ironically, her account is addressed to one for whom her quest is simply an escape, a regression to infantilism. Actually, she is the hunted animal, escaping not just from the image of violence, but also from the disintegrative rationalism of those who label her neurotic. And her flight from this destructive hunter is the more difficult because she has been part of his murderousness, has known his desire to destroy: "We have murdered spontaneity. That's what we have done. The faces of analysts, everywhere, with bits of matter on slides, saying: That's all it is. And we wonder about war and horror! About murderers . . . !" (p.28). Her flight carries her too far, just as Sandy's withdrawal from the "tribe" carries him temporarily too far, and Nan, too, gives an instinctive, self-menacing allegiance to one she thinks a murderer — the strange young man in the woods, appropriately named Adam. Her allegiance is Gunn's symbol, clearly, for the attraction of awakened anti-intellectuality to the "primitive," the "dark gods." Nan knows that her fascination may appear to derive from a "dark sex-unconscious." But she also knows that she is not that "far gone." "All this talk about escapism. . . . Not to mention the smile, the murderer's sneer, that Nan is going all D. H. Lawrence. . . . Blood and myth and stuff. But I'm not! We have to rescue the intellect from the destroyers" (p.42).

---

9 Wittig, p. 334: "there is much 'searching innuendo,' much stealthy manoeuvering, as each of the speakers in turn probes the other's mind, and tries first to draw him on and ultimately drive him into a blind corner. Doubtless this reflects an essential feature of Scots conversation. . . ."

As a hunter, Adam belongs to the world of the bloodhunt. He philosophizes brutally on a hawk's hovering and flushing a blackbird (Nan has just witnessed this), scoffs at her sentimentality, and " Presently he was telling me about a stoat and hare. . . . He was in the wood, moving quietly, searching with his eyes for wild life, when he sees the stoat and the hare going round in a circle, not a very big circle, just a few yards across. They are at opposite points of the circle so that, if you didn't know wild life, you might hardly tell whether the stoat was following the hare or the hare the stoat " (p.63). Adam " has the wild in him, a wild-animal freshness," (p.64) and Nan is hynotized like the hare, stalked like the blackbird, by one who, though not the actual murderer, is one of Gunn's destroyers, one with an infernal curiosity, a love of " Destruction, the death throe " (p.65), who is " capable of using anything and everything that will help him to get what he wants, like a wild beast stalking its prey " (p.77). But the circle makes it hard to tell hunted from hunter. Nan turns the tables, becomes herself the hunter of the atrophied part of herself that is in him—" Not to go is to *escape*. I want to go through him, to separate him and understand . . . in a dream sense to tear his chest open and separate the dark " (p.79)—just as Sandy must work through his allegiance to the murderer to win his new allegiance to life in Liz and her child.

Nan's decision carries her to a primeval country and a vision of death, and she undergoes a relapse. Gunn makes use of her temporary incapacity as central consciousness to enlarge the scene, establish a complementary point of view in Aunt Pheemie, and develop the several subordinate hunts that go on outside Nan's mind. Only at the end does Nan reassume her position; meanwhile, Pheemie's stalking of the two men, the opposed politico-erotic forces in Nan's life, gives structure and meaning. Pheemie's own experience is deeply involved, much as Sandy's is. Sandy, however, the old sailor come home to die, derives his detached view of alternative lives only from a certain breadth of experience. Pheemie has known the world of intellect as teacher and is more abstractly attached to the instinctual, pastoral life. Too, she looks at the modern world of male destructivess as an older woman, with sufficient intellectuality to comprehend Nan's struggle, and sufficient humane instinct and instinctual wisdom to help — to help a ewe through a difficult birth on a snowy night, or to help Nan through an analogous psychic process. She has the hunter's instinct, too, for ferreting out the secrets of personalities, and the mythic consciousness necessary for seeing Ranald and Adam in their archetypal forms. Throughout the middle of the book, her quest is to find out what happened with Adam to cause the relapse, and her purpose is to assess and manipulate Nan's relations with the two men, in spite of her own instinctive hatred of the destroyer Ranald and liking for the instinctual artist Adam.

With the reawakening of Nan's love for the " real Ranald," Pheemie's influence wanes, even as her narrative centrality diminishes. This point, af the end of the second part, coincides with what is—almost literally— the second murder in the book : Ranald's fight with Adam. Their struggle, the book's external climax, is the clash of instinctual man, the defiantly antisocial, primitive artist, with the logical utopian, the white-faced analytic destroyer. Adam is the " fighting wild thing," " his eyes wary as a stoat's "; Ranald is " one who would kill at his leisure, who knew he would kill at his leisure, but needed first to dominate the mind in front of him, to frighten it into gibbering bits " (pp.157-8). It is profoundly significant that no one wins. Adam steps by accident over a ledge and into the river, but miraculously survives. Ranald goes back to the women surprisingly exhilarated by this rare surrender to instinct. Nan sees " the real Ranald "; realizing the cause, our reaction, like Pheemie's, is one of horror. But we too must learn with Pheemie, during the final part, why no one can win this fight, why Nan cannot choose Adam but must go back to Ranald to work for his redemption, to save intellect from its destructive self, perhaps to free the serpent from the invading devil.

For relevance to a world of urban violence and restlessness, and for psychological sophistication, *The Shadow* might be preferred to the other two novels. The fact that it is in many ways untypical would have no bearing on such a judgment, nor would its lack of connection with the Scots Renaissance. But such facts may well imply *causes* of what I consider its relative inferiority. The special archetypal psychology, the implausible epistolarism of the first part, are productive of schematic, abstract characters, terms in a dialectical psychomachia. But is this a flaw? If we follow Frye's terminology and classify the book as romance-anatomy, we can excuse such abstractness and speak of effective personae vividly embodying ideas as operative parts of an intellectual structure. But such a process, it seems to me, ends in either total formalism or total philosophism and robs fiction of its essentials:

concreteness of texture, dramatic authenticity of experience. Hence, I don't believe *The Shadow* can be preferred by licentious reclassification. However impressive, it is inferior to *Bloodhunt*.

As for the choice between *Bloodhunt* and *The Key of the Chest*, it would be again easy to decide on *Bloodhunt* and comforting to find the latest the best. One could argue that in this latest depiction of the Highland community, all simple black-white moral distinctions are gone, and no tendency remains to idealize. *Bloodhunt's* picture of rural life is the ballad picture: unwed mother, homicidal rejected lover, amoral accomplice, brutal pursuer, a leavening of phariseeism and pettiness. By contrast, one could say, the townsmen of *The Key* have the sternly heroic, moral grandeur of Wordsworth's shepherds or Scott's Highlanders. Why not choose *Bloodhunt* on grounds of accuracy? Is the more brutal picture necessarily truer because metropolitan civilization demands a King's Row - Peyton Place myth of Hobbesian Nature in degenerate small town life? And were the brutality demonstrable, would this argue the inferiority of idealizing? Hardly. But if the reader is apt to be unconvinced by what purports to be an authentic picture of a way of life, then this does matter. And here *Bloodhunt* is the safer method, for it focuses sharply on the central figure's experience and does not try to sketch a community.

The Key does. Its community is varied, peopled with distinct characters and no mere village chorus. As its social scope is wider, so its structure risks diffuseness and generality. Moreover, there is a radical split between rural characters and sophisticated alien observers, who observe and comment. The reader finds himself at home with the urbanites, participates in their commentary, and this makes for a degree of abstractness: the reader participates through one of two general " sides." The doctor serves as a bridge; but his almost purely generic identity—only his mother calls him anything but " the doctor"—again suggests generality. Sandy would seem a much more adequate bridge. But as a matter of fact, the doctor's generality is fully functional, and he is part of an ambitious narrative and symbolic anatomy of human destructiveness at war with human brotherhood which is, for me, more impressive. *The Key*, the first Gunn novel I read, serves well as an introduction to his distinctive achievement in fiction.

Let me begin with its counterpart to Pheemie and Sandy, its involved yet detached mediator between pastoral-instinctual and urban-intellectual ways of life and modes of vision. The doctor is ideally placed as pivotal consciousness. His profession makes him a focal figure in the community; his professional affairs endow him with sad scepticism and deep compassion; he is intellectual, yet urgently practical; he is bound to his people by deep, instinctual ties. But his intellectuality draws him to the two sophisticated outsiders, Michael and his foppish, pedantic, yet wise and kindly guest Gwynn, whose own hunt for the key to modern primitive art has brought him to this traditional community and made him the most articulate mouthpiece for notions and values Gunn takes most seriously. Michael, though less intellectual, is close to Gwynn. The doctor, who would ordinarily *use* their rather academic premises to defend his people's way of life and of seeing, finds himself inclined to retreat into silence and scepticism from their rush of words and aggressive curiosity. In this perfect mechanism for dialogue Gunn has given himself an ideal means for sifting the pastoral and primitivistic attitudes or values of which his themes are often made, and at the same time given himself, in the doctor, an ironic device for backing away from any tendency to immerse narrative concreteness in such discussion. The ideas are perfectly relevant—they are usually that; but here, their excessive exposition is an integral part of narrative structure and meaning. Words, abstract formulations, cannot supply the key to any chest; the crucial facts must be seen, visualized personally and archetypally, to be properly interpreted. Such is the doctor's lesson, and his reticence is a sign of his wisdom and an effective comment on Gwynn's intellectual primitivism.

Michael is distinguished from both by his strongly creative or destructive impulses. Hence, he is associated with images rather than with ideas. His photographic hobby commits him to a central faith in the book: that the individual as concretely visualized is ultimate. Michael is a hunter. He hunts odd birds, though only as a photographer; and he hunts individual solitary human birds as well — not as the destroyer would, but in the creative way of the artist—" the one man who sees a thing whole " (p.175)—seeking the full dynamic essence of each. This is his way of hunting the key of the chest, of the mystery of the seaman's death, which is the mystery of life and death, in this traditional community.

Michael's camera is just one of many visual aids in the book; the terrain demands telescopes and binoculars. The book

is, as Charlie describes his impression of people, "Eyes, many
eyes. looking around corners" (p.251). From the beginning,
when the Procurator Fiscal tries to get a "picture of the whole
thing" (p.43), when Michael is sent to take photographs, and
Gwynn admits he has come "to spy out the land" (p.56), the
hunt unfolds as a rich texture of contrasting and complimentary
modes of perception. As, for example, the doctor analyzes the
photographs in the seventh chapter, he is made "aware of that
border line beyond which analysis is blind, and, being blind,
destructive" (p.63). The entire chapter is a scene constructed for
the expounding of contrasting ways of seeing the murder—and
ways of not seeing. The mythic way of seeing prevails in the
minister's sermon of the following chapter—a parabolic vision
of life as a sea, ending as the minister "opened his eyes and
looked upon the world, and the men were delivered from their
visions" (p.73). The next chapter ends with an almost identical
gesture, as the patriarch Smeorach "lifted his eyes to the blind
window, and it seemed to him that life was all shadows" (p.78).
The main characters are identifiable in terms of wholeness and
intensity of vision. Michael is credited "with a precision so vivid
that it gathered attributes of the mythical" (p.67); Flora is like
him, the would-be primitive artist for whom reasoning is carried
on through visualization: "Reason produced its own profound
logic in the form of images" (p.82). The minister has a mind
as sensitive and hidden as "one of Michael's plates"; the
horrible vividness of the doctor's dream has "the kind of clarity
which Michael sometimes got in his photographs" (pp.101, 169).
Michael and Gwynn, though they come (says the doctor) "with
the outsider's eye" (p.122), bring from theatrical experience a
strong sense of spectacle; the *species aeternitatis* under which
they view the unfolding tragedy of Charlie and Flora is congenial
with the community's timeless vision. Thus, the book evolves
its contrast of modes of seeing as its structure moves in circles
about the central figures with many eyes.

To what end? The end is a remarkable fusion of thematic
resolution and technical articulation. The novel is a hunt for
a key, the key is to be found only in the mystery of individual
personality, and the finding awaits the proper mode of vision.
When "the concept is all but lost in the thing itself," when
"the personal, the dangerous personal, touched the universal,"
when words are useless and images are primary, then vision can

[81]

recognize "the individual human being, the one whole being" (pp.198, 238). Those who would be whole can achieve wholeness only by achieving the capacity for seeing it.

But the problem is not just personal; it is social. The key to the mystery of the dead seaman is also to be found in the mysterious bond of the two brothers, which in turn reflects the larger brotherhood of men of the sea which Charlie, in accidentally causing the seaman's death, has violated. Brotherhood is given its widest significance by the several allusions to Cain and Abel. Both brothers are accused of wearing Cain's mark. The whole novel explores Cain's answer and poses the dependent query: how *can* one be one's brother's keeper? It is, ironically, the Cain-like figure of Dougald, the seemingly brutal shepherd, who supplies the answer—by being the answer, by being one who has instinctively known how to be his brother's keeper and who has been willing to stand and defy the destructive forces, external and internal, that threaten his brother. The doctor tries; the doctor is anxious to "fix things up." But even the doctor must learn the lesson embodied in Dugald's brotherhood and in the instinctive, unobtrusive, practical helpfulness of the other men of the community. Charlie's plight cannot be fixed up any more than Nan's illness can, any more than Allan can be hidden from moral law. Brotherhood is a matter of the most delicate tact or instinct, which acts as its brother's keeper without violating the individual wholeness of its brother. It can do this only when possessed of the most precise and operative vision of individuality.

Thus the intellectual and social imperatives are intertwined, and thus the key of the chest is recovered. It is an excellent key to what is most characteristic and impressive about Neil Gunn's remarkable achievement in fiction.

UNIVERSITY OF VIRGINIA

STUDIES IN SCOTTISH LITERATURE

VOLUME I   NUMBER 2   OCTOBER 1963

CONTENTS

STUDIES IN SCOTTISH LITERATURE

EDITED BY G. ROSS ROY
TEXAS TECHNOLOGICAL COLLEGE

STUDIES IN SCOTTISH LITERATURE is an
independent quarterly devoted to all aspects of
Scottish literature. Articles and notes are welcome.
Subscriptions are available at $5.00 U.S. per annum in the
United States and Canada, elsewhere 30 shillings.
All communications should be addressed to the
Editor, Department of English, Texas Technological College,
Lubbock, Texas, U.S.A.

PUBLISHED BY TEXAS TECHNOLOGICAL COLLEGE
AND PRINTED BY THE TEXAS TECH PRESS
LUBBOCK, TEXAS, U.S.A.

EDITORIAL

While the first issue of *Studies in Scottish Literature* was in the form of a trial, this second number finds us more firmly established. Critical reception has been encouraging, two distinguished scholars have been added to the editorial board, several interesting articles have been submitted for publication, and new subscriptions have been coming in. This does not suggest that complacency is in order: much remains to be done, especially in the area of attaining wider coverage through more subscriptions.

With the third issue, Texas Technological College will begin subsidizing the publication of *SSL*. The decision to do so was taken by the President, Dr. R. C. Goodwin, and the Editor takes this opportunity to express his gratitude to him for making the continuation of this journal possible.

The printing of *SSL* is now done by the Texas Tech Press; it is hoped that this will speed the publication of future issues.

CONTRIBUTORS
TO THIS ISSUE

William R. McGRAW: Holds the M.A. from Ohio State University and the Ph.D. from the University of Minnesota. Formerly taught at the College of Wooster, University of Minnesota and the University of Oregon. Presently Assistant Professor of Speech and Director in Theatre at the University of Michigan. Currently serving as Administrative Vice-President of the American Educational Theatre Association. Has previously published in *Modern Drama*, the *Educational Theatre Journal* and *Dramatics Magazine*. In 1961, through the courtesy of Sir Tyrone Guthrie, was a guest at the Edinburgh Festival, the Pitlochry Festival, the Old Vic and elsewhere, where he conducted interviews for the purpose of assessing current developments in the English theatre.

Mabel L. MACKENZIE: Took her Ph.D. at the University of Toronto and is teaching at the University of British Columbia. Particular interest in Scottish ballad poetry. Gave a series of lectures over the Canadian Broadcasting Corporation entitled "Talking about poetry." Spent last year in the United Kingdom doing research on ballads, especially "The Gaberlunzie Man."

Allan H. MacLAINE: Graduate of McGill University, Ph.D. from Brown University with a thesis on Fergusson. Has taught at McGill, Brown, University of Massachusetts, and Texas Christian University. Now Professor of English at the University of Rhode Island. Long a student of Scottish literature, he is the author of several scholarly articles in this field, and is currently at work on a book-length critical study of Burns to be published by Twayne Publishers. A book on Chaucer's *Canterbury Tales* is scheduled to appear soon.

William MONTGOMERIE: Born in Glasgow. Graduated M.A. in Glasgow and Ph.D. in Edinburgh with a thesis on the Scottish ballads. He published *Via* and *Squared Circle*, both books of verse; contributed an essay to *New Judgments*: *Robert Burns* which he edited; and, with his wife, edited *Scottish Nursery Rhymes*, *Sandy Candy* (traditional folk rhymes), and *Well at the World's End* (Scottish folk tales). He has contributed poems, short stories and articles to many publications. He feels that his essay "More an Antique Roman than a Dane," published in the *Hibbert Journal* (October 1961), solves the *Hamlet* problem of the play-within-the-play.

M . L . M A C K E N Z I E

A New Dimension
for "Tam O' Shanter"

To suggest a new dimension for "Tam o' Shanter," probably the most frequently discussed of Burns's poems, is at this date an ambitious undertaking. Critics have long been content to classify the work as "a narrative poem," occasionally with the qualification that it "belongs to the well known *genre* of the Wild Ride, of which Byron's 'Mazeppa' is perhaps the best example in British literature."[1] The ride, however, is only one aspect of the poem. I propose to show that "Tam o' Shanter" follows in external details the *genre* of the mock-heroic, and that in several respects it echoes the techniques and even the incidents of Pope's *The Rape of the Lock*.

While the evidence for my argument must be demonstrated within the poem, there exists corroborative material from external sources, particularly from Burns's letters. Many references in his correspondence show that he read much epic poetry, at least in translation. "Thanks many thanks for my Gawin Douglas,"[2] he writes to a friend when the book is returned to him. And to another friend:

> Dryden's Virgil has delighted me . . . I own I am disappointed in the Aeneid. . . . I think Virgil, in many instances, servile copier of Homer. If I had the Odyssey by me, I could parallel many passages where Virgil has evidently copied, but by no means improved Homer.[3]

In January 1789, he writes:

> I muse & rhyme, morning, noon & night; & have a hundred different Poetic plans, pastoral, georgic, dramatic, &c. floating in the regions of fancy, somewhere between Purpose and resolve.[4]

Six months later he composed "Tam o' Shanter," no doubt the fruition of one of these "hundred different Poetic plans."

Specific resemblances, not necessarily borrowings, between "Tam o' Shanter" and *The Rape of the Lock* make Burns's familiarity with the

---

[1] Thomas Crawford, *Burns* (Edinburgh, 1960), p. 221.
[2] *The Letters of Robert Burns*, ed. J. DeLancey Ferguson (Oxford, 1931), II, 315.
[3] *The Letters*, I, 221.
[4] *The Letters*, I 290.

works of Pope a matter of some importance. Besides the quotations from Pope which appear at the head of several poems, at least nineteen references to, or quotations from, Pope, appear in Burns's letters. The quotations, drawn from many lines, and not merely the popular aphorisms, indicate a fairly wide knowledge of the whole of Pope's canon. The following remarks in a letter to a friend make clear what Burns's intentions were. He writes:

> I very lately ... wrote a poem, not in imitation, but in the manner of Pope's Moral Epistles. It is only a short essay, just to try the strength of my Muse's pinion in that way.... I have likewise been laying the foundation of some pretty large poetic works.[5]

The poem alluded to above is, unhappily, not identified, nor is there evidence for the surmise that he appreciated Pope's jest, "Receipt to make an Epic Poem."

Reference to "Tam o' Shanter" itself clearly discloses mock epic characteristics. Without striving too laboriously to find a conscious application of the *genre,* on the one hand, or mere imitation on the other, the reader can be aware of the resemblances to an epic poem. Burns has adhered closely to Aristotle's precepts. "Tam" has fable, action, characters, sentiments, diction and metre, and the reader contemplates at one view the beginning and the end. The poet speaks in his own person as little as possible, and the intrusions when they occur, are limited to moral digressions similiar to those delivered by the epic narrator. The surprising, the improbable and the incredible are all admitted, and the impossible which appears probable is preferred to the improbable which appears possible. Finally, neither manners nor sentiment are obscured by too splendid a diction.

Besides these general resemblances, "Tam" has close affinities with the epic in many particulars, similarities too exact to be dismissed as merely coincidental and which are matters of essence and not merely of superficial qualities.

The mock epic burlesques the characteristics of the classical epic, beginning generally with an invocation to the Muse. Burns does not invoke his Muse but he makes known her existence by regretting her inadequacy to describe the heights to which Nannie rose in her terpsichorean efforts:

> But here my muse her wing maun cour;
> Sic flights are far beyond her power:
> To sing how Nannie lap and flang
> (A souple jade she was, and strang). (ll. 179-182)

[5] *The Letters,* I, 258.

A formal statement of theme is another convention of the epic. Burns makes it clear in the first twenty lines that he will write of the dire, if grotesque, fate which will overtake his feckless hero on the harrowing journey of "lang Scots miles" from the tavern to his home. Just such a journey, fraught with dangers, is of course a theme of The Odyssey and The Aeneid. The comment on the town, "Auld Ayr," is strictly in the epic tradition, as is the storm. Everywhere Ulysses goes there is a woman to minister to him. Tam is equally favoured:

> The landlady and Tam grew gracious,
> Wi' favours secret, sweet and precious;   (ll. 47-8)

The epic has its story tellers. In Burns's mock epic, "The Souter tauld his queerest stories;" (l. 49). In epics, the Olympian deities direct the destinies of men. In "Tam," inexorable fate is the master of poor mortals:

> Nae man can tether time nor tide;
> The hour approaches Tam maun ride;   (ll. 67-8)

With these words, the poem, begun conventionally in *medias res,* resumes the narrative.

The fable of an epic stresses the joy of recognition rather than the shock of surprise. Burns's fable is a folk tale that had become legend for miles around. As do events in true epics, the action in Burns's poem takes place on several levels, as the hero finds himself in Heaven, in Hell and on earth. The epic hero towers above all ordinary mortals, and is surrounded by men of stature comparable to his own. Therefore the mock epic requires an anti-hero. Burns rises to one of his best efforts here. His hero has attributes a king might envy; he is at times kingly:

> Kings may be blest, but Tam was glorious
> O'er a' the ills o' life victorious!   (ll. 57-8)

Moreover in his utter drunkenness and superb madness when "Tam tint his reason a' thegither" (l. 189) he is a truly realistic anti-hero. Nor does he stand alone; his companion in countless campaigns is equally worthy:

> And at his elbow Souter Johnny,
> His ancient, trusty, drouthy crony;
> Tam lo'ed him like a vera brither;
> They had been fou for weeks thegither.   (ll. 41-4)

Freedom of treatment is accorded to an epic poet to invent his own details and dialogue so long as he produces grandiloquent speeches, generally of a moral nature. Grandiose and moral, though ineffective is the first speech of Tam's wife, Kate, a comic Penelope, who sits at home awaiting the return of her lord:

[89]

> Gathering her brows like gathering storm,
> Nursing her wrath to keep it warm.   (ll. 11-12)
> .... She tauld thee weel thou was a skellum,
> A blethering, blustering, drunken blellum;
> That frae November till October,
> Ae market-day thou was na sober.   (ll. 19-22)

Kate very properly ends her exhortation in epic style with a warning and a prophecy:

> She prophesied that, late or soon,
> Thou would be found deep drowned in Doon;
> Or catched wi' warlocks in the mirk
> By Alloway's auld haunted kirk.   (ll. 29-32)

The sustained formality of language requisite to the epic is found in the speeches in which Burns is pointing his moral. He piles up similes in carefully stated, neo-classical language:

> But pleasures are like poppies spread—
> You seize the flower, its bloom is shed   (ll. 59f.)

and so on for the half a dozen lines of the catalogue. To take the place of the epic paean of praise, Burns gives his readers:

> Inspiring, bold John Barleycorn,
> What dangers thou canst mak us scorn!
> Wi' tippenny we fear nae evil,
> Wi' usquabae we'll face the devil!   (ll. 5-8)

The bees which appear in Homer, Virgil, Spenser and Milton are not missing from Burns's poem. They appear twice. "The bees flee hame wi' lades o' treasure" (l. 55) and again:

> As bees bizz out wi' angry fyke,
> When plundering herds assail their byke;   (ll. 194-5)

and so on to the end of the simile. Important in the true epic are the four elements. Burns introduces these when he says:

> Tam skelpit on through dub and mire,
> Despising wind, and rain and fire—(ll. 81-2)

The epic journey has been mentioned as beginning the poem. Burns surely makes his as terrifying and horrible as any in the tradition. Even Satan's journey in *Paradise Lost* is not more graphically described than Tam's visit to the Alloway Kirkyard, which achieves its macabre effect from the variation Burns produces on the theme—Tam does not descend to the underworld; it comes up to him. The recitation of horrors to be found in the ruined church burlesques the catalogue convention of the epic, as Burns enumerates the series of frightful objects adorning the unholy altar.

Nor does Burns omit the metamorphosis. Pope has the dusky Umbriel, Minerva-like, perch himself on a sconce's height to witness the battle in *The Rape*, where the reader's imagination metamorphoses him into a light. Burns, with more frightful invention, resorts to diabolical, rather than divine, apotheosis, as the corpses are transformed into the sconces or light holders:

> Coffins stood round, like open presses,
> That shawed the dead in their last dresses;
> And by some devlish cantraip slight
> Each in its cauld hand held a light.   (ll. 125-8)

A true epic has a lofty purpose. In the climactic episode of both *The Rape* and "Tam" is found the lofty purpose which is made the supreme burlesque of each poet, similar as to subject, and at the same time ludicrously different, the rape of a lock of hair. In the first poem the charming Belinda is the victim of the loss of one of her delightful curls, while in the second "noble Maggie," Tam's grey mare, "(A better never lifted leg)," is bereft of her tail.

Prophecies come true in epic poems though usually ironically or partially. In *The Rape* only one half each of the Baron's boast and prayer is realized; in "Tam," half of Kate's prophecy is fulfilled. Tam is not drowned, providentially, but only "catched wi' warlocks in the mirk." (l. 31) An ironic moral is generally presented at the appropriate moment in an epic poem. Burns, in a fine dramatic climax, presents his ironic moral as a grave admonition in which both the hero and Maggie share the last words:

> Think! Ye may buy the joys o'er dear
> Remember Tam o' Shanter's mare.

These generic resemblances of "Tam o' Shanter" to the mock epic poem have been suggested by the devices it most conspicuously uses, without questioning that the poem is essentially a "verse narrative," and that it employs other devices than the mock epic. There is as much low burlesque as high in Burns's stanzas, as he describes the adventures of his drunken hero. And for this reason he uses not the high style of the heroic couplet, but the quick succession of rhymes of the octo-syllabic couplet, long favoured by Scots poets for narrative poems, and for popular poetry of the folk epic type, and is by turns rugged, pungent, grotesque, gruesome, tender and charming. His language is chiefly the colloquial idiom of the Ayrshire peasant of his day, interspersed with diction sufficiently elaborate and formal to burlesque the epic style.

No claim is made for "Tam o' Shanter" that it has more in common with *The Rape of the Lock* in poetic terms than the generic resemblances which have been indicated. The world of Belinda and Sir Plume is far removed from that of Tam by more than time and place. Each poem reflects with almost pictorial accuracy the society from which it comes, and each has its origin in universals. Appearance and reality are as deceptive to Belinda and the Baron as they are to Tam and his cronies, and to the epic heroes, and reason and emotion in one breast produce the same conflicts. Reflecting perhaps the temperaments of the two writers, the irony which pervades both poems is warmer and kindlier in Burns's work than in Pope's.

From the time of its first publication "Tam o' Shanter" has been recognized as one of the great narrative poems of literature. By pointing out a new dimension—the resemblance to the mock heroic *genre*—I hope however to enhance an understanding of the poem. "Tam o' Shanter" is not a greater work by this addition, but the thought that Burns may have had epic poems in mind, may produce further appreciation of the poem for the sophisticated reader. It would appear that the full originality of the work has not yet completely emerged. The poem is more than a verse narrative, and this new dimension heightens the effect in an already dynamic poem. So successful is Burns's fusion of divergent elements that "Tam o' Shanter" corroborates with greater intensity Carlyle's belief that Burns left "no more than a poor mutilated fragment of what was in him."

UNIVERSITY OF BRITISH COLUMBIA

William Macmath and
the Scott Ballad Manuscripts

The student of Francis James Child's volumes *The English and Scottish Popular Ballads* may have noticed frequent references to the help given to the editor by William Macmath. It would be a pity if William Macmath continued to be remembered only in the few sentences scattered through Child's five volumes, especially as a closer examination of the evidence shows that Professor Child could not have brought his impressive collection of British ballads to its high state of completeness without the assistance of William Macmath.

Professor Child's fumbling when he tried to tap the wealth of Aberdeen oral tradition is revealed by a very superficial examination of the Alexander Keith's *Last Leaves of Traditional Ballads and Airs*. In a sense, the hundred-odd manuscript notebooks of Gavin Greig, from which Keith extracted the ballads may be seen in Child's work as a series of gaps. The mass of material supplied by William Macmath might also have been gaps in that work.

As a Scot visiting Cecil Sharpe House in London, I have often been reminded of Scottish neglect of Gavin Greig who is at least equally important. The following notes are a preliminary attempt to bring another neglected Scot into greater prominence. He is not as important as Gavin Greig but his present almost complete obscurity is due largely to the fact that he was a Scot whose countrymen have not yet discovered him.

The few facts about William Macmath's uneventful life were published in *William Macmath* (1844-1922) *A Biographical Sketch* by Frank Miller (Dalbeattie: Thomas Fraser, 1924).

William Macmath was born in Brighton, his father being Alexander Macmath, a native of the Galloway parish of Parton. In 1867, William was employed in the office of Messrs. W. and J. Cook W. S., 61 North Castle Street, Edinburgh; then in the office of Messrs. Dundas and Wilson, 16 St. Andrew Square for fifty years.

On 14th December 1874 he was elected a Fellow of the Society of Antiquaries of Scotland, and was one of the original members of the Edinburgh Bibliographical Society. He began his correspondence with Professor Child in the Spring of 1873 and continued it till Child's death in September 1869. It is from Macmath's complete record of that correspondence that the following extracts have been copied.

Professor Child and William Macmath met only once, during Child's visit to Edinburgh in August 1873.

William Macmath, from his office at 16 St. Andrew Square, Edinburgh, wrote to F. J. Furnivall on 25th April 1877. He asked the editor of the Percy Manuscript to insert the following notice "in one of the literary journals of Saturday":

Death of Mr. Geo. R. Kinloch

. . . George Ritchie Kinloch died at his residence, West Coates Villa, Edinburgh, on Sunday last, in his eightieth year, having survived by half a century the publication of his *Ancient Scottish Ballads*, . . . The strong point of Mr. Kinloch's excellence as an editor lay in his scrupulous fidelity, and in this respect he belonged emphatically to the school of Herd, Ritson and Motherwell, as opposed to that of Ramsay, Percy, Scott, Jamieson, and Buchan.

This notice was printed in the *Edinburgh Evening News* of Saturday, April 28, 1877.

In his letter Macmath added a significant statement about Scott:

The views expressed are not my own alone, but are these which I know to be held by Professor Child. Even he, however, does not yet know the full extent to which Sir Walter Scott was a sinner in the matter of ballad editing. Nothing but my reluctance to anticipate the Professor's book prevents me from exposing Scott. How necessary that we should value the men, like Kinloch, who were faithful among the faithless found.

Three years later, on 9th February 1880, Macmath repeated this charge to Professor Child:

I cannot speak with any confidence as to Jamieson's treatment of Mss., but for Scott's fidelity I would not give twopence. From what I have seen in Glenriddell's case (to which I will immediately advert) I know he made the most paltry alterations, "from tradition", . . . that he plundered one Ballad for the sake of another, that he failed in many cases to acknowledge his authority at all, and that, in short, he did almost everything which a Ballad Editor, as his duties are now understood, ought not to have done. To deal with Scott's Ballads without Mrs. Brown's Mss. would not be unlike dealing with Percy without the Folio . . . .

But even if we should fail to get Mrs Brown, we have enough, I am thankful to say, in Glenriddell, upon which to frame an indictment against Sir Walter . . . . I doubt if we will ever get a better example of Scott's style of treatment than in the Ballad which he has called (I do not say improperly, but "trusty Glenriddell" does not venture on a name himself) "Lord Maxwell's Goodnight", and which, so far as I know, does not exist elsewhere. I send a copy of eight lines, which is a fair enough sample. I told Mr. Furnivall long

---

ERRATUM: Page 94, line 3, for "1869" read "1896."

ago that nothing but my unwillingness to anticipate your edition prevented me from exposing Scott, and I think the printing of this little poem alone might make a reputation for a man! . . .

Before leaving Sir Walter I may say it seems to me worthy of your serious consideration whether you have got all the material from Abbotsford which you ought to have. . . . Every day I live I am more and more impressed with the great responsibility resting upon those who take part in the discussion of Ballad authenticity, and the danger of proceeding without clear and sufficient evidence . . . .

Ten years later, evidence begins to appear in Macmath's correspondence that he was laying siege to Abbotsford. Robert B. Armstrong wrote him that he had not heard again from Father Forbes-Leith and concluded that there was nothing to be found at Abbotsford.

This gave Macmath his opportunity. On 28th January 1890 he wrote directly to the Revd. W. Forbes-Leith, S. J., reminding him that he had consented to look through the Abbotsford Library for a copy of the Ballad of "Jamie Telfar". It had been for some years, for Macmath, a matter of great regret that Professor Child had not been in a position to use the texts of the Ballads collected by Sir Walter Scott, as taken direct from the original Mss. In the letter he lists the famous Scottish collectors already used by Child, tells him that David Laing, a number of years before, had applied to the Abbotsford Trustees on the Professor's behalf and that, at a later date, Thomas Carlyle had written to Mr. Maxwell Scott on the subject.

The reply on both occasions had been that no Ballads in Ms could be found.

It did not seem to me fitting that I should attempt to rush in where such eminent names had failed. But though silent, I have remained unconvinced and dissatisfied. Though the Abbotsford Library may contain no Ballads in Ms bound up together *as such*, the Ballads which Sir Walter collected in Ms must, I think, still be in existence, and are probably bound up with or form part of his correspondence.

In a further letter (4th February 1890) Macmath tells the Rev. Forbes-Leith that Mr. Laing had obtained from Abbotsford certain Ballads from a Ms Miscellany in Abbotsford, "Scottish Songs," which had been shown at the Scott Centenary Exhibition. They were of small value, being only "copies from the versions of Mrs. Brown of Falkland, altered and interpolated."

If it would further the Ballad cause, Macmath was willing to make a special journey to Abbotsford and arrange to take his annual holiday in the neighbourhood, copying manuscripts if necessary.

Next day (5th Feb.) Macmath wrote to Child, beginning his letter, "Abbotsford has been carried, as I believe." Forbes-Leith had just called on him and the two men were to manage the matter between them. Macmath sends Father Forbes-Leith a list of a few Ballads, "Hobbie Noble," "Jamie Telfer" etc. from the next part of Child's collection. By the beginning of June, Macmath is suggesting the first week in July as the date most convenient. Can he get into Abbotsford then to look for ballads? There are no obstacles, but Forbes-Leith is not sure if he can be at home at that time. It is probably for that reason that the date proposed for Macmath's visit to Abbotsford is postponed to 7th July.

> All I shall require will be a corner to write in, and the necessary volumes. Those I *know* of at present are (1) the volumes containing Sir Walter's correspondence. (2) the 6 small vols of stall ballads we spoke of. (3) the Bell stall ballads. (4) the Ms Vol "Scottish Songs".
> I intend to lodge at Darnick or Gattenside if I can.

It is evident, from the correspondence between Macmath and Father Forbes-Leith, that Mrs. Maxwell Scott did not wish Sir Walter Scott's correspondence to be seen by everybody, so Macmath promises not to note anything not relating to ballads.

Macmath arrived in Melrose on 7th July, on a train from Edinburgh that arrived at 10:41. From the station he walked to Abbotsford. Three days later, he was already sending copies of Sir Walter Scott's ballads to Professor Child, addressing his letter from The Library, Abbotsford.

> I have seen enough to enable me to report that the expedition is a great success,—how great I cannot yet say, as the Reverend Father is producing the chief treasures by degrees from some repository in the private part of the mansion, which no ordinary mortal is allowed to enter.

A week afterwards, he had already examined volume one of the Letters and much of the first Volume of ballads. He was able to sum up his first impressions:

> If the second volume is as rich in material as the one I have, the Abbotsford— so far from being nowhere among Collections—will take a first place, and even what I have already seen will place it pretty high.

Macmath completed his first visit to Abbotsford on the 6th of August. In a letter to Child, five weeks later, Macmath asks him to dismiss from his mind the idea that there had been anything of martyrdom in going to Abbotsford in holiday time. He had regarded the omission of Abbotsford from among the sources of material in Child's book as a very grave reproach and scandal, which he is only too glad to be able at length to wipe out. It was at Macmath's own request that there is no mention in Child's *Ballads* of Macmath's sacrifice of his summer holiday to work in the Abbotsford library. He will have to return to Abbotsford, for several reasons. One of these is that Father Forbes-Leith lives miles away, at Selkirk, and has work of his own to attend to. Another difficulty is described in this same letter:

> For instance, one small bookcase in the Library, which contains Ballads, can only be opened by the use of a screw driver! No wonder, therefore, that David Laing and Thomas Carlyle could do nothing. Writing letters is of no avail. Personal presence is required, to sit down before the place, and pointing say in effect, but more politely, "I must have that book out, please get the screw driver, as I cant go away without seeing the volume."

It is necessary at this point to quote a few lines from the same letter to clarify the business relations between Professor Child and his Scottish collaborator:

> As to money, the fair thing is to charge you the excess over what I would have been spending in ordinary course, and if you send £2 more than you have sent already, that will be enough. I had to make one or two presents, not in current coin of the realm, and for them you can send me a book or two when opportunity offers. I should like to have your volume of Religious Poetry and your Ballads for Schools.

In the following year (1891) Macmath returned to Abbotsford on the 27th of July. As before he made his arrangements through Father Forbes-Leith:

> I should like to have the volume called 'Scotch Ballad' from the private part of the Mansion, and to continue my examination of the 'Letters', beginning with Volume IV.

On 25th August he wrote Forbes-Leith from Edinburgh:

> I returned from Melrose this afternoon, having done very well at Abbotsford.
>
> I can hardly say at present whether or not I still have to claim your indulgence on a future occasion. I have secured all the important ballads I have found, and while I think there ought to be others, I am unable to point out their whereabouts.

In his report to Child (26th September 1891) Macmath is not satisfied that they have got all the Ballads in Abbotsford.

> You speak of "their" duty in telling "us" about Ballads. The position now is just the reverse,—we have to tell them. We have all that I can point out in the shelves, but the state of things at Abbotsford render it impossible for me to get, or indeed to ask, full "rummaging" powers. At the time of the year I can go, the public part of the house is held by the tourists and the private part by the tenants, and I have to do the best I can among them.

He had been unable to find "North Country Ballads" in Ms., and therefore left it an open question whether he was to be back in Abbotsford or no. He had not closed the door on himself. Father Forbes-Leith had spoken of a small volume containing the songs which were sung in Sir Walter's family, but had no idea where it was. Macmath had expected to find something of the kind from what Lockhart said in his edition of the Minstrelsy as to the tunes. He concludes:

> As to Abbotsford expenses,—if you can afford it, I would be all the better of the same as last year £7. This in full, however,—nothing extra for postage.

Macmath returned to Abbotsford at the end of July 1892 to examine the manuscript "North Country Ballads" which proved to be substantially the pieces printed in Maidment's *North Country Garland*. Some of them varied considerably from the printed form. Apart from three other unimportant volumes, there now remained the red morocco volume, described by Father Forbes-Leith as containing the pieces that used to be sung in Sir Walter's family circle. Mrs. Maxwell Scott was at Chiefswood on the estate and Macmath hung about thinking he might meet her.

Ultimately he wrote to Father Forbes-Leith about the red morocco volume. He got the informal answer that the family did not wish that volume published.

Macmath tried to find the date when the folio manuscript volume "Scotch Ballads, Materials for Border Minstrelsy" was put together. He wrote David Douglas who informed him that David Laing had something to do wih the arrangement and also Alexr Brock, Bookbinders of the North Bridge, Edinburgh. Macmath's information from them was that all the old books were packed in a cellar and it might be some time before they could send him the information he desired. No further correspondence is recorded. Macmath's expenses for this third Abbotsford expedition were £3.

After his outbursts about Scott in 1877 and 1880, Macmath did not repeat his opinion of Scott as a ballad editor. There is no evidence that he altered his opinion. The evidence is now on record in the pages of Francis James Child's *The English and Scottish Popular Ballads*. The literary critic will probably continue justifying Scott for "improving" our traditional ballads and making poems out of them. The true balladist will agree with every word of Macmath's criticism.

BROUGHTY FERRY, ANGUS

ALLAN H. MacLAINE

Robert Fergusson's *Auld Reikie*
and the Poetry of City Life

The most famous poem in British literature devoted wholly to description of city life is John Gay's *Trivia*. But this fascinating work stands by no means alone; rather it is representative of a vast body of little-known poetry in this genre, extending from the time of Chaucer to the present. William H. Irving in the final chapter of *John Gay's London* (Cambridge, Mass., 1928), an encyclopedic and eminently useful study of this kind of verse, notes that prior to the Romantic movement which brought more personal, humanitarian, symbolic, or even mystic poetic interpretations of the city into fashion, the city poetry of earlier eras is marked by more or less objective descriptive technique: the poet observes the life of the city and describes it for purposes of eulogy (as in Dunbar's *The Flour of Cities All,* or in passages of Spenser or Herrick); or for purposes of satire and exposure of folly (as in Swift's savage little sketches of street life); or for the sheer fun and fascination of it all (as in *Trivia*). A long-neglected work in this earlier tradition and a direct successor of *Trivia* chiefly concerns us here. This is *Auld Reikie,* an extraordinary portrait of life in eighteenth-century Edinburgh by the brilliant Scots poet Robert Fergusson (1750-1774). Fergusson, whose career was tragically cut short in the first flush of his genius by death in the Edinburgh mad-house at the age of twenty-four, is remembered as the author of some thirty Scots poems (mostly graphic sketches of life in his beloved city) which were destined, a decade later, to have a profound and decisive impact upon the creative imagination of Burns. *Auld Reikie,* a poem of 368 lines in tetrameter couplets, is Fergusson's longest and most ambitious treatment of the Edinburgh scene, and deserves to be recognized as one of the finest poetic renderings of city life in our literature.

Matthew P. McDiarmid, in the notes to his splendid edition of Fergusson, declares curtly of *Auld Reikie* that "the main suggestion for the poem came from Gay's *Trivia.*"[1] This statement is unquestionably accu-

---

[1] *The Poems of Robert Fergusson,* Scottish Text Soc., 3rd Ser. 4 (Edinburgh, 1956), II, 276. All quotations from Fergusson are taken from this definitive edition; for the text of *Auld Reikie* see II, 109-120.

rate, since it is clear that Fergusson was thoroughly familiar with the work of Gay[2] (and also with that of Dryden, Pope, and Swift), and that in *Auld Reikie* he was obviously trying to do for Edinburgh something on the order of what Gay had already done for London. But *Auld Reikie* bears the stamp of Fergusson's distinctive originality, and is anything but a servile imitation of Gay; in fact, the differences between the two poems are more striking than their similarities. At this point, then, a brief comparison of the two, in structure, subject matter and style, will help to elucidate the characteristics of both poems, before we turn to a more detailed analysis of *Auld Reikie*.

Gay evidently conceived *Trivia* partly as a sort of "town-georgic" adapted from the Virgilian rural georgics, and partly as a burlesque on the versified "Arts," the habit, very popular in his day, of composing pompous poetic treatises on the most mundane of arts.[3] Accordingly, he provides his poem with a subtitle, "The Art of Walking the Streets of London," though Gay's original satiric motive seems soon to have become subordinated to his zest for his subject matter. The idea of burlesquing the "Arts" poems, however, supplied Gay with a convenient framework for his material which is neatly organized in three books: "Of the Implements for Walking the streets, and Signs of the weather"; "Of Walking the Streets, by Day"; and "Of Walking the Streets, by Night." Within this overall scheme, the structure of *Trivia* is firm and satisfying.

Auld Reikie, on the other hand, suffers from a certain looseness of structure. Dealing with the same kind of miscellaneous, kaleidoscopic materials, Fergusson's poem lacks an overall structural bond such as Gay's street-walking device which gives to *Trivia* a logical pattern. Fergusson simply shifts his focus from one vignette to another without reference to any single scheme, although it is possible that a more definite structure would have emerged had Fergusson completed his original conception. The fact is that *Auld Reikie*, as we have it, is essentially a fragment. The first 328 lines were published separately in 1773, "for the author," in a slim pamphlet, with a dedication to Sir William Forbes in some of the copies, and the subtitle "Canto I" which suggests that further installments were to follow. The original design was never completed, however, presumably because Fergusson met with no encouragement from Sir William Forbes. After publication of his first "Canto," the poet merely added forty lines

[2] For evidence of Fergusson's admiration of Gay, see his poem *To Sir John Fielding, on his Attempt to suppress the Beggar's Opera* in *Poems*, II, 201-203.

[3] Among the more pedestrian of the titles cited by Irving (pp. 62-87) are John Durant Breval's *The Art of Dress* (1717), Robert Dodsley's *The Art of Preaching* (1738), an anonymous *Art of Stock-Jobbing* (1746), and *The Art of Making Hasty-Pudding* by Dr. Wm. King (1663-1712).

to round off the work, and it was reprinted in its final form five years after Fergusson's death in the 1779 edition of his poems. Hence the total design for the poem, if Fergusson had one, remains unknown.

Nevertheless, this apparent lack of an overall unifying structure in the poem as we have it does not mean that *Auld Reikie* is altogether without organization. Actually, the first half of the poem, after the introduction, is · neatly divided into morning, afternoon, and night scenes (lines 23-58, 59-66, and 67-194 respectively). This arrangement was no doubt suggested to Fergusson by Gay's separation of day from night scenes in Books II and III of *Trivia*. But at line 194 there is an abrupt break in the smooth development of *Auld Reikie* as Fergusson abandons his morning-afternoon-night scheme, and turns to treatment of other aspects of Edinburgh life which do not fit into this scheme. The second half of the poem falls into five sections on the following topics: contrasted description of the attractive vegetable market and the repulsive meat market (lines 195-230); Sunday in Edinburgh (lines 231-270); Holyrood House and poverty (lines 271-312); tribute to the late George Drummond as contrasted to the present corrupt civic leaders (lines 313-350); and a concluding eulogy on Edinburgh (lines 351-368). It should be noted, however, that the three central sections of this second half of the poem—on Edinburgh Sundays, on Holyrood and poverty, and on the city government—are ingeniously linked, one developing naturally out of the other. ' The section on the markets is the weakest part of the poem from a structural point of view, being more or less unrelated to what precedes and follows it. Thus, although *Auld Reikie* contains long passages which are carefully organized around related themes and linked by smooth transitions, the poem as a whole suffers from lack of an overall structural principle.

As for subject matter, *Trivia* and *Auld Reikie* show inevitable similarities. Many of the characters to be encountered in the streets of any eighteenth-century city are treated in both poems—bullies, fops ("macaronis" in Fergusson), housemaids, chairmen, link-boys ("caddies" in Fergusson), whores, and so forth. One brief passage on funerals in *Auld Reikie* (lines 163 ff.) is clearly modelled on *Trivia* (III, lines 255ff.). Apart from this instance of direct indebtedness and one or two other minor hints, however, Fergusson's treatment of the same characters or scenes is entirely independent of Gay's in detail and phrasing. In general, it may be said that the far greater length of *Trivia* (over three times that of *Auld Reikie*) enables Gay to present more wealth of cumulative illustration and detail than is possible to Fergusson within the scope of *Auld Reikie*. At the same time, Gay's use of the street-walking device limits his material mainly to outdoor scenes, whereas Fergusson is able to move indoors to portray the lively tavern life of old Edinburgh. For this reason, Fergusson's poem is more comprehensive than Gay's in that it attempts to recreate the whole life of the city, not just its street scenes. Finally, whereas Gay includes several extended and detailed scenes, a large proportion of his poem is taken up with brief, undeveloped illustrations or suggestive glimpses. Fergusson, on the other hand, within his narrower space tends to concentrate upon a few sharply realized vignettes.

More striking than the differences in structure and subject matter, however, are the differences in the style of these two poems. Gay chose the mock-heroic technique for *Trivia* probably for two reasons: the mock-herioc was then very much in vogue; furthermore, this style enabled his neo-classical sense of decorum to remain inviolate. He could thus render poetically a subject which might otherwise seem to his fashionable readers intrinsically unpoetic and unpleasant. For purposes of outright satire or burlesque the mock-heroic style, especially in the hands of a master like Pope (in *The Rape of the Lock,* for example), may do wonderfully well. But *Trivia,* though it does contain satiric elements, is not basically a satire. The poem is too long and too miscellaneous in subject matter, and Gay's attitudes toward his material are too varied for a consistant mock-heroic technique. As a result there is a certain sense of strain in *Trivia,* or at least so it seems to modern readers accustomed to realistic treatment of city themes. But the delicately artificial quality of his style is doubtless part of Gay's conscious purpose.[4] Through copious use of classical allusion, myth, and pseudo-myth, together with Latinate diction and euphemisms, Gay deliberately softens the harsh realities of his subject matter and achieves a gently ironic, urbane, and pleasantly humorous effect.

Fergusson's aim in *Auld Reikie* is very different. Though he brings in touches of mock heroic here and there in comic or satiric passages, for the most part Fergusson employs a far more direct and unvarnished style to render his brilliant vision of eighteenth-century Edinburgh. The contrast can be illustrated by the fact that Fergusson introduces only eight classical allusions and eight personified abstractions, whereas Gay's poem is filled with scores of these devices. Moreover, Fergusson employs a stylistic method based upon dramatic contrast, thereby achieving a style which is wholly his own and which may be unique in the poetry of city life. A detailed examination of this style will be given later. In summary, it may be said that although *Auld Reikie* was clearly suggested

---

[4] On this point see the illuminating discussion in James Sutherland's "John Gay," in *Pope and his Contemporaries: Essays Presented to George Sherburn* (Oxford, 1949), pp. 201-14.

by *Trivia* and in several ways resembles it (being like *Trivia* neither wholly satiric nor wholly eulogistic in point of view), *Auld Reikie* is distinguished from it and from other city poems chiefly by the method of dramatic contrast which Fergusson uses. And this method is perfectly suited to the unique city which Fergusson celebrates—Edinburgh.

In Fergusson's day Edinburgh was a relatively small city, squeezed within ancient walls with open country on all sides. The overflow of population to the New Town was just barely beginning in 1773; the Old Town, dramatically perched upon its narrow ridge from the Castle to Holyrood House was still the focal center of Edinburgh life. The old capital was an incredibly crowded place, a gray stone jungle of tall tenements (called "lands") huddled on either side of a single mile long street, penetrated by a fantastic network of narrow, evil smelling closes and wynds which gave access to the High Street. So cramped were housing conditions, whole families often living in single rooms, that most of the business and social life of the city had to be carried on in the High Street or in the many taverns. Tavern life was, in fact, the heart and soul of eighteenth-century Edinburgh. Despite the filth and squalor, the city had a strange and impressive kind of beauty which coexisted with this ugliness. No doubt its dramatic location on a narrow ridge with magnificent views of high hills nearby and the Firth of Forth glistening in the distance, has much to do with this impression. At any rate, this unique juxtaposition of beauty and squalor has always fascinated visitors to Edinburgh, and continues to do so. Unfortunately much of the Old Town, the ancient closes of the High Street and the Cowgate, has degenerated since Fergusson's time into something of a slum. This fact is graphically expressed by the contemporary Scots poet Maurice Lindsay in his poem entitled *In the High Street, Edinburgh*:

> Warriston's Close, Halkerston's Wynd!
> Crookit and cramped, dim, drauky, blind . . . .
>
> Fegs, and you're gey romantic places
> for thae wha ainly pree your faces![5]

In Fergusson's day, however, the Old Town was anything but a backwater. It was a dynamic community, bustling with energy, full of stirring life. Unlike London with its sprawling suburbs, Edinburgh was a compact and homogeneous kind of community in which all classes lived together in very close contact. Its intellectual as well as its social life was lively and generally uninhibited. Smollett in *Humphrey Clinker* characterized it as "a hotbed of genius." This, then, was the city full

[5] In *Robert Fergusson, 1750-1774: Essays by Various Hands to Commemorate the Bicentenary of his Birth*, ed. Sydney Goodsir Smith (Edinburgh, 1952), p. 191.

of bewildering contradictions which Fergusson attempted to recreate in all of its contrasting moods, its robust and dissipated life, in *Auld Reikie*.

In a poem of this length it is, of course, manifestly impractical to attempt to treat all of its noteworthy passages and lines in detail, but a few typical examples will perhaps be enough to illustrate the important features of Fergusson's style and method. He opens, appropriately, with a rousing salute to Edinburgh:

> AULD REIKIE, wale o' ilka Town   *best; every*
> That SCOTLAND kens beneath the Moon;
> Where couthy Chiels as E'ening meet   *sociable fellows*
> Their bizzing CRAIGS and MOUS to weet;   *parched; throats; mouths*
> And blythly gar auld Care gae bye   *make*
> Wi' blinkit and wi' bleering Eye . . .

These lines are notable for their warmth and vigor, expressing as they do Fergusson's hearty and unchanging love for the old gray city. It is significant that he begins his poem with this reference to drinking, always a dominant feature of Edinburgh social life in his time.

The next section of the poem, on morning scenes, begins with a splendid couplet portraying sunrise over the city, followed by lines describing the early activities of housemaids and the foul morning smells of sewage (which Fergusson ironically refers to as EDINA's Roses"). This passage is photographic in its terse and impressive realism, as the following extracts will show:

> Now Morn, with bonny Purpie-smiles,   *purple*
> Kisses the Air-cock o' St. Giles;   *weathervane*
> Rakin their Ein, the Servant Lasses   *rubbing; eyes*
> Early begin their Lies and Clashes . . .   *gossip*
>   . . . . .
> On Stair wi' TUB, or PAT in hand   *pot*
> The Barefoot HOUSEMAIDS looe to stand,   *love*
> That antrin Fock may ken how SNELL   *strangers; strong*
> Auld Reikie will at MORNING SMELL.
>
>   (lines 23-6, 33-6)

This passage is typical of Fergusson's comprehensive realism: he does not allow his profound affection for Auld Reikie to blind him to the city's more obnoxious characteristics; while, at the same time, his description of the foul smells and of the sordid side of Edinburgh social life and customs is softened and modified by his emotional response to the strange and unique beauty of this grimy old city, a beauty which coexists with its squalor. It is this balance, this double vision which distinguishes Fergusson's style in *Auld Reikie* from that of Swift in his fiercely realistic satires on London life. Fergusson perceives that the unique atmosphere, the essence of old Edinburgh, lies in the startling and unusual contrasts, both physical and social, which the city presents; and he recreates that atmosphere, with remarkable precision and intimacy, in terms of these contrasts. This double vision, reconciling beauty and ugliness, and unifying thought and feeling so that each modifies the other, is ever present in *Auld Reikie* and is the basic artistic principle of the poem. This principle is clearly discernible in the lines quoted above, where Fergusson, in a single charming couplet, suggests the fragile, fleeting loveliness of sunrise over the ancient spire of St. Giles, and follows it immediately with lines on the slovenly housemaids and the nauseous morning smells of the city.

In his fifth verse paragraph Fergusson makes a direct and trenchant attack on the vanity and small-mindedness of the idle "wits" of the town who gather at the Luckenbooths[6] to observe the passing crowds and sneer at all they see. The passage is worth noting for its biting sarcastic force:

> Now Stairhead Critics, senseless Fools,
> Censure their Aim, and Pride their Rules,
> In Luckenbooths, wi' glouring Eye,
> Their Neighbours sma'est Faults descry: *smallest*
> If ony Loun should dander there,   *fellow; wander*
> Of aukward Gate, and foreign Air,
> They trace his Steps, till they can tell
> His Pedigree as weell's himsell.
>
> (lines 51-8)

Fergusson, it will be seen, has no sympathy with sham, affectation, false pride, or meanness of soul; and these are the qualities which become the objects of his severest satire whenever he observes them, as in these lines and elsewhere in the poem.

The section on Edinburgh night life is perhaps the most brilliantly executed part of the poem. Here Fergusson describes in sharp, vivid detail typical characters and scenes of the city, when "Night, that's cunzied [invented] chief for Fun," begins. Out of doors in the narrow streets the "cadies" and Highland chairmen go about their respective businesses, the latter working hand in glove with prostitutes. Next we are shown the belligerent ramble of a drunken "Bruiser" or pugilest, in a passage which is a brilliant example of Fergusson's descriptive method, of his balanced realism. It begins as follows:

> Frae joyous Tavern, reeling drunk,
> Wi' fiery Phizz, and Ein half sunk,   *face; eyes*
> Behad the Bruiser, Fae to a'   *behold;foe*
> That in the reek o' Gardies fa':   *reach; arms; fall*

---

[6] A narrow range of buildings which once stood in the middle of the High Street near St. Giles Cathedral.

Close by his Side, a feckless Race   *feeble*
O' Macaronies shew their Face,
And think they're free frae Skaith or Harm,   *injury*
While Pith befriends their Leaders Arm: *strength*
Yet fearfu' aften o' their Maught,   *might*
They quatt the Glory o' the Faught   *quit; fight*
To this same Warrior wha led
Thae Heroes to bright Honour's Bed . . .   *these*
(lines 99 ff.)

In these lines Fergusson portrays the "Bruiser" from a satiric point of view, emphasizing the coarseness of the man, his crude, primitive instincts and blind brutality. The picture of him being egged on to "Glory" by the "feckless Race" of cowardly toadies is disgusting enough in itself. But Fergusson does not allow this feeling of disgust at the bruiser to develop any further in the reader's mind. He immediately modifies it in the the very next couplet, and places the bruiser's behavior in another light:

And aft the hack o' Honour shines   *often; scar*
In Bruiser's Face wi' broken Lines . . .

This is a brilliant and sensitive stroke; Fergusson, in this single couplet, controls his reader's reaction to the whole scene, and reveals his own attitude toward and judgment on the conduct of both bruiser and macaronies. The point that Fergusson is making here is that whereas the behavior of the bruiser is far from admirable, that of the macaronies who have goaded him on is a great deal worse. The bruiser is an ignorant and barbarous creature, but at least he has courage and a certain sense of honor; he is not contemptible. The macaronies, on the other hand, who take advantage of the bruiser and leave him in the lurch, have neither courage nor honor and are wholly despicable. Fergusson exposes this "feckless Race" of parasites and frauds, while at the same time he elicits sympathy for the bruiser. The passage is remarkable both for the moral judgment it implies and for the brilliant way in which Fergusson modifies and changes our original impression of the bruiser by contrasting his conduct with that of the macaronies. Fergusson's realism here, as elsewhere, is of a sane and comprehensive kind, involving both rational and emotional response to the situation, the one balancing and modifying the other.

In his next verse paragraph Fergusson portrays the macaroni in another situation. For relentless realism and sharp satiric power these lines are unsurpassed in Fergusson:

WHAN Feet in dirty Gutters plash,   *splash*
And Fock to wale their Fitstaps fash: *choose; footsteps; take care*
At night the Macaroni drunk,
In Pools or Gutters aftimes sunk:

> Hegh! What a Fright he now appears,
> When he his Corpse dejected rears!
> Look at that Head, and think if there
> The Pomet slaister'd up his Hair!   *pomatum; plastered*
> The Cheeks observe, where now cou'd shine
> The scancing Glories o' Carmine?   *shining*
> Ah, Legs! in vein the Silk-worm there
> Display'd to View her eidant Care;   *busy*
> For Stink, instead of Perfumes, grow,
> And clarty Odours fragrant flow.   *filthy*
>
> (lines 117-130)

As John Speirs very acutely observes of this passage, "the richness of this magnificent comic poetry arises from its unusual combinations of images and sharp contrasts."[7] The "Corpse" and "Gutter" associations contrast with the idea of pomatum and rouge, suggestive of elegance and finery; while at the same time Fergusson's choice of word and idiom, especially "slaister'd up his Hair" and "scancing Glories o' Carmine," conveys an impression of the messiness and unpleasantness of these cosmetics, as well as of their "Glories." These contrasts culminate, as Speirs points out, in the last two couplets, in the superbly restrained and suggestive "Ah, Legs!" image, and in final juxtaposition of "Stink" and "Perfumes," "clarty" and "fragrant." Through his skillfull use of these contrasts Fergusson succeeds, without explicity describing the scene, in rendering an astonishingly precise and powerful impression of its filth and loathsomeness as seen from a satiric and semi-humorous point of view. Perhaps the most striking thing about the passage is its admirable restraint. At least half of the power and vividness of this description lies in what Fergusson does *not* tell the reader. He merely suggests certain aspects of the scene in such a way that the reader's imagination is stirred and induced to fill in the rest of the details.

The principle of contrast operates in *Auld Reikie* on two levels: in the imagery of individual passages, as in the lines just cited, where it is an inherent characteristic of the style; and, on a larger scale, in the overall arrangement of the poem. They way in which this principle of contrast works out on the structural level may be illustrated from Fergusson's arrangement of his night scenes in this major section of the poem and of the morning scenes which follow. In his verse paragraphs on the bruiser and on the drunken macaroni rising from the gutter Fergusson is treating the more sordid and disgusting aspects of Edinburgh night life. Yet in his next passage, when he begins to tell of the clubs and societies, the mood suddenly changes as Fergusson starts to develop another side of the picture. Here the emphasis is on a more wholesome conviviality:

[7] *The Scots Literary Tradition* (London, 1940), pp. 120-121.

Now mony a Club, jocose and free,
Gie a' to Merriment and Glee . . .   *give all*
                (lines 135 ff.)

At the end of this same verse paragraph, however, Fergusson introduces
a rather ominous note in commenting on the inspiriting qualities of
liquor:

It makes you stark, and bauld, and brave,   *stout; bold*
Ev'n whan decending to the Grave.

This reference to "the Grave" casts only a momentary shadow on this
generally sunny part of the poem. In his next two paragraphs Fergusson
describes and commends the activities of two famous Edinburgh social
societies, the Pandemonium Club, and his own Cape Club. But the genial,
light-hearted mood of these passages abruptly changes once again at the
end of the lines on the Cape Club where Fergusson suddenly pauses to
describe in gruesome detail a passing funeral (lines 161-194). Even
though the poet has partially prepared for this passage in his previous
incidental reference to "the Grave," it comes as a shock to the reader,
especially since Fergusson lays on the horrid details with rather too
heavy a hand. These lines, with their references to "a painted Corp" and
the "Dead-deal" (a board for laying out corpses), and their excessive
emphasis on the frightfullness of death, smack of morbidity and are
suggestive of that neurotic streak in Fergusson which caused him to feel
an unnatural terror at the thought of sickness and death and which
undoubtedly contributed to his final mental collapse. Yet this ghastly
funeral scene is immediately followed by a charming description of the
vegetable market which was in those days held in the High Street between
St. Giles and the Tron-kirk. He then touches on the bits of pastoral
freshness, the trees and greenery, which brighten even the grimy old
city and "Ca' [drive] far awa' the Morning Smell." Next comes an
extraordinary lyrical outburst apostrophizing "Nature":

O Nature! canty, blyth and free,   *happy*
Whare is there Keeking-glass like thee?   *looking-glass*
Is there on Earth that can compare
Wi' Mary's Shape, and Mary's Air,
Save the empurpl'd Speck, that grows
In the saft Faulds of yonder Rose?   *soft folds*
                (lines 209-214)

The lyric tone and emotional quality of these lines are unusual in Fergusson and are strongly suggestive of the lyrical style of Burns. They
are followed, significantly, by a passage on the filth and nauseating smells
of the Edinburgh "flesh-market."

The summary given above of two major sections of the poem
should be enough to show how basic is the method of dramatic contrast

in *Auld Reikie*. Fergusson is attempting to catch the essential spirit of the old city and to fix it forever in terms of its strangely contrasting moods. He shows the sordidness and bestiality of Edinburgh night life side by side with its friendliness, its genial goodfellowship and spirited conviviality; he contrasts the greenery of the vegetable stalls in the High Street and the sweet freshness of trees and flowers with the foul stink and filth of the "flesh-market." The constant shifting of scene and mood and the bold juxtaposition of ugliness and beauty give the poem a high degree of actuality and dramatic force. The imagination of the reader is excited by the sharpness and suggestiveness of the poem's details, as one keenly-etched portrait after another flashes before his eyes and the whole bustling, colorful panorama of eighteenth-century Edinburgh gradually takes shape.

Two or three passages of the latter part of the poem demand special comment. Fergusson's attack on Sunday hypocrisy is one of the most biting satiric passages in the poem. It reads, in part, as follows:

> On Sunday here, an alter'd Scene
> O' Men and Manners meets our Ein: *eyes*
> Ane wad maist trow some People chose   *almost*
> To change their Faces wi' their Clo'es,
> And fain wad gar ilk Neighbour think   *make; each*
> They thirst for Goodness, as for Drink:
> But there's an unco Dearth o' Grace,   *strange*
> That has nae Mansion but the Face,
> And never can obtain a Part
> In benmost Corner of the Heart.   *innermost*
> (lines 231-240)

Fergusson here uses a more direct method of attack than is usual with him. The effectiveness of the passage is undeniable, however, and lies chiefly in its sharply satiric phrasing, skillful use of rime, and, above all, in its imaginative force, especially in the brilliant simile, "They thirst for Goodness, as for Drink." The same kind of direct, keen-edged satire is evident again a few lines later in the poem, where Fergusson derides the pretentious Sunday strollers:

> While dandring Cits delight to stray   *strolling citizens*
> To Castlehill, or Public Way,
> Whare they nae other Purpose mean,
> Than that Fool Cause o' being seen . . .
> (lines 259-262)

The terse, biting, epigrammatic quality of these touches of direct satire in *Auld Reikie* remind one of the polished couplets of the great English neo-classical satirists, especially of Pope, Swift, and Gay, to whom Fergusson is unquestionably indebted in a general way.

The poem ends fittingly on a note of inimitable wit in a short verse paragraph which is worth quoting in full:

REIKIE, farewel! I ne'er cou'd part
Wi' thee but wi' a dowy heart;   *sad*
Aft frae the *Fifan* coast I've seen,   *often*
Thee tow'ring on thy summit green;
So glowr the saints when first is given
A fav'rite keek o' glore and heaven;   *peek; glory*
On earth nae mair they bend their ein,   *eyes*
But quick assume angelic mein;
So I on *Fife* wad glowr no more,
But gallop'd to EDINA's shore.   *Edinburgh's*

(lines 359-368)

The humorous force of this farewell is irresistible. Fergusson's affection for the old gray city is here given comical, half-satiric expression through his use of a mock epic simile. In its irrepressible waggery and imaginative daring the passage seems to epitomize Fergusson's whole poetic personality. The scintillating wit of the passage, its richness in humorous suggestiveness, arise from the comic irony of Fergusson's comparison of Edinburgh and heaven in the light of what has gone before, and from the impish tone of his phrasing in such superb lines as "A fav'rite keek o' glore and heaven." The ironical force of the comparison, it may be noted, is underlined by his happy choice of the adjective "angelic." Yet, in spite of the conscious irony of his praise of *Auld Reikie*, Fergusson manages to convey in these lines the impression that he sincerely loves this strangely beautiful, historic, battered, incredibly crowded and squalid old city of his birth.

Auld Reikie is an extraordinarily attractive and powerful poem and, as Fergusson's last major work, forms a fitting climax to his poetic career. It ranks as one of his four or five very best poems, and is certainly the most comprehensive and impressive of Fergusson's many treatments of eighteenth-century life in Edinburgh. As we have seen, the poem owes much to *Trivia*, but its overall effect is strikingly different, its style far more vividly realistic though no less sophisticated than that of Gay's pleasantly artificial work. Had Fergusson been given the time and encouragement to complete his original design of the poem, it would probably have developed to epic proportions; and, in view of the quality of what he actually did get on paper, it might well have become one of the major classics of eighteenth-century poetry. As it stands, *Auld Reikie* is a little classic, and deserves to stand beside *Trivia* as one of the most distinguished treatments of city life in British poetry.

UNIVERSITY OF RHODE ISLAND

WILLIAM R. McGRAW

Barrie and the Critics

It is sometimes difficult for present-day students of the drama to comprehend the stature once accorded James M. Barrie. Most of us agree that he no longer ranks with the most popular playwrights of today, but there is some disagreement on the reasons for this occurrence. As a first step in assessing this phenomenon it might be well to review the plays with particular emphasis upon the critical reaction of his own day, which should, in turn, give some measurement of his former popularity and perhaps coincidentally suggest some causes for his current position.

The author himself remarked in an article in *The Greenwood Hat* "that perhaps the play [*Richard Savage*] had done some good after all, if only by inducing the Ibsenite and anti-Ibsenite critics to agree about something."[1] This statement, written after the one and only performance of Barrie's first serious attempt in the drama simply means both factions agreed it was a poor play. The length of the run seems to indicate that the audience concurred. But, in spite of an unsuccessful beginning, the experience planted permanently in Barrie the virus of the drama. Phelps emphasizes this when he says: "One would think that the prodigious success of *The Little Minister* [the novel] and the failure of *Richard Savage* would indicate to the author his true 'line.' But Barrie, encouraged by success, was inspired by failure, for in the same year [1891] he produced two other plays of no importance, *Ibsen's Ghost* and *Becky Sharp*."[2]

The first of these was simply a mock Hedda Gabler, which was running in London at the time, and although it would appear that Barrie was confidently launching out on his own it is significant that on opening night (May 30, 1891) the author's name was purposely omitted from the program. *Ibsen's Ghost* is important, though, for several reasons. First, it is an early example of Barrie's perfect timing. As H. M. Walbrook relates, at this period "London was divided into two camps: the Ibsenites behind William Archer and the detesters behind Clement Scott, who had coined the word 'Ibsene.' " Second, although a burlesque, it was so clever-

---

[1] James M. Barrie, quoted by W. A. Darlington, *J. M. Barrie* (London and Glasgow, 1938), p. 506.

[2] William Lyon Phelps, *Essays on Modern Dramatists* (New York, 1921), p. 13.

ly handled that the "satire, though pointed, was not barbed."[3] This, of course, served to unite the critics who enjoyed what Walbrook called "the wittiest burlesque he ever saw"[4] and the *Times*, a "clever little parody."[5] The play ran for over a month as a curtain-raiser and gave Barrie the incentive to work seriously on his first full-length play, *Walker, London.* It obviously delighted him, too, to know that he could make an audience laugh. He recalled years later the lines of Hedda: "To run away from my second husband just as I ran away from my first, it feels quite like old times;" and how on the first night a man in the pit found it "so diverting that he had to be removed in hysterics."[6]

Yet it is not with either *Richard Savage* or *Ibsen's Ghost* that Barrie's career as a dramatist truly began. *Walker, London* is the starting point; it represents Barrie working on his own, at a full-length play, with an original story. He had taken several ideas from his popular novel *When a Man's Single*, rearranged them, and set them in the unique atmosphere of a houseboat on the Thames. (The central character is a barber who after deserting his bride-to-be poses as an African explorer to spend the honeymoon money.) The play was an instantaneous success, running uninterruptedly in London from February 25, 1892, for 511 performances. It is essentially a well-constructed farce, geared precisely to the tastes of the day. The bulk of criticism can be fairly represented by Child's comment that Barrie's "skill as a craftsman is plain already in *Walker, London*" showing quite clearly that he could have been the greatest writer of well-made plays ever known.[7] It is a play of well-planned situations, exhibiting a sure sense of that which is effective on the stage. In retrospect, the consensus is that "it can only rank as a good piece of journeyman's work," but following the initial performance several critics were highly impressed, including Clement Scott, who during his day was considered "an infallible judge of what was effective in the theatre."[8] His review in the *Daily Telegraph* included the following statement: "... The brilliant author reminds one of Robertson far more than a score of Robertson's feeble imitators. There is no flaccidity about Mr. Barrie. He is a Robertson of today, a Robertson up to date—not so sentimental, but quite as human, as observant, as pungent, as laconic, and a Robertson

[3] H. M. Walbrook, quoted by Darlington, p. 57.

[4] Walbrook, quoted by J. A. Hammerton, *Barrie: The Story of a Genius* (New York, 1929), p. 240.

[5] Denis Mackail, *The Story of J. M. B.* (London, 1941), p. 178.

[6] James M. Barrie, *Peter Pan* (New York, 1928), p. ix.

[7] Harold Child, "J. M. Barrie as Dramatist," *Saturday Review of Literature*, January 29, 1949, p. 34.

[8] Darlington, p. 62.

who has that strange dramatic mastery over the simplest and apparently the most trivial details of life."[9] It is decidedly modern in its treatment of the domestic situation, its satire on the medical student, and particularly the pseudo-intellectual of the day:

> BELL—...I don't see how I can love you. I have reduced love to syllogistic form . . . (rise—they embrace)
> BELL— . . . Don't.
> KIT—Why not?
> BELL—It is so—unintellectual.
> KIT—But what if we like it?
> BELL—How can we? There is nothing in it.... You must never pay those infantile compliments to my personal appearance. If you love me, let it be for my mind alone, for all other love is founded on an ontological misconception.[10]

This and other passages, too, as Phelps points out, are also obvious burlesques on the sentimental drama.[11] It was a certain "freshness of humor, an oddness of fancy,"[12] too, which induced its popular appeal and prevented the departures from convention from making it appear radically new, as was the case, for instance, with Shaw's *Widower's Houses*, Pinero's *Second Mrs. Tanqueray*, and Wilde's *Lady Windermere's Fan*, all of which opened in London within a year of Barrie's play.

The next year was not so fortunate for Barrie since it was at this time he decided to offer the one-act play *Becky Sharp* which he had written two years previously, and a comic opera, *Jane Annie*, written in collaboration with Conan Doyle. The former was based on the last three chapters of *Vanity Fair* and according to the *Times* was "at once diffuse and obscure."[13] The critic Edward Morton said it "reproduced word for word, the language of Thackeray without reviving the spirit of *Vanity Fair*."[14] Little more can be said about it since no copy of the play is available today, but it is significant in that it taught the dramatist a lesson. In Darlington's words, "The experience was useful to him if it taught him that this kind of stage adaptation from other men's books is seldom worth a good dramatist's while; and he certainly never attempted anything of the sort again."[15]

[9] Clement Scott, quoted by Hammerton, p. 243.

[10] James M. Barrie, *Walker, London* (New York, 1907), p. 131.

[11] William Lyon Phelps (ed.), *Representative Plays by J. M. Barrie* (New York, 1926), p. xiii.

[12] Hammerton, p. 241.

[13] Mackail, p. 210.

[14] Edward Morton, quoted by Thomas Nelson Magill, "Sentiment, Satire and Fantasy in the Drama of Sir James Matthew Barrie" (unpublished M.A. thesis, Cornell University, 1937), p. 41.

[15] Darlington, p. 67.

He learned another lesson in *Jane Annie, Or the Good Conduct Prize*, and that was the fruitlessness of collaboration. Darton says: "As I remember it, it was like a baddish Gilbert and Sullivan. It did not hang well together and was neither inevitable nor surprising—two necessities of stage effect."[16] In all fairness to Barrie it should be noted, however, that after finishing the first act he had become ill and, having to meet a deadline, called in his friend Conan Doyle to finish it. But the cause was lost before it got to the stage. Doyle promised to help, but when he examined the work, as he says himself, his heart sank. He could not conceive what had made Barrie accept the commission, and he completed the "book" purely from friendship, and with no hope of success.[17] It is interesting to notice that Barrie and Doyle ironically predict the outcome in a marginal note: "Greg and Sim (two bulldogs) have a bet that the critics will quote the third and fourth lines here, and say they apply to the opera." The lines are: "plot unsystematic and very erratic."[18]

Such was not the fate, however, of the next work—a play which Phelps calls Barrie's first truly successful venture in the theater because it gave the author general public recognition as a dramatist.[19] The reactions to *The Professor's Love Story* are interestingly varied. An opening night reviewer said, "As a result of seeing *The Professor's Love Story* one steps breezily out into the night, holding one's head ever so much higher than usual."[20] William Archer, on the other hand, called it in *The World* "a calculated disloyalty to art . . . a patchwork of extravagant farce, mawkish sentiment, and irrelevant anecdote."[21] When comparing the two remarks we need not question the sincerity of either except to say that one is obviously a subjective reaction, the other highly objective or out-and-out prejudicial. Archer, we recall, in 1903, was steeped in the Shavian "social" function of the drama.

The play ran for over 500 performances in London and was similarly successful in the United States where it was produced first by E. S. Willard, who kept it in his repertoire for twenty years. Such a record certainly reveals popular appeal—an appeal which apparently came from unabashed sentiment and charm, and, although in this particular case the sentiment almost went out of bounds, Barrie had obviously stuck to a formula he knew would result in a popular entertainment.

[16] F. J. Harvey Darton, *J. M. Barrie* (London, 1929), p. 30.

[17] Darlington, p. 66.

[18] James M. Barrie, *Jane Annie* (London, 1893), p. 21.

[19] Phelps, *Essays*, p. 15.

[20] Max Beerbohm, "The Professor's Love Story," *Saturday Review*, December 12, 1903, p. 731.

[21] William Archer, quoted by Hammerton, p. 202.

This same formula was kept in mind as he went about adapting his two-volume novel *The Little Minister* for the stage, for if *The Professor's Love Story* brought the author public recognition as a dramatist the next play established him as the most financially successful of living playwrights. Under Frohman's management *The Little Minister* was to provide Barrie personally with 80,000 pounds.

This success may be attributed to one characteristic according to a present-day student, Janet Murray—it is "a straightforward romantic love story."[22] But some critics, notably those who wrote their remarks upon emerging from the theater, assessed its effectiveness differently. One of them said:

> *The Little Minister* as a play has not only story and character, but the invaluable quality of atmosphere... By some subtle magic, easier to recognize than to explain, the spectator finds himself transposed forthwith into the quaint and primitive community of Thrums, where a dour and sturdy puritanism battles other forms of human weakness. Here, to begin with is conflict, and conflict is drama. Mr. Barrie from the outset escapes the great besetting danger of the adapter, the temptation to tell some part of the story by retrospective narration. From the moment the curtain rises the story begins to live before us. *The Little Minister* in fine bids fair to rank as the best play of the year.[23]

Walbrook agreed and added that November 6, 1897, provided a signal event—"It broke down finally the barriers which had so long and so disastrously stood between Literature and the Drama."[24] George Bernard Shaw, too, in spite of his supposed antithetical position, pays tribute to Barrie's success with the play: "Mr. Barrie is a born story-teller.... He does the thing as if he likes it, and does it very well.... He has a keen sense of human qualities and he produces highly popular assortments of them.... [Gavin and Babbie] are nine-tenths fun and the other tenth sentiment which makes a very toothsome combination."[25] It is significant to note that, in spite of Miss Murray's comment in 1950 that the play "possesses neither enough power nor enough vitality ever again to bear successful revival,"[26] the National Broadcasting Company staged an extremely effective television adaptation on its *Matinee Theatre,* December 26, 1957.

The three-year period from 1897 to 1900 was unproductive as far as Barrie's dramatic efforts were concerned, but with the income from

[22] Janet E. Murray, "A Comparison of J. M. Barrie's Novel and Play *The Little Minister*" (unpublished M.A. thesis, University of Colorado, 1950), preface.

[23] J. F. N., "Drama," *The Academy*, November 13, 1897, p. 407.

[24] H. M. Walbrook, *J. M. Barrie and the Theatre* (London, 1922), p. 49.

[25] George Bernard Shaw, *Dramatic Opinions and Essays* (New York, 1906), p. 73.

[26] Murray, p. 76.

The Little Minister and his novels which were continuing to sell he was assured of a comfortable living. He apparently had time to think, too, about the direction his writing should take him, but his decision to attempt a problem play was ill advised. *The Wedding Guest* is a serious experiment in the prevalent realistic vein of Ibsen. Although the play was unsuccessful at the box office, it received mixed reactions from the critics. One reviewer found the plot trite and uninteresting but went on to say: "... We find his drama during the second act supremely touching. The play is decidedly one to be seen, and he is hard of heart who does not find a vein of true pathos and one of dramatic interest running through the whole, and combining fairly well. The treatment is imaginative and witty; there are scenes of much delicacy and there is careful psychology."[27] Another critic, Max Beerbohm, whose comment is probably more representative of the general reaction to the play, says simply, "When he tries, as in *The Wedding Guest* to try to tackle seriously the serious things around him, then his pathos runs to mawkishness, and his fun apt to jar."[28]

Quality Street, the next play, opened in Toledo, Ohio, in October of 1901. It represents the transition in Barrie's writing from Kirriemuir, or Auld Licht Scotland, to Kensington Gardens. Here is marked the "bridge from Thrums to a world of make believe."[29] The critic for *The Athenaeum* said: "The claim of *Quality Street* consists entirely in atmosphere. . . . [It is] very charming and simple. So good is it that we can not help wishing it were a little better. The spectator, however, who represses all tendency to criticism and takes Mr. Barrie's piece just as it is is not unwise."[30] This last point suggests a rather obvious premise—that the average playgoer does not maintain this "tendency to criticism" while sitting in the darkened auditorium. Such a condition is particularly fortunate for *Quality Street*, which suffers considerably more under the scrutiny of the literary critic than does, let us say, *The Admirable Crichton*. Its magic in the theater was irrefutable, however, for it ran without a break in London from September 17, 1902, to November 20 the following year. Mackail reported: " . . . An immediate and unquestioned success. Walkley, quoting French and Greek, welcomed it with hardly a word of criticism. William Archer called it a stage classic. The rest of the press—and in those days, a whole column was still considered the right length for these notices—hailed it with equal enthusiasm. *The Wedding Guest* was forgotten. This, said everyone, was real Barrie, and so in a sense

---

[27] "Drama—The Week," *The Athenaeum*, October 6, 1900, p. 451.

[28] Max Beerbohm, "Little Mary," *Saturday Review*, October 3, 1903, p. 423.

[29] Hammerton, p. 328.

[30] "Drama—The Week," *The Athenaeum*, September 27, 1902, p. 424.

it was."[31] Here again, Beerbohm evaluates the playwright's technique quite well. He makes the point that to date Barrie's "most famous mixture is one of tears and laughter," but more specifically says:

> Mr. Barrie sets out to show us, as did Miss Syrett (of *The Finding of Nancy*), the tragedy of a girl in whom joy of life is being sapped by years of drudgery—a girl growing old without benefit of girlhood. . . . Miss Syrett went straight to the root of the matter, strong and unflinching. Mr. Barrie hovers around it, smiling and sobbing. . . . Commercially, it is well for Mr. Barrie that he behaves thus, since the average playgoer loves this kind of behavior as deeply as he is disturbed and annoyed by Miss Syrett's kind. Artistically, too, it is well for Mr. Barrie. Neither his humor nor his pathos blends well with any attempt to create seriously from the materials of real life.[32]

The year 1902 was much more memorable, however, for another play, *The Admirable Crichton,* which opened at the Duke of York's theatre on November 4. The critical reaction was mixed here, too, but not in the same manner. All agreed the play was Barrie's most effective dramatic contribution to date. They did not agree about the idea presented. Some critics, like William Archer, who took the play perhaps a little too seriously, "solemnly expressed doubts of whether the dramatist had the smallest idea of the immensity of his attack upon the constituted social order of the country; another critic compared the play with Rousseau's writings which paved the way for the 'French Revolution.' "[33] Others were less wary, especially Beerbohm, who said boldly, "I think *The Admirable Crichton* quite the best thing that has happened, in my time, to the British stage." He went on to explain that the public seemed to understand what Barrie was driving at; they didn't just "cry buckets of tears over the butler." He states: "It is undeniable that the most successful modern plays are those which are most fantastically untrue to real life. But Mr. Barrie's play differs from them in that it is frankly, and of a purpose, untrue to life. . . . We are not asked to take them [these strange people] seriously. . . . Mr. Barrie has always been able to amuse us. But this is the first occasion on which he has succeeded in making us also think."[34] Of the later critics some have said, like Darlington, that the social criticism in the play was purely accidental.[35] Others believe that the play "began in Barrie's mind as a serious problem requiring serious treatment,"[36] but the

---

[31] Mackail, p. 319.

[32] Max Beerbohm, "A Pretty Play Spoilt," *Saturday Review,* September 20, 1902, p. 361.

[33] William Archer, quoted by Walbrook, p. 72.

[34] Max Beerbohm, "A Welcome Play," *Saturday Review,* November 15, 1902, p. 612.

[35] Darlington, p. 90.

[36] Hammerton, p. 331.

author, realizing that he usually failed when trying to be wholly serious, put the problem in a comic framework.

With the possible exception of *Peter Pan, The Admirable Crichton* has been Barrie's most popular full-length play, although, understandably, since it "slightly shocked" the audience it had a shorter initial run than *Quality Street.* It has been successfully revived several times in London, was translated into French and produced at the Théatre Antoine in Paris, made into a motion picture at least twice—one with the unfortunate title of *Male and Female*—and has been one of the all-time favorites of college and university theaters.

It would be difficult to conjecture just what Barrie's primary objective was in writing the play, but at least the critics had taken more notice on this occasion than before. In retrospect, too, some of them called attention to its modernity: "This play has been aptly distinguished as the first of the 20th Century English social plays and it demonstrated triumphantly that the theatre was a place where the very basis of civilization could be discussed. The play could have been written with bitterness and defiance. It would have been with Shaw. Barrie accepts the social structure as the result of human nature and satirizes the rebels in a masterly mingling of fantasy and realism contrasting natural with civilized conditions and allowing each to produce the same effect."[37] Even George Bernard Shaw, in a letter to J. T. Grein, gave Barrie credit for "the final relegation of the nineteenth century London theatre to the dust bin."[38] Perhaps Shaw recalled the social satire in *Walker, London* or the direct, Ibsenesque attempt, *The Wedding Guest;* but more than likely he was thinking of *The Admirable Crichton,* which had not only aroused the critics but had also reached the eyes and ears of a vast public as yet not ready to receive the direct preachment of Shaw.

The next play was of much less consequence. It was actually "an elaborate gastronomic joke"[39] wherein the author concludes that the source of most of the difficulties of the British people is in the fact that they eat too much. Its title was *Little Mary* and although it was not very successful—it ran for six months in London—the critics were quite happy with it. Sydney Brooks had this to say:

> . . . Here we have the mocking, whimsical, tantalizing Barrie almost, if not quite, at his best. No doubt his moral that sympathy and common sense are the best doctors is a sound one, but one does not go to Mr. Barrie to learn things. Enough that he has this happy, this unique gift of pleasing and pro-

---

[37] A. E. Malone, "The Conservatism of J. M. Barrie," *Thought,* June, 1929, p. 36.

[38] George Bernard Shaw, quoted by John W. Cunliffe, *Modern English Playwrights* (New York, 1927), p. 83.

[39] Hammerton, p. 342.

voking at one and the same time; that his shy unexpected, topsy turvy wit is still as quietly agile as ever and that in *Little Mary* he hardly for a moment "slops over." Every one will criticize and condemn the construction of the play. Every one will go to see it, and every one will like it.[40]

Another critic, according to Mackail either the *Times* or Walkley, had only one reservation in a full column of warm appreciation—a reservation which again reflects the futility of analyzing Barrie's slighter works. "Set down in black and white, the thing seems rather silly."[41]

In the case of Barrie's next play one is impressed by the strange contrast in critical reaction. Perhaps it is because there had never been anything like *Peter Pan* known in the theater before. Certain of the critics were simply baffled. The public, although a little slow in responding in New York, were not baffled; they welcomed it with open arms. One commentator asserted that the public's unqualified acceptance was due to Barrie's timing. "The play came at one of those discouraged moments when the public mind was occupied to an almost marked degree with huge and vexing problems, and with things that were going wrong. Legalized evil doing was rampant in business and politics .... Cynicism was the dominant note in literature and dramatic art, a cheerful clever twentieth century cynicism but a bitter and depressing influence, for all that."[42] Into this atmosphere came *Peter Pan* and it came with the free, untrammeled spirit of childhood. Camillo Pellizzi says, " ... It is fantasy which in its own way has become will again, not the disturbed and distorted will of post-Romantics or decadents, but the ingenuous and direct will of a child; the lyrical phantom comes to life in an epic song of liberation in childishness."[43] From those who were negative came several cryptic comments:

> Action Davis—a great disappointment . . . a conglomeration of balderdash, cheap melodrama and third rate extravaganza.
> Alan Dale—drivel and the fancies of a disordered mind. .·.. Darnton (of *The Evening World*) vowed that Barrie had finished *A Midsummer Night's Dream* by getting up out of the wrong side of the dramatic bed.[44]

Beerbohm was just as sure on the other side as he wrote following the initial production: "Undoubtedly *Peter Pan* is the best thing he has done, the thing most directly from within himself. Here at last we see his talent in full maturity." In addition he admits to the gossamer elusiveness of

[40] Sydney Brooks, "A View of Mr. Barrie," *Harper's Weekly*, January 23, 1904, p. 126.

[41] Mackail, p. 348.

[42] Louise Boynton, "Maude Adams in 'Peter Pan,'" *Century Magazine*, December, 1906, p. 320.

[43] Camillo Pellizzi, *English Drama* (London, 1935), p. 161.

[44] "Peter Pans in Rivalry," *Literary Digest*, January 17, 1925, p. 26.

the play and the futility of trying to describe it in a review. "For me to describe to you now in black and white the happening in *Peter Pan* would be a thankless task. One cannot communicate the magic of a dream. People who insist on telling their dreams are among the terrors of the breakfast table. You must go to the Duke of York's there to dream the dream for yourselves."[45] Among some of the dissenters were those who claimed Barrie had played a nasty trick and fed them a play meant only for children, but the great majority agreed with Roy, who said years later: "For Barrie the real things in life are the eternal verities—not social issues. *Peter Pan* can be appreciated by both old and young.... It embodies a profound philosophy of life which is found in the symbolic significance of Peter himself . . . the eternal boy in all of us. . . . Humanity itself is Peter Pan, eternally childish and foolish."[46]

As to length of run, the play has established several records, the most notable of which is its staging every year at Christmas time in London since 1904, running for several months on each occasion. The initial production in this country ran for 237 performances, with the most recent revival (1950) playing for 320 performances.

Magill states that Barrie wrote *Peter Pan* more to please himself than anyone else and had always considered it "a sort of private pet"[47] which would probably not be successful. This is borne out in the fact that upon Barrie's suggestion Frohman agreed to produce *Alice Sit-by-the-Fire* to recoup the losses of the more ambitious production. Darlington recounts the error in their judgment: "Barrie and Frohman could afford to smile now at the idea that the profits on this play had been relied on to pay for the losses on the bigger venture, and the smile must have grown a little ironic when the new play proved hardly able to do more than pay for itself." *Alice Sit-by-the-Fire* ran for 115 performances "which by standards of actress [Ellen Terry] and author was something far short of success."[48] What did the critics say? Walbrook maintains that their reactions were mixed: "One called it his most joyous composition, another his saddest, setting at defiance every recognized rule of dramatic craftsmanship, playing all sorts of practical jokes upon his audience, and at the same time manipulating the stops of laughter and tears with so unrivalled a mastery."[49] The critic for the *Saturday Review* said that somehow Ellen Terry seemed too big for the play just as did C.

[45] Max Beerbohm, *Around Theatres* (London, 1953), pp. 357, 360.

[46] James A. Roy, *James Matthew Barrie, An Appreciation* (New York, 1938), p. 181.

[47] Magill, p. 56.

[48] Darlington, p. 103.

[49] Walbrook, p. 108.

Aubrey Smith. At the same time he admitted to a thorough enjoyment of the performance, stating a recurrent point that "the delightfulness of 'Alice' cannot be communicated through criticism. . . . [The play] depends so little on its framework and so much on its embroidery."[50]

The consensus indicated that it is probably one of the poorest products of Barrie's maturity. He had written it for Ellen Terry, and, unlike the plays for which Maude Adams had been the inspiration, the combination was unfortunate. Its greater strength lies in the ingenious satire on the theater.

. . . . When he has told the theatre's stories with a twist, he has, one feels, been the more Barrie. Nothing could be better satire of the theatre which is for ever given up to the pursuit of some matrimonial intrigue than the play which, for two acts itself a play of matrimonial intrigue, has for its final curtain warning an "especially loud click." How many constant playgoers, Amy Greys every one of them, sat through Alice Sit-by-the Fire in the belief that it was the real article rather better done until that final fall of the curtain shocked them, perhaps into a reconsideration of the dramatic values on their way home?

Here was Barrie the modern at work, and the particular effect of the satire prompts one to wish the play, as a whole, had been better. Perhaps the characters and situations were just a little too unbelievable or the joke at the end "beaten a little too long and thin."[51]

Very little criticism is available on the next three plays, which were one-act curtain raisers. Of the first, *Pantaloon,* the best that can be said is that it is Barrie experimenting in the short play form, a form with which he was soon to become quite proficient. *Josephine* was an unsuccessful review in three scenes, "his effort to adapt himself to the French medium of political and social satire." Hammerton discloses that "the impression left on most of those who saw this so-called revue was that of a strangely ineffective skit directed at persons rather than the tendencies for which they stood."[52] Barrie himself had felt rather shaky about it as disclosed in a letter to his friend Sir Arthur Quiller-Couch: "*Josephine* is out, but whether it will do is as yet open to doubt. I've enjoyed writing it more than most things I've done of late, but for one thing a solemn burlesque calls for more from the audience than anything appealing to the feelings, and I dare say the irony is too prolonged. Nothing wearies me more I believe than satire the moment it ceases to be attractive. It is such a confoundedly unlovable vehicle."[53] The third play,

[50] Max Beerbohm, "Mr. Barrie Again," *Saturday Review,* April 15, 1905, p. 483.
[51] P. P. Howe, *Dramatic Portraits* (New York, 1913), p. 105.
[52] Hammerton, p. 393.
[53] *Letters of J. M. Barrie,* ed. Viola Meynell (New York, 1947), p. 21.

Punch, was a moderately effective dramatic skit "whose interest was derived from presenting G. B. S. in a top hat and frock coat as the rival to Punch and Judy."[54]

Barrie's next effort ranks with the most popular of his plays. *What Every Woman Knows* opened at the Duke of York's on September 3, 1908, and ran for 384 performances. The New York production, with Maude Adams, ran just as long. This play, which has "a mixture of realistic, romantic and political elements,"[55] presented the idea "that men are children, and every wise woman can manage a child."[56] Its success, however, was due to something more than such a simple idea. The London *Times'* critic suggested that "his strong point is genuine lovable character and he certainly has given us no more lovable character than that of the charming humorous little woman who modestly supposes herself to be without charm."[57] William Archer, who apparently by this time was willing to recognize Barrie as a dramatist of some consequence, said:

> The charm of *What Every Woman Knows* lies not in its probability, but its quaint improbability. We yield ourselves up, for two and a half hours to the whim of an enchanter who conjures up before us, not life as it is, but life as it is pleasant to imagine it....Everywhere life is cunningly manipulated, slightly thrown out of focus, so as to beget in the audience a mood of smiling make-believe. Not truth, but the pleasure implied in the mood, is the author's primary aim . . . . It is a fantasy worked out of materials supplied by keen, and shrewed, and subtle observation.... There is both truth and significance in the character of John Shand and Maggie . . . .[58]

A similiar note on character is struck in the following review from *The Evening Post*: "The play provided most delightful entertainment in the freshness of its incidents, its whimsical illumination of essential truths in human nature, its happy and vivid strokes of characterization, its constant play of unexpected humor, its touches of pathos and its general, though absolute, freedom from theatrical conventionalities."[59]

Such were the opinions of those shortly after seeing the play, but there were others, examining the play removed from the stage, who felt that this improbability of character and situation, which Archer

---

[54] Hammerton, p. 393.

[55] Sister Agnes Richarda Blinkhorn, O. P., "A Critical Analysis of the Plays of James M. Barrie from the Point of View of Dramatic Structure" (unpublished M.A. thesis, Catholic University, 1953), p. 39.

[56] Darton, p. 57.

[57] Blinkhorn, p. 49.

[58] William Archer, "Plays of the New Season," *Fortnightly Review,* October, 1908, p. 677.

[59] Blinkhorn, p. 47.

cites as one of its strengths, was its major weakness. Hammerton says there is just "too much to believe about Maggie."[60] Still others felt somewhat like Barrett Clark, who said years later that "*What Every Woman Knows* reveals nothing new in Barrie, only a reworking of the old" in spite of its still being "valid theatre."[61]

Of Barrie's next four plays, one-acts designed as curtain-raisers, two may be called valid theater without reservation. *The Twelve Pound Look* and *Rosalind* reveal Barrie's mastery of the short play form. The former shows the influence of Ibsen and as Phelps contends "has the depth of Ibsen without his grimness . . . . It is the tragedy of failure in success; the husband, identified by Barrie with every man in the audience, had a complacency that literally made his lawful spouse run for her life."[62] The play ran successfully in both New York and London in 1910 and has been revived successfully many times since. Its first producer, Frohman, considered it one of Barrie's greatest, perhaps second only to *Peter Pan;* "like most others, he realized that in this one act of intense life was crowded all the human drama, all the human tragedy. . . ."[63]

Rosalind was received similarly by the critics and stands out, too, as a favorite with the general audience. One reviewer said: "His one-act form has enabled him to keep many things where he wanted them, in the half light. He has recognized the peculiarities of his medium, has used them so as to achieve in *Rosalind* the special Barrie surface which pleases him and pleases us."[64]

The other two plays were the unpublished *A Slice of Life,* which was a mockery upon stage conventions of the day, and *Old Friends,* an unsuccessful attempt on the author's part to present seriously the question of hereditary alcoholism. Of the latter we may note another interesting divergence of opinion. Walbrook, writing not long after its production, called it "a ghostly story told with tragic power . . . a concentrated tragedy by a master craftsman." Hammerton labels it an "artificial melodramatic sketch."[65] Other than this there is very little published criticism of the play.

Next came a three-act play which in the final estimate would stand as one of the author's major mistakes, at least with respect to

[60] Hammerton, p. 394.

[61] Barrett H. Clark and George Freedly, *A History of Modern Drama* (New York and London, 1947), p. 180.

[62] Phelps, *Essays,* p. 49.

[63] Hammerton, p. 401.

[64] Q. K., "After the Play," *New Republic,* September 18, 1915, p. 185.

[65] Hammerton, p. 401

the London production. *The Adored One* presented the strange case of a woman who was on trial for murder. It seems she had pushed a man out of a railway car because he had refused to close the window. The woman is acquitted finally on the basis of her concern for her daughter's health. This was a rare instance where Barrie had misjudged his audience. The *Globe* the next day told the unfortunate outcome: "Baronet Booed." Walbrook asserts that the author had simply carried his tendency to "freakishness" too far—the satire and comedy did not work in a situation of murder. Barrie immediately set about to rewrite the play, changing the whole story into a dream, but the damage had been done and as far as London was concerned the play failed. Several months later, however, it opened in New York with Maude Adams under the title of *The Legend of Leonora* with a much different reception. In spite of its still being "a very queer sort of play"[66] it ran for four months and remained ever after in Miss Adams' repertoire.

With World War I came a patriotic response on Barrie's part to write for the effort of the Allies. Among these plays was *A Kiss for Cinderella*, about which Walter Pritchard Eaton said: "Here is a play which scarcely touches the earth . . . . The master of whimsy, with wings on his pen, says more to our hearts than the realists."[67] Several of the critics thought it overly sentimental; others like the *New Republic* commentator felt that *A Kiss for Cinderella* represents how the "humor saves Barrie's tenderness from the extremeties to which it leans." It prompted him to say further that: "Your attitude toward this man's genius depends altogether, I should imagine, on your general attitude toward heaven. If you believe in heaven, the peculiar kind of child's heaven that is Barrie's, you find it easy to lend yourself to him, to his general wistfulness and shy sensibility and hazel-twig gift for nostalgia. . . . Few grown persons of my own acquaintance take any great stock in heaven but when they were little all of them believed in it, not because they were told to so much as because they were able."[68]

More recent commentary seems to agree that the play is somewhat dated owing to topical references and that in terms of construction it is not, for instance, the equal of *Dear Brutus*, which was to follow the next year. Darton, too, points out a "distinct thinness of plot and characterization."[69] Perhaps the play suffered because of Barrie's reaction to the war psychology of the time, but it was another case of his gauging

[66] Mackail, pp. 459, 465.

[67] Walter Pritchard Eaton, quoted in "A Kiss for Cinderella," *Current Opinion*, March, 1917, p. 178.

[68] P. H., "After the Play," *New Republic*, January 6, 1917, p. 209.

[69] Darton, p. 86.

a play to the prevailing atmosphere. Mackail describes the response at its initial performance:

> It was drenched in the wartime background ... which as one reads it now seems, comparatively speaking, such a cozy and almost fragrant affair. But its test, of course—war or no war—was whether the knitting together of all these fancies would or could reach out over the footlights; and particularly, when the time came, whether the audience would be caught up in the drama.... Its magic and kindness, and friendly satire went straight to the public heart ... It had its addicts, immediately and throughout, for where it hit the mark it stuck and clung, and there were two Christmas revivals, at other London theatres, during the war; almost while that lasted, as if it were another *Peter Pan.*[70]

In his next war play the author seemed to correct most of the ills prominent in *A Kiss for Cinderella,* and whether or not it is true that it was the "greatest play produced by the war"[71] much can be said in its behalf. In his reaction to *The Old Lady Shows Her Medals* the critic for *Current Opinion* stresses the difference between the contributions of Shaw and Barrie at this time:

> Before the war ... Bernard Shaw could amuse and delight an audience. But with the advent of national service and active patriotism, his comic recipe fails.
> The London critics said this of Shaw's war play *Augustus Does His Bit*—"unmitigated bosh," "of no importance," "futile," "combined bad taste and puerility," "utterly silly and feeble." Contrast with this the joy with which Barrie's one-act wartime play *The Old Lady Shows Her Medals* has been received by press and public .... When Barrie achieves the pathetic without being mawkish, he is quite irresistible.[72]

Its one major weakness, strangely enough, seems to center close to what many consider its greatest strength. Darton says that "unhappily, the old lady never seems at all like a real London 'char', and the adventitious Kenneth is not much more like a real Tommy or Jock."[73] On the other hand, within these and the other characters in the play are manifested the most universal emotions.[74]

It should suffice to say here, though, that in spite of its particular application to the milieu of World War I England the play in subsequent years continued to rank second only to *The Twelve Pound Look* in popularity, among the author's short plays.

No such reference to specific time or place exists in *Dear Brutus,*

---

[70] Mackail, p. 492.

[71] Phelps, *Essays,* p. 59.

[72] "Barrie vs. Shaw in the Realm of Wartime Drama," *Current Opinion,* June, 1917, p. 405.

[73] Darton, p. 90.

[74] Hammerton, p. 414.

however, a play which has been aptly called the author's "most mature play."[75]

> ... [It] is a game of what might have been ... a game that probably all men play from youth to old age.... But the play is much more, of course,— [its] philosophy is simply a second chance changes nothing ... a pessimistic play made pallatable by a "happy ever after" ending.
>
> Barrie gives healing not by transcendent optimism like Ibsen but rather through infinite pity.
>
> A tragic scene where we wait for the painter to awaken.... "Things that are too beautiful can't last" is a line that goes to the heart of everyone capable of suffering.[76]

These were the words of a critic writing after a revival of the play in 1922 when it began to look as if *Dear Brutus* had certain qualities which would make it even more effective than at its initial production. This is particularly significant upon realizing that Barrie thought of it as a war play. In a letter to William Gillette, which the actor read to the New York opening night audience, the dramatist said:

> *Dear Brutus* is an allegory about a gentleman called John Bull who, years and years ago, missed the opportunity of his life. The Mr. Dearth of the play is really John Bull. The play shows how on the fields of France father and daughter get a second opportunity. Are not the two to make it up permanently or forever drift apart? A second chance comes to few. As for a third chance, who ever heard of it? It's now or never. If it is now, something will have to be accomplished greater than war itself. Future mankind are listening for our decision. If we cannot rise to this second chance, ours will be the blame, but the sorrow will be posterity's.[77]

Desmond McCarthy, writing somewhat later, called it another bit of excellent timing on Barrie's part when in the *Saturday Review of Literature* of June 29, 1929, he said: "*Dear Brutus* was written at a time when people cried to get away from realism—Barrie the popular, airy, sentimental playwright, whom no one considered a pioneer, did it."[78] That the play was a popular success goes without saying. In 1917 and 1918 it ran for 365 performances and at two revivals subsequently almost 400 performances. It was able, too, to gain the endorsement of certain exponents of "realism" who in other instances shied away from the Barrie appeal. Perhaps this was due to the realistic way in which the play could be produced. Watson and Pressey tell us, for instance, that Gerald du Maurier "brought to the character [Dearth] the lightest and most fluent

---

[75] Magill, p. 68.

[76] John Pollock, "Four Plays of the Season," *Fortnightly Review*, August, 1922, p. 955

[77] James M. Barrie, quoted by Hammerton, p. 441.

[78] Desmond McCarthy, "A Present-Day Dramatist," *Saturday Review of Literature*, June 29, 1929, p. 1140.

naturalism to be found among London's admirable comedians."[79] Gran-ville-Barker asserted that there is no machinery in the play to de-humanize it. "The magic of *Dear Brutus* involves none at all, and the more realis-tically the play is treated the better."[80]

On the question of theatricality Darlington tries to show "why an audience seeing *Dear Brutus* in the theatre swallows the pill and tastes only the jam."

> One [reason] is that people listening to a story have a primitive tendency to concentrate their interest on the fate of the hero and heroine, and to be quite callous about the importance of minor characters. The hero and heroine of *Dear Brutus* are Will and Alice Dearth. They are the two exceptional people of the play, who are capable of learning by their adventures in the woods. Dearth regains his self-confidence; Alice learns that she is better off as she is than she would have been if she had married the other man. ... The second [reason] is perhaps only the same one in a different dress. It is that we are all, to ourselves, the heroes and heroines of our own little dramas; we all have a conviction that if there is a chance for exceptional people there is hope for us.[81]

Barrie's next play, his last popular success, was received by the general public again without reservation, but not so by all the critics. This time the dramatist made an unequivocal assault on the emotions, and for 400 performances "beginning on April 22nd [1920] audiences wept, sniffed, swallowed, and choked without ever being able to explain what had reduced them to this state."[82] *Mary Rose*, needless to say, is an odd play and unlike *Dear Brutus*, as Granville-Barker points out, possesses strangely mixed elements. "... The real and the unreal are boldly mingled; there is neither evasion of the difficulty nor compromise. Upon the magic island she must disappear before our eyes. This is a matter for a single risky moment which is, moreover, led up to with extraordinary dramatic skill, and a sympathetic producer may compass it."[83] No such "risky moment" had occured in *Dear Brutus*, and such boldness prompted one critic to say years after its first production, "The escape into fantasy, which in *Peter Pan* and *Dear Brutus* is perfectly justified by a general epi-colyrical atmosphere, seems out of place and arbitrary in a story like that of *Mary Rose*, which should be purely dramatic."[84] On the other hand, one commentator, Maurice Baring, after having witnessed a performance

[79] E. Bradlee Watson and Benfield Pressey (eds.), *Contemporary Drama*, (New York, 1941), p. 769.

[80] Harley Granville-Barker, preface to *The Boy David*, by James M. Barrie (New York, 1938), p. xi.

[81] Darlington, pp. 124-125.

[82] Mackail, p. 546.

[83] Granville-Barker, preface, *Boy David*, p. xi.

[84] Pellizzi, p. 171.

"thought the Act III scene where Mary Rose comes back the most moving thing he'd seen on the stage." A similar impression was received by Desmond McCarthy, who simply said "never have tricks with time been played with such dexterity."[85] Another eyewitness to the opening night agreed that the tricks worked.

> Barrie has done something very rare for the stage. . . . [He has] had a fleshly ghost come off successfully.
> He has depicted for us the psychology of the spirit severed from the body. . . . We see it summoned to converse with the living by the force of thought. . . . It lives in memory. . . . We who have suffered with her find in her departure the catharsis of feelings that have been raised and troubled.[86]

More interesting, however, than this are efforts to discover the play's central meaning. The London *Times* didn't even try, stating, "It can't be explained any more than a great piece of music can be explained." Ralph Block says, writing to the *New York Times*: ". . . There is a girl who doesn't grow up and a Never-Never Land to which she flies, as well as a home that has forgotten her when she returns. But all of it has achieved so complete a trans-valuation into serious human values that what has been merely sentimental and regretful and pathetic in Barrie before becomes austere and meaningful and tragic." The critic for *Current Opinion* said: ". . . For once Barrie has made an actual impact between two powerful motives—death and life. He does not shrink from the issue, and the result is clear tragedy."[87] These and other comments prompted Barrie to say in a letter to Cynthia Asquith on December 27, 1920: "Cables from New York about the *Mary Rose* production make me doubtful about its course there. They say the audience was enthralled but the press can't make out what it means. I wish you would tell me what it means, so we can settle this for once and for all." Actually, its central meaning is nothing more than the obvious: none of us can return to this life once we have departed. It was an idea that had intrigued him for some time. In fact, in a letter to Quiller-Couch in 1911 he said: ". . . There is no doubt about its being a fine subject but the difficulty is that it seems to lead to a grim end, and rather a queer view of life altogether. I have often thought of it in 3 acts and see the first two all right. The third seems to amount to this. No one should come back, however much he was loved."[88]

---

[85] Maurice Baring and Desmond McCarthy, quoted by Cynthia Asquith, *Portrait of Barrie* (London, 1954), pp. 34-35.

[86] John Pollock, "Mary Rose," *Fortnightly Review*, June, 1920, p. 955.

[87] "Mary Rose: A Tragic Fantasy of Time by James M. Barrie," *Current Opinion*, July, 1920, p. 63.

[88] James M. Barrie, quoted by Meynell, pp. 22, 187.

Quite the opposite reception was given Barrie's last play, *The Boy David*. Most of those who witnessed the occasion attribute its failure to a combination of unavoidable circumstances, the most important of which were Barrie's ill health, the ill health of the leading actress, and the misfortune of the opening night coinciding with King Edward VIII's abdication in December of 1936.

The negative remarks seemed to revolve around the contention that Barrie had been essentially dishonest in altering the facts of the Bible story. It is difficult to conceive of such an accusation upon reading the play, but perhaps certain actors' interpretations prompted the comment. This might easily have happened since Barrie had been unable, as was his practice, to attend many of the rehearsals. On the other hand, Roy suggests that its failure was due to the fact that "it showed David too much like Peter Pan, an ineffectual one."[89]

On the positive side are statements such as Granville-Barker's: "It is one of life's fundamental conflicts that is here reduced to such deceptively simple terms and crystallized, as drama should be, into significant action and a few revealing words."[90] Harold Child felt that Barrie had finally reached his ultimate goal in *The Boy David*.

> At the very end of his career he found out what it was that he had been grop-ing after in *Peter Pan*. It was not the domination of reality by play; the mak-ing the world his toy. . . .
> Michael says in *Peter Pan,* "Wendy, I've killed a pirate!"
> David says, "Mother, I've killed a lion!" They are both children; but one is childishness as distinct from manhood, the other is the childhood at the core of all humanity. . . . Here is the intuitive wisdom of childlike humanity.[91]

In general, however, the press reacted in disfavor, and the play ran for only two months. It was the greatest disappointment in Barrie's career that his last effort should be received in this manner. As Mackail relates, "It was a wound from which there could be no recovery."[92]

The Boy David was the thirty-seventh of the dramatist's plays to reach the commercial stage; we have discussed all those for which there is available information in terms of critical and popular reaction, trying not to exclude major dissenting criticism nor to overemphasize laudatory appraisal. From this, then, what conclusions can be drawn?

First, there is evidence of Barrie's continual experimentation. He tried the problem play, the comic opera, the burlesque, and the straight

[89] Roy, p. 247.
[90] Granville-Barker, quoted by Asquith, p. 8.
[91] Child, p. 37.
[92] Mackail, p. 706.

fantasy to name some of the dominant types, and within specific forms attempted different mixtures of sentiment, humor, pathos, and satire. The critics observed a growth in his work from 1892 with the pure entertainment in *Walker, London* to 1917 and the complex art of *Dear Brutus,* and within this period perceived definite innovations commonly called "modern" which were somehow accepted by the public with little reservation. These new devices led one critic, Bernard Shaw, to remark that it is to Barrie that credit is due for relegating the nineteenth-century London theater to the dust bin. It was noted, too, how often plays of Barrie emerged at the proper psychological moment; how, on such occasions as the production of *Ibsen's Ghost, Peter Pan, The Old Lady Shows Her Medals,* and *Dear Brutus,* the public mind was ripe to accept what Barrie had to offer.

More important, however, is the recurrent stress on Barrie's facility for creating certain theatrical effects—effects of mood and atmosphere gauged so precisely to and derived from the conditions of the theater. It is under these same conditions that he makes an appeal to the emotions rather than the intellect, and wherever truth is expressed it is through the medium of character and significant action rather than through words.

Barrie's subject matter and peculiar approach are seemingly out of step with contemporary modes and manners, but all of this aside, there seems to be a more fundamental reason for his relatively minor position today. The plays are essentially theatrical pieces rather than literary works. Not that the terms are mutually exclusive, but with Barrie the appeal was primarily to the eye and too infrequently is the reader given aural pleasure. In the literary sense he was a magician; audiences, and play reviewers for the most part, have been captivated by this magic but time has disclosed the tricks, and as with any act of magic its attraction is lost when explained.

UNIVERSITY OF MICHIGAN

Notes and Documents

Scott — Byron

The following incomplete sketch of Scott and Byron by John Galt may be found as Item 000930-934 in the Dominion National Archives at Ottawa. It is primarily of interest in that it mentions a meeting between Galt and Scott. Such a meeting is not mentioned, to my knowledge, by any of the biographers of Galt and Scott. It must have taken place in late October, 1831.

FRED COGSWELL
UNIVERSITY OF NEW BRUNSWICK

My acquaintance with Byron himself was form'd accidental and I have in the memoir which I afterwards wrote of him,[1] said all that I know of that distinguished genius. It has been by some supposed that I looked askance at his merits, and because I have mentioned various limitations that are obvious in his work, that I regarded him invidiously. Those who have said so or think so do me injustice; nor are they capable of appreciating how I felt or how such rare talents should be considered. It does not follow that because a man is transcendent in some things he is great in all. The injudicious admirers of Byron however seem to think he is, and perhaps I am blamable in numbering himself among them. But in those peculiarities in which he excelled, in energy of thought, picturesque expression, and that lurid kind of sentiment derived from, what the painters would call, studying too much the cold colours, he has no superior, and accordingly while I give him praise for originality in those qualities as generously as those who see him always unspoiled can desire, am I therefore not to be at liberty to say his verse is often prosaic and his conceptions jejeune? As a poet, I place him in the very first rank, I do homage to him as such, but I cannot discern that his Lordship, more than many others has any peculiar claim upon my esteem. As for his heroism, I laugh at it, and rank his meddling with the Greek cause, instead of being the effect of moral or mental enterprise, the cramp and spurn of misanthropic indiges-

---

[1] The argument in this paragraph is one of Galt's many defences of his controversial biography, *Life of Lord Byron*, published in London by Colburn and Bentley in 1830.

tion. And I say so because I wish myself to be understood very plainly, especially as what I have said of him may be the only thing by which as a literary man I shall hereafter be remembered.

Of Sir Walter Scott I can speak less decidedly, for I knew him only as an author—our personal acquaintance was not great and except about half an hour alone with him on the day before he went abroad benumbed in his faculties with his fatal illness, I would not properly be said to have been much in his company and therefore it is only of him as an author that I can speak, in which capacity I do not, though I think him a much more agreeable poet, think him to be at all compared for a single instant with Byron. He relates his semi-epics certainly with great beauty, a vivacity quite unexampled and often gleams possessed of that fine frenzy which is the poetical element, but in general his verse scarcely rises beyond respectable mediocrity, but in romance he towers into unapproachable excellence.

Of his different novels and romances, I do not profess myself to be a proper judge—I am only sure of what pleases myself, not of its worth. Thus it happens that while I have always regarded The Antiquary as one of his happiest productions to my taste I have not been insensible to the vigour of his pencilling in what are perhaps greater works. Ivanhoe in this respect I regard as his master piece and yet if required to give reasons for saying so I could not draw them from my own feelings because I do think that its merits can only be classed, not compared, with some of the rarest efforts of the human mind, and can only be read to be duly valued by passages, for it is one of those books in which the bright truth, and the deep insights with which it abounds can be only properly seen in quotations. No writer but himself ever made the limning of crimes beautiful and yet witheld from that beauty the power of captivating. Byron in one of his freaks of genius made sensuality by giving to it benevolence in Sardanapolis almost a virtue, but Scott has never encouraged in himself the indulgence of such eccentricity; all with him is wholesome, pure, open, and robust.

Lord Byron says that all great authors are voluminous. This is not correct. Nations have constructed pyramids, but only one man has existed in all time capable of creating the Apollo.

What circulating library. . . .

"What is a Conger?"

John Dunton and Scottish Booksellers

John Dunton (1659-1733), eccentric bookseller, publisher of *The Athenian Mercury*, and tireless traveler both in fact and in fiction, is best known for *The life and errors of John Dunton* (1705;1818), the fullest known catalogue of the booksellers of his day. He first showed a strong bias against Scottish booksellers in a little-known work, *A voyage round the world* (1691). Describing a former London bookseller of Lombard Street, Dunton calls him "a Pirate ... a Cormorant,—*Copies, Books, Men, Shops,* all was one; he held no Propriety, right or wrong, good or bad, till at last he began to be known ... and our Trade ... spew'd him out."[1] This traitor to the honorable trade of booksellers was "a Conger, and *over-grown Eel,* that devours all the Food from the weaker Grigs, and when he wants other Food, swallows them too into the bargain. *A poor Fly* can't stir upon water, but—pop, he's at him." There are, continues Dunton, congers in all nations, but the worst

> are of a *North-countrey* race, much about the *Tweed* mouth .... But *Scotland* being a barren Countrey, others are rather for the *Shannon* or *Boine,* or not yet content, *ramble* further .... so slippery withal, that no Hook can catch 'em, no Hand detain 'em, no Spear strike 'em, no Wear hold 'em. Nor will they ever be quiet, and leave plaguing all the little Fry in this (*watry*) World, till they tumble down through some Vortex or other into the grand Abyss.[2]

Dunton's commercial travels to the large fairs in England, to New England, to the capitals of Great Britain, and to the Low Countries had brought him into contact with other peripatetic booksellers and created in him an antipathy for the Scots, partly because of the great numbers of them in the trade:

> Look but how *lofty and stately* they bear themselves,—you'd think 'em all *Leviathans,* and there's no coming near 'em unless you slip into their Gills. *Venus orta mavi* is a good old Observation: For some of these *same Fish* are very waggish *prolifick*—but there's room enough in the wide Sea to turn out as much Spawn as Nature has give 'em.[3]

The earliest definition, aside from Dunton's, combining ichthyological and mercantile senses of *conger* appears in *A new dictionary of the terms ancient and modern of the canting crew* (1700):

[1] III, 76-77.
[2] Ibid., III, 77-78.
[3] Ibid., III, 78.

a Set or Knot of Topping Book-sellers of London, who agree among themselves, that whoever of them Buys a good Copy, the rest are to take off such a particular number ... in Quires, on easy Terms. Also that they joyn together to Buy either a Considerable, or Dangerous Copy. And a great over-grown Sea-Eel.

B. E., Gent., the author of this work, was not strong on etymologies; the implied identity between the two senses may have been accidental. An intentional connection is plain, however, in *The universal etymological English dictionary*, Vol. II, second edition (1731), by Nathan Bailey, where *conger, congre* signifies:

a society of booksellers, to the number of 10 or more, who unite into a sort of company, or contribute a joint stock for the printing of books; so called, because as a large conger eel is said to devour the small fry, so this united body overpowers young and single traders, who have neither so much money to support the charge, nor so united an interest to dispose of books printed; tho' (according to the tradition) the foregoing was the original of the name *conger*, yet to be a little more complaisant, you may derive it of *congruere*, L. *i.e.* to agree together; or ... of *congressus* a congress.

If, as the editors of the *Oxford English dictionary* suggest, Bailey's definition and doubtful etymology refer to a contemporary joke, there is evidence that Dunton was its originator. He was well-known along Grub Street, his books were popular, and his *Athenian Mercury* enjoyed six years of prosperity in the 1690's, a long run at that time for a periodical. Most significantly, his sympathy for "the little Fry" was often expressed, in such works as his *Religio bibliopolae* (1691).

Dunton's animosity toward Scottish booksellers is aired again and at much greater length in a "three-decker" work published in 1699: *The Dublin scuffle ... The Billet Doux, sent him by a citizens wife in Dublin, tempting him to lewdness ... Some account of his conversation in Ireland.* Although he could say of Scotland in this work, "that Countrey has labour'd under discouragements, as to Learning, for many Years, tho it does not want its proportion of Learned Men," and "they are pretty well furnisht with Books; and what they buy is generally of the *Best Sort*,"[4] the central theme of the book is the author's quarrel with one Patrick Campbell, a Scottish bookseller·who lived in Dublin between 1687 and 1720.[5]

Dunton attacks Campbell for having preempted the auction room in Dick's Dublin coffee-house which Dunton had reserved before coming from London in June 1698 with "a Venture of Books"[6]. A poem by T. B. in the volume encourages the aggrieved bookseller:

[4] p. 154.
[5] Henry R. Plomer *A dictionary of the printers and booksellers ... in England Scotland and Ireland ... 1668 to 1725* (1922).
[6] *The Dublin Scuffle*, p. 5.

You must go on, this scurvy Scot
Has broke the Peace, and the proud Loon
Insults, unless you take him down.[7]

Campbell's additional crimes are his failure to pay Dunton for books sent him from London, unwillingness to meet for a glass of ale and a peace parley, and inability to spell, the last illustrated by one of Campbell's advertisements reproduced by Dunton.[8]

The Scottishness of the Scot is treated throughout as an expected concomitant of his rascally behavior in a trade which Dunton always praises for its honesty. " 'Tis true," writes Dunton, "he calls himself the *een Mon of Coonshence;* but I am afraid to tell you, what *Persuasion* he is of, seeing he has so very little either of *Justice or Humanity.*"[9] In a "character" of Campbell, the author dwells on his covetousness, pride, *"Natural Aversion to Honesty,"* equivocation, and false piety. "He'll commonly say grace over a Choppin of Ale, and the same time be contriving how to over reach you."[10] Dunton asserts that he has enough by him "to confirm every tittle of this character," by means of a history of Campbell's life sent him in London from Dublin. As a generous enemy, Dunton will say nothing of Campbell's humble beginnings selling "Thread-laces in Glascow [sic], by the name of Patrick Ure, to the time that Patrick Campbell begged Pardon of the Company in Dublin, for his pretty Experiment of turning Hodder into Cocker, &c."[11]

Ironically, the largest conger joined by the Scottish eel who swam up the Liffey included just two others. Together with Eliphal Dobson and Matthew Gun, Campbell published in 1694 a book by a Dissenting minister, J. Boyse, *Remarks on a late discourse of William, Lord Bishop of Derry.*[12] Patrick Campbell's little share of immortality has come to him chiefly through his enemy, John Dunton, who did indeed write a book.

GILBERT D. McEWEN
WHITTIER COLLEGE

[7] *Ibid.,* p. 11.

[8] *Ibid.,* pp. 99-100.

[9] *Ibid.,* p. 23.

[10] *Ibid.,* p. 337 f.

[11] James Hodder's *Arithmetic* had 20 editions, 1661-1697; Edward Cocker's *Arithmetic,* 22 editions, 1678-1700, none of either published in Dublin. Cf. Donald Wing, *Short-titled Catalogue . . . 1641-1700* (1945). The allegation was that Campbell switched title pages.

[12] E. R. McC. Dix *Books, tracts, &c., printed in Dublin the 17th century,* part IV (1905).

A Note on Spenser
and the Scottish Sonneteers[1]

Despite the disagreement of some scholars, it has been generally assumed that Edmund Spenser devised the Spensarian sonnet and that the Scottish poets James VI, Alexander Montgomerie, Thomas Hudson, and others, who used the form, were imitating Spenser. The question is raised by certain dates of publication. Spenser first published sonnets in the form graced by his name in 1590; they were the seventeen dedicatory sonnets accompanying the *Faerie Queene*. Six years earlier (1584), however, James VI had published *The Essayes of a Prentise, in the Divine Art of Poesie* which contains twenty Spensarian sonnets: one by Thomas Hudson, one by Robert Hudson, one by M. W., one by William Fowler, one by Alexander Montgomerie, and fifteen by James himself.

On the basis of these dates Oscar Hoffman argues that Montgomerie evolved the form and Spenser adopted it from him.[2] George Stevenson points out that Dr. Hoffman overlooked a sonnet inscribed by Spenser to Gabriel Harvey which is dated July 18, 1586, although it was not pub-

[1] All references to individual poems are to these editions:
New Poems by James I of England, ed. Alan Westcott, Columbia University Press, 1911.
The Poems of Alexander Montgomerie, ed. James Cranstoun, STS, 1887.
The Poetical Works of Edmund Spenser, ed. J. C. Smith and E. De Selincourt, Oxford University Press, 1912.
The numbering of the poems in Mr. Westcott's edition is much more conveniently referred to, so I have used it, but there is a newer edition of James' poetry. *The Poems of King James VI of Scotland,* ed. J. R. Craigie, STS, 3d. series 22,26, 1955, 1958. For the reader's convenience I list here the corresponding numbers of the poems cited.

Westcott	Craigie
Amatoria	
II	1
III	2
XII	5
Miscellanea	
XXI	13
XXIII	15
XXXII	20
XXXIII	21
XLVII	31
L	33
Appendix II	Uncollected Poems
IV	VIIIa

[2] Oscar Hoffman, "Studien zu Alexander Montgomerie," *Englische Studien,* xx, (1895), 51.

lished until 1592.[3] Stevenson argues that the Scots' priority of publication is therefore not great enough to be significant.[4] Herbert Cory glances at their evidence and decides for Spenser on the grounds that he was the greater and more versatile poet.[5] Allen Westcott and Stevenson, without yielding much credit to Montgomerie, assume the probability of independent invention. James Craigie attributes the invention to the circle of poets around James.[6]

Most aspects of the question have been discussed by the scholars mentioned above: the capabilities of the poets concerned, the poetic activity of Scotland and England, the probable French inspiration, the dating of the sonnets and the dates of publication, the mutual awareness of James and Spenser, and the intercourse between the English and Scottish courts and literary men.[7] Only the sonnets themselves have not been considered.

If, in addition to the rhyme-scheme, the sonnets by Spenser and James and his coterie were alike in style, subject matter, manipulation of the form, and in theme, one might discount the evidence to the contrary and assert that even though the exact exchange between the poets is not demonstrable it must have occurred. Thus the question might be opened again. An examination of the sonnets however, confirms the probability that the Scottish poets and Spenser developed and used the form without awareness of each other's activity. The poets' use of the form is very different.

There are similarities, as one would expect; all were, as far as we know, subject to similiar influences. They were reading other English sonneteers, and DuBartas, DuBellay, and Petrach. They were interested in poetic theory. And in using a common verse pattern they committed themselves to likeness, except insofar as they were able to change the form without destroying it.

The Spenserian sonnet is not a distinct form as are the English and Petrarchan sonnets, which, besides rhyming differently, move and develop

[3] George Stevenson, *Poems of Alexander Montgomerie*, Supplementary Volume, STS, 59, (1910), xlv-xlvii.

[4] Stevenson and Hoffman overlook a sonnet by Spenser which must have been written around 1582. Sometime between 1580, when Spenser left Leicester's employ to go to Ireland, and 1588, when Leicester died, Spenser addressed a sonnet to Leicester. It was published with *Virgil's Gnat* in 1591. The content and tone of the sonnet indicate that it was written nearer the earlier date. The editor of the *Variorum* dates it 1580.

[5] Herbert E. Cory, *Edmund Spenser, A Critical Study*, Berkely, (1917), p. 234-5.

[6] J. R. Craigie, *Thomas Hudson's History of Judith*, STS, third series, 14, (1941), xcii-ci.

[7] A summary discussion of all these matters is in J. R. Craigie's introduction to *The Poems of King James VI of Scotland*.

differently. The Petrarchan is a fourteen line poem composed of two quatrains and two tercets. The English is a fourteen line poem of three quatrains and a couplet. The Spenserian is also three quatrains and a couplet; structurally it is the English form, but the interlocking rhyme can blur the construction so that the poet can ignore the quatrain and write a sonnet which has more the movement of the Petrarchan (Spenser, *Amoretti* XXXVII; Montgomerie, Sonnets 1; James, *Miscellanea* XXXIII). Because Spenser never overrides the inherent construction as entirely as Montgomerie sometimes does, the logic of his sonnets usually progresses through the three quatrains to a conclusion in the couplet (*Amoretti*, II). The grammatical structure of the poems also is molded to the form. Each quatrain contains a completed sentence, and the phrasing is so arranged that it corresponds to the line. Each line, then, is end-stop and caesuras are blurred. Spenser writes few run-on lines. The verse is smooth, without great variation, never rough (except for the sonnet to Harvey). The commonest substitution is of a trochee or spondee for the initial iamb.

James' sonnets have not the consistent smoothness of Spenser's but submit to the same logic. There are a few exceptions; one, a catalogue (*Miscellanea* XXI) has only the logic and structure of a list. Spenser confines his catalogues (*Amoretti*, IX, XV) more closely within a grammatical construction. In another (*Miscellanea* XXIII) James completes the first sentence at the third foot of the fifth line, the fifth line is run on into the sixth, and the seventh into the eighth; he slurs the form as Spenser never did.

In this respect Montgomerie's sonnets resemble Spenser's even less. He is less consistent than James and Spenser in handling the form so that his sonnets vary considerably in character. Some are rough, sonnets only in scansion and rhyme. He often ignores the quatrain and melds the couplet with the preceding lines (Sonnets, I). End stop lines (XXV), each line broken into several short phrases (LV), frequent and positive caesuras (LXX), midline sentence endings (XXV), a change of cadence in the middle of a sonnet (VI); all these characteristics cause a halting, rough, staccato movement. This seems more typical of his verse than do the smoother, sweeter lines of several sonnets (*Suppl. Vol. Misc. Poems*, XXI-XXVII) which are more like Spenser's and more in the manner of the conventional love sonnet.

The ruggedness of Montgomerie's sonnets is aggravated by another characteristic which he shares with James. Both poets use alliteration indiscriminately. With each repetition of sound Montgomerie's line slows and breaks into individual words. Often a line is a list; one sonnet begins "Of Mars, Minerva, Mercure, and the Musis/" and continues "A cunning king a cunning Chanceller chuisis./" Line after line will have three or four words in alliteration. Scarcely a single poem is without instances. James is like him in this practice, following his own prescript in the *Reulis*, "The most part of your line shall run upon a letter." (*Amatoria*, II 1, 4, 5-8; III 11, 12, 13; XII 1, 7; *Miscellanea* XXXII 1).

Alliteration is not common in Spenser's sonnets. It appears frequently in the sonnet to Leicester and several times in the one to Harvey. In other instances, particularily in the *Amoretti*, it is an occasional device, useful to emphasize a parallelism (XI 14) or to form an epithet (XIII 1, 2). Whenever it occurs it is subdued. All three poets are alike in preferring masculine rhyme, but Spenser frequently employs feminine rhyme (*Amoretti* II, VI; *To Harvey*; *Visions of the Worlds Vanities* I; II) or rhymes on secondary accents (*Amoretti* III).

In content the sonnets of the three poets are not much alike. It may seem meaningful that Spenser calls one sequence *Amoretti* and James calls a group *Amatoria*; however, only twelve of the twenty poems in *Amatoria* are sonnets, and they have none of the sequential unity which Spenser gave the *Amoretti*. Several of the *Amatoria* are not on the subject of love and so are without even the unity suggested by the title. In Montgomerie's work there is no such grouping of poems at all. In the love poems of all three poets we find the time's conventional manner and imagery. That the poems are alike in this respect is not significant, but it is significant that as they differ from the conventional they continue to differ from each other. This means that the Scots poets are not imitating Spenser, nor Spenser them. As Spenser develops his own mode, he introduces into the *Amoretti* elements of neo-platonism and displaces the conventional manner and imagery (*Amoretti* XXVII, LXXVIII, LXXIX, LXXXVIII). Neo-platonism is not a theme in Montgomerie's and James' work. If their love poems move from the conventional it is toward a more personal occasional tone and manner which is typical of all their work (Sonnets L, LV). They become more concrete as Spenser becomes more abstract.

The personal and occasional character prevails in sonnets written on other subjects by the two Scots. Montgomerie uses the sonnet in the manner of the flyting (XIX, XX). He threatens his enemies (XX). He abuses a former friend (XXI), his own lawyer (XXIII), and appeals to the king to restore his pension (XIV). This is immediate, direct, open poetry of statement. James is again like his master. He writes sonnets in praise of learned men (*Miscellanea* XXIII), to give advice to his son (Appendix II, IV) and about current events (*Miscellanea* XLVII, L). Their poems do not arise out of concepts nor are they written to express the sort of abstraction which Spenser is wholly concerned with in *Visions of the Worlds Vanities.* Nor are their poems about the idea of love or about the nature of love as are the *Amoretti.* Even in his most occasional poems such as the commendatory and dedicatory sonnets and in some of the more personal of the *Amoretti* Spenser is less detailed, less specific, less concrete than the Scots.

Nothing in the character of the sonnets written by Spenser, on one hand, and two of the most important of the Scots poets would support an assertion that one imitated the other. Only in form are they alike, and it seems reasonable to assume that if the familiarity of one with the works of the other was sufficient to lead to imitation of form there would have been some imitation also of manner, subject, and structure. That Spenser and the Scots poets were not familiar with each other's work in the form increases the reliability of the conclusion that they developed this sonnet form independently.

MURRAY F. MARKLAND
WASHINGTON STATE UNIVERSITY

Reviews

P. H. Butter. *Edwin Muir*. Edinburgh and London.
Oliver & Boyd. 1962. 5 shillings.

Ever since the publication of *The Story and the Fable* in 1940 and
The Narrow Place in 1943, more and more readers have been quietly discovering that Edwin Muir is one of the few authentic "voices" (and the
even fewer authentic visionaries) who has written in English during this
century. J. C. Hall's edition of *Collected Poems: 1921-1951* and his essay on Muir in the series "Writers and Their Work" were, among other
things, public recognitions of the number of such private responses; and
those volumes introduced the living Muir to an audience much wider than
he had ever known before. Since Muir's death in 1959, there have been
an increasing number of serious appraisals of his work (those by Helen
Gardner and John Holloway seem to me among the best). Now Professor
Butter's study joins the other volumes in "Writers and Critics," a series
devoted to writers of the past century who are still felt as living pres-
ences today. It is the most extensive and substantial treatment of Muir
which we have had.

The book contains six chapters: "The Man," "The Critic: Of Literature and Society," "The Novelist and Autobiographer," two chapters
on"The Poet," and a "Conclusion." In the central section of the book,
Professor Butter considers, chronologically within each chapter, each volume that Muir published. (*The Estate of Poetry*, the posthumously published Norton lectures at Harvard, seems to have appeared too late to be
treated.) He places the works within the context of Muir's life and development as a writer. His careful scholarship gives particular weight
and interest to his comments. He has read the uncollected writings; he
has examined the manuscripts; and he is able to quote from unpublished
letters and personal reminiscences. He includes a bibliography of Muir's
published volumes, notes on the translations and occasional pieces, and a
brief selected bibliography of secondary commentary.

Although this present work is clearly (and properly) conceived as
an introductory critical survey of Muir's life and work, the bits of new
information which are modestly presented make one look forward to the
full biography of Muir on which Professor Butter is now engaged. At
first thought, to write a biography of a man who has left one of the best

autobiographies of this century would seem a thankless task; but Professor Butter has already shown by his tact and discrimination here that there is more to know about Muir's "story," if not his "fable," than we now know, and that the additional knowledge will be of value.

If one has any misgivings about the book they may be that Professor Butter pays too great attention to Muir's limitations and claims too little for him. He concludes his chapter on "The Critic" with, ". . . he gave incisive and well-balanced assessments of particular writers, which are still, and will remain worth reading. But he did not make any important contributions to the theory of literary criticism . . . It is, surely, as a poet, not as a critic, that he will live." Of the novels, he remarks: "Parts are produced by the not very powerful imagination of a novelist trying to tell stories about fictional characters, parts by the powerful imagination of a poet brooding over his own experience. Though the novels are not wholly satisfactory as fiction, the presence of the poet in them results in their containing moving and memorable passages, which make them more worth reading than many more nearly perfect works." On a number of occasions, it seems to me that his criticisms of specific poems are less generous than the poems themselves would warrant. In a day when one is used to extreme statements, when, particularly with modern poetry, critical "appraisals" usually either praise highly or damn, one may feel that Professor Butter could have allowed himself a little more extravagance. One may be afraid that, amid all the noise, this quiet and conscientious voice may go unheard.

And yet, even as one formulates the objection, one is conscious of the fact that a critic who has truly responded to Muir's own voice is probably incapable of being shrill. Professor Butter is concerned neither with mass conversions nor with "selling" Muir. He is giving the most careful and most just appraisal he can to a writer of whose greatness he is convinced, but whose occasional weaknesses or limitations he recognizes. The critic whom Professor Butter most nearly resembles is Muir himself. One feels that Muir would have liked this book. And if Muir's own voice continues to be heard increasingly today, one need not fear for the effectiveness of Professor Butter's account of it. There are, here, no extravagancies for later critics and scholars to condemn. The final paragraph is a model of the sort of modesty, honesty, and commitment which we badly need in criticism—and which will be heard:

> I have enjoyed Muir's poems more than any other new ones I have come across in the last ten years or so. I am confident that he is a genuine poet because he speaks always with an individual voice. I am confident, too, that he is a poet of major importance because of the depth and comprehensiveness of the vision which his poems collectively contain. In comparison the work of

most other modern poets seems to me fragmentary. The last time I saw him he told me he was planning a long poem. He did not live to write it, but, in a sense, he had already written it; for his poems, taken together, make up a whole.

JOSEPH H. SUMMERS
WASHINGTON UNIVERSITY (ST. LOUIS)

James Johnson (ed.). *The Scots Musical Museum.* Hatboro, Pa. Folklore Associates. 1962. 2 vol. $25.00 (Facsimile reprint).

In the last letter Robert Burns sent to James Johnson (ca. 1 June 1796), before the publication of Vol. V of the *Scots Musical Museum,* he wrote, "I will venture to prophesy, that to future ages your Publication will be the text-book & standard of Scottish Song & Music." Burns was in a position to know for he had by this time been collaborating with Johnson for nine years. From the second volume of the *Museum* on Burns was centrally concerned with it: he collected or wrote almost half the songs which appeared thereafter, he wrote the prefaces for three of the volumes, and without his enthusiasm it is more than possible that Johnson would have let fall the project after the third or fourth volume. In this last respect it is worthy of note that the six volumes appeared in the following years: 1787, 1788, 1790, 1792, 1796, and 1803. During the period 1790-1796 Burns was also busy writing and collecting for George Thomson's *Select Collection of Original Scotish Airs* (5 vol., 1793-1818). Both collections slowed down considerably after the poet's death. Upon completion of the final volume Johnson wrote of the set with justifiable pride: "it unquestionably contains the greatest Collection of Scotish Vocal Music ever published."

Burns's prophecy was correct; the *Scots Musical Museum* remains to this day a standard work on Scottish song. Collected in it one finds traditional songs and airs, as well as songs written especially to be set to tunes which either had no words or whose words were bawdy or otherwise objectionable. It is not easy to ascertain the exact number of songs Burns contributed to the *Museum* as not all of them are indicated as being his. Some have been identified through Burns's letters to Johnson but not all of this correspondence has survived. Ninety-seven songs are acknowledged as Burns's in the indexes, but over two hundred were probably collected, touched up or written entirely by him.

Of course Burns was not the only contemporary writer whose songs were printed by Johnson; others include Dr. Thomas Blacklock, Rev. John Skinner, Andrew Shirrefs, and Hector MacNeill. Also included were works by both William Hamiltons, Robert Fergusson and several by Allan Ramsay.

To any but the bibliophile the most valuable edition of this work is that of 1853, with its 512 pages of "Illustrations of the lyric poetry and music of Scotland" originally prepared by William Stenhouse. When Stenhouse died in 1827 the edition lay dormant until David Laing, Librarian of the Signet Library, took over the task of readying it for the publishers William Blackwood. With help from other qualified persons he added 228 pages of "Additional illustrations," as well as 134 pages of Preface and Introduction. Fortunately there are four indexes to this mass of editorial material (there is even one for the Introduction) and these make it relatively easy to locate any information which may be required.

The present two-volume set is a photo-facsimile of the four volumes of 1853. Henry George Farmer, Keeper of Music at Glasgow University Library, has added a short Foreword which does much to fill in the background on the variants of the *Musical Museum* to be found and on those who have been associated with it editorially. Some annoying errors in Mr. Farmer's essay: the date of Burns's Kilmarnock edition is not 1787 (p. xv); Yale's 1723 edition of Vol. I of the *Tea-Table Miscellany* (p.xi) has been known for some years; Yale also possesses the 1727 Vol. III of this collection which Mr. Farmer claims is not extant. For the record, this first edition of Vol. III contains the words "A Collection of Celebrated Songs."

The earlier editions of the *Scots Musical Museum* have long since become difficult to find and expensive. This new set will be welcomed alike by libraries and individuals.

G. R. R.

Louis Simpson. *James Hogg: A critical study*. Edinburgh and London. Oliver & Boyd. 1962. 35 shillings.

Courage of conviction should be sharply distinguished, in maturity, from courage of condescension: when another scholar takes a crack at me, I wish he would quote me entire. In my book on James Hogg I call *The Confessions of a Justified Sinner* "as greatly superior to his other prose works as *Kilmeny* is to his other longer poems . . . Badly constructed as the story is, it is sufficient to justify Hogg's boast that he had several witches among his ancestresses:—a piece that ranks with *Frankenstein* or *Eugene Aram* or even perhaps *The Turn of the Screw.*" Three pages later I note that the public ignored *Queen Hynde* "as, with far less excuse, they ignored the macabre and brilliant *Confessions of a Justified Sinner.*"

In earlier footnotes Professor Simpson dismisses H. T. Stephenson, whose " major judgements are absolutely wide of the mark," and though he praises Professor Edith Batho's "Bibliography," considers her criticism "inferior." Whereas Miss Batho frequently comments on a tale of Hogg in a sentence, Professor Simpson in his study slogs steadily through his subject's prose pieces in pages that make heavy reading until he comes to the *Justified Sinner,* which he treats with illuminating enthusiasm. (I have always felt that T. Earle Welby's "discovery" of this piece in 1924 should be remembered along with André Gide's in 1947.) "Miss Batho's criticism is often mixed with biography," he laments, "and it is evident that she has no high opinion of Hogg himself." Professor Simpson's criticism is (happily) mixed with biography, and it is evident that he has no high opinion of Hogg himself: at least on p. 152 he refers to the poet's "most pig-headed opinion" in defending his *Bridal of Polmood*; and on p. 200 to his being "apt to sound like a bragging ignoramus" when attempting to define his talent. The truth is that one cannot help condescending to the Ettrick Shepherd because with his genius went three faults: 1). wishful thinking and sloppy accounting and bad judgment in financial matters; 2). conscious or unconscious self-complacency; and 3) a gritty streak of obtuseness or insensibility combined with his otherwise lovable, generous, and sunny character. The first point may be illustrated by William Blackwood's tart retort to Hogg quoted in Mrs. Oliphant's *Annals of a Publishing House,* I, 345: "It is the first time I have been under the necessity of bringing forward a printer's account to substantiate any of my statements, either with authors or with any of my correspondents." The second point may be illustrated by Hogg's naive remark in the last of his four Autobiographies ("I like to write about myself," he admits) that the *Justified Sinner* did not sell because it came out anonymously. The third point may be illustrated by his broad intimation in his *Domestic Manners . . . of Scott* that Lady Scott was illegitimate. Professor Simpson on p. 47 seems to me quite unfair to Lockhart, who, stung by Hogg's indiscretion, yet treats him sympathetically in his own great biography.

Professor Simpson is mistaken about the "Chaldee Manuscript": "there is no doubt that he wrote most of the articles" [sic], p. 33. In "James Hogg's 'Chaldee Manuscript'," *PMLA,* September, 1950, I compute that Hogg wrote 46 of the 180 printed verses. (Whether Hogg's later satire on Constable, *John Paterson's Mare,* discussed by me in *PMLA* of June, 1937, is worth mention or not is a matter of opinion.) On p. 33 also Professor Simpson writes, "Constable set up a magazine of his own, which soon collapsed." Does he refer to *The Scots Magazine,* which was going strong before Constable was born? Such quibbles in no way detract from Professor Simpson's sound scholarship. For a time I feared that he would prove himself to belong to what may be called the Procrustean School of Critics, but on page 107 he catches himself in time: "But this is to want Hogg to have been someone else." I like Professor Simpson's warm enthusiasm for *The Witch of Fife* and I dislike his quoting the first six lines of *The Skylark* as an illustration that Hogg's "lyrical flights are aimless." Just where a skylark should aim I don't know, but in this lovely poem a Scotsman writes on a subject that he knows. Professor Simpson's thesis on his last page that Hogg, "uncertain of his beliefs ... retires into a public role, playing the buffoon to civilized man," strikes me as a very imperfect summary: I wish he had gone whole Hogg. But his stimulating—or, to give him full credit, his provocative—book offers new slants on a man who shares with Scott the distinction of being, next to Burns, Scotland's best lyric poet though so far behind Burns as to make any comparison ridiculous. Some years ago I called Miss Edith Batho's *The Ettrick Shepherd* of 1927 "the only good critical biography of James Hogg." Thirty-five years later it is pleasant to welcome Professor Simpson's "Critical Study" as the second best book on James Hogg.

A. L. STROUT
TEXAS TECHNOLOGICAL COLLEGE

STUDIES IN SCOTTISH LITERATURE

VOLUME I   NUMBER 3   JANUARY 1964

CONTENTS

STUDIES IN SCOTTISH LITERATURE

EDITED BY G. ROSS ROY
TEXAS TECHNOLOGICAL COLLEGE

STUDIES IN SCOTTISH LITERATURE is an
independent quarterly devoted to all aspects of
Scottish literature. Articles and notes are welcome.
Subscriptions are available at $5.00 U.S. per annum in the
United States and Canada, elsewhere 30 shillings.
All communications should be addressed to the
Editor, Department of English, Texas Technological College,
Lubbock, Texas, U.S.A.

PUBLISHED BY TEXAS TECHNOLOGICAL COLLEGE
AND PRINTED BY THE TEXAS TECH PRESS
LUBBOCK, TEXAS, U.S.A.

EDITORIAL

As anyone who has worked in the field of Scottish literature is aware, there is a pressing need for bibliographies. Without these essential tools for research scholars have no way of knowing what has already been written, and this in turn leads to much wasteful duplication of effort. We need bibliographies of writers' works, as well as of critical estimates of their works.

Several fine bibliographies exist already; the *Edinburgh Bibliographical Society Transactions* and the *Records of the Glasgow Bibliographical Society* are most useful and it is much to be regretted that the latter has ceased publication. William Geddie's *Bibliography of Middle Scots Poetry* (S.T.S.) is of prime importance, as is J. C. Corson's *Bibliography of Sir Walter Scott: A Classified and Annotated List of Books and Articles relating to his Life and Works, 1797-1940*. There are, however, all too few works of this sort; the student of Scottish literature discovers that checklists for minor writers are generally non-existant, and that those for the more important authors are frequently incomplete and inaccurate. The last bibliography of Robert Burns, for instance, is James Gibson's volume of 1881 — a most useful work, but sorely outdated. For information on Burnsiana subsequent to 1880 scholars have had to go to the half-dozen catalogues of Burns collections issued by libraries. Even the best of these, the Mitchell Library *Catalogue of Robert Burns Collection* (1959), is incomplete as must be any work of reference which is confined to the holdings of a single library. We are soon to have a bibliography of Burns compiled by Professor J. W. Egerer, but this will solve the problem for only one author.

Fortunately an enterprising and energetic start has been made under the direction of Dr. W. R. Aitken, as chairman and editor of a committee of the Scottish Central Library in Edinburgh, to gather bibliographic information on recent Scottish authors, the project to be called *A Bibliography of Scottish Literature, 1900-1950*. This will list the the works of about one hundred writers of the first half of the twentieth century, in a style reminiscent of H. P. Thieme's *Bibliographie de la littérature française de 1800-1930*. A full list of the authors to be included in this bibliography is to be found in the Scottish Central Library's *Annual Report* for 1960-1961. Although there have been a few additions to and deletions from this list since it was published, it still provides a general indication of intention and coverage.

The Bibliotheck, which is published by the Scottish Group of The University and Research Section of The Library Association, has to date published four extremely useful checklists (on Lewis Grassic Gibbon,

Neil Gunn, Hugh MacDiarmid and William Soutar) and it is understood that there may be more.

A forthcoming study by Duncan Glen, *Hugh MacDiarmid and the Scottish Renaissance*, is to contain a lengthy bibliography in three sections: the first dealing with MacDiarmid himself; the second with other poets, novelists, and dramatists; and the third with critical studies of the Scottish Renaissance. Another work of major importance, now in progress, is Duncan Gollan's comprehensive guide to the Scottish novel, which will contain a bibliography on the lines of Lucien Leclaire's *A General Analytical Bibliography of the Regional Novelists of the British Isles, 1800-1950*.

Finally, the editor of this journal has commenced work on a bibliography of Scottish poetry, 1700-1900. There are at present approximately 10,000 entries taken principally from the Mitchell Library "Catalogue of Scottish Poetry" (unpublished); when this work is completed titles will have been added from all significant collections of Scottish poetry.

The above-mentioned publications and projects are just a start, admittedly a good start, if we are to prepare for the systematic study of Scottish literature.

CONTRIBUTORS
TO THIS ISSUE

David CRAIG: Born in Aberdeen, 1932. Educated Aberdeen University, Ph.D. from Downing College, Cambridge. Lecturer in English, University of Ceylon, 1959-1961. Organizing Tutor, Workers' Educational Association, North Yorks, 1961-1964. Will become Lecturer in English, University of Lancaster, in September, 1964. Author of *Scottish Literature and the Scottish People, 1680-1830* (London, 1961). Has contributed essays and reviews to *New Left Review, Essays in Criticism, New Statesman,* and poetry to *New Saltire* and *Lines* (Edinburgh). Presently working on a historical analysis of British literature, 1600-1914.

John LINDBERG: B.A. from State University College at Albany, N.Y.; M. A. and Ph.D. from University of Wisconsin with a dissertation entitled "Symbolic Presentation of Ideas in Carlyle." Has published articles on Browning, Carlyle, Rossetti and Dickens in *The Victorian Newsletter* and *College English.* His main interests are rhetoric and the history of intellectual opinion. He has taught at Carthage College, Illinois, and at the University of Maine, and is at present on the faculty of the State College of Iowa.

J. B. PICK: Born in Leicester, 1921, of a Scottish mother and an English father. Educated at Emmanuel College, Cambridge. Towards the end of the War worked as a coal miner, and his first published book was an account of this life. Lived for ten years in the North-West Highlands writing. Published three books on sports and games, and four novels, one of which, *The Last Valley,* has been published in America by Little, Brown & Co. Became interested in David Lindsay in 1946 when *A Voyage to Arcturus* was republished.

DAVID CRAIG

A National Literature?

Recent Scottish Writing

Until very recently, Scottish writers went on clinging with a mad Japanese courage to the idea of their cultural separateness. A generation ago, Scottish literature *was* the poetry of Hugh MacDiarmid and the fiction of Lewis Grassic Gibbon, and these two were nationalists almost more than they were socialists. That may be why they have contributed far, far less than they should to the common idea of what *British* literature has been in recent times. This invisible barrier between Scottish and English literature is a modern development, due perhaps to that London dominance of culture that has threatened to drown the north of England as well as Scotland. Burns, for example, was fully current in England. By 1815 there were at least eight editions of his works published in the north of England (e.g. in Newcastle), and pubs were being named after him. Matthew Arnold's pages on him in *The Study of Poetry* are more perceptive, serious, and complete than anything by the Scottish critics of that time. Arnold did not fuss about the "language problems," the need for glossaries, and the like. He felt Burns as immediately as he did Chaucer, Gray, or Shelley, and he could absorb him into his critical standard, as when he says:

> For the votary misled by a personal estimate of Shelley... of that beautiful spirit building his many coloured haze of words and images "Pinnacled dim in the intense inane—" no contact can be wholesomer than the contact with Burns at his archest and soundest.

These are qualities which Scottish literature can still contribute to the British tradition. MacDiarmid especially could well stand for the "sound" as a corrective for votaries of the clever-clever Auden. Yet for British readers in general MacDiarmid has never got much beyond his extraordinary minority-esteem as a Great Poet whose great poems somehow aren't common property. Many a snatch from his lyrics should surely have joined Auden's "We must love one another or die" among the slogans of the intelligentsia, for example this from "Second Hymn to Lenin"—

> Oh, it's nonsense, nonsense, nonsense,
> Nonsense at this time o' day

[151]

> That breid-and-butter problems
> S'ud be in ony man's way.

Yet MacDiarmid is totally ignored in Kenneth Allot's Penguin *Contemporary Verse* (1950), as in the Faber anthology compiled by Michael Roberts just after MacDiarmid's heyday in the early Thirties; and English intellectuals ask one for opinions on MacDiarmid as though they were seeking otherwise unobtainable news from the North Pole.

Again, Grassic Gibbon has, like Robert Tressell, extremely high standing among working-class readers; but outside what may be called the labour-movement public—silence. In the Pelican *Modern Age* he isn't even given a mention (though Noel Coward, C. P. Snow, and Hugh Walpole get detailed entries). When I was hitch-hiking from Edinburgh to Aberdeen in the spring of 1958, I said to the lorry-driver as we came onto the red soil of Angus, "Here's the Mearns," and he replied, "Aye—Grassic Gibbon's country." He had heard the first part of Gibbon's trilogy *A Scots Quair*—surely the finest British fiction of the Slump age—more than once during its many broadcasts on the Scottish radio. No other Scottish literature of recent times has become proverbial in this way, and here is another likeness to Tressell: Brendan Behan says in *Borstal Boy* that Dublin house-painters who had never read *The Ragged Trousered Philanthropists* ("nor any other book, either") would call the foreman Nimrod.

It is a quarter of a century since Gibbon's trilogy and since the last work of MacDiarmid's that I would call creative—the *Hymn to Lenin* volumes of 1931 and 1935. There are salient aspects of their work that mark them as not of the age in which we now live. This older note can be heard, for example, at the close of Gibbon's first volume, *Sunset Song* (1932), where a country minister's sermon for the Great War dead turns into a lament for the peasantry:

And then, with the night waiting out by on Blawearie brae, and the sun just verging on the coarse hills, the minister began to speak again, his short hair blowing in the wind that had come, his voice not decent and a kirk-like bumble, but ringing out over the loch:

" FOR I WILL GIVE YOU THE MORNING STAR

In the sunset of an age and an epoch we may write that for epitaph of the men who were of it . . . It was the old Scotland that perished then, and we may believe that never again will the old speech and the old songs, the old curses and the old benedictions, rise but with alien effort to our lips.

"The last of the peasants, those four that you knew, took that with them to the darkness and the quietness of the places where they sleep. And the land changes, their parks and their steadings are a desolation where the sheep are pastured, we are told that great machines come soon to till the land, and the great herds come to feed on it, the crofter has gone, the

man with the house and the steading of his own and the land closer to his
heart than the flesh of his body . . .

"... But need we doubt which side the battle they would range themselves did they live today, need we doubt the answer they cry, to us even now,
the four of them, from the places of the sunset?"

And then, as folk stood dumbfounded this was just sheer politics,
plain what he meant, the Highland man McIvor tuned up his pipes and began
to step slow round the stone circle by Blawearie Loch . . .[1]

National feelings breathe and surge in such a passage, and the vocabulary
that comes naturally to express them is the old Romantic language—
sunsets and stars, "nothing abides," the darkness. The associations the
Romantic poets had played on to express their melancholy at what seems
now to have been their fundamental underlying subject—the spoliation
of the old craftsmen's and yeomen's England—are equally apt for Gibbon. He invokes them shamelessly, with no inhibition, so overweening
are his national fellow-feeling, grief, and nostalgia.

There is no nostalgia in MacDiarmid—his intellect is too ruthless.
But in his poetry, too, one feels the swell of nationalist ardour, as in
this lyric from a long sequence, "Ode to all Rebels," which was kept out
of *Scots Unbound* when the godly Victor Gollancz published the book in
1934:

> Scotland, when it is given to me
> As it will be
> To sing the immortal song
> The crown of all my long
> Travail with thee
> I know in that high hour
> I'll have, and use, the power
> Sublime contempt to blend
> With its ecstatic end,
> As who, in love's embrace,
> Forgetfully may frame
> Above the poor slut's face
> Another woman's name.   [2]

The remarkable unbeautiful metaphor at the close, the power of the
one intellectual conviction to sustain a single tense sentence from the
first line of the poem to the last—these qualities mark the poem as belonging to MacDiarmid's strongest vein; and the subject is *Scotland*.

Scotland—this was the richest single idea in our best writers of
that inter-war period. What caused this? The Scottish National Party
was being founded. But that is itself another symptom, rather than a deep
social cause. For MacDiarmid's generation, the Great War had shattered

---

[1] *A Scots Quair* (London, 1950), 192–3.
[2] *Stony Limits and Scots Unbound* (Edinburgh, 1956), 93.

irretrievably the old Whig and imperialist idealogy which *England* (rather than Britain) had embodied for so many. As the Twenties wore into the Thirties and the Slump deepened, many forces gathered strength on the Left: two Labour governments, organisation of the unemployed, the anti-Facist front. But in an autonomous culture like Scotland's there was also a precipitation of nationalism—the wounded morale of a Distressed Area that happened to have a national past. (Compare the Agrarian movement that the Slump produced in the American South.) Scotland was exceptionally hard hit. The industrial lop-sidedness and obsolescence that are still so crippling made Clydeside and the central Scottish coalfields one of Britain's black spots in the Thirties. Our unemployment rate averaged twice England's (as it has done ever since the Second War too), and an average of 25,000 people emigrated every year—this has recently gone up sharply.[3] So a heightened, and painful, sense of separate entity was reborn. In literature, the effects of the nationalist Thirties lasted after the economic basis had changed again. During the War and after, a second generation of poets were writing in a special literary Scots, and they constantly canvassed the idea of cultural nationhood. But cultural values cannot exist for long in mid-air, without roots in practical social life. Now that nationalism is spent, what is there to feed sap to the literature?

It might be argued that nationalism is not spent. MacDiarmid often prides himself that Scotland has its own literature once again. His poems are on school syllabuses; there is a School of Scottish Studies at Edinburgh and a Lectureship in Scottish Literature at Glasgow; one of the Edinburgh little magazines, *Lines Review*, has even published criticism written in Scots. In politics, waves of national feeling continue to rise from time to time. The Covenant in favour of Home Rule was signed by a majority of our adults; a Nationalist candidate did well in the 1962 West Lothian by-election; and now this latest and deepest of the postwar slumps has added fuel to the movement for a plebicite on self-government. Yet no mass party backs Home Rule (a majority of Labour M. P.'s did in the Twenties); and in literature the 'national' features are mostly secondary or institutional—lectureships and research projects are set up, but the literature itself is hard to find. There are good talents at work in Scotland but, unlike Gibbon and MacDiarmid, what they write isn't overtly national, and has therefore less to offer the

---

[3] As always, Scotland becomes "interesting" when things are worst for her—this latest crisis has produced a host of searching commentaries, e.g. Andrew Hargrave, "Scotland and the Common Market," *New Saltire*, No. 6 (December 1962); Lawrence Daly, "Scotland on the Dole," *New Left Review*, No. 17 (Winter 1962); James Milne, "Shall Scotland be murdered?" *Labour Monthly*, (November 1962); Gordon McLennan, *Demand a Future for Scotland* (C.P.G.B., 1962).

journals, dictionaries, and study-projects that are set up on the assumption that there is in the north a distinct, separate culture. Of course these things should all be done. But often the mill seems pretty short of grist.

If one thinks of who is writing poetry in Scotland today, there is Norman MacCaig, whom I consider largely fake, a blatantly synthetic 'Metaphysical'—yet as Scotland's most talked-about versifier he cannot be ignored, and his work is wholly in English, as is the published work of the most consistent younger poet, Iain Crichton Smith. Among the novelists, Robin Jenkins is outstanding, David Lambert should also be read, and these men go no further in the national direction than to use some Scottish settings and some Scots speech. It is rather that they happen to be Scottish citizens than that they write to any received idea of our history or separate nationhood—as had been the approach of all our significant novelists from Scott and Galt through Stevenson to George Douglas Brown and Gibbon.

This strikes me as a liberation. For generations (as I tried to show in my *Scottish Literature and the Scottish People*) our culture was neurosed with *over*-consciousness of nationality. Our writers dithered among stereotypes, theories, poses; and the faculty of perceiving life for itself was all but lost. Today, with the fading of the nationalist mirage, we can see ahead more clearly and in particular can appreciate better how our literature plays its part in struggles and developments much broader and more real than the private nationalist obsession.

Two anthologies of poetry bring out the change between pre- and post-war generations. The first, Maurice Lindsay's *Modern Scottish Poetry: An Anthology of the Scots Renaissance, 1920-1945* (1946), is a book I have been through many times, and lately I have been finding which poems stay with me on their merits, according to the sharpness of the line they leave in the imagination. Of the poems written since Mac-Diarmid, or since the Spanish War, the outstanding piece is certainly the Gaelic poet George Campbell Hay's "Grunnd na mara" ("There they lie") translated into Scots by Douglas Young. It is imagined as the reverie of an old island woman, stunned and half-disbelieving at the loss of her son at sea during the War:

> 'Thonder they ligg on the grund o the sea,   *lie*
> nae the hyne whaur they wald be.'   *haven*
> Siccan a thing has happenit me
> sin my son's been gane. When he was wee
> I dannlit the bairn like a whelpikie
> and he leuch in ma airms richt cantilie.   *cheerily*
> It's the auld weird nou I maun dree.

After a section presenting her village with its daily round carrying on, the poem reaches the kind of starkness that Scots (like all vernaculars) is so suited to evoking:

> I see your jacket on the heuk,
> but the hous is lown in ilka neuk,   *silent*
> never a sound or a word i the room,
> nae sclaffan o buits on the threshart-stane,   *scraping*
> the bed cauld and the chalmer toom.   *room empty*

Expression is stripped down to the plainest facts—yet even these can imply acute experience; and the language then intensifies to a rare pitch of unadorned tragic utterance, expressing grief that has passed through the immediate pang of loss to face death as part of normality:

> Gin it's the sych that traivels far   *sigh*
> ye'll hear my sychan whaur ye are,
> sleepan i the wrack, jundied aye,   *rocked*
> wi ugsome ferlies sooman by . . .   *terrible*
>   *monsters swimming*

The young man's reply expresses a very Scottish theme—the son struggling to shake off the clingings of mother-love:

> Wheesht, woman, wheesht, and deavena me.   *don't wear me out*
> My wae's the mair to see ye greet.   *weep*
> The ship brak doun under our feet,
> life gaed aff, and memorie wi 't.
> London slew me, weary faa 't,   *to hell with it*
> connacht the een that never saw it.   *ruined*
> Aiblins I was acquent wi you,   *maybe*
> the saut has reingit my memorie nou.   *scoured*

Finally Hay puts in a simple moral in the way of Henryson, Langland, or Shakespeare:

> Sair the price maun be dounpitten
> by the island-fowk for the greatness o Britain.

This attitude to the metropolitan country is in touch with the nationalist Thirties, yet it fits naturally into the almost timeless mode of the whole poem. It is one of those pieces whose style is untouched by recent literary developments. Subject-matter and presentment recall the ballad, yet there is not a trace of the fake antique. The fact is that the island community behind such a poem has changed so little in essentials from the pre-capitalist epoch that in this case the old songs do rise without effort to the lips. The individual death is given with poignant immediacy; yet every touch—the collective "they" of the first line, the acceptance of "the auld weird," the oddly distanced communication between mother and son—evokes general death in the individual one. This seems to me the most successful poem by any Scotsman since MacDiarmid; and I can think of few writers anywhere in the British Isles who could give so rich a value, through so unerringly simple a presentment, to one of the fundamental life-experiences.

Other of Young's versions from the Gaelic share these qualities, especially some short pieces by Sorley Maclean. He no longer publishes; he is supposed to be writing a Gaelic "epic"; and a friend reports him "disgusted" by his work of the late Thirties and the War. Yet at the time socialism led him to bitterly concentrated images of poverty that recall Brecht, e.g. these lines from "Hielant Woman":

This spring o the year is by and gane
and twenty springs afore it spent,
sin she's hikeit creels o cauld wrack
for her bairn's meat and the laird's rent.

Twenty hairsts hae dwineit awa,   harvests, dwindled
she's tint her simmer's gowden grace,   lost
while the sair trauchle o the black wark   struggle
pleud its rigg on her clear face.   ploughed, furrow

. . . Her time gaed by like black sleek   smoke
through an auld thaikit hous-rig seepan;   thatched
she bruikit aye sair black wark,   enjoyed
and gray the nicht is her lang sleepan.

The abrupt, unfluent movement, that never relaxes throughout the poem, conveys as palpably as the imagery the kind of desperately hard life that Robert Flaherty filmed in *Man of Aran*.

Nearly on a level with these for the distinctness of the mark it leaves in the imagination there is Adam Drinan's satire on an *émigré* come back rich from America—"Successful Scot":

By adding figure to figure
    you have developed never,
you have just grown bigger and bigger
    like this wee wort from the heather;
        and size is all you have got.

Your mind set towards London,
    your belly pushing to success,
from the very day that you won
    the bursary of the West,
        have flagged and faltered not.

Not much has your face altered!
    The man has the mouth of the child.
The Position you planted and watered
    expands from the lad's desires
        as if bound in a pot. . .

Here spite against success finds a complete style. We are reminded of many a Burns satire on paunchy businessmen—"Behind a kist to lie an'

sklent,/ Or purse-proud, big wi' cent. per cent.,/ An' muckle wame..."
But Drinan is typically modern, in the disenchanted dryness with which
one damaging detail after another is' put in, and in the hard punch of
the final rhymes. Such spite (as Burns, too, showed) is apt to be a shaky
basis for an integrated poetry, and Drinan does crumble at the end:
Scotland is too easily and sentimentally merged with the man's disowned
youth—"you would trample your youth in this flower/ that you have
forgotten." So many of the Scottish themes lead off into a position that
the writer cannot face without accepting those very defects in his own
country that he would like to wish away. For the fact is that most
Scots who have left their country behind them have emigrated, not out
of pushfulness or common greed, but for sheer survival.

Those, then, are the poems that stay with me from this representative book (the MacDiarmid poems in the anthology have not been considered, for the reasons given above), that continue to release into the
imagination. Each of them makes its own perfectly distinct impression,
they are not echoes or echoes of echoes. They stand out from among
poems like this:

> I go north to cold, to home, to Kinnaird,
> Fit monument for our time.
>
> This is the outermost edge of Buchan.
> Inland the sea birds range,
> The tree's leaf has salt upon it,
> The tree turns to the low stone wall...
> The water plugs in the cliff sides,
> The gull cries from the clouds
> This is the consummation of the plain.
>
> O impregnable and very ancient rock,
> Rejecting the violence of water,
> Ignoring its accumulations and strategy,
> You yield to history nothing.

This is laughably solemn. Each word, whenever the poem goes beyond
the simplest Imagist image, has such an air of saying so much, like an
old owl that fancies itself wise. But the abstractions—"consumation,"
"rejecting," "strategy"—are there only because T. S. Eliot had meditated
on history in "Gerontion." This way with the stark and simple—contrasted
with Hay's or Maclean's—seems to me "traditional" in a wholly weak
sense. "Home" is supposed to stand for a timeless, basic *pietas;* but it remains just a word.

That poem, however, (George Bruce's "Kinnaird Head") is one of
the accepted gems of the Scottish Renaissance. This lack of discrimination
between the genuine and the paste has been confusing enough in England

but still more baneful in Scotland, anxious as we are to make the most
of our scanty personnel. If we do wish to discriminate honestly between
the genuine and the paste—and thus save our little magazines from turning into mere showcases for gewgaws, unable to interest a broad-based
public—we must, I think, put in the former class Sorley Maclean, Douglas
Young in his translations, some of Adam Drinan, and in the latter class
Norman MacCaig, George Bruce, Tom Scott, Maurice Lindsay, and most
of Sydney Smith. This is very summary. But it is based on more than
ten years' constant reading in the Scottish literary media, past and contemporary and it is borne out by the post-War generation's anthology,
Honour'd Shade.[4] Before discussing that book we should note the
facts that the cream of the minor poets I have mentioned were all progressive. In their poems they spoke out against exploitation and poverty,
the neglect of the Distressed Areas, imperialism and war. Sorley Maclean
was far on the Left at that time, Douglas Young a staltwart of the
Labour Party (and a Nationalist too), and Adam Drinan (Joseph Macleod) one of the most open-minded champions of Soviet art during the
War.

Honour'd Shade contains almost nothing in the old high nationalist style and little overtly progressive work—indeed little considerable
poetry of any kind. What I called the nationalist obsession is gone and
with it, evidently, any powerful incentive to imagine and express. National
over-consciousness is still there in the form of synthetic Scots—the diction
MacDiarmid pioneered in the Twenties and hardly anyone but Young
in his translations has used to fresh effect since. Is this, for example,
creative Scots?

> My world in nether winter is the sun
> Barred in a cell, and dernit dull in yerth   *hidden*
> The cache is tint, the road unmapt
> And dumb wi babban-quaas its dule and rime—   *quaking bogs*
> Sol is dowsit dim, deid not but hapt   *wrapped*
> And hainit, close, or Cocorico bells rebirth   *kept*
> In the clean white clout o' the Lamb.

Each phrase, each noun with its adjective or participle, seems to have
to heave itself laboriously into place. This might be to evoke the numb
low-ebb of the year. But the movement is too wooden for such effects:
compare the truly nerveless lapsings and slowings of the words in Eliot's
"A Song for Simeon":

> Lord, the Roman hyacinths are blooming in bowls and
> The winter sun creeps by the snow hills;

[4] Chosen by Norman MacCaig to mark the bicentenary of Burns's birth (Edinburgh, 1959).

The stubborn season has made stand.
My life is light, waiting for the death wind,
Like a feather on the back of my hand.
Dust in sunlight and memory in corners
Wait for the wind that chills towards the dead land.

Beside this the Scots reads like a stilted translation from another language. Maybe the poet (Sydney Goodsir Smith) *was* thinking in English yet forcing himself—for the very best cultural reasons of course—to write in Scots.

Evidently the genuine rhythms and idioms are unlikely to crop up in that vein. Long ago MacDiarmid gave the slogan "Back to Dunbar". But the "aureate" or ornamental Scots that this implied is the least successful of the Scottish veins today. Again and again we seem to find our true voice in a style of extreme plainness, e.g. Young's translation in *Honour'd Shade* from a 19th-century German poet, Paul Heyse, "Eftir the Daith o a Bairn":

> I thocht I heard ye chap upo the door,
>   and rase til apen, as gin yince again
> ye stuid their speiran, like ye uisd afore,   *asking*
>   sae couthilie, "Daddie, can I come ben?"   *prettily*
>
> Ay, and yestreen stravaigan on the sand   *wandering*
> I felt your wee bit hand het i my hand,
> and whar the chad was rowan i the swaw   *shingle, rolling, wave*
> I spak out loud, "Tak tent an dinna faa."

This is so economical and so right that we want not a word more or less. Extraordinarily keen feeling arises from language that never (except perhaps in "sae couthilie") asks for our tears. The same "unanswerable" plainness shows through in English also, as in Iain Crichton Smith's fine "Old Woman":

> And she, being old, fed from a mashed plate
> as an old mare might droop across a fence
> to the dull pastures of its ignorance.
> Her husband held her upright while he prayed. . .
>
> Outside, the grass was raging. There I sat
> imprisoned in my pity and my shame
> that men and women having suffered time
> should sit in such a place in such a state . . .

Elsewhere (and especially in a sequence which has had a *succès d'estime*, "Deer on the High Hills,")[5] Smith is prone to a Yeatsian swell and flow of poetic diction along with a "Metaphysical" jargon and disruption of conventional syntax that recall the tiresome tricks of MacCaig and W. S.

[5] *New Saltire*, No. 2 (Nov. 1961) or separate ed. (Edinburgh, 1962).

Graham. Yet he never quite loses touch with that salutary starkness or trenchancy which is so strong in the Scottish tradition—in the ballads and folksongs, in Burns, in MacDiarmid.

Such a style probably has its basis in the culture of a small semination whose Establishment and genteel tradition are not so all-embracing, not so formidably sleek, armour-plated, and sure of themselves, that other sections of the culture have difficulty in making headway. In the small country no one is far from the people or from oral language not much filtered through print and therefore unlikely to be elaborate or indirect. Consider, for example, a bilingual sequence, "Poems of an Undefined Love," by a poet from Caithness, in the extreme north, where the language (as in Orkney and Shetland) is a dialect of Scots. The sequence is about an affair in which the poet hasn't seen his girl for months— their relationship has become abstract, void of real emotions. For seven stanzas this is analysed, in precise intellectual English:

> When we are apart
> We are other persons.
> We always see them
> In perspective, defined.
> But we cannot act on that.
> We obliterate the lines again
> In the cross-section
> And make grounds
> To forget the warning.

In the eighth stanza analysis stops, direct address occurs for the first time, and for this the poet needs Scots. It is as though pent-up bitterness absolutely demands release into real speech in which evasion will be impossible:

> I'm no playan the game o love.
> Ye may say
> We were no engaged
> And only going out
> Afore the public
> But in the hert
> Neither were we disengaged
> And ye lit him pit his mooth there.[6]

Every accent, stop, and switch feels perfectly timed, moving unswervingly to the implacable pinning-down effect of the close; and again the medium is almost unadorned speech.

In the last few years we have seen this strength of popular speech coming into its own as a medium in which Scottish writers can join in that triumphant renewal of the folk and vernacular forms that has dis-

---

[6] John Manson, *We Must Alter the Words* (Aberdeen, 1954), 10-11.

tinguished the present period in British cultural life—the mushrooming of the folksong clubs, the superb, pioneering creative work of Ewan MacColl and Peggy Seeger (their individual songs and, above all, their radio-ballads), and the rebirth of a drama close to folksong in the hands of John Osborne, Brendan Behan, Arnold Wesker, John Arden, Shelagh Delaney. In November 1959, Hamish Henderson (an outstanding folksong collector for the School of Scottish Studies and known already for his Poundian English *Elegies for the Dead in Cyrenaica*, 1948) wrote to the *Scotsman* to disclaim any resentment at having been left out of *Honour'd Shade*:

> ...I have come to set greater store by my songs 'in the idiom of the people' than by other kinds of poetry that I have tried to write. By working in the folksong revival, therefore, I am paying what is probably congenial tribute to the "honour'd shade" of the most famous Crochallan Fencible [i. e. Burns].

Here the difficulty arises, as with all discussion of the New Wave, that one cannot really do without live oral illustration. One of Henderson's best songs "Farewell to Sicily," can be heard on the MacColl record, *Barrack Room Ballads* (Topic 10T26), but most of them would have to be searched out from the memories of the men who sang them in Italy in 1944 or from old issues of the Workers' Music Association paper, *Sing*. As a song-writer he works close to the people's own movements, and one song that is easily available was published as a leaflet (with music) by the Associated Blacksmiths' Forge and Smithy Workers' Society, to commemorate an exchange of good wishes between workers from Leith and Kiev during a Scottish-Soviet Friendship Week. Here Henderson captures the very pulse of muscular exertion in a way that was second nature to the Scottish people's poets of the 18th century— Ramsay, Fergusson, Burns:

> Ó horo the Gillie More
> Noo's the time, the haimmer's ready,
> Haud the tangs—ay, haud them steady
> O horo the Gillie More
> Gar the iron ring, avallich!
> Gar it ring frae shore tae shore.
> Leith tae Kiev—Don tae Gairloch
> O horo the Gillie More.
>
> O horo the Gillie More
> Here's a weld'll wear for ever.
> Oor grup they canna sever
> O horo the Gillie More. . .

That is pure milk of industrial folksong, expressing downright straightforward emotions. A more complex style, still drawing on the

folk source, appears in the anti-Polaris song, "The Freedom Come-all-ye"
—printed in *Ding Dong Dollar* (Glasgow, 1961) as anonymous but in
fact by Henderson. This is struggle literature, literature of the march,
platform, and loudspeaker, and this does not preclude poetic virtues.
I admire particularly the imagery that is scaled large enough to make
us think of the whole world yet never dissolves into Shelleyan fantasy.
The superabundant freshness of the opening colours all that follows:

Roch the wind in the clear day's dawin	*rough*
Blaws the cloods heelster-gowdie ow'r the bay,	*head-over-heels*
But there's mair nor a roch wind blawin	
Through the great glen o the world the day...	
Nae mair will the bonnie callants	*lads*
March tae war, when oor braggarts crousely craw,	*cockily*
Nor wee weans frae pit-heid an clachan	*kids, village*
Mourn the ships sailin doon the Broomielaw;	
Broken faimilies in the land we herriet	*ravaged*
Will curse Scotland the Brave nae mair, nae mair;	
Black an white, ane til ither mairriet,	
Mak the vile barracks o their maisters bare.	

Henderson is "old fashioned," both in the thickness of his Scots and
in the whole-hearted drive and swing of his militancy. But a recent
poetry booklet called *Underwater Wedding*, by Alan Jackson (a member
of the Scottish Committee of 100), shows how folk styles can fertilise
verse distinctly of the younger generation in its clipped, off-hand deflation of the old hallowed symbols and values:

> I hate circles,
> Haloes, hats, the lot.
> I'm going to smash 'em
> With all I've got.
>
> I'm coming out.
> I've got a right to birth;
> To air and sun
> As well as earth.
>
> I'm gorged with the ancient
> Goody foods.
> Time now for fighting
> And the seven-league boots.
>
> Time for the Mother
> To get a big kick;
> To scatter the dark
> With a swipe of my stick.

This is the very voice of the browned-off intellectual, both the background of Freud and Jung and the hard-bitten Sixties slang—"the lot."

STUDIES IN SCOTTISH LITERATURE

It is the voice of Jimmy Porter (or Osborne himself) and of Jo in *A Taste of Honey*. What is unusual is Jackson's trick of grafting a Beat manner onto the fairy-tale, nursery jingle, and nonsense rhyme:

> Goodly godly kindly men,
> If you pour I won't say when.
>
> Wash me in the holy lather,
> Ancient as my ancient father.
>
> Scrub my toes eight nine ten,
> Goodly godly kindly men.

When Jackson tries to suggest positively the kind of freed, impulsive experience he is pitting against the prohibitions of the old Presbyterian code, he falls back on the sheerest poet diction, lush and hackneyed. But the adolescent revolt—I say that quite straight with no intention to patronise—that mainly motivates his poems is expressed with astonishing bite by that quirky, jingling style.

English or American literature could not have been discussed adequately at such length without a mention of fiction. In Scotland very few pieces of lasting value in the prose forms have appeared, perhaps (as I have suggested elsewhere[7]) because the modern novel is a town form and by the time the industrial town was being absorbed into the British imagination, Scotland had lost by emigration the bulk of her literary talent—hence our long fixation on the past, the village and the countryside. What can hardly be doubted is that the characteristic life of the millions who have spent their days in the densely built-over industrial Lowlands that stretch from Glasgow to Dundee has scarcely figured in a single piece of writing that would bear pondering and re-reading. In the Thirties there was Grassic Gibbon's *Grey Granite*. Since then we have had to content ourselves with the counterfeit coinage of a George Blake. By reputation he is a sort of Glasgow Zola; yet in his famous (and reprinted) *The Shipbuilders* (1944; 1954) he can lapse into presenting for our serious attention a vision of the lure England has for Scots folk that has no more actuality than a tweed Christmas card, no more relevance to the present than a print of pink-coated gentry riding after a fox. Scottish novelists have behind them too little tradition of writers tackling the town with full confidence that it is wholly available and wholly fitted for authentic re-creation. David Lambert's *He Must So Live* (1956) tries to render Red Clydeside—the Clydeside of Davie Kirkwood, Willie Gallacher, and the Battle of George Square. In dialogue at least he is adept—he can catch to perfection the hard-hitting back-

[7] See Craig, *Scottish Literature and the Scottish People* (London, 1961), 145-6, 222-4, 309; and letter to *Glasgow Herald*, 27.10.61.

chat of tenement dwellers. Yet in his presentment of violent experiences—battles between workers and police, physical collapse—he is, like Blake, too contaminated by the pulp novel, by sensationalistic over-writing, at once hectic and vague. As a result his own long trade-union experience (he is now General Secretary of the Foundry Workers) goes for nothing, and the natural drama of fluctuating labour struggles fails to be strongly established. It is not that the subject is intractable in itself, whatever the bourgeois-minded critics say: think of the searing vividness with which it was handled by Dos Passos, Farrell, Steinbeck, or Gibbon in the Thirties, or for that matter the more-than-documentary competence and interest with which Len Doherty and Margot Heinemann have handled it recently.

The esteemed Scottish novelists, the "quality" artists, are rooted in the countryside—Neil Gunn and Fionn MacColla. Yet there is little in Gunn beyond the simplest "nature notes" larded with the kind of laborious naïvetés and solemnities that are so often (as in the case of Edwin Muir) taken for real, even spiritually exalted creation. MacColla, a man who moved from Montrose, on the east coast, to the Outer Isles, also labours to express deep experiences, and he draws on the hallowed national subjects—the Clearances, the Troubles that harrowed Scotland from the Wars of Independence until the Reformation.[8] Yet the evident sincerity and nationalist credentials cannot conceal the truth that these works are, as fiction, stillborn—wordy, strained, gauchely melodramatic.

Gunn did write one novel that I recall reading with bated breath, it so promised to get a serious theme into an effective form of fiction. This was The Drinking Well (1946). It deals with the efforts of a lad from a Highland croft to find his feet in Edinburgh, as a lawyer's junior. Here, in the theme of a young man who has moved from manual work to a profession, we have a likeness to a whole cluster of recent books, notably Raymond Williams's Border Country, Margot Heinemann's The Adventurers, and (in an oblique way) Arnold Wesker's Roots. The peculiar interest of The Drinking Well is that Iain's new companions are restless metropolitan intellectuals, a set of drinkers, who are not flirting (as might be the case in London) with socialism, Zen Buddhism, or drug-taking but with Scottish nationalism. The atmosphere of this section is authentic (I remember it myself from student days in Aberdeen)—the "brilliant talk," fired with enthusiasm as long as the drink lasts, the plans for books that would plumb the deeps of Scottish

---

[8] See And the Cock Crew (Glasgow, 1945; 1962); Scottish Noël (Barra, 1958); Ane Tryall of Heretiks (Collieston, 1962).

experience. The theme, in fact, demands the steadiest treatment—treatment steadied by a perfectly clear realisation, on the author's part, of actual social possibilities. Gunn is too sentimental to manage this. He dissolves into evocations of the Scottish Past, the Highland Soul, etc., that are no better than the purple patches in a highclass tourist brochure. The appeal of the traditional fiddle music is described thus:

> But the slow notes—they were too profound, too terrible in their potency. There is a level at which the emotion of naked life can no more be borne, life lifting its face from the emotion of ten thousand years, its girl's singing face, pale with the generations of the dead, and the singing throat of an innocence that, at long last, is pure.[9]

Such flounderings, such weak generalizations *about* Scottish culture are no substitute for the embodiment of it in achieved drama of storytelling. Gunn's novel should be compared with a story in a recent *New Saltire* (No. 7, March 1963)—*Black and Red* by the poet Iain Smith —the best short work we have had for years. It tells in extraordinarily keen-edged impressionistic prose, supposedly in letters home, the story of a Highland lad coming to university; and the basic attitude (at the other pole to Gunn's) is one of urgent desire to grow beyond a dying civilisation with its ageing people and ingrown puritanism. One memorable passage describes his deep thrill at a music utterly new to him— a Negro jazz hymn which his friend, a medical student, puts on the gramophone.

That is a glimpse of how our writers are becoming alive to our own time. The man who has done far and away the most towards this is the novelist Robin Jenkins. He is a popular library-novelist, and he does tend to skate along the surface with a facility that sometimes disguises a failure to more than sketch the outlines of the very complex characters, especially women, that he sets out to present. Yet at his best, which means not infrequently since *The Changeling* (1958), his lightness can, as in the early E. M. Forster, serve as the attitude of an unpartisan intelligence, not too heavily invested in any one of the characters or milieux he creates and thus able to bring out the value of each. Like Forster, and like T. F. Powys, Jenkins is forever concerned with the need for tenderness and humility—that we should be ready for and open to one another, not so afraid of being thought fools by the worldly-wise that we harden ourselves off into some role of self-importance or self-righteousness that stultifies the living impulse. Jenkins is acutely aware of how people can be hurt—he evidently feels deeply the wound of the Second War and the sheer knowledge that the Glasgow slums are there. He is moved to atone by warm love, and the feelings involved

---

[9] *The Drinking Well* (London, 1946), 133.

are indeed hard to dramatise without sentimentality. In Jenkins this comes out sometimes as a quite swamping tendency to the arch and whimsical: the likeness to Forster and Powys is too often to their weakest work, the quasi-supernatural whimsies of Forster's short stories or Powys' poorest novel, *Kindness in a Corner*. In *The Missionaries* (1957), for example, about the eviction of a community of religious devotees from an old holy island in the west, there is little respite from the flow of heavily gnomic conversations, crankily oracular characters, and moments of "miracle" that are left much too nearly endorsed by the author himself.[10]

Nevertheless, the startling likeness of the style at many points to Forster and Powys is something Jenkins has a right to. Many a touch in his novels shows his Powys-like ability to note in a symbolic way the smallest symptoms of cruelty or malice, e.g. this image of a bland, treacherous shopkeeper looking at the corpse of a boy, from a novel about evacuees from Glasgow, *Guests of War*: "Michaelson dabbed now at one side of his moustache and now at the other, with his knuckle: he was imitating the swing of the gravedigger's spade."[11] The most obvious likeness to Forster is Jenkins's ability to generalise, often paradoxically, on the dramatic moments he has created, as in this passage from a novel about a Scottish girl in love with a high-born Indian—*The Tiger of Gold*:

> Remembering Chandra, with my eyes, my lips, my breasts even rather than with my intellectual memory, I was convinced he had been sincere in Isban; but even sincerity in love was not, I realised with a spontaneous gush of thankfulness, as unchangeable as those stars. If Chandra no longer wished to marry me, it did not mean he never had; and the change was insulting to neither of us.[12]

I think Jenkins's problem has been to find his way to subjects good not only for entertaining story-telling but also for the treatment of his deepest preoccupations at a level more deep-reaching than an easy opposition of the priggish and the warm-hearted, the self-righteous and the tolerant, and so forth. The *Changeling* shows him at his best—and strikes me as one of the finest things in British fiction since the War—because in it the meaning isn't issued to us in little wise mottoes and the drama stands up by itself. The theme is, characteristically, that of a man trying to do good and finding that good, as the world receives it, can turn painfully into its opposite. Forbes, a rather pompous good-

[10] For a quite different opinion of *The Missionaries*, see Alastair R. Thompson's essay on Jenkins—"Faith and Love," *New Saltire*, No. 3 (Spring 1962), 62-3.

[11] *Guests of War* (London, 1956), 260.

[12] *The Tiger of Gold* (London, 1962), 215.

hearted Glasgow schoolteacher, decides to take a slum lad on holiday with his own family, to "give the boy a chance." For though the lad is clever, well-behaved, and mature, he is reputed a rogue because no-one can believe anything else could come from so squalid a home and because authority is constantly being nettled by the impenetrable *suffisance* the lad has developed simply to survive. On the holiday everything goes wrong—Mrs. Forbes is on edge waiting for signs of criminal slumminess, the other children are jealous, Forbes can't help wanting *some* sign of warmth or oncomingness from the imperturbably civil lad. Jenkins's Forster-like ability to cut very fast, yet without any forcing or sensationalism, from the laughable to the painful—in a way that reflects the disruptive shifts of life itself—comes out in an excellent scene in which the souring and jarring of the whole group has reached a climax:

> Tom looked at Mrs. Forbes. He was astonished by the loathing in her eyes; but she nodded, and he immediately left the room.
>
> As he went through the hall to the front door he caught sight of Forbes's old raincoat hanging on a peg. It was soiled, with green paint on its seat. He had a longing to touch it, but that shy gesture could not satisfy the sudden surge of love in him, so that he crushed his face into the coat, smelling not only paint but the sea.
>
> ...Then Tom found himself not hurrying through the garden to the hut, but knocking at the dining-room door. He would confess not only to the thefts in Woolworth's but also to the others at school; and he would tell them he was going away that afternoon for good.
>
> Mr. Forbes opened the door, just enough to show his face; tear-stained, bewildered, and woebegone, it might have struck a stranger as comical. Inside the room was the sound of Mrs. Forbes weeping.
>
> "What is it?" muttered Mr. Forbes. "What d'you want?"
>
> What Tom had come to say, he found he could not; that weeping within the room demoralized him; or rather it drove him back to his old resources.
>
> "I was wondering, sir," he said politely, "if I could have a loan of the bike to go to Dunroth."
>
> "The bike?" repeated Forbes.
>
> "Yes, sir. It would save the bus fare."
>
> There was a rush inside the room. Forbes was pushed aside and his wife's face was seen, tearful, enraged, ugly.
>
> "No, you can't have the bicycle," she screamed. "You knew Gillian was going to use it; that's why you want it."
>
> Not only had he not known that, but he thought Mrs. Forbes hadn't known it either.
>
> "I didn't know, Mrs. Forbes," he murmured.
>
> "Yes, you did. You can't have it. Do you hear, you can't have it!"
>
> Then she rushed back into the room.

Forbes was left glaring miserably at him.

"Changeling," he muttered. "Changeling."

It was a word Tom did not know. Then the door was closed.[13]

Nothing could be finer than the sure way in which the novel then moves to what we feel to be its only possible end—a tragic end, which implicitly recognises the hopeless difficulties of thinking to solve dilemmas of class and inequality by single acts of kindness. The final pages are unerring, and show how Jenkins's gift as a narrator springs from his keen, loving knowledge of how people feel and behave.[14] This openhearted interest in people, the humane radicalism which gives an edge to his writing whenever it deals with privilege and inequality, the marked distrust of fanaticism—these are qualities which put him with the "liberal" tradition in modern British writing. From the Scottish point of view what is so heartening is the breadth of his interest in not particularly "national" subjects (like many an English liberal, especially Joyce Cary, he is interested in children and in the backward countries). In him we have a talent that richly typifies what I meant when I said at the end of *Scottish Literature and the Scottish People* that "a freer spirit, facing up more openly to experience at large whatever its origins, might better enable the Scottish writer to cope with the problems of living in this place at this time."[15]

RICHMOND, YORKSHIRE

---

[13] *The Changeling* (London, 1958), 119-120.

[14] *Love is a Fervent Fire* (London, 1959) would have been equally worth discussing at length. I was deterred only by the difficulty of doing justice, briefly and with little quotation, to both the power of the book and the question of whether the sharp contradictions in the make-up of the heroine are done in sufficient depth.

[15] p. 293.

The Work of David Lindsay

Writers, generally speaking, are only writers. They write not primarily because they have anything to say but because for one reason or another they want to write. Once a man has begun his book, if he has anything in him it will come out. If he hasn't much in him, and realises it, he will strike an attitude to disguise the fact. The attitude may take the form of "stylistic originality" or something of that sort, which the literati, who are easily deceived, may well admire.

It is no wonder that David Lindsay was never found generally acceptable. He had actually *seen* something, and his masterpiece *A Voyage to Arcturus* is a vivid account of the vision. We require from a witness not a display of educated sensibility but an account of what happened, and this is what David Lindsay gives us. The literati have often proved to prefer a display of educated sensibility. If nothing important has happened, to display educated sensibility is the only possible reason for only giving an account at all.

David Lindsay's tragedy—and his literary life was really that—is the tragedy of a man who has seen something, tells people and they don't listen or don't understand what he is talking about.

Lindsay had worked as a Lloyd's underwriter for fifteen years before he wrote his first novel. During this time he had filled notebooks with observations, reflections, perceptions and aphorisms, which all slanted in one direction and culminated in the explosive vision which became *A Voyage to Arcturus*, as soon as he left his job and settled in Cornwall to write. The book sold only a few hundred copies and its reception is typified by a review in the *Times Literary Supplement*, dated September 30th 1920:

> There may be an intention of allegory in what appears to be simply a riot of morbid fancy; but we doubt whether many readers will be inclined to pursue the possible hidden meaning over a quagmire and through a noisome fog. For the book is, at any rate, consistent in respect of its uniform unwholesomeness; the keynote being struck in the opening chapter, which recalls Baudelaire, or Poe in his most grisly vein. It is, no doubt, a legitimate aim of the

writer of fiction to make the flesh creep; scarcely, we think, to make the gorge rise.

The book is nothing whatever like Baudelaire or Poe, in whatever vein they may be writing, but the reviewer had several detective novels to deal with and no time for reflection. *Arcturus* was not reissued until 1945 and by that time David Lindsay was dead.

Lindsay, a strong, reserved man of Scottish Calvinist background, a solitary walker, a mountaineer, devoted to German metaphysics and to music, was not primarily an artist. He was concerned ruthlessly with his vision of truth, with his bitter and profound experience of spiritual reality. Panawe, the artist in *A Voyage to Arcturus*, says: "Nothing comes of it [art] but vanity."[1] In his notebook Lindsay writes: "The first preliminary for all metaphysical thinking is to produce within oneself the sense of *reality*."[2] Lindsay had this sense; he did not need to "produce it within himself."

If the reality behind his vision had been acknowledged on the appearance of *Arcturus*, perhaps his grip upon our human life here on earth would not have weakened so sadly in his later work. *Arcturus* proved too weird and strange both for critics and public.

No wonder. Its keywords are "wildness" and "grandeur." Its impact is powerful, its message at the same time tonic and terrible. The book is *there*, as a whole, violent and compelling. It is not anything so crude as an allegory, it is an imaginative fire in which years of thought are burned up. In *Devil's Tor* the painter says: "A symbol is a mystic sign of the Creator. An allegory is a wall decoration with a label attached."[3] *A Voyage to Arcturus* is no wall decoration.

Later books needed "composing" from scraps of discontinuous perception, from ideas and observations. None has the singleness of *Arcturus*, none gives the same impression of overwhelming, unified power. The "story" is often forced, and has insufficient means of locomotion. Lindsay in some of the books seems like a lithe, muscular man in a very ill-fitting suit. The savagery has gone, the grandeur is more abstract and the "sublimity" seems more deliberately sought.

In *Arcturus* the wildness is naked. Pleasure and pain are seen contemptuously as vulgar and trivial. Krag "made a careless and almost

---

[1] *A Voyage to Arcturus* (London, 1946), p.60. First published London, 1920. All quotations from 1946 edition.

[2] From typescript of "Sketch Notes for a New System of Philosophy," unpublished.

[3] *Devil's Tor* (London, 1932), p.145.

savage slash at Maskull's upper arm."[4] Maskull "scowls with pain." Such phrases are common.

The book begins as if Lindsay intends to set his story in the here and now. He introduces a set of characters who assemble for a seance. They are all fully described, as though they were the chief runners in a marathon. In fact they disappear like bubbles on a stream and never return after the first chapter. Two rough, wild strangers, Maskull "a kind of giant, but of broader and robuster physique than most giants,"[5] and Nightspore, "of middle height, but so tough looking that he appeared as if trained out of all human susceptibilities" enter the house just when the medium is about to conduct a materialisation. The medium succeeds in producing a beautiful, supernatural youth. A thick, muscular, ugly, yellow-faced man with an expression of "sagacity, brutality and humour"[6] bounds in and twists the youth's neck round. "A faint, unearthly shriek sounded, and the body fell in a heap on the floor... The guests were unutterably shocked to observe that its expression had changed from a mysterious but fascinating smile to a vulgar, sordid, bestial grin."[7] So much for the wiles of Crystalman, the god of this world.

From that moment everything is vision, and only occasionally does deliberate invention intrude. The story of Maskull's pilgrimage pulses and flows. The savage latecomer, Krag, who is in fact an emissary of Muspel, the hidden eternal light, and who on earth takes on the aspect of redemptive Pain, draws Maskull and Nightspore aside and persuades them to accompany him on a voyage to Tormance, one of the planets of the star Arcturus. They set off in a space-ship from the top of a high tower in Caithness. Although the means of rocket propulsion is more interesting than it would be in most space-fiction writers, what a space-fiction writer would concentrate on, Lindsay ignores, and the journey is not described.

My guess is that the characters assembled for the seance were to have been the leading figures in a novel of the same oddly polite, disturbing kind as the later *Sphinx* and *Violet Apple,* but at the point of Krag's entry, the vision exploded in a huge pattern of light, the novel disappeared, and an extravagant masterpiece took its place. From then on the tale drives forward with reckless directness.

Despite the metaphysical intention, everything is concrete. We start from fruits and colours, not from abstractions. The nature of a fruit

[4] *A Voyage,* p.40.
[5] *A Voyage,* p.20.
[6] *A Voyage,* p.23.
[7] *A Voyage,* p.24.

unknown on earth is "hard, persistent, melancholy."[8] The nature of colours unknown on earth are described like this: "Just as blue is delicate and mysterious,yellow, clear and unsubtle, so he felt ulfire to be wild and painful, and jale dreamlike, feverish and voluptious."[9] The imagery, often drawn from music, is burning and impressive. The descriptions have tremendous imaginative force, and a vivid hallucinatory quality. Lindsay uses words violently, sometimes uncouthly, is occasionally ponderous, and cares nothing for grace. "He [Maskull] was a naked stranger in a huge, foreign, mystical world, and whichever way he turned unknown and threatening forces were glaring at him. The gigantic, white, withering Branchspell, the awful, body-changing Alppain, the beautiful, treacherous sea, the dark and eerie Swaylone's island, the spirit-crushing forest from which he had just escaped. . . . "[10] This is the world of the book, which at a first reading has an effect similar to that of certain Tormance music on Maskull: "Maskull felt that something important was about to be uttered, which would explain all that had gone before. But it was invariably postponed. . .and yet somehow he did understand."[11]

Sometimes, when words have to be put into the mouths of the strange, living, symbolic figures, and the vision provides no words, he makes them up from what he knows—bald, direct and without the glow of vision. At other times their utterances have a gnomic, pithy conciseness and an aphoristic force which strike home to the heart: "If you wish to say what is *not,* many words will not suffice. If you wish to say what *is,* a few words will be enough,"[12] says Catice.

The tale itself is the account of Maskull's pilgrimage on Tormance, in search of Muspel, about which he knows nothing except that he seeks it. Maskull is a Prometheus figure who "came to steal Muspel-fire, to give a deeper life to men, never doubting if your soul could endure that burning." Krag and Nightspore desert him. He goes through a series of remarkable, violent, terrifying adventures in a world of extraordinary reality, led onwards towards Muspel by mysterious drumbeats. These drumbeats are indications that the other world of Muspel in truth exists. "The drum-beats. . . .reminded him of some place and some life with which he was perfectly familiar. Once again they caused all his other sense-impressions to appear false."[13]

[8] *A Voyage,* p.52.
[9] *A Voyage,* p.51.
[10] *A Voyage,* p.140.
[11] *A Voyage,* p.71.
[12] *A Voyage,* p.127.
[13] *A Voyage,* p.133.

Maskull is told nothing by the enigmatic Krag, but must find out everything for himself. At the very start he is warned. A voice tells him: "Nightspore is asleep now, but when he wakes you must die. You will go, but he will return."[14] Maskull's nobility and daring make it possible for him to receive intimations that beyond this world there is another, which alone is real. But Maskull is human, and can be led in many directions. Nightspore is Maskull's "new man" who awakes only when Maskull, the everyday self, dies. The nature of the true god becomes revealed after terrible suffering, for the Devil is the God of this world and idealism, philosophy, pleasure, love are all the toys with which Crystalman deceives his victims. Most forms of mysticism, too, seek union only with Crystalman (or Shaping) and never realise the existence of the hidden Muspel. "This is Shaping's world," says Slofork. "He that is a good child here, knows pleasure, pain and love, and gets his rewards. But there is another world . . . not Shaping's . . . and there all this is unknown, and another order of things reigns . . ."[15]

Polecrab says: "I live by killing and so does everybody. This life seems to me all wrong. So maybe life of any kind is wrong, and Surtur's world is not life at all, but something else."[16] In Lindsay's notebook occur the words: "In the Norse mythology, Muspel is the primeval world of fire; existing before heaven and earth, and which will eventually destroy them."[17]

When Maskull at last fights through the torments of this illusory world and reaches, with Krag, a great ocean, he is ill and dying.

> "What is this Ocean called?" asked Maskull, bringing out the words with difficulty.
> "Surtur's Ocean."
> "Where's Nightspore?"
> Krag bent over him with a grave expression.
> "You are Nightspore . . ."
> Shortly afterwards a frightful pang passed through Maskull's heart, and he died instantly.
> Krag turned his head round. "The night is really gone at last, Nightspore . . The day is here."
> Nightspore gazed long and earnestly at Maskull's body.
> "Why was all this necessary?"
> "Ask Crystalman," replied Krag sternly. "His world is no joke. He has a strong clutch . . . but I have a stronger . . .Maskull was his, but Nightspore is mine . ."

[14] *A Voyage*, p.38.
[15] *A Voyage*, p.67.
[16] *A Voyage*, p.145.
[17] "Sketch Notes."

"Do all men escape from that ghastly world .. or only I, and a few like me?"

"If all escaped, I shouldn't sweat, my friend."[18]

Nightspore reaches the Muspel tower. "All was dark and quiet as opened tomb. But the air was filled with grim, burning *passion*, which was to light and sound what light itself is to opaque colour . . ."[19]

When Nightspore ascends the Muspel tower he sees through an embrasure that light is streaming from the tower towards a luminous sphere, which is the world. Between the sphere and Muspel hangs a shadow. When the light passes through the shadow it is split.

> What had been fiery spirit but a moment ago was now a disgusting mass of crawling, wriggling individuals, each whirl of pleasure-seeking will having, as nucleus, a fragmentary spark of living green fire . . . Sometimes the green sparks were strong enough . . . to move a little way in the direction of Muspel . . . but they never saw beyond the shadow, though they were travelling towards *it*.[20]

The spirit-stream from Muspel passes through the Shadow, which is Crystalman, and the passage "caused him exquisite pleasure. *The Muspel stream was Crystalman's food*. Nightspore shuddered. He comprehended at last how the whole world of will was doomed to eternal anguish in order that one Being might feel joy."[21]

On the roof, expecting the final revelation, Nightspore sees—nothing. "Darkness was all around him .. he had the distinct impression that the darkness . . . was *grinning* . . . he understood that he was wholly surrounded by Crystalman's world, and that Muspel consisted of himself and the stone tower on which he was sitting."[22] He goes down to rebirth, to help Krag lead others toward the light.

Any description of the book must give an uncouth, bizarre impression, and this is not unjust. But what emerges after several readings is something quite other—a sense of the remarkable profundity and coherence of the vision and its message. The message is terrible in its uncompromising purity, and is more likely to repel casual readers than to attract. But the achievement of the book exactly balances the astonishing ambition of its intention. This, surely, is most exceptional.

After *A Voyage* Lindsay wrote at least seven books and published four. He never found again the ease of movement granted to him by his translation in *A Voyage* to another planet than ours. The other books

[18] *A Voyage*, p.240.
[19] *A Voyage*, p.242.
[20] *A Voyage*, p.245.
[21] *A Voyage*, p.246.
[22] *A Voyage*, p.247.

have to live in this world of Sussex downs .and drawing rooms. *The Haunted Woman* appears on the surface to be a story of intrigue. An engaged girl interested in buying an old house falls in love with a middle-aged man, its owner. But the movement of events is unusual. Isbel is not attracted to Judge in "normal" life, but only as the result of visits in his company to a part of the house which can only be reached by ascending a staircase which to most people and at most times simply isn't there. In the room where they eventually find themselves, people take on a new dimension, and become most deeply themselves.

> It was not so much that she appeared more beautiful as that her face had acquired another character. Its expression was deep, stern, lowering, yet everything was softened and made alluring by the pervading presence of sexual sweetness ... The face struck a note of deep, underlying passion, but a passion which was still asleep ... It seemed to her that no woman possessing such a strong, terrible sweetness and intensity of character could avoid accepting an uncommon, perhaps a fearful destiny.[23]

Underlying, threatening, exalting and intensifying their love, comes the music that in *The Haunted Woman* replaces the drumbeats of *Arcturus*.

> The low rich heavy scraping sound certainly did resemble that of a deep-toned string instrument, heard from a distance, but to Isbel's imagination, it resembled something else as well. She thought she recognized it as the music of that dark upstairs corridor, which she had heard on her first visit to the house. But this time it was ever so much nearer, fuller and more defined; the electric buzzing had resolved itself into perfectly distinct vibrations ... A tune was being played, so there was no doubt about the nature of the noise. It was a simple, early-English rustic air — sweet, passionate and haunting. The sonorous and melancholy character of the instrument added a wild, long-drawn-out-charm to it which was altogether beyond the range of the understanding and seemed to belong to other days, when feelings were more poignant and delicate, less showy, splendid and odourless ... After the theme had been repeated once, from beginning to end, the performance ceased, and was succeeded by absolute stillness.[24]

Each visit to the strange wing brings the musician nearer. Sometimes the music is gay, sometimes ominous. At last Judge and Isbel see the musician in a sunny landscape below the tower in which they stand.

> He sat motionless, facing the valley, with his back to the house ... Only his head, the upper half of his back and one outstretched leg were visible; but the leg was encased in a sage-green trouser, tightly cross-gartered with yellow straps, the garment on his back resembled, as far as could be seen a purple smock, and the hair of his hatless head fell in a thick, bright yellow mane as fas as his shoulders.[25]

[23] *The Haunted Woman* (London, 1947), p.50. First published London, 1922. All quotations from 1947 edition.

[24] *The Haunted Woman*, p.127.

[25] *The Haunted Woman*, p.137.

Finally, Isbel, having broken with Judge, is walking in the rainy, autumn garden of the house when she meets him unexpectedly. After some conversation, in which they are plainly at cross-purposes, Judge says:

"Tell me where you think your are?"

"I have already told you. It is *your* manner which is so very singular, Mr. Judge. Are you quite well?"

"Listen! I am talking with you here, and I am where we wished to be yesterday. Does it not seem so to you?"

"I don't understand you. Where did we wish to be yesterday?"

He gave her another searching look. "So you really are seeing differently. And have you not been up the staircase today?"

"I haven't set foot inside your house, I tell you. Have you lost your senses?"

"No; but I *have* been up that staircase today, and I have not yet come down again."

"Oh, my God!" said Isbel quietly.

"I was wretched, and could not keep away from the house. It contained all my memories. The stairs were there; I climbed them. Passing straight into that other room, I got through the window, and succeeded in reaching the ground without accident, though it was not easy . . . ."

She stared at him with frightened eyes. "And where are you now?"

"I am standing beside you in the open countryside in full sunshine — and it is spring, not autumn."[26]

Judge leaves her and she finds herself in a beautiful spring landscape. The house is gone.

Her mood was one of unutterable excitement and reckless audacity; she appeared to herself to be laughing and sobbing under her breath . . . . .

Henry and that other man were facing each other on the hillside, a little way below her. The man was tall and stout, and, in his bright-coloured, archaic garments, cut an extraordinary figure. He held his instrument against his chest, and was in the act of drawing his bow across it — the note she had heard had not yet come to an end. His back was turned towards her, so that she could not see his face, but Henry, who was standing erect and motionless beyond, was looking right into it, and, from his expression, it was as though he were beholding an apalling vision . . . . .

At that moment it seemed to her that yonder strange man was the centre around which everything in the landscape was moving, and that she herself was no more than his *dream!*[27]

Henry Judge sinks to the ground, and Isbel faints. Judge is later found dead in the east room.

Despite the rather stilted dialogue there seems to me no doubt that the power comes through.

[26] *The Haunted Woman*, pp.160-161.
[27] *The Haunted Woman*, p.167.

In *The Haunted Woman, The Sphinx* and *The Violet Apple* (unpublished) Lindsay deals again and again with the nature of man and woman and contrasts the illusory world of conventional material life with the real world in which human significance is revealed. He says in his notebook:

> One must regard the world not merely as a home of illusions, but as being *rotten* with illusion from top to bottom .... The most sacred and holy things ought not to be taken for granted, for if examined attentively, they will be found as .hollow and empty as the rest .... Behind this sham world lies the real, tremendous and awful Muspel-world, which knows neither will, nor Unity, nor Individuals: that is to say, an inconceivable world.[28]

The focal character in *The Sphinx* is Lore, a cynical, enigmatic woman composer.

> She writes pretty-pretty music, has a whole host of flabby worshippers in all parts of the country — in short, is fully conscious which side her bread is buttered on, and has gauged public taste to a hair, while all the time and in reality she drinks like a fish, habitually swallows drugs and in town never contemplates the possibility of bed before three or four in the morning.[29]

This woman herself says: "It's all very well for superior persons to insist on pure art, as opposed to money-making, but, in the meantime, who is to provide an artist's bread and butter?"[30]

The main male character, Nicholas, has invented an instrument for recording dreams. (It's typical of Lindsay's indifference to the mundane in these affairs that it appears to be made of clockwork.) "I think, that as long as the soul is present the body is alive, and when it leaves the body we die at once .... When the soul retires inside the intellectual part of the brain system, and leaves the locomotive and sensitive parts to themselves, to allow them to recover from their exhaustion, what happens is ... what I want to ascertain."[31] Throughout the book the powerful, prophetic dreams enrich and balance the willed action. Finally, Lore is drowned, and a dream of Nicholas's shows her, transformed, after death: "Quickly and unexpectedly Lore stepped, rather than jumped, up through mists and screens into a free, pure atmosphere of a light, fresh, open world."[32] Nicholas dies in his sleep and the dream record shows him embracing Lore. Significantly, in the waking action of the book, it was other women to whom he found himself attracted.

Lindsay comes nearer in *The Sphinx* than any other book to being at home with naturalistic dialogue and normal human interchange.

[28] "Sketch Notes."
[29] *The Sphinx* (London, 1923), p.62.
[30] *The Sphinx*, p.71.
[31] *The Sphinx*, p.84.
[32] *The Sphinx*, p.311.

"You haven't bored me at all. It has been very interesting."

"Interesting!" She appealed to the others. "He calls it interesting! It's a rather useful expression, and I'll make a note of it."[33]

* * *

"I'm utterly fed-up with his everlasting glittering eyes and dapper moustache. He has fairly got entangled with my nervous system. I want a complete rest."[34]

This vitality is present chiefly in the character of Lore. Elsewhere the narrative writing is careful, detailed, and a little wooden. The book contains so many facets and ambiguities that it would bear considerable weight of reflection.

Lindsay returns in *The Violet Apple*[35] to the theme that polite, conventional life, with its emotions at whatever depth, does not touch reality, which is revealed only in enigmatic signals that usually remain unheeded. This is continually related to his sense of the meaning of a true relationship between man and woman. The book has a freshness, simplicity and clarity of outline that give it mysterious depth under a deceptively quiet surface.

There was a long silence before the ambitious *Devil's Tor* was published in 1932. This book is a solid attempt to construct a fictional building which will show forth a whole view of the nature of human significance. It is again about the necessary uniting of a man and a woman through miraculous intervention to alter the course of history. The attempt is too deliberate, the miraculous intervention too insistent and heavy. The book has a stodgy feel. The light and vitality of *Arcturus*, *The Sphinx* and even *The Violet Apple* have gone. The vision is there, but less fiery. It fails to uplift the mass. There are more ideas, fewer insights, and these ideas are incorporated in a story based upon an intricate movement of fate to a given end. This notion of the pressing of a necessary fate is so much more suety and depressing than the tonic vigour or the Arcturan vision of Nightspore's *choice* on the beleagured Muspel tower, that one can see it as the work of a man himself depressed. The dialogue loses in conviction without gaining in nobility and force. Instead of showing the reader, he lectures. The less real *this* world becomes in fiction, the less real the *other* world becomes also. The one must shine through the other, as in his earlier books it often does. This decline seems to me the inevitable result of Lindsay's feeling that no one was genuinely interested in what he was trying to say.

And yet, as always, there are powerful penetrations and, in particular, descriptions of mysterious music which make one long to hear the music

[33] *The Sphinx*, p.92.
[34] *The Sphinx*, p.103.
[35] "The Violet Apple." This book was completed in 1924 but never published.

Lindsay himself might have written had composing been his gift. In no book does music fail to play a significant part. Somewhere he says: "Music is the higher speech; so that if truly there are angels and they converse with one another, it must be in music . . ."

And the theme bearing along these tones upon its back — its progress was not in *time*, but in some other incomprehensible mode of change from state to state. Its line of advancing was not between a full past and an empty future, carrying them listening upon its constant front: but they were carried by it — feeling, more than listening — towards another kind of future, already full, though this music was helping to fill it. Therefore the perpetual filling should be of intensity not substance.

These individual tones — to Ingrid, like the dropping of souls — instead of running one upon the heels of another and vanishing at the moment of their sounding, were somehow joining themselves to and increasing the next tones following . . . wherefrom only the softening by the glass made it far more beautiful. The foreground of shadowy garden was invisible except as an imaginary perspective. I repeated the attempt at the next window along the front, but again the same thing happened; I could make out nothing but the reflected trees. Then, since I could hardly undertake the circuit of the house, I gave it up. So small my curiosity had been after all, that I remained standing yet a little while to admire the fascination of wonder given back by this new glass world . . .

Now, all at once, in that mirror of the window, I became aware of a man's dark standing shape against the hollow trunk of a dead tree . . . .

His elbow rested lightly on a remaining low dead branch of the tree, the feet were crossed, the face, though it was towards me, I couldn't distinguish, because it was in rather heavy shade, and some way off. His shape was abnormally thin and exaggeratedly tall. He was in dark, tight clothes . . .

And thereupon, of their own will, came scurrying through my head a medley of illustrative superhuman figures . . . any imaginable caricature of the human male form, the most lean and long and travesty-like, that nevertheless should excite a feeling stranger than laughter. Wasn't this mirrored idler in a wood, resting against a death-touched tree, as inauspicious there as a shadow of death itself? . .

Twice, thrice and more I compared the true and the imaged woodlands to resolve the paradox. So slowly the truth dawned on me; and yet by cool and simple notice I could have grasped it in the beginning. For this presumed reflected vision of trees behind me, beyond the lane, was actually the direct view of different trees seen through the house, the background of its invisible garden. An extraordinary scene was reaching me through opposite windows of the front and back of the house — there was no impediment that couldn't be explained. These lower rooms ran from back to front, or else doors stood open between. Nothing of the inside of the house was visible, because its gloom was quite overpowered by the brightness beyond. The glass panes, the interior dusk, softened the scene to the likeness of a reflection. Only I should have seen immediately how the sinking sun in the west was shining through the trees, not on them.

If the vision of that man was intended for me, my mistake didn't go for nothing . . . I was to see neither a house nor the world, but only a human phantom in its setting . . ..A startling recoil from optical illusion to optical

[181]

ERRATUM: Page 181, line 15, from "only the softening . . ."

TO

Page 182, line 6, ". . . dead tree again, but"

should be read *after* page 182, line 24, "as reality,"

illusion was to impel me with violence past the common sight. That I was disporting myself with no mirror ... but unwittingly steadfastly beholding existence itself — the transition was to supply my mind with the momentum which should easily carry it on to receive the supernatural ...

It was a phantom ... for already its humanity was gone. With no difficulty, my eyes always found the dead tree again, but there was no light heartless stepping from one corpse to another of sound until the last corps should be reached and straightway forgotten, and all should be forgotten, as in the music of the world: but always there arrived, never again to depart, this grander and grander intensity of emotion, compounded of all the past ...[36]

When he wrote *The Witch* he was ill, deeply discouraged by the advent of the war, and had become silent and withdrawn, feeling less need than ever to relate his work to the normal life of his readers. The book is probably unpublishable, being written with an obsessive concentration on a series of speeches by an Earth-Mother figure who speaks in a strange, stilted, archaic· rhetoric quite at variance with the forceful utterance of the people in *A Voyage to Arcturus*. There is an equally obsessive solemnity of tone ·which makes some of the dialogue unintentionally comic. And yet, as.always, magnificence, vision and power break triumphantly through again and again and illuminate all that surround them.

The room I tried to see into was large, but the bright reflection in the window-glass of the sun-dappled tree behind me, across the lane, prevented my distinguishing anything whatever inside. The image of the trees was as vivid as reality, not any longer was there a man˗beside it; yet where he had been remained. A black gap, a fissure of darkness, occupied exactly his remembered outline. That, however, had been a man, this was a cleft. A cleft in what? I don't know ....

.... I was too quickly to discover that the gap wasn't opened before me in innocence. Intolerable, sightless waves from it were making nothing of the house between, in ever faster reducing my spirit to the colour of death. I mean, death in its positive character: the odour, taste, sadness of death — its utter joylessness and loneliness, the awful falling of the shadows of night ... So death swept me ... until step by step, backwards, I must have retreated to the lane ...[37]

Everything that David Lindsay wrote is the work of a man who cannot help but see what others do not, the true nature of what he calls "the vast shadow-house of earth and sky." To find an individual Scottish novel comparable with *A Voyage to Arcturus* in force and strangeness — and it is in no way comparable in depth and scope — you would have to go back as far as *The Confessions of a Justified Sinner*. It is odd that the most extraordinary Scottish novelist of this century should have been so neglected.

BILLESDON, LEICESTER

[36] *Devil's Tor*, pp.470-471.
[37] "The Witch." Typescript; unpublished.

JOHN LINDBERG

The Decadence of Style:
Symbolic Structure in
Carlyle's Later Prose

It is possible to consider Carlyle's career in three stages, an arbitrary but helpful illustration of his continuous development. His books are all masks, their structure mediating between author and material, presenting characteristic yet varied faces to their readers from stage to stage. The first stage culminates with *The French Revolution;* his work to this point is a personal interpretation which his audience accepted as their own. The second stage produced *Heroes and Hero-Worship* and *Past and Present;* continuing his personal interpretation, Carlyle still found a receptive audience as worried as he was about the manifest problems of the times. The third stage is that of *Latter-Day Pamphlets;* the personal interpretation has now become so idiosyncratic that his readers reversed their opinion of Carlyle's work. The present study concerns these last two stances of the prophetic role.

I

In the opening stage of his career Carlyle perfected a style of remarkable appropriateness. It was both a private and a public symbolism. There was yet to develop the basic clash between the prophet and the evil times on which he had fallen. That clash began to appear in *Heroes and Hero-Worship* and *Past and Present* and was made to serve a didactic end in *Latter-Day Pamphlets.* It would seem that the initial divergence arose from Carlyle's view of the social role of literature. He was a prophet first, and disclaimed any aesthetic intention in his manipulation of reality. His style began to separate itself from reality, first unconsciously, then willingly, when the times had so altered as to deprive the style of its representational role of art and to throw the style ever more dogmatically into its role of symbolism.

Carlyle was at one with his times, earnest and puritanical. His chosen audience influenced his choice of diction. Although the diction was unconventional, it was calculated to capture the minds of a literate, prosperous middle class, convinced of the importance of individual duty and social commitment. At once Carlyle divested his readers of anachron-

[183]

istic evangelical terms and invested their bourgeois code with a refreshing religiosity. And when the middle class betrayed his morality, Carlyle elevated his audience with his style, addressing ever more sacerdotal terms to a narrowing circle of the political aristocracy.

The most significant feature of the style would be an ironic reversal of values. As a philosophic radical, Carlyle would claim not to understand conduct of which he disapproved. Adopting a pose of ignorance, he would gain the satiric perspective of *Gulliver's Travels* or *Rasselas,* and would fall back on his own prepared symbols. The unity of his works would not be the expected unity of his ostensible topics but the dogmatic unity of a symbolic point of view, a unity of verbal consistency, metaphoric coherence, and structural analogies.

But with a double irony, as soon as Carlyle self-consciously employs his style for satiric perspective, he has lost the immediate inspiration of his style. He has given up imaginative description of his times in preference to egotistic prescription of the course his times ought to take. The shape of things to come will alter from the configurations of the prophetic mask prepared to receive them, and the prophet will fail of his communion, having lost the instinctive artistery that formed his prophetic style. So in Carlyle's later prose, the style achieves brilliance in public address, but the stylist is addressing a social void.

II

Heroes and Hero-Worship addresses itself to social problems through the medium of individual heroism. Heroism is the public dimension of the private personality. The book is directed toward the future, making an immediate ethical appeal to change present abuses. History is only important as a source of heroic models, an arena of the hero's conflict with the conventions of his particular era. But though history is little more than a series of static stages, the series as a whole illustrates an inverted progress of greater moral decay as people in the successive stages fail to emulate their heroes, whose energies gradually contract from public effect to introverted individualism as they strive to assert their intuitions of greatness.

The titling of the chapters explains this process of decadence. *Heroes* devolves from medieval paganism to modern revolutionism, and the book limits itself to the thousand years of modern history. The moral is clear. Two general themes unify *Heroes,* and exchange dominant roles in an X-plan, their ascendancies crossing as one theme rises and another falls in the course of the book. The first theme is the chronology from feudalism to revolution, and the second one, the important and paradoxical one, is the fact that his time forces the hero to move from the unselfconscious actions of the god to the intellectual words of the man of letters, until the hero as king brings the cycle to a close by crashing through formulas and compelling an obedience which had once been a spontaneous tribute.

The hero defines himself unconsciously in any era by his instinctive wonder and reverence. Nature figures to him as an apocalypse. He is inspired to preach a conservative evangel of return to pristine virtues. In every chapter, the natural apocalypse "glares in upon" the hero, fire-imagery burns through shams, and images of light convey the prophetic message. In his own person, every hero is sincere and sympathetic and convinced of the value of suffering to teach virtue; that is, he believes in the painful necessity of rejecting easy councils and accustomed mores. His personal sympathy combines with his intuition of perpetual values to make him a hero, larger than life, the gigantic collective embodiment of the emotions of all men in his time.

The opening of each essay explicitly links the hero of one era with those preceding, until the structure of the book builds a chain of epiphanies in history, symbolic moments among lesser affairs. Each essay then gives a brief biography stressing the hero's intellectual and moral qualities, and concludes with the relevance of the hero to Carlyle's audience. The cumulative structure builds a belief in the predominance of heroic virtue in the past, the decadence of heroic virtue in the present, and an implicit but powerful reproach.

Introducing Odin, or the hero as divinity, Carlyle opens his lecture with a metaphysical lesson drawn directly from popular interest in the theories of Comte. Pagan mythology, rather than being the superstitious allegory which rationalists think it, was actual faith, a faith that is our reproach to have forgotten: "What in such a time as ours it requires a Prophet or Poet to teach us, namely, the stripping-off of those poor undevout wrappages, nomenclatures and scientific hearsays,—this, the ancient earnest soul, as yet unencumbered with these things, did for itself."[1] So much for positivism. Carlyle substitutes his own religion of reversed progress—"that man, in some sense or other, worships Heroes ... this is, to me, the living rock amid all rushings-down whatsoever;—the one fixed point in modern revolutionary history." (V, 15)

Whether or not there was a historic Odin is irrelevant in the symbolic realm. Odin's divinity sprang less from himself than from the admiration of his fellows: "what others take him for, and what he guesses that he

---

[1] All citations are to the Centenary Edition of Carlyle's works edited by H. D. Traill and published by Chapman and Hall, London, 1896. This quotation is from *Heroes and Hero-Worship*, p. 9. All subsequent citations will give the volume and page of the Traill edition in the text.

may be; these two items strangely act on one another, help to determine one another." (V, 25) The concept of divinity is social. If there were not such a god-man, it was inevitable that men should believe him into being, because civilization springs from the urge of a culture toward a principle of order: "this light, kindled in the great dark vortex of the Norse mind, dark but living . . . is to me the center of the whole. How such light will then shine out . . . depends not on *it*, so much as on the National Mind recipient of it." (V, 26)

"Given your Hero, is he to become Conqueror, King, Philosopher, Poet? It is an inexplicably complex controversial-calculation between the world and him!" (V, 80) The hero remains unconscious and imminent in his private self, but in his urge to prophesy and in the sympathetic response he excites, he will find himself invested in shifting public roles. Beginning with "The Hero as Poet," two heroes appear in each essay, and here also begins a deliberate anachronism—both being devices for more adequate symbolic representation of increasingly diverse modern history. Poet, not priest, follows prophet, because "they have penetrated both of them into the sacred mystery of the Universe. . . . The one [prophet] we may call a revealer of what we are to do, the other [poet] of what we are to love." (V, 80, 81) Both prophet and poet are closer to God than the priest, and poetry is more influential than formal religion. Next in symbolic order though chronologically prior to Dante and Shakespeare come Luther and Knox, whose work was longer in being felt than that of the poets. From the Reformation grew modern nations with strong kings. When they abused their power, it was the role of men of letters like Johnson and Burns to adjust opinion between authority and liberty, and when that conflict of opinion bred violence, the hero as king imposed order, wisely in accord with primitive virtue like archaic Cromwell, or wickedly for personal glory like modern Napoleon. So *Heroes and Hero-Worship* makes an Epimethean and a Promethean pause halfway through. Gods, prophets, and poets are of the mighty past; priests, men of letters, and kings are though heroic yet much diminished, all too human. Prophesy must now make its way by tradition rather than instinct, words more than action. We are in the modern world.

"The Hero as Priest" turns back in time to Luther because "Protestantism is the grand root from which our whole subsequent European History branches out. For the spiritual will always body itself forth in the temporal history of men." (V, 123) The paradox begins here, that all modern revolution is a punishment for failure to practice the virtues of god, prophet, and poet: "I find Protestantism . . . to be the beginning of a new genuine sovereignty . . . a return to all old sayings." (V, 124-125) The development of separate nations, apparently radical, is the outward form of an inner regeneration: "Theocracy ... is precisely the thing to be struggled for!" (V, 152)

"The Hero as *Man of Letters* ...is altogether a product of these new ages." (V, 154) Of the three unexpected colleagues—Johnson, Rousseau, Burns— Johnson is the most noble, but his best is a maimed, hagridden heroism striving against the deism and atheism of his epoch. The eighteenth century, called a paper age in *The French Revolution*, has turned entirely from realities to formulas, and the hero's prophesy is forced into authorship—his actions must be books.

The symbolic appreciation of Johnson is among the most effective passages of *Heroes*. Johnson was his age in person, his very diseases and morbidities being appropriate to the "chronic atrophy and disease of the whole soul" (V, 174) in a skeptical time. His disabilities result from the inadequate hero-worship he receives. "Nature, in return for his nobleness, had said to him, Live in an element of diseased sorrow." (V, 178) Johnson's worst faults become virtues; his greediness and bigotry are his despair of virtue in his own time, and he completely fulfills the heroic qualifications: "Was there ever soul more tenderly affectionate, loyally submissive to what was really higher than he? ... Johnson believed altogether in the old ... The great Fact of this Universe glared-in ...upon this man too!" (V, 179-180) Carlyle takes leave reluctantly of such a sympathetic symbol: "in his poverty, in his dust and dimness, with the sick body and the rusty coat....Brave old Samuel: *ultimus Romanorum!*" (V, 184)

"The Commander over Men; he to whose will our wills are to be subordinated ...may be reckoned the most important of Great Men. He is practically the summary for us of *all* the various figures of Heroism." (V, 196) Participating in the distraught demands of the anarchic public, the kingly hero is the dominant figure in a reactionary counter-revolution, the final degradation and primary exaltation of the prophet. Carlyle's audience still considered Cromwell the "brave, bad man" of Clarendon's history, and in returning Cromwell's reputation to the historic facts, Carlyle again finds a highly appropriate symbol—the reluctant leader compelled to reform his evil times. The Civil War was part "of that great universal war which alone makes up the History of the World, —the war of Belief and Unbelief!" (V, 204) The Restoration was an arbitrary anachronism. "Puritanism was hung on gibbets,—like the bones of the leading Puritan. Its work nevertheless went on accomplishing itself." (V, 207) With Burke and with Macaulay, Carlyle understands modern English history to have begun in 1688, the inevitable resurgence of morality and intellect in politics.

Cromwell's moral biography parallels the political fortunes of Puritanism. He had the indispensible trinity of heroic traits, sincerity, sympathy, and sorrow over his times. He "spoke always without premeditation of the words he was to use," (V, 219) and far from following a premeditated progress to the Protectorship, he rose only because of the rectitude of each pragmatic decision. His own sense of duty, combined with his knowledge of men and his genius for action, made Cromwell "the one available Authority left in England, nothing between England and utter Anarchy but him alone." (V, 233) Sober scholars—Gardiner, Firth, Wedgwood, and Abbott—all concur in Carlyle's symbolic judgment. Probably the only dictator in history to call a free election, Cromwell almost wept as he dismissed his third Parliament: "You have had such an opportunity as no Parliament in England ever had . . . . God be judge between you and me!" (V, 234)

Carlyle finishes his lecture-series in a noble yet modest tone. He has always had his audience in mind and ends with words that at least momentarily must have thrilled his listeners with the present consciousness that a hero stood before them: "The accomplished and distinguished, the beautiful, the wise, something of what is best in England, have listened patiently to my rude words. With many feelings, I heartily thank you all; and say, Good be with you all!" (V, 244) Carlyle's confidence in his own mission as prophet finds its best expression in words of supreme good will.

Past and Present reverses the approach of *Heroes and Hero-Worship*. Rather than make an individual appeal, it speaks to a whole class, the working mammonites or captains of industry, and rather than offer separate heroes to emulate, it contrats the whole present with the whole past.

The style of *Past and Present* is as effective as its earlier versions because the times wanted a prophet. Writing in the winter of 1839-1840, Thomas Arnold is perplexed and shocked:

> It fills me with astonishment to see antislavery and missionary societies so busy with the ends of the earth, and yet all the worst evils of slavery and heathenism are existing among ourselves. But no man seeems so gifted, or to speak more properly, so endowed by God, with the spirit of wisdom, as to read this fearful riddle truly; which most Sphinx-like, if not read truly, will most surely be the destruction of us all.[2]

These words might be the sermon-text for *Past and Present*, especially the Sphinx-metaphor, which appears in "Proem" of the book. We know from a letter of May 19, 1842, that "Carlyle dined, and slept here on

[2] Quoted by Arthur Penrhyn Stanley, *The Life and Correspondence of Thomas Arnold* (New York, 1903), II, 125-126.

Friday last" and visited Naseby field with Arnold. It would seem plausible that they discussed "the condition-of-England question," more especially as Carlyle had published "Chartism" in 1839, and could give as reason for beginning *Past and Present*: "My heart is sick and sore in behalf of my own poor generation."[3] Once again and then no more, his times will applaud Carlyle in his role of sympathetic sorrowing hero and his book will gain in power from his confidence of that willing hero-worship.

Explicitly prophetic devices become very prominent—a parable on almost every page like Balaam and his ass or the Dead Sea apes or the stuffed goose in its magic circle; a concluding moral at the end of every chapter; frequent self-quotations or transparent personae like Sauerteig; invented epithets like Sir Jabesh Windbag, or Choctaw and buccaneer capitalism. It seems very clear that Carlyle is no longer careful to find an equivalence between subject and style but chooses his topics to suit his tone.

Instead of the X-plan of themes in *Heroes*, *Past and Present* develops a quincunx in both diction and structure. Carlyle invents five groups of terms to arrest the complexity of English society in a quincunx of diction:

Joe-Manton Aristocracy

Millocracy	Fact	Working
(Dilettantism)	(The Condition of	Aristocracy
	England)	(Mammonism)

Democracy

He varies this tension of opposites with a constellation of dyslogisms—galvanism, animalism, asphyxia, enchantment—taken from his description of the eighteenth century in *The French Revolution*. And the structural quincunx appears in the titling:

Horoscope
(Book IV)

The Ancient Monk	Tools and the Man	The Modern Worker
(Book II)	(announced theme)	(Book III)

Proem
(Book I)

The quincunx is a static device, and the book does not argue but presents a series of perspectives. Each chapter elaborates its title and repeats all of the prophetic diction of previous chapters in the special context of the new chapter. The growth of subject is internal and symbolic.

[3] *The Correspondence of Thomas Carlyle and Ralph Waldo Emerson, 1834-1872*, ed. Charles Eliot Norton (New York, 1883 and 1884), II, 10.

Upon closer reading of the text, the most striking member of the quincunx of diction is the central term—Fact. It functions in the style as a juggernaut-term around which deploy the terms for the various class levels. Tools and the Man is the central theme in the book corresponding to Fact in the diction. It is the reality for the modern worker to face, who may use the ancient monk as a model. Fact, or the theme of Tools and the Man, remains imperturbable to the frame of other terms in the quincunx and leaves the frame of the quincunx behind like a lion leaping through a series of paper hoops. The structural quincunx of the actual book, both diction and theme, is the most recent attempt to capture Fact.

"The condition of England" (X, 1) is unable to master the Fact of the times. The chapter "Midas" is a metaphor of economic deadlock. "The workhouse Bastille," "they sit there," "we sit enchanted here" (X, 2) weave through the pages to create a stylistic version of enchantment: "in the midst of plethoric plenty, the people perish." (X, 6) Alliteration adds to the effect of repeated words. And a moral recapitulates: "Midas had insulted Apollo and the gods .... What a truth in these old Fables!" (X, 6) "The Sphinx" follows Midas-enchantment with a demand for justice, being no less than "Nature, Universe, Destiny, Existence, howsoever we name this grand unnamable Fact in the midst of which we live and struggle." (X, 7)

When Carlyle turns to the past for an authentic example of hero-worship, the book moves forward in faith as it moves backward in time. "The Ancient Monk" found a better accommodation to Fact than did "The Modern Worker." A study of style has no place for more than a few words about Carlyle's philosophy of history, but "Jocelin of Brakelond" is one of the most emphatic and persuasive passages in Carlyle's work; he expends his genius for stylistic splendor on the evocation of past heroism: "covered deeper than Pompeii with the lava-ashes and inarticulate wreck of seven hundred years!" (X, 40) It is heroism that is buried, not just men and buildings, and the detritus of the burial is not even remoteness in time and space; but rather the ashes and wreck refer to spiritual decadence, more effective than ever Vesuvius was in choking off the lives of men. "But fancy a deep-buried Mastodon, some fossil Megatherion, Ichthyosaurus, were to begin to *speak* from amid its rock-swathings, never so indistinctly!" (X, 43) Carlyle exhorts the vanished Jocelin to leave more than his fragmentary chronicle of the giants in the earth of his day, for such a feeble tradition of heroic virtue poses a greater riddle than ever the fossils did about the origins of human greatness.[4]

----

[4] In *Bleak House* a megatherium wallows up Ludgate Hill. In *Hereward the Wake* Kingsley praises the courage and endurance of "the last Englishman" in "The Fens." In the idealist tradition, material progress may mean moral decadence.

"Phenomena," the first chapter in "The Modern Worker," repeats the diction of "Midas" and "The Sphinx" as a shocking contrast to the brave old world of "The Ancient Monk"——"enchanted St. Ives' Work-houses and Joe-Manton Aristocracies; giant Working, Mammonism near strangled in the partridge-nets of giant-looking Idle Dilettantism." (X, 137) Here is a political cartoon in words, varied with social absurdities reported at random, the stuffed figure of a kneeling pope, a champion in tin armor, a seven-foot hat, cheek by jowl with equal absurdities of Corn Laws and Sliding Scales. (X, 144)

"Gospel of Mammonism" and "Gospel of Dilettantism" are *tours de force* of satiric literalism. The naive pedant Sauerteig establishes English worship of money with the instructive metaphors of capitalists like stuffed geese within a chalked circle, and legislators like apes who have lost their souls in chatter.

From the apotheosis of "The English" as "the stupidest in speech, the wisest in action," (X, 160) Carlyle addresses his book to the middle class. He wishes to inspire a whole segment of the public to heroism. Every new chapter varies this basic appeal. Like Cromwell addressing Parliament, Carlyle believes the captains of industry can alter history if they respond to the challenge of Fact. Sir Jabesh Windbag and Plugson of Undershot alike are humor characters, but no more ludicrous than the selfish classes they represent. Here occurs a parable on Columbus, no digression, but another model from the past. (X, 199) "Labour" and "Reward" are shot through with syntactical references to Columbus and to Norse gods—all heroic, prophetic men of action—to prepare the climax of the book: "May it please your Serene Highnessess ... the proper Epic of this world is not now 'Arms and the Man'; how much less, 'Shirt-frills and the Man'; no, it is now 'Tools and the Man!' " (X, 209)

"Horoscope" echoes "Proem" in repeated metaphors, reiterated diction of social decay, but with the effect of the immediately preceding contrast between past and present, so that Fact gathers around itself a new frame of terms—"Aristocracies" of true merit, "The One Institution" of Parliament willing to "interfere" for justice, "Captains of Industry" and "the Landed" now by love united with the workers and themselves, not isolated by cash and privilege. The opening quincunx, viewed retrospectively through the moral kaleidoscope of the book, has changed the import of its terms.

Latter-Day Pamphlets no longer observes any distinction between diction and theme. The unity of one chapter is the unity of the whole book, or the book as a whole has no unity, no relationship between parts, and consequently no recognition of an external world to be adapted to the book. The only reality is the integrity of the diction. In short, Carlyle is no longer playing a role. He thinks of himself as a genuine prophet delivering divine oracles. The circle of his friends contracts. Indeed, he has no friends, only disciples. But the question of madness does not arise. He still controls his meaning as well as ever. Though he may live in a private world, he feels his insecurity as painfully as the sanest of anxious men. Every chapter rebuilds a symbolic whole as indefatigably as does every separate poem of Browning, another sane man whose diction became his theme, or, perhaps more to the point, as does every new letter in *Fors Clavigera*, where, as Rosenberg has said in *The Darkening Glass*, the music of the style is the music of consciousness itself.[5]

The enchanted unemployed in their workhouse Bastilles in *Past and Present* are no more than expressive metaphors of social reality. Everyone knew that it was so. But times had changed from 1843 to 1850. The Corn Laws and Sugar Duties had been repealed at the same time that Europe was convulsed with revolutions; and Sir Robert Peel in accepting Richard Cobden as a gentleman had changed the Whig party beyond recognition. England could congratulate herself for achieving a Great Exhibition and leading world commerce away from regional loyalties while her European contemporaries had as yet hardly achieved the status of nations.

Latter-Day Pamphlets then was poorly timed and impolitically titled for popular acceptance. It earned Carlyle his first public caricature as Dr. Pessimus Anticant in Trollope's *The Warden*. "They have had immense reading," wrote W. E. Forster, "but probably less effect than almost any of his writings."[6] "When I speak of the Latter Day Prophet," wrote Fitzgerald to Frederick Tennyson, "I conclude you have read, or heard of, Carlyle's pamphlets so designed. People are tired of them and of him: he only foams, snaps, and howls, and no progress, people say: this is almost true: and yet there is vital good in all he has written."[7] A hostile review in *Blackwood's*[8] accuses Carlyle of arrogating the prophetic mantle which only popular accolade can give: "What is Mr. Carlyle himself but a Phantasm of the species which he is pleased to denounce? . . . In short, we pass from the Latter-day Pamphlets with the sincere conviction that the author as a politician is shallow and un-

---

[5] John D. Rosenberg, *The Darkening Glass: A Portrait of Ruskin's Genius* (New York, 1961), p. 187.

[6] David Alec Wilson, *Carlyle at His Zenith* (London, 1927), p. 295.

[7] Edward Fitzgerald. *The Library of Literary Criticism*, ed. Charles Well Moulton (Buffalo, 1904), VII, 254.

[8] W. E. Aytoun, "Latter-Day Pamphlets," *Blackwood's Edinburgh Magazine*, LXVII (1850), 641-658.

sound, obscure and fantastic in his philosophy, and very much to be reprehended for his obstinate attempt to inculcate a bad style."[9]

To all of these animadversions and many more Carlyle would have us believe he shrugged an indifferent shoulder. His *Reminiscences* display him somewhat self-consciously adjusting his rumpled costume of goat-skins:

> In 1850, after an interval of deep gloom and bottomless dubitation, came *Latter-Day Pamphlets*, which unpleasantly astonished everybody; set the world upon the strangest suppositions ("Carlyle got deep into whiskey!" said some), ruined my 'reputation' (according to the friendliest voices), and, in effect, divided me altogether from the mob of 'Progress-of-the-Species' and other vulgar,—but were a great relief to my own *conscience* as a faithful citizen, and have been ever since.[10]

The epithet *vulgar* and the stress on individual relief of conscience (even as a citizen) betray the increasing privacy of his symbols and his desire for a select audience though few.

He found one such aristocrat in his literary executor, who ironically hurt Carlyle's reputation more by indiscreet editing than Carlyle could have done with still more excrementitious excess than in *Latter-Day Pamphlets*. Yet Carlyle probably smiled with grim approval from his repose in Abraham's bosom, for he had taught Froude to overlook facts in quest of Fact. "The question which Carlyle asked," wrote Froude, "... was not, Is it true? but Is it alive? Life is not truth, but the embodiment in time and in mortality of a spiritual or animating principle."[11] When he exposed his mentor's frailty, and did it out of duty, Froude finally accomplished what Carlyle had despaired of doing even in the violent literalism of *Latter-Day Pamphlets*—the transmutation of words into deeds.

Latter-Day Pamphlets is a tiresome book. Inversion as a means has passed into inversion as an end, and the irony has become impertinent. Carlyle deliberately makes the worse into the better cause. He might be said to write on a topic the opposite of the title of the pamphlet.

---

[9] *Blackwood's*, pp. 642, 658. A retrospective review, "Mr. Carlyle," *Fraser's Magazine*, LXXII (1865), 778-810, upon publication of *Frederick the Great*, understands the stylistic problems of the prophet: "each book has its own object and its own unity; and their author is much too considerable a writer, and far too great an artist, to ... strain them ... to any special purpose. Still this general vein [symbolic structure] does run through them all. ... these views ... run ... into poetry and metaphor." (pp. 779, 781) The reviewer calls the *Schwein'sche Philosophie* a lamentable and unfair use of a brilliant style.

[10] *Reminiscences*, ed. Charles Eliot Norton (London, 1887), p. 125.

[11] From an autobiographical memoir printed by Waldo Hilary Dunn in his *James Anthony Froude* (Oxford, 1961), p. 73.

> A discussion may consist of what might be called 'nodal' propositions, [Holloway writes of Carlyle] with a far from immediately plain sense, but introduced, familiarized, made easier for the reader to grasp, by a variety of techniques that would indeed be sophistical, if their interpretation could be nothing but logical; but not otherwise. . . . What is a paradox at one extreme, interpreted in a perfectly straightforward sense, is a truism at the other, when the special sense given to some crucial word is made fully explicit.[12]

The "crucial word" in *Latter-Day Pamphlets* is always an image of corruption modulated from paradox to truism to nausiate the reader with his seeming-comfortable world.

Because there is no thematic progression in the book, one pamphlet demonstrates the method, and "Jesuitism" demonstrates it best because it is last and serves as peroration. The inversion of "Jesuitism" is to make a truism of a paradox comprising all of the paradoxes in the book—that the most cherished formulas of social welfare are the surest means to social ruin. The essay rises to a paired climax, first of diseased inanity, then of prophetic faith, as Carlyle pursues his method of assertion and counterassertion, the only means of development left to him in his despair of finding order in life. "Like the valley of Jehoshaphat, it lies round us, one nightmare wilderness, and wreck of deadmen's bones, this false modern world." (XX, 313) The perfection of modern Jesuitism is the famous pig-philosophy, or *Schwein'sche Weltansicht,* another product of the literal pedant Sauerteig. Benthamites are Carlyle's Yahoos. The pig-philosophy in this essay is analogous to a series of impromptu addresses in the preceding pamphlets, addresses by a despairing hero to an audience who, Carlyle's stage-directions tell us, jeer and desert the hall.

Yet no man is happy in mere pursuit of pleasure, "restless gnawing ennui," (XX, 335) Carlyle arrives at saying after pages of reiterated images of sensualism, and *Latter-Day Pamphlets* concludes with eloquent pity for a country that has driven itself into a dumb intimation of faith by its very excess of prosperity:

> You are fed, clothed, lodged as men never were before; every day in new variety of magnificence are you equipped and attended to; such wealth of material means as is now yours was never dreamed of by man before:—and to do any noble thing, with all this mountain of implements, is forever denied you. . . . Mount into your railways; whirl from place to place, at the rate of fifty, or if you like of five hundred miles an hour. . . . if you would mount to the stars. . . . [t]hat prophetic Sermon from the Deeps will continue with you, till you wisely interpret it and do it, or else till the Crack of Doom swallow it and you. *Adieu: Au revoir.* (XX, 337)

If such heaped hyperboles of prophesy have become daily headlines, and they have, it is possible that the style of the prophesy is as immediate as its fulfillment. Carlyle has ended with *Adieu,* but also with *Au revoir.*

[12] John Holloway, *The Victorian Sage* (New York, 1953), pp. 51-52.

III

Who is decadent—society or the man who says it is? There is no necessary connection. It only seems that Carlyle created his most vigorous and persuasive expression in response to a society that seemed decadent to him. In judging the adequacy of that style, it is important to remember that Carlyle's purpose was expressive rather than expository. As a historian, he was an interpreter, not a discoverer nor an orderer like his contemporaries Gardiner and Green. He conceived of his task like a Greek dramatist, re-working familiar material for a didactic moral.[13] As a social critic, he never explained new principles but returned to old ones. His work accommodated the complexity of human events to large symbols of "natural supernaturalism," and the symbols at their best were susceptible to a flexible interweaving of themes.

To consider the relevance of his style to our own time, Carlyle suggests apposite contrasts with James Joyce, a modern stylist of great power. His influence on Joyce is a critical commonplace, both in the invention of metaphoric catalogues and in the parody of literary forms. But the difference is more striking. Those passages of metaphoric mastery of the face of reality that we find in Carlyle, so similar to passages in *Ulysses*, never develop into the aesthetic reduplication of reality of *Finegans Wake*, not even in *Latter-Day Pamphlets*. In the metaphor of a compass, with the artist at the apex, Joyce's compass had one foot in society and one in his conception of artistic creation, and he tried to bring the feet together; but Carlyle's compass had one foot in society and one foot in his transcendental faith, and he tried to spread his compass to infinity. Elman's biography presents Joyce as a Freudian sick man who invested his traumas with his works, but Carlyle appears to have invested himself with the ills of his era. Before he grew into a disappointed egotist, Carlyle had the courage of a responsible citizen confident of his ability to have an effect on the world around him. And if great writers are representative, we may read a lesson for our times in the contrast between these men.

STATE COLLEGE OF IOWA

---

[13] In *The French Revolution*, Carlyle explicitly develops the death of Robespierre as a mock-heroic Greek tragedy; "The Insurrection of Women" as mock-epic; the death of the Girondins as a serious tragedy with Homeric epithets.

Notes and Documents

Lockhart The Scorpion
An Unpublished Manuscript

The following article by John Gibson Lockhart (the manuscript of which is in my possession) has never, so far as I know, been printed. The Annual Fox dinner, on which Lockhart is giving a commentary, was held in the Waterloo Tavern, Edinburgh, on 24 January 1825, to celebrate the birthday of Charles James Fox. The first of these Whig dinners was held in 1821 and the last in 1826. The Tories, with their Pitt Club of Scotland, had been first in the field and the annual dinners help by the two parties helped to foment the bitter rivalry which was only too prevalent at that time. Lockhart could not have been present at the dinner even if he had wished for Cockburn tells us that the doors at the Fox dinners were carefully guarded to prevent the entry of spies and Lockhart, a well-known Tory, could hardly have eluded the sentries. The article is obviously based on newspaper reports. He sent it to William Maginn but I feel sure he did not really mean him to print it. Had it been published it would have caused almost as great a sensation as the famous Chaldee Manuscript in *Blackwood's Edinburgh Magazine* and what Scott said of that he would have said of the Fox dinner report — "Edinburgh is rather too narrow for satire so markedly personal, and there are certainly several individuals who, from their character and situation, have reason to resent having been so roughly handled." Scott had warned Lockhart more than once. "Remember," he wrote to him, "it is to the *personal* satire I object and to the horse-play of your raillery." Although Sir Walter would have strongly disapproved of this article being published he would, in private, have chuckled over it, for it is a delightful piece of satire, extremely clever, extremely witty, and as a *jeu d'esprit* must be classed as one of Lockhart's masterpieces.

JAMES C. CORSON
UNIVERSITY OF EDINBURGH

It may be thought that we are merely trifling with the reading Public, by alluding to any doings of a set of people so utterly insignificant as the Whigs of the enlightened Capital Auld Reekie, alias Modern Athens. We cannot however refuse ourselves the gratification of remarking in a single sentence on the fact that out of "the two hundred noblemen and Gentlemen" placarded as having constituted the party at their Great Annual Fox dinner last week only *seven names* belong to persons holding landed property in this ancient and illustrious kingdom. The said seven being His Grace Alexander Duke of Hamilton and Brandon, brother of the Handmaiden to her late Majesty of blessed memory, Queen Caroline, and abdicator of his hereditary mansion when it was threatened by the radicals of Glasgow in the year 1819[1]—*secundo* Lieut General the Earl of Rosslynn who holds a law sinecure of £4000 per annum in Scotland[2]—*tertio* the Lord Viscount Glenorchy who considering the structure of his lower person is addicted to wearing his philabeg too short[3]—Old Maule of Panmure "that prince of good fellows and king of old man"[4]—Angus Grant Timber-Feller in Inverness[5]—one Monteith a Lime-merchant in Galloway[6]

[1] Alexander Douglas Hamilton, 10th Duke of Hamilton and 7th Duke of Brandon (1767-1852). His eldest sister, Lady Anne Hamilton, had been Lady in Waiting to Queen Caroline and had been, according to C. K. Sharpe, "very inferior to all the other *Dames.*" (*Correspondence*, II, 93.) On the Radicals' threat to march on Hamilton Palace see Scott's amusing account in a letter to Morritt, 13 Nov. 1819. (*Letters*, VI, 16 and 25.)

[2] James St. Clair-Erskin, 2nd Earl of Rosslyn (1762-1837); Lieut. General, 1805; General, 1814. He was Director of Chancery and this is, presumably, the sinecure office to which Lockhart is alluding. According to a statement made by the Lord Advocate, Sir William Rae, in the House of Commons, March 30, 1824, "the Director of Chancery, with his clerks, might levy fees to any extent he thought proper," but that the commissioners appointed to enquire into the courts of justice of England, Scotland and Ireland, had "recommended, that at the termination of the existing interests in that office, the officers should receive a regular salary." (*Hansard*, N.S. Vol. XI, col. 24.) As there was no salary, Lockhart's "£4000" is probably no more than a guess as to the amount of fees collected by Rosslyn.

[3] John Campbell, 2nd Marquess of Breadalbane (1796-1862). As Lord Glenorchy he sat as M.P. for Okehampton, 1820-26, and as Earl of Ormelie for Perthshire, 1832-34. He became the 2nd Marquess of Breadalbane in 1834.

[4] William Ramsay Maule of Panmure (1771-1852), M.P. for Forfarshire, 1796, 1805-31; created Baron Panmure, 1831. Lockhart's calling him a "prince of good fellows" is an allusion to his well-known convivial habits. The words are slightly altered from the old song "There's auld Rob Morris" which Burns rewrote for Thomson's *Select collection of original Scotish airs.*

[5] John Peter Grant (1774-1848) of Rochiemurchus; Advocate and M.P.; knighted, 1827. The estate of Rochiemurchus is near Inverness and was valuable for its forests — hence the ironical expression "timber-feller in Inverness." See also Lockhart's *Peter's letters*, II, 84-86, and Scott's *Letters*, VI, 329.

[6] Charles Granville Stuart-Menteith (1769-1847); created a Baronet, 1838. He spent large sums developing the estate of Closeburn in Dumfriesshire which his father had purchased in 1783. Lockhart's reference to him as a "lime-merchant" would have been easily understood at the time. "The capacity of his limestone mines was greatly enlarged by the application of water-power; and he bought the estate of Mansfield on the borders of Ayrshire, to enable him to burn his lime at the smallest

— and Gibson, a writer or attorney in Auld Reekie.[7] These are their seven magnates, but even such as they are, they did not obtain the management of this grand meeting. The chair was filled by little Jeffrey, the prating Barrister whose name has been rendered at once infamous and ludicrous by the Edinburgh Review, a man of the lowest possible origin, the son of a Barber who actually walked about the streets of Auld Reekie with his Mambrino under his arm, shaving for a twopenny, and in manners a perfect caricature of vulgar pertness and dapper dandyism[8] — This was the creature whom the longtailed[9] Representative of the House of Hamilton supported upon the occasion. There were many points of contrast between the pair, but in two important particulars they agreed — they both dined in black stocks and they both clipped the King's English[10] — Jeffrey imitating his Grace's costume, and His Grace being infected, we suppose, by the neighbourhood of the hereditary Shaver for Scotland. The Croupier was a sulky looking, crack-voiced Barrister of the name of Moncrieff[11] — a man of no sort of distinction in any way and the Stewards were such folk as "Hot and heavy, Hot and heavy," some-

cost with the coal found on his own property." (C.T. Ramage, *Drumlanrig Castle,* Dumfries, 1876, p. 213.)

[7] James Gibson-Craig (1765-1850). He was a Writer to the Signet, the highest class of solicitor in Scotland, and Lockhart's "writer or attorney" is intended to be derogatory. He was originally James Gibson and on succeeding to Riccarton he assumed the additional name of Craig in 1823. By giving him only his baptismal name in 1825 Lockhart is having another dig at him. He was made a Baronet in 1831.

[8] Francis Jeffrey (1773-1850), editor of the *Edinburgh Review,* 1803-29; Senator of the College of Justice as Lord Jeffrey, 1834. Lockhart's pen-picture of him is almost diabolically clever. The epithet "little" refers to his stature, Jeffrey being short and slightly built. His father, George Jeffrey, had been a Deputy Clerk of the Court of Session but Lockhart apparently knew that the Jeffrey family had been barbers and wigmakers in Edinburgh for several generations and George Jeffrey, in his youth, had no doubt frequented, and may even have assisted in, his father's, and later, his brother's, shop. The reference to the Mambrino reminds us that Lockhart had edited *Don Quixote* in 1822. The reference is to Part I, Bk. III, chap. VIII.

[9] Cf. Scott's "touch not a hair of the long tail of his Grace of Hamilton." (*Letters,* VI, 16.)

[10] The Duke of Hamilton (see Note 1) sat on Jeffrey's right hand. The black stock had been part of the military dress in the eighteenth century but had come to be adopted by bucks and Lockhart's combination of black stocks and clipping the King's English is intended to suggest that they were a couple of dandies. In *Peter's letters* (II, 60) Lockhart had described Jeffrey's pronunciation as "wretched" and as a "mixture of provincial English, and undignified Scotch, altogether snappish and offensive."

[11] James Moncrieff (1776-1851), son of Sir Henry Wellwood Moncrieff, a well-known Church of Scotland clergyman; advocate, 1799; succeeded as 9th Baronet, 1827; Senator of the College of Justice, 1828. Although Lockhart says here that he was "a man of no sort of distinction" he had described him in *Peter's letters* (II, 79) as "the most rising man at the Scottish Bar," but he does say that his voice was "harsh" and "unmusical."

[199]

body of the name of Parlan Macparlan,[12] and another obscure little Barrister who we believe commenced his public life with a towel under his arm.[13] These are the sort of gentry that now take the lead among the Whiggery of this poor certainly, but still proud "Nation of Gentlemen." These are the illustrious statesmen who toast "radical reform," "Catholic Emancipation," Joseph Humbug, [14] and "that illustrious person" — so, God pity them, they absolutely did call him — Lord Archy.[15] These are the sages and moralists who drank the memory of the old gambling and degraded sinner Charles Fox as "the greatest of public and the purest of private men"! (Hear! Hear!) These were the heroes who heard a ci-devant Tea-boy[16] call the allied sovereigns of Europe "a parcel of rascally, swindling, Bandits!" — These — but we must not waste more words upon them. Their dinner is styled "sumptuous" in their own newspapers — and cost, toddy included, 10/6 per patriot.[17]

Only two things occurred to enliven the assemblage of dull democracy — and we must do His Grace of Hamilton the justice to say that even he laughed heartily at them when they were explained to his princely mind. Little Jeffrey, in toasting our friend Joseph of Aberdeen, said that "his greatness was bottomed on the broad basis of Arithmetic," and that "so long as CROKER[18] remained he *would* not be forgotten." Upon this some "Gentleman whose name we could not hear"[19] proposed

---

[12] John McFarlane (1767-1846), advocate. The name Parlan Macparlan was probably taken from Scott's *Rob Roy*. Parlane MacFarlane was Bailie Nicol Jarvie's maternal grandfather. (See chap. 31.)

[13] I have been unable to identify this steward.

[14] Joseph Hume (1777-1855), M.P. At the time of the dinner he was M.P. for the Aberdeen burghs.

[15] Lord Archibald Hamilton (1769-1827), younger brother of the Duke of Hamilton (see Note 1): M.P. He was absent owing to indisposition. His health was proposed by John A. Murray, advocate.

[16] John Boyd Greenshields (d. 1845), advocate; took the name Boyd on succeeding to Drum; his father was John Greenshields, a merchant in Glasgow, who presumably traded in tea.

[17] Actually, tickets cost one guinea each.

[18] John Wilson Croker (1780-1857), M.P. In 1823 a poem entitled "Vacation reminiscences" has appeared in which the following lines occurred:

> Says Joseph Hume, "Though Croker's cuts have made an alter'd man o' me, I'll still be foremost in the throng for preaching up economy."
>
> (*Spirit of the Public Journals for 1823*, p.428)

"Croker" is correct, though there might be an allusion to Cocker whose *Arithmetic* was a famous book. A writer in the *Dublin and London Magazine for 1826* (p. 80), referred to "Mr. Hume's aptitude in applying the simple rules of Cocker to the business of the state."

[19] This was Gilbert Laing Meason of Lindertis (d. 1832); adopted the additional surname Meason; brother of Malcolm Laing, the historian; in Italy in 1832 and met Sir Walter Scott a number of times; died at Rome on 13 August of the same year.

the health of Mr Francis Jeffrey — Mr Francis Jeffrey returned thanks in a speech of EIGHTY-FIVE MINUTES length [20] — sitting down as usual the moment the cramp seized his calf — whereupon up struck the waggish fiddlers

"Scots wha hae wi' Wallace *bled*"

We would say *bleeded* in such a case here, but the other is in the Doric dialect the perfect tense of this verb active.

We had almost forgotten to say that Michael Angelo[21] was present and that Jeffrey proposed his health as "one of the PRACTICAL BENE-FACTORS of his species," the said Jeffrey having dined with the great Michael only a few months back.

Dear Doctor

Accept the above and do as it seemeth good to thee

Yours

J. G. L.

[Addressed to :]
Dr. Maginn
21 Compton Street
Brunswick Square
London
[PM: 28 Jan. 1825.]

[20] Jeffrey's speech, which seems to be verbatim in *The Scotsman* report, consisted of only 121 words!

[21] Michael Angelo Taylor (1757-1834), M.P. In 1825 he represented Durham city.

Barbour, Blind Harry,
and Sir William Craigie

There is no doubt that Blind Harry's *Wallace* has suffered unduly through comparison with Barbour's *Bruce*, but the late Sir William Craigie,[1] in trying to redress the balance, upset it even further in the opposite direction, enhancing the reputation of his favourite only at the expense of denigrating those parts of Barbour's work that are in fact most worthy.

Craigie's evaluation may most conveniently be criticized under the headings of Prologue and Epilogue. Barbour's introduction, in Craigie's opinion, is coldly academic: — "Barbour opens with scholastic remarks on the pleasures of reading and a frigid distinction between truth and fiction."[2] But the opening lines of *The Bruce* are really invaluable as revealing the author's purpose and the light in which he wished his work to be regarded. The poem clearly takes its way from the French medieval romances; if these gave pleasure, reasons Barbour, how much more so would "romances" that described realistically historical persons possessing more interest than shadowy heroes of fiction. And on the other side, there was no reason why history should not aspire to be classed as literature, if presented in a style that was artistically acceptable. "He anticipated Macaulay's ambition in that his history was to differ from the most attractive literary matter only in being true."[3] It is plain that Barbour intended his work to have a two-fold appeal: —

> Than suld storys that suthfast wer,
> And thai war said on gud maner,
> Have doubill plesance in heryng.
> The fyrst plesance is the carpyng,
> And the tothir the suthfastnes
> That schawys the thing rycht as it wes:
> And suth thyngis that ar likand
> Tyll mannys heryng ar plesand.[4]

More to Craigie's taste is the beginning of Harry's poem: — "Blind Harry, on the other hand, plunges at once into the intensely national

[1] W. A. Craigie, "Barbour and Blind Harry as Literature," *The Scottish Review,* XXII (1893), 173-201.

[2] Craigie, p. 180.

[3] *The Bruce,* ed. W. M. Mackenzie (London, 1909), p. xv. All subsequent references are to this edition.

[4] *The Bruce,* I, 3-10.

tone which characterises his whole work. We neglect the noble deeds of our ancestors 'throw very sleuthfulness.' Reading this in the light of Scottish history, we fail to see in it anything but a strong and true expression of patriotic feeling, certainly not a 'ludicrous prejudice': read Barbour himself and see whether his or Harry's tone is most likely to be that of Scottish feeling in general."[5]

In fact, however, the sentiment of the two prologues is the same — "Let us now praise famous men and our fathers that begat us." The difference is that whereas Barbour can still extol the medieval and truly supranational virtue of chivalry,[6] Harry is sufficiently a man of the Renaissance to prize the narrower national quality of patriotism. Indeed, Neilson has shown[7] that Harry's intense nationalism was inspired not so much by the War of Independence itself as by events of the poet's own time.

It is rather misleading of Craigie to suggest that while Barbour requires 476 lines to get really started, Harry requires only 16.[8] At that point, Harry has done no more than complete his *apologia* for writing the work. If this constitutes the prologue, then Barbour requires only 10 more lines to finish his. Many of Barbour's 476 preliminary lines are taken up with historical background, which Harry feels quite as much to be necessary.

There is thus a certain parallelism between the two poets' methods of setting about their work: —

	Barbour	Harry
Prologue (*apologia*)	I, 1-26	I, 1-16
Introduction to the hero	I, 27-36	I, 17-40
Historical background	I, 37-476	I, 41-180

When we turn to Craigie's commentary on the Epilogue, a serious misunderstanding is revealed. After quoting *The Bruce*, XX, 611-617, and *Wallace*, XI, 1451-1458, he continues: — "The feeling of imperfection with which the old man leaves the work of his lifetime to future generations is surely something far finer than Barbour's somewhat conventional desire for the good behavior of his heroes' descendants."[9]

In fact, it is Harry's conclusion that is conventional, not Barbour's. Craigie has apparently failed to recognize the passage he quotes from Harry as a specimen of the literary device known as the *envoy* (cf. James I, *Kingis Quair*, cxciv), in which the author's profession of modesty about

[5] Craigie, p. 181.
[6] *The Bruce*, I, 21-25.
[7] G. Neilson, "Blind Harry's Wallace," *Essays and Studies* I (1910), 109-110.
[8] Craigie, pp. 179, 180.
[9] Craigie, p. 181.

his work had become more or less stereotyped. The lines from *Wallace*, *"Go nobill buk, fulfyllit of gud sentens . . ."* are interesting certainly, but only as a variation within the convention.

Even more common in medieval poetry is the final prayer, which terminates both *The Bruce* and *Wallace*. It was customary for the poet to express the hope that his hero, or he himself along with his readers, might enjoy the bliss of heaven. Lines 612-617 of *The Bruce* Book XX should therefore be considered as part of this prayer. Setting aside, then, the purely conventional termination and considering the conclusion proper (i.e. that which comes between the close of the narrative and the prayer), over against Harry's *envoi* we must place one line of *The Bruce* — *The lordis deit apon this wis* (XX, 611) which for laconic simplicity, hiding deep feeling, is comparable to Thucydides —

$$\tau\alpha\tilde{v}\tau\alpha\ \mu\grave{\epsilon}\nu\ \tau\grave{\alpha}\ \pi\epsilon\rho\grave{\iota}\ \Sigma\iota\kappa\epsilon\lambda\acute{\iota}\alpha\nu\ \gamma\epsilon\nu\acute{o}\mu\epsilon\nu\alpha\ ^{10}$$

This line also serves to refute Craigie's criticism that the poem should have ended with Book XIII after the Battle of Bannockburn.[11] Barbour, mindful of his duties as a historian, concludes not unfittingly with the death of the chief actors in his narrative. It is the passing of an age.

Craigie does not, however, confine his depreciation of *The Bruce* to Prologue and Epilogue. He finds a serious flaw in the lack of an important personage to provide a contrast to the hero, a flaw all the more lamentable because Harry for his part has shown keen literary judgment in providing for this need.[12] Unfortunately, to make such a criticism is to ignore the presence of Edward Bruce, who in Barbour's work provides a consistent contrast to his brother, not only in character, but also in action and its consequences. Edward Bruce was second to none for valour, but lacked moderation: —

> Had he had mesure in his deid,
> I trow that worthyar than he
> Micht nocht in his tyme fundyn be,
> Outakyn his brother anyrly,
> To quhom, in-to gude chevelry,
> I dar peir nane was in his day.
> For he led hym with mesure ay,
> And with gret wit his chevelry
> He governit ay sa worthely,
> That he oft full unlikly thing
> Brocht rycht weill to gud ending.[13]

[10] Thucydides, VII, 87.
[11] Craigie, pp. 179-180.
[12] Craigie, p. 200.
[13] *The Bruce*, IX, 661-671.

His failure to conquer the whole of Ireland is directly attributed to his headstrong will: —

> Couth he haf governit hym throu skill,
> And followit nocht to fast his will,
> Bot with mesour haf led his deid,
> It wes weill lik, withouten dreid,
> That he mycht haff conquerit weill
> The land of Irland everilk deill.
> But his outrageous succudry
> And will, that mar wes than hardy,
> Of purpos letit hym, perfay,
> As I heir-eftir sall yhow say.[14]

Barbour uses this contrast between the two brothers to illustrate his ideal of true leadership, which is not synonymous with animal courage: — "*For, but wit, worschip may nocht be.*"[15] Robert Bruce meets this requirement, Edward Bruce does not.

The temptation to compare the two works, in spite of their differences, is great, because they stand alone in Scottish literature, both on account of scope and of subject matter. Harry too, notwithstanding the literary sophistication of his style, is just as capable as Barbour of producing a direct realism reminiscent of the ballads, as in the account of Wallace's laconic conversation with the boy who had carried food for the five assassins: —

> Than to the chyld sadly agayn he socht.
> "Quhat did thow her?" The child, with paill face,
> On kneis he fell, and askit Wallace grace.
> 'With thaim I was, and knew no thing thair thocht.
> In to service, as thai me bad, I wrocht.'
> "Quhat berys thow her?" 'Bot meit,' the child can say.
> "Do, turss it up, and pass with me away.
> Meit in this tym is fer bettyr than gold."[16]

The archdeacon is probably just as guilty as the minstrel of exaggeration (cf. *The Bruce*, VI, 67-178), but even the sober truth about the patriots' exploits was startling enough, and both the biographers give the same reason for their success — strategy which never allowed the enemy to strike the first blow, which involved speed of movement, avoidance of pitched battles, and recognized the value of a *strenth*.[17]

Such comparison is legitimate for the purpose of evaluation; but to go further and praise one at the expense of the other is to ignore the fact

[14] *The Bruce*, XVI, 321-330.
[15] *The Bruce*, VI, 358.
[16] *Wallace*, ed. J. Moir (Edinburgh, 1889), XI, 632-639.
[17] *The Bruce*, IX, 632-635; *Wallace*, VII, 1135-1136, IX, 828.

that the poems belong to two different ages, two different genres. There is no need to search for an expressly-formulated theme, such as the triumph of freedom, in *The Bruce*. The narrative by itself illustrates the chivalric concept of nobility and honour, so that Barbour can with perfect propriety intervene to censure his own hero when he transgresses that code by the sin of sacrilege in slaying Comyn at the high altar of the Friars' Kirk: —

> He mysdyd thar gretly, but wer,
> That gave na gyrth to the awter.
> Tharfor sa hard myscheiff him fell,
> That Ik herd nevir in romanys tell
> Off man sa hard frayit as wes he,
> That eftirwart com to sic bounte.[18]

Harry, on the other hand, preoccupied with the patriotism of his own day, does not blame Wallace for inconsistency in killing his own follower Fawdoun who lagged behind, but rather attempts to justify him (*Wallace*, V, 107-122). As a narrator, he disclaims all moral prejudice in the matter, merely suggesting that in time of national peril one cannot afford to take chances with people of doubtful loyalty.

Nevertheless, though disregarding convention in one respect, Harry shows himself extremely sensitive to it in another, when he anticipates the possible criticism that his principal character was not a man of high degree and therefore unsuited for the part he had to play: —

> Wallace a lord he may be clepyt weyll,
> Thocht ruryk folk tharoff haff litill feill;
> Na deyme na lord bot landis be thair part.
> Had he the warld, and be wrachit off hart,
> He is no lord as to the worthiness;
> It can nocht be, but fredome, lordlyknes.[19]

— an interesting facet in the history of the attributes of the hero in literature.

IAN C. WALKER
UNIVERSITY OF ABERDEEN

---

[18] *The Bruce*, II, 43-48.
[19] *Wallace*, VII, 397-402.

Reviews

Robert Donald Thornton. *James Currie: The Entire Stranger and Robert Burns.* Edinburgh and London. Oliver & Boyd. 1963. 459 pp. 63 shillings.

This book is primarily a biographical study of the Liverpool physician Dr. James Currie, the "entire stranger" who became the official biographer of Burns and the editor of *The Works of Robert Burns* (Liverpool, 1800), the first comprehensive collection of Burns's poems, songs, and letters. Additionally, Professor Thornton includes a fresh interpretation of the last eight years of Burns's life which will be of interest to all serious students of the poet.

Looked at simply as a biography of Currie this is an admirable piece of work, showing the results of a great deal of careful research. Thornton gives us vivid and interesting pictures of Currie's childhood as a poor Scots lad in Dumfriesshire, of his five years in Virginia as an apprentice to a Glasgow tobacco firm, of the medical fraternity in Edinburgh and then in Liverpool, of Currie's rise to the top of his profession in Liverpool, and of his achievements as a writer of treatises on medicine and politics. The amazingly popular biography and edition of Burns, undertaken by Currie without pay in the last decade of his life, was the capstone of a distinguished career. And throughout this career, the author makes abundantly clear, Currie was plagued by chronic illness, the lingering and debilitating consumption which finally killed him at the age of forty-nine. The portrait which Professor Thornton draws is an enthusiastic, but on whole a convincing one, of James Currie as a basically good and courageous man of exceptional abilities.

In style, the book is generally vigorous and readable, but it suffers from occasional lack of clarity. Though I read the opening chapters with more than usual care, I found myself quite confused by Thornton's account of Currie's welter of family connections in Dumfriesshire. These relationships, it is true, are clarified by a set of genealogical tables in an appendix, but the description in the text could, I think, be clearer than it is. Here and there are heavy-footed passages like the following comment on the conflict in Currie between desire to serve humanity and need to conserve his waning strength: "An unkept promise became a hope defeated; a passing remark on indolence, inner recognition of lethargy out of sickness; procrastination, an hour gained for treatment. Every denial made further volition more insistent, but also more hazardous." But such labored sentences are exceptional; for the most part the book is well and interestingly written.

Readers will, I think, find little to quibble with and much to be thankful for in Dr. Thornton's portrait of Currie as a man. But the long chapter on Burns is quite another matter and is certain to arouse heated controversy. Here, it seems to me, the author goes overboard in an attempt to justify Currie. It would appear that Thornton has become a devoted admirer of his man to such an extent that he feels obliged to defend Currie's views at every point, and does so at the expense of Burns. Currie, in his biography of Burns, interpreted the last years of the poet's life in Dumfries as a period of pathetic decadence in which Burns's creative powers declined sharply and he gradually sank into the grave as a hopeless drunkard. This view of Burns's Dumfries years was fixed in the public mind by Currie's account for over a century. Not until 1932 was this idea effectively challenged, by Franklin B. Snyder in his admirable *Life of Robert Burns,* still the best biography of the poet. Snyder convincingly rejected Currie's assertion that Burns drank himself to death, arguing that Currie was biased by fanatically anti-alcoholic views, and concluding on the basis of modern medical diagnoses that the poet died of rheumatic heart trouble reaching back into his teens. Furthermore, Snyder interpreted Burns's last years not as a decadent phase, but rather as one of steady creativity and relative happiness. Since Snyder's book, modern Burns scholars have generally accepted his view of the poet's last years. Now Dr. Thornton wishes to reverse this trend and wants us to believe, despite the findings of twentieth-century scholarship, that Currie was right after all.

In one way Thornton's treatment of this subject is salutary since the generally accepted view of Burns's Dumfries period needs some modification. At least his book will reopen the whole question for further study. But most Burns students will feel that he has gone much too far. Let us look briefly at two or three of the main issues.

When James Currie was selected in 1796 as the official biographer of Burns, he modestly protested that he had been an "entire stranger" to the poet, but accepted anyway. Dr. Thornton attempts to dismiss, or at least to minimize, this plain statement by Currie. He points out that Currie was born in and deeply attached to Dumfriesshire; that he had dozens of relatives and friends there, some of whom had contacts with Burns; that he owned two estates in the shire. But the fact remains, as Thornton's own book makes clear, that Currie *was* indeed an "entire stranger" to Burns. Currie lived all of his adult life in Liverpool, visiting the Dumfries area for brief periods only three times in twenty-five years. He met Burns face to face only once for a few minutes in a casual encounter on the streets of Dumfries. What does it matter that Currie owned land in the shire? He never lived there after childhood days; *he did not know Burns personally*. His biography was composed chiefly on the basis of the letters and papers of Burns sent to him in Liverpool by John Syme, supplemented by additional personal information from Syme and Gilbert Burns. Through no fault of his own Currie's sources of information were severely limited. The extent to which he was reduced to mere guesswork is shown by his wholly unfounded insinuation that Burns had contracted venereal disease — "He who suffers the pollution of inebriation, how shall he escape other pollution? But let us refrain from the mention of errors over which delicacy and humanity draw the veil." This is an innuendo which Snyder has once and for all time flattened and disproved. Its phrasing suggests that Currie, despite his admirable qualities, was something of a prig.

Once again in support of Currie's view of the Dumfries years Thornton tends to underrate Burns's literary productivity in this final phase of his career. He is of course right in asserting that Burns in this period failed to equal the poetic achievements of 1785 and 1786; Burns never again attained the white heat of creativity of those two wonderful years. But his production in the last years was steady and copious, with no real signs of exhaustion. No doubt he wrote too much, as most established poets are apt to do; yet a man who can compose as superb a lyric as "Oh wert thou in the cauld blast" virtually on his deathbed can hardly be said to be fizzling out as a creative artist.

On the drinking question Thornton disposes of the notion that Currie was a temperance fanatic by showing that the good doctor himself indulged through most of his adult life. How then are we to explain Currie's seemingly rabid attitude in his biography of Burns where he sounds like a bigoted teetotaler, referring to drinking in such terms as "this detestable habit"? The answer perhaps lies in Thornton's own book. Currie, in the last decade of his life was forced to give up drinking, largely or wholly, because of his tubercular condition. For him any substantial indulgence became suicidal. If, then, Currie jumped to the conclusion that Burns's condition was similar to his own, what would be more natural than for him to assume that Burns's drinking drove him into an early grave? Also, Currie's own experience in the latter part of his life may well have brought about a change in his attitude as a medical man toward the "detestable habit" which he had formerly enjoyed.

At any rate, Professor Thornton sets out to show that Currie was largely right in his treatment of the devastating effects of drink upon the poet. He piles up evidence from the letters to show this. But it should be noted that by careful selection one can prove almost anything from the letters of as complex a personality as Burns. It would be easy to demonstrate from the letters, for instance, that Burns was a religious zealot, or that he was an arch conservative. All one has to do is pick the right passages and ignore all evidence to the contrary. No one doubts that Burns drank more in his last years than earlier in his life, or that he sometimes drank more than was good for him, or that his drinking occasionally got him into trouble; but that the habit was as disastrous to him as Currie and Thornton suggest is dubious indeed. Currie, in his edition, mangled many of Burns's letters, sometimes out of "delicacy," but also sometimes (and less forgivably) in order to support his interpretation of the facts. Dr. Thornton never does this, of course, but many will feel that he too readily ignores or brushes aside evidence on the other side of the question. As a result, his analysis is less than convincing.

On the positive side this book provides useful information, some of it new, on several of Burns's associates in the Dumfries area. Dr. Thornton is especially good on Robert Riddell and Francis Grose, and he throws valuable new lights on the whole provincial world of Dumfriesshire in which Burns lived out the last eight years of his life. He succeeds in creating a more vivid and better documented impression of what it was like to live in that world than has hitherto been available. Thus, whether one agrees or disagrees with Professor Thornton's interpretation of Burns, this challenging biography of James Currie is a major contribution to Burns scholarship.

ALLAN H. MacLAINE
UNIVERSITY OF RHODE ISLAND

STUDIES IN SCOTTISH LITERATURE

VOLUME I   NUMBER 4   APRIL 1964

CONTENTS

STUDIES IN SCOTTISH LITERATURE

EDITED BY G. ROSS ROY
TEXAS TECHNOLOGICAL COLLEGE

STUDIES IN SCOTTISH LITERATURE is an
independent quarterly devoted to all aspects of
Scottish literature. Articles and notes are welcome.
Subscriptions are available at $5.00 U.S. per annum in the
United States and Canada, elsewhere 30 shillings.
All communications should be addressed to the
Editor, Department of English, Texas Technological College,
Lubbock, Texas, U.S.A.

PUBLISHED BY TEXAS TECHNOLOGICAL COLLEGE
AND PRINTED BY THE TEXAS TECH PRESS
LUBBOCK, TEXAS, U.S.A.

EDITORIAL

In this day of specialization dictionaries play a particularly important role. There is a dictionary for almost anything—slang, underworld talk, even "beatnick" jargon has been considered worthy of a small dictionary. And yet there is still no adequate dictionary of Scots.

Scottish dictionaries have already been published, of course, notably John Jamieson's *Etymological Dictionary of the Scottish Language* (1808, 1825; and revised reprints). But the idea of what a dictionary should be changes with the times, and the *Oxford English Dictionary* altered the entire concept of dictionaries. It was, in fact, at the suggestion of the co-editor of the *OED*, Sir William Craigie, that work was begun under Craigie's own editorship on the *Dictionary of the Older Scottish Tongue*, a record of the Scottish language down to the Union of Parliaments (1707). The *DOST* is part of Craigie's plan to supplement the *OED* with a series of dictionaries for each of the main periods in English and Scots. In addition to the *DOST* the *Scottish National Dictionary*, under the editorship of William Grant, was commenced to cover the period 1700 to date. The first part of both dictionaries appeared in 1931, both are now up to the letter *M*, or about half completed. The expected date of their completion is 1973.

Since their inception the cost of producing these works has soared with no corresponding increase in revenue from their sale. The *DOST* and the *SND* are sold as sets at the price current when the purchase is agreed upon; ironically the early enthusiasm shown by libraries and individuals in subscribing to the dictionaries now means that later parts must be furnished at a fraction of their actual cost, although many of these subscribers have made voluntary additional contributions to help defray the increased cost of publication. Adjustments have, of course, been made in the price to new subscribers based on current costs, but past events give little hope that these costs will prevail when the final volumes go to press. At present, for instance, the *SND* requires an additional £30,000 to complete its work.

Since 1952 the Scottish Dictionaries Joint Council, consisting of the Scottish universities, the Cargenie Trust for the Universities of Scotland, and the Scottish National Dictionary Association, has co-ordinated the work of the dictionaries under the able editorship of A. J. Aitken of the *DOST* and D. D. Murison of the SND. Premises on George Square are supplied by the University of Edinburgh, appropriately beside the School of Scottish Studies. Continuing contributions are made by these bodies; in addition there have been sizeable donations in the past by the Rockefeller Foundation, the Chicago University Press, the Burns Federation, the Educational Institute of Scotland, as well as certain Scottish burghs.

But this is not nearly enough. Hundreds of dedicated voluntary workers have collected about 2 million quotations for use in the dictionaries. Trained professional workers are needed to use this material, getting it ready for publication. Grants and subscriptions are urgently required. Our readers should do all in their power to enable both these great dictionaries to meet their target date for completion.

CONTRIBUTORS
TO THIS ISSUE

Laurence L. BONGIE: Associate Professor in the Department of Romance Studies at the University of British Columbia. B.A., University of British Columbia; Doctorat d'Université, University of Paris, with a thesis on Hume in France. Has published studies of the continental reception of Hume's work and thought in *French Studies* and an article on Voltaire in *Modern Language Quarterly*. A monograph on Hume and the French Counter-Revolution has been accepted for publication by the Oxford University Press.

William GILLIS: Chairman of the Department of English at Bradley University. He took his A.M. degree at Boston University and, after further graduate work there, transferred to the University of Edinburgh where he took his Ph.D., with a thesis on Fergusson. Editor of *The Unpublished Poems of Robert Fergusson* and author of articles on literature, history, education, and foreign languages.

Rev. John MACKECHNIE: Has been for many years actively engaged in research in the various Celtic languages, the history, traditions, etc. of all the Celtic peoples. He has been Assistant in the Department of Celtic at Glasgow University and has acted as Interim-Professor of Celtic languages at Edinburgh University. His published works include *Instructio Pie Vivendi et Superna Meditandi* (2 vol., Irish Texts Soc.), *Beinn Dorain*, the highly popular *Gaelic Without Groans*, and the *Dewar MSS.*, Vol. I. He now holds the pisition of Reader in Celtic Languages at the University of Aberdeen.

Toshio NAMBA: Born in Osaka, educated at Osaka Music Academy and Nihon University. Has lived in Tokyo since 1937 where he has worked in educational circles. At present Assistant Professor in the Department of English Language and Literature at Nihon University. In addition to the articles and books on Burns mentioned in the text of his article, is author of *A Study of English Grammar* (1955) and *English Conversation in our Daily Life* (1963).

ROBERT FERGUSSON, 1750 - 1774

WILLIAM GILLIS

An Authentic Fergusson Portrait

A new portrait of the 18th century Scots poet Robert Fergusson, recently acquired by the Scottish National Portrait Gallery, is undoubtedly an authentic likeness painted from life. Its discovery dispels almost a century and a half of uncertainty. Mr. H. Cooke of Hitchen, Hertfordshire, brought the portrait to light. Late in the 19th century it had been purchased by his father, and in 1935, after his father's death, it went to Mr. Cooke's home. Not until 1960 did he see an inscription on the reverse in an early 19th century hand identifying the subject as Fergusson and the painter as Alexander Runciman.

Authentication of the portrait rests upon three factors: (1) internal evidence; (2) biographical evidence; and (3) its relationship to other hitherto questionable portraits of the poet.

I. Internal Evidence

Since we know that Fergusson was painted by Runciman, the attribution of this portrait to him is of first importance. In a letter to me the Director of the Scottish National Portrait Gallery, Mr. R. Hutchison, offers as much confirmation that Runciman painted it as is possible: "We are reasonably convinced that this is a Runciman. The painting is very like his work, but without additional evidence it is difficult to be *absolutely* certain." He has further pointed out that the brush stroke appears to be Runciman's.

As I shall show later, the portrait is perhaps a study for a series of religious paintings undertaken by Runciman. The artist may have taken some artistic liberty with his subject, romanticizing Fergusson's appearance for his own purposes. Contemporary descriptions allow only a vague comparison of Fergusson's actual appearance with the portrait.

> His forehead was elevated, and his whole countenance open and pleasing. He wore his own fair brown hair, with a massive curl along each side of the head, and terminating in a queue, dressed with a black silk riband. (Robert Chambers, *Lives of Illustrious and Distinguished Scotsmen.* (Glasgow, 1832-1835), II, p. 304.)

*   *   *

Fergusson was in his person, rather slender; his countenance expressed the vivacity of penetrative genius, yet modesty was mingled in his glance. (Alexander Campbell, *An Introduction to the History of Poetry in Scotland.* (Edinburgh, 1798), p. 300.)

* * *

The personal appearance of Fergusson is described as interesting and genteel, although not peculiarly handsome... ([Alexander Peterkin], *The Works of Robert Fergusson.* (London, 1807), p. 73.)

* * *

As to his person, he was about the middle stature, and of a slender make. His countenance, which in other respects had a tendency toward effeminacy, was rendered highly animated by the expression of his large black eyes. (David Irving, *The Poetical Works of Robert Fergusson.* (Glasgow, 1800), p. 18.)

* * *

He was in person about five feet, six inches high, and well shaped. His complexion fair, but rather pale. His eyes full, black, and piercing. His nose long, his lips thin, his teeth well set and white. His neck long, and well proportioned. His shoulders narrow, and his limbs long, but more sinewy than fleshy. (Thomas Sommers, *The Life of Robert Fergusson.* (Edinburgh, 1803), p. 45.)

Only some of this material is pertinent to the authentication of the newly discovered portrait, though its relevance will be evident in further discussion.

II. Biographical Evidence

Our first source of biographical evidence is Thomas Sommers' *The Life of Robert Fergusson*, in which he recounts the poet's first meeting with Runciman:

...That artist was... painting in his own house in the Pleasance, a picture on a half length cloth, of the *Prodigal Son*, in which his fancy and pencil had introduced every necessary object and circumstance suggested by the sacred passage. At his own desire, I called to see it; — I was much pleased with the *composition,* — *colouring,* and admirable *effect* of the piece, at least what was done of it; but expressed my surprise, at observing a large space in the centre, exhibiting nothing but chalk outlines of a human figure. He informed me that he had reserved that space for the *Prodigal,* but could not find a young man whose personal form, and expressive features, were such as he could approve of, and commit to the canvas. *Robert Fergusson's* face and figure, instantly occurred to me: Not from an idea, that Fergusson's real character was that of the *Prodigal;* by no means; but, on account of his sprightly humour, personal appearance, and striking features. I asked Mr. Runciman, if he knew the poet? — He answered in the negative, but that he had often read and admired his Poems. That evening at five, I appointed to meet with him and the Poet, in a tavern, Parliament close; — we did so; and I introduced him. The painter was much pleased, both with his figure and conversation. I intimated to Fergusson the nature of the business on which we met; — he agreed to sit next forenoon — I accompanied him for that purpose, and in a few days, the picture strikingly exhibited the Bard in the character of a *prodigal,* sitting on a grassy bank, surrounded by *swine,* some of which were sleeping, and others feeding; his right leg over his left knee; eyes uplifted, hands clasped, tattered clothes, and with expressive countenance bemoaning his forlorn, and miserable condition! This picture when finished, reflected high honour on the painter, being much admired. It was sent to the Royal Exhibition in London, where it was also highly esteemed, and there purchased by a gentleman of taste and fortune at a considerable price. I have often expressed a wish to see a print from it, but never had that pleasure; as it exhibited a *portrait* of my favourite Bard, which for *likeness, colouring,* and *expression,* might have done honour to the taste, and pencil of a *Sir Joshua Reynolds.*[1]

The meeting took place in mid-1772. Sommers errs a little in this account, for the painting sent to the Royal Exhibition was not the one he describes: it is catalogued as "Luke XV, 20-21" and therefore must have been a painting of the Prodigal's Return. There are two extant copies of the Return, one in the possession of the Honorable Steven Runciman and the other in an altarpiece in St. Patrick's Church in Edinburgh. Though these pictures differ considerably, the figure of the Prodigal is the same in both, and therefore we can assume that Runciman used the same model for the whole Prodigal series he is said to have painted.

The person depicted as the Prodigal is a robust young man, chiefly distinguished for his muscular, unstarved appearance. Although no portrait of the poet resembles the Prodigal, Sommers maintained it was the best likeness he had seen. On his testimony a portrait based on one of the Prodigal series (Lord Runciman's) was engraved for the 1821 edition of the poet's works (edited by James Gray); another impression from the same plate was sold separately.[2]

But one authoritative dissent to Sommers' opinion of the portrait is in John Kay's *Portraits:* "The engraving was shown to the late Robert Pitcairn, Esq. Keeper of the Register of Probative Writs, who was well acquainted with Fergusson, but he could trace no resemblance to the poet."[3]

I can suggest an explanation for this uncertainty. Sommers did not know Fergusson as well as he claimed to, for major errors and inconsistencies appear in his biography of the poet. Thus his accuracy must always be questioned. Sommers was also recalling the painting 29 years after the poet's death. While we do not doubt that Runciman painted Fergusson and that he at least considered him in 1772 as a possible model

[1] Thomas Sommers, *The Life of Robert Fergusson* (Edinburgh, 1803), pp. 23-26.

[2] Also reprinted in *The Poetical Works of Robert Fergusson,* ed. Robert Ford (Paisley, 1905), p. xliii.

[3] John Kay, *A Series of Original Portraits and Caricature Etchings* (Edinburgh, 1838), II, p. 239.

for his Prodigal series — and may have used him, for the artist can be quite free in his conceptions — we have too little evidence to take the Prodigal as a good likeness. Can it be that Sommers saw an artist's sketch, that is, our newly discovered portrait, and then saw a free use of it in the series? Can it be that he confused the two?

My conclusion is that Runciman painted Fergusson's head hastily, trying to see in the poet his concept of the Prodigal (hence the thick neck and the emphasized sensitivity in the eyes as in the Prodigal series). Having painted his series and having no further use for the portrait, he presented it to Fergusson. Mr. Hutchison's comments tend to substantiate this conclusion:

> Our portrait is probably a study rather than a finished picture. Those portraits of Runciman's that do survive are carefully composed and with more space used round the head.

> Our painting is on paper mounted on a board, which adds weight to the idea that it is a sketch. The head, which is not complete, gives the impression that it was done in one sitting.

III. Relations To Other Portraits[4]

While other portraits of Fergusson all differ considerably one from the other, the new portrait, which I shall hereafter refer to as the Runciman portrait, bears a strong relationship to most of them. I shall designate them as Portraits A, B, C, D, and E.

A. The Runciman portrait must have been the model for the engraving which appeared in the first issue of the 1782 edition of Fergusson's poems (published August 1781).[5] The "Codicile" to Fergusson's poetical will could explain how it came to the publisher, Thomas Ruddiman, son of Walter Ruddiman, who first printed Fergusson's poems in his *Weekly Magazine*:

> To WALTER RUDDIMAN, whose pen
> Still screen'd me from the *Dunce's Den*,
> I leave of PHIZ a picture, saving
> To him the freedom of engraving
> Therefrom a copy, to embellish,
> And give his work a smarter relish . . .

Obviously Runciman had given the portrait to Fergusson and, while the poem is nothing more than fun in the Villon tradition, it reminded

---

[4] Portraits A, D, and E in this discussion appear in Ford's edition of the poems and in *Robert Fergusson 1750-1774, Essays by Various Hands to Commemorate the Bicentenary of his birth*, ed. Sydney Goodsir Smith (Edinburgh, 1952).

[5] And if not, the following argument does not suffer, for the subject of the Runciman portrait is obviously the same as that of the 1782 portrait, and here I wish only to assert the fact that it is Fergusson depicted in both and to recreate the history surrounding the portraits.

Thomas Ruddiman that there was a portrait to be borrowed from the Fergusson family. He must have had an engraving made from it for his edition of the poems.

But Ruddiman cancelled the engraving in the second issue of the poems. John A. Fairley[6] has suggested that the cancellation was made because the portrait was a caricature and Fergusson's family objected to it. I think Fairley was partly right. The family may well have objected to this rather horrid pig-like production; and Fergusson's mother had obviously consulted with Ruddiman about other materials in the 1782 volume. The engraving, however, is no caricature; it is simply a bad job of engraving from the Runciman portrait or another sketch. Basic features are the same. The poet is depicted as having a long nose and strikingly large eyes, a peculiar ear lobe and upper lip, a massive curl at the side of his face, and a heavy jaw. Besides these telling features, he has white, or greying, hair. This feature is explained in the 1805 edition (Edinburgh) of his works: "His hair was almost pure white," a characteristic perhaps true of him just before his death. The engraver may have known Fergusson in those last days.

Because the engraving from the Runciman portrait had been botched, Ruddiman sought another portrait (or, a bare possibility, the same one for re-engraving) for the second issue of the 1782 edition. He wrote James Cummyng, heraldic painter and friend of Fergusson:

> Tho. Ruddiman's Compliments to Mr Cummyng. Begs he would look among his Papers for a Quarto Book of Drawings which T. R. left with Mr. C. some months ago. — It contains a sketch of the likeness of R. Fergusson, whose works T. R. has nearly ready for Publication and wishes to have his head engraved with all speed — If Mr. C. will leave the Book with his Son, T. R. will send for it this afternoon.
> Tuesday—
> 7 May 1782 [this last in Cummyng's hand][7]

In another letter, dated a week later, Thomas Ruddiman again urged Cummyng with the words, "The want of Fergusson's Head is an infinite Loss to us at present.—"[8] Obviously Cummyng was not sufficiently stirred to send it along in time for inclusion in the second issue of the 1782 edition and that portrait is perhaps lost; it can hardly have been the Runciman portrait.

Despite the cancellation of the 1782 engraving, new engravings were made from it for a number of editions of Fergusson's works. The

[6] John A. Fairley, *Robert Fergusson, The Published Portraits* (Aberdeen, 1932), pp. 4, 5.

[7] Edinburgh University MS. La. II 334/3.

[8] *Ibid.*

more ridiculous elements were refined, but it was not much improved. One of Fergusson's editors, David Irving, who knew the poet's family, declared that these later engravings were "suppositious." Re-engravings appeared in the editions of 1788 and 1800. Later A. B. Grosart, Fergusson's most dedicated biographer and editor before Matthew P. McDiarmid, found a "private copper-plate" of it[9] in the hands of the Ruddiman family, had that re-engraved and improved, and placed it in each of his four editions. Grosart's "private copper-plate" must have been the one used for the first issue of the 1782 edition, though he could not recognize this because he had not seen a copy of that volume. Grosart wrote to David Laing, Director of the Signet Library, on the matter of portraits and Laing was able to find substantiation for the copperplate.

> Robert Fergusson the Poet [Laing's hand]
> Mem. Mr. Spence thought the portrait with the pen in hand the best likeness, but allowed every one of the rest, except the miserable copy of the above, to be more or less like also.
> With Mr Chambers' compts.[10]

The "miserable copy" may have been any one of the imitations of the original engraving, but it was probably that of the 1788 Morison edition of the works. Further attestations to the likeness were made, says Grosart, by Miss Ruddiman, Professor Vilant of St. Andrews, and Mr. Howden, a jeweller. These attestations, however, probably related to any of the portraits of the 1782 "series" (i.e., the original engraving and any of its copies), since Professor Vilant, we know, had approved the portrait in the St. Andrews edition of 1800. It should be remembered that all of these people were very old at the time they gave testimony and may not have remembered Fergusson particularly well — just as Sommers seems to have forgotten him. But all in all, this series, most likely started from the Runciman portrait, which the series resembles, has a good basis for authentication as a likeness of Fergusson.

B. In the 1800 Glasgow edition of the works, edited by David Irving, is a stippled engraving of the poet. It bears little resemblance to the 1782 engraving or any of its successors, but yet it reminds us strongly of the Runciman portrait. Drawn by I. Denholm and engraved by K. MacKenzie, it is connected with the next portrait to be discussed.

C. We know that the lack of an available portrait led Alexander Peterkin, editor of the 1807 edition (Edinburgh and London) of the works, to use a portrait for which the poet's sister, Margaret Duvall,

---

[9] *The Works of Robert Fergusson with Life of the Author and an Essay on his Genius and Writings*, ed. A. B. Grosart (Edinburgh, 1851), p. xi.

[10] Edinburgh University MS. La. II 334/5.

had posed. She is said to have resembled her brother closely. Upon seeing the engraving, we note the resemblance to the Runciman portrait, and this leads immediately to the question: is the newly discovered portrait actually an artist's study of Margaret Duvall painted expressly for engraving? It is unlikely. Closer observation reveals rather the effeminate features of a handsome Scotswoman than those of a man, however delicate and sensitive appearing he may have been. Then, turning back to the Irving portrait, we become fairly certain that the Irving engraving and the 1807 engraving came from the same original. Irving must have arranged for Denholm to paint the sister: he knew the family. He had been unable to find an authentic portrait. But for our purposes the authenticity of these engravings is not the question. The sister resembled the brother. Engravings of her resemble the subject of the Runciman portrait. This tends to substantiate the identification of the subject as Fergusson.

D. Fergusson was a member of the Cape Club and it was the practice of the club to dub each member with a facetious title of knighthood: Sir Toe, Sir Cape, etc. On the back of each Cape Club membership petition a club artist, or artists, sketched something illustrative of the knight's title. Usually Runciman is credited with the sketches, although another artist, James Cummyng, was also a member of the club. The masterful work of Runciman seems most prevalent. In the club Fergusson was Sir Precenter and on the back of his petition is a line drawing of a long, thin, woebegone person seated and holding a book, obviously a song book. The nose is long and the chin heavy. This sketch is far below the quality of Runciman's petition drawings and reminds us more of the sketches of James Cummyng. This "portrait" has been reproduced a number of times, the first time in 1823. Since it is a cartoon, it is too slight to compare with the Runciman portrait for purposes of authentication.

E. While Grosart had very assuredly stated that his copperplate "faithfully — literally represents the poet,"[11] in 1897 he changed his mind and vouched for a painting of Fergusson he had found in the possession of the Raeburn family. The tradition of this painting was that Runciman had painted it and had given it to Sir Henry Raeburn. (It is now in the Scottish National Portrait Gallery.) The story is enticing, for Raeburn was 19 when Fergusson died and must have seen him. But the portrait was not painted by Runciman. It is not his style; it does not show his considerable skill. Nevertheless Grosart published the portrait.

[11] Grosart, Works, p. xii.

But what can be said in its defense as a portrait of Fergusson? The Raeburn tradition, if partially mistaken, must be regarded as strong evidence. It may have been given to Raeburn by Runciman; it could have been the work of one of his students. It was painted c. 1770 and it depicts a person with the physical characteristics of Fergusson: long nose, heavy chin, brownish grey hair. The hair is the color of a lock of Fergusson's hair preserved in the National Library of Scotland. The eyes are large, the lips full; the general impression is of a young, though haggard, sensitive person.

If the authenticity of the portrait must rest upon its origin, I can make a conjecture. The 1821 Deas edition of the poems presents a plausible explanation: "There were two portraits of Fergusson finished, one by the celebrated Runciman, the other by Mr. Fyfe, North Bridge, Edinburgh; but it is feared both of these are now lost."[12] Perhaps the Raeburn portrait then can be attributed to "Mr Fyfe." Who was he? One Fyfe was a Cape Club member, but there is no evidence he was an artist. Whoever he was, the portrait is a bad minor work which we cannot assign to Runciman.

As with the Cape Club petition cartoon, a comparison of the Runciman portrait with the Raeburn portrait does not serve for authentication. The only connection between the two is the common depiction of some basic features.

*　　*　　*

That the Runciman portrait was, in fact, painted by Runciman rests upon uncertain evidence of technique in the painting itself and upon the sometimes unreliable memories of Thomas Sommers. That it is a likeness is more certain. Portraits A, B, and C bear a resemblance to it. Portrait A has a strong testimony in its favor as a likeness and it was perhaps engraved from the Runciman portrait, which it resembles strongly. Portrait C (of Margaret Duvall) has a certain contemporary validity as a likeness and this, in turn, appears closest to portrait B, perhaps also taken from a painting of Mrs. Duvall. The subject in B and C resembles the subject in the Runciman portrait. Portraits D and E are of no use in authenticating the Runciman portrait, but we know the first to be a portrait of Fergusson, and the features depicted in the second lead us to the conclusion that it is a portrait of Fergusson. Little doubt can exist that the Scottish National Portrait Gallery now has an authentic likeness of Robert Fergusson by the hand of a competent artist.

BRADLEY UNIVERSITY

[12] *The Poems of Robert Fergusson with a Life of the Author, and Remarks on his genius and writings,* ed. James Gray (London, 1821), p. xi.

JOHN MACKECHNIE

The Gaelic Manuscripts in Scotland

Gaelic MSS.[1] were, as shall appear in the sequel, being written in the Highlands and Islands of Scotland down into the first half of the 18th century. The 1745 Rising and the deliberate destruction of the great houses, e.g. that of Glengarry,[2] of Ardsheil and of Keppoch, together with the furious burning and wasting of the countryside almost achieved the end the then Government had in mind, the obliteration of both the Gaelic people and their language. Possession of a Gaelic MS., especially in the disturbed areas, during the troubles of the '45, would be most dangerous. Thus it is that such a great family as that of Mackintosh of Mackintosh does not now possess a single Gaelic MS. although one might well have expected to find many in a house so famed for its zeal in the Gaelic cause. The survival of tattered fragments of a Campbell, a MacLeod and a Mackinnon Duanaire points to something of what did once exist in the great houses but of which the owners had to get rid if they would live in the new Scotland.

The flight of the most enterprising Gaelic people from the Highlands and the Islands left a country empty and impoverished and a people dispirited and listless with no ear for the poetry of old, no heart for the tales of the past. Yet some people did treasure both tale and poem and John Dewar found in the mid 19th century as did also Alexander Carmichael — both once acting under the guidance of J. F. Campbell of Islay — that all was not gone and the Dewar MSS. in Inveraray Castle as well as the great bulk of Carmichael papers in the Carmichael-Watson Collection in

---

[1] All MSS. here recorded I have read and catalogued, many being catalogued for the first time. This task would have been impossible had it not been for the help given so ungrudgingly by the Carnegie Trustees and the keepers of the various collections of MSS. This help I gratefully acknowledge.

[2] J. H. Forbes, Edinburgh, in a letter dated 20th June, 1806, to Sir John Sinclair (NLS. 73.2.11(35)) says that the Glengarry papers taken from Glengarry House were examined by Sir Edward Fawkener, Secretary to the Duke of Cumberland, at Fort Augustus and then taken to London to be used as evidence against Glengarry. Sir John Sinclair in an endeavour to find those papers got into touch with William Blake, Deputy Keeper at the Treasury, (NLS. 73.2.11(38)) but neither then nor since has anything more been heard of them.

Edinburgh are 20th century harvestings not unlike those in Ireland when Lebor na hUidhre (1106) and the Book of Leinster (1160) were compiled.

It is in the National (once the Advocates') Library, Edinburgh, and in the Library of the University there that the main collections of Gaelic MSS., especially the vellum, now lie. Glasgow, although said to be "the most Gaelic city in the world," houses in the University Library the MacLagan Collection (MacLagan was contemporary with James Macpherson of Ossianic fame), the Fernaig MSS. (1688-1693), the Ratisbon MS. together with a great mass of material belonging to the end of the 19th and the beginning of the 20th century. In the Register House, Edinburgh, are to be found the MacDonald Charter (1408), a Contract of Fosterage dated 1614 and a MS. containing an Elegy on Sir Duncan Campbell of Glenorchy (1631). What is probably the oldest Gaelic writing in the country lies in the Abbey at Fort Augustus, marginal notes on a MS. of Marianus Scotus, Abbot of St. Peter's, Regensburg (1028-1082).

James Macpherson ("Ossian Macpherson") is one to whom we are indebted for the survival of many Gaelic MSS. He had had no intention of doing anything like this. He merely published in a style that proved attractive tales that he had heard around his father's fireside in his youth and John Dewar mentioned above found a century later in Macpherson's native district old tales still surviving. The bitter feelings engendered by the '45, the plague of spies and informers throughout the Highlands stirring up trouble together with unwillingness to believe that any good could come out of the Highlands led to attacks on Macpherson's work and, naturally, those attacks added to the interest in, and popularity of, Macpherson's publications. Ossian still stood in spite of attack: indeed, it flourished on attacks and gained not merely a sympathetic, but even an enthusiastic, audience on the Continent. Nevertheless, some of these attacks demanded an answer and men such as the Reverend Dr. Blair of Edinburgh knew that old Gaelic poetry and tales existed but they also knew that they themselves were lacking in the knowledge necessary to one who would make a suitable reply to, and defence against, such attacks. The dispute circled round MSS. Macpherson was known to have had MSS. in his possession but of those MSS. Professor MacLeod of Glasgow University could write (NLS. 73.2.23(14)) to Lord Bannatyne on 21st January, 1801, that as far as he (MacLeod) was concerned they were quite illegible and, further, that he had no doubt but that they were also illegible to Macpherson. Even as late as March 1806 the Reverend Donald Mackintosh wrote (NLS. 73.2.11(7)) from Edinburgh to Sir John Sinclair that he had himself transcribed several Gaelic MSS. for the Highland

Society "which nobody else could do or even read a word of." Such was the state of Gaelic scholarship in Scotland at the end of the 18th century.

Returning now to the early days of the Ossianic dispute we find that the defenders had in 1762 sent out a questionnaire to Ministers and all likely to have any information whatever about Ossian, about Macpherson's work and about Gaelic MSS. It was the belief of many that there did exist MSS. which would completely overwhelm the attack on Ossian, for by this time Ossian, Macpherson, politics and national zeal had fallen into a hopelessly confused and confusing mass. Nobody, however, could produce such MSS. with any confidence in the result. Worse even followed. It must have been with consternation that the Reverend Dr. Blair read in his study in Edinburgh a letter (NLS. 73.2.13(4)), undated indeed, but written 1762-3 from the Reverend Lachlan Shaw, Minister at Elgin, saying that there were no MSS. of the poems of Ossian, that nobody in Strathspey (where Shaw had been brought up) could read the Irish script, in which it was presumed any Gaelic MS. must be written, but that that script was still known in the Western Isles where possibly a MS. might even be found. The Reverend Duncan MacFarlane, a most outstanding man, Minister at Drymen and the father of a future Principal of Glasgow University, wrote (NLS. 73.2.13(5)) to Dr. Blair on 28th November, 1763, that while he had himself often heard poems not unlike those rendered into English by Macpherson, yet he had never seen any MS. containing any such poems.

James Macpherson had meantime died leaving to his literary executors the task of regaining his good name and of publishing Ossian. In a letter (NLS. 73.2.10(5)) dated from London 19th December, 1797, John Mackenzie, one of these executors wrote to Henry Mackenzie (the "Man of Feeling") that the executors were highly satisfied with the proposed enquiry into the authenticity of the poems of Ossian.[3] The next step was taken in 1804 as we learn from a Minute of the Ossian Committee of the Highland Society of London held on 23rd June, 1804. It was resolved *inter alia* (1) to print at once Ossian's poems in the original Gaelic with a Latin version (2) that Bulmer in London should be the printer (3) that a new English translation be made because Macpherson's "does not do justice to the original" (73.2.24(28)). It was also arranged that the

---

[3] Macpherson made it known that he preferred to use Greek characters in the Gaelic text of Ossian but this may merely have been a device for putting off the day when he would have to produce the Gaelic text. At any rate, he nearly started a fashion of writing Gaelic in Greek letters. In NLS. 73.2.13(11) there is an extract from a letter dated 25th April, 1781, referring to a Greek translation of Ossian by Donald MacLaurin, brother of the mathematician. In 1810 the Reverend William Smith, Minister at Bower, published *Sacred Lessons and Exercises* where the Gaelic prayers are printed in Greek characters.

Reverend Alexander Stewart, a well-known Gaelic Minister and scholar, and the Reverend Dr. Smith of Campbeltown be joined in the work of correcting the proofs of Ossian as they should come from the printer (NLS. 73.2.24(48)(49)).

The general excitement and spate of discussion led to the finding of many MSS. Smith did his best to examine and report on them for the coming *Report on the Authenticity of the Poems by James Macpherson* — a book published by the Highland Society in 1805 — as did also Ewen MacLauchlan[4] of Aberdeen. How many MSS. were destroyed during this time will never be known. Macpherson in his day had to cover up his tracks and Smith [5] was in much the same position. At the same time many MSS. came into existence because the Highland Society was ready to pay for collections of poetry or MSS. — the more "Macphersonese" the better — so that "non-Macphersonese" MSS. were doomed.

The Reverend Alexander Campbell, Minister at Portree, sent to the Highland Society in London bundles of what he alleged were traditional poems, the pages being all written by himself and certified by James MacLeod J.P. These bundles were broken up and scattered so that now some are NLS. 73.2.3, others NLS. 73.2.10(6) - 73.2.10(11) and still others are in the Library at Edinburgh University. In a letter (undated but NLS. 73.2.11(18)) to Sir John Sinclair, Campbell complained that Sinclair's last letter to himself had not contained the £200 promised for his work. Again on 9th April, 1806, Campbell wrote to Sir John pointing

---

[4] P. J. Anderson, University Librarian, Aberdeen, said of his distinguished predecessor, Ewen M'Lachlan, that while it must be admitted that his English verse was poor stuff, yet his Gaelic scholarship was remarkable. M'Lachlan (he himself did not regularly use Mac) was Librarian of University and King's College, Aberdeen, from 1800 (when having just taken his M.A., he was appointed at a salary of 300 merks Scots) till 1819 when he seems to have resigned on receiving full charge of the Parish School of Old Aberdeen. He died in 1822. Of all those in Scotland concerned in the Ossianic dispute he was the only man capable of reading the Gaelic MSS. with any degree of accuracy. Cf. *Notes & Queries*, 10th Ser., XI (February 20, 1909), 90, 150, for a bibliography of his works.

[5] The two brothers, the Reverend Donald Smith, Minister in Edinburgh, and the Reverend John Smith, Minister at Campbeltown, were deeply concerned with Gaelic matters. In 1787 John published *Sean Dana le Ossian, Orrann, Ulann etc . . . Collected in the Western Highlands and Isles being the originals of the Translations sometime ago published in Gaelic Antiquities* and in the same year *Dargo and Gaul.* The Gaelic in these is foreign to the style of the language but in his efforts to outdo Macpherson, Smith got into the habit of writing in this stilted "romance" Gaelic with the result that his contribution towards the translation of the Scriptures had to be rejected. Uniting in himself a high degree of brazen audacity and profound ignorance and with the power to mislead others his influence was such that real traditional Gaelic poems were despised, since they were not in the Macphersonese tradition, till J. F. Campbell of Islay in his *Leabhar Na Feinne* pointed out this grievous error.

out that the Highland Society of Scotland now found that it had not the funds to pay for his Collection of Gaelic Poetry (NLS. 73.2.11(14)). Possibly Sir John had promised to make good any deficiency on the part of the Society: there is evidence that he did not find his patronage of Gaelic literature cheap.

In spite of the protests made by C. Stewart, Printer to Edinburgh University, to Sir John Sinclair against printing Ossian in London (NLS. 72.2.24(42)) it was reasonable that the Highland Society in London should be allowed to continue with what it had so enthusiastically started. Nevertheless, on 5th January, 1803, that Society sent on to the Edinburgh Society the MSS. now numbered NLS. 72.1.37 - 72.2.2 (some of these had been in Macpherson's possession) to swell the stock already in the hands of that Society. It seems that about this time Major M'Lachlan of Kilbride presented to the Highland Society of Scotland the MSS. now numbered 72.1.33, 72.1.34 and 72.1.36 along with another two which, if they had not been lost, would have been 72.1.32 and 72.1.35. The Reverend John Mackinnon, Minister at Glendaruel, was keenly interested in Gaelic traditions and he had obtained the MS. now romantically referred to as the "GlenMassan MS." which eventually, through the hands of Lord Bannatyne, was deposited with the Highland Society: its present number being 72.2.3.

On 4th October, 1804, Dr. Smith of Campbeltown wrote to Sir John Sinclair that Captain Sim, "the possessor of the Kilbride MSS." lives with his (i.e. Sim's) mother at the Stockwell in Glasgow. A list of the Kilbride MSS. had been made on 4th May, 1801, by the Reverend Donald Mackintosh in Kilbride House, the home of Major M'Lachlan. This List is now NLS. 73.2.24 but what happened in the intervening years is not known. Finally, in 1857 a firm of Writers, Messrs Gordon & Meek, in Glasgow handed over the Kilbride MSS. now NLS. 72.1.5 - 72.1.31.

A strange character in this world of MSS. is Peter Turner, probably a member of an extraordinarily gifted family from Inveraray. His MSS. are now NLS. 72.2.4 - 72.2.7, his name appearing in all of them: e.g. on p. 40 of 72.2.7 he has written "sgriobhta le Paruig Tuairnair, coirpleir ann an cath bhuidhinn chois Earaghaedheal ann an . . . Midhe san bliaghna 1801."

To these fall to be added NLS. 72.1.2, presented to the Faculty of Advocates by the Reverend Donald MacQueen, Minister at Kilmuir in Skye in 1784, at which date he also presented to the Antiquaries Society another Gaelic MS., dealt with later in these notes. How or when 72.1.3 and 72.1.4 came to the Library is not known but part of 72.1.1 was discovered accidentally by the historian W. F. Skene in 1834 in the Library. Additional to these are the Miscellaneous MSS. 72.2.8 - 72.2.15 of which all that can be said is that they seem to have come to Edinburgh from the London Highland Society.

Although these form the basic collection of Gaelic MSS. in Scotland it was not till W. F. Skene in 1862 determined to gather together into "some public Library for preservation" what was left of the Gaelic MSS. that they passed into the hands of the Faculty of Advocates. The Faculty of Advocates was chosen as the permanent home of the Gaelic MSS. because it had already in its possession four Gaelic MSS. NLS. 72.1.1 - 72.1.4 mentioned supra. The Advocates were not, however, very interested in their possession of Gaelic MSS. and thus Skene writes in 1862, "This collection has been formed within the last few years by the instrumentality of the writer. When he commenced the Faculty possessed four manuscripts. The Collection now consists of 65." J. F. Campbell of Islay says in a note dated 25th December, 1872 (now 73.3.24(1)), "This drawer may contain lots of queer stuff. I have examined one bundle and find that it contains important evidence as to Macpherson's Ossian, letters etc . . . and all sorts of things. It is not my work to sort all this out but it ought to be done." Immediately under this note Mr. Park of the Library and I as we "were sorting out this stuff" found a letter (73.3.24(2)) dated 29th October, 1783, from John Murray, Calcutta, to James Macpherson enclosing a bill for £600 and urging Macpherson to publish the original Gaelic text of Ossian. Along with this letter are laid up Minutes of meetings held by the Highland Society in connection with Ossian dated April, 1779, May, 1779, June, 1784, and January, 1790.

Skene himself did not know any of the Celtic languages and had therefore to depend on translators, e.g. William Hennessey and Owen Connellan for Irish and William Owens and the Reverend John Williams of Llandovery for Welsh. When Skene died many of his papers came to the Library, especially those used in compiling his historical works and also papers in connection with the Iona Club. These papers and the versions sent in by his translators are now numbered 73.1.10 - 73.1.21.

While J. F. Campbell of Islay was haunting the then Advocates' Library there were two Gaelic-speaking men on the staff; viz. Donald Macpherson, a native of Bohuntin in Lochaber and Malcolm Macphail. These men made transcriptions of a number of MSS. for Campbell; viz. 72.1.36, a MS. written in 1690 and 1691, and also of portions of 72.1.34 which had been written in 1603. Another man, one of the keenest scholars of Gaelic in his day, the Reverend Alexander Cameron, was busy transcribing and copying Gaelic MSS. in the Advocates' Library and his work will fall to be dealt with in connection with the Library of Edinburgh University.

An enquiry of some sort was set afoot in 1878 because a letter (73.2.10(12)) dated 10th December, 1878, from Donald Macpherson to the Curators of the Advocates' Library informs them that he has compared the Gaelic MSS. in the Library with Skene's list and found that nos. 1 & 13 of the MSS. and nos. 13 & 14 of the transcripts are not in the Library. He adds, "There are two drawers full of miscellaneous papers in Gaelic and about Gaelic subjects, chiefly about the Ossianic controversy, not included in Mr. Skene's Catalogue." These are the papers and the drawers referred to by J. F. Campbell and the papers are now catalogued for the first time: they are 73.1.22 - 73.3.23.

J. F. Campbell's death led to his MSS. being deposited in the Library where they number 50.1.1 - 51.2.7. These deal with his West Highland Tales, Gaelic traditions and the material that went to the compilation of his heart-breaking *Leabhar Na Feinne* as well as records of his various scientific works, e.g. papers in connection with his sun-shine recording apparatus (which was in use at Greenwich Observatory till the 1940's), papers in connection with Thermography (which he claims to have invented) and many duplicates of the contents of the Dewar MSS. at Inveraray Castle.

The next collection to reach the Library consisted of over 100 notebooks containing much valuable work done by the Reverend Charles Robertson, who died in 1927 when Minister at Kilchoman, Islay, on place-names, word-lists, etc. — generally the material collected by a highly intelligent Gaelic scholar when working as a parish Minister in various Highland parishes.

Another Minister who gathered Gaelic material when performing his parochial duties was the Reverend Alexander Pope (died 1782), Minister at Reay in Caithness. He was one of Ossian Macpherson's correspondents but it was away back in 1739 that he began to make his collection. This is now 73.1.23. Notable also is the work of the Reverend Alexander Irvine[6] but the material he collected has a history so far unexplained. Some of the collection lies in the Library at Edinburgh University and will be discussed along with the other contents of that library. In the National Library there is, however, another collection (temporary deposit No. 271) entitled *Collection of Gaelic Songs and Poems /made by/ Reverend Dr. Irvine*. This is one of the best sources for the works that go under the name of Iain Lom (John MacDonald).

[6] The Reverend Alexander Irvine in a letter dated 22nd September, 1806, to Sir John Sinclair gives an account of his own collection and comments on the collections by MacLagan and MacDonald (NLS. 73.2.11(47)). MacLagan's name is also spelled M'Lagan.

STUDIES IN SCOTTISH LITERATURE

We come now to deal with the contents of the MSS. that form the basic collection. The vellums are 35 in number, the rest of this group being on paper of various ages; e.g. the *Book of the Dean of Lismore* is said on doubtful evidence to have been written between 1512 and 1529 so that the paper is at any rate 16th century, while the Robertson Collection is on paper belonging to this century. Briefly the contents of the MSS.[7] are:

72.1.1 Genealogies and religious matter. The Teachings of Cormac Mac Airt and the Sayings of Fithil. Triads of Ireland. Coir Anmann. Skene erroneously took a marginal note 1476 as being the date of the MS. and published the Genealogies from this MS. in the *De Rebus Albanicis* as belonging to 1476.　　　　　　　　　　　　ff. 26[8]

72.1.2 Scientific matter. The planets; medical tract; tract on materia medica including "triacla." Computus. Cisio Janus. Collection of spells and charms e.g. for barrenness in women; for procuring love; to make hair grow; to take a mote out of the eye; to make the hair become golden; diseases common in the Autumn; virtutes aque Vite; table of weights and measures; blood-letting; wheel charm to be applied to a woman's breast; Teachings of Cormac Mac Airt. Chiefly medical texts.　　　　　　　　　　　　　　　ff. 104 plus
ff. 44 paper

72.1.3 Scientific matter. Materia medica; spells and charms e.g. to restore sanity, to restore sleep, to find out whether a man shall still be alive at the end of the year, to ensure the birth of a son; calendar for January and February giving a note of the lucky, unlucky and indifferent days.　　　　　　　　　　　　　　　　ff. 89

72.1.4 Tract on Definition. Miniature book measuring 1¾ x 2½ ins.
ff. 100

72.1.5 Cath Leitreach Ruide; Preface to Amra Coluim Cille; Life of St. Gregory the Great; Decollation of John the Baptist; Decapitation of St. Paul; Aided Chonchobuir; the Four Manannans; genealogies of Finn; poems from various sources e.g. Tri fotain nach sechuntar; Bec a Beind Boirchi; Mellach lem beth an ucht ailion etc.; Fulacht na Morrigna; Cormac and the Geilti Glinni; Life of St. Moling.
ff. 11

72.1.6 Gabhaltas Serluis Mhoir; inmate of Druimanach Abbey becomes a woman, bears seven children and becomes a man again; Mochaoi of

---

[7] Vellum unless otherwise specified.

[8] The number of folios or pages is the number actually containing a Gaelic text, not necessarily the number of ff. involved in making up the MS. in book form.

[2 3 0]

Nendrum and the Bird-song; genealogical tracts; the story of Ciarnat. ff. 13

72.1.7 Coir Anmann. Scota ingen Foraind rig Eigifti bean Niuil mathair Gaedil; Treide dleagar don ollam filidh; Teachings of Cormac; Triads of Ireland; Sermo ad Reges; Auraicept. ff. 11

72.1.8 Togail na Tebe; Argonautic Expedition and the Destruction of Troy. ff. 37

72.1.9 Fragmentary medical text and fragmentary genealogy of the MacDugalds of Lorne. f. 1

72.1.10 Aphorisms of Hippocrates. ff. 10

72.1.11 Aphorisms of Aristotle; crises in diseases; Lanfranc's theory of knowledge; voice production. ff. 4

72.1.12 Medical tracts on anatomy, diets, philosophy and on the soul; calendar for the year (but the fol. containing March and April has been torn out and is now lost); de operationibus occultis naturae of Thomas Aquinas. ff. 21

72.1.13 Isidore's Commentary on Damascenus; medical tracts including the Aphorisms of Hippocrates; de amore hereos; treatment of wounds; hydrophobia. ff. 38

72.1.14 Aphorisms of Hippocrates. ff. 16

72.1.15 Togail Troi. ff. 26

72.1.16 Dinnshenchas. ff. 6

72.1.17 Isidore's Commentary on Damascenus. ff. 3

72.1.18 Lilium Medicinae (fragmentary). ff. 10

72.1.19 Poems; Luid Iason na luing loir; Ardri dar gabh Erenn uill; Ceithri coimpertta caemha. ff. 6

72.1.20 Lilium Medicinae. ff. 6

72.1.21 Aphorisms of Hippocrates. ff. 8

72.1.22 Medical tract, beginning and end lost. ff. 8

72.1.23 Isidore's Commentary on Damascenus. ff. 6

72.1.24 Life of Findchua of Bri Gobann. ff. 8

72.1.25 Medical tract without heading; Fada go tuighim mo theach; Passion of Christ as related by the B.V. to Anselm; homily on the Commandments; Deasgaid gach uilc in t-uabar; La braith in Coimdi in cedain. ff 24

72.1.26 Moling and a Leper; Moling sees the Devil; a Christian and Jewish child both go to Church and eat the consecrated bread; Michael's Bit; a man lied at the Fair of Tailten after swearing by St.

Ciaran and his head eventually dropped off; a ship seen flying in the air; a priest's wife too heavy to be carried to the grave; white black-birds of Achaia; a leper comes to St. Brigit; gigantic women cast ashore on the Scots coast; Communion; Comgall and a foreign monk who seeks to match him in austerity; the devil Caincille in Armagh; Toirseach me dod chumundsa; medical tracts; diets appropriate throughout the year; passage of the moon and the sun; article on sleep; Garb Mac Stairn.   ff. 11

72.1.27   Medical tracts; music.   ff. 5

72.1.28   Synchronisms of the Irish Kings; Enna dalta Cairpri cruaidh; notes on the Calendar; A liubair ata ar do lar; Ata sunn sencas nach suaill; Cairpre Cindchait and the Revolt of the Aithech Tuatha; Nuallguba Oilill Oluim.   ff. 7

72.1.29   Poems including Gabh mh' eignech a Eoin Baisdi; Fearg an Choimdhi re clann Adhuimh; Ag so mo bragha a Dhe; Tagair red mhac a Muire; Aoighi misi ac mathair Dhe; Tairg mo mhunadh, a Mhuire; Tene arna fadadh fearg Dhe; Imdha rod direch go Dia; Beag nach tainic mo terma; Denadh Criosd comhairle a mhathar.
                                                                      ff. 13

72.1.30   Poems including Trian Connacht ar coimet aeinfir; Da coimet tech tigerna; Truagh ar n-echtra go h-Ath Truim; Ni mar chach as cainte Brian — all parts of Filib mac Briain mac Felimi hi Raighallaigh.   ff. 8

72.1.31   Poems including Mairg doni peta da cholaind; A Bhaethinn na ceil re cach; Caithreim Conghail Clairinghnigh (fragmentary)   ff. 7

72.1.32   (lost)

72.1.33   Calendar and how to find the Golden Number; rickets (The English word is used in the text which must therefore be later than 1645 when that word first appeared in an English medical text.) Bliaghuin so solus a dath; medical tracts and charms for toothache; Regimen Salernitanum; tract on urine;   ff. 8 plus as paged
                                                                by the scribe pp.84

72.1.34   (Paper)   Bruighean Chaorthuinn; Bruighean Bheag na hAlm-hain (written 1603. Dunstaffnage)   ff. 21 plus scraps

72.1.35   (lost)

72.1.36   Imtheacht Conaill Gulban for Domhan mhor; poems including Triath na nGaoidheal Giollaespeg; Rug eadrain ar iath nAlban; Bregach sin a bhen beg an seal do bhaois; Go mbenuigh Dia in tighe sa muinter; A Chonuill ca sealbh na cinn; Na maoi huaisle orum fein; Innis disi giodh be me; Soraidh slan don aoidhche reir; Mairg ni uaill as oige; Scela Muici Mic Da Tho; Sud i an thslatog; Na fuatha; Ni bfuigheadh misi bas duit; A dhuine cuimhnich an bas; Nech sin bhios corrach do ghnath; Bruighion bheg na hAlmunn; Bruighion Cheisi Coruin; An Dearg; Is maith mo leaba is olc mo shuain; Na srotha is edoimne is iad labhrus gu dana; An Ceithirneach O Domhnullan; Murchaidh Mac Brian agus an Dirioch.[9]   ff. 127

72.1.37   (paper)   The Book of the Dean of Lismore. Cf. infra.   ff. 127

72.1.38   (paper)   Cath Cnuca; Brisleagh Mhaighe Mhuirtheimhne agus Deargruathar Chonaill Chearnaigh; Cath Mhaighe Mucraimhe; Oileamhuin Conculainn agus Oigheadh Chonnlaoich; Coir Anmann; Oigheadh Chloinne Lir (the earliest extant text); An Bruighionn Chaorthuinn;

72.1.39   (paper)   Tales from the Seven Sages; Bliaghuin so solus a dath; Ata an saoghal ag seirmoir; Meisneach miledha Mic Eoin; Iomdha rod direch ag Dia;   pp. 32

72.1.40   Aided Chonchobuir; Aidid Ailella ocus Conuill Cernaig; Aidid Fergusa Maic Roich (the only extant text); Adid Medba; Aided Ceit Maic Magach (the only extant text); Aded Loegaire Buadaig (the only extant text); Aded Cealtchair Maic Uithechair (the only complete extant text); Anas mesa do rioghaibh; homily on the Life of St. Columba; Oiged Cuill maic Carbata; Tain Bo Fraich; Peannaid Adaim; Mesca Ulad; Cennach an Ruanado; Sunday Observance.   ff. 38

72.1.41   Medical tracts; Letter of Prester John; Triar ban drui ... Be Bhinn ocus Bc Cuill Cladhach ocus Be Chairncomrumach;   ff. 16

72.1.42   (paper)   Family tree of the Kings of Spain down to Phillip 4th (b. Valladolid 8th April, 1650.); Ni feas a chonach catha; Senbriathra Fithail; Udhact Morainn; Gaible mac Endamuin eigeas; Aoibhinn sin a Eire ard; Eisdigh a eigsi Banbha; Eire og innis na naem; An sith do rogha, a righ Fionngall; Ataim i gcas eider da chomhuirle; A eolcha Eirenn airdi; A Emuinn an agat fhein; Bennacht De gom dhaingensa.   ff. 26

72.1.43   (paper)   Forus Feasa ar Eirinn.   ff. 40

72.1.44   (paper)   Collection of poems including: Da gradh do fagbas Eirinn; Ein fear peisd ag milleadh Muman; Iomdha uaisle ar iath Laigen; Da roinn comtroma ar crich Neil; Dlighidh ollam uirrim riogh; Tanag aghaigh go heas gcaoille; Islig do mhenma, a Maoilir etc. etc.   ff. 85

[9] Written by Ewen MacLean, 1691, for Colin Campbell. In this same year this scribe wrote MS. H.4.21 (in Trinity College Library, Dublin) and in 1698 he wrote for Lochlin Campbell H.2.12 (No. 6) (also in Trinity College Library).

72.1.45   Aided Con Culainn.   ff. 6

72.1.46   In Cath Catharda.   ff. 8

72.1.47   An Tenga Bithnua.   ff. 4

72.1.48   (paper)   Poems including Soridh soir go hAlbain uaim;
A Ri an bheatha bi gum leighis; Dferuibh Ile nar thoill toighbhem;
Luaithe cu na cuidecht; Cethrar tainig anoir; Goll mear milenta;
Caoin thu fein a dhuine bhochd; Gabh a mhic mo mhunadh; tract
on Confession; Moran lense air aicme Ile; Se la gus an de nach faca
me Fionnd; Mairg duine bhrathis e fein;   ff. 34

72.1.49   (paper)   Poems including Ionmhuin tech re ttugas cul; Ar
hfaosamh dhamh, a Dhe Athar; Ionmhuin fert iona bfuil Brian; Mian
Chormaic thighe Temrach; Or na mban bainchenn nimhe; Slan fad
lot a lamh Aodha;   ff. 20

72.1.50   (paper)   Historical etc. notes on the descendants of John
of Islay from 1405 down to 1658; Cause of the Coming of Par-
thalon; Ataid aitheach thuatha iomorra le fiora Eirenn; Ban-shenchas
viz. Sgota ingean Foruinn bean Niail mathair Gaoidhil Ghlais;
Genealogy of King David of Scotland and of King Charles Ist;
Genealogy of the Kings of Ireland; History of the Clan Donald, a
part of the Book of Clan Ranald, written on modern paper by a
person unskilled in writing Irish, the original pp. having been given
back to Clan Ranald in 1897.   ff. 29

72.2.1   (paper)   Forus Feasa ar Eirinn.   ff. 9

72.2.2   (paper)   Campbell Duanaire, a Clan Ranald Duanaire and a
Mackinnon Duanaire; tract on grammar as in the Auraicept; geneal-
ogy of the Campbells of Argyll: Ionmhuin tech re ttugas cul;
Tugadh oirne easbadh mhor.   ff. 55

72.2.3   The GlenMassan Ms. Oidheadh Cloinne Uisneach; Fochunn
Loingsi Fergusa; Tain Bo Flidais.   ff. 27

72.2.4   (paper)   Poetry including Oisin is fada do shuan; Mo thoil si
an toil thug toil mhaith dhuit; A Phadruig in gcoula tu an telg;
Faoisidin Semuis na sronn alias Paor; Laoidh Mhna an Bhruit; Ata
faoi thonnaibh no tton; An Sioguide Romhanach;   pp. 88

72.2.5   (paper)   Eachtra Cloinn Tamais; Teamhair teach am bi Mac
Cuinn; Stair Emuind ui Cleirigh do reir Sean ui Neachtain; Cath
Lisin Ui Dhunagan; Cernn (sic) ui Domhnaill; Laoi an Deirg; A
Chleirigh chanas na phsailm; Dubhach sin a bheann Ghualann; An
Tenga Bith Nua;   pp. 310

72.2.6 (paper) Oigheadh Chloinne Tuireann; Oigheadh Chloinne Lir; Oidheadh Chloinne hUisneach; Bruighion Eochaidh Bheag Dearg.
pp. 105

72.2.7 (paper) Laoidh an Deirg; Laoidhe air Maluirt na h-oige airson na h-aoise; Gabh mo theagasg a bhean og; Innis sin a Oisin air heineach s air iongnadh; A chleirigh a leigeas gach dubh air a bhan; Teagasg Righ Arthuir do a Chloinn mhac; Plearacach na Ruarcach; Och a Mhuire nach truagh mo chas; pp. 48

72.2.8 (paper) Do Shuidhiughad do no hEirionn; tract on Gaelic grammar; contractions used in Gaelic MMS.; Cath Finntragha; Bruighean Caorthuinn; Life of St. Margaret; Cath Mucraimhe; pp. 354

72.2.9 (paper) Cath Ruis na Rig; Oided Con Culainn; Tain Bo Cuailgne (fragment); Poem on the Death of Archibald McDonald, Laird of Leargie. ff. 54

72.2.10 (paper) Aphorisms of Hippocrates; charm for producing sleep; Lilium Medicinae; Regimen Sanitatis Salernitanum; Tract on urines; treatment of bullet wounds; Gaelic version of Bernard Gordon's de Floribus Dietarum; tract on anatomy; materia medica; tract on fevers. pp. 474

72.2.11 (paper) Cath Finntraga. pp. 40

72.2.12 (paper) Poems etc. Tri Manuinn a bh'aig riogh Bretann; collection of proverbs; Tuirimh Bhrighid; Faighdoireacht amadan Emhna mhacha; Laoidh an Tailleoir; Gloir Diarmuid. (This MS. is possibly a common-place book that once belonged to Alasdair Mac Mhaighstir Alasdair.) pp. 30

72.2.13 (paper) Collection of poems by Alasdair Mac Mhaighstir Alasdair (by whom possibly the MS. was written). ff. 25

72.2.14 (paper) Collection of religious poetry by Tadhg Og, Donnchad Mor, Fpilip bocht O hIggin, Fergal Og Mac an Bhaird, Con O Cleirigh, Fergal Og O hUiginn. Aongus mac Aodha Ruaidh I Uiginn, Tuilecna mac Torna. ff. 38

72.2.15 (paper) Marbna Eignechain Ui Cellaigh; Soridh uam gu Cinntire; Moladh na pioba; Eascaoin molaidh na pioba; Nach truagh leibh na scela so deist mi di domhnuich; A chleirich chanfus na sailm; A Lachuinn scuir dod bhardachd; Cath Caphtharrus; a number of poems by Alasdair Mac Mhaighstir Alasdair followed by Caoi Mhic Ui Mhaolciarain beginning, Mac Ui Mhaolciarain mo ghradh / mo ghrianan e s mo choille chno; Satire on Dunstaffange by Angus O Daly (the Red Bard); pp. 98

(*To be continued*)

ABERDEEN UNIVERSITY

LAURENCE L. BONGIE

The Eighteenth-Century Marian Controversy
and an Unpublished Letter by David Hume

Scotland in the middle of the 18th century witnessed the beginnings of what proved to be a prolonged revival of vehement debate over the ill-fated career of Mary Queen of Scots. Focal point of the "Marian controversy," as it was already being called, was then, as it perhaps still largely remains today, the battle between Mary's detractors and partisans over the authenticity of the famed "Casket Letters."

A very summary recapitulation of the origins of these letters could go as follows: on February 10, 1567, Henry, Lord Darnley, consort of Mary Stuart, had been murdered at the Kirk-o'-Field as the result of a conspiracy in which, it was commonly said, James, 4th Earl of Bothwell, had played a leading role. Three months later, on May 15, Mary Stuart became the Earl of Bothwell's wife. The "second honeymoon" was short and troubled. On June 15 Mary surrendered to her rebellious lords at Carberry Hill while Bothwell made good his escape to the fortress of Dunbar. One week after this, James, 4th Earl of Morton, let it be known that his servants had found and seized a silver casket in the possession of one of Bothwell's retainers. The locked casket was broken open in front of witnesses and a certain number of documents were discovered including eight letters allegedly written by Mary to Bothwell proving her full complicity in Darnley's murder. Discovered too was a series of poetically irregular but very passionate sonnets from the romantic queen to her flagitious lover.

The contents of the casket were subsequently produced by order of the Regent Murray before various bodies and notably at Westminster on December 14, 1568, before a body of English commissioners appointed by Queen Elizabeth to investigate the mutual accusations of the Scottish lords and Mary Queen of Scots. Mary was then, as she remained until 1587, the year of her execution, a prisoner of the English.

It is impossible here to relate, even in the briefest of terms, the long drawn-out and probably endless controversy regarding the genuineness or spuriousness of these famous letters.[1] Suffice it to say that for all of the 18th century historians and critics who dealt with the question, the issue was almost hopelessly obscured by uncertainties concerning the actual text of the letters produced by Murray and his associates before the various investigating bodies. The originals were said to have been in France but had last been heard of in 1581 when they passed into the possession of William, 1st Earl of Gowrie, after the execution of Morton, accused in turn of complicity in Darnley's assassination. Despite the insistence of the English ambassador, Robert Bowes, Gowrie had balked at complying with Elizabeth's request that these documents be returned to England for safekeeping. With Gowrie's execution for treason in 1584, the precious papers completely disappeared.[2]

Not long after the close of the Conferences, various translations of these documents had been published; and, by a curious confusion, it was popularly assumed for almost two centuries that the well-known published French version, dated 1572, represented the original text shown to the English commissioners in 1568. It can thus be easily imagined how the cause of Mary's apologists was seen as achieving an enormous advance in 1754 when Walter Goodall proved conclusively that the printed French text in circulation was not the supposed original French at all but a vitiated translation from George Buchanan's Latin and his Latin itself a translation from what Goodall termed "the Scottish original forgery."[3]

The controversy was pretty much at that stage of development when, five years later, in 1759, two of the most celebrated 18th century historic accounts of Mary Queen of Scots appeared in Robertson's *History of Scotland* and Hume's *The History of England under the House of Tudor.*

[1] See S. A. Tannenbaum and D. R. Tannenbaum, *Marie Stuart Queen of Scots, a concise bibliography,* 3 vols. (New York, 1944-46).

[2] Robertson in 1759 stated that "after a diligent search, which has lately been made, no copy of Mary's letters to Bothwell can be found in any of the publick libraries in Great Britain." (William Robertson, "A Critical Dissertation concerning The Murder of King Henry, and the Genuineness of the Queen's Letters to Bothwell" appended to *The History of Scotland during the reigns of Queen Mary and of King James VI till his accession to the crown of England* (London, 1759, 2nd edition, II, p.35).

[3] Walter Goodall, *An Examination of the Letters said to be written by Mary Queen of Scots, to James Earl of Bothwell: Shewing By intrinsick and extrinsick Evidence, that they are Forgeries. Also, An Inquiry into the Murder of King Henry* (Edinburgh, 1754), I, p.80.

Hume and Robertson, though they worked out their positions independently,[4] and though they held opposite views concerning Mary's share of guilt in the Babington conspiracy, proved to be in fundamental agreement with respect to the authenticity of the Casket Letters.[5] Both historians were even more than willing to grant their friend Goodall[6] his premises concerning the spurious French translation. They insisted quite rightly, however, that his conclusions of forgery did not follow unless he was likewise able to prove that these French documents in the available printed form represented also a true copy of those produced by Murray and his party in the Scottish parliament, at York and at Westminster. Goodall, they maintained, had taken elaborate pains in his work of 1754 to prove something that, in fact, no one had ever denied.[7] To Goodall's

[4] Much to Hume's regret, it would seem: see *The Letters of David Hume*, edited by J. Y. T. Greig (Oxford, 1932), I, pp. 287-88, 292, 294; *New Letters of David Hume*, edited by Raymond Klibansky and Ernest C. Mossner (Oxford, 1954), p.46. See also the new letter below.

[5] Robertson's position has been described as "middle-of-the-road" and as leaving the issue "more open" than Hume's account. (See E. C. Mossner, *The Life of David Hume* (Edinburgh, 1954), p.413 and "New Hume Letters to Lord Elibank, 1748-1776" edited by Mossner in *Texas Studies in Literature and Language*, IV (1962), 449, note 6.) It is true that Robertson in his "Critical Dissertation" proposes only to "assist others in forming some judgement concerning the facts in dispute," and he makes some pretense of stating the proofs produced on each side. He makes it clear, nevertheless, in this as well as in other writings, that he himself believed Mary to be guilty. We even find some of Mary's apologists at times attacking him in terms more vehement still than they saw fit to use against Hume. (See, for example, John Whitaker, *Mary Queen of Scots vindicated* (London, 1788), III, p.8; Louise-Félicité Guinement de Keralio, dame Robert, *Histoire d'Elisabeth, reine d'Angleterre* (Paris, 1786-88), III, pp.362, 379.

[6] Who as sub-librarian of the Advocates' Library in Edinburgh and "seldom-sober" assistant to Hume once assaulted the prank-loving Scottish philosopher when awakened from a day-time nap by Hume's deafening roar in his ear to the effect that "Queen Mary was a whore and had murdered her husband" (Mossner, *Life*, p.252). Robertson acknowledges Goodall's help in obtaining documents for his own work "though," he adds, "he knew my sentiments with regard to the conduct and character of Queen Mary to be extremely different from his own" (Robertson, *History of Scotland*, I, p.vii). In a letter of 1759 to Robertson from London, Hume writes: "Tell Goodall, that if he can but give me up Queen Mary, I hope to satisfy him in every thing else; and he will have the pleasure of seeing John Knox and the Reformers made very ridiculous" (Greig, *op. cit.*, I, pp.299-300).

[7] See Robertson, "Critical Dissertation," pp.24-26; Hume in a letter to Sir Alexander Dick of August 26, 1760, wrote: "It was not surely Goodall, who forc'd Dr Robertson & me, to allow that the French Copy of these Letters was not the Original, but a Translation of a Translation. For the very Title Page of the Book bears it; and it was never conceiv'd to be other wise that I know of." (See Klibansky and Mossner, *op. cit.*, p.59.)

credit it must be noted, by the way, that he had clearly foreseen this objection but had dismissed it on the grounds that those contemporaries who were familiar with the original letters would have protested on seeing the spurious translation. "Would it not," Goodall had already pointed out, "be a very wild supposition, and equivalent to yielding the cause, to alledge that papers reckoned of so high importance, had been published in words and expressions quite different from those in which they were originally written, although in the same language, even at the very time while the dispute was hotly carried on, whether such papers did, or ever had really and actually existed in the Queen's hand-writing?"[8]

If we turn now to Hume's general treatment of the Queen of Scots in his *Tudors* we see that, despite his classical concern with painting an elegant and balanced portrait of historical personnages, his account of Mary's behaviour was largely a statement of the prosecution's case. This is not to say, of course, that his narration of her troubled career was entirely unsympathetic. Mary was indeed a proper object of compassion but the fact still remained that she was guilty of most and perhaps all of the misdeeds of which her enemies accused her. Like Voltaire,[9] Hume saw no reason to view the Queen of Scots in her misfortunes as a martyr to any noble cause. Martyred she may very well have been but hers was a martyrdom suffered because of her adultery, her guilty share in the murder of her husband and, in general, her extraordinarily unbridled imprudence. The frailties of human nature, the fury of passion had betrayed the romantic queen into actions which could with some difficulty be accounted for, "but which," Hume writes, "admit of no apology nor even of alleviation."[10] The historian goes on to conclude that, although an enumeration of her qualities might carry the appearance of a panegyric, an account of her conduct "must in some parts wear the aspect of severe satire and invective."[11] It was possible to gild Queen Mary to some extent; but to wash her white was a patent impossibility.[12] In fact the belief that he himself may have "gilded" her too much troubled Hume on at least one occasion sufficiently for him to express his fear to Robertson that they had both "drawn Mary's character with too great softening."[13] Hume's most authentically recorded unsympathetic statement on

[8] Goodall, *op. cit.*, I, p.100.

[9] See the *Essai sur les moeurs* in *Oeuvres complètes de Voltaire* (Paris, 1878), XII, pp.496-98.

[10] Hume, *The History of England, from the Invasion of Julius Caesar to the Revolution in 1688* (London, 1809), VI, p.229.

[11] *Loc. cit.*

[12] Greig, *op. cit.*, I, p.297.

[13] *Ibid.*, I, p.299.

the subject appears in a private letter to his Jacobite friend Lord Elibank in which he angrily refers to the Queen of Scots as "an old Strumpet, who has been dead and rotten near two hundred Years."[14]

As for the Casket Letters themselves, Hume comments on their authenticity in a note[15] to the *Tudors* in which he contests the forgery theory put forward by Mary's apologists with critical arguments concerning the improbabilities of their case. He notes, for example, that the letters are longer and more involved than they needed to have been in order to serve the purposes of Mary's enemies. Such length would have unnecessarily increased the difficulties of a fraudulent composition and added as well to the risks of detection if the letters had really been forgeries. The letters were carefully examined and compared with authentic specimens of Mary's handwriting not only by the Queen of Scots' enemies, but by her most devoted partisans as well. Even if it could be shown that such scrutiny was lacking in its full effect, Murray and his associates had every reason to think, before presenting the letters, that they would be canvassed with the greatest severity by able adversaries, interested in the highest degree in refuting the evidence as forged. Moreover, the Scottish lords had little reason to run the risk of exposure by such dangerous artifices since their cause, from Mary's known conduct, even without the letters, was "sufficiently good and justifiable."

Conceding nothing to what may have been the personal requirements of a spirited queen's pride, Hume based his major defense of the Casket Letters on the argument that Mary, at the time when the truth could have been fully brought to light "did, in effect, ratify the evidence against her, by recoiling from the inquiry at the very critical moment, and refusing to give an answer to the accusation of her enemies."[16] Mary's refusal to answer the charges *unconditionally* formed, for Hume, a strong presumption against her. In general it could be said that the arguments her apologists proposed against the authenticity of the letters were of "small force" but, the historian concluded, since Mary refused to answer, "were they ever so specious, they cannot now be hearkened to."[17]

We should perhaps not fail to note that this final argument presents an unexpectedly severe line of reasoning, emanating as it did from a

[14] Letter of August 14, 1764, "New Hume Letters to Lord Elibank" (1962), p.456.

[15] Volume II, pp.498-500 of 1759 edition; Note L to Volume V of the collected edition.

[16] *History of England*, V, p.503.

[17] *Loc. cit.*

man who throughout all his literary life took great and frequent pride in never answering the charges brought against him by any of his own numerous adversaries. It is perhaps not surprising, then, that in this inaugural period of apologetic literature relating to the unhappy Queen of Scots Hume's probably correct but somewhat cavalier evaluation of the controversy's merits provoked a number of heated rebuttals. Chief among these was the very popular *Inquiry*[18] of William Tytler, a work which appeared in February, 1760, and which was subsequently re-edited with additions and textual modifications in the years 1767, 1772, and 1790.

Tytler's *Inquiry,* though a less original contribution to the debate than Goodall's *Examination,* was destined to have a good deal more public success. In the eyes of many contemporary readers, it was immediately viewed as a complete vindication of Mary Stuart and one which triumphantly drove the malicious Hume and Robertson from the field. Joining in the victory with an obvious relish, Dr. Samuel Johnson contributed a review of the new apologist's work to the October, 1760, issue of the *Gentleman's Magazine.* The review's thinly-disguised introductory generalities made no attempt to spare Hume or his pretensions to impartiality and independence of mind: "The writers of the present time," Johnson pointedly decreed, "are not always candidates for preferment, nor often the hirelings of a patron. They profess to serve no interest, and speak with loud contempt of sycophants and slaves."[19] These writers, the eminent critic pursued, only delude themselves; though not the slaves of patronage they are yet the slaves of fashion and those who write for sale are tempted to court purchasers by flattering the prejudices of the public. It was only natural that the Stuarts had had few apologists; the dead, after all, cannot pay for praise. Nevertheless, Tytler had exhibited in his recent work a new zeal for truth and "a desire of establishing right, in opposition to fashion."[20]

In the body of the review itself, Johnson went on to list with fairly obvious approval most of Tytler's charges against Hume (paying, all the while, little attention to those against Robertson). He repeated Tytler's observation that assertions apparently contrary to fact are unworthy the character of an historian and may, quite justly, render his decisions with respect to evidences of a higher nature very dubious. Finally, he summed

---

[18] First published anonymously at Edinburgh as *An Historical and Critical Enquiry into the Evidence produced by the Earls of Murray and Morton against Mary Queen of Scots. With an Examination of the Rev. Dr Robertson's Dissertation, and Mr Hume's History with respect to that Evidence.*

[19] *The Works of Samuel Johnson, LL.D.* (Oxford, 1825), VI, p.80.

[20] *Ibid.,* p.81.

up in the characteristic Johnsonian manner with what must have been one of the most inaccurate predictions of his entire career: "That the letters were forged," Johnson concluded, "is now made so probable, that, perhaps, they will never more be cited as testimonies."[21]

On the continent, where Mary had never lacked support among those traditionalists who regarded her as a victim of English politics and a martyr to the Catholic religion,[22] Tytler's *Inquiry*, in the second edition, was honoured by translation into French.[23] In the preface to this work the ex-Jesuit translator, Father Louis Avril, noted with particular satisfaction that Tytler's was an apology of Mary Stuart "tracée par une plume protestante." The French ecclesiastic went on to make the charge, moreover, that both Hume and Robertson "ont affecté de mépriser les monuments qui contredisaient leurs préjugés, et l'on retrouve dans leurs Ouvrages toutes les calomnies qu'inventa ou répéta autrefois Buchanan contre sa Souveraine et sa bienfaitrice."[24]

On first hearing vague reports of a work written against him, Hume had informed his publisher that he rather felt it would do him good— meaning no doubt that it would increase readership interest in his *Tudors*.[25] He quickly assumed a much less casual attitude, however, when he had had an opportunity to look over Tytler's work. His personal correspondence soon began to bristle with angry references to the unfairness and lack of candour of "this gentleman" or rather "this author" who, he maintained, had called him almost directly "a Lyar & a Rogue & a Rascal" and who was obviously morally akin himself to the thieves and pickpockets of this world, "a very mangey Cur" indeed, for whom "a sound beating or even a Rope" was too good.[26]

---

[21] *Ibid.*, p.89.

[22] So strong indeed were official French feelings on the subject of the hapless Stuarts that in 1779 Louis XVI's council, preparing a war manifesto against Great Britain, included among its accusations the charge that the House of Hanover held its power through usurpation and also reproached the English with the assassination of Mary Stuart and Charles I. (See *Oeuvres de Louis XVI* (Paris, 1864), II, p.49.)

[23] *Recherches historiques et critiques sur les principales preuves de l'accusation intentée contre Marie Stuart, Reine d'Ecosse. Avec un Examen des Histoires du Docteur Robertson & de M. Hume, par rapport à ces preuves* (Paris, 1772). This translation was re-edited in 1860.

[24] *Ibid.*, p.vi. See also Mlle de Keralio's *Histoire d'Elisabeth*, already mentioned, III, *passim*, in which Hume and Robertson are accused not only of suppressing testimony in Mary's favour, but of actually fabricating evidence against her.

[25] See Greig, *op. cit.*, I, p.317.

[26] See *ibid.*, I, pp.318-21; Klibansky and Mossner, *op. cit.*, pp.58-64; see also the new letter presented below.

Such heat as we find expressed in the letters just cited (the most severe of which, by the way, may never have been sent) must appear somewhat unusual in a philosopher who had long before vowed never to take active notice of his literary adversaries. But Tytler's *Inquiry* had obviously stung the philosopher in an area where he was most susceptible to feeling the greatest pain: this was not, certainly, in his philosopher's love of calm; it was rather in his quite honest and entirely legitimate vanity as a man of letters. Hume, it must be admitted, worried a great deal about his literary reputation and Tytler, Hume felt and also made very plain in letters to his friends, had attacked his reputation in an underhand way.

One may speculate that Hume's anger on this occasion had yet another source: Tytler had caught Hume out on several easily verifiable points of fact, the account of which he now saw himself obliged to modify for succeeding editions of his *History*. In the first edition of the *Tudors* Hume, using his favourite argument to establish the authenticity of the Casket Letters, had asserted his belief in the validity of the confession extracted from Mary's servant Nicholas Hubert. He had even written that it was useless, at present, to seek improbabilities in this confession or "to magnify the smallest difficulty into a contradiction." It was, he affirmed, "certainly a regular judicial paper, given in regularly and judicially; and ought to have been canvassed at the time, if the persons whom it concerned had been assured of their own innocence."[27] Though he probably never gave up believing in the authenticity of Hubert's confession himself, Hume now found it necessary to admit (albeit privately) that it had come to light long after the Conferences had ended and that it was likely Mary and her commissioners had never heard of it and hence could never have had any opportunity to canvass it.[28]

Hume, as we have just seen, privately and somewhat grudgingly[29] conceded this victory to Tytler; no reference is made, however, in subsequent editions of the *History* to his reasons for suppressing this and another[30] offending passage, both of which were, in fact, dropped rather discreetly and perhaps with a certain lack of that very candour Hume

---

[27] *Tudors* (1759), II, p.500.

[28] See postscript of Hume's letter to Sir Alexander Dick, in Klibansky and Mossner, *op. cit.*, pp.63-64.

[29] "I have accordingly struck out the last Clause of the Sentence, in case of a second Edition; and shall willingly give this Triumph to the Enquirer; allowing him at the same time to call me, if he pleases, Rogue & Rascal & Lyar for it" (*loc. cit.*).

[30] See *Tudors* (1759), II, p.498.

found so wanting in his opponent. Perhaps the greatest indignity of all came some years later when the Scottish historian found it necessary even to break his long-standing vow never to answer directly in a literary quarrel. In the 1770 edition of the *Tudors* a new note appeared in which, after bitterly attacking Tytler for misrepresenting his account of the Conferences, Hume concluded as follows:

> That whole Enquiry, from beginning to end, is composed of such scandalous artifices; and from this instance the reader may judge of the candour, fair dealing, veracity, and good manners of the Enquirer. There are, indeed, three events in our history, which may be regarded as touchstones of party-men. An English Whig, who asserts the reality of the popish plot, an Irish Catholic, who denies the massacre in 1641, and a Scotch Jacobite, who maintains the innocence of queen Mary, must be considered as men beyond the reach of argument or reason, and must be left to their prejudices.[31]

No doubt more than delighted at having finally provoked the great historian to answer, Tytler in the third edition of his *Inquiry* added a 26-page *Postscript* as a rebuttal to Hume's note:

> The author of the History of England, so often mentioned in this Inquiry, has now for many years, with regard to this Essay, preserved a profound silence. But it would seem, that all this while he has been meditating vengence: he has now stept out into the world, and aimed a deadly thrust at the Inquiry and its author . . . .
>
> Let not that gentleman, intoxicated as he seems to be with popular applause, assume the character and style of infallible director of opinion, nor presume to wrest from that public, to whose indulgent favour he owes the credit he has obtained, the right which they have of judging for themselves. Had the Historian's judgement of the Inquiry been equitable, he would have found his opinion long ere now justified by the concurring sentiments of the public on his side: but that these sentiments have not concurred with him he seems tacitly to acknowledge, when now, at the distance of a dozen years since the offence, he deigns (contrary to his conduct with his other opponents) to take the offender out of the hands of the public, and to pronounce sentence himself.[32]

[31] Note N to volume V, collected edition.

[32] *An Inquiry, Historical and Critical, into the Evidence against Mary Queen of Scots. And An Examination of the Histories of Dr Robertson and Mr Hume, with respect to that Evidence. The Third Edition, with Additions and a Postscript* (Edinburgh, 1772), pp.363-64. By 1790, the *Inquiry* in its 4th edition had grown to two volumes and included this same *Postscript*, now "Addressed to the Public" (II, pp.341-74).

Other Marian apologists subsequently made much of this same point, that Hume, "who never replied to an adversary before, now replied to Mr. Tytler" (see John Whitaker, *Mary Queen of Scots vindicated* (London, 1788), I, p.v). Whitaker, after referring to Hume's note, speaks of the historian as rallying "with a seeming ferocity of spirit and with a real imbecillity of exertion . . . ," but all to no avail since Tytler's *Postscript* settled the matter decisively.

Commenting further on the recently added note, Tytler pointed out that Hume's impeachment was delivered in terms very inconsistent with his complaints concerning politeness and good manners. "If," Hume's adversary continued, "the Inquirer has, in these respects, been deficient to Mr Hume, (of which he is not at all sensible), that gentleman has now very amply retorted upon him. Who could have suspected the cool Philosopher to be so conversant in terms of the grossest and most illiberal abuse? . . ."[33]

Warming to his subject, Tytler denied Hume's charge that the anonymous Inquirer had been unfair in his use of quotations. He appealed to the impartiality of the public to judge the matter and asserted that he had not quoted "a single or detached passage from him; on the contrary, he has quoted almost the whole of the Historian's narrative concerning Queen Mary's refusal to answer, and like wise her request to be present at the trial of her cause, and that, too, in the Historian's own words."[34]

As can also be seen in the new letter presented below, the debate between Hume and his opponent was at its loudest on this very point concerning Mary's alleged refusal to answer. Tytler accused Hume of condemning Mary unheard since he formed his major presumption of guilt on Mary's "recoiling from the inquiry." On the contrary, Tytler maintained, Mary had agreed to answer but under certain reasonable, equitable and necessary conditions. Hume had, by an unfair inference and by a glaring sophism, converted this positive offer into an absolute refusal.[35] Had the Queen of Scots truly remained silent at the time Murray produced his letters, Hume's argument, Tytler admits, might have been conclusive. But Mary had not remained silent; she had accused her adversaries of producing forged writings against her and, asking that they might be inspected by her or her friends, had even undertaken to prove the forgery. What was the result of all this? The letters were hastily handed back to Murray and Morton and they themselves were sent a-packing to Scotland with their evidence. The result was too that Queen Mary to her dying hour never once saw the letters, and now they were lost, we are told—a fact, Tytler hinted darkly, from which every impartial person could draw the conclusions he thought fit.

I have not encountered any personal record of Hume's reactions to Tytler's postscript of 1772. What probably wounded the Scottish philosopher most in this respect was Tytler's harsh observation that Hume's

---

[33] *Ibid.*, p.361.
[34] *Ibid.*, pp.366-67.
[35] *Ibid.*, p.376.

boasted candour was asleep when he silently withdrew from later editions of his *History* the two major assertions of fact detected as false by the *Inquiry*. "But let me ask," Tytler continued acidly, "although the pride of an author would not suffer him to acknowledge those errors to the person who had detected them, in consistency with honour, was not something due to the public, and to the possessors of his first edition?"[36] Hume may well have regretted answering the Inquirer even to the extent that he did and the tradition is probably authentic which has it that he would not remain in the same room with Tytler (a Writer to the Signet and member of the Select Society) if they met at a common friend's.

In fact, although Hume often protested that he liked nothing more than to be reasoned with and argued against, provided such controversy could be carried out politely and according to the usual rules, the reader of his correspondence cannot help feeling at times that the great philosopher-historian occasionally protested too much on the subject. Hearing in 1764, for example, that his friend Lord Elibank was at work preparing a vindication of Queen Mary, Hume's first reaction, his very first thought, seems to have been that such a work would probably put an end to their friendship. And why was this so? Because the Jacobite Elibank might be intemperate or heated in his defense of the Scottish Queen and indulge himself in strokes of satire and in personalities as he dealt with this silly controversy.[37] Now it may be conceded that for Hume to feel such sentiments on that particular occasion is understandable; but to communicate these feelings to Lord Elibank, as he did in no uncertain terms, was quite another matter and suggests that Hume was at least as touchy on the subject, risking as he certainly did in this instance the appearance of blackmail, as any of his wrong-headed Jacobite friends. It seems fairly evident too that in the controversy with Tytler, Hume, as far as intemperance is concerned, attempted to give, both privately and publicly, at least every bit as much as he received.

*   *   *

The preceding considerations, though necessarily limited in scope, may help to throw light on the circumstances which gave rise to the following hitherto unpublished letter from David Hume to Sir Alexander Dick. Dick was a more than luke-warm defender of Mary Queen of Scots[38] and this letter is one of several which Hume wrote in 1760 con-

[36] *Ibid.*, p.381.

[37] See "New Hume Letters to Lord Elibank," p.456.

[38] See *Curiosities of a Scots Charta Chest 1600-1800. With the Travels and Memoranda of Sir Alexander Dick, Baronet of Prestonfield, Midlothian, Written by Himself.* Edited and arranged by the Honble Mrs. Atholl Forbes. (Edinburgh, 1897) pp.193-94.

cerning Tytler's *Inquiry*. It deals in particular with remarks made on this subject by John Campbell of Cawdor Castle and Stackpole Court, in letters addressed to Sir Alexander Dick but which Hume was evidently given an opportunity to examine.[39]

*   *   *

Letter from David Hume to Sir Alexander Dick, November 1, 1760.

Dear Sir

I receivd great Pleasure & Satisfaction from Mr Campbells Letter,[40] which you was so good to send me; & shoud be ashamd of being so late in answering it, had I not been out of Town almost ever since I receivd it, and have not settled so long as was requisite to consider these Matters. I own, I admire Mr Campbels Candour; and next to the Credit of converting him entirely to our Opinion (I mean Dr Robertson's & mine) I shoud be ambitious of being brought over to his. For after the Honour of being always in the Right (which is impossible) I think the most honourable thing is to be convincd (& to own it) that one has been in the wrong.[41]

I shall just mention a Remark in Mr Campbels former Letter, where he thinks that both Dr Robertson & I are in the wrong, when we lay an equal Stress on the Proofs of Darnely's Conspiracy against Murray as on those of Murray against Darnely at the Kirk of Beith. I own I am of his Opinion: The latter Proofs were certain: The former go little beyond Affirmation. But if Mr Campbell will be so good as to look into my History, he will find I there say so; & I have since had some Argument

[39] See also Letter 31 in Klibansky and Mossner, *op cit.*, pp.58-64 and notes 3 and 4 on p.58. The editors appear to be in error when they refer in note 4 to "Campbell's letter to Hume of 26 Sept. 1760"; the letter in question (see *Curiosities of a Scots Charta Chest*, pp.189-91) is addressed to Sir Alexander Dick although Dick obviously passed letters from Hume on to Campbell (see endorsement below) and letters from Campbell on to Hume. The new letter is to be found in the invaluable Bliss Collection at the Bibliothèque Nationale in Paris (Fonds Franc. Nouv. Acq. 23162, Fol. 128-31). The cover on the letter is endorsed, apparently in Dick's hand, as follows: "This Letter Sir Alexander Dick receivd from Mr David Hume Novr 8 1760 which he now transmitts to Mr Campbell in Pembrokeshire which he will please return after he has fully perusd it."

[40] See preceding note. Campbell had apparently been impressed with some aspects of Tytler's *Inquiry* and, though he took a more moderate stand than the Inquirer, he believed, contrary to Hume, that the Earl of Murray was guilty of complicity in the murder of Darnely. (See his letter of September 26, 1760, in *Curiosities of a Scots Charta Chest*, pp.189-91.)

[41] Expressions of such high-sounding sentiment are not infrequent in Hume's correspondence but that Hume really meant them in more than a conventional sense is, at least with respect to the Marian controversy, somewhat doubtful.

about that Matter with Dr Robertson, since his Publication.[42] But indeed, I have the good Fortune to agree with the Doctor in so many points, that it was natural for Mr Campbel to presume we had also agreed in that.

I do not know, whether I ever told you, that the Dr & I, tho we knew we were writing the same Period, & saw one another every day, yet we never communicated our Manuscripts to each other, except a few Books of the Doctors, which he allowd me to peruse. I proposd to him to communicate the Whole to each other, & mutually to correct our Pieces, and reason about all the Points wherein we differd. After some Deliberation, he declind the Proposal; and said very modestly, that if my Work opend any new Views or containd any remarkable Strokes, it woud be very difficult for him to pass them by without adopting them, & he woud rather be taken for an indifferent Writer than a Plagiary. After Publication, we might talk over the Matter as much as we pleas'd.[43]

I shall now mention a few particulars of Mr Campbels Letter, where I really regret we shoud differ: For as I said before, I have a great Desire to be of the same Mind with him.[44] I cannot but think, that the laying these Letters before Q. Elizabeth & her Council, and that Queen's throwing down along with them, a great Number of Mary's Letters that the

[42] Hume states in the *History* that is is difficult to clear up this question of mutual accusations but he added a note (*Tutors*, 1759, II, p.463; note G to volume V, collected edition) affirming that certain evidence served to justify the account "given by the Queen's party of the Raid of Baith, as it is called." He judged, however, that the conspiracy of which Murray complained "is much more uncertain, and is founded on very doubtful evidence." Robertson in *The History of Scotland* (I, p.285) notes as follows: "The reality of these two opposite conspiracies has given occasion to many disputes, and much contradiction. Some deny that any design was formed against the life of Murray; others call in question the truth of the conspiracy against Darnly. There seem, however, to be good reasons for believing both . . . ." Tytler had found Hume less partial on this point than Robertson. It was important for Mary's apologists to stress that Murray's early conspiracy against Darnley was real and that the Queen's marriage crossed his ambitions. The prospect of the Queen's issue, it was argued, would cut off all his future hopes. The implication of course is that these black designs lay long brooding in the heart of the Queen of Scot's natural brother, gradually unfolded as time passed, and came fully to light only with the forgery of the Casket Letters.

[43] A discussion of what are described as Robertson's "jealous suspicions" in this matter may be found in E. C. Mossner's *Life*, p.397. Robertson had actually gone so far as to request Hume not to write on the same period as himself (see Hume's letter to Robertson of January 25, 1759, Greig, *op. cit.*, I, p.294). The two historians had in fact communicated so little on the subject that Hume, who was given permission by Robertson in 1758 to look over the corrected proofs of *The History of Scotland*, found himself much relieved to discover that his friend asserted in that work "the authenticity of Mary's letters to Bothwell, with the consequence which must necessarily follow" (see letter to Robertson, November 18, 1758, *ibid.*, I, pp.287-88).

[44] See *supra*, note 41.

handwriting might be compard; I say I think this a strong external Proof of the Genuineness of these Letters. Consider that Norfolk, Westmoreland, Northumberland were of the Number; all of whom were afterwards forfeited in Mary's Cause & two of them lost their Lives. Q. Elizabeth at that time pretended to be neutral; & they ran no risque, except perhaps of a Frown, if they had said, the handwriting appeard not to be the same. And woud not something of their Sentiments on that head have transpird afterwards? But we find by Norfolks Trial, that even after that Examination, Norfolk said in private to his Friend & Confident, Bannister, that he thought Q. Mary guilty.

Besides Murray & Morton had all the Reason in the World to expect, that Lesly & Herreis & others of Mary's Commissioners woud be present at the Examination. That they were not so was entirely their own Fault; & never coud have happend, had they not known their Mistresses Guilt, & known these Letters to be genuine.[45]

I am sorry Mr Campbell has not a Copy of Goodall:[46] He woud have seen that the Enquirer has employ'd against me one of the most scandalous & dirty Tricks that ever was made use of in Controversy; but it is a Trick so frequent that one woud almost pass for ridiculous, if they conceivd any Indignation against it. It is that of mutilating the Quotations, & produc-

---

[45] This is the very essence of Hume's position concerning the authenticity of the Casket Letters.

[46] Hume, writing to Lord Elibank in 1760 after the appearance of Tytler's *Inquiry*, informed his correspondent that it was "Contempt & not Inability" which had kept him, as it had kept Robertson, from making a reply to their "common Answerer" (Greig, *op cit.*, I, p.318). He added that Goodall, though not a very calm or indifferent advocate in the cause, disowned nevertheless the Inquirer as an associate "and confesses to me & all the World that I am here right in my Facts, and am only wrong in my Inferences" (*ibid.*, I, p.321). One would, of course, like to see other evidence besides Hume's affirmation in exact support of this claim since Goodall was probably even more vehemently committed to the defense of the Scottish Queen than Tytler who in his *Inquiry* in fact popularized much of his predecessor's documentation. Goodall, for example, defends the position that "neither Queen Mary, nor her commissioners could ever obtain a sight of these letters, nor yet copies of them, tho' they several times demanded them of Queen Elizabeth and her court" (*Examination*, I, p.ix). He even goes so far as to affirm the absurd proposition that Mary Queen of Scots so far excelled all other sovereigns "who ever yet appeared on the face of the earth, that, as if she had not been of mortal nature, all the arts and contrivances of her numerous and malicious enemies have not availed to fix upon her one crime . . . nay, not one single foible, either while on the throne, or in the jail, from her cradle to her grave . . . ." (*ibid.*, I, p.xxviii). Tytler, in the 4th edition of the *Inquiry*, states that Goodall's vindication of Mary, when first published, was, without proper examination, received as a "piece of Quixotism" (*op. cit.*, I, p.20), and that his own *Inquiry* was intended to defend Goodall who, though urged at the time by several friends to reply to Hume and Robertson, "declined, from an honest indignation at the uncandid reception his book had met with" (*ibid.*, pp.23-24).

ing only what makes for one's own Side, while all the rest is suppress'd. He quotes a long Passage, where Q. Mary offers, in very stout & bold terms, to answer, & desires Copies of the forgd Letters. He takes no Notice, both that that Defiance refers to a former Letter, where it is made an express Condition that she be admitted to Q. Elizabeths Presence and also that Q. Elizabeth, before she breaks up the Conference altogether, calls Q. Mary's Commissioners into her Presence, & offers to give them Copies provided they will promise to answer without insisting on that Condition, and will get their Commission renewd: For, she tells them, that she understands it is expird or recalld and that therefore they cannot answer. This is the last Transaction at Hampton-court.

To put the Inquirer's Unfairness in a full Light to Mr Campbell, I beg him to consider that the Author never dares say, that Q. Mary offerd to answer without that Condition: Goodalls Papers are too direct a Proof of the contrary. Where then do we differ? Only in this particular as I said to you in my last.[47] He insists that *she offerd to answer provided she was admitted to Q. Elizabeths Presence.* I say, *that she refusd to answer unless she was admitted.* And for this, he insinuates or rather says plainly that I am a Rogue, a Rascal, & a Lyar. Is such a Fellow worth regarding or answering?[48]

I agree with Mr Campbell, that much Stress ought not to be laid on Huberts Confession;[49] it comes to us in such a blind way: But it may be mentioned in the heap of other Proofs. As to the long Delay of his Trial & Execution, we may suppose, that he maintaind for so long a time Fidelity to his Trust, & was at last brought by the Rack to confess. The Use of the Rack weakens a Proof from Confessions; but does not entirely destroy it; otherwise there woud be no Evidence except in this Island, where alone that Instrument of Torture is happily abolishd.

As to the Forgery of Q. Mary's Letter after the Affair of Carberry Hill, we have that Story only from Sir James Melvil, who is the most

[47] Apparently Hume's letter from Edinburgh of August 26, 1760, in which he makes much the same statement. (See Klibansky and Mossner, *op. cit.*, p.60.)

[48] Hume felt, perhaps incorrectly, that these were "positive & negative Propositions of the same Import" (see his letter to Lord Elibank, Greig, *op. cit.*, I, p.320). Hume charged that Mary's offer to answer, being grounded on a condition which the Queen of Scots did not expect to be granted, and which accordingly was denied, was "certainly equivalent to a simple & absolute Refusal" (*ibid.*, I, p.319). Tytler accused Hume of basing this major conclusion on mere conjecture and of converting "a positive offer, under a condition reasonable, equitable, and necessary, into an absolute refusal" (*Inquiry*, 3rd edition, p.376).

[49] Hume, yielding to Tytler's criticism on this point, had already struck out the passage concerning Hubert's confession "in case of a second Edition" (*supra*, note 29).

enticing deceitful Author in the World. He has throughout all his Memoirs such an Air of Candour & Sincerity that we are extremely inclind to believe him; yet is he such an idle Prater and can be disprovd in so many things, which he tells from his own Knowlege, that no Credit can be given him. However, I think, with Mr Campbel, that, if such a Letter was ever shown to Kirkaldy, it was probably a Forgery. But by whom it was shown, I think Sir James does not tell us; & Murray had at that time left Scotland.[50]

[50] Hume is here referring to a letter supposedly written by Mary to Bothwell shortly after her surrender to the Scottish lords at Carberry Hill. Mary, after a negotiation with Kirkaldy of Grange who commanded an advanced body of the enemy forces, received his promise, with the consent and in the name of the associated lords, that, on condition she dismiss Bothwell from her presence and govern the kingdom by the advice of her nobles, they would honour and obey her as their sovereign. The lords, however, on making her prisoner, considered themselves absolved from this commitment by what was alleged to be her incurable attachment to Bothwell. Melville's account is as follows:

". . . it was alledged that her Majesty did write a Letter unto the Earl of *Bothwel*, and promised a reward to one of her keepers to convoy it securely to *Dunbar* unto the said Earl, calling him her dear heart whom she should never forget nor abandon, though she was necessitated to be absent from him for a time, saying, that she had sent him away only for his safety, willing him to be comforted, and be upon his guard. Which Letter the Knave delivered to the Lords, though he had promised the contrary: Upon which Letter the Lords took occasion to send her to *Lockleven* to be kept, which she alledged was contrary to promise. They on the other hand affirmed, that by her own hand writing she had declared that she had not, nor would not abandon the Earl of *Bothwel*. *Grange* again excused her, alledging she had in effect abandoned the said Earl, that it was no wonder that she gave him yet a few fair words, not doubting but if she were discreetly handled, and humbly admonished what inconveniences that Man had brought upon her, she would by degrees be brought, not only to leave him, but e're long to detest him: And therefore he advised to deal gently with her. But they said, that it stood them upon their Lives and Lands, and that therefore in the mean time they behoved to secure her, and when that time came that she should be known to abandon and detest the Earl *Bothwel*, it would be then time to reason upon the matter. *Grange* was yet so angry, that had it not been for the Letter, he had instantly left them . . . ." (*The Memoirs of Sir James Melvil of Hal-Hill* (London, 1683), p.84.)

Though, paradoxically, embroidering to some extent in his text on Melville's description of the letter's contents, Hume had already noted in the *Tudors* (1st edition, II, p.483) that "the reality of this letter appears somewhat disputable; chiefly because Murray and his associates never mentioned it in their accusation of her before Queen Elizabeth's commissioners." It may be noted, nevertheless, that Hume made rather frequent use of the "enticing deceitful prater," Melville, as a documentary source on this whole period.

One may conjecture that an additional reason why Hume was willing to give up even the existence of this letter lay in the fact that it argued, since nothing more was heard of it, really more in defense of the Queen of Scots than against her. Mary's partisans could and did maintain that it was the crude prototype, if it existed, of

There are three Folio Volumes of Manuscripts in the Advocates Library, copyd from the Burleigh Books in the Cotton Library; & the Transcriber observes, that in the very place, where the Copies of Q. Mary's Letters shoud have been, there are evidently several Leaves cut out of the Original. It is easy to see that this must have been done after K. James's Accession; which, with what Dr Robertson has said, sufficiently accounts for the Dissappearance of the original French.[51] Q. Elizabeth never woud publish them; because she pretended always to be neutral: Murray might have done it; but the Scotch sufficd, he thought, for this Country & England; Latin for Foreigners. French was not then the general Tongue as to present.[52]

Thus I have finishd, Dear Sir, every thing material I had to say of Mr Campbells Letter; and acknowlege myself much obligd to him for the Pains he has taken, & to you for communicating his Sentiments to me. I am

Edinburgh
1 Novr 1760

Dear Sir
Your most obedient humble
Servant
David Hume

UNIVERSITY OF BRITISH COLUMBIA

all the later forgeries. Though effective enough to permit the Queen's incarceration and plausible enough in appearance to deceive the unpracticed eye of Kirkaldy, it was a hasty effort and prudently suppressed once it had served its purpose. The success of this first venture in fraud, it was argued, encouraged Mary's enemies to make, only with more skillful preparations, their grand attempt later on.

[51] Robertson in his "Critical Dissertation" (p.38) writes as follows: "Whether James VI who put the Earl of Gowrie to death, A.D. 1584 and seized all his effects, took care to destroy his mother's letters, for whose honour he was at that time extremely zealous; whether they have perished by some unknown accident; or whether they may not still remain unobserved among the archives of some of our great families, it is impossible to determine." For Hume too, the disappearance of the original documents was an argument, not in favour of their forgery as Mary's defenders insisted, but quite obviously in support of their authenticity: "That event," he states in his note on the Casket Letters, "can be accounted for no way but from the care of King James's friends, who were desirous to destroy every proof of his mother's crimes." (See item 15, note L to volume V, collected edition.)

[52] Hume, it would appear, is here clutching at straws. If French was not then "the general Tongue," it was not, for all that, the language of some primitive distant tribe; the originals, after all, *were in French*. That Latin did not suffice for foreigners is made equally clear, moreover, by the fact that, as Hume knew very well, a contemporary French "translation of a translation" had appeared in print soon after.

TOSHIO NAMBA

Robert Burns in Japan

THE MEIJI ERA   (1868 - 1911)

Immediately after the Tokugawa Shogunate restored power into the hands of the sovereign, Japan began to restore order out of chaos and to modernize as quickly as possible. The Meiji Restoration was the dawn of a new era. Its leaders were in general "samurai"[1] of the old school, brought up in the feudal system. After the Restoration, however, this system fell into disuse. A new enthusiasm swept the country, carrying all before it. Two important victories, the Russo-Japanese War and the Sino-Japanese War, gave the Japanese people a new sense of destiny.

The vision of the leaders in the Meiji Era was of modernization, although their ideas were not at that time well organized. There remained, however, a conflict between the new democracy and the old feudalistic ideas. During this era modernization meant Europeanization of thought, and the country soaked up Occidental civilization like a sponge. With the help of western countries remarkable strides were made.

A new interest developed in the literature of these European countries and the United States; among the authors studied we find Robert Burns. The door to the study of Burns was opened by Chiaki Inagaki in 1881 when he and some comrades wrote a parody on "Auld Lang Syne" for a school graduation ceremony. Its success was immediate and today "Auld Lang Syne" is almost a synonym for Robert Burns in Japan. It is now the only song of parting used in Japan. In 1908 Shogun Sakai published an article on "Auld Lang Syne" in *Eigo Sekai* (*The English Word*). Another early translation was that made of "The Cotter's Saturday Night" by Yoshifumi Yamabe in 1892 which was published in the *Japan Review*.

The earliest critical work on Burns to appear in Japan was Masahisa Uemura's "The Peasant Poet Robert Burns" which appeared in the *Japan Review* (1890). In 1895 a well-known literary critic, Tateki

---

[1] *Samurai* or *bushi*: during the feudal era, one of the class of military retainers of the daimyos (vassals of the Mikado).

Owada, included a chapter on Burns in his *Lives of Literary Men,* a book which is still widely read in Japan.

In 1896, the Burns Centenary Year, there was considerable interest in Burns. Foremost among those who helped to spread his fame was Tetsuo Kunikita, who lectured frequently on him and gave public readings of his poems. Among Kunikita's favourites was "My Heart's in the Highlands" which he frequently recited. That same year he published "The Failure of Burns" in the *National Companion,* an article based on Carlyle's *Essay on Burns.* "If we study the poetry of Robert Burns, we must be taught very deeply," he wrote in *An Honest Confession* (1909). As Kunikita was then at the height of his fame he produced a powerful effect on the people; it is not too much to say that he was a major figure in diffusing the literature of Robert Burns during the Meiji Era.

The year 1902 saw "Husband, Husband, cease your Strife" translated by Isoo Yamagata in his *Collection of English and American Poetry.* This same year Kaiseki Matsumura included a chapter "Robert Burns" in his *Critical Biography,* Ryusui Ogata wrote "Sad Fame of the Poet Robert Burns" for *Tragic History as it was,* and Reisuke Kazama devoted Chapter 18 of his *Self-Culture* to Burns. By this time the poet was well enough known to be quoted in works not dealing specifically with literature. For example, Hosui Muto quoted "Nae man can tether time nor tide" from *Tam O'Shanter* in a work entitled *Human Economics* (1902).

Mugen Ohara did a great deal to make Burns known to the Japanese reading public. In 1905 he included a translation of "To Mary in Heaven" in his *New Translations of Western Poetry.* The following year he published *Selected Poems from Burns,* the first book of translations of the Scottish poet. It contains 160 pages with the original text and the translation. There are thirty-two poems including such favourites as "To a Mountain Daisy," "The Birks of Aberfeldie," "To Mary in Heaven," "My Heart's in the Highlands," "The Vision," "A Red, Red Rose," "The Song of Death," "O Lassie, are ye Sleepin' yet," "There was a Lass, and she was Fair," "Here's the Glen," "Lament of Mary Queen of Scots," "Simmer's a Pleasant Time," and "O were my Love yon Lilac Fair."

Totan Miyamori and Senryu Kobayashi again translated "My Heart's in the Highlands" in their *One Hundred English and American Poems* (1909). This anthology, with notes, did much to familiarize the public with Burns's poem.

Such was the interest in the National Bard of Scotland that Oson Sakurai visited the land of Burns and included photographs of Burns haunts in his *European Tour* (1909). At about this time also the *Ency-*

clopaedia of Literature included an article "Robert Burns" by Shukotsu Togawa.

Although scholars of this period had few texts, they enthusiastically pursued the study of Burns; it was their early work which made possible the growth of interest in Burns during the succeeding Eras. It is not overrating the poet to say that Burns exerted a hidden, but distinct, influence on Meiji democracy.

THE TAISHO ERA   (1912 - 1926)

This short era (during the reign of the Emperor Taisho) produced one outstanding book on Burns—a selection of poems translated by Professor Yoshisaburo Okakura. It was published in 1923 by the Tokyo firm Kenkyusha, the oldest established publisher of English literature in Japan, in their *Kenkyusha English Literature* Series. Professor Okakura was an energetic scholar who had put the finishing touch to his education in England and Germany. An excellent philologist, the author took great pains over his work, adding copious notes and explanations. These helped greatly with the study of Burns in Japan, as the difficulty of understanding the Scottish dialect is very real to the Japanese student. This work, which was reprinted three times, remains one of the basic Burns texts and is widely used by Burns scholars and Burnsians throughout the country.

The last year of the Taisho Era saw the publication of three books containing items of Burns interest. The first of these was the translation by Professor Aizo Okamura of William Swinton's *Studies in English Literature*, a work which was first published in 1880. Of course this book was destined for the intellectual class only, but it has had an important effect on its small circle of readers. A more popular work was *A Collection of Stories of Genius in the World* by Professor Kyoson Asahara which went into five editions. Burns's humanity was highly praised in the brief treatment given the poet. Finally, in 1926 Professor Kenji Kaneko, who had written a thesis entitled "The View of Natural Beauty in Wordsworth and Burns," published a series of travel sketches *Uma no Kushami* (*A Sneeze of a Horse*). His four-page section devoted to Burns gives a brief description under the title "The Peasant Poet of Alloway" of how this area appeared to Japanese eyes.

THE SHOWA ERA   (1926 -)

The most important work in the early years of this era was *A Treasury of English Literature* (1928) compiled by Professor Yoshiyuki Ide. This important anthology has been instrumental in introducing English literature to Japanese students. It includes "The Cotter's Saturday

Night," "To a Mountain Daisy," "Is there for Honest Poverty" (For a' that, an' a' that) as well as Carlyle's *Essay on Burns*.

An edition of translations (printed, as with most editions, with the English and Japanese in parallel text) was published in 1934. These learned translations were made by Professor Tameji Nakamura and are still widely used. This same year a thesis, this time devoted entirely to Burns, was presented in the Department of Literature of Kyushu University— "On the Early Works of Robert Burns" by Tsuneo Takeyama.

Another significant addition was made to the literature on Burns in Japanese in 1937 when Professor Kinji Shimada published "A Study of English Literature in France: The Achievement of Auguste Angellier" in the literary bulletin of Taipeh Imperial University. This long article (it extends over 102 pages) gave a detailed analysis of Angellier's famous *Robert Burns: la vie, les oeuvres* (1893, 2 vol.). Shimada's eloquent introduction of Angellier gave Burns students new information about the poet and especially a vital new insight into Scotia's Bard. The fact that Angellier was able to interpret Burns in terms of his own country added a further dimension to the poet for Japanese readers. Professor Shimada's brilliant essay is still widely read and studied.

The first year of the latter period of the Showa Era (1951) saw the beginning of a revival of interest in Robert Burns which is still in full force. The impetus to Burns study was supplied by an article of mine on "Auld Lang Syne" which appeared in the *Come, Come Club*, an English-language magazine. Several of my translations with commentaries have since been published in such periodicals as *Albion* (the organ of the Albion Club), *Yushu,* as well as in anthologies. My *Poems of Robert Burns*, a bilingual edition with notes and commentaries, was published in 1959. It includes twenty-eight poems, among them such favourites as "Auld Lang Syne," "Afton Water," "My Heart's in the Highlands," "Coming Through the Rye," To a Louse," "Mary Morison," "Scots Wha hae," My Love is like a Red, Red Rose," "Ae fond Kiss," and "Epistle to a Young Friend." This last poem is very popular in Japan. A new translation of mine was published in the magazine *Information for the Education of Youth* (1961) for "Adults' Day" (January 15) which celebrates the attainment of a youth's twentieth year. The last stanza in particular appeals to the rational faculty in its readers. It is hoped that the advice to "Andrew dear" will be followed by many a Japanese "Andrew dear."

In 1960 I published *The Lyric Poetry of Robert Burns* in parallel text translation with notes. This work contains twenty-one poems, six of which were not included in my previous book—"The Vision," "To James Smith," "Elegy on Captain Matthew Henderson," "Address to the Unco

Good," " Epistle to John Lapraik," and "Tam O'Shanter." This was followed in 1963 by *The Gem of Burns,* which includes fourteen new translations, again in parallel text with notes. Among the poems are "Address to a Haggis," "To a Mouse," "The Rigs o' Barley," "Green Grow the Rashes," "Willie brew'd a Peck o' Maut," and "Halloween."

Coupled with translations of Burns I have published several studies of the poet. These include "A Study of 'Tam O'Shanter'" (*Bulletin of Setagaya College of Liberal Arts, Nihon University,* 1957), "On Features of Consonants in Burns's Poetic Language" (*Bulletin of the English Literary Society of Nihon University,* 1958), "On Some Vowels in Burns's Poetry" (A special issue entitled *English Studies in Japan* published by the English Literary Society of Nihon University, 1958), "Burns and Medievalism" (*Omon,* 1960), "Burns's 'Winter' and its Background" (*Shikai,* 1960), "Time, Work and Life of Robert Burns" (*The Study of English,* 1961) and others.

I have also been interested in comparing our national haiku poet Issa (1763-1827) with Burns. Issa's haiku poems are unsophisticated and deeply religious in substance. This formed the basis for a paper "A Comparative Study of Issa and Burns" which I read before the Comparative Literature Society of Japan in 1958.

Two other important pieces of Burnsiana remain to be mentioned. Dr. Yasuo Yamato, who is well acquainted with Scottish literature in Japan, edited *Essays on Burns* (1961) which contains several important articles: "Merry Devils" by Professor Osamu Miura, "Robert Burns" by Dr. Takeshi Saito, "Expediency of Scottish Enunciation" by Professor Shigeshi Nishimura and others. The volume also contains poems translated by Professor Minoru Soda. Also in 1961 Tadashi Izonu published *The Poet Robert Burns* which is concerned chiefly with Burns's country.

Finally, it may be of interest to know which Burns editions are most frequently used in Japan. By far the most popular edition of the poetry is that of the Oxford University Press, edited by J. Logie Robertson. We Japanese find the notes and glossary extremely useful. To supplement this we employ William A. Craigie's *Primer of Burns* (1896) and, of course, Reid's *Concordance.* The *Encyclopaedia Britannica* is much used for a source book of information on Burns; in schools where children are learning English the junior edition of this work is widely popular. William Jacks' *Robert Burns in Other Tongues* (1896) has been frequently consulted by Japanese who are interested in how Burns's poetry was translated in other nations. No mention is made by Jacks of the Japanese translations prior to 1896 noted above.

By far the most frequently employed critical study of Burns is Carlyle's famous *Essay.* An edition of this work with notes and some of Burns's poems was published in 1931 and is still widely used.

These volumes are what we call "Gensho" meaning source books or originals. There are, as one might expect, no true originals of Burns in Japan. I have made an exhaustive search for manuscripts in this country, but without success.

Some idea of how well Burns is now known in Japan may be had from the manifestations and publications connected with the bicentenary celebrations of 1959. The most notable of these was the establishment, under the auspices of the British Council, of the Japan Caledonian Society. Two television programmes on Burns were broadcast and I prepared a talk "Burns and Japan" which was broadcast over the Scottish Home Service. Furthermore several newspapers carried articles on Burns. The fact that the mass media took up Scotland's Bard shows that he is now known not only to a few specialists in the literature of Scotland but to a broad segment of Japan.

NIHON UNIVERSITY

Notes and Documents

The Devil and John Barleycorn:
Comic Diablerie in Scott and Burns

Sir Walter Scott's "Wandering Willie's Tale" is often praised as one of the finest short stories on a supernatural theme ever composed. Its sources and parallels have been extensively studied and its relationship to *Redgauntlet*, in which it appears, has been suggestively analyzed. But only David Daiches, to my knowledge, has ever linked Scott's tale with what to my mind is one of its most interesting analogues — Robert Burns's "Tam O'Shanter." In his essay, "Scott's *Redgauntlet*," Daiches remarks in passing that Willie's tale is "the perfect counterpart in prose, from the point of view of technique though not of content, of Burns's 'Tam O'Shanter' "[1] Why the two works have never been extensively compared, however, is not difficult to discern. For the formal distinctions between a prose short story embedded in a novel and a narrative poem suggest a limitation to the depth and success of such a comparison. But to compare them, I submit, yields interesting insights into the originality Scott shared with the older "heaven-taught plowman" poet whom Scott at sixteen had been so eager to meet. The following paragraphs explore what I consider to be the major similarities between the two narratives, similarities which confirm Daiches's observation that "Wandering Willie's Tale" is "the perfect counterpart in prose" of Burns's "Tam O'Shanter."

First, the characterization of Steenie Steenson and Tam O'Shanter provides interesting parallels in that both are honest, happy peasants who love music; Tam is a crooner of auld Scotch sonnets, Steenie a player of the bagpipes who incidentally learned "Well hoddler, Luckie" from a warlock who played it at Satan's worship. Both are favorites of their neighbors: Tam's cronies are the blacksmith, the miller, Kirton Jean,

[1] "Scott's *Redgauntlet*," *From Jane Austen to Joseph Conrad: Essays Collected in Memory of James T. Hillhouse* (Minneapolis, 1958), p. 57. See also Coleman Oscar Parsons, "Demonological Background of 'Donnerhugel's Narrative' and 'Wandering Willie's Tale,' " SP, XXX (October, 1933), 604-617; Douglas Bliss, *The Devil in Scotland* (London, 1934), pp. 26-32; and John Patterson, *Memoir of Joseph Train. F.S.A. Scot. The Antiquarian Correspondent of Sir Walter Scott* (Glasgow, 1857), pp. 44-53.

the landlady of the cosy tavern, and Souter Johnnie — his "ancient, trusty, drouthy crony." Steenie is also a favorite in the neighborhood — often called upon to play the pipes and able, if necessary, to scrape up a loan from his neighbors. Perhaps as a consequence of their genial characters, both have flaws that play important parts in the narratives. In the first place, both like to sit bousing at the nappy. Tam of course has the more notorious reputation for haunting the tavern and getting unco fou; Steenie is less given to spirits but likes a drop of brandy now and then. But both are affected identically by alcohol — they become comically rash. Tam intrudes on a dance of warlocks and witches in Kirk Alloway, and Steenie utters an intemperate oath that gets him transported off to Hell. Each has a second flaw, not identical but of like functional significance in the framework of the two narratives: though married to Kate, Tam admires too much a brawlie wench; and Steenie "hadna the saving gift." It is Tam's second flaw that brings on the chase by Nanny in her cutty sark; and Steenie's flaw precipitates the whole action of Scott's story. These common characteristics link the two principal characters of the tales.

The plots of the narratives are also strikingly similar at least in those scenes where the Devil and his gang are confronted. The most noteworthy considerations are these: both Tam and Steenie ride alone on their way home at the witching hour. Both men have been tippling to excess. Steenie has drunk enough in two draughts to put many a man under the boards. Tam, though, has been at the cups all night, "Fast by an ingle, bleezing finely." In such a condition, each encounters the Devil as he rides homeward. He appears to Steenie in two forms: as a mysterious rider who follows up Steenie's oath and boast to go one step further than the gates of Hell to get the rent receipt; and as Redgauntlet himself within the confines of Hell. Tam encounters Old Nick and his hellish crowd dancing in Alloway Kirk. The dance of witches and warlocks, in fact, occurs in both narratives. As Steenie enters the outer courtyard of the infernal Redgauntlet manorhouse, he can see "pipes and fiddles, and as much dancing and deray within as used to be in Sir Robert's house at Pace and Yule, and such high seasons."[2] Similarly, Tam sees:

> Warlocks and witches in a dance;
> Nae cotillion brent new frae France,
> But hornpipes, jigs, strathspeys, and reels,
> Put life and mettle in their heels.
> A winnock-bunker in the east,

[2] Sir Walter Scott, "Wandering Willie's Tale," *Redgauntlet* (Boston, 1892), p. 110. Hereafter, page numbers from this edition will appear in parenthesis after the quotation.

> There sat auld Nick, in shape o' beast;
> A towzie tyke, black, grim, and large,
> To gie them music was his charge:
> He screw'd the pipes and gart them skirl,
> Till roof and rafters a' did dirl.[3]

Both peasants are of course spellbound by the situations in which they find themselves. And both break the spells — Steenie by deliberately uttering "I refer myself to God's pleasure and not to yours"; and Tam by involuntarily blurting out "Weel done, Cutty Sark." Immediately supernatural darkness surrounds both. The major after-effects of these comments, however, are not alike: the warlocks and witches chase Tam out of the Alloway Kirkyard, but Steenie awakes in the dark old kirkyard of the Redgauntlet parish.

The narrative technique or point of view in both stories is also similar. Scott's tale is told by Steenie's grandson Willie many years later. By assigning to Willie a narrative of bygone days, Scott has provided himself with an effective frame for the story and the opportunity to report it in more or less native dialect by a peasant who would religiously have believed the superstitions of the district. Burns's poem is also narrated by a Scots peasant who, like Willie, comments on the action of the narrative as he tells it. One significant parallel between the points of view is the effect of the excitement of the action on the teller of each tale. Willie, as one critic has put it, "begins in a calm, unhurried tone, with only a hint of terror in his voice, but . . . grows breathless with horror and excitement"[4] as his narrative reaches the critical point. Burns's narrator not only grows breathless in narrating the chase but loses his sense of time and perspective: he gets inside the story in order to spur on the mare Meg as the witches begin gaining on Tam — as if the action and the narration of it were simultaneous events (p. 95):

---

[3] Robert Burns, "Tam O'Shanter," *The Complete Works of Robert Burns*, ed. Alexander Smith (London, 1900), p. 93. Hereafter, page numbers from this edition will appear in parenthesis before the quotation. There is a significant contrast to be pointed out here, I believe, between the portraits of the Devil in each narrative. Scott's Devil, the mysterious stranger who calls Steenie's bluff and holds him to his oath, belongs to the familiar tradition of Satan as The Adversary, the sinister embodiment of all the forces of Evil — a figure commonplace in the traditional lore of demonology. The Devil in Burns's poem, however, belongs to another tradition of diablerie more common to Scotland, perhaps, than elsewhere. He is the "tricky rascal" who, in Professor Kurt Wittig's words, "likes to enjoy himself, courts the lasses, whistles, dances, drinks, cannot get rid of his cloven hoof, and frequently disguises himself as a fisher or a workman, or in a dark suit like a kirk-elder." He is a halfway appealing Deil who goes by such familiar and affectionate names as Auld Clootie, Hornie, Nickie Ben, or (as here) Auld Nick. See Kurt Wittig's *The Scottish Tradition in Literature* (Edinburgh, 1958), p. 212.

[4] Edith Birkhead, *The Tale of Terror* (New York, n. d.); pp. 151-152.

> Ah, Tam! ah, Tam! thou'll get thy fairin!
> In hell they'll roast thee like a herrin!
> In vain thy Kate awaits thy comin!
> Kate soon will be a woefu' woman!
> Now, do thy speedy utmost, Meg,
> And win the key-stane of the brig.[5]

Both narrators, in addition, immediately develop an atmosphere of fear and supernatural danger. Burns's narrator takes great care to suggest that the sensual pleasures of life which Tam enjoys are all transitory (p. 92):

> But pleasures are like poppies spread,
> You seize the flower, its bloom is shed;
> Or like the snow-falls in the river,
> A moment white — then melts forever.

This sober reminder is deepened and intensified, moreover, by the howling storm outside the tavern which provides the proper setting for the supernatural events which are about to envelop Tam as he rides homeward (p. 92):

> The wind blew as 'twad blawn its last;
> The rattling show'rs rose on the blast;
> The speedy gleams the darkness swallow'd;
> Loud, deep, and lang, the thunder bellow'd;
> That night, a child might understand,
> The Deil had business on his hand.

[5] The narrators have, of course, their differences. Willie is thoroughly a peasant, naive in his uncritical acceptance of the supernatural story he tells. Burns's narrative, though based on the traditions of oral storytelling, betrays signs that it is primarily intended to be read rather than told ("Now, wha this tale o'truth shall read"). Thomas Crawford has argued that Burns is here "speaking with several different voices" in several different dialects [*Burns: A Study of the Poems and Songs* (Edinburgh, 1960), p. 235; but on the matter of dialects, see Wittig, p. 203]. The tension between the oral and written features of the poem may arise because there are actually two narrators in the poem. The first is the "implied narrator" whom Burns has created to speak for him. This *persona* is prudent, excitable, superstitious, and given to melancholy moralizing. He is also a Scots rhymer who knows his own poetic limitations ("But here my muse her wing maun cour; / Sic flights are far beyond her pow'r"). Like Tam he loves a lassie but is no fool for a withered beldam or hag. (In these respects the "implied narrator" is somewhat like Willie.) The other narrator is of course Burns himself, the ordering intelligence who brings comedy out of the juxtaposition of event and comment, of fact and delusion, and out of experience narrated and meaning assigned it. Although it is not easy to distinguish the voices at all points, Burns does seem at times to express his own views: "(Auld Ayr, wham ne'er a town surpasses, / For honest men and bonie lasses.)" In the moralizing lines beginning "Now, wha this tale o' truth shall read" we hear the voices of both narrators: the "implied narrator" means the moral to be taken literally; on the basis of Tam's experience, the moral contains his sober advice. An octave below, however, we detect the voice of Burns the sophisticated writer having his fun not only with Tam and the witches but also with the grave moralist and his admonition to the reader.

Willie also develops the atmosphere of fear and dread surrounding Sir Robert Redgauntlet when he remarks "our fathers used to draw breath thick if ever they heard him named." Later Willie observes, "Far and wide was Sir Robert hated and feared. Men thought he had a direct compact with Satan. . . . The best blessing they wared on him was 'Deil scowp wi' Redgauntlet' " (p. 101). When Steenie visits him with the rent money, his face looks "as gash and ghastly as Satan's." In addition, he has an "ill-favored jackanape" of a monkey called Major Weir, "named after the warlock that was burnt."

Another similar technique which Burns and Scott employ is the catalogue of horrors which accompany the Devil — a piling on, as it were, of horrible details and personages. Steenie encounters Middleton, Rothes, Lauderdale, Dalyell, Earlshall "with Cameron's blude on his hand," and Bonshaw "that tied blessed Mr. Cargill's limbs till the blude sprung." Dunbarton Douglas, MacKenyie, and Claverhouse himself are also encountered, not to speak of their wicked serving-men — all of them detested persecutors of the Covenanters. Tam likewise sees a catalogue of hair-raising sights (p. 93):

> Coffins stood round like open presses,
> That shaw'd the dead in their last dresses;
>
> A murderer's banes in gibbet airns;
> Twa span-lang, wee, unchristen'd bairns;
> A thief, new-cutted frae the rape,
> Wi' his last gasp his gab did gape;
> Five tomahawks, wi' blude red rusted;
> Five scymitars, wi' murder crusted;
>
> Wi' mair o' horrible and awfu',
> Which ev'n to name wad be unlawfu'.

The same comic moral also comes through both tales, although Burns is more explicitly writing with tongue in cheek. As a result of the horrors which he had seen, Steenie swore off pipes and brandy for a long year: ". . . it was not even till the year was out, and the fatal day passed, that he would so much as take the fiddle, or drink usquebaugh or tippenny" (p. 116). Burns's narrator also warns us, in language Scott might have remembered, that "Wi' tippenny, we fear nae evil; / Wi' usquebae, we'll face the devil!" (p. 93), and he concludes his narrative with the justly famous moral (p. 95):

> Now, wha this tale o' truth shall read,
> Ilk man and mother's son take heed;
> When e'er to drink you are inclin'd,
> Or cutty-sarks run in your mind,

> Think, ye may buy the joys o'er dear,
> Remember Tam O'Shanter's mare.

It is worth observing, finally, that the events in Scott's tale are more rationally comprehensible than those of "Tam O'Shanter." At least, Scott provides at the end of his tale logical alternatives to the supernatural explanation implied by the events. But given the factor of John Barleycorn, Burns's tale, like Scott's, can be "explained" as the hair-raising hallucination of a comic inebriate.

Although aspects of the atmosphere, characterization, and plot structure reflect the traditional conventions of the supernatural narrative in Scotland, it is worth pointing out that Scott was, as one critic has put it, not only familiar with Burns's poetry but also "probably better equipped to understand Burns's character and work than any other man of his generation."[6] Both of them shared a native Scots tradition in language and lore — and were best as writers when they worked within that tradition.[7] In view of these facts and parallels, it is perhaps not unreasonable to suggest that Burns's poem might have unconsciously shaped the composition of "Wandering Willie's Tale."

JAMES W. TUTTLETON
UNIVERSITY OF WISCONSIN

---

[6] Franklyn B. Snyder, *The Life of Robert Burns* (New York, 1932), p. 484.

[7] See Stephen Gwynn, *The Life of Sir Walter Scott* (Boston, 1930), p. 100; and Wittig, pp. 199, 203, 228-230, 235.

Reviews

William Thomson (ed.). *Orpheus Caledonius: A collection of Scots songs set to music.* Hatboro, Pa. Folklore Associates. 1962. 2 vol. in one. $10.00 (Facsimile reprint).

The historical importance of the *Orpheus Caledonius* (1725) is that it was the first collection of Scottish songs that printed music as well as words; and it appeared in London, not in Scotland, in order to "cash in on" the fashion for Scottish and pseudo-Scottish verse and music then sweeping the Court of George and Caroline. The present reprint is of the two volume edition of 1733, which contained an additional hundred songs in all; deleted the unhistorical attribution of certain melodies to David Rizzio that disfigured the 1725 edition; and replaced the original "wayward bass" with what H. G. Farmer, in his foreword to this facsimile, describes as "something better." Like the 1725 edition, Vol. I of the 1733 *Orpheus* included Thomson's original dedicatory epistle to the Princess of Wales, now the Queen, with its statement that "Your Majesty having graciously heard some of the following songs" (presumably sung by Thomson himself) "encouraged me to resolve on publishing them;" and it also printed the introductory lines *On Mr. Thomson's Orpheus Caledonius* (1725), which state quite clearly what the court and the aristocracy chose to see in Scottish song:

> Love's brightest flames warm *Scottish* Lads,
> Tho' coolly clad in High-land Plads;
> They scorn Brocade, who like the Lass,
> Nor need a Carpet. if there's Grass;
> With Pipe and Glee each Hill resounds,
> And Love that gives, can heal their Wounds.

And "kind Nature" fills the anonymous poets, composers and arrangers (in great measure, Allan Ramsay and his friends) as she fills "the gay Warblers of the Spring" with "sweet and unaffected Notes." Thus artificial verse paid tribute to simplicity and passion in 1725, as it was to do twenty-four years later, when Collins wrote his *Ode on the Popular Superstitions of the Highlands of Scotland.*

Yet the *Orpheus Caledonius* is by no means the first indication of a vogue for Scottish music in England. As Mr. Farmer points out, Henry

Playford in 1700 brought out *A Collection of Original Scotch-Tunes (Full of Highland Humours) for the Violin: being the first of its kind yet printed*; and — a point not noted by Mr. Farmer — in the second half of the seventeenth century English music publishers often included Scots airs in their compilations, such as *Apollo's Banquet* (1691), Playford's *Musick's Delight on the Cithren* (1666), and *Musick's Recreation on the Viol* (1652). As far back as 1651, John Playford printed Scottish tunes in his *English Dancing Master*; a Highlander's March and a Scots March were added to the 1665 edition; and in the 1669 edition "Johnny cock up thy beaver" appears. One of the most popular London singers in the decade before 1688 was John Abell, who included "Katherine Ogie" in his repertoire; and the references in Pepys's diary are familiar, as when on 2 Jan. 1666 Mrs. Knipp sings the "little Scotch song of Barbary Allen" or on 28 July of the same year he hears Scotch fiddle music at Lord Lauderdale's — "but, Lord! the strangest ayre that ever I heard in my life, and all of one cast." As Shakespearian and other references prove, Scottish music and song were known and valued in England from late Elizabethan times onwards. It follows, then, that William Thomson's *Orpheus* must be seen as a point along a line of development rather than as the start of an altogether new process. If Collins' *Ode* already referred to and Gray's *The Bard* (not to speak of James Thomson's *Rule Britannia*) document the eighteenth century attempt to achieve a new super-nationality that should be British rather than English or Welsh or Scottish, then so too, do Thomson's *Orpheus*, the forty Scots or pseudo-Scots tunes in d'Urfey's *Pills to Purge Melancholy* (ed. 1719-20), the many Scots songs in Gay's *Beggar's Opera* and *Polly*, and — above all — Allan Ramsay's *Tea Table Miscellany*, predominantly Scottish, but whose third volume consisted entirely of *English* songs.

Though he quotes Allan Ramsay's complaint that the words of most of Thomson's songs were really Ramsay's, Mr. Farmer does not dwell on Thomson's plagiarism, nor does he bring out that Alexander Stuart's *Musick for Allan Ramsay's Collection of Scots Songs Edinr: Printed and Sold by Allan Ramsay* was almost certainly an answer to the 1725 edition of the *Orpheus*. It is sometimes stated that a complete set of Stuart's Collection does not exist, but the late Harry M. Wilsher found copies of all the airs in Stuart's six volumes in the Wighton Collection in the Central Library of Dundee. Comparing Stuart and Thomson, Wilsher wrote: "Over ninety of the airs in the Tea Table Miscellany appear in the two volumes of the Orpheus Caledonius, but Stuart and Thomson hardly ever provide the same version of an air. Sometimes the differences are small; sometimes they are considerable. As a rule, Stuart's versions are less simple than Thomson's and are marked by a greater elaboration and ornament. About a dozen airs are found in Stuart's volumes which do not appear in the *Orpheus Caledonius*." ("Music in Scotland during three centuries (1450-1750), being contributions towards the history of music in Scotland," 3 pts. Unpublished doctoral thesis, St. Andrews, 1945, Part II, p. 58). But if Stuart's music is more elaborate than Thomson's, Thomson's is in its turn more complicated — more "art" and less "folk" — than versions of the same airs found in earlier MSS., such as the Agnes Hume MS. in the National Library of Scotland. Wilsher comments that this development is only what we would expect from the evolution of eighteenth century taste, and he criticises the *Orpheus Caledonius* because its

> fitment of words to music is sometimes indifferent, often awkward and occasionally thoroughly bad. In the Bonny Earle of Murray and others, especially where the method is one note, one syllable, the fitment is perfect: but too often elsewhere, the accent is on a weak syllable and at other times the sense of the text is killed by the angular and awkward arrangement of the musical phrases. In "Absent from the Nymph I love," the muscular accent comes on the second syllable of the word "fairer." In "Mary Scot," the definite articles and prepositions are given prominence on the first note of the bar without reason, when a little adjustment would have avoided the awkwardness: actually the version of this air chosen by Thomson with its octave leaps for the voice and commonplace "quaverings" is a poor thing compared with the version in the Agnes Hume MS. Doubtless . . . much was left to the singer's ingenuity. . . . As for the accompaniments, they are of the sketchiest and dullest sort, unless Thomson merely meant them as a guide for a skilled performer to fill in a fuller background." (*Ibid.*, pp.57-8)

Mr. Farmer's Foreword repeats the error (also found in his introduction to the 1962 facsimile reprint of the *Scots Musical Museum*) that the *Tea Table Miscellany*, Vol. I, was first published in 1724, and his rather coy approval of Ramsay's "softening" of his bawdy originals is hardly in accord with the spirit of most modern folksong scholars. He has some interesting comments on the bibliography of the *Orpheus*.

The publishers are to be commended on issuing this invaluable reprint. Every library should buy two copies — one for its literature and another for its musical collection; and it should be brought to the attention of folksingers in every part of the world.

THOMAS CRAWFORD

UNIVERSITY OF AUCKLAND

Robert Henryson. *Poems.* Selected and edited with an Introduction, Notes, and Glossary by Charles Elliott. Oxford. Clarendon Press. 1963. xxvi + 184pp. 18 shillings.

Next year will see the centenary of the first collected edition of Henryson's *Poems and Fables,* published by David Laing. In the intervening years, Henryson's stock as a poet has risen steadily, so much so that Dr. Kurt Wittig does not scruple to say that "in his assimilation of European subject matter, of Chaucer's conception of the poetic art, and of Scottish characteristics, Robert Henryson is one of the greatest poets of the whole of Scottish literature, perhaps the greatest of all, certainly the one with the most marked personality" (*The Scottish Tradition in Literature,* 1958, p.52). More judiciously, the editor of this latest volume in the Clarendon Medieval and Tudor Series assigns Henryson to a place among the "Scottish Chaucerians" and calls him "less precious and more fundamental than James I, less immediately impressive and more practical than Dunbar, less 'allegorical' and more succinct than Douglas" (p.xv). These judgments do not rest on an extensive canon of poetry—one long work, two medium-sized ones, and thirteen lesser pieces. Of this, Mr. Elliott gives a complete *Morall Fabillis* and *Testament of Cresseid,* the "Complaint of Orpheus" from "Orpheus and Euridyce," and the following short poems: "The Garmont of Gud Ladeis," "The Annunciation," "The Bludy Serk," "The Thre Deid-Pollis," "Nerar Hevynis Blys" ("The Prais of Age"), "Ane Prayer for the Pest," and "Robene and Makyne." The reasons for excluding the other poems are convincing, and in any case they are readily available in Harvey Wood's editions (1st, 1933; 2nd, revised, 1958). Whoever meets Henryson for the first time in this selection will be well served. An acceptable text, normalized on sound editorial principles, is clearly presented, while the notes and glossary are accurate and pithy: *guid gear in sma' buik.* Only the "Appreciations" seem expendable—unnecessary mock-cream on an otherwise excellent cake. Could the general editor of the series be persuaded to substitute in forthcoming volumes a section devoted to "Criticism," which would reprint spirited essays of interpretation and analysis likely to offer fruitful approaches to the texts?

As for Henryson's "marked personality," Dr. Wittig speaks confidently about this in a literary sense. Biographically, the poet is a shadowy figure indeed. Tradition has associated him with the calling of schoolmaster in Dunfermline, and he died in time to qualify for inclusion in Dunbar's "Lament for the Makaris" (written *c.* 1505, printed, 1508-9).

For the meagre facts that do exist about Henryson, Mr. Elliott refers us to David Laing's edition (*Poems and Fables*, 1865, pp.ix-xxi, xxxvii-lx). One notes that Mr. Elliott makes no attempt to describe the circumstances of a typical Scots schoolmaster of the late fifteenth century and what he might have taught and read, surely matters of some interest to Henryson's readers. In this connexion, use could have been made of the contributions to the *Innes Review* and the books that have arisen from this periodical: John Durkan and Anthony Ross, *Early Scottish Libraries* (1961) and *Essays on the Scottish Reformation 1513-1625*, ed. David McRoberts (1962). It is startling to find, in view of Henryson's realistic depiction of the ravages of leprosy, that in Glasgow in the early sixteenth century, "the grammar schoolmaster was also chaplain of the leper hospital of St. Ninian beyond Glasgow bridge," and that there is reason to believe that the Stirling schoolmaster acted in a similar capacity (*Essays*, "Education in the Century of the Reformation," pp.158-159 and *n*.118). Was this experience Henryson's too, one wonders? Then, Henryson apparently acted as a notary public in Dunfermline, and a good deal is known about this official in Scotland, whose social status was much higher than that of his counterpart in medieval England (*Essays*, "Parish Life in Scotland, 1500-1560," p.93). Henryson's breadth of contact with all walks of life becomes much more understandable in the light of such information. A critic's sensitivity to his subject's experience of life and the voices heard in his milieu can assist greatly in the work of interpretation and evaluation, as Francis Berry has reminded us recently in *Poetry and the Physical Voice* (1963). Perhaps the shadowy Henryson need not be so shadowy after all.

Aside from biographical oversights, Mr. Elliott provides a stimulating introduction. First, he addresses himself to the question, in what sense is Henryson a *Chaucerian*? He points out that the Scots poet looks to his English predecessor for some of his basic subject matter, and that in handling some of his topics he manifests a "Chaucerian protrusion of personality," either directly or obliquely or through simple extension of "area of reference," when a speaker becomes a champion for a group. Thus in "Ane Prayer for the Pest" the poetic voice takes up *our* quarrel with God, just as Harry Bailly rejects the Pardoner's claims on behalf of the pilgrims and, by natural extension, on behalf of the laity. In his attitude towards his material, Henryson also resembles Chaucer. Both poets, for example, show a capacity for disabusing their audience about easy acceptance of conventions, either literary or social. Mr. Elliott argues, too, that Henryson has the Chaucerian touch in his expression, particularly in the effective juxtaposition of rhetorical and colloquial passages. Finally, the link between Henryson's and Chaucer's forms is pointed out, for instance, those of "Anelida's Complaint," "An *A B C*," and *Troilus and Criseyde*. In sum, Mr. Elliott makes out a very good case for saying that Henryson read Chaucer with care and intelligence; if this is what being a "Chaucerian" means, then he is one.

To assert Henryson's *autonomy* and *distinctiveness* from Chaucer, Mr. Elliott elects to discuss the *Morall Fabillis* and the *Testament of Cresseid*. In the case of the first poem it is noted that Henryson is firmly committed to the medieval Christian ethos. The world is represented as a dunghill or a wilderness; sojourners in it must look beyond its "wretchitness" and "vanitee" to the "blissit hour" to come. Hence, according to Mr. Elliott, arises the "dichotomizing" or "bifurcation" of the *Fabillis*. The fable proper is customarily worked out at the narrative level in a satisfying way from the literary point of view; sharply separated from the fable is a "Moralitas" which is blatantly didactic. At all costs, temporal values must be subordinated to spiritual ones. Mr. Elliott contrasts Chaucer's easier assurance that "the Catholic faith can contain centrifugal forces." The implication, of course, is that Henryson is thereby revealed as the lesser artist. But is he, in this regard? In a recent article, Mr. Denton Fox has demonstrated convincingly, through a careful topical and rhetorical analysis of "The Taill of the Cok and the Jasp" and "The Preiching of the Swallow," that narrow assumptions about the dichotomy between the Fabill and the Moralitas will not do ("Henryson's Fables," *ELH*, XXIX, 1962, 337-356). Mr. Fox holds to the unity of Henryson's vision and insists, for example, on the literary skill displayed in the ironic elevation of the cock through his aureate speech, his deflation in the course of the speeches about him by his wives, and the mordant note struck in the Moralitas, where the cock is declared to represent stupid man, and we realize that we are involved in his particular form of stupidity, i.e. male arrogance and blindness. The "Preiching" in Mr. Fox's view, asserts through the tellingly-registered moods and tones of the poem, "the ontological superiority of God," and the Moralitas has a functional role in establishing the relationship between the actual and ideal worlds which God comprehends. The basic contention of this article is that we should take seriously Henryson's statement about the purpose and mode of the kind of poetry he is writing in the *Fabillis*; this poetry is designed ". . . to repreif the haill misleving / Off man be figure of ane uther thing" (ll.6-7). In other words, Henryson is suggesting that the *Fabillis* can be interpreted in the same fashion as his contemporaries read the Old Testament, holding that it "prefigured" the New. The Aesopian animals talk like men; men sometimes behave like animals. The Moralitas does not blunt this satirical point—it can and does direct the satire to its target with power and artistry.

Henryson's chief claim to distinction, of course, lies with the *Testament of Cresseid*, that marvel of medieval literature, an extensive poem without longueurs, a veritable triumph of poetic attack and verve. Mr. Elliott sees it as a work dealing with sin, punishment, and regeneration, which transcends the code of *amour courtois* and invokes such forces as Providence and Destiny, and ultimately Divine Reason; this is his reading of the doom pronounced on Cresseid by the *parliament* of the gods, and of her final acceptance of a fate that is self-caused. Cresseid's Pride and Anger are represented as the immediate occasion of the suffering visited on her. The "falsing" of Troilus is artfully kept in the background until Cresseid learns of his unwitting kindness to her when she is a leper, at which point she can recognise the enormity of her initial offence:

> 'Thy lufe, thy lawtie and thy gentilnes
> I countit small in my prosperitie,
> Sa elevait I was in wantones
> And clam upon the fickill quheill sa hie.
> All faith and lufe I promissit to the
> Was in the self fickill and frivolous:
> O fals Cresseid and trew knicht Troilus!
>   . . .
> Nane but myself as now I will accuse.'
>
> (ll. 547-574)

When she is finally purged of self-pity by an instructed view of her lot, Cresseid wills her body to the worms and toads, and her spirit to Diana. The importance which Mr. Elliott attaches to Cresseid's display of Anger could be supported by an appeal to medieval psychology; witness St. Thomas's treatment of the sensitive appetite and his resolution of it into the concupiscible and irascible powers (*Summa Theologica*, Q.81, Art.3). On this view, Cresseid's tragedy arises because her appetite dominates her will and reason. The poem presents her at the point when her concupiscible power is blocked ("I fra luifferis left and all forlane!" l.140) and irascibility gets full reign ("Upon Venus and Cupid angerly / Scho cryit out," ll.124-5).

As it happens, however, Mr. Elliott's interpretation has already been challenged by the criticism that it continues a long-standing confusion about the moral centre of the poem ("Cresseid in Scotland," *TLS*, 9 April 1964, p.290). It is pointed out that we are asked to believe that Cresseid is punished for the Christian sins of Pride and Anger, manifested in her chiding of the gods Cupid and Venus. Less muddled thinking, it is claimed in the *TLS* article, suggests that Cresseid's cursing of the gods and her dream-vision of the *parliament* is an allegorical representation of her life after being discarded by Diomed. The offence for which she is punished is her failure to live according to the code of *amour courtois* which had brought her happiness in the past. This is the blasphemy in *deed*, for which Cupid says she must suffer bitter pains:

> 'Lo!' quod Cupide, 'quha will blaspheme the name
> Of his awin god, outher in word [or] deid,
> To all goddis he dois baith lak and schame,
> And suld have bitter panis to his meid:
> I say this by yone wretchit Cresseid,
> The quhilk throw me was sum tyme flour of lufe,
> . . . '

(ll.274-279)

Still, a consensus of recent critical opinion is on Mr. Elliott's side in believing that more is involved in the *Testament* than the "courtly theme of the betrayal of a lover" ("Cresseid in Scotland"). Mr. Douglas Duncan, for instance, holds that the poet of the *Testament* is a Yeats-in-his-tower figure, aware of the loss of his sexuality and sympathetic to the similar, but naturally more poignant plight of a young woman: ". . . that seid [of lufe] with froist is slane," l.139). Out of Cresseid's bitterness and suffering is made a pessimistic, if guarded, exposure of a world lacking in divine justice of any merciful sort. The questioner of the social and political order in the *Morall Fabillis* now becomes the questioner of the theological order ("Henryson's *Testament of Cresseid*," *EIC*, XI, 1961, 128-135). Mr. Sidney Harth will have none of this and chooses to argue that the poem is an exercise in irony. He depicts the poet as a Noel Coward figure, drink in hand, compèring a display of typical behaviour by the pagan gods, who punish Cresseid for several transgressions—poor choice of sexual partner in an affair; prostitution; and contumacity towards themselves ("Henryson Reinterpreted," *EIC*, XI, 1961, 471-480). A more finished piece of criticism by Mr. A. C. Spearing affirms that the *Testament* is a true medieval tragedy, displaying the downward turn of Fortune's wheel as Cresseid's miseries relentlessly accumulate: betrayal, prostitution, disease, bitter self-knowledge, and death. Mr. Spearing's most penetrating insight lies in his awareness that the poem ultimately expands beyond the terms of reference of medieval tragedy and explores an "Euripidean situation": a conflict between cruel and powerful gods and an impotent, foolish, and wicked mortal, whose suffering involves the emotions of readers and engages their compassion ("*The Testament of Cresseid* and the 'High Concise Style,'" *Speculum*, XXXVII, 1962, 208-225).

[2 7 2]

Herein is the way to a richer understanding of the poem—by means of a thorough analysis of its tragic rhythm, going beyond the Euripidean model even, and taking into account the enaction of tragic rituals which call on the deepest levels of our response to mimesis. The *prologue* strikes the right portentous note, from the reference to hail showers in April, with its hint of cosmological discord, to the dramatic irony of the welcome of the priest of Venus to a daughter who has sinned against Venus: "'Thow art full deir ane gest'" (l.105). The *agon* of Cresseid's angry crying out on the gods follows. The *climax* is provided by the *parliament* of the gods, while the *peripety* is to be found in the sentence passed on Cresseid by Saturn and Cynthia, and the *recognition* comes when Cresseid looks in the glass after her dream, and again when Calchas is admitted to her presence. The *pathos* or *sparagmos* of Cresseid's suffering among the leper-folk runs its course until her encounter with Troilus. This gives rise to the *epiphany*, when Cresseid perceives what she really is, and offers herself as "mirrour" and "exempill" to those who will survive her, sharing with them the knowledge she has gained at such terrible cost. As *nemesis* overtakes *hybris*, Cresseid appears to us as a tragic protagonist, incorporating elements of the *alazon* and the *pharmakos*, the self-deceiver who becomes a scapegoat and promotes in onlookers the authentic *purgation* of pity and fear. [For a commentary on the terms used in this discussion, see Francis Ferguson, *The Idea of a Theatre* (1949), and Northrop Frye, *Anatomy of Criticism* (1957).]

Though Mr. Elliott might not sanction such an interpretation, he is certainly responsible for making us think again about Henryson by providing so admirable a text. The poet is indeed fortunate in his editor; both are true sons of Mercurius, who most assuredly can "in brief sermone ane pregnant sentence wryte."

IAN ROSS
UNIVERSITY OF BRITISH COLUMBIA

John Prebble. *The Highland Clearances*. London. Secker & Warburg. 1963. 35 shillings.

In this moving account of the diaspora of the clansmen of the North and of the Isles, Mr. Prebble has closed, it would appear, his tragic chronicles of the Scottish Highlands. In his *Culloden*, he recounted the sacrifices made in '45 by the clansmen at the summons of their chiefs; in *The Highland Clearances*, he has laid bare the shameful and ironic and tragic

consequences, not only of Lowland and English policy, but of the chief-
tains', the clan-fathers', betrayal of their own loyal children. For tragic
any chronicle of the "clearances" must be, in the strictest classical and
Aristotelian sense: one of deeds committed callously or ignorantly, out of
greed or blind pride, by fathers upon children, upon those who were, or
should have been, "near or dear" to them. Whatever inaccuracies other
historians may find in Mr. Prebble's relation, whatever callous responses
may be made by latter-day Malthusians or defenders of utilitarian "improvements" (vide, e.g., Thomas Crawford, Burns, pp. 160-164), no
humane reader and certainly no true son of the North or of the Isles can
gainsay that the primal sanctities, the archetypal ties of chieftain and
clan-children, were cruelly and repeatedly violated during the long agony
of the century of the brutally but rightly named "clearances." With restrained yet just wrath and in the saddest cadences, Mr. Prebble tells us
of the time when men and women and children bearing the proud ancestral names were burned out like vermin or bracken from lands their
chiefs and lairds had set apart for sheep and deer, and then driven perforce
to death or exile upon or beyond the Atlantic roar. During the closing
decades of this same century (1762-1856), continentals and Irishmen
fled famine and foreign oppressors; their stories are pitiful enough; but
at least they had not been betrayed and expelled by their own race and
blood, nor do their ancestral lands remain largely unpeopled today by
kinsmen of their names.

This, almost the latest of Scotland's tragic centuries, has found then
in Mr. Prebble its Holinshed, one indeed more faithful to history and
more eloquent than the chroniclers who inspired Macbeth and Henry VI.
Whether some new Demodocus or Barbour will in time to come put in
moving numbers these "old, unhappy, [not too] far-off things," we
cannot know. The lyric planctus of the Canadian Boat Song is destined,
it may be, not to be matched—surely it is not to be surpassed—in the
grander genres.

Less proleptic questions must concern sons of Scotland in our generation. Issues of retribution and reparation still confront us; their resolution Mr. Prebble has not attempted, nor is this the time and place to
weigh such grave matters. Yet the students of Scottish literature composed since 1745 may yet inquire with what fidelity to the truth, with
what insight and compassion, with what sureness of dramatic and ethical
judgment, have the "burnings of the North and the Isles" been reflected
in latter-day Scottish poetry and fiction and drama. A Samuel Maclean
can make a proud answer for the bards of the Gael. Have the bards of
the Gall shown a like insight and compassion or even awareness? Mr.

Prebble has pointed in his account of the crucial and classical instance of Glengarry, Alistair Ranaldson, chief of Clan Macdonell, to the varying degrees of understanding and ignorance manifested by Burns and by Scott. Detailed and all-inclusive accounts of the treatment of the "burnings" in Scottish literature, whether Gaelic or non-Gaelic, remain still to be written. Mr. Prebble is perhaps himself best qualified to describe the relevant but embarrassingly limited non-Gaelic literature. Nor, should he undertake such an account, need he be too sober and detached and passionless: the grave and ironic and shameful truths of this history can never be grasped by Malthusian or Benthamite theorist dead to human ties or by some scribbling gillie of a late twentieth century heir to Glengarry or Sutherland.

A. M. F. GUNN

TEXAS TECHNOLOGICAL COLLEGE

The Scottish National Dictionary. Designed partly on regional lines and partly on historical principles, and containing all the Scottish words known to be in use or to have been in use since c. 1700. Edited by William Grant, M.A., LL.D. (1929-46) and David D. Murison, M.A., B.A. (1946-). Edinburgh. The Scottish National Dictionary Association Ltd.

The *Scottish National Dictionary* goes back to a suggestion of Sir William A. Craigie, made as long ago as 1907, and is the modern counterpart to Craigie's *Dictionary of the Older Scottish Tongue.* Publication started in 1929 at King's College, Aberdeen, but *SND* has in the meantime moved to Edinburgh, where it is now under the auspices of the School of Scottish Studies of Edinburgh University.

For *SND*, a total length of 10 volumes is envisaged. The earlier volumes had four fascicules of 80 pages each, but in recent years the length has grown and the latest half dozen parts had 128 pp., making volumes of 512 pp. The pre-war subscription price was £20, payable in four yearly instalments; some ten years ago the price was raised to £30, and more recently to £40. But even so, *SND* may be the best bargain to be had anywhere on the book market: a volume of 512 pp. in Royal 4° for £4, or roughly $11! This unbelievable price can only be maintained by substantial donations, especially from the Carnegie Trust for the Universities of Scotland, the Burns Federation, the Educational Institute of Scotland, a number of town councils (Glasgow, Aberdeen), and a good many private individuals, Burns Clubs, etc. from three continents.

This year, *SND* can look back on 35 years of publication and 22 parts. Work was often held up by war and post-war difficulties, but of late the different parts have succeeded one another more quickly. Some three years ago, half-way house was reached, and at the present rate of progress, the dictionary should be completed in a little over a dozen years. Certainly all students of Scottish literature wish Mr. David D. Murison, the very efficient editor, best of luck and speedy progress in his life's work.

For there can be no doubt about the urgent need for this dictionary. Before *SND* (if we exclude works which are essentially glossaries, such as Chambers' *Scots Dialect Dictionary*) there is only Jamieson's *Dictionary of the Scottish Language* of 1808-25 (!), and this, necessarily, often makes a poor show. *SND* deals with the vocabulary of literary and spoken Scots, including the dialects of the mainland, Orkney, Shetland, and Ulster, from 1700 to the present day; it does not deal with Gaelic or Standard English as spoken in Scotland. The sources comprise some 5,000 books, whose bibliography will form part of the last volume, and a large number of correspondents, readers, excerptors, and experts. The general method followed is that of the *New English Dictionary*, while the regional treatment follows Wright's *English Dialect Dictionary*. A general introduction of 50 pp. in Vol. I gives a survey of the boundaries of Scottish speech, of Scots and dialect literature, of phonetic change, a phonetic comparison between modern Scots and modern English, and a phonetic characterisation of the dialect districts.

The aim of *SND* is twofold: it aims at being a comprehensive dictionary of the Scots tongue, and it intends to be an encyclopedia of Scottish institutions, the Church, the legal system, trades and crafts, children's games, national dishes, social history, superstitions and folklore, national games, local ceremonies, etc. This encyclopedic aspect is of immense help in understanding Scottish life and Scottish literature, especially since the definitions and sources given are highly illuminating. One need only mention some of the obvious examples (*Gretna Green; Habbie; Haggis; Halloween; hap, stap and lowp; hert of Midlothian; hogmanay; Hieland*) to indicate the scope of this "dictionary." The editors are certainly not claiming too much when they call *SND* "a history of the Scottish people arranged alphabetically."

The encyclopedic character also permeates the purely lexicographical side. The quotations given to illustrate the usage of a word can often serve as definitions and seem to be the most characteristic example from the whole of Scottish literature. The rich vocabulary of Scots has been set down with painstaking scholarship that leaves nothing to be desired. Even in so well-known texts as those of Scott, the ballads, or Burns we find many instances to show how vague or even slipshod all of the former glossaries were: in most Burns editions *leeze me (on)*—to take an example at random—is considered to be a verb "command me to"; in *SND* it is shown to be a frequent contraction of *lief is me (on)*, and this is what gives the passage its true meaning and allows a full enjoyment. Dozens of similar examples could be quoted, and in each case we not only learn the true denotation, but also see the expression in all its connotations and in its development and usage. And we finally come to enjoy a poem like Burns's "Willie Wastle," which so far all glossaries have fought shy of.

A comprehensive review of some 2,500 pp. of dictionary is not the place for detailed discussion of individual points of etymology, pronunciation (given in narrow API transcription), relationship, etc.; for more than a dozen years, *Anglia* has carried my extensive reviews of the parts of *SND* as they appeared. But I should at least add that *SND* is also a valuable help in face of all those "false friends"—the words that look so familiar and still mean a completely different thing in Scotland. If you read the word *indictment* in a Scottish newspaper, it may not mean what you think, but "the form of process by which a criminal is brought to trial at the instance of the Lord Advocate;" an *inquest* in Scotland is "a body, part jury part witness, which made inquiry into such matters as the service of heirs and cognition of the insane." Would the general reader know that *to run one's letters* means "to await one's trial," or would he understand a police statement saying that "the theft of four hens was libelled in the first charge"? Traps like these are frequent in Scottish texts, even when written in Standard English. They are a reminder that Scots is not just a dialect, but seems to aspire—in the same way as American English—to the status of a semi-independent language with its own history and traditions.

Any page of *SND* is ample evidence of this history and tradition. We see a great many direct lines from Old English, lines that no longer have parallels in modern English. We come across a substantial number of words from Latin and French that have not gone through the medium of English and remind us of the strong links of Scotland with the Continent and, under the Auld Alliance, with France especially. These close contacts must be kept in mind for a phenomenon like that of the aureation of the old Makars: this may have been no more artificial than the language of Chaucer, but while in England the development went on unbroken, the Scottish development of a higher language was abruptly cut short by the Union (and the Reformation, which translated the Bible into English, not Scots). But what makes the most fascinating study is the rich vocabulary of Gaelic and Scandinavian origin. The careful work of *SND* will enable scholars to investigate both the regional domains and the special fields of this adopted vocabulary. That the Highlands and their fringe are rich in words of Gaelic origin will surprise nobody; but it came as a surprise to me to see that Galloway and the Southwest have such a large share. The things, too, that are given Gaelic names are interesting: fish and birds and plants of course; but also feelings, trades, articles of dress, terms of endearment as well as derogatory words, food, and especially a rich vocabulary graphically descriptive of the features of a landscape or a man. Often we see traces of how the ancient Scots translated their thoughts from their native Gaelic into the language of the Sassenach: *gobhar* in Gaelic means both "goat" and "sheaf"—and the Scots word for goat, "gait," has the same secondary meaning. The Scandinavian vocabulary, too, dominant in the Orkneys and Shetlands, has its ramifications on the mainland, and its special charm seems to be a vividly descriptive faculty of all the things connected with the shore, the sea, and weather at sea. I hope that soon after its completion *SND* will give rise to studies of vocabulary of different origins in Scotland. In quite a number of cases, *SND* also points out the Scottish origin of English and American words (*Dean of Faculty, faculty, hellion, hard drink, hold it!, hold up, hastie pudding, heft, high school, janitor*).

More or less as a by-product of the dictionary, we find numerous entries concerning historical grammar, phonology, syntax, and we see the Scottish language not as a collection of words, but as a living organism. Again we come across the Gaelic substratum in sentences like "it's a rough sea that's in it" (*in*) or "I'm after telling him" (*efter*).

I may sound over-enthusiastic about *SND*, yet I am not blind to certain shortcomings—but they are few and far between: an occasional cross reference, a doubtful etymology here or there, a chance word in a modern poem not listed. But in all the years of reviewing *SND* I have always been hard put to it to find any point at all which I could raise as an issue. On the other hand, in all my studies of Scottish literature I have felt the terrible need for this dictionary. The parts already in existence have enormously facilitated—and enriched—my work. There can be no doubt that wherever Scottish literature is studied the *Scottish National Dictionary* is a must.

KURT H. WITTIG
NEUSTADT/SCHWARZWALD, GERMANY

Robert Burns. *The Jolly Beggars. A Cantata.* Edited by John C. Weston. Northampton. The Gehenna Press. 1963. $20.00. Limited to 300 numbered copies.

The study of few writers of major stature has been so hampered by the lack of good texts as has that of Burns. The standard text for his poems remains that established by W. E. Henley in the Henley & Henderson edition of 1896-7. No really significant edition of the poetry has been published since then, although there have been over one hundred of them. The situation with respect to Burns's letters is somewhat better — the DeLancey Ferguson edition (of 1931) brought together over seven hundred letters, collated from the MSS. wherever possible. Not a few letters which survived the poet were used by early editors — notably Currie, Stewart and Cromek — but have not been seen since. Most of these may be presumed to have been destroyed. This would not be so serious if we had full and accurate transcriptions in the printed versions — but we do not. In this respect Currie is particularly blameworthy: the few letters which have come to light have shown that for various reasons (prudishness, "protecting" the names of living people, or just to make them more "readable") Burns's first editor was ever ready with the scissors.

An example of the poor editing which is so common with Burns may be seen in "Tam O'Shanter." The early printed versions and the MSS. of this poem contain the following lines after line 142 ("That even to name wad be unlawfu':—")

> Three lawyers' tongues, turn'd inside out,
> Wi' lies seam'd like a beggar's clout;
> Three priests' hearts, rotten, black as muck,
> Lay stinking, vile, in every neuk.

Upon the advice of Alexander Tytler, Burns dropped these lines from the 1793 edition of his poems. Currie included them in the Appendix to his edition of 1800. The lines were printed, although never in the text, in other important editions (but not that of Robert Chambers) including Henley & Henderson. The situation has deteriorated during the twentieth century. The most ambitious edition (Boston, 1926; London, 1927; 10 vol.) does not even mention what Burns intended to be a part of the poem and removed only in order not to jeopardize the sale of his works. This instance is only one of many which could be cited to show how badly an authoritative variorum text of the poems and songs is needed.

A step in this direction has been taken by Professor John C. Weston of the University of Massachusetts with his elegant limited edition of *The Jolly Beggars*. The ribald piece, which Burns apparently tossed off, seems not to have made a lasting impression on the poet, for he wrote to George Thomson in September 1793 that he had kept no copy of it nor could he remember any of the songs in it. One may wonder whether or not Burns was in earnest: he may well have sensed that Thomson would not be willing to use any of the songs and was closing the issue.

Fortunately two holograph MSS. survived and from one of these *The Jolly Beggars* was first printed in 1799 in the famous Stewart & Meikle chapbooks. Its success must have been immediate for the pamphlet was twice reprinted that year, and again in 1800. In 1801 it was printed at least six times: in *Miscellanea Perthensis* and in five editions of Burns's poems, among them Stewart's *Poems ascribed to Robert Burns*. In 1800 and subsequent editions Currie erred on the side of prudence and omitted the cantata. In fairness to Currie it should be pointed out that Hugh Blair had eliminated it from the Edinburgh edition of 1787. But the work had its champions too — Sir Walter Scott, in reviewing R. H. Cromek's *Reliques of Robert Burns* in *The Quarterly Review* (February 1809), took Cromek (and Currie) to task for omitting the cantata which he found "inferior to no poem of the same length in the whole range of English poetry . . . It is certainly far superior to anything in the *Beggars' Opera,* where alone we could expect to find its parallel." Half a century later Matthew Arnold could safely assert that *The Jolly Beggars* had "a breadth, truth and power which make the famous scene in Auerbach's cellar, of Goethe's *Faust,* seem artificial and tame beside it, and which are only matched by Shakespeare and Aristophanes."

Mr. Weston has meticulously collated the two holograph MSS., a third MS. (not holograph), the first printed version (1799), the Earl of Rosebery's unique *Merry Muses of Caledonia* (c. 1800), and Cromek's *Select Scotish Songs* (1810) in which the editor included the work after Scott's complaint mentioned above. The reason for collating this latter is that there is evidence that Cromek had access to a MS. now lost or destroyed. The *Merry Muses* is, of course, unreliable as a text; the Burns songs it contains may well have been printed from transcriptions (at second, third or fourth hand) of the original MSS.

There are certain interesting problems connected with *The Jolly Beggars* which Weston has examined previously [see his article "The Text of Burns's *The Jolly Beggars*" in *Studies in Bibliography* (1960)]. He concludes that Burns did not intend the Merry-Andrew sequence to be included in the completed work, having discarded it as inferior to the remainder. (Weston includes the sequence in the textual notes, however.) Other characters with their songs have been lost: a sailor, a sootyman, a quack doctor (Hornbook?), and Racer Jess (Poosie Nansie's daughter who, with "twa-three whores," appears in "The Holy Fair").

In addition to the textual notes, the editor has included a section of useful editorial notes and a short Afterword. Scots words which might give the reader difficulty are glossed in the margin. One could question some of these, for instance Weston glosses "raucle Carlin" as "sturdy old girl." Today "old girl" suggests familiarity and affection (infrequently old), whereas the *S.N.D.*, in quoting this passage from *The Jolly Beggars* as an example, defines the word: "a woman, generally an old woman and often in a disparaging sense." But these are *nuances* and would in no way detract from the reader's understanding and enjoyment of this, one of Burns's greatest works. I cannot, incidentally, subscribe to Professor Weston's claim that this is *the* best in Burns.

Burns produced several outstanding satires and songs but only once did he attempt a tale like "Tam O'Shanter" or a cantata like *The Jolly Beggars*. We can only must upon why he did not leave the world more examples of such superior works.

G. R. R.

STUDIES IN SCOTTISH LITERATURE

VOLUME II   NUMBER 1   JULY 1964

CONTENTS

STUDIES IN SCOTTISH LITERATURE

EDITED BY G. ROSS ROY
TEXAS TECHNOLOGICAL COLLEGE

STUDIES IN SCOTTISH LITERATURE is an
independent quarterly devoted to all aspects of
Scottish literature. Articles and notes are welcome.
Subscriptions are available at $5.00 U.S. per annum in the
United States and Canada, elsewhere 30 shillings.
All communications should be addressed to the
Editor, Department of English, Texas Technological College,
Lubbock, Texas, U.S.A.

PUBLISHED BY G. ROSS ROY
AND PRINTED BY THE TEXAS TECH PRESS
LUBBOCK, TEXAS, U.S.A. 79409

CONTRIBUTORS
TO THIS ISSUE

Richard FRENCH: Is Assistant Professor of English at Louisiana State University in New Orleans. He has previously taught at Texas A. & M., the University of Texas, the University of South Carolina, and the University of Southern Mississippi. He received his A.B. and A.M. degrees at Louisiana State University, Baton Rouge, and his Ph.D. from the University of Texas.

Francis R. HART: Teaches English at the University of Virginia. He is a previous contributor to *SSL,* and has recently completed a book on Sir Walter Scott.

David MACAREE: Is a native of Scotland who came to Canada in 1956 as a teacher, and took an M.A. at the University of British Columbia, where he now teaches. He holds the Ph.D. from the University of Washington.

Allan H. MACLAINE: Has previously appeared in *SSL.* He is Professor of English at the University of Rhode Island. At present he is at work on a monograph on Robert Burns, and is editing, with G. Ross Roy, an anthology of Scottish poetry.

ALLAN H. MACLAINE

The *Christis Kirk* Tradition:

Its Evolution in Scots Poetry to Burns

Introduction

The continuity of literary tradition is common to all literatures, but has a peculiar force and consistency in the poetry of Scotland. The Scottish poets have always been especially tradition-bound, loath to experiment with new forms of expression, and usually content to pour new wine into old bottles, to work within the limits of old and familiar methods. The long history of what I shall call the *Christis Kirk* tradition is a most striking illustration of this general truth. Indeed, the *Christis Kirk* tradition is in some respect a unique phenomenon; for it is extremely unusual for a poetic form as highly specialized as this one to survive through generations of changing poetic fashions. The *Christis Kirk* genre began in the fifteenth century, and lived on through four centuries of almost continuous development, culminating in *The Holy Fair* and *The Jolly Beggars* of Burns. In fact, the type persisted through the nineteenth century and even into the twentieth, represented by such poems as David Walter Purdie's *The Kirn* (1885) and George Douglas Brown's untitled poem (1901) in praise of his native village of Ochiltree, Ayshire.[1] After

---

[1] Purdie's very pedestrian effort, largely derived from Burns's *Hallowe'en* and *To a Haggis*, was first published in his *Warblings from Ettrick Forest* (1885), but is more accessible in David Herschell Edwards ed. *Modern Scottish Poets*, 11th Series (Brechin [Scot.], 1888), pp. 298-300; Brown's work, which also shows the pervasive influence of Burns (especially of *The Holy Fair* and *Hallowe'en*), may be found quoted at length (10 stanzas) in James Veitch, *George Douglas Brown* (London, 1952), pp. 160-161. Among a fairly large number of *Christis Kirk* poems written in the early 19th century the following may be cited: Robert Lochore's *Walter's Waddin'*, a long (30 stanzas), mediocre piece, influenced by Burns's *Hallowe'en* and even more by Allan Ramsay's continuations of *Christis Kirk*, first printed in James Grant Wilson ed. *The Poets and Poetry of Scotland* (New York, 1876), I, 382-385; James Lumsden's *Alf and Lowrie*, describing in 25 stanzas (modified from the traditional form) a Saturday ramble of two Edinburgh schoolboys, in his *Edinburgh Poems and Songs* (Haddington [Scot.], 1899), pp. 59-65; Lumsden's *Ae Winter Nicht* in the same volume (pp. 44-56), which contains a panoramic description of Edingurgh's High Street in the *Christis Kirk* manner; and John Breckenridge's

Burns, however, the tradition entered a decadent phase, with the works written in this style tending more and more to be rather artificial and imitative poetic exercises, so that for practical purposes the significant history of the *Christis Kirk* genre ends with Burns. This important strand in the history of Scots poetry has never been studied as a whole, though many scholars have generally recognized its existence.

All poems in the Christis Kirk tradition conform more or less to a single pattern established by its two fifteen-century prototypes, *Christis Kirk on the Green* and *Peblis to the Play,* and may be defined in general terms as poems describing the humors of lower class life on some festive occasion, such as a wedding, a fair, or a country dance. The method of description is for the poet to give a total impression of the whole crowded and colorful scene of holiday merriment, confusion, horseplay, ribaldry, drunkenness, practical joking, and good-natured abandon through highlighting carefully chosen details. The poem is usually given structure and coherence through the introduction of a few rapidly sketched characters who lend specific human interest to the scene and provide the basis for a slender thread of narrative. In all cases the scene is described from the point of view of an amused spectator who takes no part in the action and is presumably on a higher social and intellectual level than the rustic merrymakers. The poem is swift-paced, with rapid and frequent transitions, full of robust movement and vivid detail. As for metrical form, most of the specimens of this type conform to a traditional and fairly complex pattern: a stanza consisting of two quatrains of alternating iambic tetrameter and trimeter, with the addition of a "bobwheel" of one or two lines at the end. The examples given below illustrate the many slight variations of this basic pattern.

Such, in brief and general terms, are the fundamental ingredients of the *Christis Kirk* formula. The purpose of this study is to trace (with some critical comment) the evolution of this characteristically Scottish genre through four centuries of development, showing what happened to it in the hands of poets of many different generations, how it was gradually modified, expanded, and adapted through the years to fit new

The Humors o' Gleska Fair in George Eyre-Todd ed. *The Glasgow Poets: Their Lives and Poems* (Paisley, 1906), pp. 204-208, a 15-stanza piece deriving chiefly from the *Christis Kirk* poems of Burns and Fergusson and from the 17th-century *Blythsome Bridal* (treated in Part II of this study). Alexander B. Grosart, in his edition of *The Works of Robert Fergusson* (London, Edinburgh, and Dublin, 1851), pp. 84-90, mentions three other early 19th-century imitations of Fergusson's *Christis Kirk* poems which I have not seen: *Leith Races* by David Vedder; *Leith Races* by George Bruce in his *Poems and Songs* (1811), pp. 105-115; and *Kern Supper* by Rev. James Nicol of Traquair in his *Poems,* I, 138-141.

social conditions and new artistic purposes, until it finally evolved into something rather different from what it started out to be, yet still retaining the unmistakable stamp of its remote ancestry. Finally, I shall try to adduce reasons for the astonishing longevity of this very distinctive art form.

The Fifteenth Century

The two fifteenth-century poems already mentioned, *Christis Kirk on the Green* and *Peblis to the Play*, are the earliest surviving specimens of the *Christis Kirk* genre, though there may well have been older poems of this type which are now lost. Indeed, this supposition seems to be highly probable, judging from a reference in the first stanza of *Christis Kirk* to two other poems of the same type, *Falkland on the Green* and *Peblis to the Play*. The latter, of course, we have, but the poem on Falkland has perished. These facts would lead one to suspect that the two surviving pieces are merely representative of perhaps a considerable number of fifteenth-century poems of the same kind.[2] However this may be, since *Christis Kirk* and *Peblis* alone were preserved for poserity and became famous in Scotland, they became for all practical purposes the prototypes of the tradition.

The dates and authorship of these two pieces have long been disputed. George Bannatyne, in his monumental manuscript collection of ancient Scottish poetry completed in 1568, assigns *Christis Kirk* to King James I of Scotland;[3] and, writing in 1521, the historian John Major credits the same author with *Peblis*, (or "At Beltayn" as he calls it, a name deriving from the first two words of the poem).[4] Since the two poems are very similar in content and style, these two bits of evidence, as T. F. Henderson has pointed out,[5] tend to corroborate each other;

[2] This conjecture is supported by the evidence of George F. Jones in " 'Christis Kirk,' 'Peblis to the Play,' and the German Peasant-Brawl," *PMLA*, LXVIII (1953), 1101-1125, who shows that these poems have many parallels in themes and satiric motifs in a group of South German poems dating from the 13th through the 15th century. This article contains an illuminating discussion of the folklore elements in *Christis Kirk* and *Peblis*, stresses the satiric intention of the author, and suggests that the peasant types portrayed in the poems reflect a literary convention for the most part, and do not necessarily correspond to reality.

[3] See *The Bannatyne Manuscript*, ed. W. Tod Ritchie, Scottish Text Soc., 2nd Ser. 22, 23, 26, 3rd Ser. 5, 4 vols. (Edinburgh, 1928, 1928, 1930, 1934), II, 268. Scottish Text Soc. is hereafter noted as STS, and this edition of the Bannatyne MS. as *Bann. MS.*

[4] *History of Greater Britain*, trans. from Latin and ed. Archibald Constable, Scottish History Soc., Vol. X (Edinburgh, 1892), p. 336.

[5] *Scottish Vernacular Literature* (Edinburgh, 1910), p. 107.

and the obvious conclusion is that both pieces were composed by James I, a cultured monarch who is known to have written poetry and to have been the author of the famous love-allegory, *The Kingis Quair*. In 1627, however, the historian Thomas Dempster assigned to King James V a poem which he described as "De Choreis rusticis Falkirkensibus, epos vernacule, lib. I. quo nihil ingeniosius aut Graeci aut Latini ostentare possunt."[6] This title has been taken to refer to *Christis Kirk*, though the assumption seems to me to be a very dangerous one in view of our incomplete knowledge of ancient Scottish poetry. At any rate, Bishop Edmund Gibson, probably taking this hint from the unreliable Dempster, credited James V with *Christis Kirk* in his 1691 edition of the poem,[7] and in so doing encouraged the growth of a tradition in favor of the later James's authorship. However, in the eighteenth century, with the rediscovery of the Bannatyne and Maitland Manuscripts there came a reassertion of James I's claims to both poems; and a full-scale critical battle ensued between the scholars favoring James I and those who stood for James V. In more recent years the controversy has been highlighted by the disagreement of two very reputable scholars, Walter W. Skeat and Thomas F. Henderson. Professor Skeat, in 1884, came out for James V or at least for his period, in a rather full treatment based mainly on internal evidence,[8] only to have his arguments very ably and, to my mind, decisively refuted by Henderson in his *Scottish Vernacular Literature* (pp. 104-111). The question has never been finally decided, however, and continues to be debated.

Though it is no part of my purpose to enter into a full discussion of this very complex and specialized problem of authorship, a brief review of the facts is necessary to substantiate my belief that these poems date from the fifteenth and not from the sixteenh cenury. The scholars who have argued for the authorship of James V have failed to convince chiefly because they have not been able to explain away satisfactorily the plain statements of fact by Major and Bannatyne. It seems hardly credible that *both* men, sound and careful men at that, writing independently of each other, could have been confused or mistaken in this matter. Indeed, those critics who, like Skeat, have argued that *Peblis* as well as *Christis Kirk* belongs to the reign of James V have simply chosen to ignore histori-

---

[6] *Thomae Dempsteri Historia Ecclesiastica Gentis Scotorum*, ed. D. Irving, 2nd. ed., Bannatyne Club Pub., No. 21 (Edinburgh, 1829), p. 382.

[7] *Polemo-Middinia . . . Accedit Jacobi id nominis Quinti, Regis Scotorum, Cantilena Rustica Vulgo Inscripta Christo Kirk on the Green* (Oxford, 1691).

[8] See W. W. Skeat ed. *The Kingis Quair*, STS, O. S. 1 (Edingurgh, 1884) pp. xvii-xxiii.

cal fact. Once we accept, as I think we must, that the poem mentioned by Major, *At Beltayn*, is *Peblis to the Play* or some variation of *Peblis*, then it becomes manifestly impossible that James V was the author. For at the time of Major's writing, 1521, James V was only nine years old. Furthermore, in assigning *Peblis* to James I (1394-1437), Major clearly believed that the poem was almost a century old in 1521. Therefore, whether or not Major was right about the author of *Peblis*, his testimony proves beyond any reasonable doubt that the poem cannot possibly have been written in the sixteenth century, that it belongs rather to the first half of the fifteenth century. Strenuous attempts have been made by critics favoring James V to shake this evidence of Major's, to cast doubt upon Major's accuracy, and so forth. But no amount of such argument can get around the fact that the poem seemed old enough to Major in 1521 for him to assign it to James I. It is inconceivable that Major could have been so utterly and fantastically wrong as to mistake a brand new work for one that was nearly a hundred years old. His testimony alone, then, establishes *Peblis to the Play* as a product of the fifteenth century, probably of the years between 1400 and 1450.

The external evidence for a fifteenth-century date for *Christis Kirk* is not so strong as for *Peblis*, but the probabilities are all in favor of it. It is, of course, conceivable that Bannatyne, in assigning this poem to James I in 1568, made a slip of the pen and wrote "first" instead of "fift." Much has been made of this possibility by Skeat and others.[9] At the same time, nearly all the authorities on both sides of the question agree that *Christis Kirk* and *Peblis*, being very similar in style and language, are at least roughly coeval, if not by the same author. Add to this the facts that Bannatyne did write "Quod K. James the first," that Dempster's evidence to the contrary came much later and is highly questionable in the bargain, that in the first stanza of *Christis Kirk* there is a familiar reference to *Peblis* as though the latter work had recently captured the public imagination, and that Bannatyne's ascription is greatly strengthened and corroborated by the independent evidence of John Major, and one cannot escape the conclusion that *Christis Kirk*, though perhaps not by James I, though perhaps not even by the same author as *Peblis*, at least belongs to the same period, namely 1400-1450.

Peblis to the Play, the older of the two poems, is a richly humorous and vivacious description of a group of country people coming into the town of Peebles to enjoy the sports and festivities held there annually at

[9] See, e.g., George Eyre-Todd ed. *Scottish Poetry of the 16th Century* (London, n.d.), pp. 150-155.

"Beltane," a Celtic holiday on the first of May.[10] The action of the poem falls naturally into five divisions, and may be summarized briefly as follows. The first eight stanzas portray in vivid detail the preparations for the day and the events of the journey to Peebles. Here we see the excited young girls getting their clothes ready for the big day with some coy embarrassment over unpressed kerchiefs and sunburnt faces; the villagers gathering on the road to Peebles, with bagpipes playing and groups singing as they march exuberantly along under a cloudless sky; and the young men meeting a group of local girls and pairing off for the day's festivities. Stanzas 9 to 14 describe a ludicrous tavern scene in Peebles itself. Having arrived at the town, the group of rustics gaily enters a tavern to order food and drink. A fight breaks out between two of the young men over the reckoning, a fight which quickly develops into a general brawl and overflows into the street outside. In the next group of five stanzas a burlesque episode is introduced involving a "cadger" (street peddler) and his wife. The cadger, at first an innocent bystander, becomes entangled in the brawl outside the tavern and gets a severe drubbing. Fiercely swearing vengeance, the cadger is finally dragged out of the gutter by his wife, who does her best to calm his rage for fear that he will suffer further damage. At this point (stanza 19) the riot is broken up, with seven of the more belligerent being thrown in the stocks. The good humor of the group is restored, however, when one of their number, Will Swane, proposes an old-fashioned dance. They all gather in a field on the outskirts of town to dance uproariously to the tune of the pipes. Finally, in the last three stanzas the joyous day comes to an end, and we are presented with a touching little vignette of the young men bidding farewell to the girls and promising to meet again on the next feast day in Peebles.

Such, in short, is the content and structure of *Peblis to the Play*. But no summary can possibly give an impression of the remarkable verve and craftsmanship which this piece displays. Two or three individual stanzas, however, will illustrate its most prominent characteristics. The opening lines are marked by a fairly elaborate pattern of alliteration, a device which is used in varying degrees throughout the poem:

[10] For the best text of this poem, see *The Maitland Folio Manuscript*, ed. W. A. Craigie, STS, 2nd Ser. 7 (Edinburgh, 1919), I, 176-183. I have slightly modernized the texts of passages quoted from the manuscripts of *Peblis, Christis Kirk*, and *Symmie and his Bruder* as follows: the "thorn" letter has been replaced by "th"; the letter "z", when it has the sound of "y" (as in "ze"="ye"), is rendered as "y"; the double letter "ff" where it simply indicates capitalization is given as "F"; all abbreviations are spelled out; and modern punctuation and capitalization are supplied throughout. Otherwise the original spelling is retained.

At Beltane quhen ilk bodie bownis	*sets forth*
To Peblis to the play,	
To heir the singin and the soundis,	
The solace, suth to say;	
Be firth and forrest furth thay found,	*by; went*
Thay graythhit thame full gay;	*clad*
God wait that[11] wald thai do that stound,	*knows; time*
For it wes thair feist day, Thay said,	
Of Peblis to the play.	

The most cursory glance at this stanza will give an impression of its extreme technical complexity. As Henderson has pointed out,[12] it is an interesting combination of the ballad and romance methods, each quatrain being rhythmically equivalent to the common four-line ballad stanza (though here the quatrains are linked within the stanza by a very exacting rime scheme), while at the same time an alliterative pattern, typical of the northern metrical romances such as *Sir Tristrem,* is superimposed on the already difficult stanzaic form. The "bobwheel" at the end is in the nature of a refrain rounding off each stanza, the last line ("Of Peblis to the play") being repeated throughout. In this arrangement, the short tag-line ("Thay said") is called the "bob," and is followed by a longer line or "wheel" which is metrically equivalent to the last line of the stanza proper.

It is obvious that the verse form as established in this opening stanza is difficult and confining for a long poem of some 260 lines. The author of *Peblis* seems to have realized this fact; for after sticking more or less rigidly to his original pattern through the first four stanzas, he begins at stanza 5 to introduce variations, using three rimes in the octave, though occasionally reverting to the two-rime scheme of the opening stanzas. From stanza 5 on, the rime scheme thus becomes fairly fluid, though it will be noted that the same rime is used for all the trimeter lines in each octave, the variations occurring only in the tetrameter lines. At the same time, the heavy alliteration of the first stanza gradually breaks down as the poem gets under way; and although alliteration continues to be noticeable here and there throughout the poem, the author seems quickly to have given up the notion of using it regularly and consistently in each stanza. The fact that the *Christis Kirk* verse form began to reveal this tendency toward a limited degree of fluidity from the beginning will be of some interest in connection with later modifications of the traditional stanza.

[11] The manuscript gives this word as "thai," undoubtedly a slip of the pen for "that."

[12] *Scottish Vernacular Literature,* pp. 111-112.

The variations noted above enabled the author of *Peblis* to achieve a degree of flexibility, to tell his story more naturally and effectively than he might otherwise have done. Even with the variations, however, the stanza remains a difficult one; and the author handles it with an ease and a technical dexterity which are altogether remarkable. Take, for example, the two stanzas below. In the midst of the brawl, the cadger leaps to his gray mare, presumably to chase an opponent. But the horse's girth breaks, and the cadger falls off into the gutter:

His wyf come out, and gaif ane schout,	
And be the fute scho gat him;	*by*
All be dirtin drew him out;	*dirtied*
Lord God, richt weill that sat him!	*became*
He said, "Quhair is yon culroun knaif?"	*low-born*
Quod scho, "I reid ye lat him	*advise*
Gang hame his gaitis." "Be God," quod he,	*ways*
"I sall anis haue at him Yit,	*once; yet*
Of Peblis to the play."	

"Ye fylit me, fy for schame!" quod scho;	*defiled*
"Se as ye haue drest me!	*see how*
How feill ye, ssir?" "As my girdin brak,	
Quhat meikle deuill may lest me?	*hinder*
I wait [nocht] weill quhat it wes,	*know*
My awin gray meir that kest me,	
Or gif I wes forfochtin faynt,	*tired from fighting*
And syn lay doun to rest me Yonder,	*then*
Of Peblis to the play."	

The robust humor of this passage is, of course, wholly delightful. But equally admirable is the skill with which the author, here and elsewhere in the poem, creates vigorous and realistic dialogue while remaining within the rigid limitations of the verse form. This deft use of dialogue, allowing us to hear the actual speech of the various characters, helps materially in bringing the scene to life, and enhances its actuality and liveliness. Frequent use of this kind of direct quotation became, indeed, one of the most distictive characteristics of the *Christis Kirk* tradition, persisting through the eighteenth century.

From what has already been said about *Peblis to the Play*, it should be clear that the piece is far from being a primitive folk poem. There is nothing primitive about it except the subject matter itself. *Peblis,* in common with the other surviving specimens of the *Christis Kirk* tradition, belongs to a broad and important classification of ancient Scots poetry which consists of art poems dealing with folk themes. Such poems are, of course, sharply distinguished from the folk poetry itself, though they were often influenced by it. In *Peblis,* the intricacy of the metrical

form alone precludes the possibility of a folk origin, whereas the skill
with which the form is handled makes it certain that the poem is the
work of an accomplished craftsman, a conscious and sophisticated artist.
There are, moreover, clear indications that the poem is aristocratic in
origin. The entire work is a burlesque, gently satiric in tone, written not
from the point of view of the rustics portrayed, but from the point of
view of an amused and superior onlooker who makes good-natured fun of
their antics. The tone of tolerant amusement comes out most strongly
in such stanzas as the following, where the poet describes the entrance
of the rustics into Peebles and the townspeople's reaction:

> Than thai come to the townis end
> Withouttin more delay,
> He befoir, and scho befoir,
> To se quha wes maist gay.   *see who*
> All that luikit thame vpon
> Leuche fast at their array: *laughed*
> Sum said that thai wer merkat folk,   *market*
> Sum said the Quene of May   Wes cumit   *was come*
> Of Peblis to the play.

Such stanzas were certainly not written for the amusement of the common folk whom they satirize, but rather for the amusement of the upper
classes, for the relatively small cultured segment of the population in
fifteenth-century Scotland.

Despite the earthiness of material, *Peblis to the Play* is a fine poem.
The passage of time and changes in language and social customs have, of
course, dulled much of its point for modern readers. The full flavor of
its wit, the subtler niceties of its phrasing are, unfortunately and inevitably, beyond our reach today. But in spite of these obstacles, the truth
and reality of the poem, its genial humor, abounding vigor, and often
brilliant execution, still shine through to us even after five hundred years.
For sheer vitality and excellence of technique, *Peblis to the Play* can
surely stand comparison with anything produced in England during the
fifteenth century; and it remains today one of the classic specimens of
ancient Scottish poetry.

Christis Kirk on the Green,[13] the companion-piece of *Peblis to the
Play*, resembles the latter very closely in most respects, but differs from
Peblis in two or three rather interesting ways. For one thing, there is a
simpler structure and much less variety of action in *Christis Kirk* than in
the earlier poem. *Christis Kirk* opens with six stanzas describing a lively
country dance on the village green, giving instances of the flirtations

[13] For the best text, see *Bann. MS.*, II, 262-268. Also in *Maitland Folio MS.*, I,
149-155.

which are being carried on among the younger men and women present. At stanza 7, two of the villagers, "Robene Roy" and "Jock," quarrel over one of the girls, and a fight ensues. In the next group of five stanzas we are presented with a burlesque archery contest, as the friends of Robene Roy and Jock reach for their bows and arrows and shoot wildly at each other. So poor are their aims that no single arrow strikes home, and the contest shifts to a hand-to-hand brawl with fists and cudgels. The final ten stanzas of the poem are taken up with the events of the barbarous free-for-all which results. *Christis Kirk* ends with the fight still in progress, and thus lacks the neatly rounded and more logical conclusion of *Peblis*. The battle is portrayed, however, in verse that has a rollicking dash, a cumulative momentum, as one vividly sketched picture after another flashes before our eyes in breathless succession. Whatever *Christis Kirk* lacks in firmness of structure is compensated for by the excitement of its action, the wealth of its barbaric and earthy detail, and the boldness of imagination it displays. In these respects it surpasses the more moderately paced *Peblis*.

Christis Kirk is written in the same distinctive meter as *Peblis*, as the famous opening stanza shows:

> Was nevir in Scotland hard nor sene
> Sic dansing nor deray,   *disorder*
> Nowthir at Falkland on the grene
> Nor Peblis at the play,
> As wes of wowaris, as I wene,   *wooers; think*
> At Chryst Kirk on ane day.
> Thair come our kitteis weschin clene   *girls*
> In thair new kirtillis of gray,   Full gay,
> At Chrystis Kirk of the grene.

Here, it will be noted, occurs the familiar references to *Peblis* and to another similar poem, *Falkland on the Green*, now lost. This opening stanza is obviously identical in form to the beginning of *Peblis*, having the two-rime scheme in the octave, exactly the same sort of "bobwheel", and alliteration. But whereas in *Peblis*, as we have seen, the author soon departs from the two-rime scheme and frequently introduces a third rime in the octave, in *Christis Kirk* the strict two-rime pattern is maintained throughout the twenty-two stanzas of the poem. In addition, in *Christis Kirk* the alliteration, too, is sustained, being employed with notable consistency in every stanza. The alliteration is particularly heavy in such lines as

> Off all thir madynis myld as meid
> Wes nane so gympt as Gillie;   *slim, dainty*
> As ony rose hir rude wes reid,   *ruddy part of face*

> Hir lyre wes lyk the lillie;   *skin*
> Fow yellow yellow wes hir heid. . . .   *full*

The exigencies of this extremely confining rime scheme and alliteration inevitably force the author of *Christis Kirk* into an occasional awkward phrase or far-fetched rime; but on the whole he manages to carry the poem through with a seeming ease, and with an apparently inexhaustible fund of rimes, which are truly extraordinary. So well does he succeed, in fact, so briskly does the poem move, that the reader tends to be swept along totally unaware of the very great technical difficulties that the author has overcome. From a purely technical point of view, *Christis Kirk* is a *tour de force* even more remarkable than *Peblis*.

Most of what has already been said concerning the artistic purposes inherent in *Peblis* applies equally well to *Christis Kirk*. It, too, is an aristocratic work, a good-natured burlesque of peasant customs and peasant character, written by a conscious and intellectual artist, and addressed to an upper class audience. The tone of its satire is very similar to that of *Peblis*, though here the humor is slightly broader and less restrained. The stanzas depicting the absurd archery contest are, of course, especially pointed in their satiric intention. Here is one of them:

> With that a freynd of his cryd "Fy!"
> And vp ane arrow drew;
> He forgit it so fowriously   *bent, forced*
> The bow in flenderis flew;   *splinters*
> Sa wes the will of God, trow I,
> For had the tre bene trew
> Men said that kend his archery
> That he had slane anew, / That day,   *enough*
>   At Chrystis Kirk on the grene.

This mockery of the rustics' bungling performance with bow and arrow is good fun. But even better are some of the later passages in the poem, where the poet explodes the false bravery and boastfulness of some of the characters and exposes them as rank cowards. The stanzas on the minstrel, on "Huchoun," and on the village "soutar" (cobbler) are all in this vein and are irresistibly funny. Perhaps best of all, however, is the final stanza on "Dick":

> Quhen all wes done, Dik with ane aix
> Come furth to fell a fidder.   *wagon-load*
> Quod he, "Quhair ar yone hangit smaix   *yon mean fellows*
> Rycht now wald slane my bruder?"   *right*
> His wyfe bad him, "Ga hame, gud glaikis!"   *stupid!*
> And sa did Meg his muder.
> He turnd and gaif thame bayth thair paikis,   *both; beating*
> For he durst ding nane vdir, / For feir,   *strike no other*
>   At Chryst Kirk of the grene that day.

It is worth nothing that in this passage, and very often throughout both *Christis Kirk* and *Peblis*, the last line of the octave together with the bob-wheel itself is used to drive home the satiric meaning of the stanza as a whole. The content of each stanza is skillfully manipulated so as to lead up to the climatic "punch line" at the end, an effect which is, of course, enhanced by a strong final rime. This device was destined to become a traditional feature of the *Christis Kirk* genre.

The broadly comic quality of the stanza just cited is typical of *Christis Kirk* as a whole. The poem is crowded with boisterous action, sly mockery, and swift, vivid characterization. Its peculiar power lies, however, not in isolated passages, but in the exhilarating cumulative impact of the whole. Though the scenes it portrays are perhaps somewhat too crude, its action too primitively brutal, for it to be wholly attractive to modern tastes, it remains an extraordinary achievement. With its incomparable vitality and realism, its breathtaking tempo, and brilliant technique, *Christis Kirk* stands beside *Peblis* as unquestionably one of the finest performances of the century in British poetry.

The popularity of *Peblis* and *Christis Kirk* seems to have gradually increased during the latter part of the fifteenth century to rise to a peak in the sixteenth. We find that *Peblis* was familiar to Major in 1521; and Sir Richard Maitland obviously considered the poem important enough to include it in his invaluable manuscript anthology of Scottish poetry completed shortly after 1586, the sole surviving source for the text of *Peblis*. *Christis Kirk* was transcribed in both the Bannatyne (1568) and Maitland Manuscripts, and was, moreover, directly imitated by Lindsay, Scott, and other sixteenth-century poets. From the first, *Christis Kirk* seems to have been the more famous of the two pieces. There are many more early references to it than to *Peblis;* and *Christis Kirk,* almost alone among Scottish vernacular poems, continued to flourish during the long winter of the seventeenth century, the "dark age" of Scottish poetry. Texts of the poems were printed in 1643, 1660, 1663, 1684, 1691, and 1706; and it was given a highly publicized revival by Allan Ramsay in no less than six separate editions which he published between 1718 and 1724.[14] *Peblis*, on the other hand, seems to have dropped out of sight during the seventeenth century, not to be rediscovered until the mid-eighteenth century when the Maitland Folio Manuscript was brought to light. *Peblis* remained in manuscript until 1783, when it was published for the first time by John Pinkerton.[15]

[14] For bibliographical data on all of these editions, see Wm. Geddie, *A Bibliography of Middle Scots Poets*, STS, O. S. 61 (Edinburgh, 1912), pp. 95-98.

[15] *Select Scotish Ballads* (London), II, 1-14.

The influence of both poems, and of the tradition they established, upon Scots poetry of the late fifteenth and sixteenth centuries was, beyond question, very powerful and pervasive. This influence was by no means limited to poems written directly in imitation of them or strictly within the *Christis Kirk* genre. Relatively few pieces of the pure *Christis Kirk* type have, in fact, survived from these centuries. But the existence of a considerable number of poems which exhibit unmistakable signs of *Christis Kirk* influence and can be located, as is were, on the fringe of the tradition attests to the enormous vitality of the genre. These borderline poems can be divided into two general categories: (1) poems which are not in the distinctive stanza but which, nevertheless, have similar themes of social satire, kinds of humor, settings, characters, methods, and artistic purposes; and (2) poems which are written in the *Christis Kirk* form, but which differ in other respects.

An interesting specimen of the latter type is a fragment recorded in the Bannatyne Manuscript and known as *Symmie and his Bruder*.[16] The date of *Symmie* is problematic, since there is absolutely no external evidence to go on beyond the mere fact that it was in existence in 1568 when George Bannatyne wrote it down. Judging from the antiquity of its language and style, however, one can conjecture that it originated in the first half of the fifteenth century, about the same time as *Peblis* and *Christis Kirk*. The fragmentary condition of the poem as it appears in the Bannatyne Manuscript would seem to support such an early dating.

Symmie and his Bruder is written in the strict form of the *Christis Kirk* stanza; and, like *Peblis* and *Christis Kirk,* it is broadly satiric in intention. Unlike them, however, *Symmie* is mainly a clerical satire rather than a purely social satire on peasant characters. It concerns two scoundrels in St. Andrews who disguise themselves as begging friars. "Symmie" and his brother thrive so well in this character, both financially and amorously, that the brother virtuously decides to marry a local widow. The rest of the fragment describes some primitive and rather obscure proceedings on the wedding day, and then abruptly ends. Here is a typical stanza:

Quhen thay wer welthfull in thair wynning,	*wealthful*
Thay puft thame vp in pryd;	
Bot quhair that Symy levit in synning,	*lived*
His bruder wald haif ane bryd.	
Hir wedoheid fra the begynning	
Wes neir ane moneth tyd;	*month's time*
Gif scho wes spedy ay in spynning,	

[16] For text, see *Bann. MS.*, III, 39-43.

Tak witness of thame besyd, / Ilk ane,   *each*
Baith *etc.* [Sym & his bruder]

From this sample it will readily be seen that *Symmie,* too, is an artistic rather than a folk poem. At the same time, and perhaps because the poem has suffered greatly in transcription, it is decidedly inferior to *Peblis* and *Christis Kirk* in technique, style, and general effectiveness. It differs from them further in being a purely narrative poem about two rascals, rather than a general burlesque of an entire group of varied peasant characters. The satire in *Symmie* is, of course, more specific and serious in its implications than in the other pieces, it being one of countless fifteenth-century poems attacking the scandalous personal and professional corruptions of the mendicant friars. In spite of these differences, however, *Symmie and his Bruder* is clearly and closely related to the *Christis Kirk* tradition by virtue not only of its identical verse form, but also of its upper class origin, its satiric overtones, and its broad and boisterous comedy.

Of the two great makers of the latter half of the fifteenth century, Robert Henryson and William Dunbar, only Dunbar seems to have been strongly influenced by the *Christis Kirk* genre. It is worth nothing, however, that Henryson, in his immortal pastoral, *Robene and Makyne,*[17] deals with country characters in a humorous way and writes in a stanza form identical with that of *Christis Kirk* minus the bobwheel, using the same meter, rime scheme, and heavy alliteration. The works of Dunbar, on the other hand, show traces of kinship with the *Christis Kirk* tradition in places. Though Dunbar wrote no poems in the distinctive stanza, or at least none that has survived, and though his social satires deal not with rustics but with the common tradesmen of the town, several of these satires, such as *The Ballad of Kynd Kittock, Amendis to Telzouris and Sowtaris,* and *This nycht in my sleip I wes agast,* bear a strong resemblance in tone, purpose, salty humor, and uproarious comedy to the *Christis Kirk* genre. Additionally, echoes of the opening lines of *Christis Kirk* ("Was nevir in Scotland hard nor sene / Sic dansing nor deray") appear in the refrain of the *General Satire* ("Sic hunger . . . Within this land was nevir hard nor sene") attributed to Dunbar, and in a phrase from the poem *On his Heid-Ake* (danceing nor deray"). The influence of *Christis Kirk* on Dunbar is most clearly discernible, however, in his scurrilous burlesque entitled *The Turnament.*[18] This amazing poem is in reality a combina-

---

[17] *The Poems of Robert Henryson,* ed. G. Gregory Smith, STS, O. S. 58 (Edinburgh, 1908) III, 89-94. Also *Bann. MS.,* IV, 308-312.

[18] For the six Dunbar poems mentioned here, see respectively *The Poems of William Dunbar,* ed. John Small, STS, O. S. 2, 4 (Edinburgh, 1884), Vol. II, poems

tion of two originally independent genres: the *Christis Kirk* genre and the mock tournament genre. The latter method of social satire seems to have been in considerable vogue in Britain at the close of the Middle Ages, being represented in Scotland by the work of Dunbar, Lindsay and Scott, and in England by the anonymous *Tournament of Tottenham*.[19] But in Scotland, the mock tournament idea seems to have been closely associated from the beginning with the *Christis Kirk* tradition, and finally to have been absorbed by it. This association undoubtedly derives from the fact that *Peblis* and especially *Christis Kirk* itself, the two prototypes of the tradition, both contain burlesque descriptions of pitched battles between rustics, battles which are suggestive of the mock tournament method of satire. Consequently, all three of the early Scottish mock tournament poems, by Dunbar, Lindsay, and Scott, are more or less closely related to the *Christis Kirk* tradition. Lindsay's *Justing* shows traces of direct imitation of *Christis Kirk on the Green* itself, while Scott's *Justing and Debait* is written in the *Christis Kirk* stanza. After the sixteenth century the mock tournament genre as such died out altogether, but it is interesting to note that slight vestiges of its early association with the *Christis Kirk* tradition continued to crop up in later *Christis Kirk* poems such as the seventeenth century *Polemo-Middinia* and Burns's *Jolly Beggars*.

Dunbar's *Turnament* is a double satire, ridiculing both the upper class custom of the tourney and the lower class characters in the mock heroic contest. His contestants are a tailor and a "sowtar" or cobbler, representatives of two trades which seem to have been in particularly bad odor and were frequently satirized by the Scottish poets. Dunbar's mockery of the uncouth manners, absurd appearance, and false courage of these tradesmen is surely typical of the *Christis Kirk* tradition. Even more striking is the emphasis he places upon the abject cowardice of the tailor and cobbler when their bombastic pretensions are put to the test, an emphasis which is reminiscent of several passages already noted in *Christis Kirk*. When the rivals march out onto the field after each has made extravagant boasts of certain victory, both the cobbler and the tailor are so frightened that the one vomits and the other befouls his saddle out of sheer terror. This notion of fear causing spontaneous bowel

numbered as follows: No. 5 (also *Bann. MS.*, III, 10-11); No. 28 (*Bann. MS.*, II, 298-300); No. 34 (*Bann. MS.*, III, 1-4); No. 14 (*Bann. MS.*, I, 79-82); No. 78 (not in *Bann. MS.*); and No 27 (*Bann. MS.*, II, 295-298).

[19] For the text of this piece, which probably dates from the 15th century, see Thomas Percy, *Reliques of Ancient English Poetry*, ed. H. B. Wheatley(London, 1836), II, 17-28. George F. Jones's "The Tournaments of Tottenham and Lappenhausen," *PMLA*, LXVI (1951), 1123-1140, is an interesting study of this poem and the mock tournament genre, but make no reference to the Scots poems of this type.

evacuation is, of course, widespread in the literatures of many nations and many periods; but it is perhaps significant that in the eighth stanza of *Christis Kirk* this same notion is broadly hinted at, where the author comments wryly after one of his characters has been missed by an arrow aimed point-black at him, "I can nocht say quhat mard him." The recurrence of this idea in Dunbar's poem would be of no importance by itself, but when added to the other marks of resemblance noted above it helps to establish a link between *The Turnament* and *Christis Kirk*, and to suggest that Dunbar's piece, though in the main a daringly original burlesque performance typical of Dunbar's astonishingly versatile genius, was, nevertheless, written under at least the partial influence of the *Christis Kirk* tradition. The tone of the satire in *The Turnament* is more devastating and less genial than in the *Christis Kirk* poems; but the rude horseplay, the uproarious comedy, and rollicking tempo of the *Christis Kirk* genre are all there.

UNIVERSITY OF RHODE ISLAND

FRANCIS R. HART

Reviewing Hay's *Gillespie*:

Modern Scottish Fiction and the Critic's Plight

The obvious, superficial things to be said about J. MacDougall Hay's *Gillespie* (1914; reprinted 1963)[1] as a novel are quickly said. It is powerful, violent, preoccupied with avarice and lust—in short, "realistic." Its titular figure is a shrewd and brutal entrepreneur in a small fishing port of the Scottish West Highlands. Its shape is the shape of his world and his wyrd. We look forward, with righteous indignation, to the day when his many enemies—strong and weak, noble and ignoble—will succeed, through his drunken, nymphomaniac wife, and his weak, hypersensitive son, in destroying him. We are asked, when that time arrives, to feel pity and terror at the spectacle of his fall. Meanwhile, we marvel at the human vividness and variety of the Argyllshire fishing village world unfolded piece by organic piece as we pursue Gillespie's fortune. We are intensely aware of the pressure of concrete circumstance on this village world: the natural circumstance of season, locale, act of God; the historical circumstance of economic cycle and political change. Such are the superficial things to be said. *Gillespie* is obviously a remarkable, and just as obviously a very confused book—confused mimetically and rhetorically. But almost as obvious is the woeful fact that we, as critical readers, are theoretically unequipped to treat of the book, in its greatness or in its confusion.

Influential voices in Scottish criticism might find the cause of our plight in the deficiency of modern Scottish literary tradition in the novel. Having saluted Scots poetry and drama, Sydney Goodsir Smith, in 1951, predicted that "the novel should be the next citadel to fall."[2] In 1962, still awaiting the trumpet blast, Edwin Morgan pronounced the novel "the most backward literary form in Scotland."[3] The indefatigable David

---

[1] London, G. Duckworth & Co., with a Preface by Robert Kemp.

[2] *A Short Introduction to Scottish Literature* (Edinburgh, 1951), p. 30.

[3] "The Novel Today" (*Programme and Notes to the International Writers Conference*, Edinburgh Festival, 1962), p. 36. It should be noted that Morgan, properly aware of the plight of "The Young Writer in Scotland," blames the novelists themselves for timidity, but finds the lamentable "backwardness" inevitable, given the views of such despotic influences as "Hugh MacDiarmid," Scotland's literary commissar, that "prose" is "non-creative" (p. 36n.).

Craig, whose uncompromising supremacy among Scottish literary theorists one admires as much as one deplores the narrowing effect on his taste of a Socialist-realist-Leavisite bias toward the "metropolitan" and "timely," still (January, 1964, *SSL*) finds "very few pieces of lasting value" in Scottish prose fiction. His reasoning is predictably at once profoundly suggestive and rigidly closed. "The modern novel is a town form"; the modern Scottish "town" is urban industrial Scotland from Glasgow to Dundee; Scottish fiction remains "rooted in the countryside," its genuine potential lost to emigration before the industrial town had been "absorbed into the British imagination."[4] One recalls in rebuttal Ortega on "the Novel as 'Provincial Life' ": "The author must see to it that the reader is cut off from his real horizon . . . . He must make a 'villager' of him . . . ."[5] And when Craig laments the absence from Scottish fiction of "town novels" in the English or Russian sense, one thinks gratefully of Edwin Morgan's refusal to ask "Robin Jenkins to write like Robbe-Grillet or Iain Crichton Smith to write like Ginsberg."[6] For Craig seems as yet unwilling to study the possibility of a legitimate Scottish variant of prose fiction mimetically and rhetorically distinct or distinguishable from English and Russian "town novels"— a variant perhaps less "novelistic," perhaps both "provincial" in Ortega's sense and "romantic" in Northrop Frye's sense, perhaps even demanding the "laborious

---

[4] *SSL*, Vol. I, No. 3, pp. 164-165; "The Novel Today," pp. 27-28; *Scottish Literature and the Scottish People* (London, 1961), especially pp. 291-293. Craig's own "Foreword" should be quoted in application to his own position (*SLSP*, p. 9): "Hugh MacDiarmid and Mr John Speirs are mentioned in this book mainly in disagreement. But we owe it to Mr MacDiarmid that Scottish literary culture in the 20th century exists at all; and Mr Speirs's *The Scots Literary Tradition* is the only book I know which shows a modern literary mind at work on Scottish literature." We no longer need Speirs's sketch; it may be argued that MacDiarmid's inspiring force has become an unbenevolent despotism. But with Craig's criticism, the theory of Scottish literature has come of age. Maturing never allows for moderation, to be sure. Though Craig in his Leavisite lack of graciousness would deny it, we also need the corrective to Craig supplied by Wittig in the pioneering theoretic passion of *The Scottish Tradition In Literature* (Edinburgh, 1958). See Craig's characteristic condemnation of Wittig in *SLSP*, p. 310, n.7. "Forced Scotticising" *may* "run amok" in Wittig; the Leavisite Craig reaction, as less ardent devotees of "Dr and Mrs F. R. Leavis" may suppose, has its comparable exaggerations. But the net advantage to Scottish literary culture of such a reanimated critical atmosphere can only be tremendous.

[5] *Notes on the Novel*, included with *The Dehumanization of Art* (Garden City, N.Y., 1956), p. 83.

[6] "The Novel Today," p. 37.

naivetés and solemnities" which, for Craig's presently limited vision, are merely "wordy, strained, gauchely melodramatic."[7]

Meanwhile, some wait with Sydney Goodsir Smith for the "one first-class novel in Scots . . . to prove that the thing can be done."[8] Others follow Edwin Muir, and, afflicted with one *dreich* cultural determinism or another, prophesy Scots culture is too narrow or too uncentered to produce the one book. Scottish literature's two most illuminating theorists stand at opposite poles: Wittig understandably, but prejudicially, excited by the imaginative peculiarities of a Scottish tradition; Craig justifiably, but exaggeratedly, hostile to all who associate the presence of an eccentric nationality with the reality of aesthetic value. And so we have no appropriate theoretic framework for the criticism of *Gillespie*.

The only materials at hand for building one are the numerous rather hasty remarks associating *Gillespie* with other notable landmarks in early modern Scottish fiction. Let us assume that a few such landmarks make an incipient tradition, and, by associating them one by one with *Gillespie*, seek to construct a useful, appropriate framework.

Robert Kemp's 1963 preface urgently proposes that Hay had no great debt to his alleged model, George Douglas Brown's *The House with the Green Shutters* (1900). Kemp's case could be even stronger: the themes, the motifs, that he asserts the books share differ profoundly in their distinct contexts. But comparison elucidates some of *Gillespie's* characteristic aspirations and confusions. Again, Wittig naturally compares Hay with his friend Neil Munro; Hay, writes Wittig, deals more honestly with Highland life.[9] Mimesis is clearly far more complex a thing than "honesty"—whether cultural, psychological, or moral. But once again, comparison in mimetic terms proves useful; and, for reasons which should become apparent, I shall use *Gilian the Dreamer* (1905) to carry it forward. Finally, every assessment of a 20th Century Scottish novel must sometime confront the orthodoxy that Scotland's one undeniably great modern fiction is "Lewis Grassic Gibbon" 's trilogy.[10] Thus, consideration of *Gillespie's* rhetorical peculiarities as fiction can find

[7] The reference is specifically to Gunn (in *SSL*, No. 3, p. 165). The terms may be accurate when applied to some of the parts of some of Gunn's novels; the terms may be equally applicable to Conrad and Lawrence. Craig has consistently failed to see the greatness of Gunn. See the present writer's essay in *SSL*, No. 1.

[8] *Short Introduction*, p. 30.

[9] *The Scottish Tradition in Literature*, p. 273: "it is a more courageous effort to deal with contemporary life in the West."

[10] *Sunset Song* (1932), *Cloud Howe* (1933), *Grey Granite* (1934), reprinted together as *A Scots Quair* in 1946. Cf. Wittig, pp. 330-333; Craig, *SLSP*, pp. 292-3.

suitable perspective through comparison with "Gibbon" 's "burgh" novel, *Cloud Howe*. Perhaps this network of kinships and comparisons can be made to evolve into a reasonably philosophical notion of the generic mixtures and modulations, the mimetic kinds and degrees, the rhetorical problems and peculiarities which constitute a definable "nature" for modern Scottish fiction. Or as least, the effort may suggest how to deal with this remarkable, confused book in itself.

The House with the Green Shutters is superficially a Scottish exile's ruthless delineation of the "unspeakable Scot," as the narrator's frequent reflections on "Scottish character" suggest. More centrally, it is "tragedy of Character" in the sense Hardy's *Mayor of Casterbridge* is: the man of brute force, energetic courage, and little shrewdness is set against more efficient "modern" forces of commercial manipulation—Hardy's Farfrae, Brown's Wilson—or social prudence. One's aweful respect goes to the heroic anachronism, though one's affections have never gone to him, in his violence, pride, inhumanity. Already an essential difference in *Gillespie* is apparent: for here, we are asked for tragic pity on behalf, instead, of the Wilson-Farfrae figure, when his own inflexible meanness speeds his downfall.

The House is concerned throughout with variants of cruelty, brutality—and, in the midst of them, memorable, though unlovely, images of human strength and endurance. What is peculiar—i.e., unEnglish or unHardyesque—i.e., perhaps "Scottish"—is the almost perverse complication of judgment of Gourlay the man: one admires his strength, fears his pride, pities his fall in the eyes of petty envy, and hates his cruelty to weakness. He is stupid enough, demonic enough, "big" enough to be tragic in the archaic sense. The superstitious fatalism with which his decline is viewed is almost perfectly dramatized, psychologized in the "town", a chorus both Greek and folkloristic (in this fusion once again Hardyesque, but reminiscent of Hardy's antecedent in *The Bride of Lammermoor*). Gourlay's "fall" is not a Scottish problem; his fate is not economic or social—*pace* Craig—but moral. Wilson may be the necessary instrument, like Farfrae; but Gourlay's fate is of his House, his infatuation, his Character, and is not of the limitations of his economic or historic position. In these terms, this Scottish *Mayor of Casterbridge* is, paradoxically, less "regional" than Hardy's, and even more truly the tragedy of a man of "Character."

Whatever reviewers may have said about the "character" of Gillespie, the first question raised by this comparison is, can the central figure of Hay's novel be treated as a "character" at all? If he is a "hero," certainly, it is purely on the "ironic" level or in a purely satiric "mythos."[11] In "himself," there is only commercial ruthlessness and ingenuity, the "humor" of avarice: a Grandet who can never truly suffer; a Dombey who can never really awaken, because his creator provides no consistent psychology for such events. As a "character," he is, true, motivated somewhat on both natural and historic levels: he is by "nature" avaricious as a George Eliot protagonist may be by "nature" "common"; he *is* the spirit—or he has in some mysterious way imbibed the spirit—of a new, more enterprising and less insular mercantilism. However, in the terms of "nature," he remains a ludicrous "humors" figure of automatic response, prudent only when provoked by avarice. And in terms of "history," it is easier to see Gillespie not as a character" but as a force, a scourge or agent of Fate or History. From his townsmen's point of view he becomes the personification of natural and economic forces which, in conflict with their puny gestures, make of their lives an heroic struggle against impossible odds. When they burn Gillespie's fleet, the destroyers merely unloose uncontrollable forces against themselves. He seems beyond human resistance: arbitrary, inscrutable, a folk-Calvinist's village God. Thus, those who try to resist—Mrs. Galbraith, Lonend— become self-destroyers, judged for their reckless folly in opposing a fatal force.

How is Gillespie delineated as a "force"? The book opens in a vaguely booming atmosphere of Highland fatalism. There is the dire threat of cultural intermarriage between utilitarian, entrepreneurial Low-lander and superstitious, traditional Highlander, the urgent, dangerous problem of cultural fusion or conciliation given as a central theme to Scottish fiction by Scott.[12] Gillespie's mother senses a doom on the house; his father is guilty of Lowland arrogance in marrying into the family, and the sign over the door of the very "Gothic" homestead, "The Ghost," a dagger pointed downwards, is not removed until the end, when it signals Gillespie's fall. Gillespie's lurid career confirms his mother's fears—to what end? To the end that *thrawn* Sassenach should not marry *fey* Gael? Her son is the punishment of the impious, the infatuated; the house and its sign prophesy the ultimate hideous triumph of some fatal rhythm. Gillespie must play his role in a mythic cycle, a cyclical family doom. Once again a son will murder his mother and in turn father a son to be murdered by a mother in his turn. Inevitability,

[11] Devotees of Northrop Frye will need no annotation here; others are invited to overlook the terms, or trace their present usage to *Anatomy of Criticism* (Princeton, N.J., 1957), pp. 34, 42, 223-239.

[12] Such, at least, is one familiar and, I believe, sound definition of the "idea" of the Waverley Novels. See, e.g., Karl Kroeber in *Romantic Narrative Art*.

ballad-like in its taste for the grisly, is mythic. This is clearly far more than the tragedy of Character in History achieved in *The House with the Green Shutters*; in its "metaphysical" ambitiousness—and this should *not* prejudge it—it seems instead to provide the connecting link between "Fiona MacLeod" and Neil Gunn. But the Gunn anticipation illuminates the confusion in *Gillespie*. Hay's characters are neither fully individual nor truly archetypal; they are culturally or regionally representative, that is all. Hence, they have no reality in a rhythm of mythic fatality. Gunn, on the other hand, at his best—at times "Gibbon," too—most perfectly fuses the individual, the regional-historical, and the archetypal, so that the "action" in which each character is caught up may be defined simultaneously in all three sets of terms. Perhaps, then, the comparative analysis of "character" in *Gillespie* implies a conception of characterization peculiar to, if not definitive of, recent Scottish fiction.

The machinery of Gillespie's downfall is also dependent on "character," where "character" is too narrowly or too abstractly motivated to support the book's pretensions to mythic fatality. One recalls Pritchett on "bad" Conrad, where Destiny is a word shouted repeatedly by a Narrator,[13] or Hardy's less successful attempts to achieve credibility for a mythic Fatality without surrendering the assumptions of a basic Naturalism. The chief character in the machinery is Gillespie's wife, whose deterioration takes up much of our attention in the book without our ever becoming convinced that Hay could dramatize the degradation of a love-starved woman. Adequate terms are present: her father's mean collaboration, then his mean warfare, with Gillespie; Gillespie's lack of sexual passion; his lack of education or refinement enough to appreciate the needs of his wife. The initial hint that she is oversexed makes us wonder at her aggressive choice of Gillespie, for the impression of him already established is of meanness, cunning, not power. Evidently, Hay was not free, perhaps not willing, to delineate the full spectacle of outraged and ultimately depraved feminine sexuality. We get only veiled hints. The stress in her degeneration is placed instead on her drunkenness, her lunatic violence. The student of American "Gothic" is accustomed to this substitution;[14] but even he may find the drawn-out horror of Mrs. Strang's razor-murder of her son, the particularizing of the boy's horrified final moments, more than enough to dissolve all moral scrutiny of Gillespie's doom in sheer horror. However violent the finale of *The House with the Green Shutters*, the precise moral inevitability of the catastrophe is never lost in sheer spectacle.

[13] *The Living Novel* (London, 1949), p. 141.

[14] See, e.g., Leslie Fiedler, *Love and Death in the American Novel*.

In both books, too, the machinery of the father's destruction depends on the sullen, yet defiant failure of an intensely sensitive, even visionary son, on whom the proud continuance of the house is to depend. Indeed, the visionary academic son as his proud, brutal, narrow father's destroyer reappears often enough in recent Scottish fiction to warrant a more general word in connection with the Scottish "reality" delineated. Moreover, the son's peculiar visionary sensibility often earns him the role of central consciousness, or at least of an essential point of view, in the rhetoric of such fiction. Hence, some notice of *Gillespie*'s Eoghan must wait, too, for our final rhetorical considerations of the book in connection with Chris and Ewan of *Cloud Howe*.

But turn first to the mimetic problem, and to the second of our associated novelists—Hay's friend Neil Munro, who dealt, we hear, less honestly with Highland life. *Gilian the Dreamer* is historically distanced, but this does not interfere with proper comparison, for, as Pritchett has said of Scott,[15] history is simply the engine of Munro's purpose—the means of imposing an order and infusing it with a characteristic and, I would argue, persuasively significant nostalgia. The entire novel is focused on the titular youth, the doomed Cinderella-hero, for whose aspirations and visionary intensities there is no adequate place in *any* historic world. It begins and ends a *coronach*, a lament for the lost, the stunted, the unrealized. Gilian, related evidently to that Marius the Epicurean so influential in the "Celtic Twilight,"[16] is the youthful dreamer for whom all realities are inward. But his is only the problem in its most lyric form. Surrounding and condemning him are old men—Black Duncan, the Campbells—who dream, too, of lost glory, lost youth. Their maiden sister Mary had watched long ago from a window as love and youth passed by; her friend, though winning the lost suitor, had died. The historic particularity of the post-Napoleonic setting is accidental; it provides the Old Soldiers with a particular past glory to lament, far on the ringing plains of any windy Troy. Gilian is the "Boy from the Glen," seen by the town as "John Hielanman," cursed with a visionary passivity. Actually, this Julien Sorel of the Celtic Twilight is motivated neither by history nor by culture; no attempt is made to do what David Craig so deplores—to see Gilian's plight in general terms simply as "the Highland problem," any more than the plight of most of Gunn's passive visionaries is seen *merely* in ecological or ethnic terms. Indeed, *Gilian* is not a "social" novel at all—thus, for Craig, perhaps not a

---

[15] *The Living Novel*, p. 44.

[16] The general fact of *Marius's* influence in this quarter was first called to my attention by Mr. John Firth, then of the Dept. of English, University of Virginia.

"novel." Its social structure of the *burgh* simply articulates, in the medium of the "town novelist," the lineaments of an elegaic state of mind, in and of history, but not historically unique. The delineation is stylized; but actually the treatment and the consequences are never falsified by sentimentality. How, then, is it possible to say that in terms of fictive "truth" this is a less honest picture of Scottish life than Hay's or Brown's? Its "truth" is this: at once, it provides an adequate "objective correlative" in "novelistic" terms for the Scottish mood whose prevalence sustains the pre-eminence of the "Canadian Boat Song"; and, in Arnoldian terms, it subjects that persistent elegaism to an authentic "criticism of life."

The "truth" or "honesty" of *Gillespie* is clearly much more complex and far less attractive—or less evocative of pathos. This fact in itself guarantees neither more "honesty" nor greater art. But were this particular kind of mimetic complexity to be demonstrably "Scottish," and were it to be adequately realized and controlled, the result would have to be termed a better Scottish "novel." The elements in the complexity should be defined first. Wittig calls the book symphonic in structure, a book of many consciousnesses.[17] But the *kinds* of consciousness are three. Gillespie's own, I have suggested, is too "humorous," too univalent and at the same time too impersonal as a "force," to serve as a consciousness. But first, there is the typical consciousness of the townsmen, or the "folk"—traditional, bluntly heroic, both naive and shrewd. Topsail Janet, Hay's favorite character, is the masterpiece of this "kind." Second, there is the kind of consciousness shared by those who know Gillespie in sufficient depth and with enough sophistication to will his destruction; and this kind is mixed. Mrs. Galbraith (widow of a man Gillespie ruined), Gillespie's wife, his son—all combine urbane (college-bred or college-infected) intelligence with a strongly mythic or ritualistic sense of their roles in some archaic tragedy of moral poison and retribution. The narrator's is a third kind of consciousness, clearly that of the "literary," liberal minister Hay himself, who combines his own sense of the archaic grandeur with a strong post-Romantic sense of Nature (Ruskin), a secular Calvinist's obsession with moral Law (Carlyle), and the Clydeside Socialist's sense of economic and ideological determinism.

Such a complex of consciousnesses is a "truth" variously rendered in Scottish fiction since the Enlightenment—and it is evidently true to post-Enlightenment Scottish culture, the culture that helped produce such curiously unEnglish Victorians as Carlyle, Mill, Ruskin, and Davidson. Such a "truth" can evidently be effectively rendered, as Hardy and

[17] Wittig, pp. 273-274.

George Eliot had shown English fiction, within the explosive confines of a provincial or "burgh" setting. Moreover, the mixing of "rationalist" shrewdness, "Romantic" pastoralism, the prophetic fervor of a secularized Kirk, and the persistent superstition of the "folk" mind marvelously particularizes the still vital tradition of violently anomalous "character" celebrated or belabored as the "Caledonian antisyzygy." The spectacle of a dour, heroic, yet often gay traditional community, confronting in naive futility the ruthless hostility of historic and economic "Law" is also "true"—true in a sense deeper and more particular than the *mere* Naturalist's "truth" of the unpleasant or anti-sentimental. And if Americans still find "truth" in the county of Faulkner or the dwindling or vanished village cultures of Frost, then the Scottish "truth" of *Gillespie* must still be recognizable to the modern Scottish experience. Specifically, the mixing in "community" of heroic but unlovely fisherfolk, with the megalomaniac entrepreneur, and with the participant but self-consciously neo-primitive or rusticated college-bred is also still a fact of Scottish community.

But mimesis is not harmony. Just as an unintegrated complexity of motivational levels and consciousnesses threatens to disintegrate the book's huge "reality," so a mixture of voices or points of view leaves it rhetorically confused. And here, clearly, the undeniable masterpiece, the touchstone, in the rhetoric of modern *Scottish* fiction is Lewis Grassic Gibbon's trilogy as manipulation of the Scottish experience, individual, historic, and mythic. Neil Gunn's latest experiments with point of view, at once communal-archaic and urbanely-distanced—*The Silver Bough, The Well at the World's End, The Other Landscape*—might also serve. But let us grant, for the sake of an already available critical orientation for *Gillespie*, that these remain to be assessed as experiments, and fall back on *Cloud Howe* (1933).

We are concerned here only with its remarkable rhetorical solution to the problem of presenting a reality demanding a potentially chaotic multiplicity of voice. No single passage will illustrate the method; the success is achieved in large and gradual manipulations. To describe briefly, the history of Chris Guthrie Colquhoun—Mearns farmer's daughter, widow of the war-dead "Highland tink" Tavendale, wife and soon widow to the burgh's liberal minister—is rendered in successive tragic retrospects, each focused in terms of, but not limited to, her point of view. Each phase of her experience—and the collective historic and mythic experience hers particularizes—is "finished," realized in elegaic memory, inevitable and appropriate in its pervasive and sometimes bitter nostalgia—again *pace* Craig.[18] The narrative is of a single style, an Anglicized lyric Scots, at once incantatory and palpably colloquial, and slipping easily between third and second person—third for externality, second for the dramatization of a single or collective point of view or consciousness:

> They saw not a soul as they passed the Mains, then they swung out into the road that led south; and so as they went Chris turned and looked back at Kinraddie, that last time there in the sun, the moors that smoothed to the upland parks Chae Strachan had ploughed in the days gone by, the Knapp with no woods to shelter it now, Upperhill set high in a shimmer of heat, Cuddiestoun, Netherhill—last of them all, high and still in the hill-clear weather, Blawearie up on its ancient brae, silent and left and ended for you; and suddenly, daft, you could't see a thing.[19]

The style easily becomes the pharisaical voice of the burgh, collective yet in "character": "And that was just daft, if Ake spoke true—that Mr. Colquhoun could mean it of folk, real coarse of him to speak that way of decent people that had done him no harm. It just showed you the kind of tink that he was, him and his Labour and socialism and all" [p. 97]. It serves the other collective voice of the proletarian, the weaver, the "tink." At times it is the dramatically neutral, yet lyrically engaged omniscient narrator's voice, a colloquial "burgh" Tiresias. And of course, for the most part, it is the voice of Chris herself, as heroine, as "Scotland," as normative point of view. Her consciousness, distinguished subtly from the narrator's own, is limited and dynamic. It sustains the book's organizing symbolism of clouds—hence, provides a poetic voice:

> She had found in the moors and the sun and the sea her surety unshaken, lost maybe herself, but she followed no cloud, be it named or unnamed . . .
> Once he'd glowered as though he would like to gut you, and thundered his politics, and you'd felt kittled up . . . . But this Sunday he blethered away in the clouds . . . [p. 128].

It gradually acquires a sense of history, adequately but not undramatically philosophical, a folk feminized version of the historic sense of the Socialist-Humanist narrator: "But she thought, as often, we saw more than that—the end forever of creeds and of faiths, hopes and

---

[18] For Craig (*SLSP*, pp. 292-3), the later two of the trilogy suffer from the "terrible nostalgia" of the émigré (cf. "The Novel Today," p. 27). Gibbon "hands over to his nostalgia, lies back and lets it carry him along. Such emotion unfits an artist to make sense of his experience even as it moves him to get it down on paper." Such is Craig's characteristically extravagant exclusiveness. It is obviously the "handing over" and not the nature of the emotion itself which does the damage, and, while this is obviously not the place to attempt it, I would argue that the "handing over" is not characteristic of *Cloud Howe.*

[19] *Cloud Howe* (in *A Scots Quair*, London, 1959), pp. 25-26; subsequent refs. are given in the text.

beliefs men followed and loved: religion and God, socialism, nationalism—
Clouds that sailed darkling into the night" [p. 138]. Thus, it provides
an historic voice. Finally, it frames poetry and history in Chris's archaizing vision of her own experience as a reenactment of the primordial in
earthly experience:

> from the earth's beginning *you yourself* had been here, a blowing of motes
> in the world's prime, earth, roots and the wings of an insect long syne in
> the days when the dragons still ranged the world . . . . And it seemed to
> Chris is was not Cis alone, her tale—but all tales that she harkened to
> then . . . [pp. 41-2, 126].

It provides, too, then, a mythic voice, in style and perspective assimilated
to the poetic and historic, and harmonized with the narrator's own lyric-
dramatic voice, and set against the related voice of a divided community.

The solution of this central rhetorical problem of modern Scottish
fiction demands the co-persistence of a mythic and an historic vision
with the colloquial dramatization of "character". The artist as interpreter
of this complex Scottish reality inherits the tradition of colloquial "character" and anecdote, and confronts on the one hand the tyranny of the
archaic, and on the other that other determinism of the historic. The
result in style and rhetorical "voicing" is bound not to be simple. Amid
the resonant stylization of Gunn's *The Silver Darlings,* or the Helleno-
Calvinistic fatalism of *Gillespie,* or the lyric neo-paganism of *Cloud
Howe,* the sacrificial hero or heroine finds an identity in historic inevitability and at the same time a doom in mythic precedent.

The "voicing" of *Gillespie* is an early groping for these truths, and
thus, is at once more confused and more uniquely promising for later
Scottish fiction than *The House with the Green Shutters* (let alone *Gilian* and other Munro). Yet it falls far short of *Cloud Howe.* It has
the possibility of a central consciousness like Chris's in both Mrs. Galbraith and Gillespie's wife—both college-sophisticated, both reintegrated
into the agrarian community, both possessed at once of historic intelligence
and archaizing vision. But the characterization of Mrs. Galbraith remains
abstract, peripheral; and, for reasons already noted, that of Mrs. Strang
can be neither honest nor stable enough to serve.

There is a further possibility, also incompletely realized. All four
books we have discussed ultimately become or provide portraits of the
anti-bourgeois Scottish artist as young man—and all four young men
are akin as sacrificial heroes to Paul Morel and Stephen Dedalus. All
four are cursed with a literalism of the imagination—"that extraordinary
vividness in the speech of the Scotch peasantry . . . . It comes from a
power of seeing things vividly inside your mind . . . ." Young Gourlay's

"mind began to visualize of its own accord, independent of his will"—
and the result is paralysis of will, destructive fatalism, a knowing "fear
of his own nature."[20] As in *Sons and Lovers*, so in *The House*, sympathies
divide between naive, heroic father and artist-weakling son; in *The
House* theirs is the ultimate, tragic battle. Gilian's curse is the same,
and it involves him in pathetic, but ironic, battle with the more masculine
fancies of his adopted fathers. *Cloud Howe* needs no such artist-hero;
the evolution and exile of Ewan belong to *Grey Granite*, the last of
Gibbon's trilogy. In *Gillespie*, the son's vision speeds his destruction, and
his is the destruction that annihilates his father's dynastic hopes. His
visionary strangeness is evident: "Old Sandy was about to take the line
from Eoghan's hand when the expression on the lad's face stayed him.
Out of the dreamland beyond Time and Space that face was growing
again into his vision . . . . Eoghan shook like the column of water on a
fall. The Spirit of the Unseen passed as breathing upon the face of the
night . . ." [pp. 320, 356]. His failure at the university is speeded by
his visionary nature: "Eoghan lived in part in a vertigo of waking, in
part in that dream state with which he had been familiar in boyhood . . ."
[p. 370]. In him, then, the book finally finds its appropriate central
sensibility.

It is too late. We have been given too many—and deprived of too
many—other possibilities. For much of the book, after all, it is Gillespie
himself who is the son, betrayer of his naive, impious father. And Gillespie's ultimate struggles are with his wife, Mrs. Galbraith, and Lonend.
Moreover—and here is the glaring rhetorical difference between *Cloud
Howe* and *Gillespie*—Hay as narrator is never willing to relinquish his
own right to the center of the novel, to dramatize or subdue his own
voice. His own narrative voice or style, at times Lawrentian in the
good sense, is too often a fusion of obscure Conradesque heroics, the
poetic verbosity of the post-Romantic Wordsworthian, and the prophetic
verbosity of the secularized Calvinist preacher. The narrator is so wholly
under the sway of the author's compulsive and confused, though powerful, imagination, that he cannot wait upon the demands of careful characterization or dramatization. And ultimately, no other consciousness can
survive for the reader. Briefly, Hay finds a dramatic spokesman in the

[20] *The House with the Green Shutters* (London, 1929), pp. 163, 214, 223. My
point here is obviously an application of Wittig's general thesis concerning the definitive peculiarities of the Scottish poetic imagination, a general poetic thesis I am not
qualified to judge. But the recurrence in Scottish fiction of a potent, yet humorous
fascination with involuntary visionary power—whether in whiskey or Second Sight—
has made the Scottish young artist as hero an easily definable type.

old schoolmaster, writing a life-book, "an epic of the obscure dead," looking down on the town below his garden:

> He imagined the people beneath projected on the face of the sky as if from a gigantic magic-lantern. The figures capered grotesquely upon the clouds, their antic gestures inspired and controlled by some passionless conjurer. *"Umbra sumus,"* he would murmur sadly, "my book will never be finished;" and the relentless clock, the unerring pilot of Time, would solemnly boom out on the hill that another hour had passed away into eternity [p. 291].

But this dramatization is brief. And there remains the same post-Romantic Virgilian pretentiousness in the narrator himself throughout *his* "epic of the obscure dead."

All of which is to say that, measured in any "novelistic" terms, *Gillespie* is an overwhelming and remarkable, a highly confused and imperfect book. But measured in terms derived from its association with other modern Scottish fiction, its imperfections may be both defined and explained, and its tremendous promise appreciated.

UNIVERSITY OF VIRGINIA

RICHARD FRENCH

The Religion of Sir Walter Scott

The stereotype notion of a Scotchman interested in religion is that of a Calvinistic Presbyterian. Sir Walter Scott does not fit that idea. In early childhood Scott was a Presbyterian, but he never shared his father's devotion to this form of Calvinism, of which he wrote:

> His religion, in which he was devoutly sincere, was Calvinism of the strictest kind, and his favourite study related to church history. I suspect the good old man was often engaged with Knox and Spottiswoode's folios, when, immured in his solitary room, he was supposed to be immersed in professional researches.[1]

This failure to share his father's interest in religion is one of the few subjects on which the two disagreed. Scott followed his father's choice of a law career, although he hated it, and became an even more ardent Tory, but he early rebelled against many of the tenets of his religion. While a child he could not openly show his displeasure, but as an adult he wrote his objection against the Presbyterian sabbath. He stated its discipline was severely strict and in his opinion injudiciously so. Later in life, he wrote he always "had a favor for" Bunyan's *Pilgrim's Progress*, Gesner's *Death of Abel*, Rowe's *Letters*, and the one or two other books which were admitted to relieve the gloom of one dull sermon succeeding to another. He thought there was far too much tedium annexed to the duties of the day, and in the end it did none of them any good.[2]

Although he could not rebel against his father as a child, he could and did against his tutor, who was a candidate for the Kirk. Of what Scott called "an excellent disposition," he permitted disputes. In these friendly arguments, Scott admitted he hated Presbyterians and admired Montrose with his victorious Highlanders. The tutor in turn championed "the Presbyterian Ulysses," Argyle. From this tutor Scott did acquire some knowledge of school divinity and church history, and a great acquaintance in particular with the old books describing the early history

[1] Citations from the *Ashestiel Memoir* are to John Gibson Lockhart, *Memoirs of the Life of Sir Walter Scott* (Boston, 1901), I, 9.

[2] *Ashestiel Memoir*, I, 27.

[32]

of the Church of Scotland and the wars and sufferings of the Covenanters.[3] This information Scott incorporated into his novels.

Whether exemplified in his father or his tutor, Scott early put behind him Calvinism and all that it implied. He neither accepted the traditional Scottish theology nor reacted against it. He simply ignored it and definitely did not let it affect him. John Buchan believes that this early rejection of Calvinism was one reason for Scott's lack of interest in philosophy. Buchan writes, "He had none of his countrymen's love of metaphysics, which was generally linked to the Calvinism of their training."[4] Lockhart insists that Scott must be numbered among the many who have incurred considerable risk in rejecting the Presbyterian form of Calvinism in consequence of the rigidity with which Presbyterian heads of families in Scotland enforced compliance with various relics of the puritanical observance.[5] In making this assertion Lockhart is correct in comparing Scott's family with other Scottish families in assigning unlimited authority to the father, but the implication that Scott's father was the typical tyrannical despot fits neither the portrait presented by Lockhart nor Sir Walter. Although no basis for this is to be found in Scott scholarship, it may have been over parental objection that Scott early in life recognized his repugnance to the mode in which public worship was conducted in the Scottish Establishment and adhered to the Episcopal Church. Lockhart implies his selection of the Episcopal Church was not only because of its less strict discipline but also because its ceremonies satisfied Scott's always-prevailing antiquarian interests:

> He . . . adhered to the sister Church, whose system of government and discipline he believed to be the fairest copy of the primitive polity, and whose litanies and collects he reverenced as having been transmitted to us from the age immediately succeeding that of the Apostles.[6]

One possibility for Scott's joining the Episcopal Church which Lockhart and scholars have not explored could be suggested by Scott's views on nationalism. He was always a champion of nationalism but his view included Great Britain and was never limited to Scotland. He believed always in the union of the two older kingdoms under one crown. In his novels he wrote of the glories of an ancient northern kingdom, but in his personal views the union was never to be separated. In almost all disagreements between the two countries, except for the one which produced his "Malachi Malagrowther" letters, Scott sided with England.

[3] *Ashestiel Memoir,* I, 25.

[4] John Buchan, *Sir Walter Scott* (London, 1932), p. 48.

[5] Lockhart, V, 456.

[6] Lockhart, V, 456.

In many respects Scott was more English than Scottish, and since the Episcopal Church was the church which represented the English view, he may have left the Scottish Establishment.

In spite of Scott's leaving the church of his parents, Lockhart insists he never rejected their moral or religious ideals. Under the eye of his parents he had received a strictly religious education. The virtuous conduct of his parents was in unison with the principles they desired to instill into their children. From the great doctrines thus recommended he appears never to have swerved.[7]

There are few passages in his diaries in which Scott alludes to his own religious feelings and practices. The most complete statement of his beliefs is recorded in the December 10, 1825, entry of his *Journal*. On this date Scott contemplated the hereafter. As every day brought us nearer that termination, one would almost think our views should become clearer as the regions we are approaching are brought nigher. But it is not so. Before we shall see things as they really are, a curtain must be withdrawn. Scott doubted that any single individual disbelieved the existence of a God. Although some have professed atheism or agnosticism, he doubts if anyone at all times and in all moods adopted these hideous creeds. Since everyone believes in a Deity, it follows that the immortality of the soul and the state of future rewards and punishments is indissolubly linked with this belief. More than these two beliefs man is not to know. However, he is not prohibited from his attempts, however vain, to pierce the solemn sacred gloom.

In projecting beyond this gloom, man has turned to Scripture. But the expressions there are doubtless metaphorical. Penal fires and heavenly melody are only applicable to bodies endowed with senses. And at least until the resurrection of the body the spirit of man, whether it is to be rewarded or punished, is incorporeal. The glorified bodies which shall arise in the last day are not destined for Mahomet's paradise. Mark xii. 25. denies this. The verse Scott refers to is translated in the King James Version:

> For when they shall rise from the dead, they neither marry, nor are given in marriage; but are as the angels which are in heaven.

Thus the glorified bodies will be incapable of the same gross indulgences with which they are now solaced and the inconsistency between the purity of the Christian's heavenly religion and Mahomet's heaven will be readily granted. Scott rejects, however, the idea of the heavenly reward consisting of nothing but hymn-singing. He cannot believe a spirit would enjoy participating in an eternal concert which would be

[7] Lockhart, V, 456.

a never-ending Birthday Ode. His only guess as to the state of a spirit in this heaven is that there would be love, unity, and a state of peace and perfect happiness.

Scott cannot conceive of it being altogether so wrong a conjecture to assume that the Deity, who himself must be supposed to feel love and affection for the beings he has called into existence, should delegate a portion of his powers. If this is accepted, one would then find reality in Milton's sublime machinery of the guardian saints or genii of kingdoms. Always anti-Roman Catholic in his theology, Scott admits the acceptance of this view approaches the Catholic idea of the employment of saints. However, it does not approach the absurdity of saint-worship, which degrades their religion. Man as a celestial being would be employed in aiding the Deity. Having been granted certain appropriate powers, he would engage in overcoming difficulties and making exertions on behalf of the Deity for other mankind. In Scott's thinking, this life of active benevolence is more consistent with his ideas than an eternity of music. He admits his and everyone else's ideas are nothing but speculation. It is impossible even to guess what we shall do in a hereafter unless we could ascertain first the equally difficult previous question of what we are to be. Almost as an after-thought, he states he would not, of course, limit the range of his genii to this confined world because there is the universe with all its endless extent of worlds.

Scott ends this discussion on his religious views of man's state after death by granting to all mankind freedom of belief. There is a God, and a just God, a judgment, and a future life. Let all who own so much act according to the faith that is in them.

A more conservative view is found in another expression of Scott on religion. In 1829 he was approached on his idea about the renewal or retranslation of the Psalmody. The reasons he gives for being adverse to such an undertaking show the conservative, sentimental, and religious side of Scott which is not found elsewhere and also indicate why he was happier in the Episcopal than the Presbyterian form of worship. In the first place, Scott, who always thought of himself as an aristocrat, believed a retranslation would be highly unpopular with the lower and more ignorant rank. Many of this class have no idea of the change which those spiritual poems have suffered in translation, but consider their old translations as the very songs which David composed. The wiser class, in turn, thinks our fathers were holier and better men than we. To abandon their old hymns of devotion in order to grace them with newer and more modish expression would be a kind of sacrilege. The somewhat bald and rude language and versification of the Psalmody gives them an antique and venerable air. Their want of the popular graces of modish poetry shows they belong to a style where ornaments are not required. Although these songs are not the words of David, they are the very words which were spoken and sung by the fathers of the Reformation, sometimes in the wilderness, in fetters, or at the stake. If a Church possessed the vessels from which the original reformers partook of the Eucharist, it would be bad taste to melt them down and exchange them for more modern. For that reason moderns are permitted, in Scott's view, to write new hymns or paraphrases if they insist, but the old must remain. Both law and religion must lose some of their dignity as often as they adopt new fashions.[8]

In 1824 Scott had occasion to write two sermons. As Lockhart humorously put it, "The announcement that the Author of Waverley had Sermons in the press [in 1828] was received perhaps with as much incredulity in the clerical world, as could have been excited among them by that of a romance from the Archbishop of Canterbury."[9] Scott had known George Huntly Gordon since 1815, when Gordon was nineteen, and had taken more than a fatherly interest in his career because of his sympathy for Gordon's deafness. Trained as a Presbyterian minister, Gordon was unable to secure a position because the Synod pronounced his deafness an insuperable objection. Scott intervened and persuaded Jeffrey to plead his case before the General Assembly where Jeffrey succeeded in obtaining a ruling in favor of Gordon. In an effort to aid him financially, Scott obtained employment for him as the transcriber of his novels for the Ballantyne press. During the autumn of 1824 Gordon was living at Abbotsford copying the manuscript of *Redgauntlet* and working at leisure hours on the catalogue of the Abbotsford library. Scott noticed Gordon was so nervous over the question of his deafness that he could not prepare two sermons which must be produced on a certain day before his Presbytery if he were to obtain a church. Unable to raise Gordon's spirits, Scott told him to continue working on the catalogue and he would write them. The difficulty of an Episcopalian writing sermons to be delivered by a Presbyterian minister apparently bothered neither of them. The next morning Scott gave Gordon the sermons he had written, but later Gordon considered it quite impossible to produce them as his own.[10]

[8] *The Journal of Sir Walter Scott*, ed. John Guthrie Tait (Edinburgh, 1950), May 28 and May 29, 1829, entries.

[9] Lockhart, V, 143.

[10] Lockhart, V, 142-147.

Scott forgot the sermons until Gordon asked him if he might dispose of them to some bookseller because he needed the money. Scott consented, and Gordon sold them to Colbourne for £250. Scott objected to Colbourne, but in his continuing efforts to help Gordon he did not stop Colbourne's printing them. He wrote of Colbourne and his wishes on the publication:

> The man [Colbourne] is a puffing quack; but though I would rather the thing had not gone there, and far rather that it had gone nowhere, yet, Hang it! if it makes the poor lad easy, what needs I fret about it? After all, there would be little grace in doing a kind thing, if you did not suffer pain or inconvenience upon the score.[11]

Just how much pain or inconvenience Scott suffered in seeing his only attempt at religious writing published for the world is not recorded. *Religious Discourses, by a Layman* was issued in the spring of 1828 with the letters "W. S." placed at the foot of a short preface. If it were not for the curiosity associated with the author's name, the *Discourses* would have remained an unimportant publication.

The interest in religion which Scott showed in his personal writings appears also in his novels. The most unusual, and indeed daring for its time, representative of a religious group is Scott's introduction of the Jewess Rebecca and her father Isaac of York in *Ivanhoe*. Basing his introduction on the tales his friend James Skene told him of Jews he had observed during his youth in Germany, Scott unknowingly helped some in curbing the prejudices and misunderstandings of his age. However, Scott was prejudiced himself. He wrote:

> The character of the fair Jewess found so much favor in the eyes of some fair readers, that the writer was censured, because, when arranging the fates of the characters of the drama, he had not assigned the hand of Wilfred to Rebecca, rather than the less interesting Rowena. But . . . the prejudices of the age rendered such an union almost impossible . . . .[12]

Scott did realize he had created "a character of a highly virtuous and lofty stamp," as he described her. His own prejudice against adherents of the Jewish religion is shown in his *Journal* after the failure of his publishers.

The introduction of Jews into *Ivanhoe* and the use as background of the Jacobite uprising, which although primarily a political issue was also religious, in such novels as *Waverley* illustrate that Scott in none of his writings attempted religious controversy. In the many instances in which he states his anti-Roman Catholic views it was not with the idea of causing religious argument but because he realized nearly his

---

[11] *Journal*, January 25, 1828.

[12] *Introduction to Ivanhoe.*

entire audience would agree with him. Scott is always sympathetic toward a character's religious beliefs. Although he left the Presbyterian Church and did not share the views of the Covenanters, he treats them with kindness whenever they appear in a novel. Scott's attitude of tolerance toward the Presbyterians is illustrated in a scene in *Guy Mannering*. Dr. Erskine delivers a sermon in which the Calvinism of the Kirk of Scotland is ably supported, yet made the basis of a sound system of practical morals. Impressed, Mannering comments that such must have been the preachers to whose unfearing minds, and acute, though sometimes rudely exercised, talents we owe the Reformation. Pleydell agrees, but insists Erskine has nothing of the sour or pharisaical pride which has been imputed to some of the early fathers of the Calvinistic Kirk of Scotland. Pleydell's position reflects Scott's view of the theological differences of opinion between the Presbyterian and Episcopal Churches in addition to pride in the history of his Scottish forefathers:

> "And you, Mr. Pleydell, what do you think of their points of difference [between factions in the Scottish Church]?"
>
> "Why, I hope, Colonel, a plain man may go to heaven without thinking about them at all;—besides, *inter nos*, I am a member of the suffering and Episcopal Church of Scotland—the shadow of a shade now, and fortunately so;—but I love to pray where my fathers prayed before me, without thinking worse of the Presbyterian forms because they do not affect me with the same associations."[13]

Pride in the fathers of the Scottish Church did not mean they always escaped criticism. Scott definitely objected to their attitude toward funerals as being unduly harsh toward the bereaved survivers. In Scott's opinion the last act which separates us forever, the creak of the screw-nails announcing that the lid of the coffin was in the act of being secured, has usually its effect upon the most indifferent, selfish, and hard-hearted.

> With a spirit of contradiction, which we may be pardoned for esteeming narrow-minded, the fathers of the Scottish kirk rejected, even on this most solemn occasion, the form of an address to the Divinity, lest they should be thought to give countenance to the rituals of Rome or of England.[14]

Scott noted that it was the present practice of most of the Scottish clergymen to seize this opportunity of offering a prayer and exhortation suitable to make an impression upon the living. This is particularly necessary and effective while the living are in the very presence of the relics of him whom they have but lately seen such as they themselves, and who now is such as they must in their time become. But this decent and praise-

[13] *Guy Mannering*, Chap. 37.
[14] *The Antiquary*, Chap. 31.

worthy practice was not adopted in 1795, the time of which Scott was treating.

Remembering Scott's lengthy objection to a Presbyterian funeral in *The Antiquary*, the reader will be glad to know that Scott received an Episcopal burial. Lockhart, who was a pallbearer, reported that his funeral was conducted in an unostentatious manner, but the attendance was very great. Few of his old friends then in Scotland were absent, and many came from a great distance. His old domestics and foresters made it their petition to carry his remains. Lockhart says the company was assembled "according to the usual Scotch fashion," but he does not explain this term. Prayers were offered by the Very Reverend Dr. Baird, Principal of the University of Edinburgh, and by the Reverend Dr. David Dickson, Minister of St. Cuthbert's, "who both expatiated in very striking manner on the virtuous example of the deceased." Mr. Archdeacon Williams read the Burial Service of the Church of England while the remains of Sir Walter Scott were laid by the side of his wife.[15]

Examples of prejudices between Presbyterians and Episcopalians occur throughout *Peveril of the Peak*. Scott refrains from sanctioning these prejudices by presenting them as coming directly from his characters. In one scene Sir Geoffrey Peveril is represented as being so fond of children and so compassionate toward the sorrows of his neighbor Major Bridgenorth that he forgot the Major was a Presbyterian until it became necessary for Alice, whom the Peverils have taken to rear, to be christened by a Presbyterian minister. The thought of Martindale Castle being violated by the heretical step of a dissenting clergyman was a matter of horror to its orthodox owner:

> He had seen the famous Hugh Peters, with a Bible in one hand and a pistol in the other, ride in triumph through the court-door when Martindale was surrendered; and the bitterness of that hour had entered like iron into his soul.[16]

Yet Lady Peveril's influence over the prejudices of her husband was such that he was induced to connive at the ceremony taking place in a remote garden-house not properly within the castle wall. The baptism was performed by the Reverend Master Solsgrace, who had once preached a sermon of three hours before the House of Commons in thanksgiving of the relief of Exeter. Lady Peveril even dared to be present, but Sir Geoffrey took care to be absent the whole day from the Castle. However, he directed the washing, perfuming, and general purification of the

[15] Lockhart, V, 439-440.
[16] *Peveril of the Peak*, Chap. 1.

summerhouse later.[17] In another scene Sir Geoffrey shows he cannot forget his friend is a member of another religious sect. When Lady Peveril explains she has heard of a love-intrigue between Bridgenorth and Mistress Deborah, he remarks:

> "It is the true end of a dissenter . . . to marry his own maid-servant, or some other person's."[18]

Religious differences separate the two friends when Sir Geoffrey believes Bridgenorth is deep in a new plot which has broken out among the Roundheads, worse than Venner's, which was the celebrated insurrection of the Anabaptists and Fifth Monarch men in London in the year 1661. Despite Lady Peveril's protests, Sir Geoffrey determines to take Bridgenorth prisoner.[19]

In David Deans of *The Heart of Mid-Lothian* Scott has presented his finest portrait of a Scottish Presbyterian. This person is practically an Old Testament patriarch, but each individual reader's opinion of this character is determined by the reader's evaluation of his action in rejecting his sinful daughter Effie. Sympathy toward the man can be excused when one remembers he held the extremely honored position of ruling elder. The conflict in his mind is best exemplified in the following passage:

> ". . . I trust to bear even this crook in my lot with submission. But, oh! . . . the kirk, of whilk, though unworthy, I have yet been thought a polished shaft, and meet to be a pillar, holding, from my youth upward, the place of ruling elder—what will the lithsome and profane think of the guide that cannot keep his own family from stumbling?"[20]

In an excellent example of writing Scott presents his knowledge of the history of the Presbyterian form of religion as it was persecuted or flourished under various monarchs from King William until 1736, the date of the action of the novel. By showing Deans's opinions of these changes and their influence on him, Scott has achieved a superb piece of narrative technique. To readers who are confused as to Scott's views on the Jacobite rebellions, Scott may have supplied an answer if his reaction is accepted as that of David's:

> Then came the insurrection in 1715, and David Deans's horror for the revival of the popish and prelatical faction, reconciled him greatly to the government of King George, although he grieved that that monarch might be suspected of a leaning unto Erastianism.[21]

[17] *Peveril of the Peak*, Chap. 1.
[18] *Peveril of the Peak*, Chap. 8.
[19] *Peveril of the Peak*, Chap. 10.
[20] *The Heart of Mid-Lothian*, Chap. 12.
[21] *The Heart of Mid-Lothian*, Chap. 18.

A similar knowledge of the history of the Presbyterian Church leaders and the doctrines and beliefs is presented when David examines Reuben Butler before his admission to Presbytery. Although he calls David's examination a very long harangue, Scott hopes the reader will share with him his interest in church history.

In David Deans Scott drew an admirable portrait, but in presenting not one but two neurotic Presbyterian ministers in his novels he seems to have held them generally in contempt. Jonathan Oldbuck in *The Antiquary* is an emotional and mental child. There is every indication throughout the novel that Scott has attempted a comic character but the humor is enjoyed by Scott rather than the reader. Scott, however, cannot be accused of maliciousness. It merely seems that he thought a bachelor minister who devotes his entire life to the pursuit of knowledge to the exclusion of all else naturally acquires such eccentric habits as indifference to dress, forgetfulness, and absent-mindedness. Even in the midst of society he is oblivious to his surroundings. Having created such a character in one novel Scott repeated the same character under the name of Josiah Cargill in *St. Ronan's Well* without, however, giving him the role of leading or title character.

Since many of his novels concern persecuted religious groups such as the Presbyterians, it is strange that Scott seldom mentions the Quakers. They do appear in his novels, and occasionally a character is given Quaker ancestors, but as a whole he seldom refers to them. In an autobiographical note to *Redgauntlet* he records with pleasure a kindness granted him as a youth during his stay at Kelso. Unable to obtain books, he became a friend of a Quaker who let him read her deceased husband's library on condition that he take some of the tracts printed for extending the doctrines of her own sect. She did not exact any promise that he read them and he does not record whether he did or not. Scott always admired the members of the Society of Friends for their benevolence and charity.

Scott wrote in his *Journal* that he thought few men were real atheists, but he has one character who not only lives but dies an atheist without Scott's converting him. Of interest in the passage is the atheist's views of his after-life. His mysterious frame of humanity will melt into the general mass of nature, to be recompounded in the other forms with which she daily supplies those which daily disappear, and return under different forms, such as the watery particles to streams and showers, the airy portions to wanton in the breeze. Scott cannot help ending the chapter with an admonition to the unfaithful:

. . . the Bohemian had gone where the vanity of his dreadful creed was to be put to the final issue—a fearful experience for one who had neither expressed remorse for the past, nor apprehension for the future![22]

The most extensive and interesting use of religion in Scott's novels is his treatment of Catholicism. For a prejudiced Protestant who knew nothing of medieval monasticism to set a novel in this rich period required study. Una Pope-Hennessy believes Scott found the necessary information for such novels as *The Monastery* and *The Abbot* in T. D. Fosbroke's *British Monachism* (1802), which is a work on the "Manners and Customs of the Monks and Nuns of England." Mrs. Pope-Hennessy also believes Scott's use of Catholicism had an important place in the development of the English novel:

> Up till Sir Walter's day the cloister decor had been used by the Monk Lewis-Mrs. Radcliffe school of writers as a background to spooky, dissolute or irreligious happenings. There had been no attempt to present it sensibly, and, as readers were prompt to swallow everything that made them shiver, the romancers got away with it without criticism. No English novelist before Scott had written about Catholics seriously or had introduced high-minded respectable papists into their books. Scott revived curiosity about Catholicism and, as Newman seems to have realised, paved the way for the acceptance of the Oxford Movement by interesting his readers in the Catholic past.[23]

Mrs. Pope-Hennessy may be correct in her evaluation of his place in this aspect of the history of the English novel, although the thought of one of England's most out-spoken anti-Roman Catholics paving the way for the Oxford Movement is difficult to accept. If correct in this thesis, she is incorrect in her evaluation of Scott's "Catholic" novels. She states that "he displays familiarity with matters ecclesiastical." What little familiarity he had came, as she readily admits, from concentrated study. And his quoting the *Te Deum* and knowing the *Stabat Mater* by heart, which she cites as evidence, hardly qualifies him to be the authority she makes him. She also argues "he knows something of the habits of monks." This, of course, would be necessary for anyone who attempted to have his characters enter a cloister. His friars and his abbots are usually anything but religious except in costume. Scott himself knew *The Monastery* was a failure. He admits this in the Introduction to the later editions, acknowledging the hurt which the critics had inflicted upon him and calling attention to the general public's lack of reception. Lockhart similarly disparages it. The success of *The Abbot*, as Mrs. Pope-Hennessy admits, is due to the introduction of Mary, Queen of Scots, rather than a better presentation of monastic life. A better description of Scott's treatment of this subject is presented by John Buchan:

[22] *Quentin Durward*, Chap. 34.

[23] Una Pope-Hennessy, *Sir Walter Scott* (Denver, 1949), p. 62.

. . . Scott had little understanding of Catholicism. This man . . . cherished a blunt Protestantism, to which he was never weary of testifying. He can describe vividly the secular aspect of Melrose, its routine, its polity and its humours, but since he had no insight into its secret things, the mystic brotherhood of an ordered community set in the heart of darkness, he cannot move us by his tale of its fall.[24]

This blunt Protestant showed anti-Roman Catholicism in almost every novel. Even *The Monastery* has, so Scott admits in the Introduction, as:

The general plan of the story . . . to conjoin two characters in that bustling and contentious age, who, thrown into situations which gave them different views on the subject of the Reformation, should, with the same sincerity and purity of intention, dedicate themselves, the one to the support of the sinking fabric of the Catholic Church, the other to the establishment of the Reformed doctrines.

Julian Peveril says of the Roman Catholic religion:

. . . I have seen Popery too closely to be friendly to its tenets. The bigotry of the laymen—the persevering arts of the priesthood—the perpetual intrigue for the extension of the forms without the spirit of religion—the usurpation of that church over the consciences of men—and her impious pretensions to infallibility, are as inconsistent to my mind as they can seem to yours, with common sense, rational liberty, freedom of science, and pure religion.[25]

Popes in *The Betrothed* are presented as unscrupulous. In this novel "the yoke of the Roman supremacy presses severely both on the clergy and laity of England." Priests are presented as fair-weather friends here, as greedy hypocrites and ready instruments of inquisitions in *The Fortunes of Nigel*. Scott pities the poor Catholics who through ignorance depend upon their religion. The Catholics invented the names Caspar, Melchior, and Balthasar for the Eastern Magi, and Scott is sorry Quentin Durward must base his reliance upon the special protection of these three invented saints. However, Scott does express hope for Quentin and other misfortunates who are sincere Catholics:

That the object of his devotion was misplaced, was not the fault of Quentin; and its purpose being sincere, we can scarce suppose it unacceptable to the only true Deity, who regards the motives, and not the forms of prayer, and in whose eyes the sincere devotion of a heathen is more estimable than the specious hypocrisy of a Pharisee.[26]

These are only a few of the many instances in which Scott shows his anti-Catholicism. Most are more vicious than those cited. And in his *Journal*, which he considered as a private diary although he expected publication, Scott is even less restrained. Two comments in a novel are

[24] Buchan, pp. 227-228.
[25] *Peveril of the Peak*, Chap. 17.
[26] *Quentin Durward*, Chap. 17.

autobiographical in explaining the reasons for this prejudice. Scott says of Nanty in *Redgauntlet* that a hatred of Popery seemed to be the only remnant of his Presbyterian education.[27] And what Scott applies to Fairford in the same work applies equally to himself:

> His line of education, as well as his father's tenets in matters of church and state, had taught him a holy horror for Papists, and a devout belief in whatever had been said of the punic faith of Jesuits, and of the expedients of mental reservation, by which the Catholic priests in general were supposed to evade keeping faith with heretics.[28]

As a result of his education and rearing Scott's interest in religion was necessarily limited. Because of his education he had a vast knowledge of the doctrines and history of Presbyterianism and Calvinism. It is assumed, although it cannot be proved, that as a convert he acquired a similar knowledge of the Church of England. In his personal and published writings Scott displays an interest in religion and shows he is a religious man. His moral and religious beliefs have impressed themselves upon almost all his writings. He himself thought that his works taught the practical lessons of morality and Christianity.

LOUISIANA STATE UNIVERSITY

[27] *Redgauntlet*, Chap. 15.
[28] *Redgauntlet*, Chap. 16.

DAVID MACAREE

Myth and Allegory in
Lewis Grassic Gibbon's
A Scots Quair

The critic who would write about *A Scots Quair*[1] is faced with a difficulty not normally encountered by those who turn their attention to the prose fiction of the twentieth century: the lack of clearly enunciated statements by the author as to his literary intentions. The only general remark that J. Leslie Mitchell ("Lewis Grassic Gibbon") permitted himself was to the effect that his novel was a symbolic representation of "the Scots countryside itself, fathered between a kailyard and a bonnie brier bush in the lee of a house with green shutters," (SS, p. 31) where the allusion to two strains of modern Scottish fiction, the oversentimental and the over-brutal, suggests that he wished to combine what was of value in each in a creation that would depict Scotland and its people without exaggerated emphasis on either extreme.

Of Gibbon's sincerity there can be no doubt, since he engaged in a race with death itself to complete the three parts of the *Quair*: *Sunset Song* (1932), *Cloud Howe* (1933), and *Grey Granite* (1934); and the race was close, for by the next year he was dead at the age of thirty-four with his one full-length work as a memorial. Despite the speed with which he wrote, however, his trilogy showed no signs of lack of premeditation; in fact, considered at the personal level as a novel of the soil dealing with the life of Christine Guthrie, daughter of a small farmer, in the years between 1911 and 1934, it has been criticised for its excessive neatness of construction with its tripartite division corresponding to youth, young adulthood, and middle age; each with its appropriate husband. farmer, minister, and poet-craftsman; in three settings: countryside, small town, and industrial city. What is more, the parallels extend even to the structure of the individual books, each of which consists of four sections with

---

[1] J. Leslie Mitchell ("Lewis Grassic Gobbon"), (London, 1946, reset and reprinted 1950). The books that make up the trilogy, *Sunset Song, Cloud Howe,* and *Grey Granite* are paged as separate entities; their references will be given in the text as *SS, CH,* and *GG* respectively, with pagination following that of the printing of 1950.

titles suggestive of the progression of the narrative. In *Sunset Song* there is the cycle of the farming year: Ploughing, Drilling, Seed-time, and Harvest; in *Cloud Howe*, the cloud formations in order of increasing gloom: Cirrus, Cumulus, Stratus, and Nimbus; in *Grey Granite*, minerals ranked by hardness and purity: Epidote, Sphene, Apatite, and Zircon. Such tidy schematization annoyed some of the novel's first critics for it suggested a preoccupation with issues wider than those they considered strictly relevant to what they saw as regional fiction dealing with lower class life on the Scottish countryside.[2]

But in fact Gibbon was concerned with a theme far greater than the personal history of Chris Guthrie as later commentators have suggested. Kurt Wittig has pointed out that "the story moves on three distinct levels: personal, social, and mythical,"[3] and Goeffrey Wagner in an article on the *Quair* as a social document has hinted at an allegorical strain lying behind.[4] The carefully balanced structure indeed, hints strongly that Gibbon was aiming not at naturalism solely, or even at a social documentation, but a myth arrived at through allegory. Besides its structure, there are elements in the story; too, that lend themselves best to such a reading. To give but one instance, Robert Colquhoun, Chris's second husband, greets the news of her pregnancy with, "Oh Chris Caledonia, I've married a nation;" (*CH*, p. 104) words that are meaningful only if we see Chris as Scotland herself, which was presumably Gibbon's intention.

His choice of "Gibbon" as pseudonym suggests also that the author of *A Scots Quair* wished us to be conscious of the wider historical perspective that lay behind the subjective account of Chris Guthrie, for what we have is a kind of "Decline and Fall of the Scottish Nation," and in the end only the land is left. But this is history by indirection; parallels between events in the life of Chris and those of Scotland's past are to be found in the fiction, presented by way of extended metaphor. At the personal level the setting is within the microcosmic society of what, with apologies to Sir Walter Scott's claim for Gandercleugh in *Tales of My Landlord*, might well be considered Scotland's heartland, the eastward-facing Howe of the Mearns. Here fertile lowlands rise from the shores of the North Sea over which came Teutonic settlers, and these rich acres merge at last with windswept uplands to the west with their remnants

[2] See, for instance, Angus Macdonald, "Modern Scots Novelists," *Edinburgh Essays on Scots Literature* (Edinburgh, 1933), p. 165.

[3] *The Scottish Tradition in Literature* (Edinburgh, 1958), p. 330.

[4] " 'The Greatest Since Galt'; Lewis Grassic Gibbon," *Essays in Criticism*, II (1952), 295-296.

of a Celtic people, themselves later comers than the builders of Standing
Stones who have long vanished from the land, leaving only these relics
to provide a sense of community with the past. For it was these incomers
whose arrival signalled the end of the Golden Age, a thought that Robert
Colquhoun puts into words as an expression of Chris's instinctive feelings:

> Once Chris and Robert came to a place, out in the open, here the wind blew
> and the ground was thick with the droppings of sheep, where a line of ancient
> stones stood ringed, as they stood in Kinraddie far west and below, left by
> men of antique time, memorial these of a dream long lost, the hopes and fears
> of fantastic eld.
>
> Robert said that they came from the East, those fears, long ago, ere Pytheas
> came sailing the sounding coasts to Thule. Before that the hunters had
> roamed the hills, naked and bright, in a Golden Age, without fear or hope or
> hate or love, living high in the race of the wind and the race of life, mating
> as simple as beasts or birds, dying with a like keen simpleness. . . . Chris sat
> on a fallen stone and heard him, about her the gleams of the wintry day, the
> sailing cloud shapes over the Howe; and she asked him how long ago that had
> been? And Robert said "Less than four thousand years," and it sounded long
> enough to Chris — four thousand years of kings and of Gods, all the dark
> mad hopes that had haunted men since they left the caves and the hunting of
> deer, and the splendour of life like a song, like the wind. (*CH*, p. 106)

It is by the Standing Stones of Blaewearie, "in Kinraddie far west
and below," that the novel has its beginning; for it is from that vantage
point that the young Chris can look over the land, with its agricultural
settlements, its small market- and manufacturing towns, and its industrial
cities. It is from there that she goes down to take up the burden of
living, as schoolgirl, wife, and widow at Blaewearie Farm on Kinraddie
Estate; as minister's wife in Segget; as widow and mother in Duncairn.
And it is on the summit of the Barmekin that the tale ends, with Chris
moving from life to death as she watches the passing of daylight west-
wards over the face of the earth. And in those moments of lonely brooding she considers in retrospect the forces that have shaped her: her family
heritage which merges in her schoolgirl's mind into that from Scotland's
past; then, as woman, her feeling that all the ideas that men have followed
over the ages are only "Clouds that swept through the Howe of the
world;" and at the end of her life, the welcoming of death as deliverer
from a world where all man-made values have been negated.

In examining the individual books of the trilogy, we find that
Gibbon has supplied us with clues to the larger time scheme that operates
in addition to the one which records the passage of twenty-odd years in
the life of the central character. Thus, both *Sunset Song* and *Cloud
Howe* open with preliminary chapters sketching the political and social
history from the Middle Ages of Kinraddie and Segget respectively. In
the case of Kinraddie, we are given its story from its beginning as a

political entity with the Norman adventurer of the twelfth century who subdued the native Picts and carved out a domain for himself by the edge of the sword, to its ending with the last survivor of the once-great family locked in a madhouse, a hopeless degenerate, and the property held by absentee lawyer-trustees. Next comes a survey of the individual holdings into which the mortgaged estate has been divided, with richly evocative sketches of the tenants and their families in which Gibbon employs subtly modulated speech rhythms to create personalities as different as Chae Strachan, Mistress Gordon, and Rob of the Mill. On this land, as tenant of Blaewearie, and among these folk John Guthrie is coming to settle at the Winter Term of the year 1911, bringing with him his family from over the hills.

And balancing this is an epilude, set in the year 1918 insofar as it has to do with the life of Chris Guthrie, who by this time is Chris Tavendale, mother of a son, a widow, and betrothed to Robert Colquhoun, the minister of the parish. She is present at the dedication of the local War Memorial which he is conducting and as the plaque is unveiled she tells over among the names of the dead almost all the men who have in one way or another played a part in her development to maturity. Thus the sense of finality is strong as the service ends with the playing of the lament, *The Flowers of the Forest*, suggesting that it is more than the end of a war that is being commemorated, it is the end of a whole way of life.

But besides the personal story of Chris as a member of a social organization which, after eight centuries of existence, has collapsed through its own debility in the face of changes in the world outside, — besides this, there is yet another time scheme in operation, for the Guthries who come to settle in the Howe of the Mearns in the year 1911 are, in a special sense, representative of all those who, over the ages, have battled natural difficulties to make their homes in Scotland and become part of the land they have created. So their journey across the hills in the blast of a Scottish winter, described in epic terms, becomes a migration of peoples moving with their possessions through darkness to an unknown destiny; and on the way Chris has her strange vision that links her people with the first voyagers to these islands:

> She fell into a drowse through the cold and a strange dream came to her as they plodded up through the hills.
> For out of the night ahead of them came running a man, father didn't see him or heed to him, though old Bob in the dream that was Chris's snorted and shied. And as he came he wrung his hands, he was mad and singing, a foreign creature, black-bearded, half-naked he was; and he cried in the Greek "The ships of Pytheas! The ships of Pytheas!" and went by into the smore of the sleet storm on the Grampian hills. (SS, pp. 41-42)

For Pytheas, according to legend, was the Grèek who sailed first out of the Inland Sea, rounded Britain, touched at Thule, and visited Scandinavia on his way to the Baltic which he penetrated as far as the Vistula, thereby quickening into life, as it were, the migratory instincts of peoples who were to settle in Scotland.

Chris the girl, then, whom we meet first by the Stones on a summer's day dreaming over the countryside from her vantage point, carries it all within herself. But she is already a Chris whose personality is split between her love for the land and her own people, and her disdain for their crudeness that her schooling fosters through its emphasis on standard English speech and southern values. In her is summed up the ambivalence of the educated Scot of every age, torn between the values of his own country that he feels by instinct and his sense of its poverty and the coarseness of its people that he has become aware of from his reading. But in the event Chris does not have to make the choice between college and home; the suicide of her mother, desperate at the thought of an unwished-for pregnancy, forces her to return as housekeeper for her father who, having driven away her brother Will through cruelty, lives alone at Blaewearie.

But just as she has epitomised the dilemma of the educated Scot, so her brother, settled as a rancher in the Argentine represents the pioneer overseas; as Sergeant-Major in the French Foreign Legion, too, he is type of the Scot who, driven from his own land, has formed the *corps d'élite* in European armies, French, German, Swedish, or Russian. In yet another way Will has a representative function: as the Scot who renounces his allegiance and tries to still his conscience with assertions of his independence of home ties, "Who'd want to come back to this country? It's dead or it's dying — and a damned good job!" (SS, p. 165)

In the years between 1911 and 1914 Chris herself has been growing from girlhood to womanhood, from the first awareness of her body and its sensual demands to readiness for marriage. Significantly, her first recognition of the prompting of sex comes through a brief but intense Lesbian attachment to a neighbour's daughter, a forewarning that no man will ever possess her utterly, though her first husband, Ewan Tavendale, comes closest to complete union. She, indeed, chooses him, for he is a landless farmhand and it is she who, by her father's death, is the landholder. In this Gibbon is historically accurate; Tavendale is Highlander as she is Lowlander, or rather he is Celt as she is Teuton, and it is this marriage that should produce the complete Scot from the fusion of the cultures that they represent. Under these circumstances, it is fitting that they plight troth among the ruins of Dunottar Castle with its mementoes of past battles between the two races. The marriage itself is consummated on a night of winter storm, appropriate symbol of the political and religious storms that have swept Scotland, and from that consummation is born young Ewan whose birth coincides almost exactly with the outbreak of a war that will engulf all that is best of the manhood of Kinraddie before it is done.

First to go is Chae Strachan whose romantic temperament makes him view war as an adventure that is preferable to the humdrum life of a farmer. Then, in due time, Ewan becomes involved in the senseless slaughter, not through any strong belief in the rightness of the cause for which he is to fight but from his inability to bear the taunts at his lack of courage that are levelled at him. And, surprisingly, Long Rob of the Mill, rationalist, atheist, and conscientious objector, after baffling all the efforts of the army authorities to impress him, enlists of his own free will because "he couldn't stay out of it longer, all the world had gone daft and well he might go with the rest." (SS, p. 176) And none of these is to return. Ewan himself is first to die, shot as a deserter when a spring breeze off the fields of Flanders awakened memories of home and made him conscious of the madness he was involved in. Then Chae throws his life away, and Rob, with a fine irony that he would have appreciated, is killed in the meaningless exchange of shots of the last few hours before the Armistice.

Once again, though he never forces the matter on the reader's attention, Gibbon has created characters who function as individuals and as typological representatives. All have been associated with Chris in one way or another: Chae is kindly neighbour who comforts her with the true story of Ewan's death; Ewan himself; and Long Rob, sharer with her in a momentary gust of passion just before his final departure. But Chae too is the romantic, amorous of the far; Ewan is the Celtic dreamer, too insecure in himself to resist public pressure and coming to self-knowledge only for reality to destroy him; and Rob is the type of philosophical rationalist whose heyday in Scotland had been the eighteenth century.

With Ewan and the others dead *Sunset Song* ends in a kind of *Vale* to the agricultural way of life for the estate as such is to be broken up and Chris herself, with young Ewan, is about to leave for Segget as wife of the minister who has been kind to her since his return from overseas. The title of the epilude, "The Unfurrowed Field," itself suggests the reversion of the land to its original state before man set his mark on it and made it serve his purposes. Chris's departure from Kinraddie, then, becomes more than an event in the life of an individual, it serves

to turn the page on one aspect of Scottish life and the characters it
fostered. Now it is the turn of the small town to receive attention.

The setting of *Cloud Howe*, then, is Segget, closer to the lowlands
than Kinraddie, though the Standing Stones are still visible from its
fort-crowned hill, The Kaimes. Once again the prelude gives the wide
sweep of political and social history of the place, spanning the centuries
from its first settlement by the Lombard, Monte Alto, who brought
his own land-hungry relatives to settle the fief he had been granted for
his services to Robert Bruce in the war against England. Then, with
vivid streaks of colour, it is recorded how the Monte Altos become
Mowats, how they and their retainers mingle with the local inhabitants,
how they become involved in the religious wars and civil tumults of the
seventeenth and eighteenth century, how, with the coming of the Industrial Revolution, they build spinning mills and provide money for
a church, though their altruism does not run to a steeple, an indication
of the emasculated faith they think proper for their employees and the
tradesmen who rely on their favours. But if this is history, it is the
oral history that passes into legend and we are aware of the rhythm of
the narrative voice dwelling on incident after incident, as in the mysterious burning of the House of Kaimes, home of the Mowats.

> a great bit fire had risen in the night and burned the old castle down to its
> roots, of the stones there stood hardly one above the other, the Segget folk
> swore they'd all slept so sound the thing was over afore they awoke. And
> that might be so, but for many a year . . . there were miekle great clocks in
> this house and that, great coverlets on beds that lay neist the floor; and the
> bell that rung the weavers awake had once been a great handbell from the
> hall of the Mowats up on the Kaimes high hill. (*CH*, p. 8)

Unlike the Kinraddie family the Mowats still have a measure of control
over their holdings, but the degenerate Alec Mowat, their last representative keeps the mills going in the difficult years that follow the First
World War only because he needs the money they bring him for his
London whores and his other sensual pleasures. Alec typifies Carlyle's
Master-Idler; he comes at the end of a process that began when the
ties between titular owner and his employees were severed, leaving only
disdain on the one hand and hatred on the other.

Segget, therefore, is depressed physically, morally, and spiritually
when Robert, Cris, and young Ewan move into the manse in 1919.
And if anything the depression has deepened by 1927 when Robert
Colquhoun dies, completely worn out by a succession of defeats that
culminates in the failure of the General Strike from which he had hoped
for improvements in the workers' conditions. But before his death the
indifference of those he had tried to help coupled with the hostility of

the middle class has caused a visionary streak in him to become obsessive. As he withdraws from the world of men he shuts out Chris also so that she rejects his faith:

> And a dreadful loneliness came over Chris, and a shivering hate for that cloud he followed, that sadfaced Figure out of the past, who had led such legions of men to such ends up and down the haughs and hills of the earth. Christ? So maybe indeed He had lived and died, a follower of clouds Himself. (CH, p. 133)

This spiritual crisis in the life of Chris has as its social accompaniment a thickening of the moral atmosphere of Segget so that what is cruelty passes for fun, and what is smut, for humour. At its worst, Gibbon depicts brutality that is sub-human or so we would like to think until we realise that he has drawn his examples from the Fascism of the twenties. It is the debasement of the human spirit that defeats Robert Colquhoun for his gospel of love is powerless against it and in seeking comfort in visions of a reincarnated Christ he loses Chris. She, in any case, has been moving away from him since the death of their infant child, and when she cannot share his visions — delusions, she thinks them — their alienation is complete. In the end he renounces her when she pleads with him to cancel his Sunday service on account of an illness caused by war-time gassing: "It's you or the kirk, Chris, and I'm the kirk's man." (CH, p. 152) Here the full force of his renunciation lies in the word "man" with its Scots meaning of "husband". By his choice of the kirk as his bride Robert is casting off Chris. But his last sermon casts off traditional Christianity too, in favour of a new faith which the Figure of his visions has disclosed to him: "a stark, sure creed that will cut like a knife through the doubt and disease — men with unclouded eyes may yet find it." (CH, p. 156) This, however, is his final effort and it is left to Chris to announce his death to the congregation in the words, "It is finished."

Read simply as an account of life in a small Scottish mill-and market town in the grim years of the twenties, Cloud Howe is fully satisfying. The personal tensions between Robert Colquhoun and Chris are mirrored in social tensions for which there seems to be no alleviation in any of the religious and political faiths that Gibbon, through various characters, explores. Colquhoun's own Christian socialism is dismissed as an unsubstantial dream; socialism as a faith for workers, independent of religion, fails also because its leaders are too easily seduced by a taste of power and because its rank and file relax as soon as they themselves are comfortable. Even fascism is examined and rejected with scorn as Chris turns on Alec Mowat, its apologist:

And what's going to happen when you and your kind rule us again as of old, Mr. Mowat? Was there ever the kind of Scotland you preach? — Happy, at ease, the folk on the land well-fed ,the folk in the pulpits well-feared, the gentry doing great deeds? . . . I've been to Dunottar Castle and seen there the ways that the gentry once liked to keep order. (*CH*, p. 81)

But just as in *Sunset Song* Chris as Scotland serves to show us the men of Kinraddie as representative Scotsmen, so in *Cloud Howe* Chris as Scotland is seen in relation to the Presbyterian Church whose close links with the nation sustained it in the troubled centuries that followed the Calvinist Reformation until the advance of science in the last hundred years or so caused a retreat into hair-splitting disputes on points of dogma on the one hand and increasing indifference on the other. In the novel the beginning of the rupture is signalled by the death, still-born, of Chris's child by Robert Colquhoun, an event that we might take as recognition that the union of Kirk and Nation is incapable of bearing lasting fruit. Chris's last words to the congregation, "It is finished," then, have a striking ambiguity about them. Besides their echo of the death of Christ on the Cross, they may suggest the end of the Kirk as a force in Scottish life and make possible the replacement of Christianity by the stark, sure creed that Colquhoun prophesied in his last sermon.

But meanwhile Chris has one child, Ewan, who is growing to adolescence in the years at Segget. He, the Scot of the future, has already grown away from the Christianity of his step-father and has come to consider God as a meaningless abstraction so that he can say to his mother, "I don't think He's worth bothering about. He can't make any difference to the world — or I think He'd have made it by now." (*CH*, p. 101) This cool self-possession that seems to subordinate feeling to thought is the face he puts on for the world, and even his own mother is taken in and tells him that he is hard and cool as grey granite, forgetting that granite is created by subterranean heat and pressure and the greater these are, the purer is the resulting rock. But this is looking ahead to *Grey Granite* and in the meantime Ewan is engaged in growing up, enthusiastic only about the past of his country, searching out his roots in the forts of the old hill peoples, and conscious, as is Chris, of a sense of identity with the land and its inhabitants. With the death of Robert, however, mother and son have to move away from Segget where signs of that past are numerous to the industrial slum that was the nineteenth century's contribution to Scottish civilisaion; there, fittingly enough, our first sight of Chris is a fleeting glimpse caught through a dense fog that stifles and restricts visibility.

Before going on to *Grey Granite,* however, it may be pointed out that, unlike *Sunset Song, Cloud Howe* has no afterpiece, perhaps an indication that Gibbon felt he had brought his records up to the present, and that *Grey Granite* was to be prophecy rather than history. This feeling is reinforced by the lack of both prelude and epilude to the last book of the trilogy, so that in a sense, *A Scots Quair* is left open-ended. The lack of a prelude can easily be explained as his recognition that an industrial city like Duncairn lacks any continuity with the past which it is burying under masonry and pavement or destroying by pollution. In it, too, the sense of national consciousness atrophies as it becomes the meeting place of many different peoples and creeds.

Engrossed in looking after the creature wants of the boarders in the rooming house that she has taken over, Chris plays a less active part in *Grey Granite* which is largely Ewan's story as he seeks a faith to live by. Faced with the brutal facts of industrial life in the troubled thirties he finds some kind of answer in Communism, which inspires him as a political creed with a mystique attached. Through participation in strikes and labour troubles, mutilation at the hands of the police, and loss of jobs, he moves steadily to dedicated membership in the Party, in the process stripping himself of all personal will. In the end, totally engaged, he has given himself into the hands of a committee and is about to leave his homeland so that any remaining vestiges of national feeling may be eradicated.

The difficulty that Gibbon faced in the last volume of his novel was the necessity of removing attention from Chris so that he might focus on Ewan. Her actions, therefore, are pushed aside by the main current of the narrative: her third marriage to Ake Ogilvie, for instance, is treated in an off-hand manner and he is shuffled out of the way as soon as possible. At the last, however, with Ewan gone the full spotlight turns again on Chris; we have a division of interest therefore, that has not been present in the first two members of the trilogy. In fact *Grey Granite* falls below these, partly for the reason just outlined, but more basically because it deals with the future and the referents which have been present hitherto are now lacking and there is no body of myth or history to which the allegory may point. Granted that Gibbon was presenting Communism as the stark, sure creed that Robert Colquhoun preached in his last sermon as a replacement for an outworn Christianity — and this appears to have been his intention — he denies in advance its efficacy by having Chris reject it as just another of the idle delusive dreams of men; "Of Robert and this faith of yours," she tells Ewan in their last conversation, "The world's sought faith for thousands of years and found only death or unease in them. Yours is just another dark cloud to me — or a great rock you're trying to push up hill." (*GG*, p. 143) Under the circumstances he can only let Ewan vanish from the scene for if his vision is a false one then all the hopes of men for a better world are idle dreams and all that one can do is to await with Chris that "Change whose right hand was Death and whose left hand was life, who might be stayed by none of the dreams of men, love, hate, compassion, anger or pity, gods or devils, or wild crying to the sky." (*GG*, p. 144)

The suggestion that *Grey Granite* suffers by comparison with its predecessors in its lack of suitable correlatives for allegory shows wherin lay their power. In them the narrative flows smoothly at the personal, social, and mythological level with the one bound to the other by extended metaphor so that the surface realism achieved by a prose style that catches the varied accents of the speaking voice or the passing of ideas through the mind easily leads on to deeper levels of meaning, and the cadences of individual utterance become representative voices of movements or types of men. And for much of the novel the effect that Gibbon achieves by this narrative method is a richness of texture that sets it far above the common run of fiction and gives it a strong claim to be the exemplar of a genre, mythic realism, which other Scottish novelists have favoured but few have employed so well.

UNIVERSITY OF BRITISH COLUMBIA

Notes and Documents

A Letter from Morgan Odoherty

One of the brightest features of William Blackwood's beloved *Maga* in its early years was the sprightly succession of parodies, epistles, poems, and mock-translations that appeared in the magazine over the name of Morgan Odoherty, the wild· Irish adjutant. Several contributors to *Blackwood's Magazine* used the name Odoherty (most notably William Maginn), but between 1819 and 1822 at least eight (and perhaps nine) of Odoherty's articles and poems were the work of David Macbeth Moir (1798-1851), a Musselburgh physician.[1]

Among the 500-odd letters from Moir to various members of the Blackwood family, now in the Blackwood Collection in the National Library of Scotland, one letter exists over Odoherty's name which was almost certainly intended for publication.[2] For reasons readily apparent the letter was not printed in the magazine, and Moir soon after gave up the character of Odoherty once and for all. Thenceforth he employed his talents in a more congenial vein and ultimately achieved considerable renown as *Blackwood's* versifying "Delta" and as the author of *Mansie Waugh*.

Obviously this letter does not represent Morgan Odoherty at his best, though with its thinly veiled allusions to contemporary writers and

[1] For a complete examination of the problem of authorship of the Odoherty papers see Ralph Wardle's "Who Was Morgan Odoherty?" *PMLA*, LVIII (Sept. 1943), 716-727 and my supplementary note, "David Macbeth Moir as Morgan Odoherty" *PMLA*, LXXII (Sept. 1957), 803-806.

[2] Through the courtesy of the National Library of Scotland, I received photostatic copies of Moir's letters several years ago. A fellowship from the Fund for the Advancement of Education (1955-56) and a grant-in-aid from the American Philosophical Society (1958) enabled me to work with the Blackwood Collection in Edinburgh.

its humorously insulting criticisms, it is typical of much of *Maga's* early wit.

EUGENE NOLTE

ARKANSAS STATE TEACHERS COLLEGE

Village of Muttonhole   1st May [1823]

My dear Fellow,

You may remember that the last time you spoke to me about having a sharp look out among the rising literary shavers, I acquainted you of my having fallen in, on board of a Steam-packet, with a young countryman of my own, whom I thought of the true sort. I have since cultivated his friendship a little more, and kidnapped (with his consent,) a half handful of his loose papers. These I send for your inspection.[3]

It is a sage remark, that all young writers are prone to imitation; parodying and bedevilling the passages of other authors, which may have most tickled their fancy. My young friend Dennis O'Brien (a half-cousin, six times removed, of the famous giant,)[4] cannot be said to be an exception to this universal law of incipient scribblerism. Originality he may have; (in the same way as Jeffrey is a poet, and Macintosh a historian,)[5] only he has not yet thought proper to show it; but, it rather strikes me, that he is a supplementary genius like Macvey,[6] or like Barry Mirandola,[7] a kind of mocking bird; taking off other bards, by cuckooing their jargon.

[3] The papers that accompanied this letter (i.e. "Jack Jenkins," the "lyrical invitation," the "Ode to the Ambrosians," and "The Fall of Stocks") were apparently never used in the magazine.

[4] Patrick Cotter (1761-1806), an Irish giant who took the name O'Brien, was a well-known figure at fairs and fetes during his lifetime. He is reputed to have been 8 feet 7 inches tall.

[5] Francis Jeffrey wrote huge quantities of verse but, of course, is remembered only as a critic. The Rt. Hon. Sir James Macintosh (1765-1832) was a famous political and moral philosopher, essayist, and orator. His attempts at history, *The History of England* and *Review of the Causes of the Revolution,* were neither ever completed.

[6] Macvey Napier (1776-1847) was Jeffrey's successor in 1829 to the editorship of the *Edinburgh Review*. Prior to that time, he was occupied in editing the 6th edition of the *Encyclopaedia Britannica* and writing much of the "Supplement" to this edition.

[7] "Barry Cornwall" (Bryan Proctor, 1787-1874) was the author of *Mirandello, a Tragedy* which was performed with great success at Covent Garden in 1821.

You have indulged Time's Whispering Gallery with his New Forest Pauper,[8] Mademoiselle C. with her broken Bridge,[9] and Delta with his Peter Ledyard;[10] shut not up, then, thy bowels of compassion on the amiable, wild Irishman, young Dennis; even although Jack Jenkins should tread too closely on the kibes of Peter Bell, Simon Lee, Goody Blake, and other eminent characters; for he is a rare fellow. Insert him, and I will speedily give you something of the kind myself, as I have done nothing for you in that line, since the days of the Auncient Waggonere, and of Billy Routing, *** *****.[11]

It is astonishing, that you have so long puzzled yourself, and the world, through the medium of Maga, with surmises about the school of poetry to which I belong. It is high time to put you on the right scent. The truth is (for out it must come,) that I have been long aiming at the accomplishment of a favourite object, which I hoped the optics of the wise of the earth would have long ago observed, which is, the title of "Patriarch of the Universal School." From this, it should follow naturally, that my disciples, dividing themselves into sections, would form distinct groupes, all acknowledging me for their head, as thus—

Universal School

Romantic School	Lake School
Artificial School	Flemish School
Leg of Mutton School	Cockney School
Satanic School	Jessamy School

Scott and Wordsworth should thus be my Lieutenant Generals; Campbell and Byron my colonels; Crabbe my Ajutant Parson O'Butterall, chaplain; Hunt and Reynolds ensigns,[12] Webbe bugleman;[13] Mother Morgan and

---

[8] "The New-Forest Pauper: A Lyrical Ballad" appeared in *Blackwood's Magazine* in Sept. 1821, the work of R. F. St. Barbe who later contributed a series of papers called "Time's Whispering Gallery" in February, March, and April 1823.

[9] C[aroline Bowles Southey's] "The Broken Bridge" appeared in the magazine in January 1823.

[10] Moir's "Peter Ledyard, a Lyrical Ballad" had appeared in August 1822.

[11] These two poems were published in the magazine in February and July 1819. The asterisks are in place of two undecipherable words in Sanscrit (?).

[12] Leigh Hunt was constantly castigated as a "Cockney" in Maga. John Hamilton Reynolds, a minor poet, was a friend of Hunt and his circle.

[13] This probably refers to Cornelius Webbe, always called "Corny" Webb in *Maga*. For many years he was a proofreader of the *Quarterly Review* and a minor contributor to several periodicals.

Maria Williams camp-suttlers,[14] and Barry Cornwall, (in green,) the Ganymede of the Mess-table.[15]

I told Dennis of my design, and asked him what school he would be of, as I wished to give him his place, amid the 1099 names in my tabular arrangement. The young dog had the assurance to answer that he was a candidate for the Universal School, and would show me his claims to that effect. He straightway exposed to me a quarto, filled with all variety of manners and measures from Shakespeare and Spenser down to Leigh Hunt and Willison Glass.[16] I doubt the Yahoo shall make good his claims of poetical relationship to me. Be it so—I am not one of those who like the Turk can bear "no rival near my throne."[17]

It appears that, when on his travels, young O'Brien resided ten days at the Cat and Bag-pipe Hotel, near Temple-bar, and that he there made an accidental acquaintance with the Centurian, who was reading the Examiner Newspaper over a Welch rabbit, and a decanter of swipes. Sonnets instantly flew between them, like Congreve rockets at the siege of Copenhagen; and now, when separated, Dennis compliments him with a lyrical invitation in his own way. Give me your notion of it.[18]

The Ode to the Ambrosians was, I strongly suspect, translated from the Sanscrit on the very same evening, that the Patriotic Ode in your

[14] Lady Morgan [Miss Sydney Owenson] (1783?-1859), an Irish lady, had a prodigious output of poetry, travel literature, novels, reform tracts, etc. throughout the first half of the nineteenth century.

Helen Maria Williams (1762-1827), also a prolific writer of verse and fiction, was best known as an interpreter of French politics and as a translator of French books. A brief critique of both women appeared in B. M., XII, 658.

[15] From a critical point of view, Odoherty's tabular arrangement of the poets compares quite favorably with Byron's "triangular Gradus ad Parnassum" in his Journal entry of 24 November 1813. See The Works of Lord Byron. Letters and Journals, II, 343-344.

[16] Willison Glass, whoever he was, appeared in the first "Noctes Ambrosianae" (March 1822) to sing a song entitled "Dialogue Between Willison Glass, Esq. of Edinburgh, and Jeremy Bentham Esq. of London."

[17] "Should such a man, too fond to rule alone,
Bear, like the Turk, no brother near the throne."

Pope, *Epistle to Dr. Arbuthnot*, 197-8.

[18] This entire paragraph is mildly satirical of Coleridge, some of whose early sonnets were written at the Salutation and Cat, a hotel near Christ's Hospital which Coleridge patronized in his early London years. A letter from Charles Lamb to Coleridge on December 2, 1796, conjures up the atmosphere: "That sonnet, Coleridge, brings afresh to my mind the time when you wrote those on Bowles, Priestley, Burke;—'twas two Christmases ago, and in that nice little smoky room at the Salutation, which is even now continually presenting itself to my recollection, with all its associated train of pipes, tobacco, egg-hot, welsh-rabbit, metaphysics, and poetry."

March N^O changed its dress from the Spanish.[19] This is a psychological curiosity. Could Mr Coleridge explain it, think you?

As I am not among the number of the Eleusinians, the male Miss McAvoy's, who see with their eyes shut,[20] mysteries are consequently to me like mill-stones, I cannot see through them. I leave such gentry to relish "The Fall of Stocks" which Dennis assured me a tip-top, table talking critic reckons equal to Cornwalls "Fall of Saturn," which (Hew! me misere,) instead of being sublime, as was too evidently intended, appeared to me only a rapsody, dedicated to a simple and silly Lamb by a horse-aping, caracoling jackass.[21]

Like a good boy, show my young friend the dexter side of thy countenance, for he is so modest and unassuming, that a rebuff would annihilate him; or at least lower him down to the calibre of the London or New Monthly.

I hope the salmon I hooked for you was good; when I may be able to send you another, Heaven knows, as fish are as scarce in the Almond as *bon bons* in Jeffreys Review. Phillpotts is true game, and nails his colours to the mast.[22]

Yours &c &—

To. C. North Esq   Morgan Odoherty

[19] "Patriotic Ode. From the Spanish Gazette of Madrid, 1st March, 1823," written by Moir, appeared in *Blackwood's Magazine* in March 1823.

[20] Margaret M'Avoy (1800-1820) was a blind lady alleged to have been able to distinguish colors by touch and to decipher letters with her finger ends.

[21] "The Fall of Saturn" was one of the poems in Barry Cornwall's *Flood of Thessaly and other Poems*, reviewed in *Blackwood's* in May 1823.

[22] The magazine for April 1823 (pp.476-478) ended with a letter from the Rev. H. Phillpotts in reply to a "Note on Dr. Phillpotts" by Jeffrey in the *Edinburgh Review*, XXXVIII (Feb. 1823), 265-269.

An Unrecorded Edition of Allan Ramsay

We are grateful to Dr. M. A. Pegg and Dr. E. F. D. Roberts, both of the National Library of Scotland, for sending the following information about a hitherto unrecorded edition of Allan Ramsay's *The Gentle Shepherd*. It would be No. 296a in Burns Martin's bibliography.

THE / GENTLE SHEPHERD; / *A SCOTS PASTORAL.* / [rule] / IN FIVE ACTS. / [rule] / BY ALLAN RAMSAY. / [vignette - woodcut - with the caption "Auld roudes! filthy fallow! I sall auld ye."] / [rule] / HADDINGTON: / PRINTED AND SOLD BY JAMES MILLER. / [rule] / 1821.

12 mo. On the verso of the title: Dramatis personae. Leaf A2 r. GENTLE SHEPHERD. Text ends on leaf F3 v. Size: 141 mm x 88 mm. Collation: A⁶ B³ C-E⁶ F³, pp. [1-]60.

This edition is bound, together with five early 19th-century [?] chapbooks, in half-calf with marbled boards. The printing and paper is of the rather inferior quality associated with such publications, but the work is excellently preserved.

ANNOUNCEMENT

The "Scottish Enlightenment" will be the subject considered by English Section 8 (1750-1800), MLA, at its meeting in Chicago December 28, 1965. Anyone wishing to contribute a paper should now communicate with the chairman for the 1965 session, Professor William B. Todd, Dept. of English, University of Texas, Austin 12, Texas.

Reviews

J. M. Reid (ed.). *Scottish Short Stories.* London.
Oxford University Press. 1963. 9s.6d.

I suppose that, given the two entities "Scotland" and "the short
story," some publisher was bound, some day, to commission an anthology
that forced a union between the two. Anything can be anthologised —
My Twenty-one Best Dog Stories. The question is whether the chosen
field is rich enough to yield a crop of any weight once the slight, ephemeral material has been sorted out and discarded. The twenty-two stories
J. M. Reid has selected have to stand for 140 years' work in shorter
fiction by Scottish authors. Six, or over a quarter, involve the supernatural. Three of the rest are mild domestic sketches (those by Cunning-
hame Graham, McNair Reid, and Dorothy Haynes) rather than imaginative creations. Neil Munro's *Hurricane Jack* and Ian Hamilton Finlay's
The Money are wee anecdotes, suitable enough to fill a page of *Punch,*
but what are they doing among the *World's Classics* (to which this book
belongs)? Of the longer pieces, Fred Urquhart's *The Last G.I. Bride
Wore Tartan* is garrulous, loose, and uncreative in its use of a modern
vernacular, and often unplausible as a story; on any evaluation it was
not worth one-eighth of the total story text. J. M. Barrie's *The Courting
of T'nowhead's Bell,* though much meatier than almost all the work by
living writers, is still in effect an insult to the countryfolk of Scotland
in its cult of the gypit — villagers presented as so dumb and thick that
they move through life in ludicrous slow-motion. Perhaps Barrie was
stylising the Angus village into pure farce, as P. G. Wodehouse later
did for the Stately Homes of England and their denizens. If so, the
story no more deserves reprinting than would Wodehouse in an anthology
of England's best.

A more detailed example will suggest the standard that I am appealing to. Eric Linklater's *The Goose Girl* is among those I have relegated to the supernatural class. Why "relegated"? Is an eery story necessarily second-class work? Perhaps not (though I can think of no exceptions); but my specific criticism of Linklater's story is this: it tells
of a man's love for a beautiful girl who turns out to be not human at
all, a flawless creature from the animal kingdom. It is most adroitly
told and full of lifelike detail from the real world of the Orkneys. Yet
what should have been the heart of the subject — the man's deep emo-

tional involvement with the woman, which is so terribly misplaced and hapless in the end — is sketched in a few pale touches: "The weeks passed with nothing to spoil our happiness . . . I came, I suppose, to take my good fortune for granted, and my happiness perhaps lost something of its fine edge . . ." The author's concern, in fact, has not been with the inner human realities of such a situation but purely with a fantastic happening for its own sake. As such, the piece can appeal to us as highly skilled entertainment, but it scarcely begins to be literature.

The criterion of "literature" implied here can best be made good from inside the anthology itself. The best story is surely Lewis Grassic Gibbon's *Smeddum*, which comes from that amazingly rich and powerful miscellany by Gibbon and Hugh MacDiarmid, *Scottish Scene* (1934). *Smeddum* tells of a smallholder's wife who brings up nine children "on that ill bit croft that sloped to the sea." Although it is only eleven pages long, its strong flow, the biting reality of every detail, are such that we feel we have been witnessing a life. The land and the work on it are potently evoked:

> Be that as it might, her man new dead, Meg wouldn't hear of leaving the toun. It was harvest then and she drove the reaper up and down the long, clanging clay rigs by the sea, she'd jump down smart at the head of a bout and go gathering and binding swift as the wind, syne wheel in the horse to the cutting again. She led the stooks with her bairns to help, you'd see them at night a drowsing cluster under the moon on the harvesting cart.

The hearty, fleering humour natural to that hard old crofting life of the north-east is always ready just below the surface, and this is conveyed (as throughout *A Scots Quair*) in a prose that catches unerringly the Scots of the north-east—broad, economical, coming down sharp on the nail every time:

> Then word got about of her eldest son, Jock Menzies that was fee'd up Allardyce way. The creature of a loon had had fair a conceit since he'd won a prize at a ploughing match—not for his ploughing, but for good looks; and the queans about were as daft as himself, he'd only to nod and they came to his heel; and the stories told they came further than that. Well, Meg'd heard the stories and paid no heed, till the last one came, she was fell quick then . . .

What is more, the story has a cumulative rhythm that beautifully reinforces the theme. One child after another leaves home and finds or fails to find the right place in the world, till finally they reassemble at the croft to pass judgement on the last unmarried daughter (a wonderfully blithe and independent figure), and self-righteousness is routed with a final comic-ironic fling worthy of Burns.

In a word, what such a story has is a concern with life itself and a medium or idiom fitted to it; the one grows out of the other, the form is not at all a stock literary mould mechanically put to use for the umpteenth time, as one too often feels with Thomas Gillespie's *The Fair Maid of Cellardykes* (the goody-goody Victorian moral story), or R. L. Stevenson's *The Isle of Voices* (the tropical fairy-tale *à la Arabian Nights*), or Neil Munro's *The Lost Pibroch* (the sad legend from the Celtic Twilight). I cannot understand why Mr. Reid, if he wanted to show the world the cream of our stories, did not drop the feebler pieces which he has presumably included because "you can't leave out John Buchan, or George Macdonald, or Barrie" and thus made room for another of Gibbon's, perhaps *Sim* or, if that were too like *Smeddum* (though it is much more sombre), then *Forsaken*, that searing story of Jesus resurrected into the Scotland of the Slump. (And as there was no objection to two stories by the same writer, surely Stevenson's weakly fanciful *Isle of Voices* should have made way for *The Two Drovers*, in which Scott at least attempted a fictional confrontation between the two Scottish societies, Highland and Lowland.)

Gibbon is part of the standard for modern Scottish fiction in that he is, it seems to me, unequalled by anyone else except the Scott of *The Heart of Midlothian* and George Douglas Brown. But there are slighter items in this anthology which can also stand for the genuine, the truly focussed on life, against the fantasy however brilliantly brought off, e.g. *Wandering Willie's Tale* or Stevenson's *Thrawn Janet*. George Scott-Moncrieff's *Number Two Burke Street* captures delicately the cheerless, dusty life of a middle-class byway in Presbyterian Edinburgh: on its smaller scale it is an image of our society as accurate and revealing as the image which George Eliot's *Scenes of Clerical Life* gave of the provincial religious community in England a century ago. And Morley Jamieson's *Madame X* is a most compassionate and touching story, the tragedy in little of an "ill-matched" couple who are devoted to each other yet cruelly forced apart at the very end; its pace and shape seem just right. This is what the short story ideally is: a phase in a life so chosen, so entered upon and left at such a point, that the implications stretching away before and after the chosen phase are suggested all the more poignantly for not being actually presented. Henry James's *Four Meetings* or *The Real Thing*, Hawthorne's *Young Goodman Brown*, D. H. Lawrence's *The Horsedealer's Daughter* or *Fanny and Annie* or *Samson and Delilah*, T. F. Powys's *Mr. Handy's Wife* or *The Lonely Lady*—these seem to me the works that give the standard in this field, and the sad yet expected disappointment of this anthology is that it found so little Scottish work of such a quality.

If it had been recognised that "the Scottish short story" did not, as a *genre*, qualify for anthologising as a body of mature art-literature, the way would then have been open for a book of stories that at least typified the vitality and variety of our popular culture. Mr. Reid is hinting at this when he says in his Introduction that "Perhaps a book of Scottish short stories should really begin with a selection of folk-tales from Gaelic and Scots" (p. ix). This doubt, if it was really there, should have been acted on. Mr. Reid should have gone to some of the recent collections of Gaelic folk-tales in translation, John Lorne Campbell's or R. Macdonald Robertson's *Selected Highland Folk-tales* (Oliver & Boyd, 1961). He should have included something by Dougal Graham, the Glasgow town-crier from the middle 18th century, who is said to have composed straight into type and thus belongs at least half to the oral tradition. *The Young Coalman's Courtship to a Creel-wife's Daughter* or *The Ancient and Modern History of Buckhaven* are much more ragged than most of Mr. Reid's choices, yet they also have a palpable drive and authenticity that shows up Thomas Gillespie and John Buchan, for example, for the stuffy fakes that they are. Mr. Reid was right to pick a piece (Crockett's *The Lammas Preaching*) that typified the extraordinary dominance of religion and the ministry in our literature; but we would have got a glimpse deeper into what Scottish Christianity was if he had excerpted that gem of vernacular story-telling, the tale of the devil coming to Auchtermuchty, from James Hogg's *Private Memoirs and Confessions of a Justified Sinner*. The stark, ballad-like tales of Orkney that George Mackay Brown has recently been publishing in *Lines Review* and the *New Saltire* would surely have represented today's Scottish fiction more adequately than some of the slight pieces mentioned at the start, and they would have shown the astonishing stamina of the folk idiom even yet.

The book I am sketching here would have seemed scrappy and "primitive" compared with what Mr. Reid has attempted. But it could have been a more valid piece of work because it would have been more in line with the cultural levels that Scotland has actually reached: that is, a very ample and vital oral-popular culture which lost its national basis before it could evolve a distinctive, full-dress, modern literature.

DAVID CRAIG

RICHMOND, YORKSHIRE

John Gibson Lockhart. *Adam Blair. Edinburgh.*
Edinburgh University Press. 1963. xxv + 287pp.
15 shillings.

The publication of Lockhart's *Adam Blair* as the first in a projected
series of reprintings of Scottish works makes available a significant novel
by an author who is best known as biographer of Sir Walter Scott and
editor of the *Quarterly Review*. In *Adam Blair*, Lockhart treated with
quiet compassion a specific instance of the conflict between the spirit and
the flesh. The plot may be outlined simply: The Reverend Adam Blair,
grieved by the loss of his wife, commits adultery with Mrs. Charlotte
Campbell and is conscience stricken. Mrs. Campbell dies from a fever;
Adam Blair resigns his position as minister and with his daughter Sarah
retires to live on a small isolated farm. There for a number of years as
he earns his living he avoids his friends and former parishioners. His days
are spent tilling the fields; his evenings in teaching his daughter. On
Sundays he and Sarah sit apart from the others of the congregation to
which Blair was once minister. Finally, in deference to the dying wishes
of an old friend, the Reverend Dr. Muir, Blair agrees to perform the ritual
of burial for him. Shortly thereafter a committee of elders from Blair's
church asks him to resume his post as minister. Blair agrees to their request and finishes out his life as a gentle shepherd to the flock from which
his sin had once set him apart.

So bare an outline can merely suggest the theological framework
around which Lockhart constructed his novel, yet the movement is
clear: from sin to public acknowledgment of sin, to repentance and forgiveness—at least to forgiveness by fellow mortals. In using the career
of Adam Blair as the focal point for depiction of this movement, Lockhart drew heavily upon his knowledge of the stern morality of Scotch
Presbyterianism. So rigidly is Adam Blair an adherent to this moral code
that the torment of his own conscience is greater than any torment caused
by condemnations his parishioners might have uttered against him. The
greatest strength of *Adam Blair* as a novel is the presentation it offers
of an individual's awareness of his weaknesses and of his sense of guilt at
having failed to live up to what he had believed to be his best self.
Lockhart succeeded admirably in presenting Adam Blair's struggle to
forgive himself so that he could hope for forgiveness from God and from
his fellow human beings.

Less successful is Lockhart's characterization of Charlotte Campbell.
She is supposed to be a woman whose unhappy marriages have caused her
to despair of love and/or honor until she can win Adam Blair. But as a

character she is never as fully realized as are two relatively minor characters who are presented with true artistic economy. John Maxwell, Adam Blair's devoted friend and an elder in Cross-Meikle Kirk, emerges as a living character of whose creation Walter Scott or Charles Dickens could have been proud. Mrs. Semple, likewise, is vividly presented as an example of the good that Lockhart evidently saw in some of the rural aristocracy of Scotland.

Despite some weaknesses in characterization and a certain awkwardness in plotting, *Adam Blair* is a significant work which merits the competent reprinting it has received by the University of Edinburgh Press. Its emphasis on the conflict between flesh and spirit brought about in part by a Puritan ethic places it early in a long series of nineteenth century novels which dealt with similar conflicts. Not all of the successors to *Adam Blair* are marked by the same type of balanced sympathy of which Lockhart was capable.

The present edition is enhanced by Dr. David Craig's perceptive introduction which establishes the background against which *Adam Blair* must be placed for fullest appreciation.

KENNETH W. DAVIS

TEXAS TECHNOLOGICAL COLLEGE

STUDIES IN SCOTTISH LITERATURE

VOLUME II   NUMBER 2   OCTOBER 1964

CONTENTS

STUDIES IN SCOTTISH LITERATURE

EDITED BY G. ROSS ROY
TEXAS TECHNOLOGICAL COLLEGE

EDITORIAL BOARD:
DAVID DAICHES
A. M. KINGHORN
HUGH MACDIARMID (C. M. GRIEVE)
A. L. STROUT
KURT WITTIG

STUDIES IN SCOTTISH LITERATURE is an
independent quarterly devoted to all aspects of
Scottish literature. Articles and notes are welcome.
Subscriptions are available at $5.00 U.S. per annum in the
United States and Canada, elsewhere 30 shillings.
All communications should be addressed to the
Editor, Department of English, Texas Technological College,
Lubbock, Texas, U.S.A.

PUBLISHED BY G. ROSS ROY
AND PRINTED BY THE TEXAS TECH PRESS
LUBBOCK, TEXAS, U.S.A. 79409

CONTRIBUTORS
TO THIS ISSUE

Anne GREENE: Associate Professor in the Department of English at Northern Illinois University. B.A., Birmingham-Southern College; M.A., University of Chicago; Ph.D., University of Wisconsin, with a thesis on Priestley, Bridie, and Fry. Author of an article on Fry in *Modern Drama*, 1962.

Allan H. MACLAINE: Of the University of Rhode Island, continues his study of the *Christis Kirk* tradition in this issue.

Witold OSTROWSKI: Chairman of the Department of English at the University of Lodz. Educated at the University of Warsaw, received his doctor's degree from the University of Lodz in 1950 for a study entitled "English Utopian Fiction from More to Swift." Prepared a lengthy introduction to the first critical edition in Polish of More's *Utopia* (1954), has written a book on Tennyson's early poetry (1957), a collection of essays on English literature (1958), and a series of papers on Scott's literary influence on Polish Romantic writers. Is a member of the Lodz Scientific Society and co-editor of its organ *Zagadnienia Rodzajow Literackich* (*Problems of Literary Genres*) a semestrial multilingual journal.

Sydney Goodsir SMITH: Was born in New Zealand and educated at the Universities of Edinburgh and Oxford. He is a freelance writer who makes his home in Edinburgh. In 1946 he received the Rockefeller Atlantic Award and in 1956 the *Poetry* (*Chicago*) Award. He is the author of the following books of poetry: *The Deevil's Waltz* (1946), *Under the Eildon Tree* (1948), *So Late into the Night* (1952), *Figs and Thistles* (1959), *The Vision of the Prodigal Son* (1960). He has written a play, *The Wallace* (1960), and a novel, *Carotid Cornucopius* (1964), as well as *A Short Introduction to Scottish Literature* (1951). He is the editor of *Robert Fergusson* (Bicentenary Essays) (1952), *Selected Poetry of Gavin Douglas* (1959) and *The Merry Muses of Caledonia* (with J. DeLancey Ferguson and James Barke) (1964).

SYDNEY GOODSIR SMITH

Trahison des Clercs or The Anti-Scottish Lobby in Scottish Letters

"The dogs bark, but the caravan moves on"

In Vol. I, No. 3, of this magazine Dr. David Craig published an article called "A National Literature? Recent Scottish Writing" to which I have been invited to reply. I would not have considered doing this, preferring to let the misbegotten thing be ignored, had it not been presented in an American magazine addressed to a wide and educated public. The article only has nuisance value, but it is a not uncommon type of nuisance and should be exposed.

It is a denigratory article. The author sees little good in his subject and one wonders why he should have chosen to write on it. This sort of thing has been happening such a lot recently in Scotland that I wish to deal with Dr. Craig, not in isolation, as a lone, unpaid hatchet man, slayer of dragons and purifier of muddy waters, but in a wider context as part of a general trend in Scottish life, literature and thought, not only today but for the last 200 years; since the Union of Scotland and England, certainly; 1745 is probably the crux, imaginatively, when the Union became firmly consolidated after the Jacobite defeat.

It is a quisling or collaborationist or simply anti-Scottish sclent of mind and it is by no means a new phenomenon, although in recent years it has had a marvellous revival. The aim is political in essence (which is why I have used those political catchwords to describe it) and seeks to deny the separate identity of the Scottish nation, to merge it in the larger "British" context and so kill its individuality, its soul, in fact: just as the larger "British" context has already throttled Scottish society by impoverishing its industries—as Dr. Craig admits, but without drawing the logical conclusions. This is not a paranoid fantasy, as I shall seek to show. Craig's thought is enslaved by the socialist dream of unity—which is a good dream, too good to have to include the destruction of any national identity of which literature is the voice and the song. Oddly enough, this particular dream of unity does not evidently include the destruction

[71]

of other national identities—the Danes, for instance, or the Indians or Africans. Whether it includes the Jews or not probably depends (for Dr. Craig) on whether or not Nasser is supported by the Kremlin. But Scotland must go! In his book *Scottish Literature and the Scottish People 1680-1830*, Craig gives away his prejudices by painfully referring to Scotland as "the Scottish part of Britain" in his efforts to deny its individuality—but he never goes further logically to refer to England as "the English part of Britain." Why not?

At the start of Hugh MacDiarmid's career in the 1920s the idea of a Scottish Renaissance, political and cultural, was merely funny to his enemies, the old and the middle-aged. In the 'Thirties just about every considerable Scottish writer of the time was an adherent of the cultural programme (which was largely concerned with the revival and intellectualisation of the Scots and Gaelic languages for poetry) and most of them also supported the political programme, which desired separation from England, the exploiter of Scotland. One or two of those writers, all of them left-wingers, even stood for political office. To the young of those days they were heroes, though still hated by the old. The war and the early postwar years saw the second wave of MacDiarmid's Renaissance and a great outburst of publishing, both book and periodical, mostly poetry, good, bad and indifferent, as one might expect, and gets, in any period anywhere. The battle, the young poets then thought, was won, or at least winning. As Craig remarks, they even got into the school books and examination papers; they were not just laughable any more.

But in the 'Fifties the Beats began exerting their attraction and the young poets coming up sheered away from the Renaissance banner; it was becoming what they called an Establishment (an Establishment, be it said, whose members found it extremely difficult to get their books published in Scotland. So much for being "established.") By the 'Sixties this had hardened into positive literary antipathy to the Renaissance or Scottish or National idea. There were even desertions by some of the chief figures of the 'Forties and 'Fifties—Maurice Lindsay in particular—and new champions of the anti-Scottish lobby appeared, among them being our own Dr. David Craig, who gained his Ph.D. from Cambridge University with a fat thesis of over 300 pages devoted, under the rose, to hammering his subject which was the above mentioned *Scottish Literature and the Scottish People 1680-1830*. Writers, hitherto friendly if not actually adherents to the cause, openly attacked Scottish, particularly Scots literature, on radio and in print, among these being Norman MacCaig and Walter Keir whom we shall quote later. Craig, however, is not *overtly*, to use a favorite word of his, against the Scots language—he rightly praises its use in the good second stanza of John Manson's poem and in those by Hay, Young and Henderson quoted in his article—so much as against the whole Scottish "thing," the movement, which naturally and specifically includes the language.

This new anti-Scottish lobby has unconnected supporters in some of the very latest generation of students writing in university magazines. One of these, a short-lived kind of post-graduate affair of 1960, even had an American title, *Sidewalk*. The position was now that all three generations were allied in opposition to what might be called the Scottish Movement: the old (who have never liked it), the middle-aged (who never like anything), and the young (who generally like the latest thing—and the Scottish thing was definitely old hat). It is a matter of curious fact that this three-headed opposition, though extremely vocal in critical opposition, is not (except for MacCaig) very productive of original, imaginative work—I am trying to avoid "creative," which is cant.

This anti-Scottish lobby is such a recurring phenomenon in the history of Scottish literature that it is really a wonder that the literature has survived its continual bashing since the 18th century. What is even more curious is that its enemies consider it worth bashing. There must be something extremely tough (or even important or significant) about it for it to occasion such continual crusades and holy wars. The horse, so the lobby always says, is quite dead, but evidently it refuses to lie down. So it must be hit again, and again, and again. I shall now give chapter and verse. Let us observe this unusual phenomenon of a sizable number of educated men in a country (we must not say nation, it seems), generation after generation, finding it imperative, or at least desirable, to expend a good deal of energy (300 pages is a long stint) in attacking its own past and present achievements (or non-achievements) in life, letters and the other arts—if any, they would say. But so it is; the curtain rises.

There is an ancient and popular sport in Scotland which consists in belittling your neighbour and his achievements, in cutting him down to size. Local boy, having made good and become a professor or a prime minister or something, is reduced by the old worthy with the words "Him? I kent his faither!" Which means he is of little account. A lot of the most characteristic Scottish literature uses this approach positively and humorously—as in the domestication of great issues to parish pump level, or in the familiar relationship with the Deity and his Opponent. Its negative use in literary matters is of respectable antiquity but does not go back beyond the Union of 1707—which is significant. Dr. Craig's article will be seen to be treading a pretty well-worn path; his heredity is impeccably bourgeois.

In the early days and for many years the anti-Scottish lobby concentrated on the language issue—for language and poetry is the expression of the soul of a people—but the drive behind their animosity was a political one. By clinging on "with a mad Japanese courage" (to quote Craig) to the Scots language, the poets were preventing complete cultural absorption into the "British" (i.e. English) totality. The lobby tried hard to discourage it.

In 1771, for instance, Dr. James Beattie (they are mostly doctors, you will notice), author of *The Minstrel* and a great enemy of "the licentious teaching" of David Hume, wrote: "To write in vulgar broad Scotch, and yet to write seriously, is now impossible." Two years later Robert Fergusson published "The Ghaists," to which I refer the reader:

> Yoke hard the poor, and lat the rich chiels be,
> Pamper'd at ease by ither's industry.
>
> . . . .
>
> I find, my friend, that ye but little ken,
> There's e'en now on the earth a set o' men,
> Wha, if they get their private pouches lin'd,
> Gie nae a winnelstrae for a' mankind;
> They'll sell their country, flae their conscience bare
> To gar the weighbauk turn a single hair.   *make the scales*
> The Government need only bait the line
> Wi' the prevailing flee, the gowden coin,   *fly; golden*
> Then our executors and wise trustees
> Will sell them fishes in forbidden seas,
> Upo' their dwining country girn in sport,   *declining; grimace*
> Laugh i' their sleeve, and get a place at court.

Serious enough, I would say. How often do you get this kind of passionate, humanitarian, social thought in 1773?[1] Thus was Dr. Beattie exploded. But the polite enemy was not deterred.

In 1786, Henry Mackenzie (the Man of Feeling), reviewing Burns's poems, advised the poet to write in English, for, he said, "even in Scotland the *provincial* dialect [my italics] . . . is now read with difficulty; in England it cannot be read at all." But lo!, as Dr. Craig reminds us in his article, "by 1815 there were at least eight editions of his works published in the North of England and pubs were named after him." And in the next century John Clare was deeply influenced by Scots poetry. Thus was Mackenzie exploded.

---

[1] It is significant that the writers of the Scots Renaissance show much greater social conscience than their opponents.

In 1787, Burns's friend, Dr. John Moore, wrote to him from London saying, "You ought to deal more sparingly, for the future, in the *provincial* dialect [my italics]. . . . You should also . . . become master of the heathen mythology . . . which in itself is charmingly fanciful." Three years later Burns wrote "Tam O'Shanter" without "heathen mythology," and in the "provincial" dialect. As a matter of simple fact, you will still hear it recited (despite what the Anti-lobby says) amid general social glee in Scottish pubs today over 150 years later. I heard it myself hilariously last summer in a pub in Orkney. Thus was Dr. Moore exploded. But still the polite enemy was not deterred.

Over a hundred years later, in 1898, T. F. Henderson, co-editor with W. E. Henley of the Burns Centenary edition and author of a history of *Scottish Vernacular Literature*, wrote: "The antecedence of Burns may also be discerned in the work of all the more characteristically Scottish writers from Sir Walter Scott to R. L. Stevenson and J. M. Barrie; but as regards vernacular poetry, his death was really the setting of the sun; the twilight deepened very quickly; and such twinkling lights as from time to time appear only serve to disclose the darkness of the all-encompassing night." Maybe in poetry, but George Douglas Brown's *House with the Green Shutters*, a key novel in modern Scots literature, appeared (in London) in 1901, three years later. It seemed the horse was not dead. But still they were undeterred.

In 1919 Professor Gregory Smith advised Scottish writers to drop the "masquing gear of Braid Scots," and suggested "a way for the freer expression of nationality in style. It may be described as the delicate colouring of standard English with northern tints." Only three years later, in 1922 in *The Scottish Chapbook*, Hugh MacDiarmid published his poem, "The Watergaw," in a Scots as rich as Burns's if more self-conscious, literary and mystical in its employment. But he was not alone; he had been preceded by several excellent minor poets, as Violet Jacob, Charles Murray, Marion Angus and Lewis Spence. Academics in their folly despise minor poets, but these are they who often manure the good earth from which the great trees spring.

Even after the dramatic appearance of Hugh MacDiarmid to prove the horse was by no means dead but kicking, the anti-Scots cry was taken up once more, notably by Edwin Muir[2] in his *Scott and Scotland* (1936). But now a new dimension opened up; the lobby extended its field of denigration to include the whole of Scottish literature. Professor R. L. Mackie in 1934 published an anthology of Scottish poetry in the Oxford

---

[2] Who himself, earlier on, had tried and failed to write in Scots.

World's Classics series. These words are from his somewhat negative short introduction (my italics throughout):

> Originality has *not* been a distinguishing feature of the Scottish poets of any age. They *seldom* innovate, *seldom* write poetry as startling and unaccountable as *The Shepherd's Calendar* or *Absalom and Achitophel* or *The Lyrical Ballads.* . . . Of the poems assembled here, the salvage of six centuries, none is conceived on a grand scale. [Not even Barbour's *Bruce* or Lyndsay's *Thrie Estaits*?] The Scot does *not* write odes and epics; he writes songs and ballads [*Auld Reikie? Tam O' Shanter? Don Juan? A Drunk Man looks at the Thistle*?]; he can achieve perfection *only* when he works within *narrow limits.* Even this perfection seems usually to be the result *not* of conscious art, but of some happy accident. . . . The Scottish poet is *seldom* subtle or profound; he lives a life of sensation, *not* of thoughts.

An odd way, this, to recommend your country's poetry to the public, surely; even if it were true it would have little critical significance. The book, by the way, is still selling happily, for its contents' sake.

In 1947, Dr. H. Harvey Wood, editor of Robert Henryson and umquhile lecturer in English Literature at Edinburgh, in *Scotland, A Description of Scotland and Scottish Life* (edited by H. W. Meikle, then His Majesty's Historiographer Royal in Scotland, and co-editor of the Penguin *Burns* and the Penguin *Border Ballads*), a book aimed at a wide general public, follows Mackie up loyally. His opening words are equally negative: "No account of the literature of Scotland can begin without making certain apparently damaging admissions." (Naturally!) He continues: "In many of the qualities that are central in the poetry of England, Spain and Italy, Scots literature is singularly poor. There is little sensuous love of beauty, little mysticism, little philosophy and high imagination. There has been no Scots Blake, no Keats or Shelley, no Traherne, no Wordsworth or Coleridge."

All of which is perfectly fatuous, for naturally the Spaniards and Italians haven't got them either, any more than the English or anybody else have a St. John of the Cross or a Dante or whoever Dr. Wood was thinking of—any more than any of them have a Burns or a Scott or a Lyndsay or a Dunbar or a Barbour. Surely there is no *competition* in any art.

Remember what Henry Mackenzie said about Burns's language in 1786? The above-quoted Prof. Mackie in that World's Classics anthology echoed his words in 1934: "The Scots of Burns has become a foreign language to the educated, as to the uneducated Scot." And on they go. It must surely be getting very foreign indeed by now.

In 1940, still on the same old tack, Dr. John Speirs, a perceptive commentator on the old poets, remarked in his *The Scots Literary Tradi-*

tion, anent Hugh MacDiarmid, "There cannot be a Scottish poetry in the fullest sense unless there is in the fullest sense a Scottish speech. What survives of such speech among what survives of the peasantry is in its last stages and is even something its speakers have learned to be half ashamed of. *That is why there has been no Scottish literature (and indeed no literature in Scotland of any kind) since the 18th century*" (my italics). A pretty sweeping but pretty silly statement about the literature, and about the speech too, but this is just how the doctors speak, who never travel by bus or take a drink in a pub. Poor souls, how can they hear the speech in a study, or among their twittering brethren in the Common Room?

Twenty years after this, in 1962 (they don't change much, these prophets of woe), Maurice Lindsay, one of the most active members of the second wave of the Renaissance in the 'Forties and 'Fifties, wrote in the preface to *Snow Warning,* his book of poems in English (as a sort of apologia for deserting Scots): "During the 'Fifties the Scots tongue receded more rapidly than ever before [it's going some speed now, praise the Lawd!] under the impact of television, and has now been reduced to a mere matter of local accent." (Lindsay, who is Programme Controller of Border Television, also never travels by bus.) He continues, "It is utterly unthinkable that this poor wasted and abandoned speech, however rich in theory its poetic potential, can possibly express *what there is to be expressed* in the Scottish ethos [my italics: note the implied denigration, that there is nothing *to* express] in the age of the beatnik and the hydrogen bomb. . . . We are all Anglo-Scots now, whether we like it or not." Dr. Craig must be cheering. Do you get the echo from Beattie in 1771: "To write in vulgar broad Scotch, and yet to write seriously, is now impossible"? A long time a-dying, indeed! Is it not amazing?

Well, there are my texts; they could be multiplied. It is a long story which seemingly has no end, for the poets continue with horrible intransigence in their unregenerate ways. Can any country match such a continued belittling of its own literature by its own literary pundits—in the face of the recurrent appearance of artists, some of them geniuses, to prove them asses?

In this procession Dr. Craig takes up his position manfully and confidently; he is going to knock another nail into the sairly battered coffin of the Scottish muse. "Until very recently," he begins his article in the third issue of this magazine, "Scottish writers went on clinging with a mad Japanese courage to the idea of cultural separateness." Four pages later (p. 155), he says in commendation of the novelists Robin Jenkins and David Lambert, "These men go no further in the national direction than to use some Scottish settings and some Scottish speech. . . . *This strikes me as a liberation* [my italics]. . . . Today, with the fading of the nationalist mirage, we can see ahead more clearly . . . ," and he talks of "struggles and developments much broader and more *real* than the private nationalist obsession." It is very real in Scotland, sir; and it is not private.

It is odd, and an index of the confusion of Craig's mind, that later, writing of the poems in Norman MacCaig's anthology *Honour'd Shade* (1959), he says that "the nationalist obsession is gone and with it, evidently, any powerful incentive to imagine and express." Well, what conclusions does he draw from that? Can he mean, adding the two "thoughts" together, that the loss of the nationalist obsession is a liberation from a powerful incentive to the imagination, so that we can now see ahead more clearly? Does he really want to "liberate" artists from incentives to the imagination? That's what he *says*.

A month after Dr. Craig's article was published he found himself among powerful allies. In February 1964, in a full dress discussion on Scottish literature on the B.B.C. Third Programme, some of the most kenspeckle names in contemporary Scottish literature devoted their time to knocking that literature—presumably always with themselves excluded. If the individual contributors complain (as they do, if taxed) that they spoke to a tape for an hour and only the negative bits of a few minutes duration were actually broadcast, one must assume that the editor, Professor David Daiches, was to blame, or the B.B.C.'s producer, Mr. George Bruce (a poet whom Craig calls "laughably solemn" and "an owl that fancies itself wise"). Whichever way you look at it, the upshot was a destructive attack on Scottish literature by the assembled hosts of the mostly bourgeois "establishment"—great word, that!

The roll included Professor Daiches and Messrs. Norman MacCaig, Walter Keir, and Edwin Morgan, all of whom hold positions in universities or schools where they instruct the young, presumably, to despise their own literature. Dr. Daiches is professor of English Literature at the new University of Sussex. He is also the author, among others, of an excellent book on Robert Burns (which Dr. Craig considers "dilute and ineffectual"—*Lines Review*, No. 20) in which he shows that the Scottish literary tradition is strongest where it is most native. That was in 1950. In 1964, however, he asked: "What are the prospects for the existence of Scottish culture? Indeed, we might go further and ask: Does anything that we can call Scottish culture really exist?" And Walter Keir, who lectures in English Literature at Aberdeen University, chimed in readily with: "I don't think there is such a thing as a Scottish culture. We have lost our identity, if ever we had one, we had several identities. I don't think they ever cohered or they will ever cohere again." (How the devil they could ever cohere *again* if they never cohered before is a bit of a puzzle.) This was the general defeatist tone of the whole discussion.

Norman MacCaig (a poet whom Craig regards as "largely fake") opined that "there hasn't been terribly much first-class poetry written by Scots of any sort in Scots." MacCaig also considered that "the language battle is over," to which MacDiarmid replied "The language battle can't be over as long as there's a poet of quality determined to write in Scots. If he succeeds in writing good poetry in Scots he vindicates the whole linguistic argument. The fact is that he manifests that great poetry can be written in Scots, and that's all that requires to be manifested." Which was one of the few sensible things said in this pathetic broadcast.

Other positive remarks came from two Scotts, both poets: Alexander Scott of Glasgow University, who holds the only readership in Scottish literature in any of the four Scottish universities, complained of the lowly place that is accorded Scottish literature in Scottish universities. "The only other literature or language that is treated in this way at Glasgow, having an ordinary graduating course and nothing else, is Welsh. I cannot well imagine in Wales that Welsh would be treated in the Welsh university colleges with one ordinary graduating course, no higher course and no honours course . . . the people who run Scottish universities do not seem to be interested in their own activities." Just before this, Tom Scott had answered a typically "slanted" or provocative question by Dr. David Daiches who had asked him, "Do Scottish universities do anything for Scottish culture? Indeed, should they do so? Is there a Scottish cultural tradition that the universities should pass on to their students?" Tom Scott's answer was direct enough: "There is no sense in our universities of there being any continuity of the Scottish tradition. The fact is that what they are not doing with Scottish children and Scottish students at Scottish universities is turning them into highly educated Scotsmen. . . . They're turning them into highly educated Englishmen. Instead of our own culture we are being offered the honour of becoming honorary Englishmen; this is pretty well what it amounts to." And he quoted another Scott, Sir Walter, "If you un-Scotch us you'll make damned mischevious Englishmen of us."

You will see from the above that the anti-Scottish lobby are not altogether friendly among themselves. Dr. Craig, in particular, doesn't seem to approve of anybody, but he will join with "laughable" Bruce, "fake" MacCaig and "ineffectual" Daiches to rally to the dear old cause of bashing Scottish literature, for the edification of the outside world. These are very sophisticated people.

In his book already quoted Dr. Craig reiterates the old rubbish once more again: "In Scotland the shrinking of distinctive speech has accompanied difficulties in using that speech seriously." (Shades of Beattie in 1771!) "The shrinking of Scots is clearly a phase [Oh, that long, long phase!] in the *development* [my italics] throughout the United Kingdom towards a more or less standardised English. We may surmise that it will take acceptance of our language change, put into practice in a realistic fiction—rather than a poetry which attempts to keep Scots as its whole medium—to put Scottish literature on a sound basis again. . . . To entertain the idea of *establishing* [my italics] Scots seems no more than a hobby, a piece of wishful thinking, or a substitute for seriously effective political interests." Hum! Let me tell you a story.

In his article Dr. Craig tells the story of the lorry-driver in the Mearns who liked the broadcast of Grassic Gibbon's *A Scots Quair*. This still goes on, this appreciation, and not only in the country districts, though he would not have it so. Scots poets are not so out of touch with what Craig and Henderson rather patronisingly call "the people" as some would make them out to be, for political reasons.

Craig knows his mystical "people" as a lecturer for the W.E.A. speaking to "working class" audiences who wish to better themselves through education so that they will be able to move out of that class into the next one up. I know them as they know me, in the pub, in the street and at home. They know me as a "gent" and as a poet and they don't think it funny-peculiar any more than I find it funny-peculiar that Bill is a navvy or Jock a night porter or Tom a boilerman whose son is a doctor. "When are we going to get another *Wallace*, Syd?" If I hear that once I hear it a hundred times. Now this *Wallace* was a play of mine in Scots verse that was put on at the Assembly Hall during the Edinburgh Festival of 1960. The critics, the academic lobby, say that poetry is dead, the future is with the novel (Craig); they say the Scots language is dead and they love to hang the unfortunate word "synthetic" round its neck, knowing full well the ambiguity in the word; they say the Scots written by the Renaissance poets—or most of them—is "bookish," not "natural" but merely translated from English (try it some time), and, of course, not understood or even understandable.

"Let them say!" say I. The fact of the matter is that that play of *The Wallace* packed "them" in in busloads. (I don't suppose Craig has seen or read it; it is not simply an adventure story). I fought hard to get the thing put on in the Assembly Hall rather than in an ordinary theatre because the Assembly Hall does not have the class association of an ordinary theatre. In the minds of the non-theatre-going public it is (at Festival time) more like a place for a "show," or a circus or a panto-mime; to them it is vaguely associated with the Military Tattoo! The audiences were very mixed indeed—which is what I had intended. I do not like this anglified habit of class distinction. Dockers and doctors and dukes—let 'em all come! Come they did.

One night in the second week, as I was walking up to the entrance, a coach arrived from Dunfermline in Fife and a gang of rowdy miners and their wives came pouring out, men who would ordinarily have been at the dog-racing or a football match. They were very cheery, having obviously had a few on the road. It was a night out. When I saw this the old heart leapt up. Ah, I thought, I've got through to them; they've heard about it and they've come to see it, the people of Scotland (not the theatre-goers from the suburbs), the ones I wrote the play for, to deliver the message. That busload seemed a justification of my efforts to stage it in that particular big hall, seating about 1500. All during those three weeks I was being surprised by the *popular* response. (The English and the Anglo-Scottish critics hated it, by the way; they said it was prejudiced and unfair; they were obviously "involved" natheless! After all, it is an "engaged" or "committed" work—which is considered admirable in a German communist, like Brecht, but not, evidently, in a left-wing Scot-tish nationalist, like Smith. Why not?) A bobby on the beat approached me once and I thought "Help! What have I done now?" He put out a hand like the proverbial hunk of meat. "It was great!" he said. "Are ye gaun to gie's the Bruce next?" That sort of thing.

Yet in the 18th century, in the 19th, and today, just yesterday, the tireless lobby is saying the language is dead, the poets have lost touch with the public and so forth. Evidently not.

I have another quite different story to prove it. A poem of mine in Scots, called "Kynd Kittock's Land," was televised with a series of bril-liant photographs by Alan Daiches (son of Professor Daiches above-men-tioned) by the B.B.C. We had worked together on the project. It lasted fifteen minutes. It was about Edinburgh—not the romantic, tourist Edinburgh, but the *real* Edinburgh, much of it done in the High Street. It was a political poem, it was joky, it was serious, it was sad, etc., etc. I had dreamed up this TV show as a means of breaking through, of getting poetry into the public *ear* again, by using the eye as a "Trojan horse." Everyone watches TV, but precious few go to "poetry readings"—also, you get paid, of course, as a professional should be.

"Kynd Kittock's Land" *took* amazingly on all sides. People didn't realize, I suppose, that they were listening to poetry, like M. Jourdain about prose. Even a certain hard-drinking commercial traveller (hardly a literary type!) was "sent" by it; he would not stop telling everyone about it. A bricklayer told me: "Ay, Syd, we want mair o' yon. No' thae awfae cowboy things." That's the sort of level. From people who would never dream of reading anything except *Racing Form* and the evening paper, and certainly not poetry. One chap, a railwayman, was furious about it. "Ye're wrang," he said, with a certain amount of passion, "yon's no' the wey o't. Yon's no' the answer!" He'd got the message, but was disagreeing. He'd listened to it seriously and he thought I was wrong. But he *had* listened and he *had* understood—both language and argument. Once more my heart leapt up.

Now regard the other side of the penny, the academic reaction.

The poem, which is about 350 lines, together with the photographs of peeling walls, children playing, old age pensioners sunning themselves on a bench, unemployed fellows lounging about, interior pub scenes full of rude mechanicals, overdressed ladies at a garden party, empty streets at dawn with a milk float, shop signs, street notices, etc., etc. was offered as a book to a Scottish University Press. By luck, when I was having lunch with the secretary, talking about the projected book, an American agent for the Press was present. He was enthusiastic. "We could *sell* this," he said, "with no trouble." But the Press turned it down, so it was reported to me, as "not the sort of thing that a University Press should publish. And it would cost too much for the pictures." So. It remains unpublished. Whom does the poet like? The people or the lobby?

To speak from personal experience is best, but I am by no means alone in having known the response to poetry or drama in Scots. The plays of Roddy Macmillan, Robert Kemp, Alexander Reid and Alexander Scott, all written in Scots, are perfectly acceptable, as is Bridie's *Anatomist,* to all classes—though in ordinary theatres you are more apt, certainly, to get a bourgeois audience. This year, 1964, at the Citizens Theatre, Glasgow, we had the première of John Arden's *Armstrong's Last Goodnight* (based on the Border Ballad of "Johnnie Armstrong") written in Scots. Here was an English playwright of esteem *choosing* to write a play in what the lobby keep on saying is a dead or dying or shrinking or incomprehensible dialect. These stories are told to show how far out of touch with real life and the real existence of a Scots poet the academic lobbyers can be. Significantly, Edwin Morgan disapproved of Arden using Scots, declaring (for an English public) "We in Scotland have had too many Scottish historical plays; we want plays in English!" (*Encore*, July-Aug., 1964).

They are wrong about the language being dead and not understood; they are wrong about the poet's language being bookish (though of course sometimes it may be intentionally so); they are wrong about poetry being a dead medium; and they are wrong, especially Craig is wrong, about the political feeling in Scotland—which has no relationship to votes cast at elections, for which there are other (i.e. English party) reasons.

Craig subtitles his essay "*Recent* Scottish Writing," but he spends most of his time discussing the 1930s (MacDiarmid, Grassic Gibbon, Gunn, Blake, MacColla) and Lindsay's Faber anthology *Modern Scottish Poetry*, of 1946. He does mention, only to dismiss, MacCaig's anthology *Honour'd Shade*, of 1959, which may be regarded as fairly recent. He then gives a page, and rightly, to Iain Crichton Smith, a bit to a ten-year-old poem by John Manson, a couple of pages to the so-called folk-song revival and Hamish Henderson's exercises therein (admirable as it well may be, "modern folk-song" is not strictly *literature*, as Henderson's *Elegies for the Dead in Cyrenaica* certainly is), one page to a couple of ditties by Alan Jackson, and ends up with four pages on the novelist Robin Jenkins. Eight pages out of sixteen-and-a-half devoted to the ostensible subject of the subtitle is somewhat short measure. However, there it is.

The thought arises, is Dr. Craig quite qualified to write on such a subject? Has he read the stuff? He tells us that he has spent "more than ten years' constant reading in the Scottish literary media," past and present, and we must believe him. But it is curious that so many of the poems he discusses happen to come out of two anthologies. Has he read the works of these authors that lie outwith the said anthologies? Who would form an idea of English literature from Palgrave's *Golden Treasury* and Yeats's *Oxford Book of Modern Verse*? But seemingly he doesn't even know all the anthologies. He mentions the fact that MacDiarmid is "totally ignored" in *The Faber Book of Modern Verse* and the Penguin anthology of *Contemporary Verse*. But MacDiarmid was included in Yeats's *Oxford Book* and also (as were some of his despised followers, mentioned or not mentioned by Dr. Craig) in such collections as Kenneth Rexroth's *New British Poets* (New Directions), *The Faber Book of 20th Century Verse* (1953), A. N. Jeffares's *Seven Centuries of Poetry* (Longman, 1955), G. S. Fraser's *Poetry Now* (Faber, 1956), and Edith Sitwell's vast *Atlantic Book of British and American Poetry* (Boston, 1958), and doubtless many others. Still being personal and apropos, it is an odd coincidence that the poem of mine which Dr. Craig hammers in his article is the same one that he hammers in his *Scottish Literature and the Scottish People*. It seems that when he finds something he really dislikes he cannot leave it alone. It must be maddening. I don't mind him hammering it at all, but it's funny that he chose the same one twice (out of hundreds published) and it also, coincidentally, is in MacCaig's anthology.

Has he read, for instance, two of the finest poets writing in Scotland at this moment, Robert Garioch of an older and George Mackay Brown of a younger generation? Or Kenneth White or Stewart Conn of a younger generation still? If so, he does not mention them even to slosh them. Of novelists, he mentions, and rightly, Robin Jenkins, but what about James Kennaway or Alexander Trocchi? He could knock them easily. Has he read Tom Scott's *The Ship and Ither Poems*? It should appeal to his socialistic principles, anyway, even if he cannot stand the language. He reminds me of a young school teacher I was talking to recently (one of those whom Dr. Craig and his fellow lobbyists have probably influenced over the years). He also hated the "Scottish thing." "And Mac-Diarmid is a lot of bunk, anyway," he said. I asked him which particular poem he was thinking of. It soon transpired or simply came out that he had never read a single line of MacDiarmid ever. Where did he get his prejudice from? It didn't drop out of the air. Or maybe it did. Or maybe he learnt it at his school or university. I am sure he is continuing the good work—in utter ignorance.

I would ask the lobby, I would ask Dr. Craig, what is their intent? Is it to prevent any Scottish writing or any agitation for Home Rule—because the two things seem to be very bound up together, as was always the aim of MacDiarmid and the Renaissance. Whatever it is, they certainly do have an effect, if a slow one, in some quarters.

Would you like to know the next stage? Having, as they have always hoped since the later 18th century, "liberated" Scottish writers from all so-called national identity, they will then say, "What is this Scottish literature? Show me it! What's so Scottish about it? It's just English really. You haven't got a literature. You've been 'liberated'!" Dr. Craig already in his book refuses to let the Scots claim Byron for their own ("Efforts to trace Scottish influences on Byron seem never to have found anything tangible"—which is one in the eye for T. S. Eliot!) despite the poet's own affirmation in *Don Juan* ("But I am half-Scot by birth / And bred a whole one." "I scotch'd not kill'd the Scotchman in my blood"). Aldous Huxley called Burns one of the greatest "English" lyric poets; Yeats is another one; and Robert Graves refers to one of the most famous Border Ballads as "English"—whose refrain of "Edinbro', Edinbro' / Stirling for aye / Bonnie St Johnstone stands upon Tay" might have given him a map reference! Why should one object, you say? Why not? In Italy, say, does an Englishman like being called an American? Or an American an Englishman? Does an American like Walt Whitman being claimed as a great English poet? Anyway, doesn't Truth *matter*?

And what is the purpose of this quisling Scottish lobby? It is a simple political aim to destroy the separate identity (as voiced in their literature and embedded deep in their souls—or "psychology," as Craig would probably call it), clung to for centuries with "a Japanese courage" against most powerful cultural pressures, of the oldest nation in Europe. It is a simple aim, but evidently difficult to achieve.

One effect they have certainly had already; it is very difficult to get a book published in Scotland today unless it is a text book. This was not so even ten years ago. Hugh MacDiarmid has to go to New York for his *Collected Poems*; Tom Scott has to go to the Oxford University Press for his *The Ship*; Robert Garioch has never had a book of his poems printed in hard covers; Iain Crichton Smith publishes in London, so does Norman MacCaig, George Mackey Brown, and all the novelists. Kenneth White, whom Craig does not mention, published his first book of poems in Paris—I'll bet if he had offered it in Edinburgh or Glasgow it would have been rejected.

I hasten to say that I am not throwing all this up against poor Dr. Craig, but articles such as the one we are talking about all add another chuckie to the cairn.

Another favourite missile is that Scottish literature does not or cannot concern itself with what are vaguely called "broader issues," as Craig says in his article *"broader* and more real struggles and developments" and, in the broadcast I mentioned earlier, he said "the real essence of Scottishness is that it loses the habit of confronting the *broader* human problems." Sometimes the cant phrase "universal themes" is used instead. What are these that Scottish literature has lost the habit of confronting? There is birth and love and death, for instance. Or is that too narrow? There is the struggle of the individual with the community (we all know about that one), the struggle of the rebel against injustice, social or national; there is the conflict between duty and self interest. There is the cycle of the seasons. There is freedom and tyranny. Has Scottish literature lost the habit of confronting these? Dr. Craig should read a bit more. I can give him a list of books.

But it is not the subject or the theme that makes literature, it is not even the attitude or the morals of the writer; it is how you write it, though Dr. Craig, as a Marxist, will doubtless disagree. I wish he would pick now on something he *likes*, to write about. Perhaps English or Russian literature would suit him better. He once said that poetry was finished and that the future lay with the novel. (I love these ex-cathedra pronouncements that critics make, for the world to attend to). Well, then, let him read novels and leave those awful poets alone. They will still be writing, and they will still be writing in Scotland, as they have been doing, despite the Jeremiahs and the Cassandras, for the last two hundred years and more. If you look into it, you will find—for all those old corncraiks tell you—a fair deal of poetry and prose that cannot be matched, in its kind, in any other literature. Yesterday, today and tomorrow.[3]

The dogs bark, but the caravan moves on, saith the Prophet.

EDINBURGH

---

[3] In January 1965, at a Poetry Conference in St. Andrews, Norman MacCaig delivered himself of these thoughts, as reported in *The Scotsman* of 25th January 1965, "There had been," he said, "a renaissance in the arts in Scotland in the last forty years, but it was now petering out and unless it changed its direction it would die. I think the future will lie in the development of a poetry in English. If the writers are Scottish it will come out in their writing." At it again!

[The above note was received as this issue was going to press—February 1965. *Editor.*]

Walter Scott in Poland

Part I

Warsaw and Vilno

According to T. S. Eliot, we cannot appreciate a poet alone; we "must set him, for contrast and comparison, among the dead."[1] In practice this often means setting the writer within the context of a national literature. But in some cases it is even more profitable to find the writer's place in the literature of an alien nationality and language. Then "contrast and comparison" may reveal some unnoticed, even surprising features in the fairly well known author. And in this process usually light is thrown on the two literatures compared. *The Heyday of Sir Walter Scott* by Donald Davie (London, 1961) offers some interesting examples of what may be gained by this kind of study.

Let this be the justification of what follows here. To set Sir Walter Scott among the Polish writers is to add something to the knowledge of the English-speaking students of the great Scotsman. It is to enlarge the literary and social scope of his writings. Perhaps, even, it is to change —to some extent—the accepted valuations.

Let us first see the general setting in which Walter Scott as a literary phenomenon appeared in Poland and then we shall pass to an analysis of his significance to the Poles.

His greatest influence coincides with the early phase of the long Romantic period of Polish literary history extending from about 1820 to about 1860. Its early phase opened with the publication of a volume of poetry by Adam Mickiewicz (1798-1855) in 1822 and ended, in one way, in 1830 with the outbreak of the November Uprising which developed into a futile Polish-Russian war. In another way this most creative and dynamic phase of Polish Romanticism continued in exile until about 1834 when it produced its finest and richest fruit.

Polish Romantic literature was shaped by following Western European literary patterns—mostly German and British—and yet it developed

---

[1] T. S. Eliot, *Tradition and the Individual Talent* in *Selected Prose* (Harmondsworth, 1955), p. 23.

an individually national character of its own. It is impossible to understand how those divergent trends have been reconciled in a synthesis or to assess the nature and the range of the foreign influence without having an idea of the historical situation of the contemporaneous Polish society.

This situation had developed towards the end of the eighteenth century when Poland had been partitioned by the three neighbouring empires of Russia, Prussia, and Austria. The imperial, absolutist, and reactionary governments of the powers did not care for any free development of the Polish nation. Consequently, the Poles started on a long period of continual, hopeful, but unsuccessful attempts at regaining political independence by force. At the same time they realized that in the absence of their own state their native language and literature might become the mainstay of the national tradition. The idea crystallized in the writings of two literary critics—Kazimierz Brodzinski and Maurycy Mochnacki.[2] They wanted a new Polish literature which would be a mirror of the national character and existence. In practice this meant turning away from the Neo-Classicist, decaying literature of the eighteenth century with its rigid rules, cold rationalism, and emphasis on the general and cosmopolitan. This also meant following the example of the Germans—Herder, Schiller, and Goethe—and of the British—Shakespeare, Scott, and Byron. These names became for the Poles symbols of fidelity to the national spirit, to the idea of liberty and humanity. Their owners had shown how to create a new, free, dynamic, imaginative literature stirring the reader's emotions and prompting him to action.

Thus Romantic literature in Poland, while modelling itself on writers like Scott and Byron, expressed the deepest aspirations of an unhappy nation whose very existence was endangered. Thus Scott's patriotism acquired in Mickiewicz almost cosmic dimensions, and Byron's hero, disgusted with society and with himself, changed on the Polish soil into a patriot who suffered because "his fatherland knew naught but sorrow"

[2] Cf. their articles in *Polska Krytyka Literacka* (*1800-1918*) ed. J. Z. Jakubowski (Warsaw, 1959), I, 125-132, 325-344.

The text by Kazimierz Brodzinski (pp. 125-132) is the final part of his larger work *O klasycznosci i romantycznosci tudziez o duchu poezji polskiej* [*Classicism and Romanticism and the Spirit of Polish Poetry*] published in 1818.

The text by Maurycy Mochnacki (pp. 325-344) consists of two articles: "O sonetach Adama Mickiewicza" ["On Adam Mickiewicz's Sonnets"] published in 1827, which ends with the words: "If ever we have an original literature and poetry, we shall owe it to him" (i.e. Mickiewicz). The second article is entitled "Mysli o literaturze polskiej" ["Thoughts on Polish Literature"] published in 1828, in which the author pleads against mechanical imitation of foreign models and for following broadly adapted ideas.

and was ready to do almost anything to change the conditions. This explains the interdependence between literature and politics, characteristic of Polish Romanticism. Writing became a political activity, shaping attitudes which culminated in the November Uprising of 1830.

The tsarist government against whom, as the greatest oppressor, the insurgents of Warsaw struck, had been aware of the interdependence even before 1830, and it began more vigorously to suppress and punish after the failure of the uprising. Most of the great poets had to emigrate. Instead of Warsaw Paris became the centre of Polish liberal and revolutionary Romanticism. St. Petersburg grouped rather conservative and less talented people who tried to save what might be saved within the narrow limits imposed by their loyalty to the tsar whom the Congress of Vienna (1815) had also made the king of the Russian-dominated part of the country ("the Congress Kingdom of Poland").

Then it was that the tragedy of 1830 became reflected in the literature of the Great Emigration. Poets became the leaders and guides of the nation, actually believed to be endowed with prophetic foresight and greatness of soul. The ancient religious Roman idea of the *vates* returned in the Polish semi-religious name of *wieszcz*. And it must be admitted that the greatest of the poets at least tried to live up to their responsibility and national dignity which far surpassed even the prestige enjoyed by Sir Walter as the representative of his nation.

But it is an undeniable fact that the Scotsman, together with the half-Scot Byron, were spiritually present at the birth of the new literary movement in Poland. They inspired, they showed some possibilities, they set up some models and standards. The form of the ballad, the poetic tale, the historical romance, the poetic travelogue, the Don Juan-like epic—these are only some of the genres which the two British writers lent to the Polish Romantics and which in some cases acquired greater literary and social significance in their new home.

It would be hardly reasonable to see mere accident in all this. Forms result from contents, contents from ideas and attitudes. Parallels point to the existence of something common to both sides.

It will be worthwhile then to investigate when, how, why, and to what extent Sir Walter Scott's literary presence in Poland affected one of the greatest developments in the literature of a country with which he had personally so little contact.

*   *   *

The first mention of the writer is to be found in Warsaw in a journal *Pamietnik Warszawski* (*The Warsaw Register*) of 1816, soon after contact between England and the Continent was re-established after the final fall of Napoleon. If we consider that the Battle of Waterloo and the end of the Congress of Vienna had taken place in June 1815, the appearance of the article entitled "A Review of the English Literature of the Last Twenty Years" in *Pamietnik Warszawski* six months later is proof of a lively interest on the part of the Poles of those times in Western European literature.

The article was a translation from the *Bibliothèque Universelle*, a French periodical providing an international forum of exchange of information and specimens of major European literatures. Its purpose was also to inform the Continental reader what had happened in the literature of the British Isles during the French Revolution and the Napoleonic wars.

The author of the article mentions "works by Mrs. Rattcliff (Radcliffe), Darblay, Maria Roche, Edgeworth—illustrious writers" and "the romances bearing the name of William Godwin," marked with "the stamp of genius;" he barely touches the contemporary English drama, and passes to poetry with a remark that "the spirit of the English language, a language bold, independent, and abounding in figures of speech, is an ally even of a mediocre talent." Among the British he sees two geniuses. One of them is "lord Biron" — "magnificent, but sombre."

> The other poet, Walter Scott, born in Scotland, provides a quick and most pleasant stimulus for the imagination. His genre combines both the poetry of the troubadours and that of the bards. He presents the manners of feudal times and decks them with brilliant colours. In his songs everything is alive, everything has breath. The strangest details seem to be true, customs quite contrary to ours seem to be our own. Men and clothes, horses and arms are made visible: we look at the chase or at battle. The background of this abundance of brilliant scenes consists of wild Nature—those mists, those silver firs, those waterfalls, rocks and lakes, which give shape to wild, but beautiful cold climes. His talent excels in the picturesque and if he does not abuse it at fruits of lesser care, he will prove worthy of the name of "the Ariosto of the North."
>
> The wonderful fecundity of this poet, always equal to himself, also deserves homage. In few years four large poems came from his pen, not to mention romances on which he did not bestow his name. (pp. 298-299)

The points raised by the quoted lines are: a connexion as regards theme and form between Sir Walter's poetry and medieval poetry; its picturesque quality and energy; his use of the romantic landscape as a background; his prolixity and a mention of his anonymous works in prose, which appeared in 1814 and 1815. It is remarkable that the poet was dubbed "the Ariosto of the North"—a designation which appears in *Childe Harold's Pilgrimage* (Canto IV, XL), which was not published until 1818.

The author of the article mentions four poetic tales by Scott and says that their features are: "profusion of thought, terseness of the narrative, charming detailed descriptions, bright and vivid colour, and—above all—this bold onrush, this fervour of a poet who, letting his pegasus loose, pierces through the clouds and ethereal regions, reaches for great effects and despises mere seductive charms." (p. 299) "Such is the mark of that Northern genius who terrifies with his audacity and captivates the imagination with the spell of his art."

The author does not dare to quote from Scott's poems "because to translate his works into French is hardly possible." But he says that it is worthwhile "to learn English in order to read Walter Scott who cannot be translated into a foreign language." At the same time it is expedient "to get to know Scotland, its history and to become familiar with the situation of the places described by him."

The whole shows that the author was well informed about Scott's works and their character down to 1815. At the same time it is obvious that the Polish translator, who signed the review with the initial S., did not read Scott's poems. He made Marmion a woman!

This early information about Scott was not lost on the readers. It was not limited to Warsaw readers either. Warsaw was the cultural centre in which the interests of all other centres of Poland, Lithuania, and the Ukraine converged, though each of them had a life of its own.

One of the cultural centres, closely connected with Mickiewicz, the most representative poet of Poland, was Vilno. The city is a well-recorded example of the intellectual trends of the times and of the contacts with Warsaw. It had been an ancient capital of Lithuania, but in Mickiewicz's times, in spite of certain provincial dislikes, the memory of the liberal Polish-Lithuanian empire or union, formed through a royal marriage towards the end of the fourteenth century and continuing until the final partition in 1795, was still very strong both among the Poles and the Lithuanians. The problem of the emancipation of Lithuanian culture from Polish cultural supremacy was as yet practically non-existent. The medium of education and creative work of the enlightened Lithuanians and Poles, who mixed freely, was Polish. And Vilno University flourished in that period before the suspicious absolutism of the tsar cut its life short.

In Mickiewicz's student days the young scholars formed all kinds of scientific and socially-ethical societies at the University. The most prominent of the organizations were the Philomaths, or the Friends of Sciences, and the Philaretes—the Friends of Virtue. Their correspondence, collected and published, gives a revealing picture of the young men's avid interest in foreign languages and literature, of their attempts to draw inspiration rather from the German and the British Romantic sources as opposed to French sources then identified with Neo-Classicism.[3]

Mickiewicz used to borrow the *Bibliothèque Universelle* from Franciszek Malewski and used the eighth volume of the series to prepare a paper which he read at a meeting of the Philomaths. In the paper he reviewed Canto III of *The Lady of the Lake* using phrases which sound like echoes of the article published in *Pamiętnik Warszawski*. The poem, he wrote, had been written "in the spirit of the Caledonian bards." Its features were "gloom and dread" and " a tenderness wild and terrifying," its heroes "taken from the age of chivalry." Its "plenty of expressions and the novelty of similes" deserved attention. The poem "might serve as a most beautiful model of chivalric serious poetry."[4]

Writing an essay on Romantic poetry, which formed a preface to his *Poems* of 1822 which, like *Lyrical Ballads*, marked the beginning of a new period in the literary history of the poet's country, Mickiewicz, as it were, repeated some statements of the French article. He wrote about the "two geniuses: Walter Scott and Byron," adding, "The former has dedicated his talent to national history, publishing folk tales of the romantic world, handled in a classic way. He has produced a repetition of national poems and has become an Ariosto for the English."[5]

Franciszek Malewski knew English, like his friend Jan Sobolewski, the translator of *The Vicar of Wakefield*. He regularly read the *Bibliothèque Britannique* and its continuation, the *Bibliothèque Universelle*,

---

[3] See Jan Czubek (ed.) *Archiwum Filomatow* (Krakow, 1913), 3 Parts in 10 vols.

The following names of English and Scottish writers are to be found in the young men's correspondence, with occasionally mentioned or implied titles of works read in French or German translations: POETS: G. Byron (*Darkness, The Siege of Corinth, Mazeppa, Marino Faliero, Sardanapalus, Hebrew Melodies*), G. Crabbe, J. Dryden (*Alexander's Feast*), T. Moore (*Lalla Rookh*), A. Pope (*Essay on Man*), W. Scott, R. Southey (*Roderick*), E. Young; NOVELISTS: O. Goldsmith (*The Vicar of Wakefield*), S. Johnson (*Rasselas*), L. Sterne; HISTORIANS: Adam Ferguson, Edward Gibbon, David Hume, William Mitford, William Robertson; William Guthrie, the geographer, and Adam Smith (*The Wealth of Nations*); PHILOSOPHERS and ESSAYISTS: Hugh Blair (*Lectures*), Dugald Stewart, Henry Home (*Essays on the Principles of Morality and Natural Religion*), William Hogarth (*The Analysis of Beauty*), the Earl of Shaftesbury.

[4] A. Mickiewicz, *Dziela wszystkie* [*Collected Works*] (Warsaw, 1933), V, 429, 435.

[5] Read: "the Britons" or even "the Scots." Polish usage, perhaps unfortunately and unthinkingly, extends the name of England and that of the English to cover all the nationalities living in Great Britain unless distinction is intended.

which he borrowed from Fryderyk Moritz, a bookseller of Vilno, as well as the *Edinburgh Monthly Review* and some "German almanachs" with translations from Shakespeare, Scott, and Byron.

Malewski's letters testify that in 1820 he knew Byron's *Mazeppa,* Dryden's ode (*Alexander's Feast*), Shaftesbury's philosophical works, and Adam Smith's *Wealth of Nations* (in French translation). In 1821 he mentions Henry Home's *Essays on the Principles of Morality and Natural Religion* and Hugh Blair's *Lectures* (again in French). In 1822 the list was extended by "an interesting palinode by Byron" published in a "revue" (most likely the *Revue Encyclopédique*). On Christmas Eve of that year Malewski sent from Berlin to St. Moritz *Lalla Rookh* and two volumes of Moore's other poems, Byron's *Sardanapalus* and *Marino Faliero,* and two volumes by Southey—all for Mickiewicz. For himself he reserved *Roderick* by Southey.

Malewski was a great reader of everything that came from England or Scotland. He used his knowledge of French, German, and English, treating German not only as a means of access to literature written in English, but also as an approach to the English language. In his letter of Sept. 9th, 1819, he encouraged Mickiewicz in the following way: "Take up German soon, even to the detriment of Greek or French. Now is the time to do it and you might read all English works in exact translations; besides, the labour will make your way to the English language itself." (I, p. 175). A month later Mickiewicz wrote to Jezowski: "I have made considerable progress in German" (I, p. 291). This statement provoked Malewski to a new challenge of April 6th, 1821: "Now, Master Adam, when you have learnt German *Leben, Geist,* and *Welt,* it is time to get to know English *comfort, blessing,* and *grief;* I leave this for you to consider" (III, p. 251). Mickiewicz accepted the advice on that occasion as well and earned his friend's exclamation: "Glory be to God for your having tackled English!" (on Feb. 13th, 1822, IV, p. 151).

The young men used Ebers' *New Hand-Dictionary of the English and German Language* (III, p. 255). Probably all the books read by Malewski were known to Mickiewicz for exchange of publications was the custom of the Philomaths. Mickiewicz was subject to urgent reminders: "Return *Bibliothèque Britannique* and other stuff!" "For Goodness' sake return *Bibliothèque Universelle!*" (I, pp. 110, 208).

The wave of interest in the liberal aspects of Western literary movements naturally brought Sir Walter's name and works to wider and wider notice. Mickiewicz read him in 1819, Malewski in 1820 and 1821, Tomasz Zan in 1822. Then Walerian Krasinski wrote from

Warsaw in November that Mickiewicz's first volume of poetry was published and that the poet "pleased Warsaw immensely; they have called him . . . the Lithuanian Walter Scott and are impatiently waiting for the second volume" (IV, p. 326).

On Christmas Eve 1821 Malewski reported from Warsaw that Karol Sienkiewicz, Prince Adam Czartoryski's librarian, who had visited Britain in search of *Polonica,* had returned and was publishing his translation of *The Lady of the Lake* into Polish. The translation appeared in 1822.

Sienkiewicz, the author of *A Diary of Travel in England 1820-1821*[6] was one of those few Poles who had seen Walter Scott. "His appearance is quite simple," he wrote after having seen the writer in the court in Edinburgh on November 24th, 1820, "neither genius, nor kindness, nor tenderness are apparent. His eyes are grey, he is blond-haired, somewhat bald, about 50, lame too, and often bows when walking. Dressed in a lawyer's gown. His face round, fat, slightly ruddy." (p. 186) Notwithstanding this almost unfriendly description, Sienkiewicz was deeply interested in everything that the Scottish writer's pen produced. The events of the day, registered in his diary under the date of Jan. 13, 1821, are: getting a letter containing the news of somebody's death, and "the new romance by Scott—Kenilworth—which has just come out from the press, still wet from the printer's ink." (p. 215)

Besides Karol Sienkiewicz, Malewski found other men in Warsaw who might have read Scott in English. They were "Jozef Korzeniowski, Zamoyski's librarian, a writer of sorts, capable, well read in English and German literature" (who later turned out a novelist) and "Chlebowski, [Count] Krasinski's tutor, the most capable of them all, I think, interested in politics, well versed in English and in German" (*Arch. Filom.,* IV, p. 103).

The Vilnian circle had contacts with Mrs. Maria Puttkammer, Mickiewicz's passionate romantic love, the "*Maryla*" of his poems. When she had decided to marry Baron Puttkammer instead of the practically penniless poet, naturally their acquaintance was broken off, but Jan Czeczot maintained an exchange of letters with the lady, occasionally providing his two friends with some information about each other. Czeczot was asked by Mrs. Puttkammer to borrow some books in town for her. On May 29, 1823, he wrote to Maryla: "The literature of romance is completely unknown to me and yet romances only are to be found in the new catalogue here. Choice is not easy anyway and here

---

[6] K. Sienkiewicz, *Dziennik podrozy po Anglii 1820-1821* (Wroclaw, 1953), the first edition!

it has become still more difficult. Fortunately I remembered, Madam, that you once wished to read Scott's *Marmion;* it was to be found in the library so I am dispatching it, taking no responsibility for the choice."

In the same letter he added: "In the new . . . catalogue . . . a historical romance by de Radklif was to be found too, describing the manners of the thirteenth century and once I heard about that woman Radklif that she had been a famous writer of romances . . ." (*op. cit.*, V, p. 24).

But Mrs. Puttkammer was better informed. She answered: "We have kept *Marmion* by Walter Scott to read it, the other two books I am returning, because I know Goethe's and I never read any romances by Radklif." (V, p. 243). Thus a distance was maintained between Scott's name and that of Mrs. Anne Radcliffe's, used by a French impostor to win readers for his imitation.

There was at least one man more in Lithuania who had mastered English well enough to be able to translate Thomas Moore and to imitate Scott's own practice. His name was Antoni Edward Odyniec, a small beer of a poet, but an ambitious man who wrote to Czeczot in May 1823: "Yesterday I wrote an original ballad based on a story told by the postillion." (V, p. 210). Here we have a hint of a fashion modelled on Scott's way of looking for literary motives in chats with postillions, country wives, and guests of wayside inns met by chance.

(*To be continued*)

UNIVERSITY OF LODZ

ANNE GREENE

Bridie's Concept of the Master Experimenter

In his essay "Equilibrium," Bridie names Calvin, Huxley, and Hegel as three "radio-active" influences on his thinking, and explains the nature of each: From Calvin he absorbed the doctrines of the Absolute, Election, and Predestination;[1] from Huxley he absorbed the idea of man as a step in an evolutionary process; and from Hegel he learned a principle of dialectic—thesis, antithesis, synthesis—by whose means he tried to reconcile the other two. Thus he evolved the concept of a Master Experimenter who is in a sense his Father, and of man as one of the experiments and a tool of the Experimenter.[2] This paper will discuss six plays in which he deals with the problem of evil in relation to these ideas.

In his first play, *The Sunlight Sonata* or *To Meet the Seven Deadly Sins*[3] (1928), the idea of man's heart as innately evil is suggested in the prologue by Beelzebub, a fatherly Devil who stands against a background of Highland scenery brooding over mankind. Beelzebub understands man's little hypocrisies and secret motives, and as he watches a group of Glasgow citizens having a picnic he knows what is in the heart of each. He knows that the Reverend Somerled Carmichael is proud of his goodness and handsome appearance, and that the avaricious Mr. Marcus Groundwater is an elder in Mr. Carmichael's church for only two reasons: it is good for trade and he is afraid of God. Beelzebub also knows that man's God is really the Devil:

> Man. Man. Man.
> You're feart o' me, you're feart o' me,
> Droll wee slug wi' the shifty e'e!
> Raise your praise to the Ancient of Days.
> I prevent you in all your ways.
> Your heavy hosannas sink to me.
> To me you pray in horrible psalm

---

[1] He should have included *Original Sin.* The omission was no doubt an oversight.

[2] James Bridie, "Equilibrium," *The London Mercury*, 39 (April 1939), 585-89.

[3] *The Switchback and Other Plays* (London, 1930). Date following title of each play is date of first performance.

[9 6]

> For the single eye and the grasping palm—
> "Play the game, Lord, play the game.
> Commit us not to the worm and the flame.
> Save us from boils and leprosy,
> Prosper our cheating and let us be!"

He sends his seven prankish little children, the Deadly Sins, to pervert the picnickers, one Sin against each. Although each mortal has his own besetting sin, all have a share of all, as indicated in the report of the Sins to Beelzebub. Superbia says, for example:

> You'd hardly believe how proud they are.
> They're proud of their accents or having a car,
> Or of knowing a knight or the name of a winner,
> Or of putting on hardboiled shirts to dinner.

Three fairies—Faith, Hope, and Charity—rescue the mortals and then wonder what can be done to improve the manners and morals of the little Sins. The problem is solved when Elsie, the minister's daughter, agrees to take them all in her personal charge.

Five years later striking changes are seen in the mortals. Groundwater has become aimless and no longer cares what happens to his business. His wife, always a lover of good food, no longer pays attention to the menu. The minister has developed an inferiority complex and is thinking of retiring. All, in fact, have become the exact opposite of what they were except Elsie, who bears the signs of *all* the sins. When the group re-convenes and the little Sins rush in, Elsie feels the "virtue" go out of her as the others return to normal.

Thus in a sparkling, nonsensical manner the play makes the point that sin is an indispensable part of humanity. When Carmichael loses his pride he loses his usefulness as a minister. When Groundwater loses his avarice he loses the quality which made him a successful business man. The epilogue, spoken by Accidia ("I suppose, strictly speaking, I am the Author of this piece"), is the dramatist's admission that he is no exception to mankind.[4] Accidia acknowledges her indebtedness to Pride, Envy, and Avarice, without whose continual encouragement the play would never have been written, and to Beelzebub, "that great Patron and Master of all young dramatists."

In including among Groundwater's charities the "Do-you-believe-in-fairies Guild," the dramatist is satirizing Barrie, of whose Peter Pan he wrote: "Barrie should have been better grounded in the doctrine of Original Sin than to have invented such a character."[5] The portrayal of

---

[4] Bridie always claimed accidia as his special sin. (James Bridie, *One Way of Living* (London, 1939), p. 25.

[5] *Ibid.*, p. 109.

the fairies supports the satire, especially Hope, with her trite, lisping optimism, and Charity, who thinks the little Sins are "such darlings" and agrees with Hope that although they are "trying" now and then, yet "naughty children make the finetht men."

The Amazed Evangelist: A Nightmare[6] (1932) approaches the problem of evil from an entirely different standpoint. It tells of a pair of Glasgow newlyweds who fall into the clutches of a Cummer who quickly calls up the Devil. When the couple assert that they do not believe in a Devil, having recently read "A Popular Synopsis of the Views of the Neo-Mechanists," the Devil feels obliged to prove his existence. But he finds that in order to do so he must explain his opposite:

> I suppose you admit an eternal purposiveness, a majestic plan, or, if you go to the theatre, a life force. You will admit that this force is making for order, righteousness, and perfection, and further, that it has been here since life began on this planet. That is a long time ago, Aggie Martin. . . . Such a long, long time it is, Aggie, that we should have had perfection long ago if there hadn't been a something. What is this something? What is this reaction to eternal action, this drag on the wheel of progress?

Thus God is explained as the evolutionary principle, or progress toward perfection, and evil as whatever hinders that progress.

In *A Sleeping Clergyman*[7] (1933) the evolutionary principle is dramatized on the biological level. It tells the story of three generations of Camerons. In the first two, evil hinders progress, but in the third the social impulses harness the anti-social ones, genius takes control, and the wheel moves forward.

The first Charles Cameron, a brilliant medical student but a moral and physical wreck, dies of tuberculosis. His illegitimate daughter, born after his death to the sister of his friend Dr. Marshall, is carefully brought up by Marshall; but following in her mother's footsteps she makes a liaison with an unscrupulous medical student, and then poisons him to be rid of him. Six months later she gives birth to twins, Hope and Charles ("C. C."), and commits suicide. Hope becomes principal secretary of the League of Nations, and C. C. becomes a brilliant bacteriologist who discovers an antivirus which ends a great epidemic of polio-encephalitis.

The thesis of the play is stated by Dr. Marshall, the mouthpiece of the playwright, who in private life was himself a physician. Marshall says that "to make for righteousness is a biological necessity." The thesis is attacked on two grounds—that of religion and that of eugenics. The religionists are represented by an elderly relative of Dr. Marshall who says

[6] *A Sleeping Clergyman and Other Plays* (London, 1934).
[7] *Ibid.*

"The fathers have eaten sour grapes and the children's teeth shall be set on edge." The eugenists are represented by two other relatives, one of whom in speaking of heredity says "it's awful. You have it running through generation after generation." The second speaks of the wretched people in slums who hand down diseases and all sorts of criminal tendencies. Dr. Marshall takes issue with her:

Marshall: There aren't many diseases they can hand down very far, Agnes; and "criminal tendency" is a very vague expression.

Agnes: Well, insanity.

Marshall: That's another vague expression.

Agnes: You can't bamboozle me that way, Uncle Will. . . . Two bad people getting married can go on and on till, after two or three generations, you've got thousands of criminal lunatics. It should be stopped by law.

Marshall: How?

Agnes: There are loads of ways. That's eugenics.

Bridie's genuine concern regarding this matter is evidenced by a letter he wrote to *The Spectator* in reply to a suggestion that the Government establish a commission to go into the question of the sterilization of the unfit. He declared that such a move would be "a fresh piece of abominable tyranny" and that those who advocated it were "cranks."[8]

In view of the play's thesis, one is surprised by C. C.'s cautious marriage proposal:

C. C.: Oh, by the way—

Katharine: What?

C. C.: You've always b-been a pretty fair sort of girl, haven't you? I m-mean you were in the Open Golf Championship or something, weren't you?

Katharine: Or something. Yes. Why?

C. C.: No fits of insanity in your family?

Katharine: What is this questionnaire? Are you doing a little life insurance on the side?

C. C.: No. I want to know.

Katharine: We're a very healthy family. Hundreds of years of us.

C. C.: I know. I thought of that. . . . I say, K., I'd like you to marry me, if you would. . . . I mean to say—you've got a small head and long legs and an eye like a good race horse. I thought with your breeding and my—

Katharine: That'll do.

But the young doctor's caution is simply a reminder that the play does not *deny* heredity. Although there are poisoners and libertines in C. C.'s ancestry, there are also genius, imagination, and talent for hard

[8] "On Sterilization of the Unfit," *The Spectator*, 151 (Nov. 3, 1933), 623.

work. The play dramatizes the possibility that the *good* traits might combine instead of the *bad* ones. Bridie's letter to *The Spectator* points out that genetics is not an exact science. Biologists, he says, know more about it than either clergymen or playwrights, but he adds that even biologists do not agree among themselves.[9] C. C.'s marriage proposal may be seen as a recognition of this uncertainty. The play dramatizes what *could* happen.

The story of the three generations of Camerons is represented as being narrated by one doctor to another in a men's club in Glasgow while a huge white-bearded clergyman sleeps in an armchair near by. Bridie explains his intention thus: "I showed a wild horse after three generations or incarnations finally harnessing itself to the world for the world's good. God, who had set it all going, took his ease in an armchair throughout the play."[10] From a dramatic standpoint the enveloping device is unnecessary and cumbersome, but it lends support to the play's thesis and is an attempt toward a synthesis of the dramatist's religious and scientific faith.

Mr. Bolfry[11] (1943) makes the point that good and evil are reciprocating opposites on both the individual and the cosmic level, and that both elements are necessary in the process of evolution. Principally, however, it attacks the joyless, repressive influences of Calvinism as Bridie had known them in the Free Kirk,[12] and presents a Blakean-Shavian Devil whose function it is to set the individual free.

The action takes place in the Free Kirk manse at Larach, in the West Highlands. Three young people are guests of the Reverend Mr. McCrimmon—his niece and two English soldiers billeted here. It is Sunday, and the young people are bored because there is nothing to do. The Minister allows no singing, smoking, or whistling, and no Sunday papers. When the soldiers think of going for a walk, Mrs. McCrimmon asks them not to go anywhere they might be seen during the evening service. "There might be talk, and you living with the Minister." She is alarmed when Jean and Cully start out as a twosome: "It's all right in England, dearie, . . . but surely you know what sort of place this is?" Jean does know, and her answer implies that the strictness of the "Wee Frees"

[9] *Ibid.*

[10] *One Way of Living,* p. 278.

[11] *Plays for Plain People* (London, 1944).

[12] *One Way of Living,* pp. 15-16. Richard West, in "No Heart in the Highlands?" *The* (London) *Sunday Times* (Nov. 11, 1962), pp. 9-13 (color section) describes the Free Kirk influence in the West Highlands much as Bridie does in *Mr. Bolfry.*

leads directly to immorality: "It's got the best record for church attendance and the highest illegitimacy rate in the Kingdom"—the charge that O'Casey made against the Catholic influence in Ireland. When the Minister finds the young people joking over their tea, he rebukes them sternly:

> I have found you eating and drinking at unsuitable hours and indulging yourselves in unseemly levity and in that laughter that is like the crackling of thorns under a pot; and this on a day that we are enjoined to keep holy.

Jean accuses her uncle of hypocrisy, and echoing Beelzebub of *The Sunlight Sonata,* she says the God he worships is really the Devil. The young people decide to perform a midnight ritual and call up the Devil so that he can speak for himself. On the stroke of midnight Mr. Bolfry walks in, a beaming little gentleman dressed exactly like the Minister. The sound of merriment brings the McCrimmons into the parlor, and for the rest of the night the Minister and Mr. Bolfry argue.

Mr. Bolfry represents the vigorous, positive qualities which the Minister lacks, his freedom from repression being symbolized by his reaching for the Minister's medicinal whiskey and leaning over occasionally to pat the knee of the maid. The keynote of his philosophy is the freedom of the individual. He refers to the war in Europe and to the "lunatic" who is trying to regiment mankind, but the war that really interests him is a "Holy War"—a war to free man from his load of guilt and his fear of Hell and make him an *individual,* no longer one of a timid, trudging horde of "Christian Soldiers." He says his war is fought also for the freeing of man's genius—for the freedom of the artist and the poet. These points of concern suggest the dramatist's affinity with Shaw, as does Bolfry's emphasis on the creative impulse. Jean and Cully are wasting time, he says; why don't they fall in love? He is interested in such experiments, and as Devil from the Machine he offers to marry them—

> Why is the blood galloping through your not unsightly limbs? Why are the nerve cells snapping and flashing in your head if you are to wrap this gift of life in a napkin and bury it in a back garden.

He claims to be a minister himself. To demonstrate his powers of exhortation he dons the Minister's second-best robe, takes a text from "the Gospel according to William Blake," and lashes the timid, negative virtues of his opponent and all his kind, scorning their hate and lies and fear, their superstition and their lack of charity. As he reaches his climax—

> How long, O Lucifer, Son of the Morning, how long? How long will these fools listen to the quavering of impotent old priests, haters of the Life they never know?—

the Minister seizes Cully's knife and starts after Bolfry, chasing him out of the house and to the edge of the precipice, where he "kills" him.

In this encounter the dramatist argues on both sides. Bolfry is his mouthpiece against the Minister's timid, repressive qualities; yet the pride of the dramatist is revealed no less than that of the Minister in McCrimmon's declaration that three hundred years of discipline in body, brain and soul has produced in Scotland "a breed of men that has not died out even in this shauchly generation." As the Minister explains the great principles of Calvinism, his language becomes that of a doctor whose long experience with human frailty has taught him to interpret these mysteries in terms of everyday life. Of Original Sin, for example, he says that anyone who has ever had a baby knows it "has every sensual vice of which it is anatomically capable with no spirituality to temper it." Of the division of mankind into the sheep and the goats—the Elect and the Damned—he tells his niece she need only look about her: "You pity the Damned—and inded it is your duty so to do. But you cannot deny that they exist." As for Predestination, if she does not believe in it, it is only because she will not face uncomfortable truths, just as she does not like the dentist's drill or the tax-gatherer's demand—for like these it is a fact.

The portrayal of the Minister is not satire on Calvinism but on what the Free Kirk has made of Calvinism, while the portrayal of Bolfry is a reminder that Calvinism originated in a spirit of freedom and rebellion which animated the sermons of John Knox but has been lost in the Free Kirk. This interpretation is supported by Bolfry's claim to have been ordained at Geneva about 1570 and to have preached, "among other places, in the High Kirk at North Berwick." It is supported by the fact that the protagonists agree on essential points of doctrine, and even by the fact that the Minister feels Bolfry to be his own heart speaking evil: "We've got the queer, dark corners in our mind and strange beasts in them that come out ranging in the night." Their reciprocal aspects are emphasized when Bolfry points to a portrait on the wall and remarks that its lineaments would not be recognizable if there were no sharp contrasts of black and white with some admixture of gray. Thus the play achieves what might be called a Hegelian synthesis.

Bridie's view of the Devil is kaleidoscopic, however, and changes within the play. Bolfry is not satisfied to be merely the Minister's other self. He reminds Jean that the Kingdom of Hell is within her as well as the Kingdom of Heaven, "and a number of other irrelevancies left over in the process of Evolution." He says she can never be happy until she reconciles these elements, but he warns her that they are irreconcilable. It is the *struggle* toward purpose that makes for progress rather than the *achievement*, he says. Denying the Minister's accusation that he is a Manichaean, "full of Dualistic sophistications," he identifies himself with that instrument of Providence who afflicted Job's body for the good of his soul; with the enemy who makes progress difficult but without whom there can be no victory. Bolfry thus represents one aspect of the evolutionary concept as defined in *The Amazed Evangelist*.

Bridie's last two plays, though rich in comic detail, show a deeper concern with evil than any of the others. *The Queen's Comedy*[13] (1950), based on the fourteenth and fifteenth books of the *Iliad*, is a sharp satire on war, the Greek soldiers being portrayed as British "Tommies" and the Greek generals as British "military brass." The play gains impact with the knowledge that during World War I the dramatist served in France as a medical officer in charge of advanced dressing stations,[14] and with the further knowledge that he lost a son in World War II.[15] It raises the question "What is God and what is man's relation to him?" Until near the end, the answer is summed up in the play's epigraph:

> As flies to wanton boys are we to the Gods:
> They kill us for their sport.

But in Jupiter's last speech there emerges an evolutionary concept in which war is seen as a temporary evil in a long process of development.

In an introductory scene, Jupiter, in the guise of an octopus, assures Thetis that he has not forgotten his promise to punish the Greeks for annoying her son Achilles. Meanwhile, in a Greek hospital tent an orderly dresses an infantryman's wounds while a dying man groans nearby. The orderly explains that a chariot wheel went over the "poor sucker." "Makes you think, doesn't it?" says the infantryman. "Makes you wonder what it's all for." The orderly answers that the Greeks have an ideal to fight for. "We got the right idea and they haven't, see? There's no place for blocks like them in the modern world." Nestor enters supporting young Dr. Machaon, great-great-grandson of Apollo. As the nurse Hecamede takes him in charge, Nestor says there has been a bit of a breakthrough and the general will have to act quickly to restore the situation. Agamemnon, Ulysses, and Diomed enter, unfold a map, and talk things over. Ajax is still holding the Y sector, says Nestor, but the Trojan chariots are concentrating behind his left flank and he is being harried by sharpshooters. As the staff officers leave, Agamemnon

---

[13] London, 1950.

[14] *One Way of Living*, p. 233.

[15] Winifred Bannister, *James Bridie and His Theatre* (London, 1955), p. 10.

notices that the soldier on the stretcher is dead. "They ought to bury him," he says. "Depressing object for a hospital."

On Olympus the gods amuse themselves. As in the *Iliad*, Juno plays a trick on Jupiter in order to give the Greeks an advantage, and as in the *Iliad*, Jupiter is furious when he discovers what has happened. But he assures Juno that he has no malice whatever toward the Greeks, and that after he has fulfilled his promise to Thetis he will put Achilles into the battle "and give your fellows a really resounding victory." Acting on Jupiter's orders, Juno restores the "status quo ante."

Suddenly a number of shadows pass over the stage—"A convoy of Shades," explains Mercury, "on their way to the Styx and Avernus." To satisfy the curiosity of Venus he goes out with a butterfly net to catch a few. Meanwhile Nestor's voice rises from below, praying to the gods, reminding them of their promises that the Greeks should return to their homes. "Turn off that horrid thing!" says Juno. Mercury returns with four torn and bloody shades—Machaon, Hecamede, the orderly, and the infantryman. Juno thinks it may be possible to do something for Machaon since he had a god's blood in his veins, but with distaste she orders Mercury to restore the others to their convoy. But the orderly interrupts, and as the shadows continue to pass he bounds up to Jupiter's empty seat and in scathing language passes judgment on the gods. Jupiter, who has entered unobserved, now speaks, but no longer in his mythological character. Remarking that the Shades have missed their convoy, he says he will turn them into three stars and call them the Rebels. "They will be very interesting to astronomers in a few thousand years."

The satire on war is expressed through the humanity of the Rebels: through the idealism of the orderly, who thinks he is fighting for a way of life; through the bewilderment of the infantryman as to what concern it is of theirs that "One of them there Trojan Gussies pinched a general's Judy"; through nurse Hecamede's lack of enthusiasm for the "victory" which passed half the army through her hospital tent. The play satirizes the callous attitude of the General Staff toward the common soldier. It satirizes the shallow heartiness of Nestor, who tells the dying boy they'll get him patched up all right, "and you can have a spot of leave at Lemnos and buck around a bit with the girls and then come back and have another slap at them." It satirizes the snobbery of Juno: "Were the other persons of any importance?" she asks Machaon. "Of no great importance, my Lady," he answers, "except to themselves and to those who held them dear." There is satire and shock in Vulcan's rambling explanation of a gadget the size of a fist, equipped with a mechanism which, when released, will "split the atom and loose enough energy to lift Olympus off its hurdies."

The Rebels express various attitudes towards the gods. The faith of the orderly knows no bounds after Juno appears to him in a vision saying, "Charley boy, take it easy. I'm here to see your push through." The infantryman, more skeptical, asks what's to keep her from coming back tomorrow and saying, "Sorry, . . . I made a mistake. Forget it." Machaon believes everything that happens is part of a chain of cause and effect, and that if we go back far enough we get a First Cause. And he believes the gods are the First Cause. But Hecamede does not believe the gods "give a damn." She thinks the creative impulse itself is a great deception of the gods:

> Hecamede: I think they make the birds sing and build their nests and the stags go crazy and the flowers blossom. And we and the birds and the stags and the flowers feel the Spring and the gaiety in us and think the gods must be good after all. Then the birds are netted and the stags are torn by hounds and the flowers are trampled, and we know what it all means.
>
> Machaon: What does it all mean?
>
> Hecamede: It means they want to make more birds and stags, flowers and people to be trapped and trampled and torn. That's really what they want. . . . What do they care?

The groping and striving and misplaced faith of the Rebels are all the more poignant in the light of the duplicity and frivolity of the gods. The character of Jupiter, however, requires special consideration. Early in the play there is a suggestion of another mythology when in response to Thetis' concern for Achilles Jupiter says he must think of all: "There are quarter of a million men in the Dardanelles, all made more or less in my image and capable of rejoicing and suffering, of foresight and afterthought." Most striking is his duality, a quality suggested by his appearing "in two minds about something" and emphasized in the words of Juno: "It is not possible to understand you. . . . You are . . . the inscrutable Master of all things. The sower, the reaper, the disheveller, the builder-up." The idea of duality is further supported by the words of the scene shifters, with implications of long centuries of building and destroying:

> We are the scene shifters.
> Ages after ages,
> Centenary after centenary
> We ha'e shifted the scenery.
> We heaved up the Pyramids;
> We dinged doon Persepolis;
> We hung the Hanging Gardens;

We made Atahualpa's Palace,
And here one for Solomon,
And there one for Semiramis.
Hamburg and Hiroshima
We blasted into shards. . . .

Finally, Jupiter speaks in the accents of a Master Experimenter—one who does not himself know the final shape of things but is compelled by his very nature to keep on experimenting. He tells of his restless childhood, and of a day when his mother pulled off a chunk of Chaos from the round on the kitchen dresser and threw it at him. "There," she said, "Sonny, take that into the yard and do whatever you like with it." He tells of moulding his bit of Chaos until it looked "something like an egg and something like a sausage." He called his little toy the Universe. But he found his Universe hard to control because it was full of "mad, meaningless, fighting forces." He kept working, however, until by arranging the forces in a certain way he got a thing called Life. "Life is very interesting," he says. "I am still working on its permutations and combinations."

On being questioned by the Rebels, he says, he does not pretend to understand these matters, but he has noticed that the little lump at the end of the spinal cord of some of the higher apes has taken on "extensive and peculiar functions," one of which "appears to consist in explaining me and my little Universe. . . . Perhaps, in time, these little objects will attain to the properties and activities of the Immortal Gods themselves." This is the concept of a Master Experimenter "who is in a sense my Father" and of man as one of the experiments and a tool of the Experimenter. "I have not nearly completed my Universe," adds Jupiter. "There is plenty of time. Plenty of time. You must have patience."

In *The Baikie Charivari* or *The Seven Prophets*[16] (1952), the evil with which the dramatist is concerned is the disorder in modern society. This disorder is viewed through the eyes and mind of Pounce-Pellott, Britain's erstwhile representative to India, who has come home to Baikie to retire. But Baikie has changed greatly since he left, having discarded its old values and adopted new ones. "Allah, the Disheveller, had been there afore him." The play dramatizes the role of Pounce-Pellott as rebel, judge, and truth-seeker as the prophets of confusion pursue him, each on behalf of his own ideology.

The play moves back and forth from naturalism to fantasy and makes considerable use of expressionistic devices. The hero is named for two of his famous ancestors—Pontius Pilate, who was both judge

[16] London, 1953.

and seeker after truth, and Punch of Punch-and-Judy fame, a born rebel against authority.[17] The wife and seventeen-year-old daughter of Pounce are Judy and Baby of the Punch legend, and the seven prophets are derived from the same source, though greatly transformed.

The pursuit theme is established in the Prologue. A devil mask appears in the moon, and the Devil, like Beelzebub of *The Sunlight Sonata*, broods over his town and its inhabitants:

> This is my Baikie. . . .
> Lulled by the wash of the waves of the Clyde
> And soothed by the sicht of white sails and the cries of the sea
> birds. . . .

When Dr. Beadle appears the devil mask vanishes, but the Devil's voice comes down to him, speaking the words God spoke to Job's Satan:

> Hae ye considered my servant Pounce-Pellott?
> There isna his marrow in a' the yerd—
> A wyse, independent, sel'saining carle,
> Wha gangs his gate and lippens to nane. . . .

Beadle supposes the voice to be that of the Almighty himself—a supposition which supports the assertion of Beelzebub in *The Sunlight Sonata* that the God men worship is really the Devil—and promises to do his best to shake Pounce-Pellott's spiritual pride.

One by one the seven prophets pay a visit to Pounce, who invites them all to a symposium at which they are to teach him how he and his family can best adjust themselves to their new life. But at the gathering five nights later confusion knows no limit. Each prophet champions his own cause and attacks the others. They interrupt and insult each other; they indulge in irrelevancies; they introduce arguments within arguments. Pounce tries to understand all viewpoints but finds no sense in any of them. Baby wails, "I didn't want to be born into this bloody world." Finally, as rainbow lights flicker to Punch-and-Judy music, Pounce lays about him with his stick and kills all the prophets. Then, as in the legend, the Devil appears:[18]

> Pounce: Have you come to take me?
> Devil: I was wondering.
> Pounce: I'm ready.
> Devil: I'm thinking you've jouked me for the moment. It may be you've
> jinked me a'thegither. Time will tell us.

[17] Bridie notes a tradition that Pontius Pilate was a Scotsman, and another tradition that Punch is a projection of Pontius Pilate. "Note on *The Baikie Charivari*," *Ibid.*, xiii–xiv.

[18] Walter Elliott notes the similarity between this encounter and that of Peer Gynt with the Button-Moulder. *Ibid.*, Preface, ix.

Pounce: Can I wait for time?
Devil: I dinna ken.

A major aspect of the play is its satire on the values of the modern world. The power of Money is represented by Mrs. Jemima Lee Crowe, an American woman publisher who offers Pounce $10,000 for the world rights of his Indian reminiscences, with more to come. The authority of Science, with emphasis on Psychiatry, is represented by Dr. Jean Pothecary, who sees Pounce's return to his mother country as a "regression to foetal life." When Pounce expresses dismay at the scientist's invention of methods to destroy mankind, she exclaims defensively, "But we don't *control* them."

Joey Mascara represents Anarchism, whether in art, morals, or government. When he nominates the artist as the truest interpreter of God's meaning, Mrs. Crowe remarks that art is "infernally unintelligible" and he had better provide them with a code. His moral anarchism is suggested by the circumstances which caused him to lose his job as organist in Beadle's church. ("What do the wee girls join the choir for?" he asks. "It's not as if they could sing.") His political anarchism appears in his debate with Mr. Copper, Controller for the Ministry of Interference, who represents the authority of Government. When Copper speaks pompously of the thousand "channels" that must be constantly checked and controlled, Mascara retorts that the Government should "let us alone." He objects especially to "wee bullies" who "take the law into their own hands." Thus the mutual recriminations of these two satirize the extremes of authoritarianism and anarchism.

The sanctions of Religion and Communism are represented by Dr. Beadle and Ketch the plumber, each of whom accuses the other of adherence to plain dogma. As the argument moves into fantasy, Mascara sums up the distortions of both ideologies:

> Old Beadle found a baby in a byre
> Who grew to be a poet and talked sense.
> Beadle forgot the sense
> And he twisted the poetry till no sane man
>   could believe a word of it. . . .
> Young Ketch found a hope for the poor and wretched
> In a system for binding the bullies in chains.
> And now, by Heavens, we're all in chains. . . .

But the main interest centers in Pounce-Pellott as he rejects all these forces that would dominate and regulate him. When he has killed all the prophets except Beadle and Ketch, he declares that he will not lie down and be crushed:

> I must stand up against the millstones.
> I must split them in four with my human hands.
> I must breathe once more.

Pounce is not only a rebel; he is a *concerned* rebel—concerned not so much for himself as for the next generation. His concern is symbolized by a dream in which he sees Baby about to be initiated into a coven of witches. Just as the Devil is about to give her the pinch that will make her membership official, Pounce awakes terrified.

As truth-seeker Pounce gets no answer but "I dinna ken." These words, usually spoken by a minor character, are frequently heard in Bridie's plays. In *The Kitchen Comedy*,[19] as a materialist, a serialist, and a traditionalist discuss theology, one turns to the village idiot and asks: "What do you think about it all, Hughie? What do you think we are here for, and what do you think is going to happen to us?" "I dinna ken," giggles Hughie. In *John Knox*,[20] someone asks a mulatto clog-dancer, "Jerry, what do you think is the meaning of religion?" "I dunno," answers Jerry. In *The Queen's Comedy* Jupiter himself does not know the answers, nor does the Devil in *The Baikie Charivari*. The pressure of time gives special urgency to Pounce's questions:

> Pounce: Can I wait for time?
> Devil: I dinna ken.
> Pounce: If you don't know, who knows? Nobody knows. Nobody knows.
> I've killed all those fools who pretended to know. And so—
> and so—
> With the soothsayers littered about the stage
> That I slew in my rage,
> Who did not know—and no more do I—
> I must jest again and await my reply.

The last line, expressing Pounce's courage as well as his frustration, makes the point that Jupiter makes with the Rebels and truth-seekers of *The Queen's Comedy*: "You must have patience."

But hope dawns as young Toby the plumber's apprentice appears out of nowhere and asks to marry Baby—

> Pounce: I don't know who you are.
> Toby: Neither does anybody, Mister. Neither do I. You see, I've no richt begun, yet.

But as Baby is willing, Pounce gives his consent. Professor Renwick sees this detail as an expression of faith in life which defeats the Devil.[21] It is the Master Experimenter's newest experiment.

[19] *Susannah and the Elders and Other Plays* (London, 1940).
[20] *John Knox and Other Plays* (London, 1949).
[21] W. L. Renwick, "James Bridie the Playwright," *The College Courant*, 3 (1951), 98.

The six plays that have been discussed show Bridie himself as truth-seeker. They show his persistent effort to synthesize the Calvinist idea of God with the Huxleian concept of an evolutionary process. They also show his effort to include in the evolutionary concept both good and evil as reciprocating opposites, thereby denying the idea of a dualistic universe with evil as an independent force. He comes near achieving a complete synthesis of these ideas in *The Queen's Comedy* with the portrayal of Jupiter as a Master Experimenter who combines the functions of creating and destroying and is in a sense his Father, and of man as one of the experiments and a tool of the Experimenter. It must be admitted that the Calvinistic aspect of this portrayal is weak. Frequent references to Calvinistic doctrine and the frequent appearance of fantasy devils reveal the dramatist's profound moral and emotional involvement with Calvinism; but the core of his thought, his experimental approach, and his suspension of final judgment are Huxleian.

NORTHERN ILLINOIS UNIVERSITY

ALLAN H. MACLAINE

The *Christis Kirk* Tradition:

Its Evolution in Scots Poetry to Burns

Part II

The Sixteenth Century

During the fifteenth century, as we have seen, the *Christis Kirk* tradition had become firmly established as a distinctive Scottish genre and had already begun to extend its influence into other kinds of poetry. Beginning as a burlesque poem describing the antics of country folk on holiday, the genre had, in *Symmie and his Bruder,* been adapted as a vehicle for a metrical tale satirizing the corruption of the friars. Moreover, by the end of the century the tradition, in Dunbar's *Turnament,* had exerted its influence upon a mock tournament poem ridiculing common tradesmen of the town. During the sixteenth century, the declining period of ancient Scots poetry, this *Christis Kirk* influence was to become steadily broader and deeper, especially in combination with the mock tournament genre.

Sir David Lindsay's entertaining piece written for the amusement of King James V and his court in 1538 and entitled *The Justing Betuix James Watsoun and Jhone Barbour*[1] is the next surviving poem to show clear signs of *Christis Kirk* influence. Watsoun and Barbour were real people, minor functionaries in the King's household; and Lindsay's poem may well be a burlesque of an actual encounter between the two. At any rate, the *Justing* is a lively performance in pentameter couplets, and, in its portrayal of the two contestants, is strongly reminiscent both of Dunbar's *Turnament* and of *Christis Kirk on the Green.* For example, Lindsay

---

[1] See *The Works of Sir David Lindsay of the Mount, 1490-1555,* ed. Douglas Hamer, Scottish Text Soc., 3rd Ser. 1 (Edinburgh, 1930), I, 113-116. Publications of the Scottish Text Soc. are hereafter referred to as STS. As in Part I of this essay, I have slightly modernized the texts of passages quoted as follows: the "thorn" letter has been replaced by "th"; the letter "z," when it has the sound of "y" (as in "ze"="ye"), is rendered as "y"; "ff" where it simply indicates capitalization is given as "F"; all abbreviations are spelled out; and modern punctuation and capitalization are supplied throughout. Otherwise the original spelling is retained.

depicts Watsoun and Barbour as being ridiculously inept and bungling in the handling of their weapons, as in this couplet:

I am rycht sure gude Iames had been vndone,
War not that Iohne his mark tuke be the mone.

The greater part of the poem is, in fact, taken up with this kind of satire on the clumsiness of the "campiouns," a satiric method which was almost certainly suggested to Lindsay by the absurdities of the archery contest in *Christis Kirk*, where precisely the same kind of effect is achieved. Lindsay's emphasis upon the essential cowardice of his mock heroes, together with the detail introduced briefly at the end to the effect that both Watsoun and Barbour have befouled themselves during the course of the battle, recalls both *The Turnament* and *Christis Kirk*. Finally, Lindsay's indebtedness to *Christis Kirk* is made indisputable by the fact that one of his couplets contains direct echoes in its phraseology and rime of the earlier poem:

Twa that wes heidmen of the heird
Ran vpoun vderis lyk rammis;
Than followit feymen rycht on affeird,   *crofters in warlike array*
Bet on with barrow trammis.   *barrow shafts*
             (*Christis Kirk*, stanza 19)

"Yit, thocht thy braunis be lyk twa barrow trammis,
Defend thee, man!" Than ran thay to, lyk rammis.
             (*Justing*, ll. 33-34)

Lindsay's *Justing*, like Dunbar's *Turnament*, is a mock tournament poem influenced by the *Christis Kirk* tradition. But whereas in *The Turnament* that influence was only partial, in the *Justing* it became important and decisive; for, as we have seen, Lindsay owed to *Christis Kirk* not merely the incidental rime and one or two other details noted above, but also (to *Christis Kirk* and *The Turnament*) the suggestion for the basic satiric method of his poem.

In yet a third poem combining the mock tournament and *Christis Kirk* genres, the *Christis Kirk* influence becomes finally dominant. The work in question is Alexander Scott's *Justing and Debait vp at the Drum betuix William Adamsone and Johine Sym*,[2] written about 1560 and preserved in the Bannatyne Manuscript. The story concerns a quarrel between two lads of Dalkeith, near Edinburgh, over a girl. Judging from the "Envoy" at the end, the girl had been seduced by William Adamson while

---

[2] *The Poems of Alexander Scott*, ed. James Cranstoun, STS, O. S. 36 (Edinburgh, 1896), pp. 9-15. The same text may be found in *The Bannatyne Manuscript*, ed. W. Tod Ritchie, STS, 2nd Ser. 22, 23, 26, 3rd Ser. 5, 4 vols. (Edinburgh, 1928, 1928, 1930, 1934), II 268; this edition is hereafter cited as *Bann. MS*.

engaged to John Sym. Discovering this, Sym challenged his rival to a tournament to decide the issue at "the Drum," a house located between Dalkeith and Edinburgh. The poem opens with an elaborate and amusing mock-heroic build-up, exaggerating the importance of the occasion and the prowess of the two champions. But after all the preparations have been taken care of, the tournament turns out to be a complete fiasco when it is discovered that one of the onlooking villagers has mischievously stolen the spears. It now being impossible to hold the tournament, Adamson and Sym return to Dalkeith with their retinues of villagers, and everyone gets thoroughly drunk. At this point, Sym, the smaller of the two men, begins vehemently to renew his challenges; but Adamson refuses to be drawn into a fight, thus incurring the jeers of the crowd at his cowardice. Some ludicrous horseplay ensues, until nightfall puts a stop to their activities and everyone goes home leaving the issue unsettled. Subsequently, according to the "Envoy," the cowardly Adamson slips out of town and goes into hiding, leaving the girl in the lurch.

It will readily be seen from this summary that whereas the opening stanzas of Scott's poem describing the preparations for the battle are clearly modeled on the mock tournament genre as developed by Dunbar and Lindsay, the greater part of the poem, with its scenes of drunkenness, horseplay, and general riot, is very similar in subject matter to *Peblis* and *Christis Kirk*. The themes and tone of Scott's satire, too, are obviously in the *Christis Kirk* tradition. His characters, though not rustics, are common folk of the little town of Dalkeith whose behavior is subjected to tolerant and good-natured ridicule—once again, for the amusement of a cultured reading public. As in Dunbar's *Turnament* and Lindsay's *Justing*, satire of boastfulness and cowardice, likewise a prominent theme in *Christis Kirk on the Green*, is present here also.

If Scott's *Justing and Debait* is akin to the *Christis Kirk* tradition in its subject matter, it is even more strikingly imitative in its form, being written in the strictly defined *Christis Kirk* stanza. Here is one of its most ingenious stanzas, wherein Scott sets up his whimsically expressed physical contrast between William Adamson and John Sym:

> Thair wes ane bettir and ane worse,
> I wald that it wer wittin;   *known*
> For William wichttar wes of corse   *stronger; body*
> Nor Sym, and bettir knittin.
> Sym said he sett nocht by his forss,
> Bot hecht he sowld be hittin,   *promised*
> And he micht counter Will on horss;   *if*
> For Sym wes bettir sittin / Nor Will,
> Vp at the Drum that day.

Here we have once again the exacting two-rime pattern in the octave, together with a consistent though moderate degree of alliteration throughout. In the metrical form of his poem, Scott clearly followed *Christis Kirk* with scrupulous fidelity. That *Christis Kirk* itself was his model is further proved by the fact that his refrains ("Up at the Drum that day" and "Up at Dalkeith that day") remind one both of the extended refrains in the second and last stanzas of *Christis Kirk* (Bannatyne text)—"At Chryst Kirk of the grene that day"—and of the "that day' 'bob lines in stanzas 6 and 9, and were certainly suggested by them. It is worth noting also that in his second to last stanza Scott changes his refrain to "Within the toun that nicht." All three refrains are significant because they were to give the hint for later modifications of the stanza.

Alexander Scott was chiefly a courtly love poet, a polished and versatile artist; and it is, therefore, not surprising that his *Justing and Debait* exhibits the sharp wit, technical competence, and easy mastery of form which characterize the work of this gifted maker. His *Justing* is a skillful and entertaining work. In spite of its obvious merits, however, one feels that Scott's poem does not quite succeed in equalling the power and charm of either *Christis Kirk* or *Peblis*. The great effectiveness of the two earlier pieces is achieved mainly through an overpoweringly realistic and lively treatment. In Scott's *Justing* this effect of simple and vivid realism is blurred by the mock-heroic treatment of the first few stanzas, so that although his poem is very similar in content its scenes lack the imaginative boldness, the feeling of truth and actuality so strikingly conveyed in *Christis Kirk* and *Peblis*. We must say then that the influence of the mock tournament genre upon the *Justing and Debait* tends to weaken its effectiveness, and that the added sophistication of Scott's style detracts from the power of his poem, making it fall short of the superb vitality of *Christis Kirk* and *Peblis*. Nevertheless, the *Justing and Debait* remains a highly creditable and amusing performance.

Although Scott's *Justing and Debait* is the latest surviving sixteenth-century poem which belongs unmistakably within the *Christis Kirk* tradition, there remains a small and varied group of other pieces which in one way or another show evidence of the pervasive influence of the genre. Foremost among these is Sir David Lindsay's massive morality play, *Ane Pleasant Satyre of the Thrie Estaits* (ca. 1640), which contains many scattered reminiscences of rimes and phrasing from *Christis Kirk*.[3] For example, the rime pattern of the final stanza of *Christis Kirk* ("aix—

[3] For a full discussion of these parallels, see my article "*Christis Kirk on the Grene* and Sir David Lindsay's *Satyre of the Thrie Estaits*," *JEGP*, LVI (1957), 596-601.

fidder—smaix—bruder—glaikis—muder—paikis—vdir") is echoed in the
following passage from the first part of Lindsay's play:

> *Sowtars Wyfe*: Cummer this is my counsall, lo: *woman*
> Ding ze the tane, and I the vther.   *beat*
> *Taylovrs Wyfe*: I am content be Godis mother,
> I think for mee thay huirsone smaiks,   *whoreson fellows*
> Thay serue richt weill to get thair paiks.   *deserve; drubbings*
>
>   (ll. 1317-21)[4]

And further echoes of this same rime pattern from *Christis Kirk* crop up
in different combinations in no fewer than six other places in Lindsay's
Satyre (lines 166-168; 185, 189; 671-673; 1868, 1870-71; 4178-79;
and 4586-87). Similarly, the "stendis-endis" rime in the sixth stanza of
Christis Kirk recurs twice in Lindsay (lines 4353-54, 4359-60) in an
almost identical context, and there is a striking reminiscence of the
opening lines of *Christis Kirk* in Lindsay's

> For quhy sic reformation as I weine
> Into Scotland was never hard nor seine.
>
>   (ll. 3721-22)

It is worth noting further that nearly all of Lindsay's borrowing from
Christis Kirk appear in the *Satyre* in scenes where the subject matter, tone,
and characters most nearly approximate those of *Christis Kirk*—that is, in
scenes of slapstick comedy and horseplay, or in comic scenes involving
the clownish "vice" characters. Lindsay's debt to *Christis Kirk* in his
great morality play is a further and most convincing illustration of the
extent to which this poem had seeped into the consciousness of cultured
Scots at least, and had become by the mid-sixteenth century a part of the
national mind and memory.

Among anonymous pieces of the sixteenth century showing *Christis
Kirk* influence may be mentioned a poem preserved in the Maitland Folio
Manuscript (and therefore written about 1580) called *Of Ladies Bewties*,
beginning "Our Lordis ar so degenerat."[5] This is a satiric attack on noble
Scottish ladies for their extravagance in dress, and as such is foreign in
theme and tone to the *Christis Kirk* genre. It is, however, written in the
distinctive stanza, without the bobwheel. Similarly, in the Maitland
Quarto Manuscript there is a song entitled *Ane ballat to be songe with the
tuine of "luifer come to luifeiris dore &c,"* beginning "O blissed bird

---

[4] All quotations and line references from Lindsay's play are taken from James
Kinsley's excellent edition, *Ane Satyre of the Thrie Estaits* (London, 1954.).

[5] *The Maitland Folio Manuscript*, ed. Wm. A. Craigie, STS, 2nd Ser. 7 (Edinburgh, 1919), I, 66-68.

brichtest of all."[6] This piece, a conventional medieval love lyric, is also written in a modified form of the *Christis Kirk* stanza. The author uses a stanza of six instead of eight lines of alternating tetrameter and trimeter, followed by a trimeter tag line which acts as a unifying refrain ("Have pitie I yow pray") and is similar in effect to the bobwheel. Judging from the language and style of the song, it probably dates from the late fifteenth or early sixteenth century. These two specimens suggest that the influence of the *Christis Kirk* stanzaic form extended in the sixteenth century to types of poetry utterly unlike the genre for which it was originally invented.

Additionally, several of the themes, artistic purposes and methods inherent in the *Christis Kirk* tradition crop up in other poems and ballads of the sixteenth century. Perhaps the best of these is the vigorous and irresistible farce called *The Wife of Auchtermuchty*.[7] Here an age-old folk theme of marital disagreement is treated in the *Christis Kirk* style, with precisely the same kind of·sharply realistic detail, robust humor, and good-natured satire presented from the point of view of an amused and superior onlooker. Similar but less effective treatments of discord between husband and wife—a theme, by the way, which appears in both *Peblis* and *Christis Kirk*—may be found in such pieces as *The Dumb Wife, Wa Worth Maryage*, and *God gif I were wedo now*, all of which are in the Maitland Folio Manuscript.[8] *The Wowing of Jok and Jynny* in the Bannatyne Manuscript[9] is a highly successful aristocratic satire on rustic marriage diplomacy, and is a very early specimen, probably the prototype, of a genre which became increasingly popular in Scotland through the seventeenth century and well into the eighteenth.[10]

The five poems noted above are merely representative of a fairly large body of such work surviving from the sixteenth century. The themes of these pieces are, of course, universal, going far beyond the *Christis Kirk* tradition and belonging rather to a common fund of folk ideas. Not the themes themselves, but rather the treatments of them are significant here. At a time when the *Christis Kirk* poems were evidently enjoying wide popularity among the reading classes of Scotland, we find

---

[6] See *The Maitland Quarto Manuscript*, ed. Wm. A. Craigie, STS, 2nd Ser. 9 (Edinburgh, 1920), pp. 112-118.

[7] *Bann. MS.*, II, 320-324.

[8] Ed. Craigie, I, 69-70, 243-244, 244-245.

[9] *Bann. MS.*, III, 15-18.

[10] For later specimens of this type, see, e.g., *Maggie's Tocher, Jocky said to Jenny*, and *The Carl he came o'er the Croft* in *The Tea-Table Miscellany*, ed. Allan Ramsay, 14th ed. (Edinburgh, 1768), I, 26-28, 70-71; II, 117-118.

a considerable number of these other poems appearing, poems which are not strictly within the tradition, but which treat a variety of folk themes in the *Christis Kirk* way. It would seem, then, highly probable that the composition of these new art poems depicting the folk ways of the Scottish peasantry from a humorous and satiric point of view was stimulated by the broad popularity and influence of the older *Christis Kirk* tradition in sixteenth-century Scotland.

The Seventeenth Century

During the latter part of the sixteenth century Scots poetry on the literary level died a slow and lingering death. With the triumph of Knoxian Calvinism there came a general stifling of poetic composition on a large scale, since poetry, along with dancing and other "lewd" entertainments, was proscribed as conducive to idleness and sin. This powerful Calvinist prohibition, together with the removal of the court (the center of poetic patronage) from Edinburgh to London in 1603, and the overwhelming influence of the great English poets of the Renaissance upon the few Scottish gentlemen who continued to cultivate the art, brought about an almost complete extinction of the old national tradition in art poetry, until the vernacular revival which took place in the early years of the eighteenth century. The seventeenth century thus represents an enormous and almost fatal gap in the natural development of native Scottish poetry, a gap which was only partially bridged in three different ways. In the first place, the purely folk literature, chiefly in the form of popular ballads and songs, continued to thrive in oral transmission in spite of Calvinist suppression. Secondly, a number of Scottish gentlemen who were genuinely interested in poetry continued to honor the names and (more important) to preserve in manuscript the works of the old makers, thus saving them from complete oblivion. And finally, the *Christis Kirk* tradition actually continued to develop through the long winter of the seventeenth century.

The persistence of the *Christis Kirk* tradition through the seventeenth century is indeed a remarkable fact, and one not easily explained except in terms of the innate vitality of the genre. Its survival during these dark years is perhaps the most dramatic illustration of its enduring and inextinguishable popularity among the Scottish people. Rigid Calvinist censorship during this century permitted the printing of only five major works of the old national poetry, four of them being of a didactic or moralistic nature. These latter were the verse chronicles of Barbour and Blind Harry, Henryson's *Testament of Cresseid*, and the works of Sir David Lindsay, the unofficial poet laureate of the Reformation in Scotland. Apart from these, the only poem of the old tradition to be consistently reprinted in the seventeenth century was *Christis Kirk on the Green*, which saw at least five separate editions, in 1643, 1660, 1663, 1684, and 1691.[11] Why this poem, rather than Henryson's *Fables*, for example, or countless other quite respectable poems of the old makers, should have escaped the Kirk's disapproval of secular poetry in general remains a mystery. One can only conclude that an insistent popular demand kept the poem alive and in print despite the official opposition to such works.

Apart from these reprints of *Christis Kirk*, there is further proof of the continued vitality of the genre during the seventeenth century in the existence of a small group of new poems written during this barren period and undoubtedly under the influence of *Christis Kirk*. The most interesting of these is a boisterous macaronic (half Latin, half Scots) poem entitled *Polemo-Middinia* ("The Midden Fight").[12] This piece has been attributed to Wililam Drummond of Hawthornden; and, although the attribution is open to some question, the probabilities seem to be that Drummond was indeed its author, as Drummond's editor, L. E. Kastner, has ably demonstrated.[13] At any rate, *Polemo-Middinia* is a seventeenth-century poem (the first known edition appears to date from the 1640's);[14] and it is significant that in at least two seventeenth-century printings of the poem, those of 1684 and 1691 (Gibson's),[15] the text was bound together with the text of *Christis Kirk on the Green*, showing that from the first the close kinship of *Polemo-Middinia* with the older poem was clearly recognized.

In the subject matter, type of humor, and general tone and purpose of *Polemo-Middinia*, the influence of the whole *Christis Kirk* tradition is obvious enough. Drummond takes as his comic situation a violent altercation between the households of two neighboring Fifeshire lairds, Scot of Scotstarvet and Cunningham of Newbarns, an altercation which may well have had its counterpart in real life. In the poem, the Scotstarvet people, rallied by their laird, attempt to assert their claim to a right-of-way across Newbarns land by arming themselves with pitchforks and defiantly escorting a string of carts laden with dung past the windows of Newbarns

---

[11] For bibliographical data on all of these editions, see Wm. Geddie, *A Bibliography of Middle Scots Poets*, STS, O.S. 61 (Edinburgh, 1912), pp. 95-96.

[12] For text and notes on this poem, see *The Poetical Works of William Drummond of Hawthornden*, ed. L. E. Kastner (Manchester, 1913), II, 321-326, 418-424.

[13] For a full statement of the evidence on this question, see Kastner, II, 418-420.

[14] See Kastner, I, xcii; II, 420.

[15] See Geddie, *Bibliography*, p. 96, for data.

house itself. The whole procession is triumphantly led by a bagpiper, and is composed of a motley crew of rustics and household servants listed in a mock heroic roll call:

> Hic aderant *Geordie Akinhedius,* & little *Johnus . . .*
> *Andrew Alshinderus,* & *Jamie Thomsonus,* & alter   *Alexander*
> (Heu pudet, ignoro nomen) slaveri-beardus homo,
> Qui pottas dightabat, & assam jecerat extra.   *wiped the pots; ashes*

Meanwhile, "Neberna," the mistress of Newbarns, observing what is afoot, decides to put up a fight and calls out her own comic crew, who are strongly reinforced by the women of the house. At the approach of the procession, "Neberna" herself rushes out furiously brandishing a "rousty gully" (large rusty knife):

> Nec mora, marchavit foras longo ordine turma,
> Ipsa prior *Neberna* suis stout facta ribauldis,
> Roustaeam manibus gestans furibunda gouloeam,   *rusty; gully*
> Tandem muckcreilios vocat ad pellmellia fleidos.   *muck-creel bearers*
> Ite, ait, uglei felloës, si quis modo posthac
> Muckifer has nostras tentet crossare fenestras,
> Juro ego quad ejus longum extrahabo thrapellum   *"thrapple"* (*throat*)
> Et totam rivabo faciem, luggasque gulae hoc   *"reeve"* (*tear*); *"lugs"* (*ears*)
> Ex capite cuttabo ferox, totumque videbo
> Heart-bloodum fluere in terram. Sic verba finivit.

The Scotstarvet folk are momentarily repulsed by this dire threat, but presently return to the attack and a mad free-for-all ensues:

> O qualis hurlie burlie fuit! namque alteri nemo
> Ne vel foot-breddum yerdae yeeldare volebat . . .   *"yerd"* (*earth*)

In the end the Newbarns women, armed with various utensils and led by the heroic "Gylla," succeed in crushing the invaders.

The *Christis Kirk* flavor of *Polemo-Middinia* is unmistakable. Here we have once again the wild and barbarous brawl between clownish country folk, the swift tempo with frequent transitions, the highlighting of details within the framework of the scene as a whole, the use of dialogue to lend reality, the brief character sketches, the robust style and uninhibited language—all of which we have noted as characteristic of the genre. The pitched battle and the comic exposure of cowardice remind one of both *Peblis* and *Christis Kirk*, while the mock-heroic build-up recalls Scott's *Justing and Debait*. In short, *Polemo-Middinia* has all the earmarks of the *Christis Kirk* tradition, except for its verse form. Above all, the general tone and point of view of *Polemo-Middinia* fit perfectly into the *Christis Kirk* pattern. The poem is a good-humored satire of Scottish country life and characters as viewed by a detached and intellecual spectator, and is obviously intended to delight the cultured minority with its incongruous combination of homely dunghill subject matter and sophisticated linguistic wit. As such, *Polemo-Middinia* is an ingenious and entertaining piece of work, a distinctive contribution to the *Christis Kirk* tradition.

Apart from the obvious connection with the *Christis Kirk* tradition, *Polemo-Middinia* has several interesting features of its own. If the poem be Drummond's (as it seems to be), it stands alone among the works of that smooth and courtly writer as a boisterous and uninhibited aberration from the norm. The conception of the poem doubtless came to Drummond as a result of his knowledge of both macaronic poetry and the *Christis Kirk* tradition. Thus, assuming Drummond's authorship, *Polemo-Middinia* proves that he was certainly familiar with the poetry of his native land, although he chose to follow the great English poets of the Renaissance in the bulk of his formal work. The poem has, moreover, two or three characteristics which are new to the *Christis Kirk* genre. For one thing, it is a tri-lingual effort—part Latin, part English, part Scots—a fact which creates difficulties for modern readers and which has, no doubt, contributed to the neglect and obscurity in which the poem has lingered. Secondly, it contains a mock epic invocation (to "nymphs" and "skippers" of Fife) and mock epic catalogues of names, devices of classical literature which had appeared in none of the earlier specimens of the *Christis Kirk* tradition.

Another notable seventeenth-century poem in the *Christis Kirk* genre is the rollicking song called *The Blythsome Bridal*, attributed (uncertainly) to Francis Sempill of Beltrees (died 1682).[16] *The Blythsome Bridal*, being in "plain braid Scots," is much better known than *Polemo-Middinia* and has been frequently anthologized. It is, however, significantly related to Drummond's piece, and not merely by virtue of belonging to the same genre. A recent re-examination of the two poems has led me to believe that *Polemo-Middinia* was, in fact, an important source for *The Blythsome Bridal*. We have already noted in Drummond's poem the mock epic catalogue of names as a feature not found in earlier *Christis Kirk* poems. There is a similar, but more extensive, comic roll call of the wedding guests in *The Blythsome Bridal*—a roll call which includes not only several of the same names that appear in *Polemo-Middinia*, but also some of the same epithets attached to the same names. Thus, "plouky-fac'd Wattie" (*Polemo-Middinia*, *l.* 38) becomes "plouckie fac't Wat"

---

[16] On the authorship question, see James Paterson ed. *The Poems of the Sempills of Beltrees* (Edinburgh, 1849), pp. 106-110 (text of poem on pp. 67-70); and Thomas F. Henderson, *Scottish Vernacular Literature* (Edinburgh, 1910), p. 393.

(*The Blythsome Bridal,* l. 23); and "gliedamque Ketaeam" (l. 85) becomes "gleed Katie" (l. 46). Similarly, the epithet "heavi-arstus" (l. 39) turns us as "happer-ars'd" in *The Blythsome Bridal* (l. 44). There are also simple repetitions of names such as "Andrew" and "Geordie;" and there is an allusion to "Mons Meg," the great cannon at Edinburgh Castle, in both poems. Finally, most interestingly and conclusively, the author of *The Blythsome Bridal* incorporates in his poem what seems to be a misreading of *Polemo-Middinia.* In the latter poem (ll. 131, 136), Drummond uses two nouns, "Gilliwyppum" and "Gilliwamphra," both meaning "a hard blow," which he unaccountably capitalizes as though they were proper names.[17] The author of *The Blythsome Bridal,* apparently misreading these words as character names, includes a "Gillie-Whimple" as one of his wedding guests (l. 42). In view of these correspondences, which cannot *all* be coincidental, it seems impossible not to believe that the author of *The Blythsome Bridal* was drawing freely on *Polemo-Middinia* for his comic roll call of names. The fact is significant in showing how firmly established, how closely knit the *Christis Kirk* tradition had become. These two seventeenth-century pieces are not only clearly related to the older *Christis Kirk* poems; they are also linked to each other.

The Blythsome Bridal certainly dates from about the middle of the seventeenth-century, and probably circulated on broadsides before it was included in James Watson's pioneering anthology, *A Choice Collection of Comic and Serious Scots Poems, both Ancient and Modern* (Edinburgh, 1706-9-11), the earliest known printing of the poem. It is a shorter and less ambitious work than most of the *Christis Kirk* poems, containing only nine eight-line stanzas, with the opening four lines acting as a refrain repeated after each octave:

> Fy let us all to the Briddel,
>   For there will be lilting there,
> For Jockie's to be married to Maggie,
>   The lass with the gauden hair.   *golden*

It will be seen from this sample that the verse form of *The Blythsome Bridal* is not that of *Christis Kirk,* but is equally distinctive with a swinging anapaestic rhythm that is well suited to the rousing mood of the song as a whole. This piece also departs from the *Christis Kirk* pattern in having literally no action and no dialogue. It is merely an extended exhortation, urging people to attend the wedding festivities, the body of the song

---

[17] See Kastner ed. *Poetical Works of Drummond,* II, 422-423, on these words. For a fuller treatment of the relationship between these two poems, see my article "Drummond of Hawthornden's *Polemo-Middinia* as a Source for *The Blythsome Bridal,*" *Notes and Queries,* N.S., I (Sept., 1954), 384-386.

being a humorous listing of the guests and refreshments one might expect to find there.

In all other respects, however, *The Blythsome Bridal* falls squarely within the *Christis Kirk* genre. Here we have the typical scene of rustic conviviality as observed from an aristocratic point of view, the satiric sketches of peasant life and character, the swift cumulative movement of the verse, the rapid shifting from one scene to another, the genial tone, the broad and robust humor. The following lines from the sketches of wedding guests will illustrate the general style of the song:

And Crampie that married Stainie,
And coft him breeks to his arse,   *bought*
And afterwards hanged for stealing,
Great mercy it hapned no worse;
And there will be fairntickl'd Hew,   *freckled*
And Bess with the lillie white leg,
That gat to the south for breeding,
And bang'd up her wamb in Mons-Meg.
Fy let us all, etc.

(stanza 4)

On the whole, and although the poem is a fairly slight and unpretentious effort, *The Blythsome Bridal* is a successful piece of work as far as it goes, a spirited and entertaining song which shows a considerable degree of artistic competence and wit. Its brief, graphic sketches of the guests and the refreshments combine to give a remarkably clear and fascinating picture of what an old-fashioned Scottish country wedding must have been like.

Another piece which deserves mention here is the song called *Hallow-fair*,[18] an imitation of *The Blythsome Bridal* which probably dates from the latter part of the seventeenth century. So confused and contradictory, however, is the evidence on the date and authorship of this poem that it has been attributed by some scholars[19] to Francis Sempill of Beltrees (?1616-1682) and by others[20] to Robert Fergusson (1750-74), authors separated by more than a hundred years. Both attributions are extremely dubious. The antiquated language and style of the song suggest a seventeenth-century date and seem to rule out Fergusson, whereas there is no really concrete evidence in favor of Sempill. Indeed, if Francis Sempill wrote *The Blythsome Bridal*, it seems almost incredible that he could also

[18] *Ancient and Modern Scottish Songs*, ed. David Herd (Edinburgh, 1776) II, 169.

[19] E.g., Geo. Eyre-Todd ed. *Scottish Poetry of the 17th Century* (Londan, n.d.), p. 260.

[20] E.g., A. B. Grosart ed. *Works of Robert Fergusson* (London, 1851), p. 92.

have written *Hallowfair,* since the latter is a conscious imitation of *The Blythsome Bridal,* set to the same meter and to the tune of "O fly let us a' to the bridal." On the whole, the probabilities seem to be that *Hallow-fair* is a late seventeenth-century song by an unknown author, a song which may have been touched up and partly rewritten by Robert Fergusson for his friend David Herd who included it in the second volume of his *Ancient and Modern Scottish Songs* (Edinburgh, 1776).

Hallowfair resembles *The Blythsome Bridal* in style and is written in the same unusual verse form, as the opening lines will show:

There's fouth of braw Jockies and Jennies   *plenty*
Comes weel-busked into the fair,
With ribbons on their cockernonies,   *snooded knots of hair*
And fouth o' fine flour on their hair.

In its content, however, this song is even more closely related to the *Christis Kirk* tradition than *The Blythsome Bridal.* It is a lively and vigorous piece, describing the antics of a group of rustics who are driving their livestock through Edinburgh on their way to the Hallow Fair held on the Calton Hill. The poem is full of boisterous action, horseplay, drunkenness, and humorous dialogue so typical of the genre. It is especially reminiscent of *Peblis to the Play.* Unlike the better *Christis Kirk* poems, however, *Hallowfair* is unequal in execution and extremely loose in structure, lacking logical arrangement and coherence. Some sections are skillfully written and full of gusto, whereas others are haphazard, careless, and disjointed. But in spite of its glaring weaknesses, *Hallowfair* remains a valuable and interesting specimen of its type.

Besides the poems already treated, there are several other late seventeenth-century songs which are more or less closely related to the *Christis Kirk* tradition, though they do not fall strictly within the genre. Among these are the immortal *Maggie Lauder,*[21] one of the undoubted classics of Scots song; the irresistible drinking song called *Toddlin But and Toddlin Ben;* and a song entitled *Muirland Willie.*[22] This last song shows striking resemblances to *Hallowfair* and, like it, was written under the influence of *The Blythsome Bridal.* These songs, and a few others like them, share several *Christis Kirk* features. They are all art poems dealing with folk themes, treating lower class life and character in a good-natured, semi-satiric way, using swift graphic description and dialogue. In view of

[21] Sometimes attributed to Francis Sempill of Beltrees. For text see Herd ed. *Ancient and Modern Scottish Songs,* II, 72-73.
[22] Both of these songs appeared for the first time in Ramsay's *Tea-Table Miscellany,* II (1725), 154; I (1724), 7-9.

these qualities and in view of the fact that at the time they were written the *Christis Kirk* genre was by far the most vital type of formal poetry being produced in Scotland, songs of this kind may safely be regarded as offshoots of the *Christis Kirk* tradition.

Looking back over the dark years of the seventeenth century, that singularly barren period when very little formal poetry in the Scots tongue was being produced, one is struck by the unique and astonishing persistence of the *Christis Kirk* tradition. At a time when virtually all of the older genres of the native poetic tradition (exclusive of folk poetry, of course) had fallen into neglect and near oblivion under the Calvinist prohibition, the *Christis Kirk* genre alone continued to flourish and develop, nurtured mainly by country gentlemen of the Drummond or Sempill type. As we have seen, the century produced at least three fairly substantial poems of the *Christis Kirk* type except for verse form—*Polemo-Middinia, The Blythsome Bridal,* and *Hallowfair*—plus a handful of related songs. In addition, at least five editions of *Christis Kirk on the Green* appeared during these years. In fact, apart from a small group of poems by the Sempills of Baltrees and a few miscellaneous songs, virtually all of the slender body of vernacular art poetry surviving from the seventeenth century is related, more or less, to the *Christis Kirk* tradition. There is further significance in the fact that four of these seventeenth-century poems—*Polemo-Middinia, The Blythsome Bridal, Hallowfair,* and *Muirland Willie*—are clearly linked to each other as well as to the earlier *Christis Kirk* poems, showing that the authors were aware of both the ancient and recent poems in this style and were consciously writing within a long established tradition. In spite of these tight interrelationships, however, each of these seventeenth-century poems is different. There is no evidence that the tradition had become static or stereotyped; on the contrary, the surviving specimens indicate a fluid and developing genre, although the later poems, after *Polemo-Middinia*, suggest a tendency toward shorter and less ambitious efforts approximating the folk song in length—a tendency which, had it not been checked, might have resulted in a gradual fading out of the genre.

(To be continued)

UNIVERSITY OF RHODE ISLAND

Notes and Documents

Douglas and Virgil

Nearly fifty years ago Pound suggested that Gavin Douglas "gets more poetry out of Virgil than any other transaltor." This is indeed possible, but it may be truer to say that the poetry Douglas "gets out of" Virgil is in fact what Douglas "puts in," those happy extensions of the original whereby an abstraction becomes colourful and particular. Of Dido in the underworld Virgil uses the phrase:

recens a vulnere   (VI 450-51)

and Douglas gives us:

The greyn wound gapand in hir breist all new   (VI vii 57)

And in his description of the fight between Dares and Entellus Virgil writes another close-packed balanced line:

Immiscentque manus manibus, pugnamque lacessunt   (V 429)

but Douglas expands this to eight lines in which the very words whack and dodge and echo:

Now, hand to hand, the dynt lychtis with a swak;
Now bendis he vp hys burdon with a mynt,
On syde he bradis fortil eschew the dynt;
He etlys yondir hys avantage to tak,
He metis hym thar, and charris hym with a chak;
He watis to spy, and smytis in al hys mycht,
The tother keppys hym on hys burdon wycht;
Thai foyn at othir, and eggis to bargane.   (V viii 10-17)

Later, Pound added to his suggestion. In "How to Read" (1929) he said that Douglas' *Eneados* is "better than the original, as Douglas had heard the sea." Then in *ABC of Reading* (1934) he referred to *Eneados* I iii 13-21 (quoted in part below) and said: "in such passages as this I get considerably more pleasure from the Bishop of Dunkeld than from the original highly-cultured but non-seafaring author."

There is a specious element in the argument here: it seems to suggest that in their descriptions of (say) the sea both Virgil and Douglas had the same intention and were using different languages in the same way and that Douglas did it better than Virgil. But is this so? When Douglas adds to his original he is localising his effects, using his language as a robust sensuous medium for exciting the eye and ear of the reader's imagination: he was surely aware that he was setting about this in a manner quite different from that of his model. For instance, one of the supreme virtues of the Scots language is its ability to describe certain types of bad weather: it is in such descriptions that we find much of the "poetry" which Douglas "puts into" Virgil. The use of language is perhaps un-Virgilian and the content is uncalled for by the standards of strict translation but without it Douglas' *Eneados* would be sadly diminished. There follow some examples from the account of the storm in Book One.

Referring to Aeolus' cave Virgil has "vasto antro" (I 52) for which Douglas gives "In gowsty cavys" (I ii 6): "gowsty" for "vasto" is singularly apt. Virgil's cave is big; Douglas' is also draughty. The winds rush out:

> terras turbine perflant   (I 83)

has its own virtues as a poetic statement but in the Scots line

> And with a quhirl blew all the erth about   (I ii 52)

the words themselves sound as if they are whirling about. This movement from the abstract to the more energetic is characteristic.

> venti velut agmine facto
> . . . ruunt . . .   (I 82-3)

becomes:

> wyndis brade in a rout   (I ii 51)

"Rout," an exploding boisterous rush, is surely more pungent than "agmen," which can hardly be divested of its connotation of military discipline. A few lines further on "ruunt" is translated "rowit," which not only preserves a close similarity in sound but also seems to me more vivid than any possible English alternative. A like use of the fortuitously vivid native word ("busteously") and the retention of some of the original sound effects (the alliteration in "vastos volvunt" and "wallis welteris") can be seen when

> incubuere mari, totumque a sedibus imis
> . . . et vastos volvunt as litora fluctus   (I 84-6)

becomes:

> Thai ombeset the seys bustuusly,
> Quhil fra the deip til euery cost fast by
> The huge wallis weltris apon hie,   (I ii 53-5)

In the next line Douglas expands and adds his own alliteration.

> strudorque rudentum   (I 87)

has within its own sound the strain and groan of tackle under stress. Douglas gives:

·The takillis graslis, cabillis can fret and frays.   (I ii 60)

But an even better piece of alliteration follows where

intonuere poli   (I 90)

becomes a line as rough as anything in *Sir Gawain and the Green Knight*:

The firmament gan rummylling rair and rout   (I ii 64)

There are occasions when Douglas' effects are more straightforward than his model's.

insequitur cumulo praeruptus aquae mons   (I 105)

has a measured inevitability and the sound and order of the words act out their meaning. The line piles up through "cumulo," explodes in "praeruptus" and thuds down on "mons." The Scots version is longer, more direct but less subtle and forceful:

Heich as a hill the iaw of watir brak
And in ane hepe cam on thame with a swak.   (I iii 21-22)

Again I think Virgil has the advantage in

furit aestus harenis   (I 107)

because

The stour vp bullyrrit sand as it war wode   (I iii 26)

loses through dilution what it gains by using "stour" and "bullyrrit"; "as it war wode" is a conventional tag.

A similar exercise in comparison directed to another sea-passage, the race in Book Five, would have comparable results. The tendency to particularise, for instance, is still there:

apricis statio gratissima mergis   (V 128)

must have been too general for Douglas for he cannot help describing what every boatman sees on a Scottish coast:

A standing place, quhar skarthis with thar bekis,
Forgane the son, glaidly thame pronye and bekis.   (V iii 49-50)

(Douglas' word for cormorant is still in use, though the form I have heard in Caithness and Sutherland is "scarf.")

Both the strength and the weakness of Douglas can be seen in his rendering of

ferit aethera clamor
nauticus   (V 140-1)

for while ferit/clamor becomes a vigorous banging line:

Vpsprang the clamour, and the rerd furth went   (V iii 72)

aethera/nauticus becomes a line quite lame, despite the alliteration:

Heich in the skyis, of mony maryner.   (V iii 73)

To say that Douglas' success in translating Virgil is of a particular and limited kind must not be taken as carping; nor must it be allowed to suggest that Douglas was unaware of the limitations of the vernacular. Like all medieval translators, he was only too acutely aware of this and his complaint is only one of many:

> Sum tyme I follow the text als neir I may,
> Sum tyme I am constrenyt ane other way.
> Besyde Latyn our langage is imperfite
> Quhilk in sum part is the causs and the wyte
> Quhy that of Virgillis verss the ornate bewte
> Intill our tung may nocht obseruyt be,   (Prol. I 357 ff.)

But as usual such complaints are not to be taken all that seriously: certainly not in face of the prologues Douglas added to the separate books of the *Aeneid*. There the energy of language which is released only now and then in the course of translation is unfettered. Has anyone else described a Scottish winter quite like this? —

> Thik drumly scuggis dyrknyt so the hevyn,
> Dym skyis oft furth warpit feirfull levyn,
> Flaggis of fire, and mony felloun flaw,
> Scharpe soppys of sleit and of the snypand snaw.   (Prol. VII)

ROBIN FULTON
THE EDINBURGH ACADEMY

Home's *Douglas* and Wully Shakspeare

Home's *Douglas* is now remembered chiefly for its coy periphrasis for pregnancy (I.i), "My name is Norval" etc. (II.i), and a remark from the audience at its first performance, which took place in Edinburgh on 14 December 1756. An example of the orthodox version of this last incident may be found in James C. Dibdin's *Annals of the Edinburgh Stage* (Edinburgh, 1888, p. 87):

> At the first performance of *Douglas*, when Young Norval was busily employed giving out one of his rodomontading speeches, a canny Scot, who had been observed to grow more and more excited as the piece progressed, unable longer to contain his feelings, called out with evident pride, 'Whaur's yer Wully Shakspere noo!'

It is difficult to establish when this story first came into being. David Hume's dedication of his *Four Dissertations* (London, 1757, pp. v-vi) to Home refers in general to the play and ends with a reference to its enthusiastic reception in the theatre:

> But the unfeigned tears which flowed from every eye, in the numerous representations which were made of it on this theatre; the unparalleled com-

mand, which you appeared to have over every affection of the human breast: These are incontestible proofs, that you possess the true theatric genius of *Shakespear* and Otway, refined from the unhappy barbarism of the one, and the licentiousness of the other.

Burns's "Prologue spoken by Mr. Woods on his Benefit Night, Monday, 16th April, 1787" also invites the comparison with Shakespeare:

> Here *Douglas* forms wild Shakespeare into plan,
> And Harley rouses all the God in man.

The earliest reference traced so far has been the following:

> During the representation of *Douglas,* a young and sanguine North Briton, in the pit, exclaimed on a sudden, with an air of triumph, 'Weel, lads; what think you of Wully Shakspeare now?'

This comes from David Erskine Baker's *Biographia Dramatica* in its 1812 edition (vol. I, p. 360 n), which had been expanded by Isaac Reed. It is not found in the 1782 edition of the book, and so it must be taken as Reed's addition. Henley and Henderson probably knew of this source, for their note on the Burns couplet quoted above refers to the Wully Shakspeare remark being made by a "pittite"[1]; however, they give Dibdin's 1888 version of the actual words used.

Home had certainly done something himself to encourage the comparison with Shakespeare. When his first play, *Agis*, had been turned down by Garrick he consoled himself in verses that contain the following:

> Image of Shakespeare! To this place I come,
> To ease my bursting bosom at thy tomb.
>
> . . . .
>
> That day and night revolving still thy page,
> I hope like thee to shake the British stage,

After the success of *Douglas* Garrick, apparently taking the point thus offered, said that there were acts in *Agis* that were more like Shakespeare than any other author had written.[2] Henry Mackenzie in his *Account of the Life and Writings of John Home, Esq.* (Edinburgh, 1822) was more cautious, feeling compelled (p. 75) to correct the impression Home's verses might have given a North British contemporary by the comment: "Shakespeare, of whose excellence he was an enthusiastic admirer, he did not think of imitating in manner or in style."

MacDONALD EMSLIE

UNIVERSITY OF LONDON

[1] *The Poetry of Robert Burns,* ed. W. E. Henley and T. F. Henderson (Edinburgh, 1896), II, 383.

[2] Henry Grey Graham, *Scottish Men of Letters in the Eighteenth Century* (London, 1908), pp. 62, 68.

Reviews

David F. C. Coldwell, ed. *Selections from Gavin
Douglas.* Oxford. The Clarendon Press. 1964. xxix
+ 164 pp. 18 shillings.

In 1959, the Saltire Society Classics series brought out a selection
from Douglas's poetry, edited by S. G. Smith and containing 70 pages of
extracts from *Eneados* together with some short pieces from *The Palice
of Honour* and *King Hart.* Previous to this edition and discounting
examples printed in anthologies, we know of only one other volume of
selections from Douglas in Middle Scots; this was a reprint of the Char-
teris edition of 1579 produced for popular consumption by the Morisons
of Perth in 1787 and characterized by their habitual inaccuracy. Now
we have a third presentation of the kind, this time a reduced version of
Dr. Coldwell's complete edition commissioned by the Scottish Text Society; its advantage over Smith's Saltire volume lies mainly in the fact that
Dr. Coldwell's text is based on his own version of the earliest MS. (the
Cambridge MS., *c.* 1515), and not on the 1874 S.T.S. edition made by
John Small from the Elphynstoun MS. (*c.* 1520). The Cambridge MS.,
owned by Trinity College, was made by Douglas's own secretary and
bears annotations possibly by the poet himself. As the copy "nixt eftir the
translation," it is the authoritative copy; Rutherford and Dundas produced a reliable transcription of it for the Bannatyne Club in 1839,
without introductory material or notes.

Dr. Coldwell organises his Clarendon volume as follows: 1) an introduction wherein Douglas's translation is compared with Dryden's as a
rendering and as poetry; 2) a biographical note on Douglas; 3) a note on
the MSS. and previous editions; 4) extracts culled from appreciations by
Warton, Saintsbury, Lewis and Tillyard, none of them, incidentally, Scotsmen; 5) the text itself, comprising about two thousand lines from
Eneados and three hundred selected from *The Palice of Honour* by Miss
Priscilla Preston and annotated by her; 6) notes, with line references;
7) a selective glossary of obsolete, dialectal or difficult words, about fourteen hundred in all, listed in the inflectional forms in which they appear.
King Hart, now reckoned to be by another hand, is not included, nor
even referred to. There is one illustration, of a woodcut by Sebastian
Brant from his edition of Virgil printed at Strasbourg in 1502; it depicts
the Romans as sixteenth-century Germans.

Dr. Coldwell's introduction takes this woodcut for its starting-point and observes that Douglas's attitude to Virgil was like Brant's—his characters are contemporary, not Virgilian or handled with the austere reverence of the translator who wants to make the personages suitably "ancient." "Douglas saw far less difference between the lives of Scots and Romans than Dryden did," he points out, and proceeds to illustrate the differences in conception by means of a number of parallel passages, concluding that "Douglas, less of a Latinist than Dryden, is largely for that reason closer to 'the common reader.'" In this Dr. Coldwell is following, rather uncritically, C. S. Lewis's argument in *English Literature in the Sixteenth Century,* from which he later prints a significant extract. Even though his method of translation, which was not line-by-line and depended on the couplet as unit rather than on the hexameter of the original greatly increased the number of lines in Virgil, Douglas was steadfastly faithful to his resolution

> . . . to mak it braid and plane,
> Kepand na sudroun bot our awyn langage,

and ignored the cold decorum of Renaissance scholarship in favour of rough-hewn equivalence in *Scottis,* as far as the limitations of that tongue would allow. Dr. Coldwell's Lewis-inspired explanation would have been rendered more acceptable had he tried to see Douglas as a *makar,* in company with Henryson and Dunbar and their predecessors Barbour and the shadowy "Blyn Hary," both of whom wrote epics in Scots; as it is, he deals with Douglas in a vacuum so far as the development of Scots poetry is concerned and nowhere enters into any discussion of the condition in which Douglas found his "bad, harsk spech and lewit barbour tong," nor about its tragic petering-out at the time of its greatest linguistic triumph. *Eneados* is a curiosity not only because later readers were conditioned by the petrified pedantry of the new learning; religious and political pressures peculiar to Scotland soon afterwards combined to bring about the disintegration of *Scottis* as a vehicle for literature of the first order. A hundred years later *Eneados* could not have been attempted:

> Yit stude he nevir weill in our tung endyte
> Les than it be by me now at this tyme.

Even in his own day the language was, on Douglas's admission, inadequate for the highest flights; its oral range was limited.

> Nor yit sa cleyn all sudron I refus,
> Bot sum word I pronounce as nyghtbours doys:
> Lyke as in Latin beyn Grew termys sum,
> So me behufyt quhilum or than be dum
> Sum bastard Latyn, French or Inglys oys,
> Quhar scant war Scottis—I had nane other choys.

When he said, therefore, that he lacked the "fowth" or abundance of language Douglas was not simply exhibiting a conventional humility in the august company of "maist reverend Virgill, of Latyn poetis prynce." The year he completed his poetical labours of eighteen months was the year of Flodden, and this national disaster may perhaps, in Dr. Coldwell's words, have "worked to Douglas's political advantage," but, as is well known, this clash of arms came to be the symbol of the end of the old Scotland and of the destruction of the young seed of her Renaissance. Political trends towards Union implied a movement in favour of anglicisation and a London-centred culture; ironically enough it was as *patria sua exul,* under Wolsey's protection, that Douglas died in 1522, proscribed in his native land as rebel and traitor. He left behind him a great translation of *Aeneid* in a language soon to become tragically unread and unreadable and in mediaeval styles technically old-fashioned in his own day. Gavin Douglas was at heart a schoolman, and although his "nature" poetry looked forward to the eighteenth century, his *Scottis* was built up on the eclectic principle of modern *Lallans,* taking its own where it could be found, from Latin, French, the literary Scots of his predecessors, and English.

The selections themselves are, of course, arbitrary, but to be "helpful to the ordinary reader" and to "the university student," one would expect the original *Prologues* to be well represented, particularly I, VII, XII, and XIII, together with sizable extracts from the actual translation, especially of the early and more familiar books of the *Aeneid.* Once these requirements have been met, one editor's choice of additional material is probably as good as another's. Dr. Coldwell's *Selections* are therefore adequate, although we should have preferred more from the *Prologues* which, after all, represent the measure of Douglas's contribution as an original poet; Dr. Coldwell leaves out *Prologues* II, III, V, VI, X, and XI. The fifth *Prologue* starts conventionally in the spring, but contains further observations on the problems of translation, while the sixth treats of Hell, as poets and philosophers have conceived it. Comparing these selections with those in S. G. Smith's Saltire edition, we are inclined to find a greater variety in the latter, which omits only II, V, and IX, though the extracts themselves are short.

The accompanying notes are extremely helpful, though aimed at the scholar rather than at "the ordinary reader" for whom, according to the statement on the dust-cover, this series of texts is intended. Ordinary readers of Douglas have in the past had his works "modernised" for their benefit; this is why the impermanence of the language in which he wrote did not affect the popularity of his works, which continued to be read, along with those of Barbour, Blyn Hary, and Lyndsay, until the nine-teenth century. Dr. Coldwell's glossary is useful but it is only a working vocabulary; a key to a translation of an epic like the *Aeneid* is obviously not going to be provided in 18 pages of dialectal and obsolete words taken from a translation in a language almost entirely dialectal or obsolete. The work is a sourcebook of what we call "Middle Scots"; no other *makar* has preserved the "wordhord" available to him so completely. For this reason the writer of the dust-jacket description deserves one bad mark for pointing out that "by some critics it [Douglas's version] has been accounted the best in *English*," and a second for drawing attention, with misquotation, to Ezra Pound's absurd claim for the translation as "actually better than the [*sic*] original." The audience for whom a text like this is intended do not need such crude salesmanship, particularly when about all it reveals is the ignorance of the seller concerning the nature of his wares. One may, of course, cut off the offending flap.

The printers have made an excellent job and it is hard to fault them. Dr. Coldwell's book is not a "populariser," but is more likely to be read or rather dipped into, than any full-scale edition of Douglas. This is the seventh in the Clarendon Mediaeval and Tudor Series and it is well up to the standard of its predecessors.

A. M. KINGHORN

UNIVERSITY OF THE WEST INDIES

Alexander Welsh. *The hero of the Waverley Novels.* New Haven. Yale University Press. 1963. xiv+273pp. $6.00.

Most careful readers of Scott have noted that there is something odd about his heroes: they are altogether too passive, they are acted on rather than act, they have an exaggerated, even a self-defeating, respect for law and public authority. This can be partly explained by interpreting the ostensible heroes of the Waverley Novels less as conventional heroes of fiction than as symbolic observers through whose innocent and law-abiding eyes the reader is allowed to see the tensions between picturesque violence and civilised order (with the latter in the end approved and victorious) that constitute the theme of most of Scott's best work. Mr. Welsh accepts this up to a point, just as he accepts and refers with gratifying generosity to my own argument about the centrality of Scott's concern with the transition from the age of heroic violence to the age of prudence. But he takes the point much further than this. He examines in perceptive detail patterns of behaviour in a widely representative selection of Scott's heroes, and he relates these patterns to the moral, social and political principles which are pointed to by the general shape of the action as well as by critical scenes and especially revealing moments. The result is a genuinely helpful book, which not only directs us towards a more perceptive reading of the novels but also demonstrates the source of the superiority of the better novels, notably of *The Heart of Mid-Lothian*.

Mr. Welsh contrasts the "passive hero" (Nigel Olifaunt, Henry Bertram, Francis Osbaldistone) with the "dark hero" (George Staunton, Rob Roy, Saladin) and demonstrates how the latter, something of a Robin Hood figure, often generous and compassionate, moved by an intuitive morality rather than by public authority, can be highly sympathetic yet must in the end be (to Scott) unacceptable. "The romantic hero has a part to play in the structure of the Waverley Novels, but he has no ethical currency. He represents, therefore, an emotional force. 'Courage and generosity' are good qualities, but in Scott they are not moral qualities. When Scott thinks of morality, he speaks in terms of regulation and restraint—rational and social functions." Thus the appearance of *two* heroes in many of the novels, the passive successful hero and the active and in the end rejected romantic hero, is related to a dualism in Scott's own attitude, a diagnosis which is convincingly reinforced by quotations from Scott's own non-fictional writings. "The proper and passive hero adheres to law or accepted morality; the dark hero boasts his own morality and places himself outside the law." This is in itself not an original insight; but Mr. Welsh develops the point with an abundance of well-chosen detail and a supporting analysis of Scott's ethical and social ideas and of the accepted ideas of his time. He also extends the analysis to include an interesting discussion of the two heroines (often a blonde—passive and good—and a brunette—romantic and wild) that appear in some at least of the novels—Rose Bradwardine and Flora Mac-Ivor in *Waverley*, Brenda and Minna Troil in *The Pirate*, and, most famous of all, Rowena and Rebecca in *The Talisman*. There are interesting variations on this. Diana Vernon in *Rob Roy* is a "dark heroine" who is not in the end relegated to exile or otherwise moved out of the novel, but actually (though in a pretty perfunctory coda to the novel) marries the hero, a destiny usually reserved for the "blonde heroine." Jeanie and Effie Deans are in fact both blonde; indeed Effie, who is morally the "dark heroine," is the fairer; but the voluptuousness of her bodily structure and the impulsiveness of her character sufficiently attest to the side on which she is ranged. In the course of his discussion of Scott's heroines, and of the heroes' behaviour towards them, Mr. Welsh pin-points some paradoxes and (in modern eyes at least) some profound inadequacies in Scott's view of the ideal relationship between the sexes. The good, passive hero marries as a rule the good, passive, fair-haired heroine, who has never been romantically impulsive enough to show her love before she has been proposed to. Marriage is a disciplined submission to the laws of society and (as Mr. Welsh very interestingly shows) of property. We knew, of course, that Scott was uncomfortable with sexual passion, but this throws a new light on the discomfort. Mr. Welsh does not go into the biographical background of this; but the story of Scott's early and unsuccessful love affair with "Greenmantle" and his marriage of moderate affection rather than love is relevant, if not to a critical assessment of the novels, at least to a study of the attitudes that underlie them.

In a careful account of Scott's view of reality as consisting of the necessity which in turn represents "the constraining relation of things and of commitments" (based on a perceptive reading of passages from *The Heart of Mid-Lothian*), Mr. Welsh takes us close to the heart of Scott's socio-moral world. I wish, however, that he had cited the confrontation between Peter Peebles and Redgauntlet in *Redgauntlet*, for that superb meeting between obsessive legal-mindedness and obsessive heroic-romantic nostalgia illuminates in one great dramatic moment not only Scott's concept of reality but also his view of the equal and opposite deviations from it (reliance on public formulas, reliance on private passion) that threaten the good society. There are other points one would have liked to see developed further. Was Scott really prejudiced against commerce in the way Mr. Welsh believes? True, in many of the novels it is the landed gentleman who represents, however tamely, the ethical centre; but the vitality of such a character as Bailie Nicol Jarvie also represents something that Scott believed in as representing an important part of Scotland's future. The defence of the Union on merchantile grounds that Scott puts into the Bailie's mouth is vibrant with genuine feeling, for all the humorous quirks that Scott introduces into the Bailie's character. Vitality, as well as social approval, can be a clue to how we are to take the activities and views of a character in a Scott novel. If Mr. Welsh had extended his study to include the minor characters—who are, after all, far more memorable and possess far more vitality than the passive heroes as well as far more psychological authenticity than most of the dark, romantic heroes—he would have seen other patterns of meaning at work in the novels. A study of Scott's heroes, however carefully and sensitively carried out, can only take us so far. To get at the true centre of Scott's world we must look closely at the minor characters of the "Scotch novels" and trace the sources of their interest and appeal. The reality of marriage contracts and legal relationships may indeed be the reality which lies beneath the world in which Scott's passive heroes surrender themselves to be acted on in the virtuous knowledge that the establishment has taken over their right to individual action and can therefore be trusted in the end to set everything right. But there is another kind of reality at work in the novels, built up by the racy Scots dialogue of characters who may in themselves (like Andrew Fairservice or the Laird of Dumbiedykes) be offensive or ridiculous; and this is surely worth some examination, for this is why the novels are read.

DAVID DAICHES

UNIVERSITY OF SUSSEX

STUDIES IN SCOTTISH LITERATURE

VOLUME II   NUMBER 3   JANUARY 1965

CONTENTS

STUDIES IN SCOTTISH LITERATURE

EDITED BY G. ROSS ROY
UNIVERSITY OF SOUTH CAROLINA

EDITORIAL BOARD:
DAVID DAICHES
A. M. KINGHORN
HUGH MACDIARMID (C. M. GRIEVE)
A. L. STROUT
KURT WITTIG

STUDIES IN SCOTTISH LITERATURE is an
independent quarterly devoted to all aspects of
Scottish literature. Articles and notes are welcome.
Subscriptions are available at $5.00 U.S. per annum in the
United States and Canada, elsewhere $4.20 U. S.
All communications should be addressed to the
Editor, Department of English, University of South Carolina,
Columbia, South Carolina, U.S.A. 29208

PUBLISHED BY THE UNIVERSITY OF SOUTH CAROLINA PRESS
AND PRINTED BY VOGUE PRESS, INC.
COLUMBIA, SOUTH CAROLINA, U.S.A. 29202

CONTRIBUTORS
TO THIS ISSUE

Andrew VON HENDY: B.A., Niagara University; M.A. and Ph.D. from Cornell University. Assistant Professor in the Department of English at Boston College. Interested in the Scottish Chaucerians.

Isabel HYDE: M.A.; M.Litt. (Cantab.). Lecturer in the Department of English at Royal Holloway College, and member of the Board of English Studies in the University of London. Wrote a thesis for the M.Litt. on figures of speech in the poetry of William Dunbar. Has published articles on Lydgate and Dunbar in *Modern Language Notes* and *Modern Language Review*, as well as articles on Shakespeare and Aristotle's *Poetics*. Is at present preparing a study of the nature and function of figures of speech in medieval poetry.

Allan II. MACLAINE: Professor of English at the University of Rhode Island. Is preparing a study of eighteenth and nineteenth-century Scottish chapbook literature.

Robert VLACH: Docteur d'Université, Lyon; Ph.D., Charles University, Prague. Associate Professor in the Department of Modern Languages, University of Oklahoma. Editor of *Books Abroad*. Interested in contemporary Slavic poetry and comparative Slavic literature.

EDITORIAL

With steadily rising publishing costs pushing up the price of books and periodicals, and with an increasingly large number of journals to interest the reader, both scholars and the general public find themselves unable to subscribe to all of the journals they read. Consequently readers have come to rely on the university or public library which serves them for all but a few periodicals.

The responsibilities of the public or institutional libraries have grown enormously in recent years, too. Their ever more complex role in training citizens for the immediate future as well as expanding to answer diversified needs of research, place a great strain on their facilities. The well-stocked library must spend large sums to keep abreast of current book publishing. Not infrequently demand is such that more than one copy of a work is needed; with increased use older volumes require replacement, and this, too, is costly. In addition the library must make a judicious selection of periodicals to which it will subscribe. There are, we suppose, few libraries which carry all the periodicals their users would wish to see on the shelves, but with union catalogues and modern inexpensive photo-duplicating processes almost any article can be had by return of post.

Because the use made through borrowing or photo-copying a periodical does not show up in subscription lists, it is difficult for an editor to accurately assess the impact his journal is having. Many highly regarded journals do not have a wide circulation beyond libraries; in fact the proportion of private subscribers some of them have is very small indeed. Yet no one would deny the essential service these journals render to the scholarly and intellectual community.

It is evident, therefore, that, with few exceptions indeed, the scholarly journal must be dependent upon outside support if it is to stay alive. (We refer to journals in the humanities, although scientific journals are, presumably, in much the same plight.) Only a small proportion of the deficit can be made up through advertising revenues; many journals prefer to carry no publicity. Very few foundations are willing to subsidize journal publication, a fact that reflects little credit on the foundations. The burden of support has consequently fallen, as much by default as for any other reason, on the universities.

Here, too, the situation has been far from ideal. Moderately well-to-do universities not infrequently support a journal while more affluent schools sit idly by. This is not to suggest that none of the larger universities does its part — Harvard and the University of Chicago are two outstanding examples of universities which support a number of highly regarded journals. In not a few universities, however, the idea persists that a good journal should be self-supporting. No college president, comptroller, or head of the board of trustees expects the multi-million dollar atomic reactor to show a profit. Its *raison d'être* is the extension of the frontier of knowledge. Is there more reason to expect the scholarly journal to pay for itself?

The continuation of *Studies in Scottish Literature* has recently been assured through the action of Dr. Thomas F. Jones, President of the University of South Carolina, in agreeing to subsidize it as a publication of The University of South Carolina Press. The enthusiasm of Drs. William H. Patterson, H. Willard Davis, and John C. Guilds, respectively Dean of the University, Dean of the College of Arts and Sciences, and Chairman of the Department of English of the University of South Carolina, played an essential part in making this arrangement possible.

At this time it is perhaps in order to sum up the substantial progress which has been made by *SSL*. This journal is sent to twenty-one countries. Most major universities and public libraries in this country and the United Kingdom, Australia, Canada and New Zealand subscribe to it. In addition we are fortunate in having a larger than usual proportion of private individuals on our mailing list.

With its future assured, the Editor hopes to be able to make *SSL* even more useful for those who are interested in Scottish literature. An annual bibliography of books and articles of Scottish literary interest is to be added, and it is hoped that a survey of poetry, fiction and belles lettres can soon become an annual feature.

ANDREW VON HENDY

The Free Thrall: a Study of
The Kingis Quair

The Kingis Quair is an unusually underrated poem. Modern commentators, from Skeat on, have been so distracted by its glamorous author that they have paid little attention to the literary conventions which shape the poem.[1] They generally write it off as James I's charming but only partially successful attempt to break through the "conventions" of allegory by talking about himself. C. S. Lewis, for example, says that in *The Kingis Quair* "the poetry of marriage at last emerges from the traditional poetry of adultery; and the literal narrative of a contemporary wooing emerges from romance and allegory."[2] If one reads the poem, however, without presupposing that the King wrote it about his own courtship, one finds no hint of marriage and no wooing, "contemporary" or otherwise. In fact, it is highly questionable whether the narrator and his beloved communicate at all. Any "literal narrative" which "emerges from romance and allegory" eludes the reader of this poem quite as much as it does the reader of, say, *The Parlement of Foules*. I mention Chaucer's work because I think the poem the author of *The Kingis Quair* did write resembles in kind *The Parlement of Foules*. I think it can best be understood, not as botched autobiography, but as a carefully designed, serious and lovely whole.

Like many medieval dream-visions, *The Kingis Quair* concerns a man's education, the moment in his experience when he discovers, however dimly, the rationale of the universe. Its author combines a literal imprisonment with the tradition of the *donna angelicata*. He combines,

[1] Skeat influenced all subsequent criticism of the poem by his editions for the Scottish Text Society in 1884 and 1911. In them he accepts the two manuscript ascriptions of the poem to James I, together with the assertion that the poem was "maid quhen his Ma[jestie] was in Ingland." He then ignores or distorts much in the poem itself not consonant with his external evidence. For a general critique of Skeat's lapses see W. M. Mackenzie's edition of the poem (Faber & Faber, 1939), pages 17-20.

[2] C. S. Lewis, *The Allegory of Love* (Oxford, 1936), page 237. Ironically, the sentence I quote caps the finest appreciation of *The Kingis Quair* in print.

so to speak, the examples of Boethius and Dante. On the one hand, he represents himself as being, like Boethius, a captive, unaware of the true nature of his captivity. Both incarcerations are things of the mind; the prisoners are victims of their own subservience to Fortune. On the other hand, in *The Kingis Quair,* as in Dante's *Commedia,* the narrator is led, in a sense, from love to Love. The Lady Philosophy is first of all an earthly lady; without erotic passion there would be no mental enlightenment. The poem deals with the Boethian paradoxes of necessity and free will, fortune and fate, time and eternity. Experience of love, which seems at the same time fated and freely willed, enables the narrator to discover his place in the universe. All men are prisoners, bound in the golden chain of love; yet, by understanding and willing their bondage they are free. At the end of his vision the dreamer climbs again on the Wheel of Fortune, to enjoy the high honor of a successful suitor, but we know that he is no longer Fortune's prisoner; he is now the free thrall of Love.[3]

The poem begins with astrology. Caught in his prison of years and days, the poet reads in the book of the heavens the unknown language of his destiny. The old paradoxes are already on his mind when, like Chaucer in *The Book of the Duchess,* he picks up some bedtime reading to wear away his sleeplessness. As in Chaucer's *Book of the Duchess* and *The House of Fame,* the reading of the book serves a purpose somewhat analogous to the *exemplum* of a sermon. The narrator meditates upon Boethius' *Consolation of Philosophy:*

> Upon the writing of this noble man,
> That in himself the full recover wan
> Off his infortune, pouert, and distress,
> And in tham set his verray sekerness. (5)[4]

Boethius triumphed over Fortune because "the vertew of his youth before/ Was in his age the ground of his delytis"(6). But the narrator's youth was more typical; Fortune's Wheel threw him easily because "youth . . . seildin ought providith"(9).

---

[3] In some of my subsequent remarks about the early part of the poem I have profited from the essay by John Preston, "Fortunys Exiltree: a Study of *The Kingis Quair" RES* (VII, 1956), 339-346. Preston seems to me admirable up to the point where the dream-vision begins. He then ignores some of the commonest elements of that convention, including the geography of the dream, and he does not refer at all to the dreamer's visit to Minerva, the climax of the poem. He concludes, as a result, with a strangely post-Romantic reading of this medieval poem.

[4] All subsequent quotations are similarly identified in the text by stanza number. I follow Mackenzie, except where otherwise noted.

As he rolls to and fro, "forwakit and forwalowit" (11), reviewing, as he puts it, "all myn aventure" (10), he hears the matins bell say, " 'Tell on, man, what thee befell' " (11). C. S. Lewis justly compares this fine effect to Sidney's " 'Fool,' said my Muse to me." Like Sidney, the author of *The Kingis Quair* records a new source of inspiration; he has found his subject. As Preston points out, Boethius is crucial in this awakening; the *De Consolatione* organizes the narrator's experience. He is going to tell us (I think) how Reason led him, by way of love, to amend his improvident youth, to rise above Fortune as Boethius did.

After making his cross, he launches into an apostrophe to his own "youth, of nature indegest" (14). Life was for him (as several times in the *De Consolatione)* a sea upon which he sailed rudderless. Because his comfort stood "in unsekerness" (15), he was "to fortune both and to infortune hable" (14).

> The rypeness of resoun lakkit I,
> To governe with my will; so lyte I couth,
> Quhen stereles to travaile I begouth,
> Amang the wawis of this warld to drive. (16)

When the narrator commences to tell about his youth, this metaphor of life as a sea-voyage gives way to a literal journey. "In ver, that full of vertu is and gude" (20), the narrator is captured at sea. "Fortune it schupe non othir wayis to be" (24). The literal "weltering" (24) which casts the poet to his foes parallels his figurative drifting "stereles . . . amang the wawis of this warld." This comparison and contrast between physical and mental bondage is the central piece of wit in the poem.

The imprisoned youth did not realize the double nature of his bondage. His formal complaint reveals his naivete:

> The bird, the beste, the fisch eke in the see,
> They lyve in fredome everich in his kynd;
> And I a man, and lakkith libertee;
> Quhat schall I seyne, quhat resoun may I fynd,
> That fortune suld do so? (27)

For the first time in his life, as one might say, he thinks. He is driven to question not merely Fortune but even Providence:

> Than wold I say, 'Gif God me had devisit
> To lyve my lyf in thraldome thus and pyne,
> Quhat was the caus that he [me] more comprisit
> Than othir folk to lyve in suich ruyne'? (28)[5]

---

[5] I have added *me* in the third line for the sake of clarity, following Skeat rather than Mackenzie.

"Bewailing" in his "chamber thus alone"(30), (like Troilus), the prisoner indulges a healthful impulse. He walks to his window and gazes down into the "herber"(31) where on the "small grene twistis"(33) nightingales sing of love. Their hymn of praise, reminiscent of the "roundel" at the end of *The Parlement of Foules,* attracts the prisoner. He offers desperately to worship Love if Love can answer his distress.

> Can I nought elles fynd, bot gif that he
> Be Lord, and as a God may lyve and regne,
> To bynd and lous, and maken thrallis free,
> Than wold I pray his blisfull grace benigne. (39)

Readers have frequently noted that the scene which follows is inspired by *The Knight's Tale.* Having made his vow to Love, the narrator receives a prompt challenge. His Rose walks into the garden. The blood drives from his heart and rushes back:

> sudaynly my hert become hir thrall
> For ever of free wyll. (41)

In this "beautiful oxymoron," as C. S. Lewis calls it *(Allegory of Love,* p. 236), the prisoner commits himself to the earthly love which will teach him ultimately about the Love which moves the sun and the other stars. In the apostrophe which follows, the prisoner combines the initial reactions of both Palamon and Arcite:

> 'A! suete, are ye a warldly creature,
> Or hevinly thing in likeness of nature?' (42)

He asks the vision if she is Cupid's princess come to loose him out of hand, or the goddess of nature who made the garden, or, in case she be a "warldly wight,"

> Quhy lest God mak you so, my derrest hert,
> To do a sely prisoner thus smert? (44)

These questions are conventional rhetoric, of course, the final and most striking one being in this case imitated from Lydgate's *The Temple of Glas* (lines 223-228). But they are not mere hyperbole: it seems to me the speaker discovers by stages that his lady is indeed Cupid's princess come to free him, the goddess of nature and an agent of Providence.

The lady is the conventional heroine of fifteenth-century romance, decked with plumes and precious stones, a chaplet on her head, a hawk on her wrist. She has "Beautee eneuch to mak a world to dote"(47), and about her white neck a gold-work chain, a faint echo, as it were, of the golden chain of love which the narrator will discover binds the universe. As she walks under the boughs, the prisoner addresses ecstatically

first her "lytill hound/ That with his bellis playit on the ground"(53),
and then, with agreeable humor, the now-silent nightingale.

> 'Now, suete bird, say ones to me "pepe";
> I dee for wo; me think thou gynnis slepe . . .
>
> Sluggart, for schame! lo here thy goldin hour,
> That worth were hale all thy lyvis laboure!' (57-8)

This address ends in lines of considerable lyric power. We can feel the
intensity of hushed wonder in the man:

> 'Bot blawe wynd, blawe, and do the levis schake,
> That sum twig may wag, and mak hir to wake.' (60)

When the birds do sing, the poet identifies with them in a striking
variation on his central paradox:

> my spirit was so light,
> Me thought I flawe for joye without arest,
> So were my wittis boundin all to fest. (61)

When the lady withdraws from the garden, the "thrall" makes a
short, formal complaint; then the poem moves swiftly into dream-vision.
With his head twisted on the cold stone the dreamer sinks into a swoon.
A light shines in his chamber window. He is addressed by an unidentified voice, and

> hastily, by bothe the armes tueyne,
> . . . araisit up in-to the air,
> Clippit in a cloude of cristall clere and fair. (75)

The cosmology of a dream-vision is always significant: in this poem
it is crucial to the meaning. The dreamer is lifted "fro spere to spere"
into the circle of the fixed stars and the Zodiac. His arrival in "the
glade empire/ Off blisfull Venus" is marked by a wonderful mysterious
touch: "ane cryit now/ So sudaynly, almost I wish noght how"(76).

He finds in this place a curiously modified version of the groups of
plainants before the Lady in Chaucer's *House of Fame*. Chaucer's Fame,
as H. R. Patch demonstrated, can be identified closely both with Venus
and with the goddess Fortuna.[6] Chaucer's rapidly displacing groups represent the abstract possibilities of fortune in love. They remind one of
the allegories of Love and Fame in fifteenth century Italian painting.
The crowd of lovers in *The Kingis Quair* was imitated, too, from Lyd-

---

[6] For medieval associations among Fame, Venus and Fortune (amounting
frequently to confused identification of the three), see H. R. Patch, *The
Goddess Fortuna in Medieval Literature* (Harvard, 1927), pages 90-98, 110-
129, 161-162. For Chaucer's poem specifically, see page 111 and the notes on
pages 43, 110, 134 and 145.

gate's *Temple of Glas.* Lydgate's Venus, however, like Chaucer's Fame, is equivalent to Fortune. The monk does not distinguish reward according to degrees of fidelity. But in *The Kingis Quair* Venus' court seems to be patterned as a courtly love analogue to heaven, purgatory and hell: disposition of the lover is not arbitrary; it depends on his earthly fidelity. The voice explains that the old lovers, warriors and poets who comprise the "heaven" were "the folk that never change wold/ In lufe" (83), even though they died for it, some in sorrow, some in arms, some in despair, and so on. In "purgatory" are "folk of religioun" (88) who served love truly, but were ashamed to admit that they did so. The "warld of folk" (82) in "hell" appear at first to suffer unjustly (as the dreamer had complained he did). They are people who never had a chance. At least that is the way they feel about it, "compleynyng there/ Upon fortune and hir grete variance" (93). But they are the same classes of human destiny which appear in the first two groups. The "voice" leaves the moral implicit: these sufferers complain of the variance of Fortune because they did not rise above it; they drifted rudderless, not steering by their ever-fixed mark. Fortune does indeed have a part, a predestined part, in determining the lover's fate, but faithfulness seems to depend on his will, and his will is free. We are back at the central paradox.

Venus, in this scheme of things, is a higher power than the goddess Fortuna. The author reaches back for precedent past the rather degenerate fifteenth century cosmology, past even the *Parlement of Foules,* to the *Romance of the Rose,* and behind that to Alanus de Insulis' *De Planctu Naturae.* As Mackenzie points out, this is the Lucretian Venus, for whom the daedal earth blossoms in flowers. The author does leave Venus some of her most frivolous conventional trappings, but they are conspicuously out of place. In this case adherence to "convention" may justly be said to betray him.

The astonished lover falls on his knees to pray, acknowledging by his trope that Venus is to love as Reason is to life:

> in the huge weltering wawis fell
> Off lufis rage, blisfull havin and sure;
> O anker and keye of our gude aventure. (100)

Venus hastens to explain that she must work in cooperation with other universal forces. She cannot grant the captive's full desire because, for example, his "persone standis noght in libertee" (108). We can see why Venus chooses his imprisonment to illustrate the limits of her authority, because she refers the lover's "spirit" (112) to Minerva. Physical freedom alone will not suffice to make the thrall free; he must learn another kind.

Before Venus sends him off to Minerva, however, she somewhat gratuitously commissions the dreamer to be her prophet before men, "sin thou hir servand art"(114). Venus commands the lover, that is, not in her own name but in that of his Rose. She complains that unrepentant men neglect her laws, "breken lous, and walken at thair large"(115). Constrained by such unkindness, she weeps; her tears fall as rain (as they do in *Lenvoy de Chaucer a Scogan*). In spring, when she exiles all her wrath and rancor

> 'of my cristall teris that bene schede,
> The hony flouris growen up and sprede. (117)

She offers two proofs "in takin of this pitous tale"(118). First, when flowers spring folk renew their service to love, and, second,

> 'Quhen so my teris dropen on the ground,
> In thair nature the lytill birdis smale
> Styntith thair song, and murnyth for that stound.' (118)

This charming plaint confirms Venus' status as a universal agent. She concludes with a threat and a promise. If men do not revert to her "observance" (121), she will league against them with her "fader old Saturne"(122). Saturn, as in *The Knight's Tale*, seems to personify the violent misfortunes which appear to subvert the order of the universe. But if men renew Venus' law, the law of kind, she will accept them in a sort of Dantesque *terzo cielo*, the "heaven" of faithful lovers.

> 'Ressave I sall your saulis of my grace,
> To lyve with me as goddis in this place.' (123)

Good Hope (guide also in Lydgate's *The Temple of Glas*) immediately leads the dreamer to Minerva, in a nearby "palace"(124). Minerva's interview with the dreamer is the climax of his vision. She is, after all, the Lady Philosophy herself. She tells the dreamer that love not set on virtue is folly (as Reason does in *The Romance of the Rose*). She advises him to pray to the "purveyance" of God "thy lufe to gye."

> 'Tak him before in all thy governance,
> That in his hand the stere has of you all.' (130)

The "stereles" dreamer has found his Helmsman at last. Minerva then excoriates inconstancy in love, returning, in effect, to the moral taught by the three states of lovers at Venus' palace. In the next five stanzas the dreamer and Minerva engage in a dialogue modeled significantly on the *De Consolatione*. The lover succeeds in convincing Minerva that he does indeed love his "flour"(139) according to "Goddis law"(138), that his desire is "set in Cristin wis"(142).[7] Minerva promises to sue Fortune for him, for, as she explains, Fortune determines the "wele" and "wo" of "all ye creaturis/ Quhich under us beneth have your duellyng" (145). Fortune, as the Lady Philosophy told Boethius, rules only as vice-regent in the sublunary world. Minerva then launches into a brief discussion of fate and free will, fortune, necessity and choice. In my opinion these four stanzas are the core of the poem.

Minerva explains that some clerks believe in strict necessity; Fortune governs all, its diverse workings being preordained "heigh in the hevin" (146). (This phrase recalls the first and last lines of the poem.) Unlike the similar passage in *Troilus and Criseyde,* however, the argument in *The Kingis Quair* proceeds to an orthodox, more or less Boethian, solution:

> Bot othir clerkis halden, that the man
> Has in himself the chos and libertee
> To caus his awin fortune, how or quhan
> That him best lest, and no necessitee
> Was in the hevin at his nativitee,
> Bot yit the thingis happin in commune
> Efter purpos, so cleping thame Fortune.

> And quhare a persone has tofore knawing
> Off it that is to fall purposly,
> Lo, fortune is bot wayke in suich a thing,
> Thou may wele wit, and here ensample quhy;
> To God, that is the first caus onely
> Off every thing, there may no fortune fall:
> And quhy? for he foreknawin is of all.

> And therfore thus I say to this sentence:
> Fortune is most and strangest evermore,
> Quhare leste foreknawing or intelligence
> Is in the man. (147-9)[8]

[7] In keeping with his autobiographical bias, C. S. Lewis takes these two ambiguous phrases to mean that Minerva speaks of the marriage of James I with Joan Beaufort. But there is no more mention of marriage in *The Kingis Quair* than there is in the conclusion of *The Romance of the Rose.* The later author is concerned, like Jean de Meun, with a more general topic, the religious basis for sex. In the prisoner's dream marriage, as usual in the courtly tradition, bears little relationship to Venus' reward.

[8] This passage, like the one in *Troilus* (IV, 958-1078), is a faint and, as it were, debased version of Boethius. The *De Consolatione* is organized to expand toward these ultimate questions; Boethius rises to a meditation on the neoplatonic One. The authors of *Troilus and Criseyde* and *The Kingis Quair,* however, utilize the Boethian topics for their own poetic ends. I think that

"Tofore knawing/ Off it that is to fall purposly" means, in effect, planning the future. According to Minerva, God's absolute foreknowledge guarantees His freedom from Fortune. He wills freely all that is to happen. Obviously, these stanzas are no impressive contribution to medieval philosophy, but they are, in context, effective poetry. It seems to me the dreamer is taught to regard both sides of the paradox: he is provided with "foreknawing" and "intelligence" that even God may be said to be bound in freedom, free in bondage. In her first speech Minerva told the dreamer to trust in God's "purveyance" and to remain faithful in love. The two acts are analogous. As God wills freely that things be what they are, so the lovers will freely to remain eternal thralls of their ladies. In thus "foreknawing . . . purposly," the lover rises above Fortune. He becomes worthy to enter the heaven of Venus.

These central stanzas serve a double purpose. Minerva teaches the lover a personal philosophy, but she does it by instructing him in the ultimate rationale of the universe. God's foreknowledge is not cited merely as a helpful analogy. Before he heard the birds sing of love the dreamer had questioned uneasily the justice of Providence. Now he has an answer within his grasp. Suspended under God's "purveyance" in the golden chain of love, the natural forces, Venus and Minerva, Love and Reason, guide the universe; under them, Fortune rules the world of man in time.

Having reached this pithy climax, Minerva demonstrates that she is Wisdom by making a swift end. She returns the dreamer to the inferior sublunary world where he is to "pray Fortune" (150).

> als straught as ony lyne,
> Within a beme, that fro the contree dyvine
> Sche, percyng throw the firmement, extendit,
> To ground ageyne my spirit is descendit. (151)

He finds himself in, an earthly paradise, the garden of love which Dante puts just below the moon. It is the type of the literal "herber" in which he saw his lady. The conventional description of its flora and fauna signifies the abundance of nature in the chain of being.[9] The author of

meditations on the mysteriousness of human destiny are characteristic of romance as a literary mode. If that is true, it would not be surprising that the authors of the two poems conduct the Boethian argument to opposite conclusions: the convention would suggest consideration of the issue, but not a set solution.

[9] See J. A. W. Bennett, *The Parlement of Foules* (Oxford, 1957), especially pages 140-142. I feel generally indebted to this model study in medieval literary convention.

[149]

The Kingis Quair works here in a very rich tradition, stretching at least from the school of Chartres to Spenser's Mutabilitie Cantos. In this garden Fortune, like Venus in *The Parlement of Foules,* has only a corner of God's paradisal foison.

The author revivifies the stock description of Fortune, and particularly of her wheel "that sloppar was to hold"(163). Its "sudayn weltering"(163) dismays him.

> And they were war that long sat in place,
> So tolter quhilum did sche it to-wrye. (164)

The dreamer does not gaze long on Fortune's varying face and her coat of "divers hewis"(160) before she calls him out by name. The scene reminds one of Chaucer's appearance before the God of Love in the Prologue to *The Legend of Good Women.* Fortune accedes immediately to the narrator's stammered request, and masterfully helps the feeble lover get situated on her wheel. For all his newly acquired wisdom, the dreamer cannot decline the ride; no sublunary creature can do that, but least of all a lover. The difference lies in what he now knows about Fortune's place in the scheme of things. Fortune herself, before she sends the dreamer up, admonishes him of the nature of the wheel, takes him by the ear and, abruptly, he wakes.

Vexed in waking "by twenti fold"(174), the narrator humbly begs the "goddis"(176) for the grace of further enlightenment; till then, he remains without "sekernes"(174). The appearance of the "turtur quhite as calk"(177) immediately confirms his vision. According to the branch of red gillyflowers "in the hevin decretit is the cure" (179). The narrator hastens to tell how inexorably and swiftly the prophecy is fulfilled. Fortune bears herself well. The narrator utters a bidding prayer, like the somewhat similar one in *Troilus and Criseyde,* for those who "servandis ar to lufe"(184), and even for those ignorant as he was.

> And eke I pray for all the hertis dull,
> That lyven here in sleuth and ignorance,
> And has no curage at the ros to pull. (186)

The poet praises his lady's succor, and thanks in descending order the agents of fate (189-191): the "goddis all," "fortunys exiltree/ And quhile," the nightingale, the gillyflower, the "castell wall" over which he looked, the very saints of March (the month when he was imprisoned), even the arbor boughs under which he first saw his beloved. He has found in the human realm "the gyd and stere"(195) who gives his life direction, the jailor through whom he comes again to his "larges" (183).

> Unworthy, lo, but onely of hir grace,
>   In lufis yok, that esy is and sure.   (193)

He has learned in his dream-vision, however, that the sure and easy yoke of love, by which men transcend their fortunes, depends on a universal order ruled by God Himself. The prisoner, bound in both senses of the word, had demanded before his enlightenment why "God me had devisit/To lyve my lyf in thraldome thus and pyne?" Now, to the possible objection that his story has been trivial, he replies in moving lines.

> Eke quho may in this lyfe have more plesance,
>   Than cum to largess from thraldom and peyne,
> And by the mene of luffis ordinance,
>   That has so mony in his goldin cheyne?   (183)

The form of *The Kingis Quair* imitates the poet's realization that all things are encircled in the golden chain of love: the free thrall concludes where he began; the first line of his narrative is the last, and it recalls the paradox of human fate suggested by the stars.

> And thus endith the fotall influence
>   Causit from hevyn, quhare power is commytt
> Of govirnance, by the magnificence
>   Of him that hiest in the hevin sitt;
>   To quham we think that all oure hath writt,
> Quho coutht it red, agone syne mony a yere,
> 'Hich in the hevynnis figure circulere.'   (196) [10]

The formal design of *The Kingis Quair* matches the beauty of its verse and the sophistication of its theme.

BOSTON COLLEGE

---

[10] Compare Boethius' famous figure of the circle whose center is God and whose circumference is Destiny (IV, prosa 6, lines 115-145 in Chaucer's *Boece*). The poem actually concludes in a conventional envoy (stanza 197). The obscurity in stanza 196 can be clarified most economically, I think, if we accept Mackenzie's suggestion that "oure" may mean " 'all that is ours,' that is, our destiny" (page 125).

Robert Burns Through Russian Eyes

Few serious books about Robert Burns have attracted as little notice as A. Elistratova's *Robert Burns* which was published in Moscow in 1957. The book was not listed in the *PMLA Annual Bibliography*, nor was it reviewed in the *Burns Chronicle*.

To review a book to which few scholars have access, and which is written in a language which (unfortunately) few of them read serves little purpose. The Editor therefore decided to publish a synopsis of the book rather than to have it reviewed. Professor Robert Vlach of the University of Oklahoma, Editor of *Books Abroad,* graciously agreed to write the synopsis.

**Anna Arkadevna Elistratova. *Robert Burns*. Moscow. 1957
158 pages. 3r.40k.**

INTRODUCTION

The author visits places reminiscent of Burns and witnesses to his living popularity: Ayr, Kilmarnock, Dumfries, Glasgow, Edinburgh, Carradale, where the writer Naomi Mitchison is her hostess. The verse and songs by Burns live in the hearts of the Scottish people. They represent, since long ago, not a literature in books, but something as usual and necessary as bread and air. Already Goethe had understood the national character of Burns's poetry — he spoke about it to Eckermann. Burns felt the same already when writing the preface to the first edition of his poems. Byron, too, saw in his national character the basis of his greatness. Burns's love for folklore was creative. With zeal he collected and learned old songs, ballads, traditions, melodies of popular dances, and ancient battle-marches, but in his works he was able to breathe a new life into them, renewing traditional texts, blending old with new; and, though deeply national both in spirit and form, his work is, at the same time, independent, marked by his individuality. This progressive man of his time had a great understanding of new, contemporary literary and social-political development: isn't his "Scots, Wha Hae" called the "Scottish Marseillaise"? Burns's inspiration is equally national, social, and political because he was able to grasp the economic motives behind the English oppression of Scotland. The theme of individual human dignity, too, permeates his entire work from "The Jolly Beggars" to "Is There for Honest Poverty." Here he went much further than most writers of the Enlightenment: their ideal stood on abstractions, while Burns derived his inspiration from poor and exploited toilers. He expressed (with a few exceptions, like "The Cotter's Saturday Night") the opposition between happiness in poverty and unjust riches, in an aggressive fighting spirit.

Burns's lyric is, from the beginning, inseparable from Burns as a satirical poet. He had learned much from the progressive literature of the eighteenth century, with its democratic pathos and the deep insight that the Enlightenment showed in the laws of human nature and reason. Yet, Burns's work differs greatly from the English and Scottish poetry of his immediate predecessors and contemporaries. Young, Thomson, Gray, Goldsmith, Cowper, Mackenzie, etc., were descending to the village theme, as Burns ironically remarked in the preface to his first edition. The suffering of the people inspired the sentimentalists to reflections about celestial justice — a tendency which was deplored already by Belinskij in his criticism of Goldsmith. Burns, who early became acquainted with their works, never let himself be limited by their narrowness. He liked, for instance, Gray's "Elegy Written in a Country Churchyard" because of the compassion shown by the author to simple people; however, he could not accept his humility and resignation. Not even the one-sided and incomplete heroes of the realists of the period (like Fielding and Smollett) can stand up to those of Burns, who was the only writer who knew them as real people — not only as objects of purely poetic sympathies. This is why he so surpassed the models of his youth.

Some utopian traits can be found in Burns's social-political views. Paine's "political summer," expected after the French Revolution, did not come, but time confirmed Burns's revolutionary enthusiasm because it was in agreement with the progressive direction of society. The poet's faith in the transforming role of the people in the social-historical development adds a particular depth to his realistic poetry.

Burns's poetry is full of movement; in the best works, its interior drama dominates the description. Scenes of drama — or comedy — are contained in poems like "The Jolly Beggars," "Tam O' Shanter," or "The Holy Fair." Allegorical but humorous and full-of-life poems like "Twa Dogs" or "The Brigs of Ayr" take the form of a dispute in dialogue. The living intonations of the popular language may be found in "Findley," [sic][1] "My Collier Laddie," etc. In a century of rhetorical amplifications and paraphrases, Burns brought to a peak the mastery of laconism in poetry. The fundamental idea in his work is the dignity of simple people and their right to happiness. He did not share with the sentimentalists their distrust of reason and their cult of irrational feeling. In him, feeling and reason are wonderfully balanced. His acceptance of the world is elemental and materialistic. He is the first who, in the English poetry of the eighteenth century, bridged over the conflict of "soul" and "flesh," and the entire world cherishes his work as a hymn of glory to the great possibilities of work, struggle, and pleasures of life which are contained in man.

CHAPTER I

1

The "honest poverty" of a poor peasant family representative of the Scottish people of the eighteenth century — that of Burns's parents — is still attested by the house built in Alloway near Ayr by the poet's father in 1757. The taxes on windows forced the poor to economize even on sunshine, and were responsible for there being only one window in the room where Robert was born January 25, 1759. A double oppression marked his youth: national, as a consequence of the uprising of 1745-1746; and economic, because at that time the rich landowner still was the central figure in the Scottish village and opposed even attempts to emigrate to Canada on the part of his dependents. New forms of bourgeois exploitation appear with the beginning of industrialization.

For a long time the Burns family had not possessed the land they cultivated. When Robert was born, his father had a job as gardener for a landowner from whom he rented a strip of land on which he built a house. When Robert was six years old, his father rented a farm in Mt. Oliphant; in 1777, another one in Lochlea. Yet only debts and a long lawsuit were the result of his striving, and these hastened the old man's death. The children proclaimed themselves his creditors in order to save some money, claiming their salary as stable-boys and servants.

Robert, the eldest of seven boys and girls, had to manage the greatest part of the work. At thirteen or fourteen, he was an experienced ploughman. Yet he found time to learn to read and write not only

[1] Fintry (?) i.e. "Election Ballad at the Close of the Contest for Representing the Dumfries Burghs, 1790." — *Editor.*

English, but also French. Folklore was another school for him: both his mother and an old servant saw seeds of poetry in him. With his teacher he read Shakespeare and Addison, but the first books he read by himself were the biographies of Hannibal and of Sir William Wallace, a hero of wars for Scottish independence in the thirteenth century. In November of 1780, he founded, in Tarbolton, the Bachelors' Club, where young farmers and artisans discussed such matters as marriage to a rich or to a poor but loving woman, or whether a savage or a peasant is happier in a civilized country — a little naïve but progressive thought for the late eighteenth century.

In 1781 Burns became a member of the Masonic Lodge in Tarbolton, but the religious, mystic motives of the Masons left no traces in his work — probably they remained foreign to him. However, they inspired him by their social-utopian tendencies ("Farewell to the Brethren of St. James's Lodge, Tarbolton").

The reading list of young Burns was not long but diverse. It was composed not only of Pope, Richardson, Smollett, the sentimentalists, and his Scottish contemporaries Ramsay and Fergusson, but also of theological works, Biblical history, physics, Locke, etc. His aesthetics were formed by reflections over a songbook (of 1746) in which he tried to distinguish the true poetry from affectation.

He wrote his first verse in the fields during the harvest ("Handsome Nell")[2] on the melody of a reel when he was fifteen years old. In the beginning, he wrote not for print but for circulation among friends. Long before the idea of a publication came to his readers, Burns became progressively aware of his talent. His *First Commonplace Book,* started in 1783, begins with a kind of social and literary program. The embryo-motives of his poetry are the consciousness of his own dignity as poet of the working people, contempt for egoistic success in life, and desire truly to express the feelings and passions of simple working men. Their life, not the Enlightenment ideas about "human nature," becomes for him the measure of humanity. His prose notes reveal his great interest in the Scottish literary traditions and poetic forms; the nature and history of Scotland make a unity; the rhythm and metrics of national songs show national character. Social motives like those in "Man Was Born to Mourn," "My Father Was a Farmer," "John Barleycorn," etc., point to what was exciting the young poet.

[2] "O, once I lov'd a Bonie Lass."

2

Burns's popularity as a poet, though in his immediate surroundings only, is connected with his first satirical poems on church and religious themes. Scotland at that time was Calvinist and the clergy powerful. The Bible was most often the only book that ever came into the hands of people, and they became accustomed to thinking in its language. Questions of religious orthodoxy continued to inflame the thoughts of all, including Burns. This "heretical" spirit is reflected in two poems that were among the first of his works to achieve wide popularity: "The Twa Herds" and "Holy Willie's Prayer." Though directed against real "pillars" of the Church, they are, at the same time, remarkable for their satirical generalization. They constitute the beginning of the poet's anti-clerical creation, which progresses with "The Holy Fair," "Address to the Deil," "Epistle to Davie, a Brother Poet," "Scotch Drink," "Epistle to The Rev. John M'Math." "The Holy Fair," incidentally, is one of the first social-realistic works of the poet; Burns appears here as a *national* poet, proving with all the riches of popular wisdom and humor the incompatibility of the Presbyterian orthodoxy with popular common-sense. In "Epistle to The Rev. John M'Math," however, he reveals his religious feelings, as he does in "A Prayer in the Prospect of Death," where God in the deistic way is called "unknown, Almighty Cause" of human hope and fear. His God is a sort of pseudonym for "Nature" as the Enlightenment understood this word.

His ethical views in this first period are best developed in "Address to the Unco Guid" (1786). Satire on the clergy is here connected with a deeply human attitude: one can judge one's neighbor only when one understands what causes his faults. Social-political inspiration fills the "Address of Beelzebub," who embodies the dark and cruel forces opposed to working people.

The poem crowning this period of Burns's creation is "The Jolly Beggars." In "Beelzebub," the heroes had maintained their connection with earth; here, they have nothing more to lose — they have reached the Gorkyan "bottom." (Some heroes of Walter Scott descend as low, too.) Burns's originality resides in his realistic approach to his protagonists, which is without the slightest embellishment or sentimentality. Gay in *The Beggar's Opera,* Fielding in *The Covent Garden Tragedy,* and Defoe in *Moll Flanders, Colonel Jacque,* and *Roxana* had introduced "low heroes," but, with Burns, they become poetically attractive beings for the first time. Poosie-Nansie's and its visitors are depicted as they were in reality, with their offended, humiliated, but living humanity.

Burns's poetry here is full of humor, but also of anger; yet he is not a singer of anarchy, as has been said by some critics: he only lets, quite righteously, the victims of society be its judges. He is a revolutionary.

Society did not pardon him for that. He had a bitter time when his natural daughter was born, when his marriage to Jean Armour could not take place. His intention to emigrate to Jamaica, however, was abandoned because of the unprecedented success of his first book.

3

It would have been too dangerous to include all poems Burns had written in the Kilmarnock edition. Still, those thirty-five pieces that constitute the volume are enough to make clear Burns's original tendencies. He dared to put in both "The Holy Fair" and "Address to the Deil." A magnificent realistic satire, "The Twa Dogs," opens the collection. An important place is given to epistles which by free composition and language, as well as unconstrained tone, greatly differ from the rhetorical and pedantic epistles by the classicists modeled on Horace. "A Dream" is a kind of literary manifesto, with its expression of the independent, popular, and national character and tendency of his creation. The same idea, without allegory this time, is contained in the "Epistle to Davie, a Brother Poet," the "Epistle to William Simson" (in particular), and in the epistles to J. Lapraik. Aesthetic problems are already social problems for the young Burns: his identification of true poetry with laborious poverty is more than an autobiographical motif; it is clear to him that art can exist only where there is no exploitation of man by man.

"To a Louse" demonstrates Burns's ability to transform a vulgar detail into a serious though humorously expressed generalization — a dissection of social pseudo-magnitude. In the same way he found pure poetry in situations unacceptable to the official school, as in "The Auld Farmer's New Year's Salutation to his Mare Maggie," "To a Mouse" (Steinbeck found a title in this poem), "The Death and Dying Words of Poor Mailie," "To a Mountain Daisy." In all these poems we also have the theme of the "social Union of Nature" — in Burns's terms — so important for this as well as for the future work of the poet. He knew and loved nature as a man who toils in it, but there is also a philosophical context in his perception: wise, living, poetic understanding of the mutual bonds between all forms of the material, earthy life; Burns's man is active, thinking, and feeling his participation in the eternal material movement of nature.

Love of life is the essential poetic mood of Burns. The exceptions in his first collection are "The Lament" and some other poems such as "Despondency," "Winter," "A Prayer under the Pressure of Violent Anguish,"[3] etc., but above all "The Cotter's Saturday Night," so dear to bourgeois critics. This static picture of the Scottish village is a utopia turned to the past, a dream of William Burnes, an idyl irrevocably bygone in Robert's time. Even the form — Spencer's — is of the past, and Burns will nevermore use it. All this is the "meditative" poetry of the early sentimentalists.

Burns's attempts to have a second book published brought him twice to Edinburgh — two periods of extrème importance for the poet: his acquaintance with the aristocracy and intelligentsia confirmed fully the ideas he had formed about the "higher" society.

CHAPTER II

1

Walter Scott, forty years later, wrote a portrait of Burns as he saw him in Edinburgh; Cromek and Lockhart give other details. Nothing, not even the advice of his friend John Ramsay, could stop Burns from making enemies. His "Lines Written by Somebody on the Window of an Inn at Stirling"[4] confirms his satirical vein and is a precursor of Shelley's "England in 1819." Though he has some illusions about the Stuarts, he does not write elegies about the past like Walter Scott, but expresses his anger against the ruling dynasty. A plebeian in aristocratic salons, a fashion of the season, Burns felt sharply the tension of this social contradiction. Yet his two stays in Edinburgh proved helpful both to his poetry, extending its horizons, and to him, affirming the militantly democratic principles of his aesthetics. More and more Burns feels he is a poet-citizen. He demonstrates it by his initiative to honor the memory of Fergusson ("Inscription for the Headstone of Fergusson the Poet")[5] or in his epigram addressed to Dr. Samuel Johnson. In Edinburgh, he became still more conscious of his being a *national* poet.

Finally he achieved his purpose, the second edition of his poems. It contains twenty-two new pieces — some rhetorical and cold like the "Address to Edinburgh" as well as versification and translation of Psalms, but also the anti-clerical "Ordination" and "The Calf," or humorous pieces like "Death and Dr. Hornbook," "Address to a Haggis," etc.

---

[3] This poem appeared first in the Edinburgh, 1787, edition. The author doubtless referred to "A Prayer in the Prospect of Death."—*Editor.*

[4] "Here Stewarts once in glory reign'd."

[5] "No sculptur'd Marble here, nor pompous lay."

The most important among the humorous poems is "The Brigs of Ayr," though its final part is artificial. "John Barleycorn" included here belongs among Burns's masterpieces; it is based on folkloric conceptions but is interwoven with themes of immortality of life and work and with revolutionary pathos of the invincibility of the national spirit.

In Edinburgh an opportunity offered itself to Burns to turn in the direction of folklore — an event that marked his creation in a decisive way: James Johnson won him for coöperation with his own *Scots Musical Museum*. Burns contributed more than two hundred songs, among them some of his own, to the second and succeeding volumes, of which he was, in point of fact, both contributor and editor.

The Edinburgh sojourns also taught Burns that he had to earn his living otherwise than through writing: thus his Ellisland years began. Having brought to an end his romance with "Clarinda" and married Jean Armour, he also became an exciseman. The farm proved to be a bad business, and he finally moved to Dumfries.

The best result of the Ellisland period is "Tam O' Shanter," a verse tale which was, curiously, published in Grose's *Antiquities of Scotland*. Burns achieved in it full union between the traditions of Scottish folklore and the sceptical, ironical realism of the Enlightenment. The story is almost Voltairian. In Russian literature, the same spirit can be found in Gogol's "Propavshaja gramota" ("The Lost Letter"). Also Burns attained virtuosity of form.

In "Tam O' Shanter" satire is secondary, though attacks against clergy and lawyers continue his anti-clerical and social line. Yet his main theme at that time is the power of money, dealt with before in "Lines Written on a Bank Note" and now in the "Ode Sacred to the Memory of Mrs. Oswald." The importance Burns ascribes to his social satire is evident from his having sent it for publication, under a pseudonym, to *The Morning Star* in London. In a similar way he had contributed to *The Edinburgh Evening Courant* in 1788, showing his democratic ideas already *before* the bourgeois French Revolution.

The Jacobite theme, popular in the Scottish folklore of the eighteenth century, took, in the songs of Burns, not the traditional legitimist-monarchist, but a democratic turn. Burns lets simple people speak, allowing them to express even naïve hopes and illusions about the Stuarts, "really Scottish" kings ("The Highland Widow's Lament," "The White Cockade," etc.)—though it was perfectly clear to the poet that the Stuart cause was hopelessly lost; the legends and sentimental memories had for him—as later for Walter Scott—mostly historical and aesthetic interest.

In Dumfries Burns made an effort to establish a local library and continued to work for George Thomson's *Select Scottish Airs*—a coöperative venture started in 1792 that gave us, besides many songs, a most important correspondence.

Among Burns's rich and thematically wide-ranging songs, the political ones take a particular and significant place. Also his songs of everyday life usually have a social connotation. Not an individual, egoist happiness, but a great one encompassing all, is heard in "Auld Lang Syne" and many other songs. The Scottish national character marks Burns's songs with humor, reflection, sorrow, sometimes mutinous passion. The rhythm of national melodies enabled the poet to break down the conservative rhythmics of the eighteenth century and give them, instead of an arithmetical symmetry, a great emotional expressiveness ("O, My Luve is Like a Red, Red Rose"). In lexical richness, only Shakespeare and Milton surpass Burns. His originality appears also in blending English and Scottish, as well as songs and social-political poetry.

2

Political events abroad as well as in Scotland itself had a great influence on Burns. The bourgeois French Revolution of 1789-1793 has to be named in the first place. By all his past, Burns was ready for this influence. A legend claims he bought contraband cannons at auction from a captured boat and sent them to France. This, together with his famous toasts and other circumstances, caused him troubles with the authorities and an investigation. The political activities of the Scottish democrats increased in 1792-1793, but Burns was not able to take part in them because his family depended on his excise income. His favorite book of this time was Thomas Paine's *The Rights of Man*. Its influence is felt in "Is There for Honest Poverty." Burns's letter to John Francis Erskine contains an important comment on his political lyrics and his situation in the Nineties. Also his letter of January 2, 1793, to Mrs. Dunlop reveals the audacity of his thoughts. We can easily sum up his ideas: he was against war of conquest, but he accepted and justified the revolutionary struggle for liberation led by France against her enemies. His ideas on the revolutionary comradeship of nations found full expression in the poem "The Tree of Liberty." The allegory was clear enough. The reaction of 1794 inspired him. "For Those Who Are Far Away," [6] though taken from an old song to honor the Stuarts, presented a new version understood as referring to the exiles.

At that time, Burns began publishing in *The Morning Star* in

[6] "Here's a Health to them that's awa."

London. On May 8, 1794, his "Scots, Wha Hae" appeared there, which he had sent to Thomson a year before with a letter, proving its contemporary inspiration. In his conception of national history as an organic unity of past, present, and future, Burns is a precursor of the revolutionary romantics Byron and Shelley.

"Is There for Honest Poverty" can be considered his last word to posterity. It represents a kind of summing up of his ideas and poetical motifs of many years. It may be seen as a democratic manifesto of progressive social thinking in Scotland at that time.

Deceived by the turn the French Revolution took, he wrote a song for the Dumfries Volunteers, of which he became a member. He had to ask Thomson and his cousin James for money in order to pay for his uniform when he was in danger of going to prison because of this debt.

His last song is "Fairest Maid on Devon Banks." He died July 21, 1796. The day of his funeral his wife gave birth to their fifth son. Many months of the family's life could have been made less unhappy if they had had only a part of the costs of the military burial.

EPILOGUE

Already in the beginning of the nineteenth century, Burns was translated into many languages. In the Museum in Alloway, there is now also a book of Samuel Marshak's translations; and the USSR participated in the Burns Festival in 1955.

The national individuality of Burns's work was not an obstacle to his international fame; on the contrary, Lafargue witnesses that he was among the favorite poets of Marx.

Burns's influence on English Romanticism is enormous. Modern British authors, too, liked him (for instance, Shaw)—and even found inspiration in him (like Sean O'Casey). The reactionary critics try in vain to mask the progressive spirit of his work. James Barke is right in saying that only people with clean hands should dare to approach the poet's memory.

One of the first evaluations of Burns in Russian is by Professor I. Sreznevskij in *Sobranie obraztsovykh russkikh sochinenij . . .* [*Collection of Model Russian Works . . .*] published in 1821. In 1800, the journal *Ippokrena* carried a prose translation of the "Address to the Shade of Thomson." Among the first Russian translators of Burns is I. T. Kozlov who, in 1829, published *Selskij subbotnij vecher v Shotlandii* [*Peasant Saturday Evening in Scotland*] which he called "free imitation of Burns." He finished with an enthusiastic address to "Holy

Russia" wishing her prosperity and peace. In 1835, he translated "To a Mountain Daisy." A discussion in the press developed around these works which is dealt with by the Soviet literary historian S. A. Orlov in his essay "Berns v russkikh perevodakh" ["Burns in Russian Translations"].

In 1837, the journal *Biblioteka dlja chtenija* published an article, "Robert Borns" whose author was probably O. I. Senkovski. It was accompanied by a translation of "John Barleycorn" in the style of a Russian *bylina*.

In 1832, Lermontov—eighteen years old—translated the four lines of Burns's "farewell" [7] that Byron used as motto to his *Bride of Abydos*.

Belinskij names Burns with Shakespeare and the English Romantics among the poets whose works constitute the treasury of lyric poetry.

Taras Shevchenko, in the manuscript preface to his *Kobzar* confiscated upon his arrest by the gendarmes in March 1847, evokes Burns in justification of his own work. Also Ogarev points to him as an example of a truly national poet, in the preface to an anthology, *Russkaja potaennaja literatura* [*Russian Secret Literature*], published in London in 1861.

Nekrasov and Turgenev had different plans concerning Burns, as we learn from their exchange of letters; however, nothing came from them. Nekrasov's journal *Sovremennik* carried translations from Burns by Kurochkin, Mikhajlov, and others.

The one-hundredth anniversary of Burns's death was remembered by P. I. Veinberg, who wrote an essay on him, and his translations appeared in book form in Moscow in 1897.

In 1904, a collection, *Robert Borns i ego proizvedenija v perevodakh russkikh pisatelej* [*Robert Burns and his Works in Translations of Russian Writers*], appearing in the *Deshevoj Biblioteka* [*Cheap Library*] for twenty kopeks, was readily accessible. It was a very representative selection.

After the Revolution, Samuel Marshak devoted half of his life to his beloved poet. His first translation was published in 1924. He never stopped translating Burns. As the poet A. Tvardovskij put it, Marshak "made Burns Russian, although letting him be a Scot." Marshak's translation exceeded 600,000 copies. Other poets, like T. L. Shchepkina-Kupernik and E. Bagritskij, have translated Burns also.

[7] "Ae fond Kiss."

ALLAN H. MACLAINE

The *Christis Kirk* Tradition:
Its Evolution in Scots Poetry To Burns.

Part III

The Early Eighteenth Century:
Allan Ramsay and his Followers

The eighteenth century dawned inauspiciously for Scotland. She was an economically poor country, suffering from a sense of injured pride and political betrayal as a result of the parliamentary Union with England (1707), which cancelled out at a stroke of the pen the cherished independence for which Scots had been fighting and dying for a thousand years. But although the Union, having reduced Scotland politically to the status of a British province, did not immediately bring the hoped-for material benefits, it did produce a remarkable cultural renaissance. The causes of this renaissance were, of course, complex. It was made possible partly by the gradual growth of a literate middle class, partly by the development of a fine system of local schools which eventually turned Scotland into a nation of educated farmers and tradesmen generations ahead of England. But this cultural resurgence resulted largely from the desire of a small, politically impotent nation, threatened with assimilation by its larger neighbor, to reassert its ancient cultural identity among the nations of Europe.

Eighteenth-century Scotland's urge to assert itself culturally found expression in several, often apparently contradictory, ways. One of these ways was through a great upsurge of interest in the national poetic heritage. That interest had, of course, continued to thrive on the folk level; but on the educated level it had been largely dormant for over a hundred years, showing itself only sporadically among the landed gentry, as we have noted. The first tangible sign of the new movement was the publication in Edinburgh of the earliest of a formidable series of anthologies of Scots poetry, James Watson's *Choice Collection of Comic and Serious Scots Poems, both Ancient and Modern,* a truly epoch-making work which appeared in three parts in 1706, 1709, and 1711. Watson's publication proves that by the time of the Union a considerable reading public interested in Scots poetry had developed.

[163]

Significantly enough, Watson gave the place of honor in his collection, as the first poem in the first volume, to *Christis Kirk on the Green.*

The work of Watson in publicizing Scots poetry was almost immediately taken over by the versatile Allan Ramsay, who started life as a wigmaker and rapidly developed into a successful poet, editor, and bookseller. Ramsay soon became, in fact, the leading light, the prime mover and pioneer of the entire vernacular revival, giving it both its original impetus and its final direction. Though Ramsay was by no means a first-rate poet himself, the historical importance of his work, both as poet and editor, can scarcely be overestimated. And among his many and extremely versatile contributions to the development of Scots poetry, his work in the *Christis Kirk* tradition was of profound importance.

Allan Ramsay's contribution to the *Christis Kirk* genre was a twofold one: he acted both as an indefatigable editor and publicizer and as an original poet within the tradition. As an editor, Ramsay's work began in 1718 [1] when he brought out a new edition of *Christis Kirk on the Green,* to which he added a supplemental canto of his own composition (written in 1715). Then, later in the same year, Ramsay produced another new canto and reissued the poem in three cantos, Canto I being the original fifteenth-century poem, while Cantos II and III were continuations of his own. So successful were these first two editions of *Christis Kirk* that Ramsay continued to bring out successive editions of all three cantos. In 1720 he repeated the 1718 edition; in 1721 and again in 1722, he reprinted the entire work as part of *Poems by Allan Ramsay.* Finally, in 1724, he included the original fifteenth-century poem in his *Ever Green,* a pioneering anthology exclusively made up of ancient Scottish poems.[2] For this collection Ramsay transcribed the text directly from the Bannatyne Manuscript instead of from the more or less corrupt seventeenth-century printed sources, and was thus responsible for the earliest printing of the Bannatyne text of *Christis Kirk.*

These labors of Ramsay in editing and publicizing the text of *Christis Kirk on the Green* made it unquestionably the best known and loved of ancient Scottish poems, if it had not been that before. And his lead was followed by a host of other editors and publishers, who continued to reprint the poem (sometimes with, and sometimes

[1] On this date, formerly thought to be 1716, see Andrew Gibson, *New Light on Allan Ramsay* (Edinburgh, 1927), pp. 107-111.

[2] For data on all of these editions, see Wm. Geddie, *A Bibliography of Middle Scots Poets,* Scottish Text Soc., O.S. 61 (Edinburgh, 1912), pp. 96-98.

without Ramsay's additions) throughout the century, other editions appearing in 1748, ca. 1750, 1763, 1768, 1782, 1783, 1783, 1786, 1786, 1794, 1796, and 1799.[3] In thus giving the poem broad publicity and spreading its fame throughout the educated classes in Scotland, Ramsay gave tremendous new impetus to the whole *Christis Kirk* tradition at a time when it might, quite conceivably, have declined altogether. But Ramsay did more than this: through his original continuations of the poem, he demonstrated that this ancient genre was still adaptable as a vehicle for modern Scots poets, and he reversed the late seventeenth-century tendency of the tradition to dwindle into songs of *The Blythsome Bridal* type.

The contents of Ramsay's two *Christis Kirk* cantos (twenty-four stanzas each) may be summarized briefly.[4] In Canto II he picks up the story at the point where the original leaves off, with the brawl still in progress. In his four opening stanzas Ramsay introduces a terrible figure, "the bauld Good-wife of *Braith*," who rushes into the fray armed with "a great Kail Gully" (cabbage knife) and calls upon the men to desist on pain of dire injury. After some discussion and some brandishing of the persuasive "Kail Gully," the good-wife prevails and peace is restored. At this point a fiddler is called in, and the next section of the canto (stanzas 5 to 10) describes a lively dance on the green. There is some grotesquely comic and occasionally coarse commentary here on a few of the village characters who participate, including the foppish tailor who had seen court dancing and fancied himself as an expert:

> *Furth* started neist a pensy Blade,   *dapper*
>   And out a Maiden took,
> They said that he was *Falkland* bred,
>   And danced by the Book . . .

At stanza 11 night falls and the party retires indoors to the alehouse where the fun goes on, some continuing the dance while others, including "Tam Lutter" (a character carried over from the earlier poem) and the self-important parish clerk, get thoroughly drunk. In stanzas 18 to 20 we see the weary folk enjoying a late festive supper; while the last four stanzas portray the ceremonial "bedding" of the bride,[5] with some general remarks on the aftermath of late drinking and courting

---

[3] For bibliographical data, see Geddie, pp. 98-101.

[4] For the best text of Ramsay's *Christis Kirk*, see *The Works of Allan Ramsay,* edd. Burns Martin and John W. Oliver, Scottish Text Soc., 3rd Ser. 19 (Edinburgh, 1950), I, 57-82. This edition is hereafter cited as *Works.*

[5] Ramsay assumes that the village celebration has been occasioned by a wedding, though there is no indication of this in the 15th-century poem.

among the villagers. Canto III opens with a very humorous description of the folk rising groggily next morning, suffering from the after-effects of the celebration. This canto, which is rather miscellaneous in content and loosely organized, is perhaps best summed up in Ramsay's own note:

> Curious to know how my Bridal Folks would look next Day after the Marriage, I attempted this third *Canto*, which opens with a Description of the Morning. Then the Friends come and present their Gifts to the new married Couple. A View is taken of one Girl (*Kirsh*) who had come fairly off, and of *Mause* who had stumbled with the Laird. Next a new Scene of Drinking is represented, and the young Good-man is creel'd.[6] Then the Character of the Smith's Ill-natured Shrew is drawn, which leads in the Description of riding the Stang.[7] Next *Magy Murdy* has an exemplary Character of a good wise Wife. Deep drinking and bloodless Quarrels make an end of an old Tale.[8]

Ramsay's continuation of *Christis Kirk on the Green* is an entertaining and skillful piece of work. Ramsay equals the original poem in the sharp realism of his description; however, he fails to achieve the magnificent rollicking tempo and verve of his model. His verses tend to move more slowly, to be somewhat gossipy, and to appear contrived in spots. This effect was perhaps inevitable when we consider that Ramsay was writing in what might be called an antiquarian spirit. He was attempting to compose a sequel to a poem already three hundred years old, to imitate its subject matter, style, and, to some extent, its language. (Though Ramsay did not try to write in fifteenth-century Scots, he did affect a slightly archaic diction.) Under these circumstances, it is no wonder that his added cantos lack the spontaneity of the original. Furthermore, Ramsay slightly overemphasized the coarseness inherent in his material. The element of coarseness is present, of course, in all of the earlier *Christis Kirk* poems, and necessarily so— otherwise they would not be true to the kind of life they portray. But

---

[6] "For Merryment, a Creel or Basket is bound, full of Stones, upon his Back; and if he has acted a manly Part, his young Wife with all imaginable Speed cuts the Cords, and relieves him from the Burthen. If she does not, he's rallied for a Fumbler." (Ramsay's note in *Works*, I, 78.)

[7] "The Riding of the Stang on a Woman that hath beat her Husband, is as I have described it, by one's riding upon a Sting, or a long Piece of Wood, carried by two others on their Shoulders, where, like a Herauld, he proclaims the Woman's Name, and the Manner of her unnatural Action." (Ramsay's note in *Works*, I, 80.)

[8] *Works*, I, 74.

at times Ramsay pushes this element too far, and occasionally seems to verge on the merely vulgar.

Despite these weaknesses, however, Ramsay's continuation of *Christis Kirk on the Green* is a remarkable achievement. Though not a great poet, Ramsay was a clever and competent one who produced several very good things, this being one of his best. Certainly it was a daring and ambitious undertaking, beset with difficulties. And although Ramsay did not have the genius to recapture quite the tone, the movement, the exhilaration of his model, he did turn out a reasonable imitation. For the most part, he handles the difficult stanza form with a deftness that is wholly admirable, though there are a few rough spots here and there. The opening stanza of Canto II, for example, is brilliantly done, making a swift transition from the end of the earlier poem:

BUT there had been mair Blood and Skaith,	*hurt*
Sair Harship and great Spulie,	*mischance; spoil*
And mony a ane had gotten his Death	
By this unsonsie Tooly:	*unlucky fight*
But that the bauld Good-wife of *Braith*,	*bold*
Arm'd wi' a great Kail Gully,	*cabbage knife*
Came bellyflaught, and loot an Aith,	*swooping down; oath*
She'd gar them a' be hooly	*be quiet*
Fou fast that day.	

These vigorous lines will perhaps suffice to illustrate the style of Ramsay's poem at its best. It should be noted that he departs from the stanza form of the original *Christis Kirk* in two respects. Ramsay makes no attempt, of course, to carry on the elaborate alliteration of his model, a device which had long since disappeared in Scots poetry, though he does retain the difficult rime scheme in the octave. More important, Ramsay, in all three cantos, changes the bobwheel ending of the original stanza, doing away with the two-line bobwheel refrain of *Christis Kirk, Peblis, Symmie and his Bruder,* and Scott's *Justing,* and replacing it with a simple dimeter tag-line which ends always with the words "that day." This simplified form of the *Christis Kirk* stanza Ramsay took from James Watson's printing of the poem in his *Choice Collection* (1706). The form had first appeared fifteen years earlier in Bishop Gibson's edition of 1691. Where Gibson got his text is unknown, but he probably used an ephemeral broadside version of the late seventeenth century which incorporated this innovation in the stanza form. The suggestion for the new and briefer "that day" refrain certainly came from Scott's *Justing.* We have already noted how Scott used the refrains "Up at the Drum that day" and "Up at Dalkeith that day," which he in turn adapted from stanzas 2 and 22 of *Christis Kirk* (Bannatyne test), where the two words "that day" are added to the normal refrain, and from stanzas 6 and 9 of the same poem where "that day" occurs as the bob line. At any rate, the simplified bobwheel, which Ramsay took over and popularized, is extremely effective with this verse form. It immediately became the standard eighteenth-century form of the *Christis Kirk* stanza, and was adopted by all of Ramsay's successors in the genre.

Ramsay's contribution to the *Christis Kirk* tradition may be summed up briefly. The widespread publicity which he gave to the genre through his repeated publications of both the original *Christis Kirk* and his own sequels helped to develop a new and broader audience for such poems. Ramsay's own cantos are, as we have noted, marked by a rather affected antiquarian flavor; and as such his work is a symptom of a nation on the defensive against cultural assimilation, turning back to its past for inspiration and for refreshing its sense of national identity. But in the hands of succeeding generations of poets who were attracted to the *Christis Kirk* form by the great success of Ramsay's venture, the genre gradually lost this antiquarian emphasis, and eventually, with Fergusson and Burns, became completely adapted to contemporary themes and artistic purposes. Had it not been for Ramsay, however, these later developments would probably never have occurred. The length of Ramsay's cantos was also significant. After *Polemo-Middinia* the *Christis Kirk* poems had been getting shorter and less substantial. Ramsay, by writing two ambitious sequels comparable in length to the prototypes of the tradition, reversed this trend and re-established the *Christis Kirk* type as a major genre. Finally, by adopting an adroit simplification of the bobwheel, Ramsay modified the traditional stanza and thus made it a more attractive and manageable medium for modern Scottish poets.

The example set by Allan Ramsay was soon followed by other writers of less note. In the generation between Ramsay and Fergusson two minor poets, David Nicol and John Skinner, tried their hands at the *Christis Kirk* genre. Nicol, an obscure schoolmaster, composed a sequel to Ramsay's sequel, entitled *Christis Kirk on the Green, Canto IV,* which he published in a volume of his collected poems in 1766.[9] The time of actual composition is unknown, but the piece probably dates from about 1750. Nicol's poem takes up where Ramsay's Canto III left off, and describes the events of the following day: the "kirking" of the bride and groom, and the post-nuptial banquet at which a rather forced and

9 *Poems on Several Subjects, Both Comical and Serious* (Edinburgh), pp. 47-53.

insipid altercation ensues between several of the villagers before harmony and general good will prevail at the end.

Poetically speaking, Nicol's canto is a dull and worthless performance, as the tortured opening stanza shows:

> When Phoebus, wi' his gauden beams,
> Bang'd in the light of day,
> And glittering on the silder [sic] streams   *silver*
> That thro' the valleys stray,
> The couthy carles, frae their dreams,   *affable old men*
> Began to rax, and say,   *stretch*
> Up drowsy herds; herds Phoebus blames
> That made so short a stay
> Away that day.

The preposterous way in which Nicol introduces neo-classical "poetic diction" into this context hardly needs comment, to say nothing of the ungrammatical use of "glittering" instead of "glittered," and the absurdity of his having the "herds" (shepherd lads of the village) blame "Phoebus" for staying away for too short a time. The poem is full of this kind of appalling artificiality, Nicol's clumsy English style clashing agonizingly with his Scots vernacular. At one point in the dialogue (stanza 9) he even has the good-wives of the village talking about embracing "Venus' laws!" In everything but his style, Nicol follows Ramsay slavishly, and manages to drag into his poem, very self-consciously, virtually every character mentioned in both the original *Christis Kirk* and in Ramsay, with all kinds of allusions to things that have happened in the earlier cantos. But Nicol's style is all his own.

As a continuator of the *Christis Kirk* tradition, the Reverend John Skinner was a good deal more successful than his contemporary David Nicol. Through most of his long lifetime (1721-1807), Skinner was an Episcopal minister at Longside, Aberdeenshire, and an amateur poet of considerable ability, being the author of, among other things, the famous song of *Tullochgorum*. He was an ardent student of Scots poetry from a very early age, as he reveals in a letter to his friend Robert Burns, dated November 14, 1787, where he declares: "It is as old a thing as I remember, my fondness for 'Chryste-Kirk on the Green,' which I had by heart ere I was twelve years of age, and which, some years ago, I attempted to turn into Latin verse." [10] Skinner's Latin translation of *Christis Kirk* here referred to, was a work of his later years. But much earlier in his career Skinner had produced a more important and original 'contribution to the tradition in the form of a long poem called *The*

---

[10] "Biographical Sketch" by H. G. Reid in *Songs and Poems by the Rev. John Skinner* (Peterhead, Scotland, 1859), p. xxx.

Monymusk Christmas Ba'ing,[11] written about 1739 when Skinner was seventeen and assistant schoolmaster at Monymusk, Aberdeenshire. Skinner makes no mention of this work in his letters to Burns; but Burns certainly knew the poem well, since there is a distinct echo of it in *Tam O'Shanter*.[12]

The Monymusk Christmas Ba'ing is a substantial poem of some thirty-four nine-line stanzas. The ideas for the poem was undoubtedly suggested to Skinner by Ramsay's continuations of *Christis Kirk*. Skinner uses Ramsay's form of the stanza, with the simplified bobwheel ending in "that day;" but, unlike Ramsay, he frequently introduces alliteration, probably because of his fondness for the original fifteenth-century *Christis Kirk* with its heavy alliterative pattern. For his subject, Skinner takes a typical *Christis Kirk* activity, a rough-and-tumble football game which was traditionally played by the villagers of Monymusk in the local churchyard during the Christmas season. The poet describes a long series of personal encounters during the game as a result of which most of the players end up with barked shins, sprained ankles, bloody noses, bruised heads, and so forth. These incidents are related briefly one after another, and are all of the same kind, becoming, in fact, a little monotonous toward the end. In its style, *The Monymusk Christmas Ba'ing* is generally competent and fairly vigorous in spots, though its wit and spirit flag from time to time. One of the interesting features of Skinner's manner is that he introduces touches of local Aberdeenshire dialect, as in his use of "bleedy" for "bloody" in this final stanza, which may serve as a fair sample of the whole:

> Has ne'er in Monymuss been seen
> Sae mony weel-beft skins: *beaten*
> Of a' the bawmen there was nane   *football players*
> But had twa bleedy shins.
> Wi' strenzied shouders mony ane   *sprained*
> Dree'd penance for their sins;   *endured*
> And what was warst, scoup'd hame at e'en,
> May be to hungry inns,
> And cauld that day.

In this stanza, and throughout the poem, Skinner indicates an Aberdeenshire pronunciation in his spelling only very sparingly, and only in words such as "bleedy" where the meaning would be clear to the general reader. He carefully avoids broader northeastern dialectal forms, such

11 *Songs and Poems*, pp. 1-12.

12 Compare Skinner: "Like bumbees bizzing frae a byke,/ Whan hirds their riggins tirr" (stanza 2), with Burns: "As bees bizz out wi' angry fyke,/ When plundering herds assail their byke" (*Tam O'Shanter*, ll. 193-194).

as "fat" for "what," so that his poem is in standard Scots with only a judicious sprinkling of Aberdeenshire. *The Monymusk Christmas Ba'ing* is a very creditable work for a young man of seventeen. It shows a solid artistic competence and is infinitely superior to Nicol's poem. Once this has been said, however, one must admit that on the whole the work is little more than competent. Though there are a number of good humorous touches, such as the picture of the absent-minded "dominie" (Skinner himself) wandering onto the field of play and being promptly bowled over, the poem lacks the brilliance and the tempo necessary to sustain interest in so long a work. In boldness and vigor of execution, Skinner falls somewhat short of Ramsay and far short of the original *Christis Kirk,* though he borrows occasional phrases and special effects from both.

But although *The Monymusk Christmas Ba'ing* is only a fair performance artistically, from a historical point of view it has interest and importance in two respects. In the first place, and quite obviously, it is an ambitious poem in the pure *Christis Kirk* tradition, written under the influence of Allan Ramsay. As such, it helped to perpetuate the genre, to further Ramsay's work in giving new impetus to the whole tradition. Secondly, Skinner's poem represents an attempt to domesticate the *Christis Kirk* tradition in eighteenth-century Scotland. Ramsay and Nicol had used more or less generalized scenes and characters with an antiquarian emphasis. But Skinner here portrays a specific celebration (which he has actually witnessed), in a specific place (Monymusk), with some touches of the local dialect actually used there. In other words, Skinner is here working away from the Ramsayesque continuations of the original *Christis Kirk,* and instead is using the genre as a vehicle for a specific, local, and contemporary subject. He does not go all the way in this direction, as we have seen exemplified in his timid introduction of Aberdeenshire dialect; but the tendency is certainly there, a tendency which was to have great importance in rejuvenating the whole *Christis Kirk* tradition, in making it a fresh and vital instrument in the hands of Fergusson and Burns.

Robert Fergusson

The first half of the eighteenth century, then, had seen the vigorous revival of vernacular Scots poetry, stimulated by the pioneering work of Allan Ramsay and the anthologists, and, along with it, a marked upsurge of creative activity in the ancient *Christis Kirk* genre in the hands of Ramsay, Nicol, and Skinner. But although the generation after Ramsay brought forth a host of new writers in the mother tongue, no single poet of Ramsay's stature emerged during the long period from about 1730 to 1770. As a result, by 1770 the whole movement initiated by Ramsay appeared to be in danger of disintegration in the absence of powerful new leadership. This danger, however, was wiped out in the year 1772 by the sudden rise of a compelling new voice in Scots poetry. In that year in Edinburgh an obscure young lawyer's clerk named Robert Fergusson (1750-74) began to publish in Ruddiman's *Weekly Magazine* a series of brilliant Scots poems which brought him almost immediate recognition as the legitimate successor to Ramsay. Fergusson's splendid contribution to Scots poetry, achieved in the incredibly brief span of two years, 1772-73 (he died in 1774 at the age of twenty-four), is only today beginning to be recognized at its full value. Eclipsed as he was almost immediately by Burns, Fergusson has long been slighted by critics and historians of literature, treated most often as an obscure "forerunner" of Burns. Under recent revaluations,[13] however, Fergusson's rare genius is finally coming into its own; and he is being given his rightful place as, second only to Burns, the most brilliant and powerful of eighteenth-century Scottish poets.

Fergusson wrote three major poems on the *Christis Kirk* tradition —*Hallow-fair* (to be clearly distinguished from the song *Hallowfair* treated earlier), *Leith Races,* and *The Election* [14] —all of which deserve detailed attention. The *Christis Kirk* genre was, in fact, an ideal medium of expression for Fergusson since it called for the lively, swift-paced method of description at which he particularly excelled.

Hallow-fair, Fergusson's first attempt in the genre, was composed in the fall of 1772 and first published in the *Weekly Magazine* on November 12. The poem is a substantial one of thirteen stanzas, describing the bustling goings-on at a fair which was held annually in

---

[13] E.g., John Speirs, *The Scots Literary Tradition* (London, 1940); David Daiches, *Robert Burns* (New York, 1950), and "Eighteenth-Century Vernacular Poetry" in *Scottish Poetry: A Critical Survey* (London, 1955), ed. Jas. Kinsley; *Robert Fergusson, 1750-1774* (Bicentennial Essays) ed. Sydney Goodsir Smith (Edinburgh, 1952); Matthew P. McDiarmid ed. *The Poems of Robert Fergusson,* Scottish Text Soc., 3rd Ser. 21 (Edinburgh, 1954), Vol. I (Introduction); and Kurt Wittig, *The Scottish Tradition in Literature* (Edinburgh, 1958).

[14] For the best texts of these poems, see *The Poems of Robert Fergusson,* ed. Matthew P. McDiarmid, STS, 3rd Ser. 24 (Edinburgh, 1956), II, 89-93, 160-167, 185-190.

November near Edinburgh. It is organized structurally in four main sections: the first stanza briefly introduces the subject and sets the scene; in stanzas 2 to 8 the poet sketches the various characters at the fair and their activities: young girls seeking boy friends, "browsters" (brewers), country farmers, "chapmen billies" (peddlers), recruiting sergeants, horses, and so forth; stanzas 9 to 12 deal with the notorious City Guard of Edinburgh (a favorite object of Fergusson's satire) and their rough treatment of "Jock Bell," a drunkard; and the poem ends with a whimsical stanza warning against the consequences of overindulgence. Fergusson presents these animated scenes one after the other with dazzling rapidity. Almost before the reader has time to relish one lively little sketch he is rushed on to the next, and the next. The effect is cumulative; the individual pictures pile up to create a wonderfully rich impression of the fair as a whole, full of life, motion, color, noise, and general confusion. *Hallow-fair* is cleverly organized to give this overall effect, though there is a somewhat overly abrupt change of pace and subject in the second stanza. The transition at the beginning of stanza 9, however, from the fair itself to the later activities of the evening and to the City Guard, is smooth and adroit.

Fergusson's opening stanza is one of the most beautifully balanced in the poem, and demonstrates his facile mastery of the difficult *Christis Kirk* stanza:

> At *Hallowmas,* whan nights grow lang,
>   And *starnies* shine fu' clear,   *stars*
> Whan fock, the nippin cold to bang,   *defeat*
>   Their winter *hap-warms* wear,   *mantles*
> Near Edinbrough a fair there hads,   *holds*
>   I wat there's nane whase name is,
> For strappin dames and sturdy lads,
>   And cap and stoup, mair famous   *cup; drinking jug*
>   Than it that day.

This stanza is notable for its lightness, for the easy natural flow which Fergusson achieves in spite of the complexity of his sentence structure. The poet makes skillful use of the rime scheme to clarify his grammatical pattern: the rime of "whase name is" and "mair famous," an ingenious and playful stroke in itself, pulls together the basic structure of the sentence after a series of interrupters, and helps to make its meaning instantly clear. This stanza, incidentally, is similar in content to the openings of both *Christis Kirk* and *Peblis.* Fergusson was certainly familiar with the original *Christis Kirk,* together with Ramsay's sequels and *Polemo-Middinia,* and probably also with Scott's *Justing, The Blyth-some Bridal,*[15] and, possibly, with the work of Nicol and Skinner. But although Fergusson had apparently studied the earlier *Christis Kirk* poems with care, his own handling of the form is fresh and independent. Ramsay, Nicol, and Skinner had all exploited suggestions and stylistic effects from earlier works in the genre; but Fergusson's effects are inimitably his own. In this connection, it will be seen that Fergusson here introduces an important modification of the stanza. Though he uses Ramsay's simplified bobwheel, he breaks with tradition in having four instead of two rimes in the octave, that is, ABAB/CDCD/E, instead of ABAB/ABAB/C, an innovation which Burns was to adopt in *Hallowe'en* and *The Holy Fair.*

Stanza 2 begins with a precise and suggestive image depicting sunrise over Edinburgh, but is marred by a sudden shift in the middle from the "trig made [spruce] maidens" to the "browsters rare" (brewers), which is slightly disconcerting in its abruptness and constitutes the single structural blemish in the poem. The lines on the "browsters," taken by themselves, are, however, inimitable:

> At *Hallow-fair,* whare browsters rare
>   Keep gude ale on the gantries,   *shelves*
> And dinna scrimp ye o' a skair   *share*
>   O' kebbucks frae their pantries,   *cheeses*
>   Fu' saut that day.   *salty*

The internal rime in the first line combines with the artfully placed alliteration in the second and third to give the passage a swinging, rollicking dash, while the sudden change of pace and pitch in the tagline is effected with superb artistry. Apparently, the brewers of Edinburgh during the festive season of Hallow Fair had a trick of providing free snacks of cheese especially prepared for the occasion and highly seasoned with thirst-provoking *salt,* to whet the appetites of their customers. Hence the phrase, "Fu' saut that day." Fergusson's handling of the tag-line in this and in the preceding stanza reveals, moreover, his technical versatility and his sure control of the *Christis Kirk* form. In stanza 1, the tag-line, "Than it that day," is necessary to complete the sense of the stanza, and rounds it off smoothly and effectively. In stanza 2, however, the tag-line is not an integral part of the grammati-

---

[15] Fergusson must have read *Christis Kirk,* Scott's *Justing,* and *The Blyth-some Bridal* either in Watson's *Choice Collection* (1706-1711) or in Ramsay's *Poems* (1721) or *Ever Green* (1724). That he was familiar with *Polemo-Middinia* is certain from his use of a passage from it as motto for his poem, *The King's Birthday in Edinburgh.* Of all the major *Christis Kirk* poems only *Peblis* was inaccessible to Fergusson (it was not printed until 1783).

cal structure; it gives the impression of an afterthought following a long pause, and involves not only an abrupt slowing down of the rapid rythm of the stanza, but also a change in pitch. The words, "Fu' saut that day," should be viewed as a kind of dramatic "aside," and should be enunciated slowly, in a low, insinuating tone of voice so as to bring out the rich flavor of the satire. The irresistibly comic effect which Fergusson here achieves is, of course, only one out of many brilliantly imaginative touches in *Hallow-fair*; but it is worth analyzing and emphasizing as an example of Fergusson's cunning sense of style. It is in just such details that his peculiar charm and distinction as a poet lie. The line bears the unmistakable stamp of Fergusson's literary personality; he takes the reader into his confidence, as it were, and comments intimately and imaginatively on the scene.

Space does not permit a full discussion of this fascinating poem, but a few further points may be made. Fergusson makes good use of sound effects throughout his poem to create a lively impression of the general noise and tumult of the fair. We hear the peddler's crying of his wares, the shrill voice of a girl being forcibly kissed by a clumsy farmer, the screeching of the recruiting sergeant, the roaring of drunken men, the gabbling of women and children, the guardsmen's barking of orders. Often Fergusson uses direct quotation (a traditional feature of *Christis Kirk* poems) to render the sound of these voices more concrete and vivid. In stanza 3, for example, the pretended indignation ·of the girl, Meg, who is being chased and kissed by "country John," is suggested in her cry—

> Ye silly coof!   *fool*
> Be o' your gab mair spairin . . .

Similiarly, Fergusson reproduces the cry of the Aberdeen peddler:

> Here Sawny cries, frae Aberdeen;
> "Come ye to me fa need: *who*
> "The brawest *shanks* that e'er were seen
> "I'll sell ye cheap an' guid . . ."

Here we find Fergusson making expert use of the Aberdeenshire or Buchan dialect, which he had learned from the speech of his parents. This stanza is full of broad Aberdeenshire forms: "fa" instead of the Lowland "wha;" "guid" given the northeastern pronunciation, "gweed;" "leem" and "teem" for "loom" and "toom," and so on. He does equally well with the Highland dialect of the City Guard, most of whom were recruited from Highland regiments, as in stanza 11:

> Out spak the weirlike corporal,   *warlike*
> "Pring in ta drunken sot."

In this full blown use of local dialects Fergusson surpasses the cautious introduction of Aberdeenshire which we have noted in Skinner's *Monymusk Christmas Ba'ing*. Finally, the poet renders beautifully the ludicrous comment of Jock Bell, the drunkard who has been brutally felled by a blow from a "stark Lochaber aix," the dread weapon of the City Guard:

> "Ohon!" quo' he, "I'd rather be
> "By *sword* or *bagnet* stickit,   *bayonet*
> "Than hae my crown or body wi'
> "Sic deadly weapons nicket."   *such*

The conclusion to *Hallow-fair* is equally effective. In stanza 12 Fergusson clinches his cutting satire of the Guard, urging "good fock" to "bide yont frae this black squad;" and in a final brilliant stanza he recommends moderation:

> A wee soup drink dis unco weel   *sip; does very*
> To had the heart aboon;   *hold; above*
> It's good as lang's a canny chiel   *shrewd fellow*
> Can stand steeve in his shoon.   *steadily; shoes*
> But gin a birkie's owr weel sair'd,   *if; fellow; served*
> It gars him aften stammer   *makes; stagger*
> To *pleys* that bring him to the guard,   *tricks*
> An' eke the *Council-chawmir*,   *also; chamber*
>   Wi' shame that day.

These lines show Fergusson in his finest vein. They have the natural rhythm, and racy colloquial diction of living speech, and yet conform exactly to the metrical pattern. His collocation of vowel sounds in this stanza give it a sprightly lilting effect which contrasts pleasingly with the harsher sound patterns of the preceding stanzas, bringing the poem to a happy close on a note of whimsical humor.

Of all Fergusson's works, *Hallow-fair* is certainly one of the best and most characteristic. It is filled with vigor, dash, and pulsating life, and with Fergusson's typical gaiety, his rich humor. The imaginative brilliance of the poem never falters; there are virtually no stylistic blunders. And in the history of the *Christis Kirk* tradition, *Hallow-fair* is important in three respects. For one thing, Fergusson here makes a major change in the rime scheme of the traditional stanza, a change which gives it greater flexibility, makes it less confining. Secondly, and most significantly, Fergusson in *Hallow-fair* extends the subject matter and changes the emphasis of the *Christis Kirk* genre. All of the earlier poems in the tradition had dealt exclusively with rural or village life and peasant character. *Hallow-fair* is the first to portray city life. Edinburgh in Fergusson's time, of course, with its small area and incredibly crowded conditions, was open to the country on all sides; it was a peculiarly intimate community in which folk of all classes rubbed shoulders and shared cramped lodgings in the tall "lands" or tenements. And life in "Auld Reekie," closely related as it was to the surrounding farming area, was a far cry indeed from life in our great, aloof, mechanized cities of today. Nevertheless, it was a more complex and infinitely more varied kind of life than we find portrayed in any of the *Christis Kirk* poems before Fergusson. Furthermore, Fergusson here breaks completely with the Ramsay tendency to portray generalized characters and old-fashioned manners with a nostalgic or antiquarian emphasis, and gives us instead a lively picture of contemporary life in his beloved Edinburgh as he observed it, keenly and imaginatively, hitting off real characters, making his bold satiric thrusts at the City Guard, and so forth. In short, Fergusson in *Hallow-fair* brought the *Christis Kirk* tradition up to date. Finally, in *Hallow-fair* Fergusson produced a poem which, in its imaginative boldness, sensitive humor, and technical brilliance, surpasses, I think, any single poem in the *Christis Kirk* tradition before it with the exception of the original *Christis Kirk* and *Peblis*.

Fergusson's two later efforts in the *Christis Kirk* genre—*Leith Races* and *The Election*—are, if anything, even more impressive as works of art than *Hallow-fair*. *Leith Races*, which appeared in the *Weekly Magazine* on July 22, 1773, is a kind of companion piece to *Hallow-fair*, but is considerably longer (20 stanzas). Like Fergusson's earlier masterpiece, the poem describes a festival in Edinburgh. The Leith Races, the social highlight of the summer season in Auld Reekie, were an annual series of horse-races held during an entire week in July, with elaborate civic ceremonies, on Leith Sands about three miles from the city. The citizens of Edinburgh flocked *en masse* down to Leith in holiday mood to witness the festivities, and Fergusson here gives a vivid and exuberant picture, touched with inimitable satire, of the whole crowded and boisterous scene.

In structure, *Leith Races* falls into four main divisions. The first five stanzas form the introduction, and present the poet's meeting and conversation with "Mirth," the mythological figure who offers to take him to the "Races" and show him the amusing sights to be found there. In stanzas 6 to 13 Fergusson depicts the various types of people preparing to go to the Races or on their way there: the fashionable ladies dressing up for the occasion; the barking peddlers hawking "true an' faithfu' lists" of the horses running that day; the City Guardsmen being shaved and inspected for the Races; the drunken "tinkler billies" reeling down Leith Walk; and, finally, the "browster wives" busily getting out their cheapest and sourest ale and whiskey, which, in spite of its poor quality, is sure to sell during this thirsty season. In stanzas 14 to 19 we are given vivid glimpses of the tumultuous scene on Leith Sands, where "Buchan bodies" cry their fish through the crowds, dishonest gamblers huddle over games of dice and "rowly powl" (ninepins), horses and carriages dash to and fro in every direction, the townguard lines up the horses for the races, and young fellows from the Robinhood debating club engage in "lang and dreech contesting." In stanza 20 Fergusson closes the poem, describing the drunken aftermath of the Races and ending on a humorous note of warning against the City Guard. The structural method here is Fergusson's usual one of lighting up carefully chosen dramatic details picked out from the general confusion with unerring skill to give a lively and concrete impression of the whole. More specifically, it is the method he had used with great success in *Hallow-fair,* though here he gives a fuller and more detailed picture.

Though *Leith Races* is too long and complex a poem to permit a thorough-going analysis, one or two typical stanzas may be singled out for comment. It is no wonder that Burns was fascinated by the vision of "Mirth," for the passage is one of the most delightful ones in all Fergusson. The poet gives to this abstraction a most engaging and natural character perfectly adapted to the humorous context of the piece as a whole. His "Mirth," a charming, vivacious creature, contrasts significantly with the pompous abstract figures usually found in philosophical "vision" poetry, a poetic tradition which Fergusson may here be incidentally satirizing. At any rate, the fifth stanza, where Fergusson agrees to accompany "Mirth" to the Races, is especially vigorous, full of zest and sparkle:

A bargain be't, and, by my feggs,	*faith*
Gif ye will be my mate,	
Wi' you I'll screw the cheery pegs,	*tune the fiddle*
Ye shanna find me blate;	*shy*
We'll reel an' ramble thro' the sands,	
And jeer wi' a' we meet;	
Nor hip the daft and gleesome bands	*miss*
That fill EDINA'S street	*Edinburgh's*
Sae thrang this day.	*crowded*

These lines have a swift, exhilarating rhythm to them; they sing their way into the memory, aided by the alliteration in lines 1 and 5 and the recurrence of the "ee" sound throughout. The superb craftsmanship of this stanza is matched in the passage (stanzas 8 to 10) on the inevitable City Guard. Stanza 8, describing the guardsmen getting spruced up for the Races, demands quotation:

To WHISKY PLOOKS that brunt for wooks	*pimples; burned; weeks*
On town-guard soldiers faces,	
Their barber bauld his whittle crooks,	*razor*
An' scrapes them for the races:	
Their STUMPS erst us'd to *filipegs,*	*legs; kilts*
Are dight in spaterdashes	*dressed*
Whase barkent hides scarce fend their legs	*encrusted*
Frae weet, and weary plashes	*splashes*
O' dirt that day.	

This stanza shows Fergusson at his liveliest, lashing out at his old enemy, the Guard, in bold and irresistibly comic style. His use of internal rime in the first line, "To WHISKY PLOOKS that brunt for wooks," deftly sets the tone of impish mockery, a tone that is sustained through his alliterative phrases ("barber bauld," "weet and weary," "dirt that day"). The reference to "their barber bauld" is a fine artistic touch, a perfect choice of epithet, striking as it does the precise note of mock-heroic satire which Fergusson is aiming at. The entire passage on the Guard is powerfully and imaginatively conceived and executed with subtle artistry. Though Fergusson does not sustain this high level of excellence in all twenty stanzas of his poem, he never drops far below it; *Leith Races* is, in fact, the most consistently brilliant of his longer poems. Fergusson's facile mastery of Scots idiom and his sensitive grasp of poetic technique are nowhere more evident.

In *Leith Races* Fergusson produced a comic extravaganza of Edinburgh social life, similar to his earlier *Hallow-fair.* But soon after, in *The Election,* his last contribution to the *Christis Kirk* tradition, he broke new ground in adapting the genre as a vehicle for political as well as social satire. This fine poem, which is not as well known as it deserves to be, first appeared in Ruddiman's *Weekly Magazine* on September 16, 1773, over the signature: "R. Fergusson. *Auld Reikie, Sept.* 13." The poem contains fifteen *Christis Kirk* stanzas with a further modification of the form. We have noted that Fergusson broke with tradition in using a four-rime octave in *Hallow-fair* and *Leith Races.* In this piece he attempts a compromise, introducing three rimes instead of two or four in the octave, thereby linking the rime schemes of the two quatrains as follows: ABAB/ACAC/D. None of Fergusson's critics and commentators seems to have noticed this interesting variation in *The Election.*

This poem describes part of a complicated municipal election in

Edinburgh—the choosing of the fourteen "deacons," each of whom represented one of the incorporated "trades" of Edinburgh on the Town Council.[16] Fergusson here employs the same structural method which he had used successfully in *Hallow-fair, Leith Races,* and other poems. He introduces his theme in the first stanza, suggesting the wild conviviality of the election. In stanzas 2 to 5 he draws two masterly sketches of tradesmen getting ready to go to the customary feast at "Walker's" given by the victorious deacons. Stanzas 6 to 8 describe the uninhibited goings-on at the feast itself; then in the next group of four stanzas Fergusson illustrates the drunken aftermath of the affair as deacons and tradesmen stagger home. In stanzas 13 and 14, we see unscrupulous politicians bribing voters, and new deacons being formally instated. And in his final stanza Fergusson comments whimsically on the tremendous strain which all the heavy drinking of election time puts on the constitutions of those involved, especially the deacons themselves.

The style of *The Election* may be illustrated briefly. The opening scene of the poem (stanzas 2 and 3), where we see and hear the pompous, domineering citizen getting dressed up for the deacons' dinner, is among Fergusson's most delightful and inimitable passages:

Haste, EPPS, quo' John, an' bring my gez,	*wig*
Take tent ye dinna't spulzie:	*heed; spoil*
Last night the barber ga't a friz,	*curl*
An' straikit it wi' ulzie.	*stroked; oil*
Hae done your PARITCH lassie *Liz,*	*porridge*
Gi'e me my sark an' gravat;	*shirt; tie*
I'se be as braw's the Deacon is	
Whan he taks AFFIDAVIT	
O' FAITH the day.	

Whar's *Johnny* gaun, cries neebor BESS,	
That he's sae gayly bodin	*furnished*
Wi' new kam'd wig, weel syndet face,	*combed; washed*
Silk hose, for hamely hodin?	*homespun*
"Our Johny's nae sma' drink you'll guess,	
"He's trig as ony muir-cock,	*spruce*
"An' forth to mak a Deacon, lass;	
"He downa speak to poor fock	*cannot*
Like us the day."	

Here, in a few masterful strokes, and entirely through dialogue, Fergusson suggests the whole character of the man, his ludicrous vanity and

[16] For a complete account of the procedure for Edinburgh municipal elections in the 18th century, see Hugo Arnot, *The History of Edinburgh* (Edinburgh, 1816), pp. 391-394.

self-importance. The taunting remarks of the neighbors in stanza 3, as Johnny steps forth starched and spruce in his unaccustomed finery, sound authentic and are perfectly calculated to drive home the satiric point of the sketch. The whole passage is concrete and dramatic in effect, showing Fergusson's astonishing ability to create lively characters in a few short lines. Equally remarkable is the superb naturalness of the dialogue, which rings true in spite of the exigencies of the difficult stanza form. This picture of "Johnny" contrasts neatly with the succeeding sketch of the "canty cobler" in stanza 5, where Fergusson's style takes on a kindlier, almost pathetic tone, without losing anything of its trenchant, objective force. Here he pictures the poor fellow's enthusiasm as he looks forward to a hearty meal at the deacon's banquet, a refreshing change after months of drudgery and malnutrition. On this day alone he suddenly and temporarily becomes a person of importance, "a pow o' WIT and LAW," and can afford for a few triumphant hours to "taunt at soals an' heels," the humble symbols of his trade. The splendid verve of this opening section is well sustained through the description of the feast and its aftermath. The whole scene of enthusiastic gluttony, rowdiness, freakish wit, and bestiality is laid before us with relentless realism. In stanza 13 occurs one of many fine imaginative touches, where Fergusson pictures dishonest voters taking half-crown bribes from politicians. He observes that the recipients of this tainted money never stop to check the coins for correct weight:

> They pouch the gowd, nor fash the town   *gold; bother*
> For weights an' scales to weigh them
> Exact that day.

In this ingenious way Fergusson suggests to the imagination of his reader the darkness and furtiveness of these nefarious transactions: the voter quickly pockets his half-crown and slinks guiltily off. This kind of suggestiveness is highly characteristic of Fergusson's style in general.

On the whole, *The Election* is a very impressive piece of work, a daring satire full of exuberance and creative vitality. It is more purely satirical in purpose than either *Hallow-fair* or *Leith Races,* and gives evidence of Fergusson's characteristic fearlessness, his clear-sighted, objective vision in criticizing political as well as social abuses. The poem is, of course, primarily entertaining rather than didactic; but it does show that Fergusson was very much aware of the short-comings in the politics and society of his day and made conscious efforts to expose them in the light of his satiric imagination.

All in all, Fergusson's work in the *Christis Kirk* tradition has tremendous historical importance. For one thing, by writing three daringly original major poems in this genre Fergusson refreshed the whole tradition and demonstrated conclusively that the age-old *Christis Kirk* form was still a vital and adaptable one for modern Scots poets. Additionally, he modified the stanzaic form and extended the traditional subject matter of the genre to include town life and political satire; and he rescued the tradition from the Ramsay antiquarian tendency by showing how powerful the *Christis Kirk* medium could be for the treatment of specific contemporary scenes and issues. Finally, and perhaps most important of all, Fergusson produced three poems of really high artistic quality, poems which are distinguished for their vigor, gaiety, and compelling artistry, and which remain eminently readable today. He was, in short, the first eighteenth-century Scots poet to reveal the full potentialities of the genre, to show that first-rate, sophisticated poetry could be written in this form. In this respect, Fergusson left Ramsay and the others far behind, and established a new standard of high quality craftsmanship. And all of these features of Fergusson's work in the *Christis Kirk* tradition were to have a profound influence upon the practice of his immediate successor, Robert Burns.

(*To be continued*)

UNIVERSITY OF RHODE ISLAND

ISABEL HYDE

Poetic Imagery:
a point of comparison
between Henryson and Dunbar.

That two of the Middle Scots poets, Henryson and Dunbar are writers of considerable stature, each with a clearly defined individuality within a convention, is a fact that has sometimes been overlooked by such critics as have worked in these comparatively untrodden fields, because they have so often been pre-occupied with the poets' relations to English writers, to the exclusion of a consideration of their poetic individuality.[1] When we cease to compare these Scottish poets primarily with Chaucer and his followers and view their work together and as an individual contribution to literature, a very interesting comparison presents itself, particularly in the field of figurative writing (or poetic imagery) which, in medieval poetic includes description ("descriptio") and moral sayings ("sententiae"). Concerning the lives of Robert Henryson and William Dunbar very little is known for certain though some assumptions have been made but, in the corpus of their poetry, their personalities stand out clearly and appeal to the twentieth century reader by qualities which are frequently complementary. It is, again, pointless to enter the contest over which of these two poets is, in fact, the greatest, for this is a matter of taste and therefore not to be disputed, but there is no doubt that each is a great poet in a way which is, ultimately, entirely individual, once we have made allowance for their indebtedness to the medieval common stock of concepts and terms. Some of these shorter examples may be illustrated here and now and the poets' work within the field of the longer conventional "descriptio" and "sententiae" will be examined later in this article.

[1] See, for example, P. H. Nichols "William Dunbar as a Scottish Lydgatian," *PMLA,* XLVI, 214-224 and "Lydgate's Influence on the Aureate Terms of the Scottish Chaucerians," *PMLA,* XLVII, 516-522.

[183]

Of the shorter common stock figures used by both poets we have for example:

> O, fair Creisseid! the flour and *A per se*
> Of Troy and Grece, . . .[2]

> London, thou art of townes *A per se.*
>   Soveraign of cities, semeliest in sight,[3]

> *Lyke to ane Bair quhetting his Tuskis kene,*[4]

> Agane thai tirvit him bak and syde,
>   *Als brim as ony baris woid;*[5]

> And till hir hoill scho went *as fyre on flint:*[6]

> The sparhalk to the spring him sped,
>   *Als fers as fyre of flynt.*[7]

> Lyke till *a flour that plesandly will spring,*
> *Quhilk fadis sone, and endis with murnyng.*[8]

> Thy lustye bewte and thy youth
>   *Sall feid as dois the somer flouris;*[9]

> Beyonde this Mure he fand a ferefull strete,
>   *Myrk as the nycht,* to pass richt dangerous,[10]

> The sone obscurit of his licht;
>   The day wox *dirk as ony nycht,*[11]

> For thay ar sad as *Widdercock in Wind,*[12]

[2] Henryson, "The Testament of Cresseid," ll. 78-79. Quotations throughout are from the S.T.S. editions of the Poems of Henryson and Dunbar, unless otherwise stated. Italics are mine throughout. Some letters have been normalized, e.g. "th" for the thorn character and "y" for the yoke and the Middle Scots "v" has been changed to "u" where necessary and "I" to "J."

[3] Attributed to Dunbar. "London, Thou Art of Townes A Per Se," ll. 1-2.

[4] Henryson, "The Testament of Cresseid," l. 193.

[5] Dunbar, "Ane Ballat of the Passioun of Christ," ll. 57-58.

[6] Henryson, "The Two Mice," l. 328.

[7] Dunbar, "Of the Fenyeit Freir of Tungland," ll. 79-80.

[8] Henryson, "Orpheus & Eurydice," ll. 90-91.

[9] Dunbar, "Memento, Homo, Quod Cinis Es," ll. 25-26.

[10] Henryson, "Orpheus & Eurydice," ll. 303-304.

[11] Dunbar, "Ane Ballat of the Passioun of Christ," ll. 84-85.

[12] Henryson, "The Testament of Cresseid," l. 567.

Of this fals failyeand warld I tyre,
That ever more flytis *lyk ane phane;*[13]

In these examples we see that Henryson and Dunbar, like many other medieval poets, such as Chaucer and the anonymous authors of secular and religious lyrics and the lengthy romances, used these common stock comparisons neatly but with very little individuality. In these examples we shall look in vain for the characteristic stamp of one author or another. They might well have been written by any medieval poet, English or Scottish. For an individual, contrasting and complementary use of imagery or figures of speech in our two poets we must look further.

In a comparison of the work of Henryson and Dunbar, we find that their achievements lie within a certain clearly defined poetic territory. In justly appreciating Henryson's work, one needs to be really familiar with the whole of it as, unlike Dunbar, he does not produce brilliant pyrotechnic displays in individual poems, although he can attain to considerable achievements of a different kind in the *Fables* and *The Testament of Cresseid.* Henryson's achievement consists of the sum total of the *Testament,* the individual Fables from Aesop and the other moralizing poems, including *Robene and Makyne, The Bludy Serk* and *The Three Deid Pollis.* Here we have nothing akin to the variation between aureate, vernacular, secular and religious poems such as we find in Dunbar. Henryson is more all of a piece, with hardly any marked contrasts of tone or style. Henryson uses, too, fewer figures of speech or images than does Dunbar and this seems to be one of the outstanding and significant differences between these two poets. Dunbar's poems are crowded with figures which are often clearly visualized, vigorous and marked by an effect of glittering light and dazzling colour. Henryson's figures, though they have their own particular charm, seem generally less visual and lack the blaze of colour so characteristic of Dunbar's work. This is no doubt due to the fact that there are also fewer passages of description in Henryson's poems and less of the aureate language than in Dunbar's work, but this in itself is simply another aspect of the difference between the two poets so clearly manifested in their use of images. It is difficult to illustrate this point in a comparatively short article but a fair comparison of characteristic examples can be made. Both poets use the common stock phrases to express colour, such as "as white as whale bone;" "as wan and wallowed as the Leid;" "reid as Rois" and "Roys red and quhit." Henryson also has "als quhyte as milk" and "quhyter than the snow"

13 Dunbar, "Of the Warldis Instabilitie," ll. 94-95.

and "grene as leif" but he seldom shows the wild delight in light and colour which is characteristic of Dunbar. For example, Henryson has:

> Exempill tak be thir Jolie flouris,
> Richt sweit of smell and plesand of *colouris,*
> Sum *grene,* sum *blew,* sum *purpour, quhite,* and *reid,*
> This distribute be gift of his godheid.[14]

This passage is one of conventional description and not much more than that. We find the same common stock description in Dunbar but with a difference:

> Me thocht fresche May befoir my bed upstude,
> In weid *depaynt of mony diverss hew,*
> Sobir, benyng, and full of mansuetude,
> In *brycht* atteir of flouris forgit new,
> Hevinly of *color, quhyt, reid, broun* and *blew,*
> Balmit in dew, and *gilt* with Phebus *bemys,*
> Quhill all the houss *illumynit* of hir *lemys.*[15]

In this aureate description of May, for example, Dunbar does not simply enumerate the colours of the flowers as does Henryson but adds the rays of the sun and the effect of light in "brycht," "gilt," "bemys," "illumynit" and "lemys." Furthermore, there is nothing in Henryson's work like the first six verses of *The Goldyn Targe* where gold, silver, crystal, beryl, pearl, ruby, sapphire and emerald burn, with red, white, purple, green, rose, azure and gold colours, in a blaze of light, as one figure merges into another. Henryson's characteristic figures have their own individual beauty and poetic power in a softer and sadder tone:

> Quhen that aurora, with hir curcheis gray,
> Put up hir heid betuix the nicht and day.[16]

and:

> The morrow come, and phebus with his bemis
> Consumit had the mistie cluddis gray;
> The ground was grene, and als like gold it glemis,
> With gres growand gritlie, gude, and gay;
> The spyce thay spreid to spring on everie spray;
> The lark, the maveis, and the merle full hie,
> Sueitlie can sing, trippand fra tre to tre.[17]

---

14 Henryson, "The Swallow and the Other Birds," ll. 1646-1649.

15 Dunbar, "The Thistle and the Rose," ll. 15-21.

16 Henryson, "The Cock and the Fox," ll. 500-501.

17 Henryson, "The Trial of the Fox," ll. 858-864.

We may compare with this Dunbar's setting of a similar scene in the same convention:

> The purpour sone, with tendir bemys reid,
> In orient bricht as angell did appeir,
> Throw goldin skyis putting up his heid,
> Quhois gilt tressis schone so wondir cleir,
> That all the world tuke confort, fer and neir,
> To luke upone his fresche and blisfull face,
> Doing all sable fro the hevynnis chace.[18]

In Henryson's lines the figure is obviously little more than a conventional phrase. "Phebus" could be translated into "the sun" without making any difference to the rest of the stanza which is restrained in its description of the sunbeams touching with gold a grey-green landscape. Dunbar, however, obviously develops the personification with far more delight in the opportunity which it affords for the interweaving of colour, movement and the atmosphere of youthful freshness and tenderness which prevails throughout the poem, in honour of James IV and the Princess Margaret. In these set pieces of "descriptio," each poet achieves a poetic effect which is individual while it is within the convention. Were they anonymous one might surmise that the first in its unsophisticated and sober colouring was by Henryson, the second with its energy and bursting radiance by Dunbar. And in noting this we must conclude that the individuality of tone and the essential poetic achievement is ultimately more important than the Chaucerian or other influences which lie behind it. We note the debt to the convention while going on to enjoy the creation from it of poetry which is successful in its own right, as distinct from the uninspired copying of Chaucer's stock expressions by such less gifted writers as Lydgate.

The images based by Henryson on the medieval common stock in which the time and season and weather are personified or depicted have a particular quality which is a part of Henryson's poetic genius and distinguishable from that of any other medieval writer, English or Scots. In another stanza we find an equally subdued and tender descriptive figure, in the same style.

> 'Na,' quod the taid, 'that proverb is nocht trew;
> for fair thingis ofttymes ar fundin faikin.
> The blaberyis, thocht thay be sad of hew,
> Ar gadderit up quhen prymerois is forsaikin.'[19]

The whortleberries and primrose of the last figure are also part of

---

[18] Dunbar, "The Thistle and the Rose," ll. 50-56.
[19] Henryson, "The Paddock and the Mouse," ll. 57-60.

the more simple country setting of Henryson's poems which contrasts with the predominantly urban life of Dunbar's settings and the lovely subdued colouring is akin to that of a much later treatment of the same theme, in a similar stock convention, some lines which were set to music at the end of the sixteenth century:

> Brown is my Love, but graceful;
> And each renowned whiteness
> Matched with thy lovely brown loseth its brightness.

> Fair is my Love, but scornful;
> Yet have I seen despised,
> Dainty white lilies, and sad flowers well prized.[20]

Henryson's berries are "sad" of hue too and his whortleberries and primroses are not just conventional. As we have remarked, the background of Henryson's poetry is rural and this element of country life may be traced in many of his images and descriptions. These figures, indeed, form some of his most beautiful lines and represent a quality in Henryson's poetry which is neither medieval nor modern but ageless: as, for example, in the following:

> In Metaphisik Aristotell sayis
> That mannis Saul is lyke ane Bakkis Ee,
> Quhilk lurkis still als lang as licht of day is,
> And in the gloming cummis furth to fle;
> Hir Ene ar waik, the Sone scho may not se:
> Sa is our Saull with Fantasie opprest,
> To knaw the thingis in nature manifest.[21]

and in the description of the month of June:

> Thus passit furth quhill Iune, that iolie tyde,
> And seidis that war sawin of beforne
> Wer growin hie, that hairis micht thame hide,
> And als the quailtye craikand in the corne;[22]

which has none of the literary formality of the conventional medieval "May morning" descriptions and is obviously based upon a loving observation of the passage of the seasons. There are too, in Henryson's poetry, a few figures which are drawn from the seasonal labours of

---

[20] *The Oxford Book of Sixteenth Century Verse,* p. 845, No. 428, Song set by Nicholas Yonge.

[21] Henryson, "The Swallow and the Other Birds," ll. 1628-1634.

[22] Henryson, "The Swallow and the Other Birds," ll. 1768-1771.

gardeners or farmers though they may owe something to convention as well; as, for example, the figure of grafting:

> Fals titlaris now growis up full rank,
> nocht ympit in the stok of cheretie,[23]

and the figure of the weeds, or "vetches" in the corn:

> Freindis, ye may find, and ye will tak heid,
> In to this fabill ane gude moralitie;
> As fytchis myngit ar with noble seid,
> Swa intermynglit is aduersitie
> With eirdlie Joy; . . .[24]

and of the seed killed by frost; from *The Testament of Cresseid*:

> The seid of lufe was sawin in my face,
> And ay grew grene throw your supplie and grace.
> Bot now, allace, that seid with froist is slane,
>
> (ll. 137-139)

These figures and descriptions, with their delicate and knowledgeable observation of the bat, hares, quails, wildflowers and the seeds and frost of the Scottish countryside are characteristic of Henryson's work.

It is interesting to note now that Dunbar's naturalistic images, like his aureate or conventional ones, are rather different. They range from the exuberance of the simile describing "James Dog, Kepar of the Quenis Wardrop":

> Quhen that I speik till him freindlyk,
> He barkis lyk ane midding tyk,
> War chassand cattell through a bog:[25]

and of another simile describing the "Maister Almaser," who danced in the Queen's Chamber "Lyk a stirk stackarand in the ry," [26] through the frank and vigorous lines describing the unfortunate husbands of the "Tua Mariit Wemen and the Wedo":

> He feppilis like a farcy aver, that flyrit on a gillot.[27]

and

> He dois as dotit dog that damys on all bussis,[28]

---

[23] Henryson, "Aganis Haisty Credence of Titlaris," ll. 1-2.

[24] Henryson, "The Two Mice," ll. 365-370.

[25] Dunbar, "Of James Dog, Kepar of the Quenis Wardrop," ll. 13-15.

[26] Dunbar, "Of a Dance in the Quenis Chalmer," l. 17.

[27] Dunbar, "Tua Mariit Wemen and the Wedo," l. 114.

[28] Ibid., l. 186.

to the beauty of the new moon (a figure which is used with no romantic intention but which is, nevertheless, very lovely):

> And, as the new mone, all pale, oppressit with change,
> Kythis quhilis her cleir face, through cluddis of sable,
> So keik I through my clokis, and castis kynd lukis
> To knychtis, and to cleirkis, and courtly personis.[29]

and of the conventional comparison of the blossoming bough:

> I saw approch agayn the orient sky,
> A saill, als quhite as blossum vpon spray,[30]

The coarseness and vitality of the first four of these figures and the lovely effects of light and shadow of the last two, with their evidence of Dunbar's intense delight in visual beauty, are quite unlike the tender delicacy of those of Henryson's figures which are drawn from nature, of which we have examined seven examples and to which we may add the following to demonstrate the point more fully:

> In lyke maner as throw the bustious eird,
> Swa it be laubourit with grit diligence,
> Springis the flouris and the corne abreird,
> Hailsum and gude to mannis sustenence,
> Swa dois spring ane morale sweit sentence
> Out of the subtell dyte of poetry,
> To gude purpois, quha culd it weill apply.
>
> The nuttis schell, thocht it be hard and teuch,
> Haldis the kirnell, and is delectabill.
> Sa lyis thair ane doctrine wyse aneuch,
> And full of frute, vnder ane feinyeit fabill.[31]

In these figures, from the "Prolog" to the Moral Fables we find an attitude to nature and the life of the countryside and the figurative parallels and illustrations which may be drawn therefrom which is characteristic of Henryson and quite different from Dunbar's approach. For instance, Henryson's "bustious" or "rough" or "fresh" earth has to be "laubourit" or tilled with devotion before natural flowers and corn can "spring" from it. In Dunbar's more conventionally aureate, though equally beautiful and effective figurative descriptions, the beauties of the earth in their energy and richness are not those of the naturalistic Scottish

[29] Ibid., ll. 432-435.

[30] Dunbar, "The Goldyn Targe," ll. 50-51.
c.f. Chaucer, "The Miller's Tale," ll. 3323-3324.

> And therupon he hadde a gay surplys
> As whit as is the blosme upon the rys.

[31] Henryson, "Prologue to the Fables," ll. 8-18.

countryside which we have found in Henryson's poems and the examples from them already quoted, but are rather akin to the medieval illuminations from calendars and Books of Hours, showing the labours of the Seasons in fields and gardens where Nature is fecund indeed and rather idealistic than naturalistic. Everything burgeons but in a conventional fashion and we are no longer conscious, as we are with Henryson, of the painful tilling of the earth to produce this abundance. This may be illustrated by the following lines from Dunbar's "The Tretis of the Tua Mariit Wemen and the Wedo":

> Apon the Midsummer ewin, mirriest of nichtis,
> I muvit furth allane, neir as midnicht wes past,
> Besyd ane gudlie grene garth, full of gay flouris,
> Hegeit, of ane hughe hicht, with hawthorne treis;
> Quhairon ane bird, on ane bransche, so birst out hir notis
> That neuer ane blythfullar bird was on the beuche harde:
> Quhat throw the sugarat sound of hir sang glaid,
> And throw the sauar sanatiue of the sueit flouris,
> I drew in derne to the dyk to dirkin eftir myrthis;
> The dew donkit the daill, and dynarit the foulis.   (ll. 1-10)

This passage of figurative "descriptio" and the lines which follow comparing the "thre gay ladeis" in their beauty to flowers:

> Thair mantillis grein war as the gress that grew in May sessoun,
> Fetrit with thair quhyt fingaris about thair fair sydis:
> Off ferliful fyne favour war thair faceis meik,
> All full of flurist fairheid, as flouris in June;
> Quhyt, seimlie, and soft, as the sweit lillies;
> New upspred vpon spray, as new spynist rose,
> Arrayit ryallie about with mony rich wardour,
> That nature, full nobillie, annamalit fine with flouris
> Off alkin hewis under hewin, that ony heynd knew;
> Fragrant, all full of fresche odour fynest of smell,   (ll. 24-33)

are formalized, conventional and idealistically un-natural and they contrast strongly with Henryson's laboriously tilled earth and his tough-shelled nuts with their sweet kernels in the "Prolog" to the Fables or with the Country Mouse's hole, in the very realistic, cold, harsh countryside, which was nevertheless "Als warme as woll." There are no such homely, small creatures as field mice in Dunbar's poems, though he refers to dogs and "stirks," and "Als warme as woll" is a comparison typical of Henryson's close and loving observation of a daily life, even that of a mouse, in the small town and a countryside which knew nothing of the court. The primroses and violets, too, of one of Henryson's more conventional "descriptio" are also markedly different from

Dunbar's roses and lilies of the aureate figurative passage which we have examined already:

> In middis of Iune, that sweit seasoun,
> Quhen that fair Phebus, with his bemis bricht,
> Had dryit up the dew fra daill and doun,
> And all the land maid with his bemis licht,
> In ane morning, betuix mid day and nicht,
> I Rais, and put all sleuth and sleip asyde,
> And to ane wod I went allone but gyde.
>
> Sweit wes the smel of flouris, quhyte and reid,
> The noyes of birdis richt delitious,
> The bewis braid blomit abone my heid,
> The ground growand with gers gratious;
> Of all plesance that place wes plenteous,
> With sweit odouris and birdis harmonie,
> The Murning Myld: my mirth wes mair for thy.
>
> The Rosis reid arrayit on Rone and Ryce,
> The Prymeros, and the Purpour Uiola;
> To heir it wes ane poynt of Paradice,
> Sic Mirth the Mavis and the Merle couth ma.
> The blossumis blyith brak up on bank and bra;
> The smell of Herbis and of foullis cry
> Contending quha suld haif the victorie.[32]

This, again, is the conventional "May" or "June" morning passage of "descriptio" but, in distinction from those of Chaucer and Dunbar, we notice in Henryson's lines again a more homely and naturalistic element. His flowers are conventionally "quhyte and reid" but his roses grow on "Rone and Ryce," real thickets and twigs of brushwood, his primroses and violets owe little or nothing to convention and his birds however conventional are also real thrushes and blackbirds, unlike the usual anonymous "fowls" of these aureate "descriptions," just as, in another spring "descriptio," he has a homely flower, a columbine, growing in real clay soil:

> Synne cummis Uer, quhen winter is away,
> The Secretar of Somer with his Seill,
> Quhen Columbie up keikis throw the clay,
> Quhilk fleit wes befoir with frostis fell.
> The Mavis and the Merle beginnis to mell;
> The Lark on loft, with uther birdis small,
> Than drawis furth fra derne, over doun and daill.[33]

[32] Henryson, "The Lion and the Mouse" (Prologue), ll. 1313-1333.

[33] Henryson, "The Swallow and the Other Birds," ll. 1698-1704.

and notes the condition of the earth with a countryman's shrewd eye for these things when he adds:

> I passit furth, syne lukit to and fro,
> To se the Soill that wes richt sessonabill,
> Sappie, and to resaif all seidis abill.[34]

and goes on to comment upon the seasonal work of the countryside. Few medieval poets indeed have made so much local and homely use of the "May morning" "descriptio" as has Henryson. Dunbar's are more brilliant and he has certainly energized this romance convention, as we have seen, with his dazzling colour effects but Henryson has succeeded in a different achievement, that of giving the conventional description "a local habitation and a name" in the Scottish countryside of his daily observation.

His poems are also not without their coarseness and harshness (as, for example, the conclusion of the fable of *The Paddock and the Mouse*), but it is not apparent in the figures which attain their effect less through dynamic energy and visual clarity than by a kind of faithful and loving power of observation of the aspects in the countryside which are in a minor key or which are observable by one who was at heart a countryman.

It is interesting to note, though, that, in another field, that of the moralizing figures of the type of "pulvis et umbrae sumus" and "dust unto dust and ashes unto ashes," Henryson has his own vigorous note to strike and it is one which is more macabre and arresting than that of Dunbar, fine as are his achievements in this line. Both poets provide the conventional type of imagery or figurative description:

> peure and riche, sal be but differenss,
> Turnit in ass, and thus in erd translait.[35]

> Remembir that thow art bot ass,
> And sall in ass return agane:[36]

> Memento, homo, quod cinis es!
> Think, man, thow art bot erd and ass![37]

> Now cled in gold, dissolvit now in ass;
> So dois this warld transitorie go:[38]

---

[34] *Ibid.*, ll. 1709-1711.

[35] Henryson, "The Thre Deid Pollis," ll. 39-40.

[36] Dunbar, "All Erdly Joy Returnis in Pane," ll. 6-7.

[37] Dunbar, "Memento Homo, Quod Cinis Es," ll. 1-2.

[38] Dunbar, "O wreche, be war! this warld will wend the fro," ll. 22-23.

In the first of Dunbar's "sententiae" he makes use of repetition and this is perhaps a use of the biblical figure in the simplest form, but the alliteration of the "a's" makes it sonorous and effective. In the second example from Dunbar we find that he quotes the Latin phrase and follows it with the vernacular version and this again is effective with its contrasted re-iteration and suggestion of an inescapable fate. In the last example, we find another innovation: ash is contrasted with gold; the bright, hard, rich metal and the dull, soft, worthless substance. But although, in this particular instance, Dunbar has made a greater use of the "memento mori" "sententia" than Henryson, we find that Henryson deals with a similar theme in a very different but extremely effective series of figures:

> Allace! quhat cair, quhat weiping is and wo,
> Quhen saule and bodie depairtit ar in twane;
> The bodie to the wormes keitching go,
> The saule to fire, to everlestand pane.
> Quhat help is than this calf, thir guidis vane,
> Quhen thow art put in luciferis bag,
> And brocht to hell, and hangit be the crag?[39]

and similarly in the following lines:

> Richt swa this warld with vane gloir for ane quhile
> Flatteris with folk, as thay suld failye never,
> Yit suddandlie men seis it oft dissever;
> With thame that trowis oft to fill the sek,
> Deith cummis behind and nippis thame be the nek.[40]

There is nothing quite like this in Dunbar's poetry, though he has many figures representing Death and Satan, and here, for a change, Henryson's tone and style is more striking and immediate. His images, "the wormis keitching," "luciferis bag," and the "hanging by the neck" seem to belong to the same tradition as the more literal and macabre passages of the miracle and mystery plays, as for example:

> Ther is none so styf on stede,
> Ne none so prowde in prese,
> Ne none so dughty in his dede,
> Ne none so dere on deese,
> No kyng, no knyght, no wight in wede,
> ffrom dede have maid hym seese,
> Ne flesh he was wonte to fede,
> It shall be Wormes mese.[41]

[39] Henryson, "The Swallow and the Other Birds," ll. 1923-1929.
[40] Henryson, "The Fox, the Wolf, and the Cadger," ll. 2212-2216.
[41] *Towneley Plays*, EETS. "Lazarus," p. 396, ll. 111-118.

from *Lazarus* in the Towneley cycle. The same quality is apparent in the many "memento mori" lyrics of the fourteenth and fifteenth centuries:

> For beo ur mouth crommed with clay,
> Wormes blake wol us embrase —⁴²

which (as Carleton Brown has remarked of the Marian Laments and complaints of Christ, in his collection of fifteenth century lyrics) may well have been influenced by the religious drama. Dunbar's figures of Death, Hell and the Devil, though they may have been drawn from similar sources, seem to lack the almost crude, unsophisticated but extremely effective dramatic quality so apparent in Henryson's figures. In Dunbar's poems there are many images of Death devouring and pursuing and of Satan with his snares, as for example:

> Done is a battell on the dragon blak, ⁴³

and

> O duilfull death! O dragon dolorous!
> Quhy hes thow done so dulfullie devoir . . .⁴⁴

and again in the following lines:

> Syne Deid castis up his yettis wyd,
> Saying, "Thir oppin sall ye abyd;
> Albeid that thow were never sa stout,
> Undir this lyntall sall thow lowt:
> Thair is nane uther way besyd."⁴⁵

But despite this insistence on the mortality of man and on the constant pursuit by Death and Satan, in Dunbar's figures there is none of the macabre dwelling on the corruption and decay of the body which is characteristic of many medieval artists including Henryson. We find this throughout the latter's work as, for example, in such images as those of *The Thre Deid Pollis:*

> Behold oure heidis thre,
> Oure holkit ene, oure peilit pollis bair:

> (ll. 3-4)

and in *The Ressoning Betuix Deth and Man:*

> Dispone thy self and cum with me in by
> Edderis, askis, wormes meit for to be;

> (ll. 37-38)

⁴² *Religious Lyrics of the Fourteenth Century,* ed. Carleton Brown, p. 129, no. 95, ll. 113-114.

⁴³ Dunbar, "Done is a Battell on the Dragon Blak," l. 1.

⁴⁴ Dunbar, "Elegy on the Death of Bernard Stewart," ll. 17-18.

⁴⁵ Dunbar, "Meditatioun in Wyntir," ll. 36-40.

and in the strain which runs through *The Testament of Cresseid:*

> Heir I beteiche my Corps and Carioun
> With Wormis and with Taidis to be rent;
>
> (ll. 577-578)

But if this grim, macabre element is especially characteristic of some of Henryson's figures, so too is its counterpart, an ingenuous humour which is quite different from Dunbar's own well-developed but again more sophisticated jesting. This humour can be clearly seen in the poets' handling of commonplace or conventional figures. Henryson uses a conventional tag in a delightfully humorous juxtaposition in his fable of the "repentant" fox.

> Me think that hennis ar sa honie sweit,[46]

a characteristically dry Scots humour, in which the conventional phrase "honie sweit," so unexpected in relation to "hens," exactly expresses the Fox's "repentance" which consists only of regret that he had not committed the crime more frequently. Another example of this delightful form of humour can be found in a similar use, by Henryson of another conventional figure, that of "the sleep of God":

> I may tak hennis and caponis weill aneuch,
> For god is gane to sleip; as for this nicht,
> Sic small thingis ar not sene in to his sicht;[47]

A figure which Henryson can also use seriously and with effect in another context:

> Quaikand for cauld, sair murnand ay amang,
> Kest up his ee unto the hevinis hicht,
> And said: 'lord god, quhy slepis thow sa lang?
> Walk, and decerne my caus, groundit on richt;
> Se how I am, be fraude, maistrie, and slicht,
> Peillit full bair: 'and so is mony one
> Now in this warld, richt wonder, wo be gone![48]

In his edition of the poems, Harvey Wood has remarked, in a note on the former passage, that "the Sleep of God was a common expression for times of hardship and oppression" and he quotes, from the Peterborough Chronicle ". . . the land was al fordon mid suilce daedeas, and hi saeden openlice that Christ slep and his halachen." The humour of Henryson's use of the figure, in the first instance, lies in the application of this solemn expression to the affairs of the Fox, while in the second

[46] Henryson, "The Fox and the Wolf," l. 692.

[47] Henryson, "The Fox, the Wolf, and the Husbandman," ll. 2324-5.

[48] Henryson, "The Sheep and the Dog," ll. 1286-1292.

passage there is no humour; the Sheep who laments "the Sleep of God" is too closely identified with the suffering peasant whom he represents and there is no jesting on this subject.

Dunbar's humour, in his use of figures, is quite different in temper though it is sometimes created from similar material, that is from conventional figures and tags used in a slightly unexpected sense, as, for example, the description of "Myne awne deir cusing," in *The Testament of Mr. Andro Kennedy*:

> Qui nunquam fabricat mendacia,
> Bot quhen the holyne growis grene.   (ll. 63-64)

or of the appearance of the "fulis nyce" who were present at "Colkelbie's feast" amongst those who were rewarded by the King, while Dunbar himself was neglected. The humour of these lines and of Dunbar's poems in general, is more sophisticated and ironic and has none of the dryness nor the tenderness which we have found to be characteristic of Henryson's humorous use of conventional figures. This distinction will be found, moreover, to apply not only to the poets' use of figures but to their poetic achievement as a whole.

Although "Maister Robert Henrisoun" is included in Dunbar's list of dead poets, there is no trace of any direct influence by Henryson on the younger poet. As we have seen, they share the common stock material of medieval imagery but achieve their own characteristic effects in accordance with their individual poetic genius. Dunbar's figures of speech differ from Henryson's in being more numerous, more clearly visualized and, if we examine them as a whole, of a somewhat wider range.[49] Henryson's figures are generally more subdued, more naturalistic and, sometimes, more homely and dramatic. It is evident that Dunbar's poetic genius found greater scope in the field of imagery than did Henryson's. But Henryson has impressed his own individual quality upon most of the figures which he has used. In the work of these two poets then differences of temperament and creative ability are marked and these differences are nowhere to be seen more clearly defined than in their use of figures of speech.

ROYAL HOLLOWAY COLLEGE
UNIVERSITY OF LONDON

[49] We find, for example, such vivid and wide ranging figures as "Reistit and crynit as hangit man on hill," "gorgeit lyk twa gutaris that war with glar stoppit" (of eyes), "And merchands at the stinkand Styll/ Ar hamperit in ane hony came," "Kirkmen so halie ar and gude,/ That on thair conscience, rowme and rude,/ May turn aucht oxin and ane wane" and in general a far wider range and more extensive use of figure than appears in Henryson's poems.

Review

Adam Smith. *Lectures on Rhetoric and Belles Lettres* (Delivered in the University of Glasgow by Adam Smith. Reported by a student in 1762-63). Edited with an Introduction and Notes by John M. Lothian. Edinburgh and London. Thomas Nelson and Sons, Ltd. 1963. Pp. xl + 205. 42 shillings.

Some five or six years ago rumors began to circulate that Adam Smith's lectures on rhetoric and belles lettres, about which the scholarly world knew no more than that they had been delivered in one form or another from 1748 to 1763, had at long last been discovered. But it was not until the appearance of two articles in *The Scotsman* (Edinburgh) of 1 and 2 November 1961 that the public was more fully informed; the articles are entitled "Long-Lost MSS. of Adam Smith" and "A New Side to Adam Smith." The author, John M. Lothian, Reader in English in the University of Aberdeen, adds further details in the introduction to the present volume. The story is a combination of serendipity and dogged research.

At an auction in Aberdeen in 1958 of the country-house library of Whitehaugh, Mr. Lothian bought two sets of lecture notes presumably made by students. The first consisted of five octavo volumes of lectures on jurisprudence. Though the lecturer is unnamed in the notes, Mr. Lothian was able to determine that they are a version of the same lectures on jurisprudence by Adam Smith which had been edited, also from student notes, by Professor Edwin Cannan in 1896. Exciting search by Mr. Lothian in the junkshops of Aberdeen was rewarded by the discovery of a missing first volume to complete the set. It is to be hoped that in due course this "differently arranged and often more fully illustrated and explained" (p. xii) version of the notes on the lectures on jurisprudence will be made available.

Our immediate concern, however, is with the second set of lecture notes in two volumes inscribed on the spine of each volume, "Notes of Dr. Smith's Rhetorick Lectures," which were given in 1762-1763 as part of a course in Moral Philosophy at Glasgow University. The "Cannan" jurisprudential lectures of 1763 consist of a fair copy dated 1766. The "Lothian" rhetorical lectures, on the contrary, bear evidence of being, at least in part, the actual notes scribbled by a person or persons present at the time of delivery. Neither set is Smith's actual manuscripts, which presumably were destroyed in accordance with instructions issued first to David Hume, and repeated after Hume's death to Joseph Black and James Hutton, when in 1790 Smith was on his deathbed. Black and Hutton, however, were authorized to publish the posthumous *Essays on Philosophical Subjects* of 1795.

Before examining the "Lothian" lectures, it will be well to review briefly the few known facts about Adam Smith as lecturer on literature and literary criticism. During the years 1748-1751, Smith gave two such public courses of lectures before an unspecified forum in Edinburgh (not the University, but quite possibly the Philosophical Society) for which he received above £100 a year. (He also gave a course of public lectures on jurisprudence during these same years.) Virtually nothing directly is known about the content of Smith's Edinburgh literary lectures. After Smith's· removal to Glasgow in 1751, Robert Watson gave a (presumably) similar (and also unknown) literature course at Edinburgh. And upon Watson's removal to St. Andrews in 1756, the public course was resumed in 1759 by the Reverend Hugh Blair. Blair's success eventually led to the creation in 1762 of the Regius Chair of Rhetoric and Belles Lettres at Edinburgh University, the first such chair in Britain, North or South. And Blair was publicly to acknowledge his debt to Smith, who had lent him part of his manuscript treatise on rhetoric.

Smith went to Glasgow in 1751 as Professor of Logic, transferring the following year to the Professorship of Moral Philosophy. There is clear evidence that Smith introduced into his philosophical courses lectures on his system of rhetoric and belles lettres. In the "Method of Editing the Text," at the conclusion of the introduction, Mr. Lothian scrupulously details the editorial process: "I have endeavoured to make a more-or-less continuous text from the three sources available: (a) the great bulk of the lectures, written nearly always on the *recto* of the leaves of the manuscript, but sometimes continuing on to the *verso*; (b) very numerous additions in the same hand and ink as (a), written on the *verso* of the preceding leaf, occasionally marked for insertion at particular points in (a), but frequently not so marked; (c) occasional additions in a different hand or the same hand at a later date, made either at the end of a lecture or on the *verso* of the leaves opposite the point where (presumably) they were meant to be inserted or used as additional comment. When not otherwise indicated, the text is from (a); all passages from (b) and (c) are so marked. The printed text is thus made to include the whole of the manuscript."

In thus setting out to provide a diplomatic edition of the notes, Mr. Lothian seems to be committed to two assumptions: (1) That the Glasgow lectures of 1751-1763 were substantially, if not entirely, identical with or elaborations of the Edinburgh lectures of 1748-1751 (e.g., pp. xii, xvi, xvii); and (2) That, with some misgivings and reservations, the lecture notes were made by a student "scribbler" or "scribe" on the occasion of the actual delivery of the lectures (e.g., pp. xix, xxii, xl, and footnotes throughout). Dr. T. I. Rae, who has contributed an appendix, "Description of the Manuscript of Adam Smith's Lectures on Rhetoric," is perhaps even more strongly committed (p. 195): "The writing, the gaps in the text, and the existence of certain comments, seem to suggest that these are the original notes written at speed in the lecture room, not a fair copy." The lectures numbering thirty, the first of which is missing, were given on Mondays, Wednesdays, and Fridays and are dated from 19 November 1762 to 18 February 1763.

Unexceptionable, and even mandatory, as these two editorial assumptions appear to be at first sight, upon study they actually raise at least as many scepticisms and problems as they settle. It will be well to examine some of these doubts and contradictions, not in the spirit of carping criticism, but rather to illustrate the complexity of the situation.

To begin with, there is the problem of the manuscript itself. In the printed version the lectures vary in length all the way from two and a half pages (No. 10) to fourteen and a half pages (No. 30). If the former could have been delivered in ten minutes, the latter would have required a full hour, presumably the actual time of a classroom lecture. What, then, becomes of the assumption of a stenographic auditor copying down the lectures at top speed? No. 18, after six and a quarter pages, breaks off abruptly with the exasperated comment of the auditor: "Not a word more can I *remember*" (my italics). Again, No. 21 opens: "N.B. This lecture was delivered entirely without book," which, as Mr. Lothian candidly acknowledges, "would seem to suggest that this lecture, at least, had been copied from another MS." And No. 24 opens: "Sine libro, *except what he read from Livy*," which would seem to require a similar comment. Yet, as a matter of fact, the lecture does not quote from Livy; the last sentence reads: "The first is seen exemplified in the oration of Titus Quinctius Capitolinus, and the latter in that of Appius Claudius Crassus, in Livy." We are, it is apparent, dealing not only with an almost incredibly fast copyist (e.g., No. 30) but also with remembrance of things past (e.g., Nos. 18 and 21).

How did Smith lecture? We are informed that early in his career at Glasgow he graciously granted permission to students to take notes. But, unlike some eighteenth-century professors, it would appear that he did not dictate his lectures slowly, sentence by sentence, and, indeed, on occasion spoke extemporaneously and emotionally. We are further informed that somewhat later in his academic career he grew jealous of the property of his lectures and that when he saw anyone taking notes, he would interrupt his discourse to say that he "hated scribblers" (p. xxii). When this change took place remains unknown, but he left Glasgow toward the close of 1763 and resigned his chair early the following year.

Smith's absent-mindedness was notorious. In No. 15 where he is speaking of La Bruyère's character of Menalcas, the absent-minded man, the scribbler or copyist commented on the *verso* (p. 77), "mutato nomine de te fabula narratur, said Mr Herbert of Mr Smith." Now this Mr. Herbert later became Lord Porchester and still later Earl of Caernarvon and as a student at Glasgow was one of several gentleman-boarders in Adam Smith's house—which introduces a further complexity. It is well known that Smith conversed informally with such students and it is not unlikely that he allowed them to read some of his notes or manuscripts or even possibly lectured to them privately. Mr. Lothian considered this possibility (p. xl) but concluded that "since there were occasional failures to recognise names of persons or titles of books in these comments [Source (c)], this hypothesis had to be abandoned." Nevertheless, need it be *entirely* abandoned?

A few examples may serve to illustrate the problems involved. The notion of the "scribbler" copying down at breakneck speed the oral lectures and in so doing making occasional slips in the names of persons or the titles of books is based, of course, upon possible errors of hearing. In No. 18, for example, "Dionysius of Halicarnassus" appears uncorrected (except by the editor) as "Diodorus of Halicarnassus" but "Tacitus" is corrected to "Thucydides." In No. 3 "rythme" is uncorrected (except by the editor) to "rhyme." In No. 7 Dr. Mandeville" is mistakenly corrected to "Machiavel." In all of these instances —to mention no more—the aural explanation is not fully acceptable. "Dionysius" does not *sound* like "Diodorus," "Thucydides" like

"Tacitus," "rhyme" like "rythme," "Dr. Mandeville" like "Machiavel." The "Thucydides"—"Tacitus" switch, indeed, as well as the "Dr. Mandeville"—"Machiavel," seem well nigh impossible. A non-aural explanation may perhaps be more acceptable, namely, that the writer was copying from another set, or sets, of notes or manuscripts and that he was incorrectly expanding some one else's abbreviations, such as *Dio, T,* and *V.* As a matter of fact *Dio* actually does appear in No. 19 where it is followed by a blank of half a page, the only such hiatus in the text. The "other" set of notes or manuscripts might be those of another student or, better yet, of the professor himself to whom the expansion of the abbreviations would have been perfectly obvious.

The two editorial assumptions noted above are not, to be sure, mutually exclusive; but so far I have been dealing mainly with the second, that of the scribbling student at the lectures themselves. In turning now to the first assumption, that the Glasgow lectures of 1751-1763 (most importantly those of 1762-1763) are virtually identical with the Edinburgh lectures of 1748-1751, we encounter difficulties both in acceptance and in refutation. In any event, we must constantly bear in mind that we have no precise information whatsoever about the Edinburgh lectures.

That many professors of whatever century repeat the same lectures year in and year out cannot, unhappily, be denied. And that Smith, because of his sudden move from Edinburgh to Glasgow with the consequent necessity of lecturing on logic and moral philosophy, relied heavily on his original lectures on rhetoric is probable enough. But there are other factors concerning the 1762-1763 series that seem most improbable. At the close of No. 20, dated 12 January 1763, for instance, Smith deals with British History. "Clarendon and Burnet are the two English authors who signalized themselves chiefly in writing history," he remarks, and shortly thereafter adds, "Rapin seems to be the most candid of all those who have wrote on the affairs of England." A marginal note, presumably in the same hand, comments, "10 years ago. A better now," and Mr. Lothian's footnote comments without discussion: "The first volume of Hume's *History* appeared in 1754; the last in 1761." Yet discussion is vital. As pure hypothesis, Smith may have added the comment as an aside during the lecture itself, or as a reminder to himself to bring the lecture up-to-date, or as an observation to one or more of the students living in his house. Surely the comment could hardly be that of a student scribbler referring to ten years ago when presumably he was still a child. Indeed, in this particular instance, it boggles the imagination that Smith was still using the very words of the 1748-1751 Edinburgh lectures or possibly that delivered in one of the first rounds at Glasgow. Since about 1750 Hume and Smith had become friends and, indeed, Hume's first known letter to Smith (24 September 1752) is in answer to a missing one from Smith discussing "the best Period to. begin an English History," and the tone is already intimate. That Smith did not know and, in general, approve of Hume's *History* is unthinkable.

Along with the failure to mention Hume is the extreme paucity of references to any literature between 1751 and 1763. Gray's *Elegy* (1751) is mentioned and there is also a possible allusion to Shenstone's *Pastoral Ballad* (1755). Yet William Robertson's two-volume *History of Scotland during the Reigns of Queen Mary and King James VI. till his Accession to the Crown of England* (1759) goes unmentioned. In 1758, as Dean of Faculty, Smith had recommended Robertson for the Degree of D.D. Macpherson's three translations from the Erse, 1760, 1762, and 1763 are alluded to (p. 131) but unspecified. Neither Dr. Johnson nor his *Dictionary* (1755) is mentioned, and certainly it would have been appropriate to refer to the *Dictionary* in No. 2 where Smith is dealing with the meanings and the changes in the meanings of words. Rousseau is named (p. 8) but the work alluded to, *Origine de l'Inégalité,* Partie première, also of 1755, is not. The cases of Johnson and Rousseau are the more curious because Smith had reviewed the *Dictionary* at great length and had considerable to say about the *Origine de l'Inégalité* in the only two issues of the ill-fated *Edinburgh Review* of 1755-1756.

A final skepticism about the "scribbler" theory is to be noted, namely, that the "scribbler," while often erring badly and even grotesquely on proper names, is remarkable for the sustained flow and finish of the text with exceedingly little of the stumbling and garbling so natural to an auditor taking notes in the classroom. No. 3, "Of the origin and progress of language," offers an excellent example because in 1767 it was published in an expanded form as an appendix, "Considerations Concerning the First Formation of Languages, and the Different Genius of Original and Compounded Languages," to the third edition of *The Theory of Moral Sentiments.* The text of the lecture itself is such that it could have been handed to the printer almost without correction. Nos. 3, 21, and 30 (the last and longest) seem, at least to this reviewer, much more likely to be fair copies than notes, even expanded and corrected notes, taken down on the occasion of the lectures.

The above strictures have been presented in considerable detail because they illustrate the complex problems of editing the notes of the lectures diplomatically. No easy solutions will be offered here because this reviewer knows of no easy solutions—only of the existence of problems. It may be asserted with some confidence, however, that the notes are not all of a piece. Some are evidently the work of the "scribbler." Others are evidently the work of the copyist, piecing together several sets of notes including, likely enough, those of the lecturer himself. And, perhaps most perplexing of all, is the indication that, by and large, exceedingly few changes were made in the lectures over the course of some sixteen years. This hardly fits in with the abundant evidence of Adam Smith as a good scholar and a popular lecturer. The "Cannan" lecture notes, interestingly enough, were updated. Why not, then, the "Lothian"? Perhaps all that can be done is to repeat the words of Smith's skeptical friend: "The whole is a riddle, an aenigma, an inexplicable mystery."

Mr. Lothian has provided in his introduction a learned account of the development of the rhetorical tradition in Scotland and of the beginnings of the reaction against the old tradition of mere categorizing. His account of the Scotland of the Enlightenment provides interesting reading and is invaluable for background. As titles are provided by the student (or students) to only three of the lectures, it would have been a kindness, however, on the part of Mr. Lothian to provide titles for the other twenty-six. It is also regrettable that Mr. Lothian did not deem it fit to provide sample photographic reproductions of the handwritings of the three sources of the lectures as well as of Smith's own. The footnotes throughout are almost always concise, erudite, and reliable. For all of this, due praise.

No praise, however, to the compiler of the index. This book will be read in its entirety by all students of Adam Smith and of the history of literary criticism in the eighteenth century and will be constantly used as a reference work. It will also be referred to by many others who wish to know what Smith had to say about a given author or topic. A full and accurate index, therefore, is not only useful but indispensible. A few random checks led to a growing skepticism on the part of this reviewer and to a careful check (restricted to the texts themselves) of a select group of British authors beginning with the period of the Renaissance. Here are some of the results. Of four references to Spenser, only one in indexed; of fourteen to Milton, only nine; of ten to Bolingbroke, only five; of eleven to Shaftesbury, only five; of eleven to Pope, only four. Shakespeare fares better with ten of twelve; Addison with eight of ten; Swift with fourteen of seventeen; Thomson, with six of eight; Gray, with two of three. Sir Philip Sidney, Samuel Clarke, and Colley Cibber never make the index at all. An index so patently capricious is no index, and the user of it gains little idea of the vastness of Smith's literary knowledge.

"Dr. Smith's Rhetorick Lectures," as they were called by the copyist, might with some justice be called Lectures *against* Rhetoric, taking rhetoric as the ancient logic of multiplicity of divisions and sub-divisions. On two occasions, in particular, Smith goes out of his way to gibe at this concept of rhetoric; "It is rather reverence for antiquity than any great regard for the beauty or usefulness of the thing itself which makes me mention the ancient divisions of rhetoric" (p. 59), and again, "The rhetoricians divide all these topics into many orders and classes. (These will be found in Quintilian by those who incline to read them. For my part I'll be at no further trouble about them at present)" (p. 167). The two passages reveal at once his Classicism, in the sense of "reverence for antiquity," and his Neo-classicism, in the sense of a drive for "beauty or usefulness" to be found through simplicity of style. This drive was much more characteristic of the Scottish universities of the eighteenth century than of the English. The doctrine of simplicity supplies the essential unity to Smith's lectures. The lectures, them-selves, may be divided into five general topics. A brief recapitulation follows.

I. The meanings of words in sentences to achieve the plain style (Nos. 2-5). Thus Swift is praised for his perspicuity and his abhor-rence of neologisms, indeed, "his language is more English than any other writer we have" (p. 2). On the contrary, Shaftesbury is condemned for deliberately going out of the common and simple road and ending in "a dungeon of metaphorical obscurity" (p. 5).

II. The attack on rhetoricians and on the ornate style (Nos. 6-15). Tropes and figures of speech are generally, but mistakenly, conceived as giving the chief beauty and elegance to language. "Figures of speech give no beauty to style: it is when the expression is agreeable to the sense of the speaker and his affection that we admire it" (p. 30). Scot-land is found to be in the paradoxical position of speaking a corrupt dialect while attempting to form the idea of a good, simple prose style.

III. The principles of historical writing (Nos. 16-18). A general rule is "That when we mean to affect the reader deeply we must have recourse to the indirect method of description, relating the effects the transactions produced both on the actors and spectators" (p. 82). Such a method arouses sympathy in the reader. Chronology is to be followed with no gaps permitted even when there are no remarkable events during that period. Dissertations and digressions within the text obscure the chronological development.

IV. History of historians (Nos. 19-20). The earliest historians were poets. They were followed by poets writing in prose but still employing subjects altogether poetical, such as elves, fairies, dragons, griffins, and other monsters. Herodotus extended the plan of history but was more interested in amusing than instructing. Thucydides, in his history of the Peloponnesian War adopted a proper design of historical writing by providing facts, the causes of the facts, and by supplementing military history with civil. Of all the Latin historians, Livy is rated as without doubt the best. Tacitus is notably successful in dealing with the knowledge of the motives by which men act. Of all the modern historians, Machiavelli is the most impartial. Among the English, both Clarendon and Burnet are too close to the events to be other than party men. Rapin is candid but is concerned more with "the lives of the princes than of the affairs of the body of the people" (p. 112).

V. Expository writing in poetry and drama; the oratorical style (Nos. 21-30). Neo-classicist that he was, Smith insists on the dramatic unities, finding Shakespeare deficient on all three counts of action, time, and place. He is also guilty of offending the propriety of character. As for the oratorical style, Smith, despite his ridicule of rhetoricians, follows Quintilian in dividing it into three varieties: the Demonstrative (or panegyrical), the Deliberative (or didactic, subdivided into the Socratic and the Aristotelian), and the Judicial (or argumentative). After long discussions of the eloquence of the Ancients, Smith rises to the defence of the English. Foreigners find the English deficient in gesticulation and in musical tone. As opposed to the French and Spanish idea of politeness, the English requires "composure, calm and unruffled behaviour" (p. 192). Violent gesticulation and display of passion are avoided and "if there is any art thoroughly understood in England, it is music. The lower sort often evidence a great accuracy of judgement in it, and the better sort often display a thorough and most masterly knowledge of it" (p. 192).

To judge Adam Smith as literary critic solely on the basis of these fragmentary lectures would be injudicious. To condemn him for being a Classicist and a Neo-classicist in an age of Neo-classicism would be unhistorical. Somewhat disappointing it is, however, at least to this reviewer, to find no sign of the aesthetic sensibility of Hume displayed in such essays as "Of Tragedy" and "Of the Standard of Taste," both of 1757, essays which Smith had read in manuscript. The philosopher of *The Theory of Moral Sentiments* is present throughout, as well as hints of the economist of the *Wealth of Nations*: "Prose is naturally the language of business, as poetry is of pleasure and amusement" (p. 132). Whatever ultimate judgment is made of Smith as literary critic, the verdict of Wordsworth will surely be disclaimed: "Adam Smith, the worst critic, David Hume not excepted, that Scotland, a soil to which this sort of weed seems natural, has produced." Hume and Smith were men of letters of a breadth incomprehensible to Wordsworth, and only blind anti-Scottish prejudice could have produced such absurdity.

ERNEST C. MOSSNER

UNIVERSITY OF TEXAS

STUDIES IN SCOTTISH LITERATURE

VOLUME II   NUMBER 4   APRIL 1965

CONTENTS

STUDIES IN SCOTTISH LITERATURE

EDITED BY G. ROSS ROY
UNIVERSITY OF SOUTH CAROLINA

EDITORIAL BOARD:
DAVID DAICHES
A. M. KINGHORN
HUGH MACDIARMID (C. M. GRIEVE)
A. L. STROUT
KURT WITTIG

STUDIES IN SCOTTISH LITERATURE is an
independent quarterly devoted to all aspects of
Scottish literature. Articles and notes are welcome.
Subscriptions are available at $5.00 U.S. per annum in the
United States and Canada, elsewhere $4.20 U. S.
All communications should be addressed to the
Editor, Department of English, University of South Carolina,
Columbia, South Carolina, U.S.A. 29208

PUBLISHED BY THE UNIVERSITY OF SOUTH CAROLINA PRESS
AND PRINTED BY VOGUE PRESS, INC.
COLUMBIA, SOUTH CAROLINA, U.S.A. 29202

CONTRIBUTORS
TO THIS ISSUE

Mabel L. MACKENZIE: Holds the Ph.D. from the University of Toronto, and teaches at the University of British Columbia. Her particular interest is in Scottish ballad poetry, and she has spent a year in the United Kingdom doing research on this subject. She is a previous contributor to *SSL*.

Allan H. MACLAINE: Concludes his study of the *Christis Kirk* tradition in Scottish poetry with this issue. The parts will shortly appear in book form. He has recently completed a monograph on Robert Burns.

THE

MERRY

MUSES

OF

CALEDONIA;

A COLLECTION OF

FAVOURITE SCOTS SONGS,

Ancient and Modern;

SELECTED FOR USE OF THE
CROCHALLAN FENCIBLES.

Say, Puritan, can it be wrong,
To dress plain truth in witty song?
What honest Nature says, we should do;
What every lady does,---or would do.

PRINTED IN THE YEAR
1799.

PLATE II — HALF TITLE
(Actual size)

PLATE II — L4 (p. 127)
(Shown with 3x enlargement)

G. ROSS ROY

The Merry Muses of Caledonia

A fine copy of one of the most important editions of Robert Burns has recently come to light—the first edition of *The Merry Muses of Caledonia,* an illustration of the title page of which appears on Plate I.

Hitherto this edition was known only through the Earl of Rosebery's copy which has the lower part of the title page, including the date, torn away, but watermarks on the paper bearing the dates 1799 and 1800 had permitted the volume to be approximately dated. The Rosebery copy belonged at one time to William Scott Douglas, and was the copy used by Duncan McNaught to prepare the 1911 edition of the *Merry Muses* issued by the Burns Federation. As Sidney Goodsir Smith has pointed out in his "Merry Muses Introductory" to the 1959 edition of the *Merry Muses,* McNaught (whose principal concern was to disassociate Burns from this work as far as possible, as the sub-title of the 1911 edition, *A Vindication of Robert Burns,* clearly shows) did not accurately reproduce the text, but incorporated changes by William Scott Douglas as well as some of his own. In fact, the first faithful transcription of the text of the early volume was not available until Smith, James Barke and Professor DeLancey Ferguson published their edition privately in 1959. This work has now been publicly reissued in New York (1964) and London (1965).

The present copy measures 17.0 cm. high. It is in an unsigned tree calf binding with marbled end-papers. The binding appears to be *c.* 1840. Bound in was a steel engraved erotic plate and six crude woodcuts of an erotic nature, each with a ten-line bawdy poem. These seven plates have now been removed from the volume. Presumably two other plates were present but had been removed earlier leaving short stubs bound in.

As will be seen from Plate II, the name of the printer has been scraped from L4 (p. 127). A small hole in the half-title at the same position on the leaf raises the question whether the printer's name was not systematically removed in the shop after the gatherings had been assembled, but before the cover (presumably paper wrappers) had been

[211]

affixed. Thus the hole in the half-title of the present copy would be explained by too great a pressure having been exerted in removing the printer's name from the last leaf of a copy piled on top of the present volume, with the result that not only the last leaf of that volume, but also the first leaf of the present volume were mutilated. The printer's name has been trimmed away in the Rosebery copy.

As with the Rosebery copy, the paper in this copy is watermarked 1799 and 1800; although they are not always on the same leaves, the watermarks in individual gatherings are of the same year as those of the Rosebery copy. There is no half-title present in the Rosebery copy. Watermarks are as follows:

> Rosebery copy—
> 1799 — B3, C3.
> 1800 — D1, E3, F3, H1, I1, K3, L1.

> Present copy—
> 1799 — A3, B3, C3.
> 1800 — Half-title, D3, E1, F3, G3, H3, I1, K3.

As in the Rosebery copy K2 is mislabelled H2.

This copy was purchased, through Bertram Rota Ltd., by the present writer for his own collection.

UNIVERSITY OF SOUTH CAROLINA

M. L. MACKENZIE

The Great Ballad Collectors:
Percy, Herd and Ritson

The assigning of specific dates to a literary age is often misleading. It may impose arbitrary limits not only undesirable, but inaccurate. The most I wish to do here is to indicate some of the signs that point to the third quarter of the eighteenth century as the centre of the transition period between the classical age, characterized by what Cazamian calls its "lucid self-mastery," and the romantic age with its rich self-expression; and to consider, both from a historical and a critical point of view, the part played in the transition by Thomas Percy, David Herd and Joseph Ritson, the three most important ballad collectors to arise in the second half of the century.

One of the important signs of the transition was the interest taken in translations from poetry of writers remote in time, place and spirit. Ker has shown the importance of Temple's essay, "Of Heroic Virtue," where Temple "notices the song of Ragnar because it explains something of the past, and contributes something to the experience of the human race."[1] And further, in the essay, "Of Poetry," Temple "takes up 'runic' literature";[2] but his remained a more or less isolated voice until Gray observed in "The Progress of Poesy," 1754, that it was possible to find the poetic muse in the untutored verses of Laplanders and South American Indians; and Macpherson in 1760 began to publish the Ossianic poems which, "whatever one may think of them now, exercised a European influence, making Scotland, in the eyes of the world, the true and only home of Romance."[3]

To read today Macpherson's "Dissertation concerning the Poems of Ossian," and Hugh Blair's "Critical Dissertation on the Poems of Os-

[1] W. P. Ker, "The Literary Influence of the Middle Ages," *Cambridge History of English Literature* (London, 1934), X, 222.

[2] *loc. cit.*

[3] Sir Alexander Gray, ed. *18th-Century Scottish Books* (Edinburgh, 1951), p.vi. A catalogue of exhibition at Signet Library, Edinburgh.

sian" is a valuable aid to understanding the literary climate which produced the great ballad collectors, particularly Percy and his circle, the climate wherein two widely disparate beliefs were held at the same time. *Ossian* is an epic poem, classical in effect, which the author and his admirers astonishingly affirmed was simpler than Homer, as full of sensibility as Virgil. Nevertheless in his dissertation Macpherson set down his ideas:

> The nobler passions of the mind never shoot forth more free and unrestrained than in the times we call barbarous. That irregular manner of life, and those manly pursuits, from which barbarity takes its name, are highly favourable to a strength of mind unknown in polished times. . . . The human passions lie in some degree concealed behind forms and artificial manners; and the powers of the soul, without an opportunity of exerting them, lose their vigour.[4]

Blair advanced to his argument through a discussion of the way in which the understanding gains ground over the imagination: "Hence poetry, which is the child of imagination, is frequently most glowing and animated in the first ages of society."[5] As an example of untamed imagination he turned back to the illustration used by Temple, "The Death Song of Ragnar," as preserved by Olaus Wormius, which he transcribed and commented upon:

> This is such poetry as we might expect from a barbarous nation. It breathes a most ferocious spirit. It is wild, harsh, and irregular; but at the same time animated and strong; the style, in the original, full of inversions, and, as we learn from some of Olaus's notes, highly metaphorical and figured.[6]

But a poem of this kind could not commend itself wholeheartedly to one steeped in the sensibility of the age, and it is not surprising to find that Blair wrote:

> But when we open the works of Ossian, a very different scene presents itself. There we find the fire and enthusiasm of the most early times, combined with an amazing degree of regularity and art. We find tenderness, and even delicacy of sentiment, greatly predominant over fierceness and barbarity. Our hearts are melted with the softest feelings, and at the same time elevated with the highest ideas of magnanimity, generosity and true heroism. When we turn from the poetry of Lodbrog

[4] James Macpherson, trans. *Poems of Ossian, to which are prefixed, a Preliminary Discourse, and Dissertations on the AEra and Poems of Ossian* ["Dr. Blair's Critical Dissertation,"] (London, 1825), pp. 49-50.

[5] "Dr. Blair's Critical Dissertation," p. 79.

[6] *Ibid.*, p. 84.

to that of Ossian, it is like passing from a savage desert into a fertile and cultivated country.[7]

Ossian has a "Solemn and awful grandeur," and

[I]n point of humanity, magnanimity, virtuous feelings of every kind . . . not only the heroes of Homer, but even those of the polite and refined Virgil, are left far behind by those of Ossian.[8]

Although the reaction from the artificiality of the classical age was not yet well established, the transition was in progress. "The public has seen all that art can do," wrote William Shenstone to John MacGowan in 1761, "and they want the more striking efforts of wild, original, enthusiastic genius."[9] In view of Shenstone's work at this time in pruning the ballads to make them suitable for men of taste, this statement is typical of the inconsistencies of the age.

The "more learned antiquaries" who succeeded Ramsay, did not confine their interest only to Gaelic, Norse, Iselandic [*sic*] and Welsh. They began to turn their attention to the neglected treasures of their own language. After publishing his "Five Pieces of Runic Poetry," Percy borrowed from Allan Ramsay's son the transcripts of David Lyndsay's *Interludes,* which Ramsay had begun in 1724 and had returned to after twenty years.[10]

I do not wish to oversimplify here; to maintain that all writers and scholars in Britain were interested in antiquities in general and ballads in particular. It is nevertheless true that the vivid emotions of the time called for adequate expression, and this could not always be found in the "order" and "reason" of the neo-classical poets. Readers were no longer satisfied with a composition wherein one "might suppose that the poem was written for a wager, to prove that country life might be described, and nothing called by its name."[11] Simplicity of diction was sought, but fervour and passion must accompany the simplicity. The primitivism which had spread to nature in both philosophy and gardening, was, as Lovejoy pointed out, extended to literature.[12]

[7] *loc. cit.*

[8] *Ibid.,* p. 97.

[9] Duncan Mallam, ed. *The Letters of William Shenstone* (Minneapolis, 1939), p. 423.

[10] George Neilson, "A Bundle of Ballads," *Essays and Studies by Members of the English Association,* VII (1921), 163.

[11] C. V. Deane, *Aspects of Eighteenth Century Nature Poetry* (Oxford, 1935), p. 12.

[12] A. O. Lovejoy, "The Discrimination of Romanticisms," *PMLA,* XXIX (1924), 241.

The necessary qualities were not to be found in the contemporary poetry of a literate people. But they were found in ballads.

Among the distinguishing features of ballad poetry are its vocabulary, rhetoric and complete freedom from fashionable poetic diction. The "wan water" and the "lily lee," "the black steed or the brown" belong to no period—they are ballad epithets. But also peculiar to this kind of poetry is the point of view found in a ballad, a point of view which is direct, simple, primitive. Love, sex, jealousy, violence, superstition and death are all presented with a matter-of-fact directness, uncomplicated by orthodox moralizing, although ballads have their own moral values. The result of this directness is a dramatic compression, which brings to the reader a sudden sense of different standards. As C. V. Deane has said in his *Aspects of Eighteenth Century Native Poetry*, "the ballads came to be powerful dissolvents of eighteenth-century poetic complacency."[13] In them was found the freedom from rules, and from the false wit which Addison had deplored: here was the "painting of nature" described by Joseph Warton. Deane has a paragraph on ballad phraseology which is pertinent at this point:

> If their work points in many ways to a transitional state of taste, it can hardly be said that the eighteenth-century ballad editors were conscious of preparing the way for a grand revolution in poetic aims. They did not hold that the taste for the polished verse of their contemporaries was likely to be dispelled by the appeal of these more roughly moulded treasures of the past. It does not seem unjustifiable to suppose, therefore, that their evident appreciation of the formal elements in the oral poetry — or, as Percy put it, 'a cast of style and measure very different from that of contemporary poets of a higher class; and many phrases and idioms, which the minstrels seem to have appropriated to themselves' — may have been quickened by the fact that an equally conventional phraseology was prevalent in the verse of their own age.[14]

On to the stage then, thus adequately furnished, in 1765, and with a receptive audience already assembled, came treading delicately, but firmly, Thomas Percy. Percy was a man of his time. Few can regret that it fell to his lot to rescue the old folio MS. from Humphrey Pitt's housemaid. Hecht, whose assessment of Percy's contribution is very just, praised his "knowledge and art." Professor Clawson in his article, *Percy's Reliques of Ancient English Poetry*, showed how susceptible Percy was to the literary currents and tendencies of his age,

[13] Deane, p. 25.

[14] *loc. cit.*

while attributing to him more originality than is generally accorded today:

> His literary ambitions, facile pen, assimilative and sympathetic power of appreciating and reflecting what he read, delicate but somewhat narrow literary judgment, and slender but genuine poetic talent made him capable of presenting this popular material in a form which would arrest public attention.[15]

That Percy appreciated the "poetry in a state of nature" which he found in the folio, is beyond doubt, and his desire to share it was genuine; but equally strong was his anxiety to conform to the standards of contemporary correctness. Here was the conflict already evident in the dissertation of Macpherson and, later, of Blair. Despite his real enthusiasm for his subject Percy felt the need to apologise for the collection he offered to the public. True, Watson in 1711 and Ramsay in 1724 had both prefaced their collections with deferential explanations; but these men had been pioneers, and the time not ripe for their kind of offering. Percy, on the other hand, published his selections from the folio MS. not only with the blessing of "the author of the 'Rambler' and the late Mr. Shenstone," but indeed on the "importunity of several learned and ingenious friends."[16] The preface to the first edition of the *Reliques*[17] shows how fortunately situated Percy was to undertake his chosen task. Watson had been a busy printer, Ramsay a wig-maker, but Percy was a scholar and a gentleman. As chaplain to the Earl of Sussex he had means and some leisure; as a man he had a lively curiosity, and as a literary connoisseur he had scholarly friends who were all ardent admirers of this "new, irregular poetry." He was even able to protest that "To the friendship of Dr. Samuel Johnson he owes many hints for the conduct of the work." Despite the assistance of scholars who supplied him with manuscripts and annotations, Percy cautiously says that "he was long in doubt whether, in the present state of improved literature, they [the ballads] could be deemed worthy

[15] W. H. Clawson, "Percy's Reliques of Ancient English Poetry," *Report of the Ontario Educational Association* (Toronto, 1913), p. 4.

[16] Thomas Percy, ed. *Reliques of Ancient English Poetry,* 3 vols. (London, 1765), I, ix.

[17] The date of the first edition of the *Reliques* is 1765, but notice must be taken here of an edition in 3 vols. in the Bodleian Library catalogued under the date 1764. These have no title page or preliminary leaves, but on the spine is the legend *Percy's Ancient Poetry*. These volumes are in Douce's Collection, and inside one volume Douce has noted that he bought them at D. Farmer's sale, as supposed waste, but that they contain some pieces not in the published editions.

the attention of the public."[18] That his admission was not from naiveté becomes evident from an examination of some of his voluminous correspondence.

An adequate estimate of Percy's position in the world of letters of the second half of the eighteenth century has not yet been made, although as Watkin-Jones pointed out thirty years ago:

> It seems that a thorough biography is necessary to do justice to a man of so many activities. Such a biography would also do inestimable service as a guidebook or map to this abundant period, revealing much information about the literary and social activities of the time.[19]

Realization of the fundamental importance in literary history of an inquiry into the diaries and vast correspondence left by Percy, who, having a sound idea as to its value caused much of it to be collected during his lifetime, has led David Nichol Smith and Cleanth Brooks, as general editors, to publish some of this fund of material; though some MS. material remains untouched as yet.[20]

It is an anomaly that the very qualities for which Professor Clawson praised Percy are those which damned him in the eyes of his contemporary, Joseph Ritson, critical student, historian and antiquarian, but only occasionally a man of taste. Percy was at all times willing to sacrifice accuracy and fidelity on the altar of good taste as he understood it. He was frank about this characteristic, and hardly found it a defect. An indefatigable worker, he carefully collated transcripts with their originals, and spared no pains to pick up information. However, "to edit" meant "to improve," and the notion of "improving" or "refining" the ballads was a constant subject of his correspondence. And if Dr. Johnson pontificated that the "reading of ancient books is probably true, and is therefore not to be disturbed for the sake of elegance, perspicuity, or mere improvement of the sense,"[21] Percy gave no sign that he heard. He believed himself to be not only sufficiently honest in his editing, but deserving of praise for his methods, and even for his disarming, if mistaken, modesty in the preface:

---

[18] Percy, I, ix.

[19] A. Watkin-Jones, "Bishop Percy and the Scottish Ballads," *Essays and Studies by Members of the English Association, XVIII* (1933), 110.

[20] Six volumes have been completed of this correspondence: *Percy and Malone, Percy and Richard Farmer, Percy and Thomas Warton, Percy and Dalrymple, Percy and Evan Evans, Percy and George Paton.*

[21] Samuel Johnson, ed. "Preface" *The Plays of William Shakespeare* (London, 1768), p. lxiii.

[W]hen, by a few slight corrections or additions, a most beautiful or interesting sense hath started forth . . . the Editor could seldom prevail on himself to indulge the vanity of making a formal claim to the improvement; but must plead guilty to the charge of concealing his own share in the amendments under some such general title as a "Modern Copy," or the like. . . . His object was to please both the judicious antiquary and the reader of taste; and he hath endeavoured to gratify both without offending either.

Until the publication of the Percy-Shenstone correspondence by Hans Hecht, the reasons for the individual amendments were a matter for conjecture, although the publication of the *Folio Manuscript* by Hales and Furnivall in 1867 enabled Child to set down a comparison of the MS. texts with those of Percy, taken, as he said, from the folio, a task not possible for the early editors, who had not been permitted a glimpse of the folio. The Percy-Shenstone correspondence, first edited by Hecht, shows Percy's mind at work. For example, in November 1757, some months after the production in London of John Home's *Douglas,* the tragedy founded on "Gil Morice," Percy wrote to Shenstone to tell him that he had a MS. version of "Gil Morice" which Johnson urged him to publish, although Boswell reported of *Douglas* that Johnson had said angrily that there were not "ten good lines in the whole play."[22] Two months later Shenstone wrote back quoting stanzas of the same ballad, which he believed were an improvement on those in Percy's copy:

> His hair was like the threeds of gold
> Shot frae the burning sun,
> His lips like roses dropping dew,
> His breath was a perfume.[23]

Shenstone's version is oddly reminiscent of lines in a short poem by an anonymous author which appeared in *The Edinburgh Miscellany,* 1720, wherein a lady's hair is described as: "Of shining Threed, shot from the Sun,/ And twisted into line."[24] Percy expressed his gratitude for Shenstone's help, finding that the versions "differ in a surprising manner; scarcely two lines are found alike."[25] The ballad remained uppermost in his mind. Again he wrote:

> I can think of no rhyme for Sun in the 14th Stanza of the additions to Gil Morrice — but what if you find one for *perfume lin. ult.* Query?

[22] James Boswell, *Life of Johnson,* 6 vols. (Oxford, 1934), V, 360-2.

[23] Hans Hecht, ed. *Thomas Percy und William Shenstone. Ein Briefwechsel aus der Entstehungszeit der Reliques, Quellen und Forschungen* (Strassburg, 1909), p. 6.

[24] *The Edinburgh Assembly: by various Hands* (Edinburgh, 1720), p. 3.
[25] Hecht, p. 8.

Threeds of Gold drawn from Minerva's Loom — or something infinitely better.[26]

One need not conclude that Shenstone approved of the version Percy finally published in the *Reliques*:

> His hair was like the threeds of gold,
> Drawne frae Minervas loome:
> His lipps like roses drapping dew,
> His breath was a' perfume.

Even the simple perfume has now become "all perfume." He had now confirmed his belief that if being Scots tended to make a ballad good, being more Scots would make it better. An example of superlative understatement occurred in the notes Percy appended to this ballad:

> As this Poem lays claim to a pretty high Antiquity, we have assigned it a place among our early Pieces: though, after all, there is reason to believe it has received very considerable Modern Improvements.

Percy had indeed reason to believe so! This same remark is repeated in all subsequent editions of the *Reliques,* but with additional notes.

An early letter from Percy to Shenstone makes it clear that the collaborators did not always agree:

> By Mr. Dodsley I rec'd the favour of your Corrections of the Rhymes you were so good as to look over: to your Pen they are now indebted for Beauties they were not before possess'd of. You will notwithstanding (I flatter myself) make Allowances for the foolish Fondness of Scribblers, if you sh'd find I have now and then ventur'd to retain the old Reading, in Defiance of your superior Judgment.[27]

They were equally culpable, however, in their editorial methods, and equally deserving of the scorn and censure Joseph Ritson was soon to pour out. That there was as yet no formula or specific criterion for a ballad is obvious throughout the correspondence, although Shenstone attempted a very simple definition in a letter to Percy: "I . . . am apt to consider a Ballad as containing some little story, either real or invented."[28] It remained for Ritson to differentiate clearly between song and ballad, and to make the now accepted statement that a ballad is a lyrical narrative.

[26] *loc. cit.*

[27] *Ibid.,* p. 4.

[28] Mallam, p. 409. Letter from Shenstone to Percy.

Percy's correspondence with Scottish antiquaries, begun in 1762, is illuminating. In January 1763 he wrote to David Dalrymple (later Lord Hailes) suggesting the mingling of two ballads, "Adam Carre" and "Edom O' Gordon," in order to make "one elegant ballad." And in the same letter he said:

> [S]hould any improvement either in Sentiment or Expression occur, I should not scruple to insert it, provided it were not inconsistent with the general Plan or style of the Poem.[29]

His complacency here regarding his ability to improve the poems is rather remarkable, considering that he was to write to Dalrymple a few months later: "[I]n some of the Scottish Ballads I meet with expressions which the Glossaries I have at hand either wholly omit, or do not explain to my satisfaction."[30] And a year later, regarding "Scottisms," he wrote:

> Mr. Johnson (Author of the 'Rambler') who has been with me for 2 months past on a Visit & left me but last week, gives them up as inexplicable: and as he has a good deal of *Glossarizing* knowledge, it will be some honour to succeed, after he has given them over.[31]

Obviously Percy and his correspondents found nothing reprehensible in using Procrustean methods on the old poems. John Wotherspoon, the able printer of the collection of ballads published in 1769 by David Herd, not only agreed with their methods, but offered approval. Herd was the most faithful and trustworthy editor of old songs and ballads yet to appear on the scene. Lacking the "facile pen" and "poetic talent" of Percy, but with far less concern for the sensibilities of the man of taste or feeling, Herd succeeded in pleasing the latter, as well as the judicious antiquary. After reading Herd's volume with pleasure, Percy proposed through an intermediary, George Paton, friend of contemporary Scots scholars and writers, to use Herd's MS. in a forthcoming volume. Wotherspoon replied to Paton:

> My friend, Mr. Herd, obliged me with a sight of Dr. Percy's letter to you respecting the Scottish Songs, &c., which I now return. — Be pleased to inform that gentleman, that we chearfully consent to his making the use he proposes of our MS. vol. by extracting such fragments as he thinks proper to adopt into his plan. These mutilated antiques thus perfected and restored by Dr. Percy, will give us a pleasure resembling that which we should feel from beholding the injuries of time on a

[29] A. F. Falconer, ed. *The Correspondence of Thomas Percy and David Dalrymple, Lord Hailes* (Baton Rouge, 1954), p. 24.

[30] *Ibid.*, p. 58.

[31] *Ibid.*, p. 85.

statue of Phidias or Polycletus repaired by the hand of Buonarruoti [sic].[32]

Today few readers would disagree with Hodgart that as "scholarship the collection [the *Reliques*] is useless, and . . . highly uneven in literary value"; but most would concur, as would have even the redoubtable Ritson, when he added, "it is nevertheless a remarkable achievement."[33] The publication of the *Reliques* resulted in a furore similar to that caused by *Ossian*. In Britain within two years the demand resulted in a second edition, similar to the first but not identical with it. Ancient manuscripts were turning up; "old women and nurses" were persuaded to remember and recite or sing other versions than those "purified" by Percy; and the excellent chapbooks of Robert and Andrew Foulis were increasingly circulated. Sudden retribution did not fall upon Percy, but criticisms of his first edition were not lacking. In the second edition he found it necessary to make changes, add explanatory notes, and sometimes modify or amplify the notes he had already given. But these changes did not necessarily make for improvement or more accuracy. Sometimes Percy, like Dr. Blair, had too much sensibility; a condition regretted by Dr. Johnson, when he pronounced that Mrs. Percy "had more sense than her husband."[34]

It was reasonable that Dr. Johnson should be mild in his strictures. He had greatly encouraged Percy in the early days of their mutual interest in ballads. Indeed Irving Churchill declares that only Johnson's preparation of his edition of Shakespeare prevented him from being co-editor.[35] But Percy's severest critic was not a gentleman. Today Ritson's thunder perhaps tells us less about Percy than it does about Ritson, although one admits that the thunder was justifiable:

> The history of Scotish poetry exhibits a series of fraud, forgery, and imposture, practised with impunity and success. The ballad of *Gil Morrice*, was printed, for the second time, at Glasgow [by the brothers Foulis], in 1755, with an advertisement, setting forth "that its preservation was owing to a lady, who favoured the printers with a copy, as it was carefully collected from the mouths of old women and nurses;" and

[32] Hans Hecht, ed. *Songs from David Herd's Manuscripts* (Edinburgh, 1904), pp. 22-23.

[33] M.J.C. Hodgart, *The Ballads* (London, 1950), p. 148.

[34] J. Pickford, "Life of Bishop Percy," *Bishop Percy's Folio Manuscript, Ballads and Romances* ed. J. W. Hales and F. J. Furnivall (London, 1867), I, xxxii.

[35] Irving L. Churchill, "William Shenstone's Share in the Preparation of Percy's *Reliques*" PMLA (1936), LI, 960.

"any reader that can render it more correct or complete," is desired to oblige the public with such improvements. In consequence of this advertisement, as we learn from Dr. Percy, no less than sixteen additional verses were produced and handed about in manuscript, which that editor, though he conjectures them after all to be only an ingenious interpolation, has inserted, in their proper places. . . . The doctor assures us, that in his ancient folio MS. "is a very imperfect copy of the same ballad: wherein, though the leading features of the story are the same, yet the colouring here is so much improved and heightened, and so many additional strokes are thrown in, that it is evident the whole has undergone a revisal. . . ." The original stanzas, even as the ballad is now printed, may be easily distinguished from the interpolations; great part of the latter being a[n] . . . evident and pitiful forgery.[36]

Ritson saw no chance of being allowed to examine the folio MS. It was easier for Hales to be amiable eighty years later, when he and Furnivall had the precious document in their possession:

> The extent to which Percy used his Folio MS. in his *Reliques* has been concealed by his misstatement, that of the pieces he published "The greater part of them are extracted from an ancient folio manuscript in the Editor's possession, which contains near 200 poems, songs and 'metrical romances'."

> The *Reliques* (1st ed.) contains 176 pieces, and of these the Folio is used only in 45; so that for Percy's "greater part" we should read "about one-fourth," and, if his term "extracted" is to be taken strictly, "not one-sixth." It is perhaps too bad to follow Bp. Colenso in applying the test of numbers to poetical statements, but the result may as well be known.[37]

One illustration of Percy's technique may suffice here. The edition of 1775 followed more or less the same lines as the text of 1767, with re-touching and re-editing still the order of the day, and misleading statements set down as facts. The old Scots song "John Anderson my jo" suffered particularly reprehensible changes. It was given in the edition of 1765 as follows:

Woman.
John Anderson my jo, cum in as ze gae bye,
And ze sall get a sheips heid weel baken in a pye;
Weel baken in a pye, and the haggis in a pat;
John Anderson my jo, cum in, and ze's get that.

[36] Joseph Ritson, "A Historical Essay on Scotish Song," *Scotish Song,* 2 vols. (London, 1794), I, lxx-lxxi.

[37] F. J. Furnivall, "Forewords" in *Bishop Percy's Folio Manuscript, Ballads and Romances,* ed. J. W. Hales and F. J. Furnivall (London, 1867), I, xxii-xxiii.

> Man.
> And how doe ze, Cummer? and how doe ze thrive?
> And how mony bairns hae ze? Wom. Cummer, I hae five.
> Man. Are they to zour awin gude man? Wom. Na, Cummer, na;
> For four of tham were gotten, quhan Wullie was awa'.

The accompanying note explained:

> It is a received tradition in Scotland that at the time of the Reformation, ridiculous and bawdy songs were composed by the rabble to the tunes of the most favourite hymns in the Latin service. . . . *John Anderson my jo* was [one of these].

The edition of 1767 followed that of 1765 as to text, but in the edition of 1775 the sea change occurred. The five bairns were turned into seven, and Percy appended the following:

> In the present Edition this song is much improved by some new readings communicated by a friend; who thinks the "Seven Bairns," in st. 2nd allude to the Seven Sacraments; five of which were the spurious off-spring of Mother Church: ae [misprint for as] the first st. contains a satirical allusion to the luxury of the popish clergy.

Percy gave no authority for his changes, and he was not convincing as to the satirical allusion. Nor was there any proof for his "received tradition" with regard to the music of the song; indeed the opposite was true, and sacred words were given to the secular tunes, a fact which Ritson seized on eagerly. Too much blame, however, should not be attached to Percy in this case. Even William Tytler, an acknowledged authority on Scottish music, had fallen into the same error, and Ritson's wrath descended upon him also. But in this case Percy went his unrepentant way, and the notes and the bairns remained uncorrected. It is a small pleasure to add that Ritson nodded for once, and misquoted Percy, turning Percy's four bairns into three.

By the time Percy's third edition reached the public, David Herd's anonymous volume of 1769 had achieved so much favourable notice that Herd felt justified in issuing his collection rearranged and extended into two volumes, which appeared in 1776. Stern critical faculties were not yet brought to bear on ballads, but Herd earnestly strove for accuracy, and he was not troubled overmuch by the delicacy of feeling admired by Percy. Considering Herd's importance in the ballad history of the eighteenth century, it is unfortunate that so little has been done to rectify the neglect which has been his portion. Hans Hecht's *Songs from David Herd's Manuscripts,* published in 1904, remains the best available source for facts on "the most indefatigable and the most conscientious of the old Scots collectors." Hecht drew largely on James Maidment's publications of the correspondence of George Paton, Herd's friend and one of the original members of the Society of Antiquaries of Scotland.[38] Paton is worthy of notice; as Hecht wrote:

> [H]is influence on the men of letters of his day must not be underrated. His comprehensive knowledge equally with his celebrated library was common property, and he imparted it with a liberality which gained him wide influence with the best intellect of his time. . . . The total number of his correspondents amounts to fifty-four, amongst whom are Lord Hailes, Thomas Percy, Joseph Ritson, David Herd, James Cummyng, Gilbert Stuart and Lord Buchan.[39]

Hecht added his regret that no editor has undertaken to finish the task so well begun by Maidment, but rejoiced that such a widely read book as Pennant's *Tour in Scotland* made enthusiastic acknowledgment of Paton's unselfish and faithful assistance to the literary undertakings of his friends.[40]

It is clear that Herd had scant literary ambition. His first volume, *The Ancient and Modern Scots Songs, Heroic Ballads, &c.,* was published anonymously. The preface is important historically, and as giving evidence of the trend ballad collecting had begun to follow:

> The only collection upon our plan, consisting entirely of Scots Songs, is the *Orpheus Caledonius,* published by William Thomson in 1733; but this is confined to a small number, with the music, and now become very scarce; for Allan Ramsay's *Tea-Table Miscellany* cannot be termed *A Complete Collection of Scots Songs;* they are, as he himself entitles them, — *A Choice Collection of Scots and English.*
>
> The valuable collection of Percy has furnished some songs, and more perfect copies of several ballads, than those formerly printed; and when modern words could only be given to ancient tunes, these are, however (*to speak en Ecossois*) composed by Poets natives of North Britain.
>
> After the manner of Percy, it was at first intended to have prefixed notes to the more ancient and historical poems in this Collection; but the volume would have been thereby too much swelled; and as the Editor hath already some prospect of materials for a second, he is of opinion that these notes will come in with more propriety at the conclusion where they may be by themselves perused.

In 1776 the collection was issued again, in two volumes, with "The Second Edition" on the title page of the second volume. The work was

[38] James Maidment, ed. *Letters from Joseph Ritson, Esq., to Mr. George Paton* (Edinburgh, 1829).

[39] Hecht, *Songs,* p. 7.

[40] *Ibid.,* p. 8.

again anonymous, and T. F. Henderson is not accurate when he says in *Scottish Vernacular Literature* that Herd's name was given as editor of the volumes.[41]

There were improvements, additions, modifications and omissions in the edition of 1776. It was enthusiastically received, and no dissenting voice appears to have been raised save only that of John Pinkerton. The statement in *Chambers' Cyclopedia of Literature*, 1903, that "Herd did for Scottish song what Bishop Percy had done for English Ballads" does not over-state the importance of Herd's collections. Their influence can be clearly seen. Burns's debt to Herd is made clear in the notes in Henley and Henderson's Centenary Edition of *Burns's Poems*. Scott made no secret of his respect and admiration for Herd as a collector as well as a man. As the introduction to *Border Minstrelsy* shows, Scott was indebted to Herd for much valuable material:

> To the politeness and liberality of Mr. Herd, of Edinburgh, the editor of the first classical collection of Scottish songs and ballads . . . the editor is indebted for the use of his MSS., containing songs and ballads, published and unpublished, to the number of ninety and upwards.

In *Familiar Letters of Sir Walter Scott* is a pen portrait of Herd, composed by Scott after Herd had been dead for fifteen years.[42] But it could be argued that years are kind and Scott was not always discriminating. Perhaps more critical praise came from Ritson, of whom Scott had written: "As bitter as gall, and as sharp as a razor,"[43] but whom even his enemies acclaimed as an acute and just critic:

> To this [collection], though not so judiciously selected or arranged as it might have been, and containing many confessedly English songs, a few supposititious ballads, and several pieces unworthy of preservation, we are certainly indebted for a number of excellent and genuine compositions, never before printed, as the author of the present collection is bound in gratitude to acknowledge.[44]

Ritson's indebtedness to Herd included the loan of Herd's MS., and interesting sidelights on the characters of the two men appear in the correspondence regarding it.

[41] T. F. Henderson, *Scottish Vernacular Literature* (Edinburgh, 1910), p. 339.

[42] Sir Walter Scott, *Familiar Letters of Sir Walter Scott*, 2 vols. (Edinburgh, 1894), II, 353-354.

[43] Sir Walter Scott, "One Volume More," *Poetical Works*, ed. Robert Ford (London [n.d.]), p. 734.

[44] Ritson, p. lxxiv.

Ritson is nowadays so much in the forefront of ballad discussions, that his position in literature may well be defined here. Henry Alfred Burd, who in 1915 published *Joseph Ritson, A Critical Biography,* puts the case for Ritson into the first paragraph of his preface:

> Joseph Ritson is a minor figure in the literary history of the latter half of the eighteenth century. But he was one of the chief instruments in bringing about the changes in that period of remarkable transition. Although a potent factor in reviving the interest in ballads and old poetry and in hastening the acceptance of advanced standards of editorship and criticism, he has been largely ignored in the historical appraisement of the romantic movement. This neglect was not altogether unnatural. Ritson's method of criticism was so invidiously personal and his beliefs and habits were so eccentric that attention was attracted primarily to his peculiarities, while his stable qualities were overlooked by the majority. As a consequence of the silence which early enshrouded his name, an adequate estimate of his literary place has, up to the present, been impossible.

To appraise Ritson, as in the case of any writer, it is best, generally, to go to the fountainhead, to the writer himself; and for this appraisal an examination of the Percy-Ritson controversy is illuminating. To this end a dissertation written by Ritson in 1783 will serve as a beginning. Ritson was a collector of literary antiquities, and one of his earliest publications was *A Select Collection of English Songs,* to which he prefixed a dissertation entitled "A Historical Essay on the Origin and Progress of National Song." This was inspired directly by the essay "On the Ancient English Minstrels," with which Percy had prefaced his *Reliques* almost twenty years earlier, and which had appeared unchanged in two subsequent editions. Percy's essay was designed to show that minstrels were composers, musicians, poets and singers, quite often all four functions being combined in one person; and as such they held an exalted position not only in the Anglo-Saxon court, but continued to do so for hundreds of years after the Conquest. Percy embellished his essay with the fruits of scholarship in the form of lavish quotations, anecdotes and conjectures; and as proof positive, he quoted a letter from an eye-witness of an entertainment given in 1575, where one of the entertainers was garbed as "an ancient MINSTREL." A note of modern verisimilitude was injected into the romantic picture: "A pair of pumps on his feet, with a cross cut at his toes for corns: not new indeed, yet cleanly blackt with soot, and shining as a shoing horn." The pleasant discursive essay accorded well with the agreeable texts and notes of the *Reliques.* Pinkerton loudly admired it in 1776, repeated his admiration in 1781, and again in 1783, just before he read Ritson. But Ritson had not been idle. Unimpressed by either Percy's romance or his realism, and with the fanatical zeal and painstaking labour which characterized him in all his undertakings, Ritson, in his "Historical Essay" refuted and ridiculed Percy's cherished theories. His method was to give facts, not to make generalizations, and he gathered together a store of references, all to show that Percy was gravely misinformed. According to Percy:

> The Minstrels seem to have been the genuine successors of the ancient Bards, who . . . sung verses to the harp, of their own composing. . . . Our Saxon ancestors . . . had been accustomed to hold men of their profession in the highest reverence. Their skill was considered as something divine, their persons were deemed sacred, their attendance was solicited by kings, and they were everywhere loaded with honours and rewards.

This indiscriminate use of the term "minstrel" to cover a whole group of entertainers was summarily dismissed by Ritson in his "Observations on the Ancient English Minstrels":

> Under this comprehensive term *minstrel* . . . we are to include the *trouveur*, or poet, the *chanteur* or vocal performer, and the *menêtrier*, or musician; not to mention the *fablier, conteur, jugleur, baladin,* &c. all which were sometimes distinct professions, and sometimes united in one and the same man.

Ignoring the evidence Percy had amassed, Ritson declared that Percy's statements were pure conjectures. Like Hume, he asked for testimonies.

Percy was not the only author to feel the sting of Ritson's jibes. Pinkerton also was attacked, with vehemence bordering on brutality, for his collections of songs and ballads, and particularly for his observations on his material. Burd believes that the attack was intensified because of Pinkerton's nationality, since it is true that to "Scotchmen [Ritson] entertained an aversion as pronounced as that of Dr. Johnson."[45] But Thomas Warton had been castigated in like manner years

before, for his *History of English Poetry* (1774-81), the history in which he gave three chapters to Scottish verse, thus being the first Englishman to discuss critically and historically the work of Scottish poets. No attack, however, was more scathing or vindictive than Ritson's uncompromising denunciation of well-meaning Percy. Percy, declining to take public action, tried through private intervention to make explanations to his critic, but in vain. Ritson would not be silenced, neither could he be ignored. Ritson was embarrassingly

---

[45] Henry Alfred Burd, Joseph Ritson, *A Critical Biography,* reprinted from *The University of Illinois Studies in Language and Literature* (Illinois, 1916), p. 164.

convincing. Even Percy's admirer, John Pinkerton, although one who had also suffered at the hands of Ritson, had finally gone over to the enemy's camp, and in a letter to Percy admitted the error in his thinking:

> I must confess myself thoroughly convinced that Minstrel only implied Musician, and was never used for a bard, maker or poet; were I reprinting any former production in this way I would retract all my opinions to the contrary, though often repeated.

After suggesting a rearrangement of Percy's essay to distinguish the minstrel proper from the poets and reciters, Pinkerton added:

> Even granting all the passages cited in your favour, you must contend against hundreds on the opposite side. For a part, Ritson's book may be referred to.[46]

In 1791 a third edition of *Ancient and Modern Scotish Songs, Heroic Ballads, etc.* appeared, which Thomas Wilson Bayne, writing in the *Dictionary of National Biography*, describes as being "manifestly without Herd's supervision." No fewer than forty-one of Herd's songs were omitted, and their places supplied by modern compositions, some of them popular songs by Burns. There was no preface, and Herd's notes were omitted. While there is no evidence that Herd offered any objection to this pirating of his text, or to the misspelling of the word "Scottish," in the title, it would appear that some readers found the new edition unsatisfactory, and hoped for another. George Chalmers wrote to a friend: "You talked of a new edition of Mr. D. Herd's Songs, to be edited by Mr. W. Scott. Is this almost ready for the public? I hope Mr. Scott will not touch the text."[47] Scott's edition, if it had ever been projected, did not appear—it will be remembered that he acknowledged the use of Herd's MS. in his own *Minstrelsy*. More than a hundred years went by before a page-for-page reprint of the edition of 1776 was published.

In the meantime, three years after the publication in 1791 of Herd's *Songs* in its mutilated form, a fourth edition of the *Reliques* was released, but not under the editorship of Bishop Percy. The task of editing, explaining and apologizing had been left to a nephew, who was also a namesake, Thomas Percy.

Do we find once more that Johnson is a dangerous person to disagree with? Was it his criticism that hurt Percy? We remember

---

[46] *Ibid.*, pp. 163-164.

[47] Archibald Constable, *Archibald Constable and his Literary Correspondents,* 3 vols. (Edinburgh, 1783), I, 414.

that it was for the convenience of the great man that Percy had had the folio bound in the first place; and the sad mishap caused by the binder. But we remember also:

> Dr. Johnson resisted to the end what he considered a deplorable deviation from neo-classical standards. In 1777, "he observed that a gentleman of eminence in literature had got into a bad style of poetry of late. . . . Boswell: That is owing to his being much versant in Old English Poetry. Johnson: What is that to the purpose, Sir? If I say a man is drunk and you tell me it is owing to his taking much drink, the matter is not mended. No, Sir — — has taken to an odd mode." (And he then produced his famous parody: 'Hermit hoar, in solemn cell')."[48]

In 1794 Percy's nephew found it still necessary to defend his relative, and stated in his introduction:

> The appeal publicly made to Dr. Johnson in the first page of the following Preface, so long since as the year 1765, and never once contradicted by him during so large a portion of his life, ought to have precluded every doubt concerning the existence of the Manuscript in question.

The indifference may have been due to the venom with which Ritson had attacked, or it may, though less probably, have been due to private acknowledgment on the part of Bishop Percy of the superior quality of Herd's variants of ballads. It may even have been caused by grief suffered on the death of his young son, the son for whom he had destined the folio MS. and of whom he had great hopes for assistance in this work. Whatever the cause, the younger editor explained in the "Advertisement" to the fourth edition:

> Twenty years have nearly elapsed since the last edition of this work appeared. But, although it was sufficiently a favourite with the public, and had long been out of print, the original Editor had no desire to revive it. . . . More important pursuits had, as might be expected, engaged his attention; and the present edition would have remained unpublished, had he not yielded to the importunity of his friends, and accepted the humble offer of an Editor in a Nephew.

Posterity has not accorded importance to the pursuits in which the Bishop was engaged in Dromore; his fame rests solely on the *Reliques*.

The text of 1794 was a great improvement on that of all previous editions. Percy had not held out against his critics; and the edition of 1794 is a lesson in how gracefully a gentleman who considers it more important to please the reader than to instruct him will accept correction. The famous essay on minstrels was changed, although all mention of the changes was relegated to a footnote:

[48] Hodgart, p. 148.

Wedded to no hypothesis, the Author hath readily corrected any mistakes which have been *proved* to be in this Essay; and considering the novelty of the subject, and the time, and place, when and where he first took it up, many such had been excusable. — That the term *minstrel* was not confined, as some contend, to a mere *musician*, in this country, any more than on the Continent, will be considered more fully in the last note . . . at the end of this Essay.

The title of the essay was subtly altered from "An Essay on the Ancient English Minstrels," to "An Essay on the Ancient Minstrels in England," and the difficulties of the Anglo-Saxons and the Normans thus gently overcome. Nor did Percy any longer insist on the greater antiquity of the minstrels. The essay began:

> The Minstrels were an order of men in the middle ages, who subsisted by the arts of poetry and music, and sang to the harp verses composed by themselves, or others. They also appear to have accompanied their songs with mimickry and action; and to have practised such various means of diverting as were much admired in those rude times, and supplied the want of more refined entertainment.

In this way he encompassed the undiscriminating term "minstrel."

Unfortunately not enough changes were made. The preface was couched in the same polished eighteenth-century diction the Bishop was accustomed to use, and the younger Percy was equally addicted to ambiguity and half-statement:

> These volumes are now restored to the public with such corrections and improvements as have occurred since the former impression; and the text in particular hath been emended in many passages by recurring to the old copies. The instances, being frequently trivial, are not always noted in the margin, but the alteration hath never been made without good reason; and especially in such pieces as were extracted from the folio Manuscript so often mentioned in the following pages, where any variation occurs from the former impression, it will be understood to have been given on the authority of that MS.

Some of Percy's methods of amending the text have been shown. That he was conscious of the lack of accuracy is clear from the defence he made of his errors in advancing lack of proof-reading in extenuation; but as Ritson had acidly observed, "[Percy] would perceive the justice of confining this excuse to the first edition."[49] It is manifestly clear today that Ritson, without access to the folio MS. was justified in declaring that Percy had "fairly and honestly printed scarcely one single poem, song or ballad."[50] Nor was this state of affairs materially mend-

---

[49] Burd, p. 160.

[50] [Joseph Ritson, ed.,] "Dissertation on Romance and Minstrelsy," *Ancient Engleish Metrical Romancees,* 2 vols. (London, 1802), I, 70.

ed by 1794; Percy's position remained in the end what it was in the beginning — he believed that the pieces had to be polished that they might "in the present state of improved literature be deemed worthy the attention of the public."

The honours on the score of the minstrels are today as evenly divided as when Scott wrote in the supplement to the *Encyclopedia Britannica*:

> [U]pon a recent perusal of both these ingenious essays, we were surprised to find that the reverend editor of the *Reliques* and the accurate antiquary have differed so very little as in essential facts they appear to have done. . . . [H]ot arguments, and on one side, at least, hard words are unsparingly employed; while . . . the contest grows warmer in proportion as the ground concerning which it is carried on is narrower and more insignificant. In reality their systems do not essentially differ.[51]

Percy's theory of antiquity was not wholly wrong, nor was Ritson's theory of the Elizabethan origin of the ballads wholly right. There is perhaps less unanimity regarding Ritson's criticism of Bishop Percy's methods of editing the ballads.   Ritson had said:

> If the ingenious editor had published all his imperfect poems by correcting the blunders of puerility or inattention, and supplying the defects of barbarian ignorance, with proper distinction of type, it would not only have gratified the austerest antiquary, but also provided refined entertainment for every reader of taste and genius.[52]

In this Burd agrees with Percy:

> Modern critics and historians of literature following [Percy's] lead, declare with one accord that the plan pursued was the only one which would have insured a kindly reception to these rude remains of antiquity.[53]

Nevertheless one can say with Ritson, while apologizing for his syntax, "As a publication of uncommon elegance and poetical merit, I have always been, and still am, a warm admirer of Bishop Percy's *Reliques*,"[54] and continue to agree with him when he says more strongly:

> To correct the errors of an illiterate transcriber, to supply irremediable defects, and to make sense of nonsense, are certainly essential duties of an editor of ancient poetry, provided he act with integrity and publicity;

[51] Thomas Percy, *Reliques of Ancient English Poetry*, 3 vols. (London, 1767), I, xiv.

[52] Burd, p. 162.

[53] *loc. cit.*

[54] *Ibid.*, p. 159.

but secretly to suppress the original text, and insert his own fabrications for the sake of providing more refined entertainment for readers of taste and genius, is no proof of either judgment, candor, or integrity.[55]

Proof that the public was not quite so tender-minded with regard to its ballads as Percy and Burd might have us believe, is found in the reception accorded to Herd's first volume, which was so rapidly sold out that augmented volumes were published a few years later; and when Herd did not accede to public demand and issue a third edition, the pirated volumes of 1791 went on the market. Herd was, in the particulars given above, an editor after Ritson's own heart. More proof is found in the fact that Ritson's own collections, *Ancient Songs, Pieces of Ancient Popular Poetry, English Songs* and *Scotish Songs,* all *unbowdlerized* and without poetic effort on the part of the editor, were also given a warm welcome. If the charming woodcuts by John and Thomas Bewick which illustrate the first edition of *Pieces of Ancient Popular Poetry* are adduced as reason for the popularity of Ritson, it may be noted that they are not present in his other volumes. The popularity of the chapbooks by Robert and Andrew Foulis, and nearer the end of the century, of the "penny numbers" published by Brash and Reid, indicate also that the climate of opinion was favourable to "the rude remains of Antiquity" in their unpolished state.

UNIVERSITY OF BRITISH COLUMBIA

---

[55] *Ibid.,* p. 162.

ALLAN H. MACLAINE

The *Christis Kirk* Tradition:
Its Evolution In Scots Poetry To Burns

Part IV
John Mayne

Before we turn finally to consider the work of Burns, two pieces by the little-known poet John Mayne (1759-1836), entitled *Hallowe'en* and *The Siller Gun,* deserve mention.[1] Although both of these poems are in the famous six-line *"Habbie* stanza" or "Burns stanza," in all other respects they are closely related to and strongly influenced by the *Christis Kirk* tradition. *Hallowe'en,* a brief and undeveloped description of a rural Hallowe'en celebration, has added historical interest in being the germ of Burns's poem of the same name. *The Siller Gun,* a much more ambitious work, portrays in the distinctive *Christis Kirk* way an annual shooting competition or "Waponschaw" held in Dumfries on the King's Birthday (June 4), in which the townspeople competed for the prize of a silver gun. Mayne began work on *The Siller Gun* about 1777, when he published the first version, a short poem of twelve stanzas, in Dumfries. After this modest beginning, Mayne gradually expanded the poem, working on it at intervals through most of his long lifetime, publishing four long cantos in 1808, and finally completing the work in five cantos (1650 lines) in 1836, the year of his death. Although the later versions fall outside the strict limits of this study, since they were written in the early nineteenth century, after Burns, all versions are deeply indebted to the *Christis Kirk* tradition, as Mayne himself acknowledges by using the first four lines of the original *Christis Kirk* as his motto. The following, from Canto IV of the final version, is a typical stanza. In the midst of the shooting competition, which Mayne describes with humorous and satiric comment on the bragging and the

[1] The text of *Hallowe'en* is available in Geo. Eyre-Todd ed. *Scottish Poetry of the 18th Century* (London, n.d.), II, 162-164. For *The Siller Gun* in 4 and 5 cantos, respectively, see Mayne, *The Siller Gun* (London, 1808 and 1836). A lengthy and enthusiastic contemporary review of *The Siller Gun* may be found in *Blackwood's Magazine,* XXXIX (June, 1836), 842-856.

bungling of the marksmen, a brawl breaks out between the tailors and the "sutors" (cobblers):

> Frae Johnny Groat's house to the Border,
> Was ne'er sic tumult and disorder:
> Here Discord strave new broils to forder: *further*
>   There, Beagles flew   *constables*
> To haud the Sutor-lads in order,   *hold*
>   But nought wou'd do.

Here Mayne is dealing with the typical *Christis Kirk* situation, viewing it from the typical satiric point of view, and using a rhetorical pattern strongly reminiscent of the famous opening of *Christis Kirk* itself ("Was nevir in Scotland hard nor sene/ Sic dansing nor deray," etc.). Though at times Mayne's style takes on a stiff artificiality, on the whole *The Siller Gun* is a spirited and competent piece of work and deserves to be better known.

Robert Burns

It would seem almost inevitable that Burns, ardent student of Scots poetry that he was, would sooner or later try his hand at the *Christis Kirk* genre. As a matter of fact, he produced six substantial poems more or less closely related to the genre, a group of poems which, taken together, represent the last brilliant flowering and culmination of the *Christis Kirk* tradition. These poems were all composed in the years 1785 and 1786, the period of Burns's greatest creativity, as follows: *A Mauchline Wedding* (August, 1785), *Hallowe'en* (November, 1785), *The Jolly Beggars* (ca. November, 1785), *The Ordination* (ca. November, 1785), *The Holy Fair* (autumn, 1785), and *A Dream* (June, 1786).[2] Three of these, *A Mauchline Wedding, The Ordination,* and *A Dream,* may be treated briefly.

A Mauchline Wedding seems to have been Burns's earliest experiment in the *Christis Kirk* genre. He enclosed the manuscript of this

---

[2] For the best texts of these poems, see *The Poetry of Robert Burns,* edd. Wm. E. Henley and T. F. Henderson, The Centenary Ed., 4 vols. (Edinburgh, 1896, 1897), II, 42-4; I, 88-99; II, 1-19; I, 210-215, 36-47, 68-74. This edition is hereafter cited as *Poetry.* It should be noted that a later ephemeral production of Burns, the second of his four *Ballads on Mr. Heron's Election, 1795,* entitled *Ballad Second: The Election* (*Poetry,* II, 193-197), and beginning, "Fy, let us a' to Kirkcudbright," is modeled on *The Blythsome Bridal* and is, therefore, remotely related to the *Christis Kirk* tradition.

fragment in a letter to Mrs. Dunlop of August 21, 1788,[3] but the piece was almost certainly composed in August of 1785, at the time of the actual wedding which it portrays. Slight though it is, *A Mauchline Wedding* is of considerable interest as a very early example of Burns's developing satiric style which was shortly to flower in masterpieces like *Holy Willie's Prayer*. The poem is a burlesque description, mildly bawdy and high-spirited, of a local wedding in Burns's own country town of Mauchline. Written in the traditional stanza form, *A Mauchline Wedding* strikes the reader as a hastily written occasional piece, not intended for publication, but nevertheless marked by Burns's characteristic skill and vitality. Both in subject matter and form it obviously belongs to the *Christis Kirk* genre, and is even more closely tied into the tradition by the fact that Burns echoes passages in all three of the *Christis Kirk* poems of Fergusson.[4] The opening lines of Burns's first two stanzas, for example, read as follows:

> When Eighty-five was seven months auld,
>   And wearing thro' the aught,   *eighth*
> When rotting rains & Boreas bauld   *bold*
>   Gied farmer-folks a faught . . .   *struggle, fight*
> The rising sun o'er Blacksideen   *name of a local hill*
>   Was just appearing fairly,
> When Nell & Bess get up to dress
>   Seven lang half hours o'er early!

These lines are clearly similar in conception to the corresponding lines in the first two stanzas of Fergusson's *Hallow-fair*:

> At *Hallowmas,* when nights grow lang,
>   And *starnies* shine fu' clear,   *stars*
> 'Whan fock, the nippin cald to bang,   *folk; defeat*
>   Their winter *hap-warms* wear . . .   *mantles*
> Upo' the tap o' ilka lum   *chimney*
>   The sun began to keek,   *peep*
> And bad the trig made maidens come   *spruce*
>   A sightly joe to seek . . .   *sweetheart*

A picture of girls rising earlier than usual on a festive day also appears in stanza six of *Leith Races*. Much more conclusive than these passages,

---

[3] See *The Letters of Robert Burns,* ed. J. DeLancey Ferguson (Oxford, 1931), I, 248-9. An excellent critical discussion of this poem may be found in Thomas Crawford, *Burns: A Study of the Poems and Songs* (Edinburgh, 1960), pp. 112-5.

[4] For a fuller discussion of these parallels, summarized here, see Allan H. MacLaine, "Some Echoes of Robert Fergusson in Burns's 'A Mauchline Wedding,'" *Notes and Queries,* N.S. VIII (July, 1961), 265-6.

however, are the final lines of *A Mauchline Wedding*, depicting the emergence of the bride's father:

<table>
<tr><td>And auld John Trot wi' sober phiz</td><td>face</td></tr>
<tr><td>As braid & bra's a Bailie,</td><td>portly and finely dressed</td></tr>
<tr><td>His shouthers & his Sunday's giz</td><td>shoulders; wig</td></tr>
<tr><td>Wi' powther & wi' ulzie</td><td>powder; oil</td></tr>
<tr><td>Weel smear'd that day.</td><td></td></tr>
</table>

Here Burns is unmistakably recalling the sparkling second stanza of Fergusson's *The Election*:

<table>
<tr><td>Haste, EPPS, quo' John, an bring my gez,</td><td>wig</td></tr>
<tr><td>Take tent ye dinna't spulzie:</td><td>heed; spoil</td></tr>
<tr><td>Last night the barber ga't a friz</td><td>curl</td></tr>
<tr><td>An' straikit it wi' ulzie.</td><td>stroked; oil</td></tr>
<tr><td>Hae done your PARITCH lassie Liz,</td><td>porridge</td></tr>
<tr><td>Gi'e me my sark an' gravat;</td><td>shirt; tie</td></tr>
<tr><td>I'se be as braw's the Deacon is</td><td></td></tr>
<tr><td>Whan he taks AFFIDAVIT</td><td></td></tr>
<tr><td>O' FAITH the day.</td><td></td></tr>
</table>

There can be no doubt about these verbal parallels, which clearly show that Burns, in this first casual attempt, was writing not only within the general limits of the tradition but also in direct imitation of Fergusson's masterpieces in this genre.

The Ordination is a daring satire on Ayrshire church politics.[5] In general, it is concerned with the struggle within the Kirk between the rigidly orthodox Calvinists or "Auld Lichts" and the Moderates or "New Lichts," Burns, of course, favoring the latter. More specifically, the poem was occasioned by the presentation of James Mackinlay, a staunch "Auld Licht," to the Laigh Kirk in Kilmarnock, where he succeeds a series of Moderates and where he will be counted on by the orthodox, including Russell (a fellow minister in Kilmarnock), to extirpate the former heresies and restore the pure faith. Burns's method of attack in *The Ordination* is to write an ironic celebration of this victory of orthodoxy. He portrays, with mock approbation, the vulgar, gloating triumph of the "Auld Lichts" in such a way as to make them appear as repulsive and ridiculous as possible. He makes his poem read like a wild, bacchanalian celebration, and uses the swinging folksy

[5] For helpful commentaries on this poem, see David Daiches, *Robert Burns* (New York, 1950), pp. 198-200; and Crawford, pp. 62-5.

rhythm of the *Christis Kirk* stanza, with conscious irony, to depict this theological victory over "common sense."

> Curst Common-sense, that imp o' hell,
>   Cam in wi' *Maggie Lauder*:6
> But Oliphant aft made her yell,
>   An' Russell sair misca'd her:
> This day Mackinlay taks the flail,
>   An' he's the boy will blaud her!   *slap*
> He'll clap a shangan on her tail,   *cleft stick*
>   An' set the bairns to daud her   *pelt*
>   Wi' dirt this day.

The Ordination lacks the kind of universal significance which has made *Holy Willie's Prayer* (also written on a local and ephemeral issue) one of the classic satires of all time. The poem is not great, but is very effective as far as it goes; and it remains quite readable today. Burns's satiric method here is a brilliant conception in itself, the product of a shrewd and powerful intellect, and serves the author's purpose admirably. One could scarcely think of a better way of ridiculing the "Auld Lichts" on this occasion. Burns here uses Ramsay's form of the *Christis Kirk* stanza, but he manipulates it deftly to suit the special effects he intends, using feminine rimes in the trimeter lines throughout to reinforce the tone of witty mockery. The execution of the poem as a whole is, in fact, masterly and highly original. This hard-hitting satire represents, indeed, a bold new departure in the *Christis Kirk* tradition, which is here for the first time adapted as a vehicle for an attack on local church politics, an extension of the genre which was probably suggested to Burns by Fergusson's success with *The Election,* a political satire.

A Dream, the other political piece which Burns composed in the *Christis Kirk* stanza, is less successful than *The Ordination* and deserves only cursory comment. Apart from meter, *A Dream* bears little resemblance to the *Christis Kirk* type. It is really a monologue in which the poet addresses in a dream King George III and other members of the royal family at the birthday levee of June, 1786. The poet's remarks are not in the best taste, combining some rather forced expressions of respect and good wishes with condescending advice and unpleasantly familiar comments on the King's family. Stanza 5, in an admonishing vein, will illustrate the general tone:

> Far be't frae me that I aspire
>   To blame your legislation,

6 Maggie Lauder was the wife of an earlier "New Licht" minister.

> Or say, ye wisdom want, or fire
> To rule this mighty nation:
> But faith! I muckle doubt, my sire,   *greatly*
> Ye've trusted ministration
> To chaps wha in a barn or byre   *cow-shed*
> Wad better fill'd their station,   *would have*
>   Than courts yon day.

Burns, of course, handles the *Christis Kirk* meter here with his usual skill and vigor (note the feminine rimes as in *The Ordination*); but the poem as a whole fails to ring true.

Hallowe'en, Burns's second poem in the *Christis Kirk* genre, was written about November, 1785. This is a very ambitious piece, Burns's longest work in the *Christis Kirk* stanza, and was, as might be expected in an early attempt, strongly affected by the work of both Ramsay and Fergusson, though the immediate suggestion came from Mayne's *Hallowe'en.* Fergusson's influence shows up in Burns's use of four rimes in the octave, a modification of the traditional stanza which, as we have seen, was introduced by the Edinburgh poet. There are, moreover, one or two verbal echoes of Fergusson in the poem.[7] But although Fergusson was undoubtedly the model for the skillful technique of the poem, Ramsay's influence on its content was decisive and unfortunate. We have noticed in Ramsay's sequels to *Christis Kirk on the Green* the antiquarian emphasis and the introduction of old-fashioned marriage customs, such as the "bedding" of the bride, the "creeling" of the groom, and "riding the stang." In *Hallowe'en* Burns builds his entire poem around the Ayrshire folk customs connected with this festival. As a result, *Hallowe'en* is a paradise for the folklorist, but rather a bore for the lover of poetry. Burns crams his twenty-eight stanzas with Hallowe'en superstitions recorded one after another. This self-conscious antiquarianism makes his description of a merry gathering of country folk on this night seem unnatural and forced; the characters are inadequately sketched and are made to go through a long series of superstitious rites. They do virtually nothing else in the poem. Burns simply puts them through their Hallowe'en paces, failing to render a really convincing impression of what such a celebration must have been like. Many of the customs he describes, morover, are very much of a kind and become monotonous. That Burns was fully aware of the studied antiquarianism of his poem is clear from his own foreword: "The passion of prying

---

[7] Compare, e.g., Burns's "Great cause ye hae to fear it" (*Hallowe'en,* stanza 14) with Fergusson's "Great cause he had to rue it" (*Hallow-fair,* stanza 9). A penetrating analysis of *Hallowe'en* may be found in Crawford, pp. 123-130.

into Futurity makes a striking part of the history of Human Nature in its rude state, in all ages and nations; and it may be some entertainment to the philosophical mind, if any such should honour the Author with a perusal, to see the remains of it, among the more enlightened in our own."[8] Since the poet had this objective in mind, it is no wonder that *Hallowe'en* gives the impression not so much of an actual party at which Burns had been present, but rather of an artificial conglomeration of all the Hallowe'en rites he had ever observed or heard about. And many of the customs he describes are of so specialized and local a nature that they are apt to be entirely lost on the general reader. Take, for example, stanza 4:

Then, first an' foremost, thro' the kail,	
Their stocks maun a' be sought ance;	
They steek their een, an' grape an' wale	shut; eyes; grope; choose
For muckle anes, an' straught anes.	big; straight
Poor hav'rel Will fell aff the drift,	foolish; lost the way
An' wandered thro' the bow-kail,	cabbage
An' pow't, for want o' better shift,	pulled; choice
A runt, was like a sow-tail,	stalk
Sae bow't that night.	bent

Burns apparently realized that such a stanza would be utterly unintelligible to many readers, and he was therefore obliged to prepare an elaborate set of notes to explain his poem to the uninitiated. His explanatory note[9] on the stanza cited above, for instance, is much longer than the stanza itself.

It is unfortunate that Burns insisted on packing this poem with folklore, for in many respects *Hallowe'en* is an excellent piece of work. It is, of course, strictly within the *Christis Kirk* tradition, embodying most of the characteristics of the genre. We have here the typical peasant celebration as the subject, the use of dialogue, the frequent transitions, the satire of cowardice, the lighting up of individual characters and incidents, the broadly humorous treatment, and the point of view of the amused spectator. Notwithstanding the touches of genial satire, Burns's attitude toward the superstitious country folk in the poem is, of course, wholly sympathetic.

Hallowe'en is of further interest for its experimental technique. Burns takes the hint from Fergusson not only in his use of Fergusson's four-rime octave, but also in his attempt at internal rime. We have noted that Fergusson introduced internal rimes sparingly and judicious-

[8] *Poetry*, I, 356-357.
[9] *Poetry*, I, 358.

ly, once in *Hallow-fair* (stanza 2) and once in *Leith Races* (stanza 8). Burns in *Hallowe'en* tries this technique on a more ambitious scale, working internal rimes into the tetrameter lines throughout stanza 1, and in the first quatrains of stanzas 3 and 6. After stanza 6, he wisely gives up the attempt. In these passages Burns seems to be exercising his technical virtuosity for its own sake, without a sound artistic reason. Consequently, the internal riming in stanzas 1 and 3 appears heavy and forced. In stanza 6, however, where the internal rimes do not interfere with the natural development of the thought, he achieves a pleasing effect:

The lasses staw frae 'mang them a',	*stole*
To pou their stalks o' corn;	*pull*
But Rab slips out, an' jinks about,	*dodges*
Behint the muckle thorn.	

Despite this largely unsuccessful experiment with internal rime, *Hallowe'en* is, on the whole, brilliantly executed. The rhythm and movement of the poem are brisk and spirited; Burns handles the complex verse form with accomplished skill. As Ramsay and Fergusson had done before him, Burns frequently changes the pace of his stanzas by using feminine endings in the trimeter lines of a whole stanza or the second quatrain of a stanza. This device tends to vary the tempo and is often quite effective.[10] In view of this fine craftsmanship, *Hallowe'en* might have been a first-rate poem had Burns been less self-conscious in the handling of his folk materials.

We come finally to two of Burns's greatest masterpieces, *The Jolly Beggars* and *The Holy Fair*. In the immense variety of its materials, the multiplicity of its sources, and in its dazzling synthesis of distinct poetic styles, *The Jolly Beggars* is certainly the richest and most complex of all Burns's works. This unique poem (there has never been anything quite like it before or since) has had its sources traced, its main features clarified, and its extraordinary appeal analyzed by a host of commentators, including Henley and Henderson, who, in a now famous sentence, epitomized it perfectly as an "irresistible presentation of humanity caught in

[10] Later, as noted above, Burns used feminine rimes exclusively in the trimeter lines of *The Ordination* and *A Dream*.

the act and summarized for ever in the terms of art."[11]   It is not my
purpose here to launch into a full discussion of this many-sided "cantata,"
but only to demonstrate its connection with the *Christis Kirk* tradition.
Surprisingly enough, this connection has been neglected in the numerous
critiques of *The Jolly Beggars,* except that the bare fact that three of the
stanzas are in the *Chrisis Kirk* form is usually mentioned.   But the relationship to the genre is much closer, as I will try to show.

Let us look first at the verse forms of *The Jolly Beggars.*   Burns, in
this piece, employs a great variety of meters, including the pure *Christis
Kirk* meter in the three stanzas mentioned above which comprise the
seventh *Recitativo.*   Here Burns uses Ramsay's two-rime octave, but replaces the "that day" refrain with "that night" in the bob line as he had
done in *Hallowe'en.*   The influence of the *Christis Kirk* meter, however,
extends beyond this single passage.   In addition, there are three other
stanzas in the *Recitativo* sections which are in the *Christis Kirk* form
without the final tag line: the single stanza of the second *Recitativo*
(Ramsay's two-rime octave), and the two stanzas of the sixth *Recitativo*
(Fergusson's four-rime octave).   Taking all six stanzas together, we find
that nearly half of the total lines of the *Recitativo* sections are in the
Christis Kirk stanza or in a modified form thereof.   Finally, the caird's
song is also in this stanza, without the bob but with the internal rimes
in the tetrameter lines which Burns had experimented with in. *Hallowe'en.*   Altogether, some sixty-seven lines of *The Jolly Beggars* are in
the pure or modified *Christis Kirk* stanza, a total which makes it by
far the most important verse form in the poem, the *Cherrie and the Slae*
stanza being second with forty-two lines.   The full significance of this
metrical influence from the *Christis Kirk* tradition upon *The Jolly Beggars* has never been recognized.

Secondly, I am convinced that Burns's careful study of the *Christis
Kirk* poems had much to do with the original conception of *The Jolly
Beggars* and with the handling of the materials in the poem.   The
obvious and immediate sources of the poem are, of course, well known.
First of all, there was the beggar theme, which came to Burns from his

[11] *Poetry,* II, 291. See also on *The Jolly Beggars,* Max Meyerfeld,
Robert Burns: Studien zu seiner dichterischen Entwicklung (Berlin, 1901),
55-58; Otto Ritter, *Quellenstudien zu Robert Burns* in *Palaestra,* XX (Berlin,
1901), 84-93; Jas. Logie Robertson ed. *The Poetical Works of Robert
Burns* (London, 1910), pp. 558-559; Daiches, pp. 215-232; Christina Keith,
"The Jolly Beggars," *Burns Chronicle,* 3rd Ser. II (1953), 72-82; Allan H.
MacLaine, "Burns's *Jolly Beggars*—A Mistaken Interpretation," *Notes and
Queries,* CXCVIII (1953), 486-487, which corrects Miss Keith's essay; and
Crawford, pp. 130-146.

keen observation of real beggars about the Ayrshire countryside and also, undoubtedly, from his reading of parts of the vast liteature about beggars, a literature which had its roots deep in the medieval past. Burns certainly knew several specimens of this beggar-poetry, including *The Gaberlunzie-Man* and *The Jolly Beggar,* ascribed to King James V of Scotland; *The Merry Beggars* and *The Happy Beggars* in Ramsay's *Tea-Table Miscellany;* and Gay's *Beggar's Opera.* As for his "cantata" form, Burns clearly got the idea for this from *The Merry Beggars* (which, incidentally, he echoes in several phrases of his poem), and from Ramsay's worthless effort, *A Scots Cantata,* with probably additional suggestions from Gay and from Ramsay's *Gentle Shepherd.*[12] But in putting his beggar theme and cantata form together, Burns had another large body of poetry to draw upon — the *Christis Kirk* tradition. Burns had in the *Christis Kirk* poems, which he knew intimately and had already followed in *A Mauchline Wedding* and *Hallowe'en,* a wealth of precedent for an ambitious and artistic poem of social description. In these poems he had observed descriptions of boisterous lower class celebrations, presented within a narrative framework and interspersed with dialogue. In *The Jolly Beggars* the cantata scheme required formal songs, which take the place of dialogue; but, except for dialogue, most of the ingredients of the *Christis Kirk* formula are there. We have the usual opening stanza, setting the season and the scene, and then move swiftly into the first brilliant little vignette, that of the "sodger" and his "tozie drab." In *The Jolly Beggars* as in all of the *Christis Kirk* poems, the technique is to light up an individual character (or group of characters) picked out from the general confusion of the celebration, show him in action, and then go on quickly to the next and the next. Through this highlighting of specific details, a vivid impression of the whole is achieved. A study of the *Recitativo* sections of *The Jolly Beggars* reveals that Burns here uses precisely the same kind of brief characterization, rapid transition, rollicking tempo, and broad humor which we have observed as typical of the *Christis Kirk* genre. The drunkenness, the horseplay, the tolerant satire are here, too, and the point of view of the superior and detached spectator. (It should be noted, though, that Burns's detachment is not complete: he seems at times to be putting his own sentiments into the beggars' mouths.)

Although there is no evidence that Burns had any particular *Christis Kirk* poem in mind when he wrote *The Jolly Beggars,* the general influence of the *Christis Kirk* genre that he knew so well is, I think,

---

12 See Meyerfeld, Ritter, and Robertson (above, note 11) for these echoes of earlier works.

undeniable. It is true that Burns found suggestions for his theme, his cantata form, and for specific details elsewhere; and it is equally obvious that there are many elements in this rich and complex poem that have nothing to do with the *Christis Kirk* tradition. Nevertheless, in view of the broad general resemblances noted above, it seems clear that in his overall conception of *The Jolly Beggars* and in his handling of the *Recitativo* sections Burns had his favorite *Christis Kirk* poems in mind and followed their traditional pattern as far as his cantata form would allow. The fact that he uses the *Christis Kirk* stanza more than any other verse form in the poem supports this position. In short, the *Christis Kirk* tradition is an important part of the background of *The Jolly Beggars;* and *The Jolly Beggars,* uniquely different though it is, may legitimately be considered as part of the *Christis Kirk* tradition.

Apart from the trivial *Dream* (June, 1786), *The Holy Fair* was Burns's final effort in the *Christis Kirk* genre; and this magnificent poem makes a fitting culmination of the ancient tradition.[13] *The Holy Fair* is a socio-religious satire, happily combining the familiar type of satiric social description with the new kind of anti-clerical religious satire on local themes that Burns had already tried in *The Ordination* and other works. The poem falls strictly within the *Christis Kirk* pattern, being in the traditional stanza, dealing with a rural celebration, and having all the other distinctive features of the genre. It describes a "Holy Fair" in Burns's village of Mauchline, an important religious occasion on which congregations from several parishes gathered together to hear their various ministers preach in turn. That most of the folk who came to this religious festival also took advantage of the opportunity for some hearty socializing is made delightfully clear in the poem.

In writing *The Holy Fair* Burns leaned heavily on earlier *Christis Kirk* poems, especially on Fergusson's *Hallow-fair* and *Leith Races,* though there are also a few verbal echoes from elsewhere.[14] But the vital stimulating influence behind *The Holy Fair* was unquestionably Fergusson. Burns here uses the four-rime octave of *Hallow-fair* and *Leith Races* once again, and, significantly, parallels Fergusson's opening references to the season:

> *Hallow-fair:*
> At *Hallowmass,* whan nights grow lang,
> And *starnies* shine fu' clear . . .

[13] For excellent discussions of this poem, see Daiches, pp. 124-131; and Crawford, pp. 67-75.

[14] Compare, e.g., Burns's "An' snuff the caller air" (stanza 1) with Ramsay's "To snuff the cauler air" (*Gentle Shepherd,* I. i). There are also some very effective Biblical references: compare 1. 104 with Job i.5.

Leith Races:
In July month, ae bonny morn,
    Whan Nature's rokelay green . . .   *cloak*

Holy Fair:
Upon a simmer Sunday morn,
    When Nature's face is fair . . .

Hallow-fair provided Burns with several other scattered suggestions, including his opening description of sunrise ("The rising sun, owre Galston Muirs,/ Wi' glorious light was glintin"), which follows Fergusson's ("Upo' the tap o' ilka lum/ The sun began to keek"). Similarly, Burns's portrait of country farmers coming into the fair ("Here farmers gash, in ridin graith") parallels *Hallow-fair* ("Here country John in bannet blue"), while his reference to Sunday clothes ("'I'll get my Sunday's sark on'") echoes the same poem ("And eke his Sunday's claise on"). But more important than these incidental suggestions from *Hallow-fair* was Burns's imitation of the entire opening section of *Leith Races*. Burns takes over Fergusson's introductory machinery, transforming his "Mirth" into "Fun" and adding two extra mythological figures, "Superstition" and "Hyprocrisy." The two poems parallel each other with extraordinary closeness in these opening stanzas. Burns's "Fun" performs precisely the same function in the poem as her counterpart in *Leith Races*: she is a fresh and jolly girl who offers to accompany the poet to the fair for the fun of observing and laughing at the sights to be seen there, especially the antics of Superstition and Hypocrisy:

> "I'm gaun to Mauchline Holy Fair,
>   To spend an hour in daffin: *fooling*
> Gin ye'll go there, yon runkl'd pair,   *wrinkled*
>   We will get famous laughin
>   At them this day."

Moreover, as in *Leith Races* Burns's "Fun" sets the tone of light-hearted observation and tolerant satire which prevails throughout the poem. It should be noted further that, in addition to incorporating Fergusson's introductory method, Burns also follows in a general way the structure of *Leith Races*: after the mythological introduction, Burns portrays the various folk on their way to the fair, then the activities at the fair itself, and finally the aftermath. Burns's final stanza, incidentally, resembles in content the last stanza of *Leith Races* and, more closely, the ending of Ramsay's *Christis Kirk*, Canto II. These extensive borrowings from Fergusson and others in *The Holy Fair* are significant in showing that in this poem Burns was fully aware of the tradition in which he was writing and was consciously modeling his work on earlier masterpieces in the *Christis Kirk* genre.

Yet in spite of the fact that Burns here followed the traditional pattern in a general way, that he borrowed machinery and other suggestions from Fergusson and elsewhere, *The Holy Fair* remains inimitably Burns's own—a fresh, daring, and original piece of work. In *The Holy Fair* Burns recreates the age-old *Christis Kirk* tradition in terms of his own experience and special purposes; and he does so with superb artistry. Perhaps the most important feature of the poem, which sets it apart and makes it a different experience, is its mixture of religious and secular satire, its delightful emphasis on the paradoxes and incongruities emerging from the intensely human scene at the fair.

> Here some are thinkin on their sins,
>   An' some upo' their claes;   *clothes*
> Ane curses feet that fyl'd his shins,   *soiled*
>   Anither sighs an' prays:
> On this hand sits a chosen swatch,   *sample*
>   Wi' screw'd-up, grace-proud faces;
> On that a set o' chaps, at watch,
>   Thrang winkin on the lasses   *busy*
>   To chairs that day.

Notice the gay mockery of the Calvinist doctrine of Election implicit in the phrase "a chosen swatch." The whole poem is, in fact, brilliantly organized to show this glaring contrast between the ostensible religious purpose of the fair and the boisterous and thoroughly irreverent activities which go on there. Burns focuses attention in one stanza on the pulpit where the preachers are thundering out hell-fire sermons, and in the next stanza on the crowd of country folk round about, many of whom are thoroughly enjoying themselves, eating, drinking, gossiping, napping, and making love, utterly uninhibited by the sound of the preacher's voice bringing "tidings o' damnation." The poem flashes back and forth, illuminating the religious and social aspects of the fair in turn, as Burns makes hilarious fun of the different preachers and lights up humorous scenes in the crowd with breathtaking verve and rapidity. The final stanza, where the poet comments on secular love-making and drinking in terms of the theological jargon of the preachers, brilliantly sums up the point of the whole poem:

> How monie hearts this day converts
>   O' sinners and o' lasses!
> Their hearts o' stane, gin night, are gane   *by nightfall*
>   As saft as onie flesh is:

There's some are fou o' love divine;
  There's some are fou o' brandy;
An' monie jobs that day begin,
  May end in houghmagandie   *fornication*
    Some ither day.

The fact that *The Holy Fair* is based on this two-fold satiric theme
and skillfully arranged to illustrate a single, fundamental contrast gives
it firmer structure, more clear-cut direction, sharper emphasis, and more
profound significance than either *Hallow-fair* or *Leith Races*, or, for
that matter, any other of its predecessors in the pure *Christis Kirk* tradition. And the execution of the poem is equally brilliant. Burns had
learned much from his study of the fine craftsmanship of Fergusson, and
here he surpasses the Edinburgh poet in the incisive force and incomparable expressiveness of his style. *The Holy Fair* is an almost faultless
poem, bursting with vitality, rich in its texture, delightful in its humor
— every stanza a work of art. Take, for example, Burns's uproariously
comic portrait of the preacher Moodie:

Now a' the congregation o'er
  Is silent expectation;
For Moodie speels the holy door,   *climbs*
  Wi' tidings o' damnation:
Should Hornie, as in ancient days,   *the Devil*
  'Mang sons o' God present him;
The vera sight o' Moodie's face
  To's ain het hame had sent him   *hot*
    Wi' fright that day.

Hear how he clears the points o' Faith
  Wi' rattlin and thumpin!
Now meekly calm, now wild in wrath,
  He's stampin, an' he's jumpin!
His lengthen'd chin, his turn'd-up snout,
  His eldritch squeel an' gestures,   *unearthly*
O how they fire the heart devout—
  Like cantharidian plaisters
    On sic a day!

The Holy Fair is certainly one of Burns's very greatest performances, and
it is also, in my opinion, the most perfect single poem in the long history of the *Christis Kirk* tradition.

It should be clear from what has been said above that Burns, in his
Christis Kirk poems, followed the lead of Fergusson in making the genre
a vehicle for social criticism, for the treatment of local and contemporary issues. But Burns went farther than Fergusson in this direction,
treating political questions (*A Dream*), for example, even more specif-

ically than Fergusson had done, and extending the subject matter of the genre in *The Ordination* and *The Holy Fair* to include religious satire. Additionally, in *The Jolly Beggars* he used the genre to expound revolutionary social ideas. Only in *Hallowe'en* does he hark back to a kind of Ramsayesque antiquarianism. Before Burns, all of the *Christis Kirk* poems (even Fergusson's) had been intended almost exclusively as entertainment; most of them were seasoned with good-natured social satire, it is true; but by and large they were meant only to delight and amuse the educated classes. Burns was the only poet to employ this ancient poetic tradition to attack what might be called "burning questions" of the day. His treatment is always, of course, comic in mood; but its implications are serious and pointed to an extent unapproached by any of the earlier practitioners in the genre with the possible exception of Fergusson in *The Election*. We find, then, a new kind of emphasis which gives Burns's poems added significance and power, a kind of undertone of vitality and passionate interest. Burns gives us something more than robust humor and whimsical observation. And in doing this as brilliantly as he has — at least in his three best poems in the genre, *The Ordination, The Jolly Beggars,* and *The Holy Fair* — Burns added a new dimension to the whole *Christis Kirk* tradition.

Conclusion

Looking back over four centuries of the *Christis Kirk* tradition, one is struck by the remarkable versatility and vitality of the genre. Beginning with genial social satires of peasant manners, the *Christis Kirk* form was early adapted to anti-clerical satire (*Symmie*) and then combined with the mock tournament genre by Dunbar, Lindsay, and Scott. In the seventeenth century it turns up again, slightly disguised, in Drummond's *Polemo-Middinia,* a mock-heroic macaronic poem satirizing country life. Then, after declining into songs of the *Blythsome Bridal* and *Hallowfair* type, the genre was revived and restored to its original status by Allan Ramsay and his followers, Nicol and Skinner. At the hands of Robert Fergusson, the old tradition underwent change and adaptation once again, its subject matter being extended to include city life and political satire. Finally, with Burns the genre reached its most versatile development, being used for social, political, and religious satire as the occasion demanded. As we have seen, the *Christis Kirk* tradition was adapted through the ages by many different poets to a wide variety of artistic purposes. This ready adaptability of the form was certainly one of the most important reasons for its amazingly long life.

Another reason was surely the innate vitality of the genre itself.

The rollicking tempo, broad humor, exciting action, good-natured satire, and abounding vigor of the *Christis Kirk* poems made them beloved favorites of the Scottish people. The lasting popularity of the early poems, especially of *Christis Kirk on the Green,* encouraged later poets to follow the same pattern, thus giving the tradition renewed momentum. And the genre itself had a kind of universality of appeal which made it largely independent of changes in poetic fashions. Many of the older Scottish genres, such as the allegorical love-poem (James I's *The Kingis Quair*), or the various types of moral allegory and dream-vision poems (Dunbar's *Golden Targe*), were essentially medieval in character, and simply died with the Middle Ages. The major changes which took place during the Renaissance in European thought and art made such genres outdated, no longer usable because no longer pertinent to the new artistic purposes and interests. But the *Christis Kirk* tradition was mainly unaffected by these great intellectual movements. A good poem satirizing country life and characters has a kind of human appeal which makes it interesting in any age. Thus the *Christis Kirk* genre was able to survive the death of the old tradition and the barren years of the seventeenth century.

Its survival was aided further by the characteristic fondness of Scottish poets for traditional forms of expression, and by the fact that a number of good poets chose to write in this form. The better *Christis Kirk* poems, including *Peblis* and *Christis Kirk,* Scott's *Justing,* Drummond's *Polemo-Middinia, The Blythsome Bridal,* Ramsay's *Christis Kirk* sequels, Fergusson's *Hallow-fair, Leith Races,* and *Election,* and Burns's *Ordination, Jolly Beggars,* and *Holy Fair,* are still eminently readable today, and represent a large body of good poetry. The high level of performance in many of these poems certainly had much to do with perpetuating the tradition.

We can, then, discern five major reasons for the almost continuous development of the *Christis Kirk* tradition through four centuries of Scots literature: (1) the adaptability of the genre; (2) its innate vitality and popular appeal; (3) its universality of interest; (4) the Scottish fondness for traditional poetic forms; and (5) the high quality of many of the poems themselves.

Taken as a whole, the *Christis Kirk* genre is a magnificent illustration of the principle of continuity in Scots poetic tradition. It is a distinctively Scottish genre (there is nothing like it in English poetry), and well demonstrates that ability to make distinguished poetry out of the most ordinary stuff of life, out of seemingly "unpoetic" materials, which has always been a feature of Scots poetry. The *Christis Kirk* tradition represents, further, one of the major strands in the poetry of Scotland, extending through four tumultuous centuries of Scottish history; and the study of its development has the advantage of affording a long-range view, a kind of vertical section of the history of Scots poetry through Burns.   Finally, the study of the long growth of this extraordinary genre reveals the tremendous wealth of traditional materials which lay behind Burns's creation of masterpieces like *The Jolly Beggars* and *The Holy Fair*, and provides, as well, a graphic illustration of just what use Burns made of such materials.

UNIVERSITY OF RHODE ISLAND

Notes and Documents

Two Versions of Ulysses' Last Voyage

A minor poet translating the work of a minor poet has at least some chance of success: he may well produce a version as good as his original, though its goodness will necessarily be of a different kind, and with luck he may effect an improvement. But anyone who tries to translate Dante is fighting a losing battle from the start: what gives the battle its fascination is the virtual impossibility of maintaining a balance between the effort to make a representation of as many as possible of Dante's qualities and the effort to write a contemporary verse which is not only "acceptable" in a negative sense but also satisfying in a positive sense. Scholarship and craft, teaching and creating, are odd bedfellows. When a sympathetic scholar translates a foreign poet the result is rarely admirable as verse; and verse cannot even be said to be readable if one has continually to make allowances, if one never forgets that it is "just" translation. But on the rare occasions when a good poet who is also a competent scholar translates a foreign poet the result is quite different from translation as such. A man who is a good poet in his own right is too much of an individual not to transform the original into something manifestly his own. A good poet's version or adaptation of another good poet is worth any amount of everyday "translation," yet when translation as such is being considered it is as irrelevant in one direction as the explanations of the scholar are in another.

I want to compare two fairly recent translations of the last voyage of Ulysses, from the second half of Canto 26 of the *Inferno*. The first is by a scholar—Dorothy L. Sayers—and is to be found in her Penguin translation (Harmondsworth, 1949); the second is by a poet—Tom Scott—and is to be found in his Oxford University Press volume *The Ship and ither poems* (London, 1963). I must emphasize that I am not comparing Miss Sayers and Mr. Scott *as translators of Dante* for we would need much more by Mr. Scott to support such an exercise: I am simply comparing two versions of half a canto. Both versions are good of their kind, both achieve a certain balance between the claims of scholarship and the claims of verse-writing, and a comparison illustrates two of the many fundamental problems of translating Dante—the problems of verse-structure and of diction.

In terza rima, verse-structure means rhyme. The rhymes anchor each line and give the verses their shape. Miss Sayers wrote in her introduction:

> By overrunning and light rhyming, the terza rima can be made to run almost continuously; or, by end-stopping and conspicuous rhyming, it can be broken at will into stanza-form; and it can be carried from the one rhythm to the other by the linked rhyme without for a moment losing the strong forward movement of the verse . . . (P. 56).

So Miss Sayers came down for "terza rima or nothing" and argued her case cogently. She denied the allegation that sufficient rhymes cannot be found in English and cited the Spenserian stanza as an even more exacting form. I have two doubts here. For one, Spenser's verse has on the whole a much looser texture than Dante's and Spenser made much more use of certain little tags which while not adding a great deal in the way of meaning were useful to call in when rhyming difficulties became awkward. More important, the kind of words which rhyme in Italian are often more functional than the kind of words which rhyme in English: inflected verbs and nouns with gender endings, for instance, supple rhymes which are ideal for terza rima in that the rhymes (already prominent per se) can be made to carry the action of the verse. The result can be a stanza with a firm backbone and a clearcut shape; sometimes, even, Dante's rhymes by themselves can give a summary of what is happening.

For:

> Quando
> mi diparti' da Circe, che sottrasse
> me piu d'un anno là presso a Gaeta,
> prima che si Enea la nomasse,   (90-93)

Miss Sayers gives:

> When I came
> From Circe at last, who would not let me go,
> But twelve months near Caieta hindered me
> Before Aeneas ever named it so,

For the first rhyme she succeeds in getting the verb into the prominent position, but at the expense of turning the positive "sottrasse" into the negative and weaker "would not let . . . go." In l. 93 in the Italian the words are ordered quite naturally in relation to the rhyming verb "nomasse": Miss Sayers gets the rhyme but has to be content with a much less important word and consequently a line which feels less inevitable.

> . . . nè 'l debito amore
> lo qual dovea Penelopè far lieta,
> vincer poter dentro da me l'ardore
> ch' i' ebbi a divenir del mondo esperto,　　　　(95-98)

"amore" and "ardore" not only rhyme, not only operate as key-words, but also in this context make emphatic the contrast between what holds Ulysses back and what drives him forward. A translation which sacrifices this point sacrifices a great deal.

> . . . nor the wedded love
> That should have comforted Penelope
> Could conquer in me the restless itch to rove
> And rummage through the world exploring it,

At the cost of a slight juggle Miss Sayers manages to keep the point.

> L'un lito e l'altro vidi infin la Spagna,
> fin nel Morrocco, e l'isola de' Sardi,
> e l'altre che quel mare intorno bagna.　　　　(103-105)

L. 105 moves inevitably to the rhyming verb and the action of the water is what the line principally makes us aware of.

> Far as Morocca, far as Spain I scanned
> Both shores; I saw the island of the Sardi,
> And all that sea, and every wave-girt land.

The echo of "l'un . . . e l'altro" is well caught in "far as . . . far as," but the verse ends weakly. For the sake of a rhyme with "scanned" (a good word here) we have to make do with "land," and the action of the sea, so important here, is lost in the archaic cliché "wave-girt." The loss is not made good by letting the sea, a subject to Dante's "bagna," stand as object to Miss Sayers' extra "saw."

Mr. Scott decided to do without rhyme. In theory I would not agree with this because rhyme is so fundamental to the texture and movement of Dante's verse, but in practice, if there are compensating virtues, the absence of rhyme may be justified. The three instances I have given from Miss Sayers should indicate the kind of sacrifices which often have to be made simply to achieve a rhyme. In any kind of verse, rhymes must feel inevitable, as if they had simply grown in the places they were meant to grow in, despite any difficulties the poet may have encountered in achieving this. But if these difficulties are apparent in the finished work, if the verse feels as if it has been pulled out of shape, even slightly, to manoeuvre the rhyme-word into place, then the rhymes merely stick out like sore thumbs. Considering the vast quantity of rhymes that Miss Sayers had to handle in the entire *Divine Comedy* it is a tribute to her skill and industry that she succeeded as far as she did.

In the half canto that he gives us, Mr. Scott uses an unrhymed, three-line stanza: it keeps pace with Dante's verse, often line for line, and the frequent pause at the end of the third line keeps the verse in shape. Lines run on, of course, as they do in the original, but this needs careful control: when Dante runs on there is always a rhyme to counteract this and preserve balance.

Here are Mr. Scott's equivalents for the passages already quoted:

> When
> I took my weygaein frae thon Circe, wha
> Near Gaeta, had abuin a year backheld me,
> Lang or Enie gied the place its name,   (90-93)

> . . . nor yet the aucht love
> That should hae made Penelope sae crouse,
> Could get the better in me o the yare
> I had for mair experience o life,   (95-98)

> I saw baith the shores as hyne as Spain
> And as Morocco, and the inch Sardinia,
> And ither isles that thon sea synds around.   (103-105)

In each case the movement of the verse is easier and smoother, the clauses slip into place more inevitably, and without the necessity to fit into a rhyme-scheme the crucial words find the right places more readily. "Amore" and "ardore" become "love" and "yare" (yearning, longing): the two abstract nouns remain abstract nouns and keep their important places, sacrificing the rhyme but preserving much else. In l. 105 the action of the sea is predominant, as it is in the original, and again this compensates for the loss of rhyme.

In the translation of any poet who lived in another age, the problem of diction is the most vexing. Miss Sayers, as could have been expected, states her position clearly:

> I have considered the whole range of intelligible English speech to be open to me, excluding, however, at one end of the scale, words and forms so archaic as to be incomprehensible, and, at the other, 'noncewords' and up-to-the-minute slang . . . I have tried to avoid, as far as possible, Latinized inversions (especially when they involve ambiguity), poetic clichés, and sudden drops into slang or bathos — bearing in mind, however, that Dante's own style moves continually from the grand manner to the colloquial, and that nothing could be more unfair to him,

or more unlike him, than to iron out all his lively irregularities into one
flat level of dignified commonplace. (Pp. 60-61)

The intention could not be better and no great blame should be
attached to a performance which does not quite live up to such an
ideal. In the lines already quoted "wave-girt" (105) is a poetic cliché
as dead as any. In 97-98:

> ...the restless itch to rove
> And rummage through the world exploring it,

"rummage" seems wrong for two reasons: there is no need to be colloquial here, and anyway the word has the wrong associations—you rummage through an untidy drawer for something you have lost.

> a divenir del mondo esperto

is simple and direct; so is Mr. Scott's line.

How Mr. Scott's language reads to an Englishman I could not
say: I find it highly satisfactory. It avoids the two extremes apparent
in much Scots writing of the present century: on the one hand the
thickly wrought, synthetic, avowedly literary language of those who
have tried to write in a modern equivalent of Dunbar's idiom, and
on the other hand the dilute, Anglified language of those who think
in English but go through the motions of writing in Scots. I doubt
(despite the opposition) if Scots has much future as the language of a
possible body of literature—as distinct from good individual works,
of which this century has seen not a few. But as a secondary language,
a language for translation and adaptation, I believe it still has great
potentialities. Scots is vivid and particular in a way which English
cannot be; the sheer physical force of the elements, the touch and
colour of landscape, the energy of wind and water, are alive in Scots
vocabulary in a way which frequently shows the English equivalents
to be quite pale. This is what makes Gavin Douglas' version of, say,
the sea passages and storms, from Virgil so much more concrete and
energetic than any English translation has done.

It would be absurd to argue that Scots is a better language than
English to translate Dante into—in general—though I would like
someone to prove me wrong. In the present case at any rate some ad-
vantages are certain. In 112-4 Miss Sayers gives:

> 'Brothers,' said I, 'that have come valiantly
> Through hundred thousand jeopardies undergone
> To reach the West . . .

If they have "come valiantly through" then "undergone" is superfluous; "jeopardies" seem very distant and abstract.

> 'O brithers,' said I, 'wha hae throu a hunder
> Thousant dangers raxt the wast wi me . . .

I doubt if there is an English word that would fit here as well as "raxt," a short pithy verb combining ideas of struggling and achieving.

> Li miei compagni fec' io si aguti,
> con questa orazion picciola, al cammino,
> che a pen poscia li avrei ritenuti;   (121-3)

Note the tension again between the rhyming verbs—the holding back and the surging forward. Miss Sayers gives:

> My little speech made every one so keen
> To forge ahead, that even if I'd tried
> I hardly think I could have held them in;

The rhyme requires "in" but surely "back" is more to the point? "So keen to forge ahead" seems more chatty than "si aguti" demands and it is certainly weaker than the Scots phrase:

> Wi this short speak I make my companie
> That yare and aiverin for it, that
> Gin I'd seyed, I couldna hae held them back;

Both versions lose the force of the contrasting rhyming verbs; Mr. Scott at least gets the "back" into the right place.

The "folle volo" of l. 125 becomes respectively "witless flight" and "skeery flicht": "witless" suggests something aimless and negative but "skeery" has the more positive force of something wild and irresponsible. The mountain that appears out of the sea is "bruna per la distanza," "grey with distance," "blear wi hyneness": "blear" is much more dim and indistinct. The storm breaks; Dante calls it simply "turbo," Mr. Scott translates this directly as "storm," but Miss Sayers oddly produces "foul weather," a weak equivalent which suggests to me umbrellas and wet trouser turnups. Dante's l. 139 is finely balanced:

> Tre volte il fè girar con tutte l'acque:

(rhyming with l. 137 . . . un turbo nacque). Miss Sayers gets a stir into her line:

> And three times round she went in a roaring smother
> With all the waters;

though "went" is colourless and "roaring smother" rather vague and generalised. Mr. Scott's line really swirls:

> And gart her birl three times round wi the swaw;

I know of no words in current English with exactly the kind of force expressed by "birl" and "swaw."

The last line of the canto needs care; there must be no anticlimax.

> infin che'l mar fu sopra noi richiuso.

Miss Sayers' line

> And over our heads the hollow seas closed up.

sounds effective so long as one does not enquire too closely in what respect the seas were hollow and how this "hollow" thing "closed." Mr. Scott's line both sounds as it ought to and is free from ambiguity:

> Until the ocean gurled abuin our heids.

In "gurled" we hear and see the waters. In Miss Sayers' line the description is generalised and sounds as if the figure had been worked out by Ulysses retrospectively, but in Mr. Scott's we feel that Ulysses is experiencing yet again what happened when his ship went down. In "gurled" we see and hear with him.

ROBIN FULTON

THE EDINBURGH ACADEMY

Some Problems Regarding A Series of Letters Between Francis Hutcheson and Gilbert Burnet

The first reactions in print to the first edition of Francis Hutcheson's *An Inquiry into the Original of Our Ideas of Beauty and Virtue* (published at the end of February or the beginning of March, 1725) seem to have been a letter from "Philopatris" in the *London Journal* of March 27, 1725, and a series of letters exchanged by "Philaretus" and "Philanthropus" between April and December, 1725, also in the *London Journal*. The letters were collected and published as *Letters Between the Late Mr. Gilbert Burnet, and Mr. Hutchinson* [*sic*], *Concerning the True Foundation of Virtue or Moral Goodness. Formerly published in the London Journal* (London, 1735). The preface to this collection, supposedly, and probably, written by Burnet, the son of the bishop of Salisbury, reveals that "Philaretus" was Burnet and that "Philanthropus" was Hutcheson. However, there is cause for much confusion over these letters.

First, the initial letter in the collection is signed "Philopatris," who remains unidentified. The letter is merely an objective, uninvolved, though careful, account of the purpose of Hutcheson's *Inquiry* as described in its preface, and of the content of Treatise II of the *Inquiry*. It is possible that "Philopatris" was either Burnet or Hutcheson.

JOHN J. McMANMON

UNIVERSITY OF NOTRE DAME

Reviews

Otta F. Swire. *The Highlands and Their Legends.* Edinburgh and London. Oliver & Boyd. 1963. viii + 290 pp. 30 shillings.

This pleasant, unpretending pilgrim's journey through the parishes of Inverness, Ross and Cromarty, and Sutherland, must leave in grateful indebtedness to Mrs. Swire all Highland men and women of the North and their kin and guests from the shires of the South and overseas. No solemn, pedantic contribution to the taxonomy of Scottish folklore is her "legendary." It is rather a joyous and yet often a saddening evocation of the tales of Northern Pict and Maormor and Celtic missioner and Jacobite and banished clansmen, of bard and prophet and witch and glaistic. Simple and even homely is Mrs. Swire's manner of relation; obvious—although surprisingly effective—is the "travelogue" mode of her narrative's progression. Yet one is moved from the opening account of her so justly lauded and beloved Inverness, by the intimacy of her knowledge of the North, her unaffected devotion to the land and its people, her fine balance of a primitive and poetic faith and a Scotswoman's canniness and clarity of vision. (This balance is perhaps only once disturbed, in a passage giving credence to certain donnish speculations concerning ties between the Pythagoreans and the Druids. See pp. 33-34. More credible and more creditable is the honor paid to the seer of Brahan and Strathpeffer and of all the North.)

Pleasantly and simply recounted and yet richly storied as is each stage in Mrs. Swire's pilgrimage, its greatest value is the distilled essence it offers, the afterglow it casts, of the long centuries of wonder and terror and courage, of piety and fidelity and betrayal, of cruelty and passion and love—which are the grand, the tragic, the heroic, yet all-too-human past of the now tourist-haunted burghs and lonely straths of the North.

ALAN M. F. GUNN

TEXAS TECHNOLOGICAL COLLEGE

Coleman O. Parsons. *Witchcraft and demonology in Scott's fiction, with chapters on the supernatural in Scottish literature.* Edinburgh and London. Oliver & Boyd. 1964. x + 363 pp. 63 shillings.

The title of this book is somewhat misleading, for better and for worse. For better, because the text discusses not only witches and demons but also many other manifestations of the supernatural in Scott's own fiction; for worse, because Scott's achievements as a craftsman of the novel tend to get lost in the shuffle. Professor Parsons has proceeded on the following plan: first, a section on the philosophical, historical, and biographical background of Scott's dealings with the wonder-world; next, a critical catalogue of examples found in the Wizard's prose fictions; then, a summing-up of the functions performed by these materials in the Waverley novels; and finally, a rapid survey of samples of supernaturalism and their uses in the works of Scott's contemporaries and of his successors (Scottish writers of prose fiction), and the usual scholarly apparatus.

This bill of fare promises God's plenty, with a threat of repletion implicit in the opening and closing courses. The reader interested in exploring Scott's practice of the art of fiction will find that the first three chapters serve up an assortment of history of ideas, of literary history, and of biography; only in connection with the third of them do critical considerations begin to emerge. The pièce de résistance is brought on in the chapters on "The Waverley Novels" and "Scott's Methods and Achievements." The former surveys Scott's variety of supernatural materials "in a topical arrangement of Waverley lore. As far as possible, the sequence in which the topics are discussed will be that of Scott's arriving at his fullest or most significant use of each superstition." These topics are displayed in sixteen main categories, from "The Warning Spirit" to "Assorted Spirits and Superstitions," and some are subdivided, to isolate sixteen sub-species. Particularly for the earlier topics, the emphasis is on origins and sources; eight or more sources are suggested for the "German *Diablerie*" in *The Antiquary,* and this in the face of an assurance that "the concentration of this study [is] on the novelist's use, rather than on the provenience, of supernatural materials." But concurrently some conclusions are suggested as to Scott's own developing attitudes and opinions on such materials, and the effective employment of them for the purposes of his novels.

It appears that Scott's early addiction, random and uncritical, to the lurid supernaturalism of inferior German models was relieved by a more wholesome diet of Scottish legend; his taste was matured, in part, by the native influence of the folk ballads he collected for the ·*Minstrelsy*. As he grew older, his own credulous acceptance of the supernatural was chastened into imaginative sympathy; this in turn gave way to common-sense skepticism. His typical response to the marvelous was "an enthusiastic curiosity followed by an urge to discover the natural cause," until in his decline he relapsed into uncritical use of the supernatural to gain artificial effects—"an artistic second childhood."

The novelist perceived a certain relationship between degrees of religious fervor and acceptance of the supernatural: the more devout, the more credulous. But serious religion was in its supernatural aspects "too solemn" for use in novels; only when it merged "into the superstition of a later day," did it become "more properly matter of fiction." Un-heroic commoners accept the superstitions of their age; highborn heroes are forced into a more critical attitude by the conflicting loyalties imposed upon them. Recognition of the interplay of human and supernatural circumstances was incumbent upon Scott as "national and cultural historian, the greatest of his fictional capacities." In the final analysis he is "much more interested in [a character's] response to the ghostly than in the ghostly *per se*."

Thus Professor Parsons suggests certain strictly novelistic functions of the supernatural: to control the personality or, temporarily, the mood of a character, or to explore it psychologically; Scott's "object is not to excite fear of supernatural things in [his] reader, but to show the effect of such fear upon the agents in the story." The supernatural can heighten the impact of the action by foreshadowing events; it can establish a link between past, present, and future. On a more superficial level, with the help of seemingly miraculous agents, "the hurried plot-maker slips out of many a tight place." A fictitious character's belief in supernatural phenomena is a part of the manners of his period, and enriches the frame of reference and the setting; the phenomena themselves objectify the environment of natural forces disposing of man's proposals, and they intensify moods conditioning characters' (and readers') responses to fictitious circumstances. A supernatural event may in itself generate an isolated (and inorganic) interest in the reader, or it may deepen his involvement in the central issue of a novel. Implicit moral values are made explicit by their objectification on a non-human level; supernatural intrusions expose with a frightening clarity the human predicament. Contrariwise, they may evoke the saving sense of humor. And, as Professor Parsons points out in two brilliant passages analyzing "Wandering Willie's Tale," the "demonry, . . . fusing details from a large body of tradition," may help to integrate the multiple elements that compose *Redgauntlet* as a whole.

The chapter of Professor Parsons' study to which the student of literature will most eagerly turn is probably that entitled "Scott's Methods and Achievements." He will find in it an organized summary, with valuable additions, of Scott's various uses of the supernatural for novelistic purposes, which in the body of the book have been worked out through analysis of the novels. As a bonus, there is an interesting exploration of the basic plot-patterns employed by the novelist, though these are not always strictly related to elements derived from "witchcraft and demonology."

An honest recognition of the virtues of the central chapters of this book must take account of certain incidental lapses. There appears to be a slackness not only in the definition of the terms employed but also in the observance of their limitations. Too many of the passages cited as illustrative of "demonology and witchcraft" are mere hollow phrases with no more supernatural significance than the "God" in "goodby." Nor does Professor Parsons sufficiently discriminate against mere counterfeit appearances of supernaturalism; pages are devoted to the poltergeist of *Woodstock* before the whole subject is dismissed as a matter of "hobgoblin impersonators." It sometimes seems that any recollection associated with a supernatural phenomenon or with a Scott novel, but not necessarily with both, is fair game for the critic. In further discussion of *Woodstock,* the story of Fair Rosamund (which is not a matter of witchcraft or demonology) is adduced to motivate an attempted seduction by Charles II. This incidental item accompanies an accumulation of evidence supporting a psychoanalytic hypothesis, of the novelist's own sexual confusion.

More questionable is the treatment of figurative uses of the supernatural. To begin with, they are virtually renounced: "figurative ghosts contribute little." Immediately thereupon, ten figurative examples are cited within the compass of two pages. A distinction might properly have been made between different classes of figures of speech—the simile puts the reader on warning that the supernatural allusion is mere rhetoric; the metaphor invites him to accept the supernatural as real (at least in the speaker's mind). This minor stricture is really only one phase of a major one: the insufficiency of inquiry into the relative degrees of belief among the parties concerned in the novel. In the course of such inquiry questions might be raised as to how far Scott's narrators (as in *Tales of My Landlord* and *Chronicles of the Canongate)* adopt a fictitious position more or less credulous than his own, and how far the narrator (or Scott) offers, and presumably for the moment accepts, his supernatural material at face value (for instance, the White Lady of Avenel), without volunteering any realistic escape from acceptance (as with the Bodach Glas). And how far reader (and Professor Parsons) are committed to going along with him in acceptance. Furthermore, since the impact of the novels on the reader depends heavily on the extent to which disbelief is suspended for the moment, a critic may properly examine the devices by which the suspension is achieved.

An extension of the considerable attention already directed toward these problems by Professor Parsons might be welcomed by some readers in place of the examination of Hogg and Galt, and of the final chapter, on fiction after Scott. This last is really an appendix to the central subject and comes as somewhat of an anticlimax to the thorough analysis of Scott's choice of supernatural materials, and to the conclusions derived therefrom. In contrast, the materials for this appendix seem to be treated rather casually (in, at the most, three pages per author); no continuity of tradition is established.

To return to Scott: it would be picayune to dispute with Professor Parsons a few of his readings of passages in the novels, or a few of his conclusions. In sum, his work is an impressive achievement in focusing attention on the nature of the supernatural elements in Scott's novels. That this was his real intent appears to be obvious, in the light of the implications of his text, and of the evidence of his extensive bibliography (at least 30% of its general items deal primarily with folklore and related topics) and of the index of subjects discussed in the text, re-arranging and expanding the list of categories presented in Chapter iv (only one-tenth of the index has to do with literary topics, five-sixths with supernatural). The impression arises that Professor Parsons is primarily interested in what the novelist has done with the supernatural, rather than in what the supernatural does to the novels. His book probably provides the last word on Scott as folklorist; its contributions to our understanding of Scott as artist are in some respects disappointing.

NELSON S. BUSHNELL

WILLIAMS COLLEGE

Christina Keith. *The Author of Waverley: A study in the personality of Sir Walter Scott.* London. Robert Hale. 1964. 189 pp. 25 shillings.

"There is no Mistress Quickly in Scott," and this lamentation is at the center of Miss Keith's study. The response to so lively and prejudiced a book must be lively and prejudiced. But one's liveliest response is undercut by the sad caution that the author did not live to revise her typescript. Had she done so, to be sure, this would not have become another *Russet Coat* (her 1956 study of Burns' poetry). It would have remained in the shadow-land of "personality" study, haunted by the odd suspicion that Scott's "personality" can be preserved only at the price of his "dust-covered" novels. But whatever changes might have been made, the book as is should not be treated to *nil nisi bonum* pap. It is much too alive. Scott seems more alive for her vigorously idiosyncratic study—and this in spite of the fact that Miss Keith repeats every dead and deadening cliché ever inflicted on the meteoric fame of the Author of Waverley.

Take her at her word, quote her out of a sometimes baffling context, and you puzzle why she wrote at all. Certainly in her condescensions she outdoes Muir and Craig and Welsh and Mrs. Van Ghent. The novels have "a marked absence of passion" (the old French complaint), "the whole air as sterile and as icy as the North Pole itself." They manifest their author's "determined refusal to think out moral questions for himself—to think out anything at all." He did not like people, could not make plots, and "the vast majority of the characters in the Waverley Novels are today sawdust—or worse." He was an amoralist; he lacked the great artist's "understanding of sin"; the "spot of adultery" Byron prescribed was, alas! denied him. His genius was throttled by everything: Calvinism ("the colour of the Catechism's dread contents and of its ghoulish atmosphere"); Kirk and Law; "this severe new Edinburgh," whence "his imagination fled to warm Glasgow"; his literary advisers—the "two purblind moles" Ballantyne and "the equally stupid Erskine," the "prim," the "priggish" Lockhart (as unfairly used as in *The Russet Coat*); finally and most startling, the "banal, deadening, suffocating" influence of his cruelly dull, Philistine children and wife. In short, "George Square and Castle Street between them defeated Scott." There is no Mistress Quickly in the Calvinistic early novels, and the later ones are overcome by a pagan and brutal taste for blood. Throughout is a "flatness" that "makes him largely unreadable today." But then, "no one, perhaps, reads Scott today."

Often, then, what she calls the "enigma" of Scott's personality, garishly drawn in the picturesque mode of Caledonian antisyzygy, is nothing to the mystery of Miss Keith's motive. But a solution is hinted by the mode and by Scott's own sustained love of picturesque contrast. A "remarkable dualism . . . with fatal effect, eventually spread over and coloured his entire personality." Placidity and passion, benevolence and (to his sons and Constable) brutality, intellectual vacuity and creative vigor, the rough Borderer's directness and the deceit and duplicity of the stifled child—"antinomies like these, at once so deep-seated and so violent, range through every cranny of Scott's being . . . the deeper you dig into his personality, the more profound the chasms that open to your reeling gaze—the more furious the hidden fires that burn, rending and tearing him." He is, when we are done, a flamboyantly contradictory creature of his own picturesque imagination, worthy company for his imaginary kin—the shrewd and sentimental Oldbuck, the vengeful Romantic snob Mannering, the ruthless mercenary pedant Dalgetty, the wise fool James VI of *Nigel* and the superstitious cynic Louis XI of *Durward*. Scott has, it is true, "a certain affinity with the queer streaks in human nature" (like Browning); and if he was the tormented walking anomaly Miss Keith makes him, all of these vividly ambiguous figures take on new life as self-projections. Attracted "so fatally all his life" by the "queer streaks" and the "illicit," the rowdy Border reiver is liberated at last from what Una Pope-Hennessy called the "urbane dignity" and "the magnificent monument designed by his son-in-law."

It is not so simple, unfortunately. And in this decade of new books and new perspectives on the Author of Waverley it is startling to find an interpretation redolent of the Carswell generation of thirty years since, when debunking was the day's sport and a kind of swashbuckling uncritical anti-Calvinism sounded the voice of liberation in Scottish studies. Neither Scott nor the "priggish Lockhart" can be blamed if Mistress Quickly is really hard to find outside of Hal's immature Eastcheap, and one suspects that the causeway gaiety of "ancient pre-Reformation" Scotland, however indispensable a myth for the Modern Makars, was much less sentimentalized by the Enlightened Author of Waverley than by his recent liberators. (Miss Keith forgot that in *The Russet Coat* the 18th Century was Scotland's Golden Age.) To make the patriarchal stability of Dandie Dinmont's Liddesdale into a "Bohemian world, of no fixed values, and where no one, mercifully, had heard of John Calvin" is fair neither to Calvin nor to Scott, any more than it is fair to Morritt or Erskine or the devoted Lockhart to say that Sheriff Shortreed was "the best companion [Scott] ever had or was ever to have."

Sentimental, exaggerated, *The Author of Waverley* nonetheless is often remarkably suggestive and richly perceptive. One may be startled to hear that Sir Piercie of *The Monastery* is Scott's finest Englishman, or that the imaginative parts of "Wandering Willie's Tale" are plagiarized from "Tam o Shanter," or that spiritual pride "oozes from every pore" of Jeannie in a book whose "point and kernel" is the passion of Effie and her lover. But the recognition of psychological and ethical mastery in *The Bride of Lammermoor* is fine, as is the recognition of *The Fair Maid of Perth* as "the last great novel." The Aristotelian attention given tragic crises in *Old Mortality* is due acknowledgement of a third novel superior to *The Heart of Midlothian*. The view that "the whole mise-en-scene" of the "later and pagan novels" is "by far the most original of Scott's work" is welcome corrective to the "theatrical pasteboard" prejudice still current. The extended demonstration of Scott's "naturally pictorial" genius, through "colour-studies" of numerous vivid scenes, is an illuminating appendix to Ian Jack's recent chapter (*English Literature, 1815-1832*). The analysis of the use of Scots—"invariably with its quality telling out against the quieter tones of the English"—is a suggestive beginning on a little studied topic. And most interesting, because most corrective of notions that Scott is not truly Scottish, is the linguistic and stylistic link of Scott with Knox, raconteurs in the same tradition, historians thematically harnessed to the same "great central clash of Kirk and State," narrators like Carlyle animated by the same spectacle of turbulent personalities and the "heady mixture of religion and fighting."

We marvel Miss Keith could have found the Waverley Novels "almost unreadable" or could have thought their Author's "personality" a separable being. For she has read the novels closely and energetically, and her enjoyment of them needs no defensive maneuvers. We can only regret that her vigorous spirit had found no company among the increasingly numerous new enthusiasts of the Author of Waverley, some of whom surely would have found the courage to reassure her that Scott is neither unreadable nor unread.

FRANCIS R. HART

UNIVERSITY OF VIRGINIA

Robert Burns. *The Merry Muses of Caledonia.* Ed. by James Barke and Sydney Goodsir Smith, with a Prefatory Note by J. DeLancey Ferguson. New York. G. P. Putnam's Sons. 1964. 224 pp. $5.00.

One of the effects of the maudlin sentimentality which surrounded Burns for over a century was the deliberate suppression of anything which might take him from the pedestal on which the idolators had placed him. The result was a wholly unreal picture of the poet. Other illustrious men were allowed their mistresses, but any liaison in which Burns was involved was kept as secret as possible. Burns's own frankness about these "transgressions," and the generous arrangements he made (including adoption) for his bastard children furnish ample proof of his own honor. It was not until DeLancey Ferguson's collected edition of Burns's *Letters* (Oxford, 1931, 2 vols.) and Franklyn Bliss Snyder's *The Life of Robert Burns* (New York, 1932) that there was an unexpurgated edition of the correspondence and a biography which did not either try to vindicate the poet at almost every turn or, as some of the earlier critics had done, try to show how Burns's death was hastened by intemperance and incontinence. It is worth noting, incidentally, that contemporary reports of Burns's death make no mention of its being "early" or that Burns had died young. To die before one's thirty-eighth year in the Scotland of the eighteenth century was not at all uncommon; that Burns lived as long as he did in view of the hardship of his early life and the then state of medicine is what is perhaps remarkable.

For a generation after Ferguson's edition of the correspondence (at times every bit as racy as any of the poetry) had been published scholars waited for a reliable edition of the bawdy poetry. Since James Currie published his first edition of *The Works of Robert Burns* (Liverpool, 1800, 4 vols.) it had been known that Burns collected bawdy songs, but a conscientious effort was made by the "establishment," including Currie himself, to suppress the songs and to claim that Burns had only collected, not written, most of them. These efforts went so far on the part of Currie that he falsified one of Burns's letters.

At about the same time as Currie was preparing his edition of Burns a book bearing no printer's name or year (but *c.* 1800) was printed—*Merry Muses of Caledonia; a Collection of Favourite Scots Songs, Ancient and Modern; selected for use of the Crochallan Fencibles.* With it the *Merry Muses* controversy was born, a controversy by no means settled. Supposedly Dr. Currie still had all the Burns MSS.

in his possession in 1800, including the collection of bawdy songs Burns mentions in a letter, so the question arises how the printed version was set up. It is unthinkable that Currie would have allowed this to be done could he have prevented it. Prof. DeLancey Ferguson in his introductory "Sources and Texts of the Suppressed Poems" argues that the texts for this edition were not taken from the holograph copy in Currie's hands, but were supplied by someone who had had them from Burns. This would explain inaccuracies, omissions and untypical additions. The whereabouts of the original MS., of course, remains a mystery. Perhaps it was destroyed by Currie or some other zealot.

If Currie indeed had the MS. collection, and the printed version was not taken from it, he must nevertheless have known that a published version of the *Merry Muses* had (or was about to) come out. Thus one might argue for dating the work late 1799 or early 1800. Sydney Goodsir Smith in his "Merry Muses Introductory" notes that two leaves of the unique copy of this edition, now in the collection of the Earl of Rosebery, are watermarked 1799 while eight are watermarked 1800. This would point to a probable date of publication some time during December 1799 or January 1800—there is little to choose between these dates, the likelihood of a printer over-estimating his needs and having 1799 paper left over is as great as it would be that he underestimated it and had to dip into his 1800 stock prematurely. It is unlikely, however, that his estimate would be out by much more than a month. If, then, the *Merry Muses* was out by January 1800 Currie would have had time to alter Burns's letter of December 1793 to John M'Murdo in which he, Currie, interpolated the sentence (Burns was writing of his bawdy song collection) "A very few of them are my own," as Currie's edition of Burns came out only in June of the year, with the dedication dated May 1, 1800. Had Currie not known that an edition of Burns's bawdry had been, or was about to be, published, rather than add the above noted sentence he would surely just have discarded the entire letter, which he was under no compunction to print. This point has been developed at some length because this reviewer does not feel that Ferguson, in his "Sources and Texts of the Suppressed Poems" goes far enough in his conclusions concerning this earliest edition of *The Merry Muses*.[1]

[1] Since writing the above a copy of the first edition of *The Merry Muses* has come into the possession of the reviewer. It is dated 1799. For a description of this volume see pp. 211-212 of this issue of *Studies in Scottish Literature*.

The next important edition of *The Merry Muses* placed Burns's name on the title page. The work is dated 1827 but an examination of the book (especially type and paper) suggests that 1872 would be more accurate; the book was carelessly printed but it seems incredible that such an error on the title page could be unintentional. (Egerer, in his bibliography, suggests earlier dates for two undated editions.) As the 1827 was an almost clandestine production the editor showed little preoccupation with accuracy, and the Burns texts are badly garbled. But worse was yet to come.

Several privately printed, and frequently undated, editions followed, one as inaccurate as the next. Genuine Burns bawdry was often dropped to make space for poems which Burns in his wildest flights could not possibly have written. Take the following example, from an edition in this reviewer's possession entitled *The Merry Muses of Robert Burns* (N.P., n.d., but post-1907):

> As Sylvia on her arm reclining,
> In a shady, cool retreat,
> All in dishabille, designing — fal, lal, &c.
> To elude the sultry heat;
> All in dishabille, designing
> To elude the sultry heat.

And so on for five more stanzas. Surely Burns could never have written this! Scholars, of course, were not taken in by this type of publication, and to the prurient minded it little mattered whether the name on the title page was that of Burns or someone else.

A far greater disservice was rendered by Duncan McNaught, who, as Editor of the *Burns Chronicle*, brought out a sort of "official" edition of *The Merry Muses* under the auspices of the Burns Federation in 1911. The title page bears the words *A vindication of Robert Burns* and it is plain that this thought was uppermost in the editor's mind. (Once again, incidentally, there is no place of publication listed, and the editor has not signed his work.) Instead of reproducing the 1800 version, as the edition claimed it was doing, McNaught took readings from the 1827 edition (highly suspect) or from emendations made by William Scott Douglas which McNaught must have known were not Burns's, or, even worse, at times the editor appears to have inserted his own changes. Apparently no bibliographical study mentions that the 1911 *Merry Muses* was originally to have included Burns's famous letter to Robert Ainslie of March 3, 1788, first published in the 1827 edition. The letter was even printed (it was to have formed pp. 137-138 of the book) but was withdrawn before issue. Obviously it would be more difficult to "vindicate" a man who could write such a letter, and it would be incompatible with Currie's "A very few of them are my own," which found its way into the introduction to the volume.

The present edition (which was first privately issued in Edinburgh in 1959) presents Burns's lyrics without hypocrisy or exaggeration; the words which we know Burns wrote are printed exactly as he wrote them, those which he copied from other sources are faithfully reproduced, and those which he did not write are so indicated. This work is particularly important in view of Burns's dedication to collecting and refurbishing or rewriting the folksongs of his country. Many of the versions to which he put hauntingly beautiful words had been too "earthy" to be publicly printed in their earlier versions; here we have those originals.

In addition to the scholarly essays by Professor Ferguson and Sydney Goodsir Smith there is an essay on "Pornography and bawdry in literature and society" by the late James Barke (not Sir James, as the jacket would have it). In his essay Barke covers Scottish folksong and bawdry in a broad sweep which, while it adds little to our understanding of Burns or *The Merry Muses*, provides an example of that lively style which made his fictionalized life of Burns so popular.

Much still remains to be done in this area of Burns scholarship. Some questions will not be answered until Burns's "Merry Muses" MS. turns up (if it ever does); other questions arise on which a close study of early song-books and chapbooks would doubtless shed much light. Any such study would necessitate reference to a standard text. This edition of the *Merry Muses* establishes it.

G.R.R.

Studies in Scottish Literature

Index to Volume I

July 1963 - April 1964

Studies in Scottish Literature

Index to Volume II

July 1964 - April 1965